P9-DYB-346

EXAM ✓ CRAM

The CompTIA A+ Cram Sheet

This cram sheet contains the distilled, key facts about the CompTIA A+ Core 1 (220-1001) and Core 2 (220-1002) exams. Review this information as the last step before you enter the testing center, paying special attention to those areas in which you think you need the most review.

220-1001

1. Laptops are smaller, portable versions of desktop PCs with replaceable items such as keyboards and touchpads. Include Fn key for implementing secondary key functions. Contain 2.5" or 1.8" hard drives (SSD, HDD, or hybrid). Use M.2 and Mini PCIe cards. Have SODIMM RAM: DDR (200-pin), DDR2 (204-pin), DDR3 (204-pin), DDR4 (260-pin).

2. Smartphones and tablets are mobile devices that have ARM-based CPUs, internal flash memory, multitouch displays, and Li-ion batteries. Often IP68-compliant (dust and water tight). Android = USB-C or microUSB; iOS = Lightning connector.

3. GPS and geotracking provide location information about mobile devices.

4. Mobile devices connect to Internet via cellular WWAN (example: GPRS, EDGE, 4G, LTE, 5G) and Wi-Fi (WLAN).

5. LAN = local area network. WAN = wide area network. MAN = metropolitan area network. WMN = wireless mesh network.

6. Switches connect computers in a LAN. Routers connect two or more LANs and connect LANs to the Internet. Firewalls protect individual computers and networks from unwanted intrusion. IDS = intrusion detection system. IPS = intrusion prevention system.

7. **Networking connectors:** Twisted pair (RJ45, RJ11); fiber optic (SC, ST, and LC); coaxial (RG-6, F-connector).

8. **568B standard:** 1. White/orange, 2. Orange, 3. White/green, 4. Blue, 5. White/blue, 6. Green, 7. White/brown, 8. Brown. 568A reverses the orange and green. (Straight-through cable = 568B to 568B; crossover cable = 568B to 568A.)

9. IPv4 addresses are 32-bit dotted-decimal numbers (example: 192.168.1.1) and can be statically (manually) inputted or dynamically (automatically) assigned (DHCP).
   127.0.0.1 is the loopback address.
   APIPA is 169.254.x.x (also known as link-local).

10. IPv6 addresses are 128-bit hexadecimal numbers (example: 2001:7120:0000:8001:0000:0000:0000:1F10).
   ::1 is the loopback address.
   Link-local addresses begin with FE80::/10 prefix.

11. Common network speeds are 1000 Mbps (gigabit Ethernet) and 10 Gbps (10 Gb Ethernet).

12. **Networking protocols include**
   - FTP (File Transfer Protocol); port 21
     Secure versions: FTPS on port 989/990 and SFTP on port 22
   - SSH (Secure Shell); port 22
   - Telnet; port 23 (*not secure*)
   - SMTP (Simple Mail Transfer Protocol); port 25
     Secure version uses SSL/TLS on port 587 or 465
   - DNS (Domain Naming System); port 53
   - DHCP (Dynamic Host Configuration Protocol); port 67/68
   - HTTP (Hypertext Transfer Protocol); port 80
   - POP3 (Post Office Protocol); port 110
     Secure version uses SSL/TLS on port 995
   - NetBIOS/NetBT (NetBIOS over TCP/IP); ports 137–139
   - IMAP (Internet Message Access Protocol); port 143
     Secure version uses SSL/TLS on port 993
   - SNMP (Simple Network Management Protocol); port 161/162
   - LDAP (Lightweight Directory Access Protocol); port 389
     Secure version uses SSL/TLS on port 636
   - SLP (Service Location Protocol); port 427
   - HTTPS (HTTP Secure); port 443
   - SMB/CIFS (Server Message Block/Common Internet File System); port 445

MFA = multifactor authentication. Ex. A password and a smart card.

UAC (User Account Control) in Windows requires administrative login to perform higher tasks.

32. Security techniques: Mantrap (quarantine area with two doors and surveillance), one-time password (OTP, card with changing code), RFID (radio frequency ID) badge, biometric reader, smart cards, DLP (data leak prevention), and ACLs (access control lists).

33. Encryption: The act of changing information using an algorithm known as a cipher to make it unreadable to anyone except users who possess the proper "key" to the data.

- **Encrypting File System (EFS):** Encrypts one or more files or folders directly within the Properties window.

- **BitLocker:** Encrypts an entire drive in Windows. Requires TPM (Trusted Platform Module). BitLocker To Go encrypts USB drives and other removable devices.

34. Hard drive disposal: Clearing (drive to be reused in-house), purging (sanitizing with Secure Erase, several passes of zeroing out data), and destruction (pulverizing/shredding, drilling holes in platters, incineration, degaussing). Acquire certificate of destruction when complete.

35. BIOS security includes administrator and user passwords, DriveLock passwords, disabling removable media, UEFI Secure Boot (helps prevent rootkit access), and setting the boot device priority to hard drive first.

36. Permissions: The more restrictive takes effect (NTFS vs. share); inheritance/propagation: If you create a folder, the default action it takes is to inherit permissions from the parent folder. (So, the parent propagates to the child.) If you move a folder within the same partition, it retains the permissions. If you move or copy a folder to another partition, the (new) folder inherits from the new parent.

37. Mobile device security: Screenlocks (pattern, PIN, password), invalid attempts lockout, remote wipe, remote backup, and antivirus. Rooting and jailbreaking: removing limitations to Android and iOS, respectively, to gain super-user capabilities.

38. Wireless security: Change admin password, change/disable SSID, reduce radio power, disable WPS, use WPA2/AES, enable MAC filtering, update firmware, enable firewall, disable ports, enable content filtering.

39. Safety: Do not open power supplies; test AC outlets before use; use Class C CO2-based or BC fire extinguisher on electrical fires and call 911. Employ cable management, MSDS = material safety datasheets, and consult when encountering a product with chemicals (toner cartridges, cleaners).

40. ESD (electrostatic discharge): Prevent with antistatic strap, mat; touch chassis; use antistatic bags; unplug computer; and increase humidity.

41. UPS has battery backup for protection during electrical outages.

42. Incident response: First response, identify what happened, report through proper channels, preserve data and devices, document, and set up chain of custody (chronological paper trail).

43. Regulated data includes: PII (personally identifiable information), PHI (protected health information), PCI-DSS (Payment Card Industry Data Security Standards), and GDPR (General Data Protection Regulation). Store regulated data in a secure area with encryption, data loss prevention (DLP), proper permissions, and lockouts.

44. Professionalism: Punctuality, listen to customer, take notes, clarify problems, positive attitude, speak clearly, project confidence, be culturally sensitive, set and meet expectations, avoid distractions (phone calls, texting, social media), and avoid confidential data.

45. An integer is a whole number that can be positive, negative, or zero. For example, 2, –2, 0, 201, –201. A string represents text rather than numbers. It is enclosed with quote marks like "This is a short string."

46. Basic loops let a program execute the same statement several times.

47. PowerShell will always place a **$** before a variable—for example, **$i**.

48. Scripting types: Windows PowerShell (.ps1); batch file (.bat); Linux Bash (.sh); Python (.py); Visual Basic script (.vbs); JavaScript (.js).

49. Remote access: RDP (Remote Desktop Protocol, port 3389), SSH (Secure Shell, port 22, ex. PuTTY), Virtual Network Computing (VNC).

Good luck! And be confident! You can do this!

1. Windows 10 min. requirements: CPU = 1 GHz; RAM = 1 GB for 32-bit, 2 GB for 64-bit; free disk space = 16 GB for 32-bit, 32 GB for 64-bit.

2. Common system tools include Device Manager, System Information tool, Task Manager, and **msconfig**.

3. Remote Desktop (RDP) software enables a user to see and control the GUI of a remote computer.

4. Workgroups are for small networks (20 maximum inbound sessions to a Windows client). Domains are for larger networks and are controlled by a domain controller that has Active Directory installed.

5. The %systemroot% (or %windir%) is C:\Windows by default.

6. Windows boot files include Bootmgr, Winload.exe, BCD.

7. In Windows, **DIR** is the directory command. Navigate with the **CD** command, including **CD..** and **CD**.

8. Files can be manipulated with **del** (deletes), **copy** (copies files), **robocopy** (robust file copy, copies multiple files and directory trees).

9. Drives can be manipulated with **format** (writes new file system), **diskpart** (does everything Disk Management does but in Command Prompt).

10. File checking command-line tools that can be used in Windows include **Chkdsk** (**/F** fixes errors; **/R** locates bad sectors and recovers info) and **SFC** (System File Checker). **SFC /scannow** is common.

11. A hard drive using GPT (GUID Partition Table) can have 128 partitions and go beyond MBR's 2 TB limit. GPT is stored in multiple locations. Requires UEFI-compliant motherboard. A hard drive using MBR (master boot record) can have four partitions: up to four primary partitions but only one extended partition. Logical drives are sections of an extended partition. The Active partition is the one that is booted from; it usually contains the OS. Any section of a drive with a letter is called a volume. Volumes in dynamic drives can be resized, but not in basic drives. NTFS is the most common file system in Windows. exFAT for flash drives.

12. Backups can be accomplished in Windows 10/8 with File History, and in Windows 7 with Backup and Restore.

13. System Restore can fix issues caused by defective hardware or software by reverting to an earlier time.

14. F8 brings up the Advanced Boot Options Menu (ABOM) that includes options such as Safe Mode, enable low-resolution video, and Last Known Good Configuration. Safe Mode boots the system with minimal drivers. (Needs to be enabled in Windows 10/8.)

15. The Windows Recovery Environment (Windows RE) includes System Recovery Options such as Startup Repair, System Restore, and Command Prompt.

16. The Event Viewer warns about possible issues and displays errors as they occur within three main log files: System, Application, and Security. Security displays auditing information.

17. A stop error (also known as a Blue Screen of Death or BSOD) completely halts the operating system and displays a blue screen with various text and code. Can be caused by faulty hardware or bad drivers.

18. Processes can be stopped in the Task Manager or with the **taskkill** command in the Command Prompt. **tasklist** displays a list of currently running processes.

19. The registry is a database that stores the settings for Windows. It can be accessed via **Run > regedit.exe**. Hives store settings; a commonly modified hive is HKEY_LOCAL_MACHINE.

20. DISM tool repairs, or prepares and services, Windows OS images.

21. GPresult displays policy information for the user/computer. GPupdate updates policies without having to log off and on.

22. Common Windows networking command-line tools include

   - **ipconfig:** Displays current TCP/IP network configuration values; **ipconfig/all** shows additional Information such as MAC address.

   - **ping:** Tests whether another host is available over the network (example: **ping 192.168.1.1**). **ping 127.0.0.1** or **ping ::1** to test the local computer. **ping -t** is continuous, **ping -n** is a set of pings. **ping -l** changes the size of each ping, **ping -a** resolves IP address to hostname.

   - **tracert:** Sends packets to test destinations beyond the local computer's network.

   - **netstat:** Shows the network statistics for the local computer. Displays TCP and UDP sessions by computer name (or IP address) and port.

   - **nslookup:** Used to query DNS servers to find out DNS details, including the IP address of hosts.

CAD/CAM design workstations (need high-end video cards, SSDs, maximized RAM); gaming PCs (high-end video/specialized GPU, HD sound, SSD, high-end cooling); thin client (basic applications, low resources, meets minimum requirements for OS, relies on server, diskless, embedded OS, network connectivity); virtualization workstations (maximum RAM and multicore CPU).

31. The laser-printing imaging process is: Processing, Charging, Exposing, Developing, Transferring, Fusing, and Cleaning.

32. Printer configuration settings: Duplexing = printing on both sides; collating = print multiple jobs in sequence; orientation = portrait or landscape; quality = DPI (600 or 1200).

33. Virtual printing: Print to file (.prn), print to XPS, print to PDF, print to image.

34. Cloud types: SaaS (software as a service), IaaS (infrastructure as a service), PaaS (platform as a service).

35. Measured services: Provider monitors the services for proper billing.

Metered service: Only the services accessed are paid for.

On-demand: Services available at all times when requested.

Rapid elasticity: Ability to scale the network quickly.

Resource pooling: Servers/infrastructure shared by a community of businesses.

36. Virtualization: Type 1 hypervisor is native or bare metal. Type 2 is hosted; runs on top of OS. Examples: VMware, Hyper-V, VirtualBox. Network connectivity: bridged (direct access to Internet), NAT (separated access), host-only (private, no Internet), or no networking.

37. CompTIA six-step *Troubleshooting Methodology:*

   1. Identify the problem.

   2. Establish a theory of probable cause (question the obvious).

   3. Test the theory to determine cause.

   4. Establish a plan of action to resolve the problem and implement the solution.

   5. Verify full system functionality and, if applicable, implement preventive measures.

   6. Document findings, actions, and outcomes.

38. Power is good but no display? Check the big four: video, RAM, CPU, and motherboard.

39. Time/date resets to earlier date? Check lithium battery.

40. Trouble with CPU? Check CPU fan, heat sink and thermal compound, overclocking setting in BIOS, and whether CPU is secure.

41. Noisy computer? Check CPU fan, case fan, power supply fan, and use compressed air and vacuum.

42. RAM issue? Reseat modules; clean with compressed air. Overheating? Try RAM heat sinks. BIOS beep codes or displayed errors? Consult motherboard docs and analyze POST beep codes and numbers.

43. Power issues? Test AC outlet with receptacle tester. Test power supply with PSU tester: A power supply tester tests 3.3 V, 5 V, −5 V, 12 V, and −12 V. Do not open power supply; it is an FRU (field replaceable unit).

44. Slow hard drive? Defrag it, use Disk Cleanup, and scan drive with AV software. Drive isn't recognized? Check connections, check in BIOS/UEFI, initialize, partition, and format in Disk Management.

45. No second screen on laptop? Check Fn key. Laptop display blank? Check resolution settings, inverter, backlight, or damage to LCD.

46. Printer paper jam? Power cycle, check paper tray, rollers, paper type, fuser, and entire paper path. Blank paper? Check toner cartridge and transfer corona wire. Lines or smearing? Check drum, primary corona wire, and replace toner cartridge. Toner not staying on paper? Check fusing assembly. Garbage printout? Check driver. Ghosted image? Check drum and toner cartridge. No connectivity? Check power, network connection, whether printer is shared, proper IP address, and whether printer is set up as default in Windows.

47. Test network connections with patch tester, LAN cable tester, tone and probe kit. Test NIC or RJ45 jack/switch port with loopback plug.

48. No network connectivity? Check link light, patch cable, disabled NIC, wireless switch is off, IP configuration, and Windows Network Diagnostics. Limited connectivity? Ping localhost, then move outward, and use **ipconfig/all**. Poor wireless signal? Check distance, placement, antennas, and update hardware and software. APIPA or IP conflict? **ipconfig/release** and **/renew**; check DHCP server.

- AFP (Apple Filing Protocol); port 548
- RDP (Remote Desktop Protocol); port 3389

13. Twisted-pair cabling standards (maximum 328 feet/100 meters):
- Category 5: Rated for 100 Mbps
- Category 5e: Rated for 100 Mbps and gigabit networks
- Category 6/6a: Rated for gigabit and 10 Gbps networks
- Category 7: Rated for gigabit and 10 Gbps networks
- Plenum-rated cable: fire-resistant cable designed for airways, conduits, and areas sprinklers cannot reach

14. Wireless Ethernet:
- 802.11a: 5 GHz, 54 Mbps
- 802.11b: 2.4 GHz, 11 Mbps
- 802.11g: 2.4 GHz, 54 Mbps
- 802.11n: 5 and 2.4 GHz, 300/600 Mbps
- 802.11ac: 5 GHz, 1.7 Gbps and beyond
- 2.4 GHz channels: 1–11
- 5 GHz channels: 36, 40, 44, 48, 149, 153, 157, 161, 165

15. Bluetooth is a short-range technology aimed at simplifying communications and synchronization among network devices. **Bluetooth classes: Class 1** maximum transmission range: 100 meters; **Class 2** (most common) range: 10 meters; **Class 3** range: 1 meter; **Class 4** range: .5 meter. Bluetooth Version 1 has a maximum data transfer rate of 721 Kbps; Version 2 is 2.1 Mbps; Version 3 is 24 Mbps.

16. NAT (network address translation): Process of modifying an IP address as it crosses a router. Translates from one network to another.

17. Port forwarding: Forwards an external network port to an internal IP address and port.

18. DMZ (demilitarized zone): Area of network for servers, not within LAN, but between it and the Internet.

19. QoS (quality of service): Prioritizes computers or applications.

20. PoE (Power over Ethernet): 802.3af PoE devices send Ethernet data *and* power over twisted-pair cable to compliant devices (for example, a PoE injector).

21. Video cards connect to motherboards by way of x16 PCIe expansion slots. Video connector types include DVI, VGA, HDMI, Mini-HDMI, DisplayPort.

22. USB (Universal Serial Bus): Type A/Type B connectors are used by desktops/laptops; microUSB and USB-C connectors are used by tablets/smartphones, etc.

USB 2.0 (high-speed) = 480 Mbps. USB 3.0 (SuperSpeed) = 5 Gbps. USB 3.1 (SuperSpeed+) = 10 Gbps. USB 3.2 = 10/20 Gbps (requires USB-C).

23. Thunderbolt: Ver. 1 = 10 Gbps and uses DisplayPort; Ver. 2 = 20 Gbps (also DisplayPort); Ver. 3 = 40 Gbps and uses USB Type C. Apple mobile devices use 8-pin Lightning connector (USB 3.0 speeds).

24. RAM (random-access memory: DIMMs include DDR2 (240 pins), DDR3 (240 pins), and DDR4 (288 pins). Example of DDR transfer rate: DDR4-2666 = 21,333 MBps. Dual-channel is double width, 128-bit bus. Quad-channel is 4x the width, 256-bit bus. Parity performs error detection. ECC detects and corrects errors.

25. Hard drives are nonvolatile devices that store data. Types of hard drives include
- **HDD:** Hard disk drive (magnetic-based).
- **SSD:** Solid-state drive (flash-based). Can be SATA or M.2.
- **SATA:** Serial ATA uses a 15-pin power connector and 7-pin data connector. Rev. 3 = 6 Gbps; Rev. 3.2 (SATA Express) = 16 Gbps.

26. RAID (Redundant Array of Independent Disks): RAID 0 = striping (not fault tolerant), RAID 1 = mirroring, and RAID 5 = striping with parity. RAID 10 is mirrored sets in a striped set.

27. ATX 12V 2.x power supplies connect to motherboard (24-pin cable), CPU (4-pin/8 pin), PCIe video (6 or 8 pin), SATA (15-pin), Molex (4-pin).

28. BIOS/UEFI identifies, tests, and initializes components and boots to hard drive, optical disc, USB flash drive, or network via PXE. CR2032 lithium battery provides backup power.

BIOS/UEFI configurations: Time/date, boot device priority (boot order), passwords, power management, WOL, monitoring, clock and bus speeds, virtualization support (Intel VT or AMD-V), enable/disable devices, and intrusion detection. For BIOS/UEFI update, flash it with new firmware.

29. The central processing unit (CPU) or processor takes care of most calculations. Typical speed = 3.5 GHz. PGA (AMD) = Pin Grid Array. LGA (Intel) = Land Grid Array. L1/L2 cache in each core. L3 cache is shared among entire CPU. Thermal compound (paste) is required whenever heat sink is installed. TDP = thermal design power, ex. 140 watts.

30. Custom PCs include audio/video editing workstations (need special A/V cards, fast hard drives, multiple monitors); graphics/

- **net:** Used to map network drives (**net use**), view computers (**net view**), start/stop services (**net start** and **net stop**), and synchronize time (**net time**).

23. **Troubleshooting Windows:** Use WinRE startup settings, advanced boot options, Msconfig Safe Boot, use the Troubleshooter tool, restart services in services.msc (and with **net start**/**net stop**), end tasks in Task Manager (and with **taskkill**), remove/repair applications in Programs and Features, enable/disable Windows components (such as Hyper-V and Telnet) in Windows Features. Analyze and remove certificates in certmgr.msc.

24. **macOS (previously OS X) uses:** Dock (icons on the bottom), Finder (for locating applications and files), Key Chain (protected passwords/certificates), Mission Control (larger desktop perspective), Spotlight (the search tool), iCloud (for cloud storage, sync, and backup), Screen Sharing (view and take control of remote systems), Boot Camp (dual-boot to Windows), Time Machine (backup program/system state), and Terminal (similar to Linux).

25. *Linux* typically uses the ext4 file system. Paths use slashes, ex: /Downloads/PDFs or /bin/bash. Distros include Red Hat, CentOS, Ubuntu, Kali, and Mint. Find the distro version by typing **cat /etc/os-release**.

    - Linux Terminal tools:

      ifconfig: Linux and macOS wired equivalent of **ipconfig**. (Being replaced by **ip**.)

      iwconfig: Linux wireless equivalent of **ifconfig**.

      ls: lists directory contents; **chmod**: modifies permissions; **chown**: changes file ownership; **ps**: displays process information; **apt-get**: installs packages; **sudo**: executes commands as admin; **vi**: opens text editor; **passwd**: changes password; **pwd**: displays full path/filename of working directory; **shutdown**: brings system down; **kill**: terminates processes; **grep**: searches for matching information.

26. Wireless encryption protocols include
    - WEP (Wired Equivalent Privacy); 64-bit key size, deprecated
    - WPA (Wi-Fi Protected Access); version 2 is 256-bit
    - TKIP (Temporal Key Integrity Protocol); 128-bit, deprecated
    - AES (Advanced Encryption Standard); 128-bit, 192-bit, and 256-bit
    - Best combination is WPA2 with AES (as of writing of this book)
    - PSK (pre-shared key) is stored on AP; RADIUS server is used (port 1812) for external authentication

27. Malicious software: Known as malware, this includes
    - **Virus:** Code that runs on a computer without the user's knowledge.
    - **Worms:** Much like viruses except that they self-replicate whereas a virus does not.
    - **Trojan horses:** Appear to perform desired functions but are actually performing malicious functions behind the scenes.
    - **Spyware:** Type of malicious software that is either downloaded unwittingly from a website or is installed along with some other third-party software.
    - **Rootkit:** Software designed to gain administrator-level access to the core of a system without being detected.
    - **Keylogger:** Hardware or software that captures the keystrokes of a keyboard.
    - **Ransomware:** Software designed to hold the computer hostage, encrypting files or locking the computer until the user pays the attacker. Often propagated by a Trojan.

28. **Best practice for malware removal:**
    1. Identify and research malware symptoms.
    2. Quarantine the infected system.
    3. Disable System Restore (in Windows).
    4. Remediate the infected systems: update anti-malware, scan and use removal techniques (safe mode, pre-installation environment).
    5. Schedule scans and run updates.
    6. Enable System Restore and create a restore point (in Windows).
    7. Educate the end user.

29. **Social engineering:** The act of manipulating users into revealing confidential information or performing other actions detrimental to the user. Know phishing, spear phishing, impersonation, shoulder surfing, tailgating, and dumpster diving!

30. **Network attacks:** Know MITM (man-in-the-middle), spoofing, zero-day, dictionary, and brute force. DDoS (distributed denial of service): enabled by a botnet (a group of compromised computers known as bots or zombies).

31. **Authentication:** The verification of a person's identity; helps protect against unauthorized access.

    Broken down into: 1. Something the user knows (password or PIN); 2. Something the user has (a smart card or other security token); 3. Something the user is (biometric reading: fingerprint or retina scan); or 4. Something a user does (signature or voice print).

EXAM✓CRAM

CompTIA® A+®
Core 1 (220-1001)
and
Core 2 (220-1002)

David L. Prowse

CompTIA® A+® Core 1 (220-1001) and Core 2 (220-1002) Exam Cram

ISBN-13: 978-0-7897-6057-9

ISBN-10: 0-7897-6057-6

Library of Congress Control Number: 2019944169

1 2019

Trademarks

Warning and Disclaimer

Special Sales

Editor-in-Chief
Mark L. Taub

Product Line Manager
Brett Bartow

Executive Editor
Paul Carlstroem

Development Editor
Christopher A. Cleveland

Managing Editor
Sandra Schroeder

Senior Project Editor
Tonya Simpson

Copy Editor
Bill McManus

Indexer
Ken Johnson

Proofreader
Abigail Manheim

Technical Editor
Chris Crayton

Publishing Coordinator
Cindy Teeters

Cover Designer
Chuti Prasertsith

Compositor
codeMantra

Contents at a Glance

Part II: Introduction to Core 2 (220-1002)

Core 2 (220-1002) Domain 1.0: Operating Systems

Core 2 (220-1002) Domain 2.0: Security

Core 2 (220-1002) Domain 3.0: Software Troubleshooting

Core 2 (220-1002) Domain 4.0: Operational Procedures

Table of Contents

Part I: Introduction to Core 1 (220-1001)

Core 1 (220-1001) Domain 1.0: Mobile Devices

Core 1 (220-1001) Domain 5.0: Hardware and Network Troubleshooting

CHAPTER 17:
Computer Troubleshooting 101 . . . . **329**

CHAPTER 18:
Troubleshooting Motherboards, CPUs, RAM, and Power **337**

CHAPTER 19:
Troubleshooting Hard Drives and RAID Arrays **353**

About the Author

David L. Prowse is the author of more than a dozen computer training books and video products. He has worked in the computer field for 25 years and loves to share his experience through teaching and writing.

He runs the website https://dprocomputer.com, where he gladly answers questions from readers and students.

Acknowledgments

I'd like to give special recognition to Paul Carlstroem, Chris Cleveland, Chris Crayton, Tonya Simpson, and Bill McManus. Without you, this book wouldn't have made it to the presses. I'm serious here, writing a book is tough work, and this edition of the A+ Exam Cram was the toughest to date. Thank you.

Publishing a book takes a team of professional and talented people. My thanks to everyone else at Pearson for your expertise and help throughout this project.

About the Technical Reviewer

Chris Crayton (MCSE) is an author, technical consultant, and trainer. He has worked as a computer technology and networking instructor, information security director, network administrator, network engineer, and PC specialist. Chris has authored several print and online books on PC repair, CompTIA A+, CompTIA Security+, and Microsoft Windows. He has also served as technical editor and content contributor on numerous technical titles for several of the leading publishing companies. He holds numerous industry certifications, has been recognized with many professional teaching awards, and has served as a state-level SkillsUSA competition judge.

We Want to Hear from You!

As the reader of this book, *you* are our most important critic and commentator. We value your opinion and want to know what we're doing right, what we could do better, what areas you'd like to see us publish in, and any other words of wisdom you're willing to pass our way.

We welcome your comments. You can email or write to let us know what you did or didn't like about this book—as well as what we can do to make our books better.

Please note that we cannot help you with technical problems related to the topic of this book.

When you write, please be sure to include this book's title and author as well as your name and email address. We will carefully review your comments and share them with the author and editors who worked on the book.

Email: community@informit.com

Reader Services

Register your copy of *CompTIA A+ Exam Cram Core 1 (220-1001) and Core 2 (220-1002)* at www.pearsonitcertification.com for convenient access to downloads, updates, and corrections as they become available. To start the registration process, go to www.pearsonitcertification.com/register and log in or create an account.* Enter the product ISBN 9780789760579 and click Submit. When the process is complete, you will find any available bonus content under Registered Products.

*Be sure to check the box that you would like to hear from us to receive exclusive discounts on future editions of this product.

Introduction

Welcome to the *CompTIA A+ Core 1 (220-1001) and Core 2 (220-1002) Exam Cram*. This book prepares you for the CompTIA A+ Core 1 (220-1001) and Core 2 (220-1002) certification exams. Imagine that you are at a testing center and have just been handed the passing scores for these exams. The goal of this book is to make that scenario a reality. My name is David L. Prowse, and I am happy to have the opportunity to serve you in this endeavor. Together, we can accomplish your goal to attain the CompTIA A+ certification.

Target Audience

The CompTIA A+ exams measure the necessary competencies for an entry-level IT professional with the equivalent knowledge of at least 12 months of hands-on experience in the lab or field.

This book is for persons who have experience working with desktop computers and mobile devices and want to cram for CompTIA A+ certification exams—*cram* being the key word. This book does not cover everything in the computing world; how could anyone do so in such a concise package? However, this guide is fairly thorough and should offer you a lot of insight…and a whole lot of test preparation.

If you do not feel that you have the required experience, have never attempted to troubleshoot a computer, or are new to the field, then I recommend the following:

- ▶ Attend a hands-on A+ class with a knowledgeable instructor.
- ▶ Consider purchasing the CompTIA A+ Core 1 (220-1001) and Core 2 (220-1002) (Video Training) (9780136526643), which goes into a bit more depth than this text and shows technology concepts from a hands-on perspective.

Essentially, I have written this book for three types of people: those who want a job in the IT field, those who want to keep their job in the IT field, and those who simply want a basic knowledge of computers and want to validate that knowledge. For those of you in the first group, the latest version of the CompTIA A+ certification can have a positive career impact, increasing the chances of securing a position in the IT world. It also acts as a stepping stone to more advanced certifications. For those in the second group, preparing for the exams serves to keep your skills sharp and your knowledge up to date, helping you to remain a well-sought-after technician. For those of you in the third group, the knowledge within this book can be very beneficial to just about any organization you might work for—as long as that organization uses computers!

Regardless of your situation, one thing to keep in mind is that I write my books to teach you how to be a well-rounded computer technician. While the main goal for this book is to help you become A+ certified, I also want to share my experience with you so that you can grow as an individual.

A person might be tempted to purchase a study guide solely for the practice exams, but I recommend against studying from practice questions *only*. This book was designed from the ground up to build your knowledge in such a way that when you get to the practice exams, they can act as the final key to passing the real exams. The knowledge in the chapters is the cornerstone, whereas the practice exam questions are the battlements. Complete the entire book and you will have built yourself an impenetrable castle of knowledge.

About the CompTIA A+ Core 1 (220-1001) and Core 2 (220-1002) Exams

This book covers the CompTIA A+ 220-1001 and 220-1002 exams, also known as Core 1 and Core 2 respectively. There are quite a few changes and additions to these versions of the A+ exams compared to the previous versions, including the following:

▶ Increased content concerning the troubleshooting of computer hardware and software

▶ Addition of Windows 10 content

▶ Addition of Chrome OS content

▶ A large increase in operational procedures content

▶ Addition of basic scripting

▶ Addition of remote access technologies

▶ Increased virtualization concepts

This book covers all these changes and more within its covers. It does so in a concise way that allows you to memorize the facts quickly and efficiently.

For more information about how the A+ certification can help your career, or to download the latest official objectives, access CompTIA's web page at https://certification.comptia.org/.

About This Book

This book is organized into two parts comprising 43 chapters, each chapter pertaining to one or more particular objectives covered on the exams. The first part of the book—Chapters 1 through 22—applies to the Core 1 (220-1001) exam. The second part of the book—Chapters 23 through 42—applies to the Core 2 (220-1002) exam. At the beginning of each of those parts you will find a handy checklist you can use as you prepare for the exams. Chapter 43 discusses how to get ready for the real exams and gives some tips and techniques for passing the exams.

For this edition of the book I decided to organize the content based on the order of the official CompTIA objectives. Typically, you will find one to three objectives per chapter. The corresponding CompTIA objective or objectives are listed verbatim in the beginning of each chapter and in the subsequent major heading(s). By organizing the book this way, you can easily locate whatever objective you want to learn more about. In addition, you can use the index or the table of contents to quickly find the concept you are after. Some chapters (such as the troubleshooting chapters) are shorter than others; this is done by design so that you can better absorb the information.

Regardless of your experience level, I don't recommend skipping content. This book is designed to be read completely. The best way to study is to read the entire book. Then, go back and review the 220-1001 portion, and take the real CompTIA 220-1001 exam. Afterward, review the 220-1002 portion, and take that exam. The reason for this is because the two exams are inextricably linked. It's a good idea to get the whole picture first, and then break it down by the exam. While this might not be possible based on time constraints, I still must strongly recommend it as the best study method.

> **Note**
>
> I do *not* recommend taking both exams on the same day. Instead, space them apart by at least a week to give you time to prepare.

Chapter Format and Conventions

Every Exam Cram chapter follows a standard structure and contains graphical clues about important information. The structure of each chapter includes the following:

▶ **Opening topics list:** This defines the CompTIA A+ objective(s) to be covered in the chapter.

▶ **Topical coverage:** The heart of the chapter, this explains the topics from a hands-on and a theory-based standpoint. This includes in-depth descriptions, tables, and figures geared to build your knowledge so that you can pass the exams.

▶ **Cram Quiz questions:** At the end of each topic is a quiz. The quizzes, and ensuing explanations, are meant to help you gauge your knowledge of the subjects you have just studied. If the answers to the questions don't come readily to you, consider reviewing individual topics or the entire chapter. In addition to being in the chapters, you can find the Cram Quiz questions within the book's companion web page at www. pearsonitcertification.com. The questions are separated into their respective 220-1001 and 220-1002 categories for easier studying when you approach each exam.

▶ **Exam Alerts, Sidebars, and Notes:** These are interspersed throughout the book. Watch out for them!

> **ExamAlert**
>
> This is what an Exam Alert looks like. An alert stresses concepts, terms, hardware, software, or activities that are likely to relate to one or more questions on the exams.

Additional Elements

Beyond the chapters, there are a few more elements that I've thrown in for you. They include

▶ **Practice Exams:** These are located at the end of Part I and Part II. There is one for each CompTIA A+ exam. These practice exams (and additional exams) are available as part of the custom practice test engine at the companion web page also. They are designed to prepare you for the multiple-choice questions that you will find on the real CompTIA A+ exams.

▶ **Real-World Scenarios:** These are located on the companion web page as PDFs. They describe actual situations with questions that you must answer and potential solutions with supporting videos and simulations. These are designed to help prepare you for the performance-based questions within the real CompTIA A+ exams.

▶ **Cram Sheet:** The tear-out Cram Sheet is located in the beginning of the book. This is designed to jam some of the most important facts you need to know for each exam into one small sheet, allowing for easy memorization. It is also in PDF format on the companion web page. If you have an e-book version, this might be located elsewhere in the e-book; run a search of the term "cram sheet" and you should be able to find it that way.

The Hands-On Approach

This book refers to two different computers as the following:

▶ *VM-House:* I built this rackmount server computer in September of 2018. It is a Xeon-based system that is designed to house all of my virtual machines and serve them to my workstations.

▶ *AV-Editor:* I built this desktop computer in July of 2015. It is an Intel Core i7 system and is designed to act as a powerful audio/video editing workstation. It has been my main workstation since then.

> **Note**
>
> The previous edition of this book included computers known as *Media PC* and *Tower PC*. Those were built in 2012 and 2009, respectively, and as such are based on older technologies. I have removed references to them from this edition of the book, but you can find information about them at my website: https://dprocomputer.com.

I built these systems using components that are good examples of what you will see in the field. These components are representative of the types of technologies that will be covered in the exams. I refer to the components throughout the book because I like to put things into context whenever possible. By referencing computers in actual scenarios presented in many of the chapters, I hope to infuse some real-world knowledge and to solidify the concepts you need to learn for the exams. This more hands-on approach can help you to visualize concepts better. I recommend that every computer technician build their own computer at some point (if you haven't already). This can help to reinforce the ideas and concepts expressed in the book.

You should also work with multiple operating systems while going through this book: namely Windows 10, Windows 8.1, and Windows 7. (Not to mention macOS, Linux, Android, iOS, and Chrome OS.) Or you might attempt to create a dual-boot on a single hard drive. Another option is to run one computer with one of the operating systems mentioned and virtual machines running the other operating systems. However, if at all possible, the best way to learn is to run individual computers. This will ensure that you discover as much as possible about the hardware and software of each computer system and how they interact with each other.

This book frequently refers to various support websites. Have a browser open all the time and be ready to perform more research as you read through the book.

Goals for This Book

I have three main goals in mind while preparing you for the CompTIA A+ exams.

My first goal is to help you understand A+ topics and concepts quickly and efficiently. To do this, I try to get right to the facts necessary for the exam. To drive these facts home, the book incorporates figures, tables, real-world scenarios, and simple, to-the-point explanations. Also, in the introductions for the Core 1 and Core 2 sections, you will find preparation checklists that give you orderly, step-by-step approaches to taking the exams. Be sure to complete all items on the checklists! For students of mine who truly complete every item, there is an extremely high passing rate. Finally, in Chapter 43, you will find some important test-taking tips that I've developed while sitting dozens of exams over the years.

My second goal for this book is to provide you with an abundance of *unique* questions to prepare you for the exams. Between the Cram Quizzes and the practice exams, that goal has been met, and I think it will benefit you greatly. Because CompTIA reserves the right to change test questions at any time, it is difficult to foresee exactly what you will be asked on the exams. However, to become a good technician, you must know the *concept*; you can't just memorize questions. Therefore, each question has an explanation and maps back to the chapter covered in the text. I've been using this method for more than a decade with my students (more than 3000 of them) and with great results.

My final goal is to provide support for this and all my titles, completing the life cycle of learning. I do this through my personal website (https://dprocomputer. com), which has additional resources for you, including an errata page (which you should check as soon as possible), and is set up to take questions from you about this book. I'll try my best to get to your questions ASAP. All personal information is kept strictly confidential. Check my site frequently for upcoming live webinars, new videos, articles, and quiz questions, and consider signing up to my mailing list to find out about the latest updates.

Good luck in your certification endeavors. I hope you benefit from this book. Enjoy!

Sincerely,

David L. Prowse
https://dprocomputer.com

Figure Credits

Figure 1-1 from David Prowse.
Figure 1-2 from David Prowse.
Figure 1-3 from David Prowse.
Figure 2-1 from David Prowse.
Figure 2-2 from David Prowse.
Figure 3-1a, Mini-USB Type B port, from David Prowse.
Figure 3-1b, Micro-USB Type B port, from David Prowse.
Figure 3-1c, USB-C port, from David Prowse.
Figure 3-1d, lightning connector, from David Prowse.
Figure 3-1e, USB-C connector, from David Prowse.
Figure 3-1f, Micro-USB Type B connector, from David Prowse.
Figure 3-1g, Mini-USB Type B connector, from David Prowse.
Figure 4-5 from David Prowse.
Figure 5-2, screenshot of RDP © Microsoft 2019.
Figure 6-3, screenshot of Wireless Properties © Microsoft 2019.
Figure 6-4 courtesy of Cisco Systems, Inc. Unauthorized use not permitted.
Figure 7-1, screenshot of Windows configuration © Microsoft 2019.
Figure 8-2a, wire stripper, from Pearson Education.
Figure 8-2b, punchdown tool, from Pearson Education.
Figure 8-2c, cable tester, from Pearson Education.
Figure 8-2d, RJ45 crimper, from Pearson Education.
Figure 8-2e, patch tester, from Pearson Education.
Figure 8-2f, tone generator, from Pearson Education.
Figure 8-2g, RJ45 lookback plug, from Pearson Education.
Figure 8-3, screenshot of Wi-Fi Analyzer © 2019 Adrian Granados.
Figure 9-1, wires organized for the 568B standard, from Pearson Education.
Figure 9-2a, RJ45 plugs, from Pearson Education.
Figure 9-2b, RJ11 plugs, from Pearson Education.
Figure 9-3a, ST connectors, from Pearson Education.
Figure 9-3b, SC connectors, from Pearson Education.
Figure 9-4a, DVI Typical video ports, from David Prowse.
Figure 9-4b, VGA, from David Prowse.
Figure 10-1 from Pearson Education.
Figure 10-2 from Pearson Education.
Figure 10-3 from Pearson Education.
Figure 10-4, screenshot of Task Manager © Microsoft 2019.
Figure 10-5 from Pearson Education.
Figure 10-6 from David Prowse.
Figure 10-9 from Pearson Education.
Figure 11-1 from Pearson Education.
Figure 11-2 from Pearson Education.
Figure 11-3 from Pearson Education.
Figure 11-4a from Pearson Education.
Figure 11-4b from Pearson Education.
Figure 11-5, screenshot of Boot Manager © Microsoft 2019.
Figure 12-1 from Pearson Education.
Figure 12-2 from Pearson Education.
Figure 13-1 from David Prowse.
Figure 13-2, screenshot of Task Manager © Microsoft 2019.
Figure 13-3 from David Prowse.
Figure 13-4a, 24-pin ATX CPU connectors, from David Prowse.
Figure 13-4b, EATX12V 8-pin CPU connectors, from David Prowse.
Figure 13-5a, SATA power connector, from David Prowse.
Figure 13-5b, Molex power connector, from David Prowse.
Figure 13-5c, PCIe power connector, from David Prowse.
Figure 13-6 from Pearson Education.
Figure 14-1, screenshot of VMware Workstation © 1998-2014 VMware, Inc.
Figure 14-2, screenshot of Task Manager © Microsoft 2019.
Figure 15-1, screenshot of configuring printing © Microsoft 2019.
Figure 16-1, screenshot of Windows Features © Microsoft 2019.
Figure 16-2, screenshot of Hyper-V Manager © Microsoft 2019.
Figure 16-3, screenshot of Virtual VM VirtualBox © Oracle.

Introduction to Core 1 (220-1001)

Welcome to the Core 1 (220-1001) section of this book. This portion of the CompTIA A+ certification focuses on: computers such as laptops, smartphones, tablets, and PCs; computer networking; virtualization and cloud computing; and the troubleshooting of hardware and networks. That's a great deal of things to know—but you can do this. Take it slow, study hard, and stay positive. Do these things, and you will succeed.

The Core 1 content of this book comprises Chapters 1 through 22. For the most part, I've written the content to match the order of the objectives. This way, you can follow along with the official CompTIA A+ objectives and mark them up as you wish while you progress through the book. After Chapter 22 you will find a practice exam that is designed to test your knowledge of the 220-1001 objectives.

Core 1 (220-1001) Domains

The CompTIA A+ Core 1 exam objectives are broken down into five domains:

- ▶ 1.0—Mobile Devices
- ▶ 2.0—Networking
- ▶ 3.0—Hardware
- ▶ 4.0—Virtualization and Cloud Computing
- ▶ 5.0—Hardware and Network Troubleshooting

After this introduction, we'll go through these in order, starting with Chapter 1, "Laptops, Part 1." Be sure to study each of the domains! To do this properly, I suggest that you get your hands on as much technology gear as you can: PCs, laptops, mobile devices, printers, SOHO routers, and so on. Look for older equipment that still works to save money. Work with as much of this technology as possible so that you can learn how the hardware and devices really work. Then apply that knowledge to the objectives and the content in this book.

Core 1 (220-1001) Checklist

You must be fully prepared for the exam, so I created a checklist that you can use to make sure you are covering all the bases as you study. Take a look at the table below and make sure you check off each item before attempting the 220-1001 exam. Historically, my readers and students have benefited greatly from this type of checklist. Use the table as a guide for ordering your studies. I suggest you bookmark this page, and refer back to it as you complete each item.

Exam Preparation Checklist

Step	Item	Details	220-1001 Status
1.	Read the Core 1 (220-1001) content.	Thoroughly read Chapters 1 through 22.	
2.	Review the Exam Alerts.	The little boxes with Exam Alerts are interspersed throughout the book. Review these and make sure you understand every one.	
3.	Review the Cram Quizzes.	Cram Quizzes are categorized by exam. You can review them in the text or on the companion website.[1]	
4.	Complete the practice exam in the book.	Directly after Chapter 22 is a 220-1001 practice exam. Your goal should be to get at least 90 percent correct on the exam on the first try. (100 percent would be preferable!) If you score less than 90 percent, go back and study more!	
5.	Study the Core 1 Real-World Scenarios.	These can be found on the companion website. Complete these by reading and answering the scenarios and questions within the PDFs, and accessing the corresponding videos and simulations.	
6.	Create your own cheat sheet.	Although there is a Cram Sheet in the beginning of this book, you should also create your own. The act of writing down important details helps commit them to memory. Keep in mind that you will not be allowed to take this or the Cram Sheet into the actual testing room.	

Step	Item	Details	220-1001 Status
7.	Register for the exam.	Do not register until you have completed the previous steps; you shouldn't register until you are fully prepared. When you are ready, schedule the exam to commence within a couple days so that you won't forget what you learned! Registration can be done online. Register at Pearson Vue (https://home.pearsonvue.com/). It accepts payment by major credit cards for the exam fee. You need to create an account to sign up for exams.	
8.	Read the test-taking tips.	These can be found in the last chapter of the book and on the companion website.	
9.	Study the Cram Sheet and cheat sheet.	The Cram Sheet is a fold-out in the beginning of this book. It is also on the companion website. Study from the Core 1 portion of this and your cheat sheet during the last 24 hours before the exam. (If your exam is delayed for any reason, go back to step 3 and retake the Cram Quizzes and practice exam 24 hours prior to your test date.)	
10.	Take the exam!	When you pass, place that final check mark in the hard Good luck!	

[1]Some electronic editions of this book do not have access to the practice test software.

ExamAlert

Do not register for the exam until you are thoroughly prepared. Meticulously complete items 1 through 6 in the table before you register.

Note

Remember: It's not mandatory, but I always recommend going through the entire book (Core 1 and Core 2). Then, return to the Core 1 portion and review it carefully, going through the steps in the table. It takes more time, yes—but this is a proven method that I have used with CompTIA A+ exams since the turn of the millennium!

CORE 1 (220-1001)

Domain 1.0: Mobile Devices

CHAPTER 1

Laptops, Part 1

This chapter covers the following A+ 220-1001 exam objective:

▶ 1.1 – Given a scenario, install and configure laptop hardware and components.

Welcome to the first chapter of this book! In this chapter we focus on laptop hardware only. Software will be covered later in the book. The core of this chapter deals with laptop hardware and device replacement. By that I mean hard drives, memory, batteries, keyboards, speakers, and so on. You might come into contact with laptops old and new that need to be repaired and/or upgraded. This chapter addresses many of those scenarios. Let's get to it.

1.1 – Given a scenario, install and configure laptop hardware and components

ExamAlert

Objective 1.1 focuses on the following concepts: keyboard, hard drive, memory, smart card reader, optical drive, wireless card/Bluetooth module, cellular card, video card, Mini PCIe, screen, DC jack, battery, touchpad, plastics/frames, speaker, system board, and finally the CPU.

Note

Don't forget, a complete list of the Core 1 (220-1001) objectives can be found on the companion website of this book (see the introduction for details) and on CompTIA's website: https://certification.comptia.org/certifications/a.

Ah, the laptop. The beauty of laptops is that they are portable, and all the connections are right at your fingertips. However, quite often there is a trade-off in performance and in price—that is, in comparison to PCs. This chapter assumes a basic knowledge of laptops and jumps straight into how to install and configure laptop devices.

Laptops were originally designed for niche markets but today are often used in businesses and at home. Laptops (also known as notebooks or portable computers) have integrated displays, keyboards, and pointing devices, making them easy to transport and easy to use in confined spaces.

Keyboards

The keyboard is the most important input device on a laptop (or a PC). One of the great things about the keyboard is that you can use it exclusively, even if you don't have a pointing device or a touchpad available (or functional). You can do just about anything within the operating system and within the Basic Input/Output System (BIOS) or Unified Extensible Firmware Interface (UEFI) with the keyboard.

> **Note**
>
> The BIOS and the newer UEFI are the firmware and software that are used to bridge the gap between a computer's hardware and the operating system that runs on the computer. Older systems only use BIOS, whereas newer systems will use UEFI or a combination of the two. Normally I will refer to them collectively as BIOS/UEFI unless I need to discuss one specifically. We cover the BIOS/UEFI more in Chapter 11, "Motherboards and Add-on Cards."

Figure 1.1 shows an example of a typical laptop keyboard. Take a look at the keyboard on your laptop and identify the various keys. Also, look for similarities and differences between the keyboard in the figure and yours. If you don't have a keyboard, go to the Internet and search for images of current laptop keyboards.

FIGURE 1.1 **A typical laptop keyboard**

I have had a dozen people I know approach me telling me that their laptop's keyboard wasn't working properly. Over time I've noticed several culprits: overuse, loose ribbon cables, spilled coffee, or users simply pounding the tar out of the keyboard! It happens—the telltale signs include bent or warped keyboards and missing keycaps. Whatever the cause, here are a couple of actual problems you might encounter:

▶ **Stuck keys:** Sticking keys could be a result of overuse, damage to the individual key's switch, or liquid spilled on the keyboard. (And if a stuck key is the worst that happens due to a liquid spill, consider yourself lucky!) A stuck key can be identified by the key failing to work in the operating system or the BIOS/UEFI reporting an error. Use an external keyboard or mouse if the BIOS/UEFI and laptop is designed for it. By removing the keycap and cleaning the keyswitch underneath, you can usually fix the problem. If not, the entire keyboard will probably have to be replaced.

▶ **Loose connection:** If the laptop is moved around and jostled a lot, as many laptops are, it could possibly cause loose connections. One of these is the ribbon cable that connects the keyboard to the motherboard. To fix this, the keyboard must be lifted away from the laptop and the ribbon cable attached securely.

▶ **Damaged keyboard:** Users who inadvertently drop heavy items onto the keyboard or operate the keyboard with a heavy hand might cause a warped or bent keyboard. Some brands of laptops suffer from this more than others. This is usually impossible to repair; the keyboard often needs to be replaced.

When replacing a keyboard, be sure to shut down the laptop, unplug it, and disconnect the battery. Then employ electrostatic discharge (ESD) prevention measures. That means using an antistatic strap and antistatic mat. I speak more to this in Chapter 40, "Safety Procedures and Environmental Controls." You'll need a very small Phillips-head screwdriver and/or small Torx screwdriver—as low as T8 or even T6—some things to add to your computer repair toolkit!

> **Note**
>
> ESD can occur when two objects with different voltages come into contact with each other.

Try to document the process as you go. Write down what you see and how and where cables and screws were attached. Also make note of how devices were oriented before they were removed. Label any parts that you remove for easier identification later on. Take pictures with your smartphone or other camera as you go through the disassembly process. If available, refer to the manufacturer's documentation that came with the laptop.

When you are done with the repair, verify that the new keyboard works by testing every key using Notepad or another text editor or word processor and by testing Fn-enabled keys as well.

If a user needs access to a laptop right away (before it can be repaired), a temporary solution would be to connect a USB external keyboard. This *should* be recognized automatically by the operating system, though a BIOS/UEFI configuration might be necessary.

Touchpad

Whereas a PC uses a mouse, the laptop uses a built-in pointing device. The bulk of laptops come with a pointing device known as a touchpad. By gliding a finger across the touchpad surface, a user can move the cursor on the screen. Touchpads might also come with two buttons that take the place of a mouse's buttons. In portable computing lingo, the word "click" is replaced with the word "tap." In addition to using the buttons, many touchpad surfaces can also be tapped or double-tapped upon, just by tapping with the finger. Touchpads can be replaced, though it is uncommon to do so; they are often connected by two cables similar to the flex cable that connects the keyboard. However, you might have to remove other devices first to get at the touchpad. You might also have to work from the bottom and from the top of the laptop; this depends on the brand of laptop. Some touchpad buttons can be replaced the way keys on the keypads are. Touchpads are sometimes referred to as track pads as well.

Now and again you will encounter users reporting that when they type on the keyboard, the mouse pointer scrolls across the screen. This is sometimes referred to as a "ghost cursor" or "pointer drift." It could be because a part of the user's hand, or even the user's sleeve, is brushing against the touchpad. To remedy this, pointing devices can be turned off within the operating system, usually through the laptop manufacturer's software. Watch out for situations in which the entire device might have been disabled or perhaps just the pad portion of the touchpad was disabled. It can be disabled in the OS and with a function key (Fn) on some laptops. It's also possible to disable tapping capability of the touchpad while still allowing movement of the cursor. In rarer cases, a ghost cursor occurring while working in the operating system or in an application can be caused by an incorrect or bad device driver (a device driver is a small program that controls the device and acts as a software interface between the device and the OS) If you suspect a driver issue, then reinstall or update the mouse/touchpad driver, the video driver, and update the OS as well,

> **Note**
>
> Another type of pointing device is the pointing stick, known within Lenovo laptops as the TrackPoint. This device manifests itself as a smaller rubber cap (that looks like an eraser head) just above the B key or as two buttons that work essentially the same as a touchpad's buttons.

Of course, external mice can be connected to the laptop or its docking station as well. These would be connected to USB ports or could be wireless devices.

Hard Drives

Hard drives will fail; it's just a matter of when. Laptop hard drives are even more susceptible to failure than desktop computers due to their mobility and the bumps and bruises that laptops regularly sustain.

Many laptops come with Serial ATA (SATA) hard drives which incorporate two connectors—a 7-pin data connector and a 15-pin power connector. The bulk of the hard drives in laptops are 2.5 inches wide, though ultra-small laptops and other small portable devices might use a hard drive as small as 1.8 inches. See Figure 1.2 for an example of a 2.5-inch SATA solid-state drive (SSD). Note the smaller data connector and larger power connector.

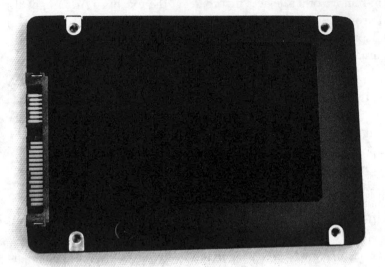

FIGURE 1.2   **A typical 2.5-inch SSD**

SATA drives are broken down into three categories: SSD, magnetic disk, and hybrid. An SSD is one that has no moving parts and generally uses NAND-based flash memory to store data. A magnetic-based drive uses an actual mechanical disk and an arm with a read/write head to store data to the disk. A hybrid drive combines the two by using a magnetic disk as well as SSD cache memory—so it combines the capacity of a magnetic disk with the performance of an SSD. We discuss the various types of hard drives in Chapter 10, "RAM and Storage."

> **ExamAlert**
>
> Know that laptop hard drive types include SSD, magnetic disk, and hybrid. Also, be aware they have either 2.5- or 1.8-inch form factors.

One of the ways to make an older laptop run faster is to replace the hard drive. For example, if the laptop contains an SATA magnetic disk, you might opt to replace it with an SSD or perhaps a hybrid drive, or perhaps even an M.2 drive, if the laptop has an M.2-compatible slot on its motherboard. These options can offer greater data transfer rates as well as improvements in overall system efficiency. Upgrades such as these might also need to be performed if the original drive fails. At that point, you'll probably need to rescue some data from the original drive.

> **Note**
>
> Be careful with M.2 drives. They create a lot of heat, and in a laptop's tight environment it could lead to overheating.

Of course, to rescue data from a hard drive, you first must remove it. Laptop hard drives can be accessed from one of three places. The first, and maybe the most common, is from the bottom, by removing either the entire bottom cover or an access panel. The second is from underneath the keyboard. And the third is from the side of the laptop where the drive is located in some kind of caddy. Those last two options are much less common. In any of the three scenarios, there is usually some kind of rubber molding or bracket that has to be removed or unscrewed from the drive when replacing it. Hold on to this item for the new hard drive. In any case, I employ antistatic measures and *use care* when working around any connections inside the laptop—they are more fragile than their PC counterparts.

Memory

Laptops use double data rate (DDR) memory that in laptops it's miniaturized and is known as a small outline dual inline memory module (SODIMM). Table 1.1 shows the four types of SODIMMs and their pin formats you should know for the exam. Different versions of SODIMM memory are not compatible. For example, normally you can't put a DDR4 SODIMM into a DDR3 SODIMM slot. SODIMM DDR speeds are similar to their PC equivalents. We'll discuss the different types of DDR and their speeds and data transfer rates in Chapter 10.

TABLE 1.1 **SODIMM Versions**

Memory Type	Module Format
DDR	200-pin
DDR2	200-pin
DDR3	204-pin
DDR4	260-pin

ExamAlert

Memorize the types of SODIMMs and understand the pin format differences between them and DIMMs.

Random-access memory (RAM) has a center notch that helps to orient the RAM during installation. This notch will usually be in a different location depending on the SODIMM version.

Before installing any new RAM, check compatibility. Remember to consult the laptop's documentation to find out exactly how much RAM and which type of RAM the laptop will accept. When you have purchased compatible RAM, installing it to a laptop is usually quite simple. RAM is often located on the bottom of the laptop, underneath an access cover. In other laptops, it might be underneath the keyboard or there could be one stick of RAM under the keyboard and a second (usually for add-ons) under an access cover underneath the laptop. Consult your laptop's documentation for the exact location of the RAM compartment. Table 1.2 shows the steps involved in adding RAM to a laptop. Keep in mind that SODIMMs, and their corresponding memory boards, are more delicate than their counterparts in a desktop computer.

TABLE 1.2 **Installing a SODIMM to a Laptop**

Step	Procedure
1. Prepare the laptop for surgery!	Shut down the laptop, unplug it, and disconnect the battery. Then employ ESD prevention measures.
2. Review your documentation.	Review your documentation to find out where RAM is located. For this step, assume that the RAM can be added to an area underneath the laptop.
3. Locate the memory.	Quite often you will need to remove the bottom cover of the laptop. Be ready to document and store the many screws somewhere safe. On older laptops there might be two screws that you need to remove to open a memory compartment door. Often, these are captive screws and will stay in the door. But if they are not, store them in a safe place and label them.
4. Remove the old RAM.	If you are upgrading, remove the current RAM by pushing both of the clips out. The RAM should pop up. If it does not, lift the RAM at a 45-degree angle. Gently remove the RAM, holding it by the edges.

Step	Procedure
5. Insert the RAM.	There could be one or two slots for RAM. One of them might already be in use. Many laptops support multichannel memory. If this is the case and you install a second memory module, the best option is to select one that is identical to the first, though that is not always necessary.
	Insert the memory module at a 45-degree angle into the memory slot, aligning the notch with the keyed area of the memory slot. Press the module into the slot; then press the module down toward the circuit board until it snaps into place (GENTLY!). Two clips (one on either side) lock into the notches in the side of the memory module. Press down again to make sure it is in place. See Figure 1.3 for an example of an installed SODIMM. Note the locking clips holding the memory module into place.
6. Close the laptop and then test.	Attach the cover (or compartment). You might want to wait on screwing it in until you test the laptop. Then boot the computer into the BIOS/UEFI and make sure it sees the new memory module(s). Finally, boot into the operating system and make sure that it sees the new total amount of RAM, and then verify whether applications work properly.

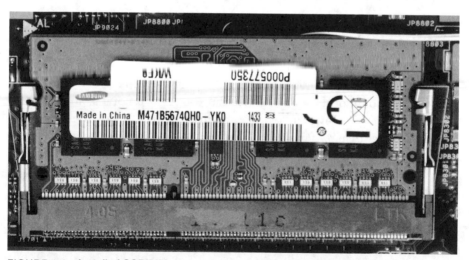

FIGURE 1.3   Installed SODIMM

Sometimes upgraded memory fails to be identified by the BIOS/UEFI. This usually means that the memory was not installed properly. Turn off the computer, reseat the RAM modules, and then reboot. This usually fixes the problem.

Occasionally a laptop fails to boot, emitting a series of continuous beeps. This could be due to faulty memory. However, it could simply be that the memory contacts are dirty. As mentioned before, laptops are often mistreated and are used in a variety of environments. Pop the memory hatch and inspect the RAM modules. If they require cleaning, use compressed air or try Stabilant 22 or similar cleaners. Plug the modules back in and verify functionality by rebooting the system several times. If they still don't work, try swapping out the RAM with known good modules.

Smart Card Readers

A smart card reader is a device that connects to a laptop, often via USB, that is designed to accept smart cards used for authentication of the user: including magnetic stripe cards, optical cards, or microprocessor cards. Some of these cards (and readers) are certified for usage with the Federal Information Processing Standard (FIPS) Publication 201—a United States federal government standard that specifies strong Personal Identity Verification (PIV) requirements. We'll talk more about these concepts in Chapter 31, "Physical and Logical Security."

Optical Drives

As of 2015 or so, it has been uncommon to see optical drives built into laptops. A few have them, or they might use an external USB-based drive if necessary. Due to the amount of abuse a typical laptop receives, it is not uncommon to see an optical drive fail. However, optical disc drives are usually easy to replace on a laptop—easier than on a desktop PC, in fact. Most of the time there will be a couple screws on the bottom of the laptop that hold the optical drive in place. When removed, the drive can be slid out of the side of the laptop. Check your laptop's documentation for a compatible replacement (or upgrade), or check the bottom of the drive for part numbers that you can use to find a replacement drive online. We'll talk about optical drives more in Chapter 10.

Communications

Communicating quickly and efficiently with other computers and wireless devices is key in business and home environments. To do so, laptops use a variety of different devices, including the following:

> ▶ **Wired and wireless networking:** Most laptops today come equipped with wired Ethernet and Wi-Fi to connect to a local area network (LAN) or a wireless local area network (WLAN). The wired connection presents

itself as an RJ45 port and can typically transfer data at 1000 Mbps, auto-negotiating its speed to the network it is connected to. Wireless networking connections are made with an internal Mini PCIe card that can potentially connect to 802.11ac, n, g, and b networks. It is also possible to connect wired or wireless network adapters to USB ports or on older systems, to ExpressCard slots. Otherwise, these technologies work the same on a laptop as they do on a desktop computer. For more information on wired and wireless LAN technologies, see Chapter 5 through Chapter 8. There is often a WLAN button (or Wi-Fi button) that can enable/disable the wireless adapter. It will often share a function key. Keep this in mind when troubleshooting. If this is disabled, the laptop cannot connect wirelessly, even if the device is enabled in the operating system. If a wireless adapter is enabled but is detecting a weak signal even though it is in close proximity to the wireless access point, check the antenna and make sure it is connected and/or screwed in properly. Many laptops use proprietary software for the configuration of wireless network connections instead of using the built-in Windows WLAN AutoConfig program. In some cases, it might be easier to disable the proprietary application and use Windows instead.

ExamAlert

If the laptop can't connect to the wireless network, try pressing the Wi-Fi button, either associated with a function key, or a standalone button near the keyboard.

▶ **Bluetooth:** Bluetooth modules enable a laptop to connect to other Bluetooth devices, such as headsets and phones, over short distances, thus joining or creating a personal area network (PAN). A Bluetooth module might be included inside the laptop as an individual card or as a combo Bluetooth/WLAN card. External USB and ExpressCard Bluetooth adapters and remote controls are also available. For more information on Bluetooth, see Chapter 3, "Smartphones, Tablets, and Other Mobile Devices." Many laptops come with WLAN and Bluetooth capabilities; however, the two technologies can possibly compete over frequencies. If the WLAN connection runs at 2.4 GHz, you might need to recommend that a user make use of only one technology at a time if possible. Function keys or individual buttons are often available on the laptop for enabling/disabling Wi-Fi and Bluetooth. If not, it can be done within the operating system; for example, in the Notification Area in Windows.

▶ **Cellular:** Wireless wide area network (WWAN) cellular connections can be done in a variety of ways. Telecommunications providers offer cellular connections via USB-based travel routers, and WAN ExpressCard technology, an older external expansion bus that you might see on legacy laptops; it comes in 34-mm and 54-mm wide form factors (known as /34 and /54). Some laptops are designed with built-in Mini PCIe or M.2 cellular modules.

> **ExamAlert**
>
> Know the various ways that a laptop could communicate with other computers, including wired and wireless Ethernet, Bluetooth, and cellular WAN connections.

Video

A laptop's video subsystem is composed of a screen and a video card, also known as a graphics processing unit (GPU). Common screens include LCD, LED, and OLED, and they are usually active-matrix, flat-panel displays. Active-matrix means that each pixel of the screen is attached to a transistor and capacitor—each pixel maintains its state because it is driven by this circuitry. We'll discuss these screens more in Chapter 2, "Laptops, Part 2," and Chapter 13, "Peripherals and Power." The GPU is the processor for video. On laptop computers, namely more powerful laptops, it is a separate processor that has its own memory and possibly is situated upon its own circuit board; for example, a separate Mini PCIe card. Usually, these attach to the main board with two screws. However, the GPU can also be integrated with the motherboard. In some cases, it is part of the chipset and utilizes RAM as shared video memory.

A laptop screen could be damaged in a variety of ways. Sometimes, the damage could be minor, perhaps caused by the keyboard scratching against the display due to worn or missing rubber bumpers or rubber screw cover inserts. Simply attach new ones with adhesive or by snapping them into place. But the damage could be more extensive. For example, you might see a crack in the screen or you might notice a portion of the screen doesn't display properly. Or you might notice dark, irregular lines that run the width of the display in all video modes. If any of these are the case, the screen will have to be replaced.

Laptop video screens require some work to replace. Often, they have some kind of plastics involved such as frames or bezels. These have to be removed with a shim and other tools. The screen might connect to the main portion of the laptop via a power connector and flex connector, or a combination connector. It's important to be careful when disassembling LCD displays because of the charge that is contained in the inverter. We discuss the inverter more in Chapter 2.

But sometimes, the issue has nothing to do with the screen. In some cases, it could be due to the LCD cutoff switch (also known as a lid switch). This is a switch or other mechanism designed to turn off the display when it is depressed or moved, meaning when the laptop is closed. If it fails, it could either leave the screen on all the time, even when the laptop is closed, or it might cause the screen to turn off when the laptop is open. In this scenario, you would need to locate the switch (be it a button or slider), which might require that you disassemble the laptop and screen. Once you find the cutoff switch, test it with a multimeter to verify that it is working properly.

Laptops' active-matrix screens are sometimes set to run at one specific resolution (for example, 1366×768, or 1920×1080). If the resolution is changed to something else, the laptop usually scales the resolution, making the picture unclear and perhaps not even fitting on the screen correctly. Or, in the worst-case scenario, the laptop displays a blank screen. Because of this, you're pretty much stuck with the default resolution. Sometimes this default resolution can be a bit tough on the eyes (for example, when the laptop's display runs at Full HD 1920×1080 but the screen size is only 14 inches). When users plan to use laptops for long periods of time, they should consider using laptops that have larger displays or perhaps external displays that are connected via HDMI, or another video port, or through the use of a port replicator/docking station.

> **ExamAlert**
>
> Remember, a laptop's video subsystem consists of a screen (example: LED) and a video card (example: Mini PCIe card).

Power

Laptops are designed to run on battery power, but laptops can run only several hours on these batteries. So, the laptop comes with an AC power adapter to plug into an AC outlet; these adapters should always be carried with the laptop. How many times have I heard users who forgot their power bricks! Recommend to users that they always put the AC adapter back in the laptop case.

The worst-case scenario is when a laptop won't turn on! Without power, a user can't do anything. When troubleshooting power problems, envision the entire chain of power in your mind (or write it on paper); from the AC outlet to the AC adapter to the DC jack and all the way to the Power button. There are a few things you can check if it appears that the laptop is not getting any power.

▶ **Check the power LED:** Check the power light on the AC adapter. If this is off, not only will the laptop not get power, but the battery won't charge as well. Most laptops also have a power LED on the front of the case, or just above the keyboard. If this lights up, then maybe it isn't a power problem at all. For example, the user might start the laptop, see nothing on the display, and determine that the laptop has no power—when, in reality, it is a display issue.

> **Note**
>
> Many laptops also have hard drive and wireless LEDs, which can tell you more about the status of the laptop without seeing anything on the screen. Use them!

▶ **Check connections:** Verify that the laptop is firmly connected to the AC adapter and that the AC adapter is firmly connected to the AC outlet. Sometimes a user presses the Power button, expecting the laptop to start, without realizing that the battery is discharged and that the AC adapter is not connected. Also, check for damage. Inspect the DC jack that is on the side of the laptop—it is soldered onto the motherboard of the laptop. Make sure it isn't loose or damaged. Sometimes the battery only charges if the output cord of the AC adapter is held at an angle— probably because the laptop was transported while the output cord was plugged into the laptop, causing damage to the DC jack. Also make sure that the user is attempting to connect to the actual DC jack, and not an audio port, security port, or something else. The DC jack is labeled (often underneath the laptop) with an image similar to Figure 1.4. In the figure you can see that there is a negative sign, and then a dot connecting to a positive sign. That means that the DC jack uses positive polarity, which is the most common, and the plug that is part of the AC adapter must conform to that. (Negative polarity would simply have the plus and minus signs reversed.) Also, it shows that it requires 19-V DC. This must be exact, which is covered by using the correct adapter—explained in the following bullet.

DC IN 19V

FIGURE 1.4 **DC jack diagram showing positive polarity**

▶ **Make sure the user uses the right power adapter:** Swapping power adapters between two different laptops is not recommended, but users try to do it all the time. Two different laptop models made by the same manufacturer might use what appear to be similar power adapters, with only one or two volts separating them; however, the laptop usually won't power on with that "slightly" different power adapter. Laptop AC adapters are known as fixed-input power supplies, meaning they work at a specific voltage. The adapter is not meant to be used on another model laptop. Unfortunately, a user might have plugged in the incorrect power adapter; the laptop then worked fine for 4 or 5 hours because it was actually running on battery power, but the user might not have noticed the laptop wasn't charging, even though the system should have notified the user when the battery was low (and critical). If you do suspect that an AC power adapter is faulty, consider testing your theory by swapping it out with an *identical* power adapter. That means that it was made for that specific laptop and that the voltage and amp ratings are exact. Chances are, a company will have extra power adapters or will have several laptops of the same make and model. Another power adapter–related issue could be that the user is trying to work in another country. To do this, the user needs an auto-switching AC adapter, meaning that it can switch from 120 to 240 VAC automatically. Some laptops do not come with auto-switching AC adapters, but after-market versions can be purchased for many models of laptops. Remember that an additional adapter might be necessary to make the actual connection to the AC outlet in foreign countries.

▶ **Check the battery and voltage:** It might sound silly, but check if the battery has been removed for some odd reason. Also, check if the battery is fully inserted into the battery compartment. There is usually a locking mechanism that should hold the battery in place. Finally, test the battery's voltage. Batteries last a finite amount of time. They can be recharged (known as cycles) by the laptop only so many times before failure. After a few to several years, the battery won't hold a charge any longer or will lose charge quickly. In some cases, you can try discharging and recharging the battery a few times to "stimulate" it, but in most scenarios, an extremely short battery life means that the battery must to be replaced. An old or failing battery can cause the system to overheat or could cause operating system freeze-ups or slow performance. In general, lithium-ion batteries last longer when the laptop is operated and stored at the right temperature ranges. Acceptable operating range for laptops is from 50–95°F (10–35°C), and acceptable storage ranges are from –4 to 140°F (–20 to 60°C). Watch out for swollen batteries, which could be caused by age, overcharging, or manufacturer defect. If it is user-removable, use great caution in attempting to remove it and be sure not to puncture it. Store it in a dark, cool container until you can recycle it. If it is a non-user-serviceable battery, bring the device to the nearest authorized repair center and, as before, keep the entire device within a cool container that light cannot get to.

> **Note**
>
> For more information on how to prolong lithium-ion batteries (the most common laptop battery), visit https://batteryuniversity.com/index.php/learn/article/how_to_prolong_lithium_based_batteries. It's a great site, by the way, if you work with mobile devices on a regular basis.

▶ **Check whether standby, sleep/suspend, or hibernate mode has failed:** If users regularly put their laptops into standby or hibernate modes, they could encounter issues once in a while. In some cases, the Power button needs to be held down for several seconds to reboot the machine out of a failed power-down state. This might have to be done with the battery removed. If either of these modes failed, check within the OS for any relevant information and possibly turn off hibernation and/or standby mode until the situation has been rectified. (On a slightly different note, sometimes laptops take a long time to come out of standby mode and it's not necessarily an issue with standby, it's a case of the lid switch being stuck. It looks like a power issue, but it's a simple hardware fix.)

▶ **Reconnect the Power button:** In rare cases, the Power button might have been disconnected from the system board, or a new one is required because the button mechanism failed. To fix this, the laptop must be opened, but often the power button is easily accessible once you do so.

▶ **Discharge the motherboard:** Another uncommon scenario is when there is a charge stored in some capacitance somewhere in the laptop—most likely the motherboard. This can cause the laptop to fail to turn on. LEDs do not light, even when it is plugged in. It could be due to a power surge or other irregularity, or an issue with the laptop's power system. You can discharge the motherboard by disconnecting the power, removing the battery, and then pressing and holding the Power button for 30 seconds or so. This will remove any residual voltage from the motherboard, and depending on the laptop, might reset some BIOS settings, which would have to be reconfigured later. Some people call this the *30-second trick* (could be less or more), or a laptop *hard reset*, though that is not really an accurate term. What you are really doing here is discharging the motherboard, but be ready for other terms used by various technicians in the field.

▶ **Check the AC outlet:** Make sure the AC outlet that the user has plugged the laptop into is supplying power. A simple test would be to plug a lamp, clock, or other device into the outlet, but a more discerning and safer test would be to use a receptacle tester or circuit analyzer. For more information on testing AC outlets, see Chapter 13.

ExamAlert

Power is crucial! When troubleshooting, go through the entire power system step by step; including the power button, battery, DC jack, AC adapter, and AC outlet.

However, you can't run on batteries forever! So, Windows includes alarms that can be set to notify the user when the battery is getting low and real low (known as critical). These alarms are set in Power Options. We'll discuss that more in the software sections of this book.

Speaker

Most laptops come with two speakers, allowing for stereo reproduction of sounds and music. This makes them output devices. These speakers are small, but through clever engineering of the speaker housings and the plastic frame of the laptop, they can offer a surprising amount of volume and bass (that is to the average user, not the audiophile).

Generally, each speaker housing is fastened with two screws, and is wired to a single 7-pin connector or something similar. It is uncommon, but sometimes the connector can be shaken loose, resulting in no sound or intermittent sound. The good news is that this connector is often easily accessible once the laptop's bottom cover is removed. However, disconnecting it can prove to require some work—a super-thin but strong plastic shim is best for the job. If both speakers need to be replaced or upgraded, it is fairly easy to do. Remember to purchase speakers made for that specific model of laptop. Also, you might find that the speaker wires are fastened to the motherboard with some type of sticky tape. Attempt to reuse it if at all possible. However, sometimes it is simply worn out, or has had coffee or some other liquid spilled on it, and needs to be replaced. Consider adding a roll of some kind of heat-resistant, nonconductive tape to your toolkit. Good candidates among the variety of types available are cotton friction tape and Kapton (which has several other uses inside of mobile devices). In a pinch, heat-resistant, electrical tape can work also. Steer clear of Scotch tape, duct tape, and other tapes you might find lying around the house or office. They could melt over time, causing damage to the laptop. This goes for PCs as well.

System Board and CPU

As mentioned before, the worst thing that could happen to a laptop is that it doesn't start. Let me rephrase: that would be the worst thing that could happen to a *user*. The worst thing for a tech would be if the system board failed. This is because it would require almost a complete disassembly of the unit to repair it, a process that is time-consuming and requires heavy documentation to get all the parts back together properly when done. CPU replacement (and upgrading) is not quite as difficult but still requires removing at least the keyboard and likely a few other components that will be in the way. Documentation is still important when replacing a CPU.

Sometimes a system board's lithium battery needs replacement. This is done in the same manner as it is within a desktop computer; however, you need to remove the keyboard, and perhaps other devices and connections, to gain access to the battery. Some laptops come with the same CR2032 battery that desktop models use; however, a few laptops (and other handheld devices) come with a rechargeable system board lithium battery that has a shelf life of up to 10 years. Other laptops simply make use of the main lithium-ion battery.

Before you do decide to take this type of plunge into a laptop, one thing to keep in mind is that a lot of companies will purchase 1- to 3-year warranties for the laptops they use. Even though there is a cost involved in purchasing warranties, it is usually the wise choice. If the laptop did fail, the alternative would be to have a technician spend several hours (at least) disassembling, testing, replacing, and reassembling the laptop—all of which could cost the company more money in man hours than it would have cost to just purchase the warranty. Warranties are a type of insurance, and this type of insurance is usually acceptable to a company. So, check your company's policies and procedures first before doing these types of repairs.

Before removing a CPU or other internal components, employ ESD prevention measures. If the CPU is surface-mounted, you cannot remove it. If it has failed, the entire system board would need to be removed. But if it is socketed with either a Pin Grid Array (PGA) or Ball Grid Array (BGA), it can be removed. Usually there is some kind of locking arm mechanism that must be unlocked to remove the CPU from the socket. Upgrade ranges for laptop CPUs are usually quite narrow. If a CPU fails, it is usually best to install an identical CPU. If you do plan to upgrade a CPU, check the documentation carefully to make sure that the exact model laptop (and its motherboard) can support the faster CPU. After removing the CPU, be sure to place it in an antistatic bag with the pins facing up. When installing CPUs, employ the same delicate procedure as you would with a desktop PC. These CPUs require no force to insert them into the socket. We'll discuss CPUs more in Chapter 12, "CPUs."

Fans

Laptops need to exhaust hot air just like PCs do. To accomplish this, a laptop uses a fan that blows the hot air out of the system. Often, the CPU will have a heat sink that leads to the fan's airway or conduit, just past the fan, helping to cool the CPU. The fan and the conduit can get clogged easily—more easily than PC fans, given the abuse that laptops receive and the various environments in which they may be used. Indicators of a clogged fan include a clicking sound or, worse, an unusually high-pitched noise. The first thing to do in this case is to use a vacuum to suck dust and debris out of the fan slots. Be sure not to blow air into the system, and I recommend doing this outside; you never know what will come out. If this doesn't work, consider checking whether something is obstructing the fan. Use a penlight to look through the fan and inside the system if possible. If not, you'll have to open the system to see what is causing the problem. If necessary, while the laptop is open, blow compressed air through the fan slot and out of the computer. Be careful not to touch the compressed air canister against anything in the laptop, and do not use a vacuum inside the laptop. The worst-case scenario is that you would have to replace the fan.

> **ExamAlert**
>
> If the fan makes a high-pitched noise, try using a vacuum (from the outside) or blowing compressed air (from the inside).

Wrap-up of Chapter 1

That wraps up this first chapter. I recommend you review the ExamAlerts and any notes that you have taken before you continue to the Cram Quiz. Do this for the rest of the book as well.

What follows is your first cram quiz. This will help to reinforce the concepts you learned. Good luck!

Cram Quiz

Answer these questions. The answers follow the last question. If you cannot answer
these questions correctly, consider reading this chapter again until you can.

1. What kinds of hard drives are used by laptops? (Select all that apply.)

   ○ **A.** SSD

   ○ **B.** M.2

   ○ **C.** Magnetic disk

   ○ **D.** DVD-ROM

2. What is the module format for a stick of SODIMM DDR4 RAM?

   ○ **A.** 200-pin

   ○ **B.** 204-pin

   ○ **C.** 260-pin

   ○ **D.** 1.8-inch

3. You just added a second memory module to a laptop. However, after rebooting
   the system, the OS reports the same amount of memory as before. What should
   you do next?

   ○ **A.** Replace both memory modules.

   ○ **B.** Run Windows Update.

   ○ **C.** Replace the motherboard.

   ○ **D.** Reseat the laptop memory.

4. Which of the following are ways that a laptop can communicate with other
   computers? (Select all that apply.)

   ○ **A.** Bluetooth

   ○ **B.** WLAN

   ○ **C.** DC jack

   ○ **D.** Cellular WAN

5. Which of the following are possible reasons that a laptop's keyboard might fail
   completely? (Select the two best answers.)

   ○ **A.** A key is stuck.

   ○ **B.** A ribbon cable is disconnected.

   ○ **C.** The user spilled coffee on the laptop.

   ○ **D.** The keyboard was disabled in the Device Manager.

6. A user doesn't see anything on his laptop's screen. He tries to use AC power and thinks that the laptop is not receiving any. Which of the following are two possible reasons for this? (Select the two best answers.)

   ○ **A.** He is using an incorrect AC adapter.

   ○ **B.** The AC adapter is not connected to the laptop.

   ○ **C.** Windows won't boot.

   ○ **D.** The battery is dead.

7. One of your customers reports that she walked away from her laptop for 30 minutes. When she returned, the display was very dim. She increased the brightness setting and moved the mouse but to no effect. What should you do first?

   ○ **A.** Replace the LCD screen.

   ○ **B.** Check the operating system for corruption.

   ○ **C.** Connect an external monitor to verify that the video card works.

   ○ **D.** Check whether the laptop is now on battery power.

8. Which are the most common laptop hard drive form factors? (Select two.)

   ○ **A.** 5.1

   ○ **B.** 2.5

   ○ **C.** 7.1

   ○ **D.** 1.8

9. You are helping a customer with a laptop issue. The customer said that two days ago the laptop was accidentally dropped while it was charging. You observe that the laptop will not turn on and that it is connected to the correct power adapter. Which of the following is the most likely cause?

   ○ **A.** The battery

   ○ **B.** The power adapter

   ○ **C.** The hard drive

   ○ **D.** The DC jack

   ○ **E.** The BIOS/UEFI

Cram Quiz Answers

1. **A, B, and C.** Solid-state drives (SSDs), M.2 drives, and magnetic disk drives are all found on laptops. Which drive the laptop uses will depend on its age and whether or not it has been upgraded. DVD-ROM drives are not hard drives, they are optical drives, and as of 2015 or so, are not commonly found on laptops.

2. **C.** DDR4 SODIMM modules have 260 pins. DDR (known as DDR1) and DDR2 are 200-pin. DDR3 is 204-pin. 1.8-inch is the size associated with smaller hard drives used in some laptops.

3. **D.** The next step you should take is to reseat the memory. SODIMMs can be a bit tricky to install. They must be firmly installed, but you don't want to press too hard and damage any components. If the laptop worked fine before the upgrade, you shouldn't have to replace the modules or the motherboard. Windows Update will not find additional RAM.

4. **A, B, and D.** Some of the methods that laptops use to communicate with other computers include: Bluetooth, WLAN, and cellular WAN wireless connections, plus wired connections like Ethernet (RJ45) and, for older laptops, dial-up (RJ11). The DC jack is the input on the laptop that accepts power from the AC adapter.

5. **B and C.** A laptop's keyboard could fail due to a disconnected or loose keyboard ribbon cable. It could also fail if a user spilled coffee on the laptop, by being dropped on the ground, and so on. One stuck key will not cause the entire keyboard to fail, and on most laptops, the keyboard cannot be disabled in the Device Manager. It can be uninstalled, but not disabled.

6. **A and B.** An incorrect adapter will usually not power a laptop. The adapter used must be exact. And of course, if the laptop is not plugged in properly to the adapter, it won't get power. Windows doesn't play into this scenario. And if the battery was dead, it could cause the laptop to not power up, but only if the AC adapter was also disconnected; the scenario states that the user is trying to use AC power.

7. **D.** It could be that the laptop is now on battery power, which is usually set to a dimmer display and shorter sleep configuration. This indicates that the laptop is not getting AC power from the AC outlet for some reason. The battery power setting is the first thing you should check; afterward, start troubleshooting the AC adapter, cable, AC outlet, and so on. It's too early to try replacing the display; try not to replace something until you have ruled out all other possibilities. A dim screen is not caused by OS corruption. There's no need to plug in an external monitor; you know the video adapter is working, it's just dim.

8. **B and D.** The bulk of the hard drives in laptops are 2.5 inches wide, though ultra-small laptops and other small portable devices might use a hard drive as small as 1.8 inches. 5.1 and 7.1 refer to speaker surround sound systems, not hard drive form factors.

9. **D.** The DC jack was probably damaged when the laptop was dropped. That's because it was plugged in (charging) and it probably fell on the plug that connects to the DC jack (which is easily damaged on many laptops, by the way). The customer probably used the laptop until the battery became discharged before noticing that the laptop wouldn't take a charge anymore—that's why it won't turn on at all. So the battery is probably not the issue. A power adapter can be damaged, but the DC-in jack is more easily damaged. The hard drive and the BIOS normally will not affect whether the laptop will turn on.

CHAPTER 2
Laptops, Part 2

This chapter covers the following A+ 220-1001 exam objectives:

▶ 1.2 – Given a scenario, install components within the display of a laptop.

▶ 1.3 – Given a scenario, use appropriate laptop features.

In this chapter, we get into the laptop display and some of the common features of a laptop. It's important to understand the types of displays available to you, as well as what an inverter is, and how to handle it properly. You'll also learn about additional components such as Wi-Fi antennas, webcams, touchscreens, and special function keys. We'll close it out with add-on connectivity and security for laptops. Let's go!

1.2 – Given a scenario, install components within the display of a laptop

ExamAlert

Objective 1.2 focuses on the following concepts: LCD, OLED, WiFi antenna connector/placement, webcam, microphone, inverter, and digitizer/touchscreen.

Note

The CompTIA A+ objectives list important concepts that you need to know for the exam, but the list is not *finite*. By this, I mean that there might be other associated technologies that are not listed, but which you might be tested on. So, at times, I add content to this book that goes further than the listed objectives. Be ready to study beyond the objectives to fully prepare for the exam, *and* for the real world.

For the exam, you should understand the differences between the various laptop display types, including LCD, LED, and OLED. Going further, you need to know the basics about the display's inverter and digitizer technology. Finally, be sure to know how other components are installed that might be located in the display area of a laptop; for instance, webcams, microphones, and Wi-Fi antennas.

Display Types

A laptop might use one of a few types of displays, depending on the age and the price of the laptop. These include LCD, LED, and OLED.

▶ **LCD:** The liquid-crystal display (LCD) is a flat-panel display that consists of two sheets of polarizing material surrounding a layer of liquid-crystal solution. It connects to the motherboard by way of a flex ribbon cable, or an all-in-one power/signal cable, and gets its power from an inverter board. Most of today's LCD screens are thin-film transistor (TFT) active-matrix displays, meaning they have multiple transistors for each pixel. These transistors are contained within a flexible material and are located directly behind the liquid-crystal material. In general, LCDs generate a small amount of heat, and cause little in the way of interference and emissions. However, they use more electricity than newer types of displays because they utilize a high-powered bulb, quite often a cold cathode fluorescent lamp (CCFL).

▶ **LED:** Light-emitting-diode (LED) monitors utilize two-terminal electronic components known as diodes to display images. These diodes are red, green, and blue (RGB); the "primary" colors when it comes to computer monitors. They use less power than traditional LCDs and are therefore more efficient. LED monitors use a different backlight than traditional LCD monitors. Whereas the older LCD monitors use a CCFL as the illumination source, LED monitors use light-emitting diodes, which release photons; this process is known as *electroluminescence*. It is so much more energy efficient that you will find many hybrid designs known as LED-backlit LCDs. In that case, we are not using a CCFL, and instead utilize diodes but with an LCD screen.

▶ **OLED:** OLED stands for *organic* light-emitting diodes. The main advantage of OLED over LED is manufacturing cost; OLEDs can be printed onto just about any substrate using simple printing processes—and they can be incredibly small (even one per pixel), all lighting individually. The technology uses an organic compound to emit light in response to an electric current. OLED displays have the best black levels, but you might opt for LED if you are more concerned with brightness and some other specifications.

Inverter and Backlight

A typical laptop's LCD display incorporates a backlight and an inverter. The backlight is a bulb; for example, a CCFL. It emits light through the screen so that you can see the images that the computer is attempting to display. The inverter, or more accurately the *screen* inverter, is a device that converts direct current (DC) that comes from the motherboard into alternating current (AC) to be used by the display's backlight. This section focuses on LCDs because LEDs (and OLEDs) don't need an inverter—they are DC only by design—and don't use a CCFL or similar lamp.

> **ExamAlert**
>
> Know that a screen inverter's job is to convert DC voltage from the motherboard into AC voltage to be sent to the backlight.

The video display in laptops is integrated; however, while being a main feature of the portability of laptops, it can be a point of failure as well. Minor issues such as intermittent lines on the screen suggest that the display cable needs to be reconnected or replaced. However, complete display failures suggest a worse problem that will take longer to repair. Aside from a damaged screen, LCD display failures can be broken down into a couple categories: a damaged inverter or a worn-out backlight.

Damaged Inverter

To review, on a laptop with an LCD-based screen, the LCD is usually lit by a CCFL (basically a bulb); it is that LCD backlight which requires AC power. The backlight is driven by a high-voltage inverter circuit. Because the inverter runs at high voltage, and possibly at high temperatures, it is prone to failure. If the inverter fails, the display will go dark; however, an external monitor should work properly. Another possibility is that the backlight has failed. You can verify if it is an inverter/backlight issue by shining a flashlight directly at the screen (best in a dark room). When you do this, you should be able to make out the operating system! This means that the display is getting the video signal from the motherboard and the problem, most likely, is indeed the inverter or the backlight. If the display's cable that connects the LCD to the motherboard was loose or disconnected, or if the video adapter failed, then nothing would show up on the screen at all. The inverter circuit is usually situated on its own circuit board. The inverter often has two connectors: one for the high-voltage connection that leads to the power source and one for a cable that connects to the display. Disconnect these and carefully remove the inverter. As always, hold circuit boards by the edges and try not to touch any actual circuits or chips.

> **ExamAlert**
>
> Warning! The inverter should not be handled if the laptop is on! Be sure to turn off and unplug the laptop and remove the battery before removing an inverter.

Worn-Out Backlight

A laptop's backlight usually lasts a long time. However, at some point the lamp starts to wear out. You might notice a dimmer screen than before, or a reddish/pinkish hue to the screen, or maybe a loss of color. All of these things indicate the possibility of a worn-out lamp.

To replace either the inverter or the lamp, you need to disassemble the display. This usually means removing a screen bezel and taking the screen out, which gives way to those items. Be ready to have mobile device tools on hand, especially a thin but strong plastic shim. Consider purchasing a pry tool repair kit that includes a variety of shims, prying tools, and so on. Don't forget to keep a variety of small screwdrivers on hand.

> **Note**
>
> As you can guess, LED and OLED screens do not suffer as many failures as CCFL-based LCDs do, mainly because LEDs and OLEDs do not incorporate (or need) an inverter or a lamp. Consider that when making laptop purchases.

Digitizers and Touchscreens

A touchscreen—also known as a *digitizer* screen—is a screen that allows for tapping or writing on the screen. Many allow users to simply use their finger, while others also allow for the use of a stylus. A *stylus* is a writing tool, usually a thin plastic "pen" type of device used to take the place of a mouse; it enables you to tap and "write" on the digitizer with great accuracy.

These methods are widely used in smartphones, tablets, handheld computers, Chromebooks, and some laptops. For example, usually, when you sign for a package from a shipping company, you sign with a stylus on a touchscreen/digitizer. This takes the place of pencil and paper.

More accurately, the digitizer is the device that converts tapped or written impulses (analog) on the screen into instructions (digital) for the operating system to follow.

Removal of a touchscreen is much the same as a regular screen, as described in Chapter 1. There will be some disassembly required: screen bezels, plastics, and so on will have to be removed before the screen can be unscrewed and disconnected.

> **Note**
>
> Be prepared to have very small screwdrivers available. Laptop and mobile device repair kits often come with these types of screwdrivers. But, also be prepared for more "proprietary" types of screws that require fewer common screwdrivers.

There are also digitizer overlays that can be added on to a laptop screen. Generally, these touchscreens or kits are strapped on to the display with Velcro and connect via USB. Be ready to install custom drivers and perform touchscreen orientation and/or calibration.

Webcam and Microphone

Webcams are great for communication but sometimes they fail, and in some cases are considered a security vulnerability. In the case that the webcam has to be replaced, or just removed altogether, you can follow a few simple steps. First, employ antistatic measures. Then, remove the bezel from the display. The webcam module should then be visible above the display screen. Often, it is just connected with a small plug, and no screws or attachment of any kind. Next, *carefully* disconnect it with your shim or other thin prying tool (non-metal), place it in an antistatic bag, and label the bag for later use. Hold on to any tape or sticky material that keeps the webcam in place. Next, replace it with an identical part. Be very careful when connecting the power for the new webcam;

the plug is often delicate. Use (or reuse) tape to fasten the webcam in the right spot (if necessary). Then, attach the bezel to the display once again. Finally, test the webcam's video and audio with an application such as Windows' built-in Camera program.

Some people use tape to cover the webcam for security or privacy purposes, but depending on the policies of your organization, this might not be enough, and you will have to remove it altogether. Some companies offer filler items to fill the gap where the camera lens normally goes.

A laptop might have a function key that can disable the webcam. It can also be disabled in the operating system, so be sure to check those options before replacing the webcam.

The microphone on a laptop is often part of the webcam module (for example, to the left of the lens). So, removing the webcam module removes the microphone. The microphone could also be disabled in the operating system. For example, in Windows you would do this in the Recording tab of the Sound dialog box. As mentioned, some people use tape to cover the webcam, and the microphone openings as well; however, depending on the type of tape, it might muffle the recorded sound, but not eliminate it. Once again, for security purposes, it is better to disable the webcam altogether, or remove it.

> **ExamAlert**
>
> Know where to find the webcam and microphone within a laptop display, and know how to disable them.

Some companies opt to disable the webcam (and associated microphone) and instead use external USB-based webcams to achieve better security as well as better performance, while allowing the user to physically disconnect the webcam when it is not in use.

Wi-Fi Antenna Connector and Placement

Wi-Fi antennas are used to connect to a wireless network, also known as a wireless local area network (WLAN). Wi-Fi antennas can be found inside the laptop as well as externally. If the antenna is inside the laptop, it will usually be some type of module; either an M.2 card (as shown in Figure 2.1) or a PCI Express Mini Card (also known as a Mini PCIe card).

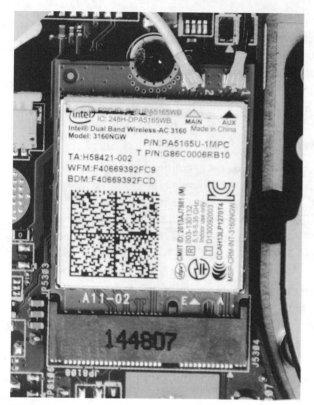

FIGURE 2.1   A typical internal Wi-Fi module using the M.2 form factor

ExamAlert

Be able to identify M.2 and Mini PCIe cards by name and by sight.

Usually, this module can be identified quickly by removing the bottom cover. It is often easily found, is connected to a slot, and is attached with either one screw (for M.2) or two screws (for Mini PCIe). M.2-based cards have up to 67 pins and might use the 2230 standard (22 × 30 mm) or the 1216 standard (12 × 16 mm), among others. The one in Figure 2.1 uses the 2230 standard. Full-size Mini PCIe cards are 30 × 50.95 mm and use a 52-pin edge connector. There are also half mini cards that are the same width, but are 26.8 mm long. This is also known as "half height," though this name isn't quite accurate. Both of these are about half the width of the older Mini PCI standard.

Be careful when installing an M.2 or Mini PCIe card; the contacts can be easily damaged. Place even pressure on both sides and press the card into the slot evenly so it goes in straight without any side-to-side movement. If a Wi-Fi antenna cable already exists in the laptop, reuse it by connecting the wire ends to the contacts on the card; usually there are two, one for Wi-Fi and one for Bluetooth (BT). If there is no antenna, install a new one, and route it through the laptop hinge and around the display as far as it can go. The longer the antenna, the better the reception.

Of course, external Wi-Fi adapters can be used, connecting to USB or an RJ45 port. If that is the case, then the antennas (if there are any) can be pointed in the direction that you desire. Or, the adapter can be moved from one USB port on one side of the laptop to another USB port on the other side. Just remember to consider using USB 3.0 or higher (blue ports or better). Also, keep the module away from any sources of interference. If it has actual antennas that you can move, first attempt a 90-degree angle, and then if that doesn't work, experiment! However, many external Wi-Fi modules that connect via USB are small, self-contained devices and the actual antenna is embedded inside. So, the choice of USB port is really your only option in that scenario when it comes to antenna placement.

Wi-Fi transmissions rely on the IEEE 802.11 standards, including 802.11ac, n, g, and b (going from fastest to slowest). We'll discuss those protocols more in Chapter 6, "SOHO Networks and Wireless Protocols."

Every Wi-Fi adapter has its own unique media access control (MAC) address, also known as a MAC ID. This identification number is usually printed on a sticker on the Wi-Fi adapter, and it is programmed into the ROM of the adapter. It differentiates the Wi-Fi adapter from all other network adapters on your network and around the world. Regardless of the type of network adapter, the MAC address is a 48-bit number, described in the hexadecimal numbering system; for example, 68-05-CA-2D-A4-B3. The number is also referred to as a physical address in the Windows command-line interface. If you have an internal Wi-Fi adapter, you can find out the MAC address in Windows by typing **ipconfig /all** in the Command Prompt or the PowerShell. (In macOS or Linux you can use **ifconfig** or **ip a**.) We'll discuss the MAC address more in Chapter 6.

Cram Quiz

Answer these questions. The answers follow the last question. If you cannot answer these questions correctly, consider reading this section again until you can.

1. Which kind of video technology do most laptop LCDs use?
   - ○ **A.** TFT active matrix
   - ○ **B.** Passive matrix
   - ○ **C.** OLED
   - ○ **D.** MAC ID

2. Which of the following uses an organic compound that emits light?
   - ○ **A.** TFT active matrix
   - ○ **B.** IPS
   - ○ **C.** OLED
   - ○ **D.** LCD
   - ○ **E.** LED

3. Which of the following are two possible reasons why a laptop's LCD suddenly went blank with no user intervention? (Select the two best answers.)
   - ○ **A.** Damaged inverter
   - ○ **B.** Damaged LCD
   - ○ **C.** Burned out backlight
   - ○ **D.** Incorrect resolution setting

4. Which of the following allows us to access a WLAN?
   - ○ **A.** LED
   - ○ **B.** Webcam
   - ○ **C.** Digitizer
   - ○ **D.** Stylus
   - ○ **E.** Wi-Fi card

Cram Quiz Answers

1. **A.** TFT active-matrix displays are the most common in laptops that use LCDs. Passive-matrix screens have been discontinued, but you *might* see an older laptop that utilizes this technology. OLED technology is a newer and different technology that is not based on TFT displays, but instead uses emissive display technology, meaning that each dot on the screen is illuminated by a separate

diode. OLED displays can, however, be passive-matrix or active-matrix controlled. The MAC ID is the hexadecimal address associated with a network adapter, such as a Wi-Fi adapter or network card.

2. **C.** OLED (organic light emitting diode) displays use an organic compound or film that emits light. TFT active matrix implies LCD, and neither of them uses organic compounds the way OLED does. In-plane switching (IPS) is a type of LCD technology that increases the available viewing angle compared to older technologies such as twisted-nematic (TN) matrix LCDs. However, IPS is generally considered inferior to OLED screens when it comes to brightness and contrast ratio when viewed from an angle. LED screens use a film and diodes, but not organically in the way that OLED does, and not at such a small size.

3. **A and C.** A damaged inverter or burned-out bulb could cause a laptop's display to go blank. You can verify whether the LCD is still getting a signal by shining a flashlight at the screen. A damaged LCD usually works to a certain extent and will either be cracked, have areas of the Windows interface missing, or show other signs of damage. An incorrect resolution setting can indeed make the screen suddenly go blank (or look garbled), but that scenario will most likely occur only if the user has changed the resolution setting—the question specifies with no user intervention.

4. **E.** A Wi-Fi card, also known as a Wi-Fi network adapter, allows us to connect to a WLAN (wireless local area network), which is essentially another name for a Wi-Fi network. LED is a type of display. A webcam is used to communicate visually and audibly with others, or to record oneself. A digitizer is the device that converts tapped or written impulses on a screen into digital information that the operating system can use. A stylus is a writing device used with a digitizer or touchscreen.

1.3 – Given a scenario, use appropriate laptop features

> **ExamAlert**
>
> **Objective 1.3** focuses on the following concepts: special function keys, on/off keys, docking stations, port replicators, physical laptop locks, cable locks, and rotating/removable screens.

We'll close out the laptop portion of this book with laptop features. A laptop will have many special function keys. Generally, these are secondary functions of the F1 through F12 keys, but in addition, they can be altogether separate buttons on the top of the laptop. These allow us to enable and disable and to adjust many of the important features of a laptop, such as enabling/disabling Wi-Fi, Bluetooth, or GPS; enabling/disabling the touchpad; and adjusting the brightness and volume. Docking stations and port replicators allow us to enhance laptops to be more like workstations, adding monitors, keyboards, and mice, as well as network connectivity and storage capabilities. A user might have a need for a more adjustable laptop, such as one that has a screen that rotates, flips over, or is removable. Or perhaps the user is interested in physical security. This section covers all of these laptop features and functionality that go beyond the core physical devices.

Special Function Keys

Some laptops have keyboards similar to the 101-key keyboard found on a PC and include a numeric keypad; these laptops are larger than most and are known as desktop replacements. However, most laptops are designed with a small form factor in mind, and this means a smaller keyboard. For example, the keyboard shown in Figure 1.1 in Chapter 1 has 86 keys. But as shown in Figure 2.2, a user has the option of using the Fn key (Function key). The Fn key is a modifier key used on most laptops. This is designed to activate secondary or *special* functions of other keys. For example, in Figure 2.2, the F12 key has the secondary function that turns the wireless connection on or off, but only if you press the Fn key at the same time you press the F12 key. To make it easier to read, Figure 2.2 breaks up the Fn key and the F1–F12 function keys, so you can see each of them better. But remember that the Fn key is usually toward the lower-left corner of the keyboard, and the function keys (F1–F12) are situated at the top of the keyboard.

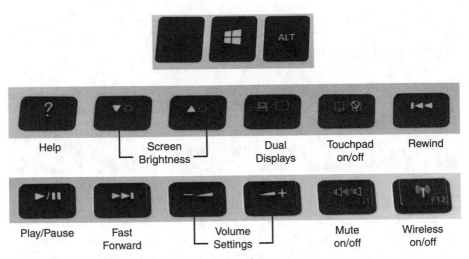

FIGURE 2.2 **Typical function keys and their tasks**

Using this method, much more functionality can be incorporated into the keyboard without the need for additional keys. This idea has since grown to include all kinds of controls; for example, using media player controls (play/pause/fast forward/rewind); putting the computer to sleep; enabling Bluetooth, the keyboard backlight, the touchpad, GPS, cellular connections, and airplane mode; adjusting screen orientation; and a variety of other functions, including enabling an external monitor. On this laptop, the F4 key seconds as a display toggle between the built-in display and an external monitor. Take a look at Figure 2.2 and attempt to identify what each of the function key images represents.

> **ExamAlert**
>
> Use the Fn key in combination with F1–F12 function keys to configure many things, including media options, Wi-Fi access, brightness, the touchpad, and an external monitor.

But all this key configuration is up to the manufacturer, and any key can be given a secondary function. That enables things like the numeric keypad, and the number lock key, which might be abbreviated as Num Lock, or num lk. (This could also be an individual key.) Sometimes, users forget about the Num Lock key, and when they try to type, strange garbled code comes out! This is because the numbers are sharing keys used by letters and symbols. Simply press the Num Lock key once to fix the problem. This is also common if the user works with an external keyboard at the office and disconnects it when leaving the office. However, today's operating systems and programs are pretty good at sensing things such as an enabled Num Lock or Caps Lock key.

> **ExamAlert**
>
> If available, press the Num Lock key to enable/disable the numeric keypad on a laptop. If the Num Lock indicator light is on, then the numeric key is enabled.

> **Note**
>
> Sometimes a laptop will have separate buttons near the Power button or elsewhere that aren't considered part of the regular function keys. These might be called special keys, special buttons, hot buttons, hotkeys, or corner keys. They might not function properly without a special keys driver. This driver can be separate from the main keyboard and touchpad drivers. It is a setup that is more common in older laptops. It can be a bit confusing because the F1–F12 keys are also referred to as *special* function keys sometimes. Be ready for the word "special" to be used with either type.

External Monitors

Most laptops have the capability of sending video signals to an external monitor. Some people refer to this technology as *screen switching* and/or extending the display. Most laptops come with an external connection (for example, HDMI or DisplayPort) for a second monitor or for a projector. When this monitor is plugged in, it can be enabled by pressing the display toggle key (otherwise known as the secondary monitor button). On the laptop used in this chapter, this can be done by pressing Fn+F4 simultaneously. However, on other brands of laptops, this key might be a different key than F4. The icon on the key usually looks like an open laptop with a monitor to its right. Normally, you have several options: display the desktop to the laptop, display the desktop to the external monitor, display a copy of the desktop to both screens, or "extend" the desktop across both monitors. These last two options are also known as using *dual displays*. In addition to using the display toggle key, you can configure your video for any of these scenarios in Windows, macOS, or Linux, which we'll discuss later in the book.

If the external monitor won't display anything, make sure that the cable is firmly connected to the external port, verify that the external monitor is plugged in and on, and then try cycling through the various video options by pressing the button several times, waiting a few seconds each time. Make sure you are holding down the Fn key while doing so. Finally, restart the computer if necessary. This can get a little trickier when you are using a projector as the second display. Sometimes, the projector might need time to warm up or might need to be configured via its on-screen display (OSD). You might also need a video adapter if your laptop's ports and projector's ports don't match up. Identify the projector's ports, and locate the projector's documentation for more details.

> **ExamAlert**
>
> If nothing shows up on an external display, then try cycling through the different display modes by using the Fn key and the appropriate special function key.

Docking Stations and Port Replicators

The docking station expands the laptop so that it can behave more like a desktop computer. By connecting the laptop to the docking station and adding a full-size keyboard, mouse, and monitor, the user doesn't actually touch the laptop any more except perhaps to turn it on. Some laptops can *hot dock*, meaning they can connect to the docking station while powered on. The docking station recharges the laptop's battery, and possibly a second battery, and has connections for video, audio, networking, and expansion cards. Docking stations might even have an optical disc drive, additional hard drive, and additional display and USB ports; it all depends on the brand and model. If all these extras aren't necessary, a user might require only a *port replicator*, which is a similar device but has only ports (for example, video, sound, network, and so on). Sometimes these are just referred to as docking stations as well.

> **ExamAlert**
>
> Note the difference: A laptop is placed or "docked" into a docking station. However, a port replicator is connected to the laptop simply to provide additional ports.

Rotating and Removable Screens

Some laptops come with rotating screens that not only open up, but can swivel from side to side. Other laptops (and some mobile devices) have screens that are removable altogether. While this can be great for the user that needs more mobility and/or the ability to use the device as a tablet, the probability of failure increases. In fact, any moving or connecting parts in any device will increase the chance of failure, such as a blank display or intermittent video issues. One of the things you can check is the connection itself. Perhaps it is dirty and needs to be blown out with compressed air, or perhaps a pin or connector is bent or damaged. In some cases, these ports can be fixed or replaced, but in many cases they have to be repaired by an authorized repair center. More reason to have good warranties and possibly insure the laptops in your organization. Remember to educate users on how to gently connect displays, and how to work with them properly to avoid these problems in the future.

While some laptops do incorporate these types of technologies, it is also common to see them integrated with mobile devices that aren't necessarily classified as laptops—and might be classified as hybrid laptops, or simply mobile devices. These devices can have rotating screens, or displays that can be folded completely over, or ones that can be removed altogether. In some cases, these devices are displays to which you can connect a keyboard. So, the lines get a bit blurred. We'll discuss other mobile devices such as tablets, smartphones, and so on, in Chapters 3 and 4.

Securing Laptops with Cable Locks

One way to physically secure a laptop is to use a cable lock. This works in a similar fashion to a bicycle lock (if you have ever used one). It consists of a very strong cable that is difficult to cut through—often galvanized, multi-stranded steel—with a lock on one end and a loop on the other. This allows the user to secure the laptop in a variety of ways, such as to a table, desk, and so on. Some companies incorporate metal loops or eye bolts near workstations to use with the cable lock for increased security. The lock itself will often adhere to lock-picking protection standards, and is usually a tubular cam lock, which can be keyed individually, or keyed for use with a master key. Many laptops come with a security slot to be used with cable locks; the tubular lock is inserted into the slot and turned 90 degrees to lock it or unlock it. This, of course, is only one anti-theft solution for laptops, but it is one that is commonly used by organizations, corporations, and individuals.

> **Note**
>
> Know that you can increase the security for your laptop but there is never a 100 percent secure solution, because any security technique can be bypassed given time, persistence, and ingenuity. So, a cable lock can help, but don't rely solely on that, or any other single security precaution.

Cram Quiz

Answer these questions. The answers follow the last question. If you cannot answer these questions correctly, consider reading this section again until you can.

1. Which of the following keys should you press to enable a secondary display on a laptop? (Select the two best answers.)

   ○ **A.** Fn key

   ○ **B.** Caps Lock key

   ○ **C.** Num Lock key

   ○ **D.** Special function key

   ○ **E.** Insert key

2. When a user types, a laptop's screen displays letters and numbers instead of only letters. What should you check first?

   ○ **A.** Fn key

   ○ **B.** LCD cutoff switch

   ○ **C.** Num Lock key

   ○ **D.** Scroll Lock key

3. You are required to install an anti-theft solution for a customer's laptop. Which of the following should you perform?

   ○ **A.** Install a docking station.

   ○ **B.** Install a cable lock.

   ○ **C.** Install Windows.

   ○ **D.** Configure a password in the BIOS/UEFI.

   ○ **E.** Use a port replicator.

4. You are helping a project manager with a presentation using a laptop which feeds video to a projector. During your tests, the projector's image begins to flicker. The laptop's display does not have any problems. You attempt to change the resolution on the laptop, but the issue continues. Which of the following should you do next?

   ○ **A.** Change the projector settings.

   ○ **B.** Check the connectivity of the video cable.

   ○ **C.** Change the aspect ratio of the laptop.

   ○ **D.** Check the connectivity of the power cable.

Cram Quiz Answers

1. **A and D.** To enable a secondary, or external, display on a laptop you would use the Fn key (called the Function key) and a special function key (for example, F3 or F4, whichever one corresponds to screen switching). It's this combination of keys that allows you to make use of displays plugged into HDMI or other ports on the laptop. The Caps Lock key enables a user to type in all uppercase letters. The Num Lock key (if available) turns on the numeric keypad (if the laptop has one). The Insert key is often used by programs such as word processors in one of two modes: overtype, where anything that is typed is written over any existing text, and insert mode, where typed characters force the existing text over.

2. **C.** The Num Lock key can enable or disable the numeric keypad. This might be necessary if the user inadvertently turned it on or disconnected an external keyboard from the laptop. Some laptops require you to press Ctrl+Num Lock to enable or disable the numeric keypad. Laptops are usually color-coded (for example, white options might require the Ctrl key and blue options might require the Fn key). In this scenario, pressing the Function (Fn) key is not necessary when pressing the Num Lock key. The LCD cutoff switch is used to turn off the bulb that lights the LCD. The Scroll Lock key is not often used but is meant to lock any scrolling done with the arrow keys.

3. **B.** Install a cable lock to increase the security of a laptop and decrease the chances of theft. Docking stations and port replicators offer increased functionality for a laptop but do not increase security; the laptop can be easily disconnected from them. Installing Windows is not an anti-theft solution, nor any type of security precaution. Configuring a password in the BIOS/UEFI is a good security practice, but it will not help avoid theft. However, if the laptop is stolen, a user password (and administrator password) that is configured in the BIOS can help prevent a person from accessing what is on the laptop.

4. **B.** Check the connectivity of the video cable. If it is flickering, chances are that the cable is loose, or the cable's quality is lacking. Screen flicker is more common with VGA cables, but it can happen with just about any connection. Remember, always check the basic stuff first: connectivity, power, and so on. It is unlikely that the projector settings will make a difference based on this particular problem. You cannot change the aspect ratio by itself on most laptops; however, when you change the resolution (which was already done in the question), you might be changing the aspect ratio as well, depending on the resolution selected. If the power cable was loose or damaged, it would probably result in more than just screen flicker; the projector might power off and power back on, which would prevent the image from being displayed for at least several seconds while the projector powers back up.

Great job so far! Two chapters down!

CHAPTER 3

Smartphones, Tablets, and Other Mobile Devices, Part 1

This chapter covers the following A+ 220-1001 exam objectives:

▶ **1.4** – Compare and contrast characteristics of various types of other mobile devices.

▶ **1.5** – Given a scenario, connect and configure accessories and ports of other mobile devices.

Welcome back! Now we'll think small; I'm talking about mobile devices such as tablets and smartphones. These are designed to be smaller than laptops, but with a limited loss of productivity in comparison to their larger brethren. For some work-related tasks—and for the general public—a laptop can be a bit unwieldy, and is a lot less "mobile" than a typical tablet or smartphone. That said, you will find that some organizations will opt to provide smaller devices for some of their users. What does this mean for you? It means that you need to know the different types of mobile devices available to users, but more importantly, you must be well-informed about those devices' connection types and accessories, and how to go about connecting and configuring them. So, think small, but remember the amazing power, and limitations, of these mobile devices. Onward!

1.4 – Compare and contrast characteristics of various types of other mobile devices

ExamAlert

Objective 1.4 focuses on the following concepts: tablets, smartphones, wearable technology devices (such as smart watches, fitness monitors, and VR/AR headsets), e-readers, and GPS.

This objective requires you to understand the differences between tablets, smartphones, e-readers, GPS devices, and wearable tech devices. You should be able to distinguish between one and another by looking at them, by analyzing the ports they use, and by being familiar with the uses for each type of device. Remember this: instead of thinking in terms of manufacturers, think in terms of technology types and uses. By this I mean don't worry too much about the popular brands of the day and instead think more in terms of what and how a device is supposed to perform for the user.

Tablets

A tablet computer, or simply "tablet," is a thin, mobile device that is operated with a touchscreen and generally measures between 6 and 11 inches diagonally. It can be used for simple tasks such as reading books and browsing the Internet, but can also be used for more complex tasks such as word and spreadsheet processing, audio and video recording/editing, multimedia live streaming, photo editing, collaboration, and even programming. The more complex the task, the more powerful the tablet that is required.

A typical tablet as of the writing of this book might have hardware specifications similar to what you see in Table 3.1.

TABLE 3.1 **Typical Tablet Hardware Specifications**

Hardware Component	Description
1.85-GHz ARMv8 CPU	64-bit system on a chip (SoC)
	Example: A9 CPU + M9 motion coprocessor
	Note: This is as of early 2019. Also, there are more powerful models. This is just one mid-range example.
2-GB LPDDR4 RAM	Mobile DDR—similar DDR standard to what PCs use, but a much smaller form factor, and is included in the SoC
32- or 128-GB flash memory	Similar to solid-state flash memory in a USB flash drive
	Used for permanent storage
Multitouch touchscreen	Capacitive touchscreen that responds to one or more fingers and proprietary stylus devices
9.7-inch display (diagonal) LED-backlit widescreen multitouch display with in-plane switching (IPS) technology	Quad Extended Graphics Array (QXGA), 2048×1536 resolution
	4:3 aspect ratio

Hardware Component	Description
Lithium-ion polymer battery (nonremovable)	Similar to lithium-ion batteries in laptops
	Can be made into any shape
	8827 mAh (milliamp hours); 32.4 watt-hour; lasts for 10 hours on a full charge (typical usage)
High-definition cameras	Main camera: 8 megapixel, 1080p video recording
	Second camera: 1.2 megapixel, 720p video recording

ExamAlert

Be able to read and understand the typical specs of a mobile device.

As you can see from the table, the whole concept of this hardware configuration is based on portability and ease of use. Therefore, tablet computers are generally less powerful than desktop computers and laptops, but the hardware is matched to the type of applications the device will be used for.

The two main goals for tablets are to be highly portable and have powerful processing capabilities. One way this is accomplished is by using a system on a chip (SoC), which combines the CPU, RAM, storage, and more on one single substrate—essentially it is a system unto itself. The most common microarchitecture used for the SoC of a tablet is called ARM, which is a type of reduced instruction set computing (RISC). An ARM-based CPU uses fewer transistors than a CPU found in a PC or laptop, which makes it a great choice for portable systems that need lower power consumption while still maintaining a decent amount of processing power.

Apple iPads run iOS as their operating system and make use of the proprietary Lighting connector, or the USB-C connector, to charge and to transmit data. Similar tablets that are Android-based often use standardized USB-C, or Micro-USB, ports for charging and synchronization of data. iPads are well-known as some of the most powerful tablet computers on the market, and as such have been used heavily for media creation and editing. This type of work would not be possible on a lesser tablet. So, choose the right tool for the job, and choose wisely!

Smartphones

A smartphone is a type of mobile phone that has much more processing power and greater hardware capabilities than a basic feature phone. A basic feature phone is designed primarily to place voice calls and do texting, but a smartphone is essentially a high-powered computer in the palm of your hand, allowing for desktop-like web browsing, high-definition playback of videos, and the downloading and usage of apps that can do just about anything you can think of. Smartphones also act as high-powered cameras, recording devices, music players, and personal assistants, among many other things. Remember, they are computers (though small), and as such, you are required to be able to troubleshoot and repair them.

A typical smartphone as of the writing of this book might have hardware specifications similar to what you see in Table 3.2.

TABLE 3.2 **Typical Smartphone Hardware Specifications**

Hardware Component	Description
2.45-GHz ARM CPU	Snapdragon 835
	64-bit system SoC
4-GB LPDDR4 RAM	Mobile DDR version 4
32-, 64-, 128-, or 256-GB flash memory	Similar to solid-state drives' flash memory
Multitouch touchscreen	Capacitive touchscreen
Lithium-ion polymer battery (aka li-ion or li-po)	3300 mAh (nonremovable)
	Typically 20 to 25 hours (talktime)
6.0-inch display	Quad HD+ (QHD+), 2880×1440 resolution
	18:9 aspect ratio
Dust and water proof	IP68 compliant

ExamAlert

Memorize the basic types of hardware used by a smartphone.

Those are just some of the specs of a typical smartphone. Here's an assignment for you: Go on the Internet and research the specs for *your* phone. Try to understand all of the terminology being used on the spec sheet. If you don't know a term, look it up and then try to relate that technology to your own device.

Just about all smartphones come with cellular access, be it 3G, 4G, LTE, 5G, and so on. This differs from tablets in that a tablet often will *not* come with cellular access, but it can be added with an upcharge.

IP Code

Some smartphones and other handheld computers are certified as being ingress protection (IP) compliant. Ingress protection means protection against dust and water, which are tested separately. There are a lot of different IP ratings, but let's use the IP68 example in the last row of Table 3.2. The first digit, 6, deals with dust and means that the device is dust tight and that no ingress of dust can occur. The second digit, 8, means that the device can be immersed in water up to and beyond 1 meter, generally for 30 minutes, though this can vary. The exact depth and length of time is up to the manufacturer, so IP68 could be slightly different from one smartphone to the next. You might also see IP67-compliant devices, which is very similar but means immersion only *up to* 1 meter for 30 minutes.

Other devices might be listed as IP65 compliant, which means they are dust tight and can protect from water jets for up to 3 minutes. The number associated with water protection is not cumulative, so if a device needs to be protected from water jets *and* immersion in water, it would, for example, have to be tested for IP65 *and* IP68 compliance. Many specialized handheld computers in the military (as well as in the medical, transportation, and surveying markets) meet both of these requirements, whereas consumer products might only meet IP68 or IP67 (depending on their age). What does this mean to the customer? Don't bring the device in the shower or spray it with a hose! It might survive, but it probably won't because it isn't tested for that type of abuse. You should also remember that some consumer smartphones do not meet any IP requirements and must be treated accordingly. In that case, if a device is damaged during use in a dusty environment or sprayed with or immersed in water, the warranty might become void. Familiarize yourself with the IP code. You can find it in various locations on the Internet, and you can get the authorized standard from the International Electrotechnical Commission (IEC).

ExamAlert

Understand what IP68 and similar IP ratings mean.

Note

Military usage often requires that devices are compliant with the MIL-STD-810 standard. This describes the lab testing of devices based on environmental conditions that are expected over the lifespan of the device. This standard is used commercially also.

Wearable Technology Devices

Moving outside of mobile devices, let's briefly discuss wearable technology. This concept has become quite the trend in recent years. One of the most common (as of the writing of this book) is the smartwatch. Initial product offerings required that a smartphone be nearby (with the watch connecting via Bluetooth), but newer versions are network-ready, meaning that you can use the smartwatch on Wi-Fi networks, and possibly cellular networks, increasing the usability (and range) of the device. Most of these allow a user to answer calls and communicate by e-mail and text. (If you like obscure references, you could say that Dick Tracy technology has finally arrived!)

Another common example of wearable technology is a fitness monitor, which is worn on the wrist or elsewhere and used by people who want to track their exercise routines and for physical rehabilitation purposes. They connect to compatible smartphones and tablets. However, most smartwatches also include fitness monitoring apps. Other wearable technology includes enhanced glasses (which can take photos and send them to your mobile device), specialized Bluetooth earpieces and headsets, and virtual/augmented reality headsets. Virtual reality (VR) headsets are used for gaming, watching movies, simulations, and so forth. Augmented reality (AR) headsets and glasses use holograms and other technology to overlay images on top of what a person actually sees (in the real world, that is—I know it's getting hard to tell what's real and what's not!).

The list keeps going when it comes to how you can add on to your mobile device. As a technician, you should understand that many of these wearable tech devices connect via Bluetooth (which might require a PIN code) and that Bluetooth has a limited range—usually 33 feet (10 meters). Some can work independently of the mobile device, but you would need to configure them to connect to Wi-Fi and/or cellular. You would do so by setting up a connection profile and/or by allowing automatic connections to "open," which means using unsecured Wi-Fi networks. We discuss Bluetooth, Wi-Fi, and cellular in more depth later in the book, but for now, remember that wearable devices' wireless connections can fail and at times need to be troubleshot like any other wireless device.

E-readers

By far the most common e-reader is the Amazon Kindle, but there are other brands as well. A true e-reader uses electronic paper technology—which is generally black and white—making longer-term reading easier on the eyes when compared to reading on a tablet or a smartphone. However, e-readers are not great when it comes to surfing the Web, though some do have Internet access. For some people, the e-reader is the only way to go because of how easy it is on the eyes, and because it displays text well both in dark environments and in sunlight. Plus, battery life is far superior to tablets and smartphones. Most manufacturers of these devices also allow users to read their digital libraries by installing a reader app to their tablets or smartphones (or PCs) and synchronizing between the devices. E-readers are often charged via Micro-USB, and many can connect via Wi-Fi or with a cellular connection to facilitate the downloading of book files.

GPS Devices

If you have a smartphone, you probably use some kind of Global Positioning System (GPS) app, but there are also dedicated smart GPS systems for your car that can work independently, and possibly integrate with your smartphone and social media via Wi-Fi and Bluetooth. The beauty of these is that the bulk of the CPU in the device is dedicated to GPS. If you have ever run GPS on a smartphone while other apps are running—and you experience slow performance—then you can understand why a dedicated GPS system might be a valid option for delivery drivers, those in the transportation industry, or those who simply want more accurate and efficiently presented GPS data.

Many vehicles offer navigation with touchscreens that can integrate with a person's smartphone. Basic versions are enabled via Bluetooth and can perform voice and text services. But in some cases, depending on the model and version of the vehicle, they will allow connectivity of CarPlay (Apple) and Android Auto. These are smartphone screen-mirroring programs that can display the GPS app for easier viewing. They can also control voice calls, text messaging, music playing, and more. Aftermarket head units are available as well. To utilize these systems, the vehicle must be compatible, the smartphone must have the correct app installed, and it is often connected in a wired fashion via USB. In this scenario, a technician should make sure that the vehicle's firmware and software are updated, that the smartphone's vehicle connectivity software and GPS software are updated, and that a *quality* cable is used.

The Internet of Things (IoT)

Collectively, tablets, smartphones, e-readers, and other mobile devices—not to mention their wearable counterparts—make up a portion of the "Internet of Things" (IoT). The IoT is the global network of physical objects which have embedded processors (of some sort) that can communicate with computers across the Internet. IoT devices also include household appliances such as smart refrigerators, digital thermostats, home automation devices, and so on. I've simplified the concept greatly, but for the purposes of this book, it should suffice. This is a buzz term that you will no doubt encounter more and more. But know that the IoT isn't limited to just personal devices; it also includes devices used in the medical, manufacturing, and transportation industries, among others. Depending on the organization you work for, you will need to install, configure, secure, and trouble-shoot a specific subset of IoT devices. Regardless, if you apply the methods and techniques in this book, you will be able to work with any device—in any market.

Cram Quiz

Answer these questions. The answers follow the last question. If you cannot answer these questions correctly, consider reading this section again until you can.

1. Which of the following is *not* a mobile device?
   - ○ **A.** Tablet
   - ○ **B.** Smartphone
   - ○ **C.** Desktop PO
   - ○ **D.** E-reader

2. Which type of memory do most mobile devices store long-term data to?
   - ○ **A.** LPDDR4
   - ○ **B.** SATA magnetic disk
   - ○ **C.** SATA SSD
   - ○ **D.** Solid-state flash memory

3. You have been tasked with connecting a wireless earpiece to a smartphone. Which technology would you most likely use?
   - ○ **A.** Wi-Fi
   - ○ **B.** NFC
   - ○ **C.** 3.5 mm
   - ○ **D.** Bluetooth

4. You have been tasked with setting up a device for a salesperson's vehicle. It should be able to display maps and give directions to the person while driving. Which of the following devices would perform these tasks? (Select the two best answers.)

○ **A.** GPS

○ **B.** Smart camera

○ **C.** Smartphone

○ **D.** E-reader

○ **E.** VR headset

Cram Quiz Answers

1. **C.** The desktop PC is not a mobile device. It is a stationary computer that is meant to stay at a person's desk. Tablets, smartphones, and e-readers are all examples of mobile devices.

2. **D.** Most mobile devices store their long-term data to solid-state flash memory. They do not use SATA as the method of connectivity. LPDDR4 is a common type of RAM used in mobile devices for short-term storage.

3. **D.** When connecting an earpiece (those little cricket-looking devices) to a smartphone, you would most likely use Bluetooth—just remember that most of them have a 30-foot range (10 meters). Wi-Fi is less likely to be used; it is more likely to be used to connect the smartphone to the LAN and ultimately to the Internet. NFC (discussed in the next section) is used to transmit data between mobile devices in close proximity to each other. 3.5 mm refers to the audio port on a mobile device. It is quite possible that a user will utilize a wired headset, but the question focuses on wireless.

4. **A and C.** A standalone GPS device or a smartphone (equipped with a GPS app) would do the job here. Both can display maps and give directions to a person while driving. The other devices are not designed to function in this manner.

1.5 – Given a scenario, connect and configure accessories and ports of other mobile devices

ExamAlert

Objective 1.5 focuses on the following concepts: wired connection types such as Micro-USB, Mini-USB, USB-C, and Lightning; wireless connectivity such as NFC, Bluetooth, and IR; and accessories such as memory cards, credit card readers, headsets, speakers, game pads, batteries, protective covers, and more.

Mobile device connectivity is imperative. For the exam, you need to know the physical ports used for charging and synchronizing, and for communicating with external devices. Then of course there are various wireless connectivity options available on today's mini-powerhouse computers. Let's not forget that people love to accessorize: headsets, speakers, add-on memory, the list is too long.... To simplify: be ready to provide support for a plethora of ports and gadgets!

Connection Types

Depending on what you need to accomplish with your mobile device, you might require a wired or a wireless connection. Let's discuss these now.

Wired Connections

Wired connections use physical ports. If you have ever plugged in a mobile device to charge it, then you have used a wired connection.

The most common wired connection is USB. USB has been around for a long time and has gone through several versions and port changes. USB is used by devices that run Android (among others). However, aside from USB-C, iOS-based devices from Apple use the proprietary Lightning connector or the older 30-pin dock connector (which is much wider). Figure 3.1 shows examples of the ports and connectors that you should know for the exam, including Mini-USB, Micro-USB, USB-C, and Lightning.

1.5 – Given a scenario, connect and configure accessories and ports of other mobile devices

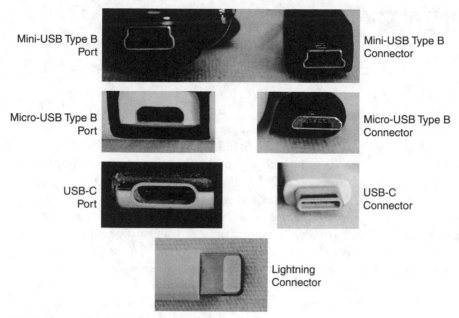

Mini-USB Type B Port — Mini-USB Type B Connector

Micro-USB Type B Port — Micro-USB Type B Connector

USB-C Port — USB-C Connector

Lightning Connector

FIGURE 3.1   **USB and Lightning ports and connectors**

If you charge a device, almost all charging cables will use a standard Type A USB port on the other end, regardless of the connector type that is used to attach to the device. That allows connectivity to the majority of charging plugs and PCs and laptops in the world. However, there are tons of adapters out there, so be ready.

At the time of writing, USB-C has become common for many Android-based smartphones and some tablets. Most likely, USB-C (and other ports) will continue to gain acceptance compared to Micro-USB, which was used by Android devices almost exclusively for a decade. For example, after years and years, and several generations of devices to use Micro-USB, the Samsung S8 was the first of that series to use the USB-C port, and in 2019 the iPad Pro began using USB-C as well. On the other hand, Mini-USB is quite uncommon, but you might see it on older devices, especially accessories for smartphones.

ExamAlert

Know your mobile device ports and connectors. Remember that Android devices will generally use USB-C or Micro-USB, and iOS-based devices will use USB-C, Lightning, or the 30-pin dock connector.

> **Note**
>
> We'll cover more about ports and connectors in Chapter 9, "Cables and Connectors."

Another purpose of the wired port is to have the ability to tether the mobile device to a desktop or laptop computer (usually via the computer's USB port). This tethering can allow a desktop computer or laptop to share the mobile device's Internet connection. Tethering functionality can be very useful in areas where a smartphone has cellular access but the PC/laptop cannot connect to the Internet. Once the physical USB connection is made, the setting for this can be found in **Networking > Tethering > USB Tethering**, or something similar (you will usually find the Mobile Hotspot option there as well). Keep in mind that Wi-Fi capability on the smartphone will usually be disabled when USB tethering is enabled, and that the user must have hotspot service with their cellular provider for USB tethering to work. Also, depending on the operating system, the PC or laptop that is connected to the smartphone might need a driver installed to communicate with it via USB. Finally, the tethered connection might render current LAN connections on the PC inoperable.

> **Note**
>
> Older versions of smartphone operating systems allowed for the reverse, where a smartphone would use a PC's Internet connection—this is known as USB Internet and is still a possibility, though it is not commonly used.

Wireless Connections

Wireless technologies are what really make a smartphone attractive to users. It's a fact, most people would rather do without cables, so technologies such as Bluetooth, NFC, IR, and hotspots make a smartphone functional, and easier to use.

Given the inherent mobility of smartphones and tablets, most technologies regarding communications and control are wireless. If designed and configured properly, wireless connections offer ease of use, efficiency, and even great speed. We'll discuss Wi-Fi, cellular, GPS, and similar data-related wireless technologies later in the book. For now, let's focus on wireless connections used by mobile devices to communicate with accessories and other mobile devices.

One of the most common technologies used is Bluetooth. This is a technology that allows users to incorporate wearable technology (such as headsets, earpieces, earbuds, and smartwatches) with their existing mobile devices. But the technology goes much farther; for example, it allows for the streaming of music to external speakers and an automobile's music system. However, Bluetooth is usually limited to about 33 feet (10 meters), which is the maximum transmission distance for Class 2 Bluetooth devices.

Another commonly used wireless technology is the mobile hotspot. When enabled on a properly equipped smartphone or tablet (with 4G or faster connection), it allows a user to connect desktops, laptops, and other mobile devices (wirelessly, of course) through the device running the hotspot, ultimately allowing access to the Internet. This can be a great way to connect your laptop or other computer if Wi-Fi goes down, often with speeds rivaling wired Internet access. But remember, there's usually a catch! Many providers charge for data usage (unless you have a corporate plan). Because of this, it is often used as a secondary connection or as a backup plan. In addition, the further the hotspot-enabled mobile device is from a cell tower, the lower the data transfer rate. So know the pros and cons of running a hotspot on your mobile device.

> **ExamAlert**
>
> Understand the difference between configuring USB tethering and creating a mobile hotspot.

Next, let's discuss near field communication (NFC). This allows smartphones to communicate with each other via radio frequency by touching the devices together or, in some cases, by simply having them in close proximity to each other. NFC uses the radio frequency 13.56 MHz and can transmit 100 to 400 kb/s. It doesn't sound like much—it transfers slower than Bluetooth for example—but it's usually plenty for sending and receiving contact information, MP3s, and even photos. Besides working in peer-to-peer mode (also known as ad hoc mode), a full NFC device can also act like a smart card performing payment transactions and reading NFC tags. If you are not sure whether your device supports NFC, check the settings in the mobile OS. Most smartphones incorporate NFC technology.

> **ExamAlert**
>
> NFC is used for close-proximity transactions, such as contactless payments.

Another wireless technology used by some smartphones and tablets is infrared (IR). Though it is not included on many flagship smartphones as of 2017, some mobile devices come with an IR blaster that can take control of televisions and some other devices (given they have the proper app installed). Infrared works on a different (and higher) frequency range than Wi-Fi, Bluetooth, and cellular connections, so it does not interfere with those technologies when it is used. Because so many appliances and electronics are "smart" enabled, the IR blaster becomes less important on today's smartphones.

Accessories

Well, a person has to accessorize, right? It almost seems a requirement with today's mobile devices. Probably the number one thing that people do to augment their device is to protect it. That means using protective covers or cases, plastic or glass-based screen protectors, waterproofing, car mounts, and so on.

Then there's add-on storage. You can never have enough memory, right? Adding long-term storage is usually accomplished with the addition of a microSD card, for example 32, 64, or 128 GB. It is common for people who shoot a lot of videos (or a whole lot of photos) to need more memory than the mobile device comes with when purchased. Some devices allow for add-on storage via a slide-out tray on the side of the device. Others don't allow upgrades. Older devices that can have the back cover removed can be upgraded internally.

Next on the list are audio accessories. The 3.5 mm audio jack (*if you have one*) allows a user to connect headsets, earbuds, or small speakers. Or you can connect a 3.5 mm to 3.5 mm cable from your phone to the auxiliary port of your car radio or your all-in-one music device—though Bluetooth is usually the easier option. When it comes to music, you can connect a mobile device to anything (given the right cable or adapter): stereos or TVs, and you can even use the device when performing live. The possibilities are endless. And today's mobile device audio ports can be programmed in such a way as to accept special credit-card readers and a host of other devices. Appliance repair persons and other maintenance workers that need to be paid onsite will often make use of this technology, though that can also be accomplished in a wireless fashion.

Getting a bit more advanced, you will also see devices such as game pads that can connect to the Micro-USB port using On-The-Go (OTG) USB technology. However, most game pads will connect wirelessly, either via Bluetooth or through Wi-Fi.

Most of today's devices cannot be opened by the consumer without voiding the warranty. So, replacing a battery is not as easy as it once was. To do this, a heat gun and proper shims are required. However, if not done correctly, it can defeat the IP rating. That's why manufacturers require that battery replacements be done by an authorized repair center. More important when it comes to accessories are battery chargers. Smartphones and tablets can be charged with their included AC chargers, or possibly with wireless chargers, where the unit is laid down directly on the charger. A user might also opt to use a power brick which stores a charge for a long time. Keep in mind that these "bricks" (also known as battery packs or battery charges) take a long time to charge up themselves.

We could go on for days about the accessories available for mobile devices, but that should be enough for the exams. Remember, protecting the mobile device and memory capacity are crucial. The rest of the things we discussed enable a user to increase functionality, or just plain make it more fun, but these things are usually not essential to the device performing its job. Plus, in a bring your own device (BYOD) or choose your own device (CYOD) environment, the users will often be quite limited when it comes to accessorizing. This is to prevent compatibility issues, which lead to lower productivity, and to avoid security vulnerabilities.

Cram Quiz

Answer these questions. The answers follow the last question. If you cannot answer these questions correctly, consider reading this section again until you can.

1. Which type of charging connector would you find on an iPad?
   - ○ **A.** Micro-USB
   - ○ **B.** Lightning
   - ○ **C.** Thunderbolt
   - ○ **D.** IP68

2. You are required to add long-term storage to a smartphone. Which type would you most likely add?
   - ○ **A.** DDR4
   - ○ **B.** microSD
   - ○ **C.** LPDDR4
   - ○ **D.** SSD
   - ○ **E.** SIM

3. The organization you work for allows employees to work from their own mobile devices in a BYOD manner. You have been tasked with setting up the devices so that they can "beam" information back and forth between each other. What is this known as?

   - ○ **A.** Mobile hotspot
   - ○ **B.** IoT
   - ○ **C.** CYOD
   - ○ **D.** IR
   - ○ **E.** NFC

4. Which of the following can be useful in areas where a smartphone has cellular access but the PC (or laptop) cannot connect to the Internet?

   - ○ **A.** Proprietary vendor-specific connector
   - ○ **B.** Accessories
   - ○ **C.** IP codes
   - ○ **D.** Tethering

Cram Quiz Answers

220-1001 Answers

1. **B.** The Lightning connector is one of Apple's proprietary charging and synchronization connectors used by iPads and iPhones, although Apple also uses USB-C. Micro-USB is used by older Android-based mobile devices—while USB-C is more common on newer devices. Thunderbolt is a high-speed hardware interface used in desktop computers, which we will discuss more in Chapter 9. IP68 deals with ingress protection from dust and water jets.

2. **B.** You would most likely add a microSD card (if the smartphone has a slot available for add-on or upgrading). This is the most common method for adding long-term storage. DDR4 is a type of RAM; it is not used for adding long-term memory storage. Some smartphones will use LPDDR4 as their main memory, but this is part of the SoC, and not accessible to the typical user. An SSD is a solid-state drive, which generally means a hard drive that is installed to a PC or laptop, connected either as SATA or M.2. These are too large for smartphones and tablets. A SIM is a subscriber identity module, usually represented as a small card (mini-SIM) used in smartphones that securely stores authentication information about the user and device, such as the international mobile subscriber identity (IMSI), which we will discuss more in the following chapter.

3. **E.** "Beaming" the information back and forth can be accomplished in a couple of ways, primarily by using near field communication (NFC). This can only be done if the devices are in close proximity to each other. NFC is commonly used for contactless payment systems. Another potential option would be Apple's AirDrop, but this relies on Bluetooth (for finding devices) and Wi-Fi (for transmitting data), and of course relies on using Apple-based devices. A mobile hotspot enables a

smartphone or tablet to act as an Internet gateway for other mobile devices and computers. IoT stands for the Internet of Things. In the question, it said employees can use their mobile devices in a BYOD manner, but CYOD is a bit different. This means that employees can *choose* a device to use for work purposes (most likely whichever type they are more familiar with). Whether or not the employees can use those for personal purposes is usually defined by company policy. IR stands for infrared, which is less commonly found on smartphones as of 2017.

4. **D.** Tethering can allow a desktop computer or laptop to share the mobile device's Internet connection. Tethering functionality can be very useful in areas where a smartphone has cellular access but the PC/laptop cannot connect to the Internet. Mobile device accessories such as headsets, speakers, game pads, extra battery packs, and protective covers are useful, but they are not used to connect to the Internet. IP codes are used to classify and rate the degree of protection against dust and water (for example, IP68). A perfect example of a proprietary, vendor-specific connector is the Apple Lightning connector that can only be used on iOS devices.

Chapter 3 is in the books, so to speak. Excellent work, keep going!

CHAPTER 4

Smartphones, Tablets, and Other Mobile Devices, Part 2

This chapter covers the following A+ 220-1001 exam objectives:

▶ 1.6 – Given a scenario, configure basic mobile device network connectivity and application support.

▶ 1.7 – Given a scenario, use methods to perform mobile device synchronization.

Nice to see you again! This is the last chapter dealing with mobile devices. We'll be discussing networking and synchronization. Ask yourself: What do users need? They need Wi-Fi, Bluetooth, and e-mail. They need cellular connections for voice calls as well as for data. And let's not forget the need to synchronize data to computers, automobiles, and the cloud. That's what this chapter is all about. Now that you know, it's time to begin.

1.6 – Given a scenario, configure basic mobile device network connectivity and application support

ExamAlert

Objective 1.6 concentrates on the following concepts: wireless technologies, Bluetooth setup, e-mail configuration, radio updates, and VPNs.

This objective expects you to know how to set up wireless connections such as Wi-Fi, hotspots, and Bluetooth, and also wired connections such as USB tethering. Be ready to understand configurations for the various types of e-mail, including POP3, IMAP, and cloud-based e-mail configurations. Finally, prepare to learn how cellular connections work, and the various updates, identification codes, and technologies used by smartphones' mobile connections.

These are the basics of network connectivity when it comes to mobile devices, but it's still a lot to know—and much of it is unknown to the typical end user. That's where you, the tech, come in. Support those mobile devices!

> **Note**
>
> For simplicity, most of the time I use the term *cellular* to refer to smartphone connectivity to a telecommunications provider, meaning 3G, 4G, 5G, and so on.

Enabling Wireless Functions

You will most definitely be called upon to enable and disable various wireless and cellular functionality. In this section we'll discuss how to connect to Wi-Fi, set up a mobile hotspot, and turn on airplane mode.

Cellular connections such as 3G, 4G, LTE, 5G, and beyond are commonplace on smartphones. If you purchase a smartphone from a telecommunications provider, then you get cellular access. It is enabled by default, unless you turn on airplane mode. We'll talk more about cellular technologies later, but for now keep in mind a couple things:

- ▶ Cellular connections can be slow when transmitting data. That could be due to the distance from the nearest cell tower, or a general lack of service availability.

- ▶ Cellular connections can cost the customer money. That's why all mobile devices are equipped with an embedded wireless antenna to connect to wireless LANs (WLANs). This Wi-Fi antenna can potentially allow access to 802.11a, b, g, n, and ac networks. The wireless connection works similarly to a wireless connection on a PC, laptop, or tablet. See Chapter 6, "SOHO Networks and Wireless Protocols," for a detailed description of connecting to wireless networks.

In general, the mobile device must first search for wireless networks before connecting. On a typical mobile device, this is done in **Settings > Wi-Fi**, or **Settings > Network > Wi-Fi**. Figure 4.1 shows a typical Wi-Fi settings screen.

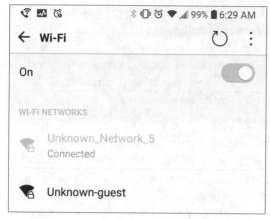

FIGURE 4.1 **Wi-Fi settings screen in Android**

In the Wi-Fi settings screen, perform the following general steps:

1. Most devices usually scan for wireless networks automatically, or you can tap **Add Wi-Fi Network** (or similar name) to add one manually.

2. When adding a network manually, enter the Service Set Identifier (SSID) of the wireless access point (WAP) in the Add Wi-Fi Network window.

3. Enter the passcode for the network. If the code is correct, then the wireless adapter in the mobile device gets an IP address, allowing it to communicate with the network. If a wireless network uses Wi-Fi Protected Access Version 2 (WPA2) and the mobile device isn't compatible, you should search for an update to the operating system to make it WPA2-compliant or consider a newer device!

4. Check for the universal wireless icon at the top of the screen (in the notification bar) to verify connectivity.

ExamAlert

Understand how to connect to a Wi-Fi network in Android and iOS.

If you bring your mobile device into a secure area or on to an airplane, you will most likely be asked to place the device in *airplane mode*. This is a mode that will disable all wireless connectivity, including (but not limited to) cellular, Wi-Fi, and Bluetooth. This can be done by pressing and holding the power button and selecting airplane mode, or by swiping down on the notification bar and accessing the quick settings drop-down menu.

Once in airplane mode, you should see the airplane icon in the notification bar. However, keep in mind that this is primarily designed to disable cellular access. On many devices, a user can still re-enable Wi-Fi or Bluetooth even when airplane mode is on. Sometimes a user might complain that there is no wireless connectivity. Always check if the device has been placed in to airplane mode and disable it from the same locations mentioned previously.

So, you know how to set up Wi-Fi. But what if you want to share that connection with other computers such as laptops or tablets? That's where the mobile hotspot comes in. When you configure a *mobile hotspot*, the mobile device shares its Internet connection with other Wi-Fi-capable devices. For example, if a user has a smartphone that can access the Internet through a cellular network, it can be configured to become a portable Wi-Fi hotspot for other mobile devices (or desktops/laptops) that are Wi-Fi capable but have no cellular option. Beware of the hotspot option; most providers have a fairly low consumer bandwidth cap (data transmission limit) for data transferred through the hotspot by default, even if the plan is called "unlimited."

Enabling hotspots is easy and is often done in **Settings > Network** (and possibly in a section called "tethering"). Figure 4.2 shows an example. The first time, you will be asked to supply a password and the wireless protocol to be used, which can be modified later. As of this writing, it is recommended to use WPA2 and, of course, set a strong password. An example of the configuration screen is also shown in Figure 4.2.

Enabling a HotSpot

Configuring a HotSpot

FIGURE 4.2   **Hotspot configuration in Android**

When a hotspot is enabled on a smartphone, Wi-Fi is automatically disabled. So, the smartphone will only be able to connect via the cellular network—but it is designed this way on purpose, expecting to only be used when there is no Wi-Fi connection available. Other Wi-Fi-ready systems (laptops, PCs, tablets, etc.) need only look for, and connect to the Wi-Fi network that was created (for example, *Hotspot-dpro* in Figure 4.2). Running a mobile hotspot can also be a great backup option in case the main Internet connection in a small office or home office fails temporarily.

USB Tethering

USB tethering is when a mobile device is connected to a desktop or laptop computer via USB; that desktop or laptop (running Windows or macOS) can then share the phone's mobile Internet connection. So, USB tethering is the wired equivalent of a mobile hotspot—but it's designed for just one computer to share the Internet connection. The option for USB tethering is displayed in Figure 4.2—it is grayed out (disabled) until a USB cable is plugged in. As with mobile hotspots, turning on this feature will automatically disable the mobile device's Wi-Fi connection. That means that Wi-Fi-based services, such as Wi-Fi calling, will be unavailable while USB tethering is activated.

> **ExamAlert**
>
> Remember that a mobile hotspot shares a smartphone's Internet connection wirelessly, and USB tethering shares the connection in a wired fashion. In both cases, Wi-Fi and Wi-Fi–related services will be shut down while the hotspot or tether is active. Normally, a hotspot and USB tethering cannot run at the same time.

Bluetooth

Bluetooth is a wireless standard for transmitting data over short distances. It is commonly implemented in the form of a headset or printer connection. It is also used to create a wireless personal area network (WPAN) consisting of multiple Bluetooth-enabled mobile devices.

To connect a Bluetooth device to a mobile device, Bluetooth first needs to be enabled. Then the Bluetooth device needs to be synchronized to the mobile device. This is known as *pairing* or *linking*. It sometimes requires a pin code. Once synchronized, the device should automatically connect and should function at that point. Finally, the Bluetooth connection should be tested. Following are the steps involved in connecting a Bluetooth device to a typical mobile device. Before you begin, make sure the Bluetooth device is charged (if applicable). The typical procedure for making a Bluetooth connection is as follows:

1. Turn on Bluetooth in the Settings of the mobile device.

2. Prepare the device by turning it on and pressing (and sometimes holding) the Bluetooth button.

3. Scan for devices on the mobile device.

4. Pair to the desired device.

5. Enter a pin code if necessary. Some devices come with a default pin of 0000.

When finished, the screen will look similar to Figure 4.3. Note the Bluetooth icon at the top of the screen. This icon indicates whether Bluetooth is running on the device. It will remain there even after you disconnect the Bluetooth device, but in a grayed-out state. To disconnect or reconnect the Bluetooth device, simply tap the device on the screen. It will remain paired but nonfunctional until a connection is made again. (Typically, devices are listed in bold if they are connected.) You can also unpair and/or forget the device in the settings for that device. Unpairing removes the link between the smartphone and the Bluetooth device, but the mobile device will remember the Bluetooth device. "Forgetting" removes the connection altogether.

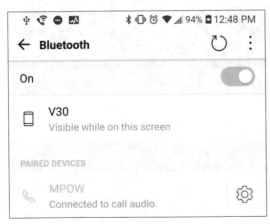

FIGURE 4.3   Bluetooth paired devices screen in Android

Bluetooth devices can be connected to only one mobile device at a time. If you need to switch the Bluetooth device from one mobile device to another, be sure to unpair or disconnect it or, going further, "forget" it from the current connection before making a new one.

> **ExamAlert**
>
> Know how to configure Bluetooth devices in Android and iOS.

> **Note**
>
> Troubleshooting is just as important as configuration. We'll discuss Wi-Fi and Bluetooth troubleshooting in Chapter 20, "Troubleshooting Video Issues and Mobile Devices," and Chapter 22, "Troubleshooting Wired and Wireless Network Problems."

E-mail Configuration

Although there are many other types of communication available to mobile users, e-mail still accounts for an important percentage. You should know how to configure a mobile device for web-based e-mail services such as Gmail, Yahoo!, and so on. You should also know how to configure Post Office Protocol Version 3 (POP3), Internet Mail Access Protocol (IMAP), and connections to Microsoft Exchange Servers.

Integrated Commercial Provider E-mail Configuration

Mobile devices can access web-based e-mail through a browser, but this is not necessary nowadays due to the "app"—most commercial providers offer integrated e-mail configuration for Android and iOS. For example, most Android-based devices come with a Gmail application built in, allowing a user to access Gmail directly without having to use the browser. Devices also might have a proprietary e-mail application. Apple iOS devices allow connectivity to Gmail, Yahoo!, and a host of other e-mail providers as well. Apple users might also connect to the iCloud for mail features. Users of other devices might use Microsoft's Outlook on the Web, or for more users and for collaboration a company might opt for Exchange Online. As you can see, there are a lot of options when it comes to mail services for mobile devices.

Connecting to these services is simple and works in a fashion that is similar to working on a desktop or laptop computer. Choose the type of provider you use, enter a username (the e-mail address) and password (on Apple devices, an Apple ID is also required), and the user will have access. In more advanced cases, a user may have to select the protocol and ports to be used. That's where you as the administrator come in—we'll discuss those in a little bit.

When troubleshooting user issues with e-mail, make sure that the username and password are typed correctly. Using onscreen keyboards often leads to mistyped passwords. Also make sure that the mobile device is currently connected to the Internet.

Corporate and ISP E-mail Configuration

When you need to connect a mobile device to a specific organization's e-mail system, it gets a little more complicated. You need to know the server that you want to connect to, the port you need to use, and whether security is employed. Look at the following e-mail configuration information and Figure 4.4 for an example.

▶ Incoming server name: secure.dpro42.com

▶ POP3 port (SSL/TLS): 995

▶ Outgoing server name: secure.dpro42.com

▶ SMTP port (SSL/TLS): 465

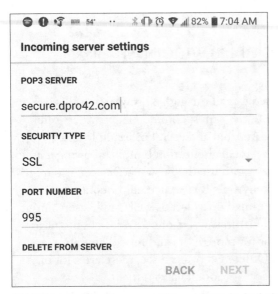

FIGURE 4.4   E-mail server settings screen in Android

The figure shows a manual configuration of an e-mail client in Android. At this stage, the e-mail client is asking for the incoming server, meaning the one we use for receiving mail. It just so happens that the same server takes care of incoming mail and outgoing mail: secure.dpro42.com; but sometimes it could be two different servers. So, we added the name of the server into the POP3 Server field. Then we specified the security type. In this case we selected Secure Sockets Layer (SSL) instead of "no security," which is important. Most of the time we want to have encrypted e-mail sessions to our e-mail server so as to avoid eavesdropping and tampering. This could be SSL or Transport Layer Security (TLS) depending on the server configuration. Then we select the port, which according to our previous documentation is 995. That is the default secure port for POP3 e-mail connections that make use of SSL/TLS. However, this can vary depending on what protocol you are using for e-mail and what type of security you implement. As a technician configuring the client e-mail, you have to go by the documentation provided by the network administrator. As an admin, it's generally a good idea to go with the default secure port numbers, but in reality you can choose which port to use (within reason), and as long as the client configures that port to connect, it should be successful. See Table 4.1 for a list of original and secure ports used by the various e-mail protocols.

TABLE 4.1 **Example E-mail Configuration**

E-mail Protocol	Original Port Number	Secure Port Number
SMTP	25	465 or 587
POP3	110	995
IMAP	143	993

ExamAlert

Know the e-mail protocols and default ports like the back of your hand!

In Table 4.1, I say "original" port number because these are what we used for many years until encrypted e-mail sessions became necessary. The secure port numbers are defaults, but it can vary. This will depend on whether you have to select SSL or TLS, or if another secure technology is used, or if the admin simply decided to go with a different port number. Here's the thing: most ports can work in a secure fashion—if configured properly—but it's the most common defaults in Table 4.1 that you should know for the exam. These are what e-mail server programs and client applications will typically default to.

> **Note**
>
> Another protocol you might implement when setting up secure e-mail is S/MIME (Secure/Multipurpose Internet Mail Extensions). This is used for authentication and message integrity and is built into some e-mail clients.

Cellular Radio Technologies

Hey, listen! Without a properly working radio in your smartphone, you won't hear anything. This section is designed to teach you the basics about cellular voice calls and data transmissions. You see, most people can't live without their radios—and ultimately, that's what the phone is.

Originally, cellular phones used the Global System for Mobile Communications (GSM) to make voice calls and GSM or the General Packet Radio Service (GPRS) to send data at 2G speeds through the cellular network. Extensions of these standards—the Universal Mobile Telecommunications System (UMTS) and Enhanced Data rates for GSM Evolution (EDGE)—are used to attain 3G speeds. 4G and 4G LTE speeds can be attained only when a mobile device complies with the International Mobile Telecommunications Advanced (IMT-Advanced) requirements, has a 4G antenna, and is in range of a 4G transmitter. Devices manufactured during the writing of this book most commonly use 4G and LTE (which builds on 4G by using an updated radio interface/antenna in the mobile device and by utilizing core network infrastructure improvements). However, the fifth generation of cellular (5G) is also available. This is known as the ITU IMT-2020 standard, and has data transfer rates of up to 20 Gbps.

Most devices cannot shut off the cellular antenna by themselves (unless you shut down the device itself). However, every device manufactured now is required to have an "airplane mode," which turns off any wireless antenna in the device, including disabling the connection to the cellular network, and disabling Wi-Fi, and Bluetooth. This can be accomplished by either going to **Settings > Airplane Mode** or by holding the Power button down and selecting Airplane Mode. You will find that some airlines don't consider this to be acceptable and for security purposes will still ask you to turn off your device altogether, either for the duration of the flight or at least during takeoff and landing. Some devices can also limit or disable cellular *data* usage—often known as "mobile data."

> **ExamAlert**
>
> Know what airplane mode is and how to configure it on Android and Apple devices.

Let's get a little more into it and briefly discuss some additional mobile technology and acronyms, such as PRL updates, baseband updates, radio firmware, IMEI versus IMSI, and VPN.

PRL stands for preferred roaming list. It is used by cellular providers (such as Sprint, Verizon, and U.S. Cellular) that utilize code division multiple access (CDMA) technology instead of GSM. It's a database that contains information about the provider's radio bands, sub-bands, and service provider IDs. Ultimately, it allows a phone to connect to the correct tower; without the database, the phone might not be able to roam outside the provider's network. When necessary, PRL information is sent as an update over the air. However, you can also update it manually by dialing a number that is unique to each provider. You can find out the PRL version number you are using within the About section on some phones.

When a phone uses GSM, that technology and its radio functions are controlled by a chip and software package that is collectively referred to as "baseband." Baseband updates are necessary to communicate properly with GSM cell towers. If an older phone won't update properly, it must be taken to the provider for a wired, manual update. Baseband is also referred to as radio firmware in that it controls network connectivity for GSM. Other wireless antennas such as Wi-Fi and GPS are controlled by the operating system's drivers.

> **Caution**
>
> Do not attempt a radio firmware (baseband) update if your phone does not require it. A faulty update can easily make the phone inoperable.

> **Note**
>
> A less commonly used acronym on the CompTIA A+ objectives is PRI, which stands for product release instructions. This is an over-the-air informational update defining what to expect from an operating system update, and in the past for mobile devices it may have included settings and codes.

Now on to IMEI and IMSI—these are both identification technologies. IMEI stands for International Mobile Equipment Identity and it identifies phones used on 3GPP-based networks (GSM, UMTS, and LTE). You can find this ID number in **Settings > About > Status** (or something similar), or on older phones it is printed inside the phone either on or near the battery. It is used only to identify the device. However, International Mobile Subscriber Identity (IMSI) is used to identify the user. For GSM, UMTS, and LTE networks, this ID is loaded into the subscriber identity module (SIM) card. For CDMA networks, the ID is loaded directly into the phone or to a removable user identity module (R-UIM), which is similar to a SIM card.

ExamAlert

Know that the IMEI ID identifies the device and the IMSI ID identifies the user of the device.

Today's mobile devices can also use virtual private network (VPN) technology to make secure connections—tunneling though the provider's radio network. The VPN data is also updated frequently as updates to mobile operating systems are released, as well as for security purposes. For more information about VPNs as they relate to computers and networks in general, see Chapter 7, "Networked Hosts and Network Configuration."

You can find the versions of most of these technologies (and the types of radio technology used) within the About (or About device) section. Take a look at your own mobile device's settings; for example, the radio technologies you are connecting to, the baseband version, and the IMEI.

Note

Sometimes, finding the information you are looking for can be a bit of a chore; the level of difficulty varies according to the device and the version of OS installed in it. Plus, the various IDs, signal levels, types of technologies used, and so on can be dispersed among different areas of the phone. Consider using a cell tower analyzer, radio signal analyzer, or network signal information app to see this data in a more visual and centralized manner.

All of these radio network technologies can be affected by a mobile phone update, such as a version update. To prevent network connectivity issues, consider waiting until a new mobile OS version has been thoroughly tested before you update your phone.

Cram Quiz

Answer these questions. The answers follow the last question. If you cannot answer these questions correctly, consider reading this section again until you can.

1. Which of the following connections require a username, password, and SMTP server? (Select the two best answers.)

   ○ **A.** Bluetooth connection

   ○ **B.** Wi-Fi connection

   ○ **C.** POP3 connection

   ○ **D.** Exchange connection

   ○ **E.** IMAP connection

2. When manually configuring a Wi-Fi connection, which step occurs after successfully entering the SSID?

   ○ **A.** Select POP3.

   ○ **B.** Check whether the device is within range of the WAP.

   ○ **C.** Enter a passcode for the network.

   ○ **D.** Scan for networks.

3. Which of the following allows other mobile devices to wirelessly share your mobile device's Internet connection?

   ○ **A.** NFC

   ○ **B.** Airplane mode

   ○ **C.** IMAP

   ○ **D.** Mobile hotspot

4. Which of the following identifies the user of the device?

   ○ **A.** IMSI ID

   ○ **B.** IMEI ID

   ○ **C.** S/MIME

   ○ **D.** VPN

Cram Quiz Answers

1. **C and E.** POP3 and IMAP e-mail connections require an incoming mail server (either POP3 or IMAP) and an outgoing mail server (SMTP). Bluetooth and Wi-Fi connections do not require a username or SMTP server. Bluetooth might require a PIN, and Wi-Fi will almost always require a passcode. Exchange connections require a username and password, but no SMTP server. The Exchange Server acts as the incoming and outgoing mail server.

CramQuiz

1.6 – Given a scenario, configure basic
mobile device network connectivity and
application support

2. **C.** After you enter the SSID (if it's correct) you would enter the passcode for the network. POP3 has to do with configuring an e-mail account. If you have already entered the SSID, then you should be within range of the wireless access point (WAP). Scanning for networks is the first thing you do when setting up a Wi-Fi connection.

3. **D.** Mobile hotspot technology (sometimes referred to as Wi-Fi tethering) allows a mobile device to share its Internet connection with other Wi-Fi-capable devices. Another possibility would be USB tethering, but that is done in a wired fashion. NFC stands for near field communication—a technology that allows two mobile devices to send information to each other when they are in close proximity. Airplane mode will disable all wireless connectivity including (but not limited to) cellular, Wi-Fi, and Bluetooth. IMAP is another e-mail protocol similar to POP3.

4. **A.** International Mobile Subscriber Identity (IMSI) or IMSI ID is used to identify the user of the device. IMEI stands for International Mobile Equipment Identity and identifies the phone used. In other words, the IMEI ID identifies the device itself. S/MIME (Secure/Multipurpose Internet Mail Extensions) is used for authentication and message integrity and is built into some e-mail clients. In other words, it is used to encrypt e-mail. Virtual private networking (VPN) technology is used to make secure connections—tunneling though the provider's radio network.

1.7 – Given a scenario, use methods to perform mobile device synchronization

In this section you learn how to synchronize mobile devices to other computers either on the local area network, on the Internet, or located in a vehicle. You should be well versed in synchronizing many data types, including contacts, e-mail, calendars, and even passwords if the user desires it. It's also important to know both how to authenticate to networks using the single sign-on (SSO) method and what SSO is and how it operates.

Synchronization Methods

A person might want to synchronize a mobile device's data somewhere else so that he or she can have availability to that data from anywhere. It also offers peace of mind in the case that the mobile device is lost or stolen—that data will be available on the other system when a new mobile device is procured. And of course, even though mobile devices today can store a lot of data, there's always the need for more. External systems allow for a much greater amount of storage, and redundancy of data.

A person can choose to synchronize data to an individual computer that is physically nearby, or to an automobile, or to the cloud, which is the most common.

Synchronizing to the Cloud

For simplicity, we can refer to the cloud as any computer that you synchronize to on the Internet. Generally, this means using some type of service. You might synchronize your mobile device's data to Google Drive, Microsoft OneDrive, iCloud, Dropbox, or one of several other services. Making this happen entails creating an account, installing the appropriate app on the mobile device (if not already there), and specifying what folders, files, and other data you would like to synchronize. The first time you synchronize your device's data, the application will copy the data over to the cloud recipient. Subsequent synchronizations will copy new files and append changed files.

When it comes to popular services such as Gmail, you might question whether you really are "synchronizing" anymore. You are, it's just that the data is all stored on the service's servers and you are simply accessing it from a mobile device, or PC, or laptop. A person who signs up for a Gmail account allows Google to automatically synchronize mail, contacts, and the calendar so that the information can be viewed on the mobile device or on the PC (when connected to the Google website). However, because the data is stored on a Google server, security should be a concern. If you choose to use Gmail (or another service such as this), you should use an extremely strong password, change it every month or so, and use a secure browser when connecting to Gmail from a desktop computer. On the mobile device side, make sure the Gmail app is updated often to patch any security vulnerabilities. The same concepts hold true for other similar services. Utilizing the cloud presents many configuration and security concerns, which we will discuss more in the networking chapters of this book.

> **Note**
>
> Keep in mind that you might also *back up* your data, but this is different than synchronization. For example, you might back up an Android-based device's apps, call history, contacts, device settings, SMS text messages, and other items that are normally stored locally. You could back up this data to a server on the cloud owned by the manufacturer of the mobile device, or you could use a separate service such as Google Drive. Either way, this is done separately from synchronization.

Synchronizing to the Desktop

Today, synchronizing to the desktop is not nearly as common as syncing to the cloud. But it might be necessary, or desired, by some users. When you connect mobile devices to a Windows PC via a USB connection, they are typically seen automatically and are represented as a device in File Explorer under This PC in Windows 10 and 8 (and in Windows Explorer under Computer in Windows 7). On the mobile device you might have to change the USB options from Charging to File Transfer or another similar option in order to see the device in Windows. At this point, you can copy files back and forth between the mobile device and the PC manually or rely on automatic synchronization software from the manufacturer of the mobile device or from a third party. This software can be configured to synchronize the folders of your choice automatically when the mobile device is connected.

If you use the mobile device's built-in contacts and e-mail programs, the information within those programs can be transferred to the PC's corresponding programs. For example, the calendar and contacts can be synchronized with Microsoft Outlook.

There are third-party tools available when a user wants to synchronize an Android device with a PC or Mac via Bluetooth or Wi-Fi. On another note, Google Sync (using Exchange ActiveSync) can be used to synchronize e-mail, contacts, and calendars between a variety of devices (iOS-based devices, Windows devices, etc.) with an Exchange Server. Android-based devices use G Suite and don't require Google Sync to make connections to Exchange Servers.

ExamAlert

Know the various ways to synchronize data between an Android and a PC.

When you plug in an iPad/iPhone to a PC via USB, Windows should automatically recognize it and install the driver for it. At that point, you can move files between the PC and the device. The device shows up in File Explorer as Apple iPad or Apple iPhone directly inside of the This PC/Computer location of File Explorer/Windows Explorer.

To synchronize data such as contacts, calendars, and so on, PC users need to use iTunes for Windows. From iTunes, a user would select Sync Contacts or Sync Calendars, for example. This information can be synchronized to Microsoft Outlook and Windows Contacts. Mac users benefit from the simplicity of synchronization across all Apple products. They can use iTunes, or they can use iCloud to store, back up, and synchronize information across all Apple devices. This can be done by USB or via Wi-Fi (when the various Apple devices are on the same wireless network). Calendar items can also be synced from the Apple-based device (such as an iPad) by going to **Settings > Mail, Contacts, Calendars**. Then scroll down and select **Sync**. iCloud can also be downloaded for Windows.

Windows 10 devices can be synchronized together with the Sync Center (**Control Panel > All Control Panel Items > Syn Center**). This allows you to choose individual synchronize settings such as Theme, Passwords, Language preferences, Ease of Access, and other Windows settings, but a user would have to sign in with a Microsoft account in order to synchronize.

ExamAlert

Know the various ways to synchronize data between mobile devices and PCs or Macs.

Synchronizing to the Automobile

It had to happen—computers in cars. Not only that, but people want to harness the power of their smartphone in conjunction with their automobile's computer and display. It's easy with tools such as Android Auto and Apple CarPlay. These apps can be used independently on the mobile device or can be synchronized to an automobile's computer that has the proper firmware/software installed. Then, the user can make use of the automobile's larger screen for easier accessibility, better viewing, and increased safety. Generally, these platforms are supported on higher-level trims of a vehicle. For integration of these platforms, the mobile device usually has to be plugged in via USB, and a high-quality cable should be used to avoid interruptions.

In reality, this isn't as much "synchronizing" as it is screen sharing. The larger screen in the automobile is used to display, and control, the common apps you might need: phone, maps, music player, and so on—Apple CarPlay and Android Auto will limit the amount and type of apps you can use in the automobile for safety reasons.

Take a look at Figure 4.5 for an example of Android Auto running on a smartphone connected to an automobile via USB. Of course, most smartphones can multitask, so you can potentially use both screens at the same time with different apps running on each—of course, only when parked!

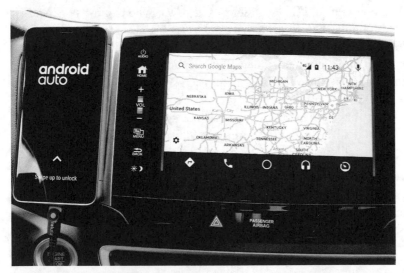

FIGURE 4.5   **Example of Android Auto**

If a vehicle does not support Android Auto or Apple CarPlay, it might support Bluetooth (BT). If that is the case, then a smartphone or tablet can be synchronized to the vehicle via BT by pairing the automobile to the device in the same manner described earlier in the chapter. Then the user can operate voice calls and texting hands-free. If the vehicle is not equipped with any computer or BT integration, then a replacement head unit (stereo) could be purchased allowing BT and USB integration as well as Apple CarPlay or Android Auto.

Types of Data to Synchronize and Authentication

There are all kinds of data types that you might be interested in synchronizing. For the average worker, the three that usually come to mind are e-mail, contacts, and calendar. The typical employee needs to be able to access these quickly and from various locations. That's why services such as Google, Yahoo!, and so on are so enticing—they allow integration of many services under one roof with one login. This is an example of single sign-on (SSO). SSO is when a user is authenticated to multiple services simply by logging in with a single username and password. The services might be accessed with separate apps, but it is all linked together. This suite of apps utilizes mutual authentication in the form of SSO, which is a type of federated identity management (FIM).

However, there is a lot more to synchronize when it comes to mobile devices, some of which a user might not want synced up. For example, location data, social media data, recorded voice data, and other information that can tell a lot about the user—data that the user might not want to share. These things are often enabled by default in most of today's services. To disable them, a user has to dig through the settings of the mobile device, and in some cases has to log through a web browser to do so.

Then there's pictures, videos, music, and plain-old documents in general. Most services such as the ones that Google and Apple provide will have a location to store files such as these (for example, Google Drive) and it is often associated with the SSO account. Or, a user might decide that for security purposes, the data should be stored locally at home or at a small office: enter the NAS—network-attached storage. These boxes can be set up to synchronize this data from a mobile device automatically. The benefit is that the data is stored at the home or office and behind a firewall, not on the cloud, which might be desired in some cases. Or, the user might decide to sync up this data to a desktop system. In that case, the desktop computer needs to meet several requirements, including OS version, hardware specs, and drivers, and perhaps needs a special program installed to communicate with the mobile device.

It seems like anything can be synchronized: website bookmarks, e-books, you name it. Even passwords. Every web browser out there has the ability to store and possibly synchronize passwords. There are also third-party programs that act as password vaults that you can access anywhere because they are stored on the cloud. However, most organizations frown at this practice because of the security implications. Generally, if a password vault is to be used, a locally saved one will be the most secure. But even locally stored vaults (such as KeePass) can be set up on the Internet. If a password vault has to be used for synchronization purposes, and it has to be on the cloud, then some additional security procedures should be implemented. For example, use a very strong master password to open the vault. Store the vault in an encrypted fashion on a secure server (which is a chapter unto itself). Update any password-storing software often. Limit the people who have access to the master password, and add that information to any offboarding scheme. Audit the vault so that you will have a log of *who* accessed the vault, *what* they did, and *when*. Remember the three Ws!

ExamAlert

Implement strong master passwords for any password vaults.

Cram Quiz

Answer these questions. The answers follow the last question. If you cannot answer these questions correctly, consider reading this section again until you can.

1. Which of the following is the most common connection method when synchronizing data from a mobile device to a PC?

   ○ **A.** Wi-Fi

   ○ **B.** Bluetooth

   ○ **C.** USB

   ○ **D.** Lightning

2. Which of the following is used to synchronize contacts from an iPad to a PC? (Select the best answer.)

   ○ **A.** Gmail

   ○ **B.** Google Play

   ○ **C.** iTunes

   ○ **D.** Sync Center

3. What is it known as when a user connects to several services using several apps
   but with only one username and password?

   ○ **A.** Android Auto

   ○ **B.** SSO

   ○ **C.** iTunes

   ○ **D.** BT

   ○ **E.** Exchange ActiveSync

Cram Quiz Answers

220-1001 Answers

1. **C.** USB is the most common connection method used when synchronizing data
   from a mobile device to a PC. Though Wi-Fi and Bluetooth are also possible, they
   are less common. Lightning is the port found on some of Apple's mobile devices,
   but the cable's other end is still USB when connecting to a PC or Mac.

2. **C.** PC users need iTunes to synchronize contacts and other data from an iPad to a
   PC. While Gmail can work to synchronize contacts, it is all based on web storage;
   nothing is actually stored on the iPad. Google Play is a place to get applications
   and other items for Android. Sync Center is a Control Panel utility that enables
   synchronization across Windows 10 devices.

3. **B.** SSO (single sign-on) is a type of authentication where a user logs in once but is
   granted access to multiple services. Android Auto is a screen sharing/synchroniz-
   ing app used on Android based mobile devices to communicate with a properly
   equipped automobile. iTunes is a music/media program that can be used to sync
   up a mobile device to a PC or Apple device. BT is short for Bluetooth. Exchange
   ActiveSync is a client-based protocol that allows a user to sync a mobile device
   with an Exchange Server mailbox.

Domain 2.0: Networking

CHAPTER 5

Ports, Protocols, and Network Devices

This chapter covers the following A+ 220-1001 exam objectives:

▶ **2.1** – Compare and contrast TCP and UDP ports, protocols, and their purposes.

▶ **2.2** – Compare and contrast common networking hardware devices.

We're back. Welcome to Domain 2: Networking. Knowing how to build computers and configure mobile devices is all well and good—but they have to communicate with each other, or very little gets done. That means you as the technician should have a good understanding of networking connections between computers on the local area network (LAN) and over the Internet. These next four chapters will set the foundation for your networking knowledge.

Let's talk. This first networking chapter discusses the TCP/IP ports and protocols that you should know for the exam; for example, the Domain Name System (DNS) on port 50. We'll first get into the most common networking devices such as switches, routers, wireless access points, and plenty more. It's these protocols and network devices that are at the core of network communications between computers.

2.1 – Compare and contrast TCP and UDP ports, protocols, and their purposes

To prepare for this objective we'll discuss the differences between TCP and UDP, why you would use each, and which protocols use them. Then we'll get into the individual protocols such as FTP, HTTP, RDP, and many more. It's imperative that you know this section—for the exam, and for the real world. That doesn't just mean knowing the acronyms and port numbers; it means understanding how the protocols work in real-world scenarios with real hardware and software. We'll try to incorporate these "use cases" as often as possible.

TCP vs. UDP

Network sessions on an IP network are normally either TCP or UDP. Let's briefly discuss these two.

Transmission Control Protocol (TCP) sessions are known as *connection-oriented sessions*. This means that every packet that is sent is checked for delivery. If the receiving computer doesn't receive a packet, it cannot assemble the message and will ask the sending computer to transmit the packet again.

TCP establishes network connections with a *3-way handshake*, a process that includes three steps:

1. **SYN:** The client computer attempts to initiate a session to a server with a synchronize packet of information (SYN packet)

2. **SYN + ACK:** The server responds to the client request by sending a synchronization/acknowledgment packet (SYN-ACK packet).

3. **ACK:** The client sends an acknowledgment packet (ACK packet) to the server.

Once the server receives that ACK packet, it acknowledges the session, and the network connection is established. This is also known as a *TCP socket connection*. With TCP, the synchronization, acknowledgment, and sequencing of packets guarantees delivery. Not a single packet is left behind! Not only that, but TCP uses a method known as *flow control*, which means that the sender does not overwhelm a server by sending too many packets, too quickly.

User Datagram Protocol (UDP) sessions are known as *connectionless sessions*. One example of UDP usage is with streaming media sessions. In these cases, if a packet is dropped, it is not asked for again. Let's say you were listening to some streaming music and you heard a break in the song or a blip of some kind. That indicates some missing packets, but you wouldn't want those packets back because by the time you get them, you would be listening to a totally different part of the music stream! Because of the nature of UDP, it does not use a handshake process or flow control, unlike TCP. It's expected that you might lose packets in UDP streams, but not when making TCP connections.

Both TCP and UDP utilize protocols and ports to make connections. Let's further discuss these protocols and ports now.

Ports and Protocols

There are many ports and protocols that computers will use to transmit information. The protocol used is based on the type of data to be transmitted and the application being used. We'll begin with HTTP and HTTPS.

HTTP vs. HTTPS

For two computers to communicate, they must both use the same protocol. For an application to send or receive data, it must use a particular protocol designed for that application and open a port on the network adapter to make a connection to another computer.

For example, let's say you want to visit a website. You type the name of that website into the address bar of a web browser and one of two protocols will be initiated: HTTP or HTTPS. Take a look at Table 5.1.

TABLE 5.1 **Comparing HTTP and HTTPS**

Protocol	Full Name	Default Port Number
HTTP	Hypertext Transfer Protocol	80
HTTPS	Hypertext Transfer Protocol Secure	443

HTTP and HTTPS both use TCP as their connection mechanism. HTTP was used for decades, but that practice has been reduced drastically in favor of the more secure HTTPS. For security reasons, most websites that you connect to today will use HTTPS. Primarily, HTTPS is designed to keep a user's information private and to prevent tampering and eavesdropping. Try connecting to some of your favorite websites and identify which protocol is being used. Most of them should be HTTPS, and those that are not should be avoided.

Let's say you connected to one of my websites by typing **dprocomputer.com**. When you do so, it will automatically be changed to **https://dprocomputer. com/blog** or something similar (which is known as a redirect). The important part is that it is using HTTPS for security. That is the protocol that makes the connection to the dprocomputer.com web server. The HTTPS protocol selects an unused port on your computer (known as an *outbound port*) to send and receive data to and from dprocomputer.com. On the other end, dprocomputer. com's web server has a specific port open at all times ready to accept sessions.

In most cases the web server's port is 443, which corresponds to the HTTPS protocol. This is known as an *inbound port*. Figure 5.1 illustrates this.

FIGURE 5.1 **HTTPS in action**

The local computer on the left in Figure 5.1 has been given the IP address 10.252.0.141. This is a private, internal address. It uses port 3515 to go out to the Internet and start a session with dprocomputer.com. For security purposes, this is a dynamically assigned port and will be different every time you connect to another web server, but it will normally be somewhere in the thousands. The session is accepted by dprocomputer.com's web server, using the public IP address 216.97.236.245, using inbound port 443. Conversely, if you want to run your own web server at home and sell widgets and such, that web server would need to have port 443, or the less secure port 80, open to the public at all times. If it were ever closed, you would lose sales! Computers that connect to your web server would use dynamically assigned ports.

HTTPS is used by the majority of websites today. It is recommended because of the secure connection it makes. It does this by connecting via a secure protocol such as Secure Sockets Layer (SSL) or Transport Layer Security (TLS) and using an encrypted certificate. We'll discuss this process more in Chapters 31–35 that focus on security.

ExamAlert

Use HTTPS for web servers whenever possible—usually on port 443.

E-mail Protocols

For people who share written communications with each other, e-mail protocols are a must. E-mail is sometimes accomplished using a web browser (HTTPS) or within an app that works in the same manner. This is great for the home user and for small businesses. However, for larger organizations using desktop computers, or if you simply need to connect directly to specific e-mail servers, you'll have to configure e-mail protocols. When setting up an e-mail client, you might need to know the protocols and ports involved. E-mail can be sent and received, so you will have to configure an outbound and an inbound server—which could be one and the same. Generally, the outbound server will be SMTP and the inbound server will be either POP3 or IMAP.

▶ **SMTP:** Simple Mail Transfer Protocol sends e-mail. When you send e-mail from the e-mail client, it goes to an SMTP server and is then sent off to its destination. The e-mail server could be at an ISP or could be supplied by the organization you work for, either in-house or in the cloud. A good way to remember this acronym is by using the mnemonic device *Send Mail To People*. The original default port for SMTP was 25, but in order to make use of an SSL- or TLS-encrypted session, you would use either 587 or 465, the choice depending on the type of encryption used and which protocol your ISP or administrator (or *you*) have selected.

▶ **POP3:** Post Office Protocol Version 3 is very common, and is used by e-mail clients to retrieve incoming e-mail from a mail server. The original POP3 server port was 110, but for secure transmissions, the default port is 995.

▶ **IMAP:** Internet Message Access Protocol is an e-mail protocol that enables messages to remain on the e-mail server so they can be retrieved from any location. IMAP also supports folders, so users can organize their messages as desired. IMAP e-mail servers used port 143 for many years, but for secure transmissions they use 993 by default.

On the client side, we must specify the server name and the correct ports for both the sending and receiving of e-mail. The protocols and ports must match exactly to the configuration of the e-mail server(s). E-mail clients include Outlook, Thunderbird, and a host of others. You can also use the Gmail application to connect to separate accounts using these protocols.

On the server side, there are several options available; for example, Microsoft Exchange can handle SMTP, POP3, and/or IMAP, as well as HTTPS connections from web browsers and from mobile devices by using Exchange Active-Sync, part of Exchange Online. Configuration of e-mail servers goes beyond the scope of the A+ exams.

FTP, SSH, and Telnet

If you need to communicate with an external host to send and receive files and/ or run commands on the external host, then you might be interested in FTP or SSH. Telnet, on the other hand, is deprecated, insecure, and should be avoided.

▶ **FTP:** The File Transfer Protocol allows computers to transfer files back and forth. When you connect to an FTP server, that FTP server will have port 21 open. Some type of FTP client software is necessary to connect to the FTP server; this could be done in the command line within the FTP shell or by using a GUI-based application (such as FileZilla). However, default FTP is not considered secure today. Instead, organizations usually prefer SFTP (discussed in the next bullet), or FTP Secure (FTPS), which uses SSL/TLS and utilizes port 989 and 990.

▶ **SSH:** Secure Shell enables data to be exchanged between computers on a secured channel. This protocol offers a more secure replacement to FTP and Telnet. The Secure Shell server housing the data you want to access would have port 22 open. There are several other protocols that use SSH as a way of making a secure connection. One of these is the commonly used Secure FTP (SFTP). As mentioned, regular FTP can be insecure. SFTP combats this by providing file access over a reliable data stream, generated and protected by SSH.

▶ **Telnet:** Short for Telecommunication network, this provides remote access to other hosts using the command-line interface (CLI). It uses port 23 but is an insecure and somewhat deprecated protocol. However, because some companies *might* still use it to access routers and other hosts, and to test and manage network connectivity, you might see a question about it on the exam. Generally, Telnet is disabled, if it even exists, in the OS. If you are wondering if it is enabled in Windows, you can do a quick check for it in the Services console window (**Run > services.msc**). If it is not listed, then it is not enabled. It can be enabled or disabled here: **Control Panel > Programs and Features > Turn Windows features on or off**.

DHCP

The Dynamic Host Configuration Protocol (DHCP) is used to automatically assign IP addresses to hosts. These hosts could be computers, printers, servers, routers, and so on. In most small office/home office (SOHO) networks, a router will use DHCP to assign IP addresses to the client computers. However, your ISP will also use DHCP to assign an IP address to you; usually your router gets this. The DHCP service makes life easier for the network administrator by automatically assigning IP addresses, subnet masks, gateway addresses, DNS servers, and so on, from a central location. If you get your address from a DHCP server, you are getting your address assigned dynamically, and it could change periodically. Computers that do obtain IP addresses from a DHCP server have the advantage of automatically getting new addressing when they are moved to a different network segment. However, some computers require a static address, one that is assigned by the network administrator manually. It is better in many situations for servers and printers to use static addresses so you know exactly what the address is and so it won't change.

By default, a DHCP server needs to have inbound port 67 open, and a DHCP client uses port 68 to connect out to that DHCP server. By the way, DHCP is also referred to as *bootp*—short for Bootstrap Protocol.

DHCP servers use a four-step process to assign IP addresses to clients—it is most commonly known as DORA. Table 5.2 briefly describes each of these steps. The first letter of each step forms the acronym DORA.

TABLE 5.2 **DHCP Four-Step Process—DORA**

Step	Description
Discovery	The client looks for and discovers a DHCP server.
Offering	The server offers an IP address to the client (or more than one).
Request	The client "picks" an address and requests that it be assigned.
Acknowledgment	The server acknowledges the request and the client can then use the IP address for a set amount of time, which is known as a *lease*.

Note

The DORA process happens in a flash. And sometimes, only half of the process is necessary. For example, if a client computer temporarily uses a static address and then goes back to a dynamic address. The original dynamic address is remembered by the computer, so the computer simply requests that same IP address, which means only the request and acknowledgment steps are required.

DNS

The Domain Name System (DNS) is the group of servers on the Internet that translates domain names to IP addresses. For example, a domain name such as *dprocomputer.com* might translate to the IP address 216.97.236.245. When you connect to a website by name, the DNS server takes care of resolving the name to the IP address so that your computer and the web server can communicate via IP. To find out the DNS server that your Windows computer talks to, type the command **ipconfig /all** in the Command Prompt.

A DNS server has inbound port 53 open by default. We'll discuss DNS servers more in Chapter 7, "Networked Hosts and Network Configuration."

LDAP and RDP

The Lightweight Directory Access Protocol (LDAP) is used to access and maintain distributed directories of information (such as the kind involved with Microsoft domains). Microsoft refers to this as Active Directory, and also directory services or domain services. It includes the user accounts, computer accounts, groups, and the authentication and permissions involved with those accounts. To have this in a domain, at least one Windows Server must be promoted to a domain controller. When you do this, LDAP is installed and runs on inbound port 389. A more secure version of LDAP (Secure LDAP) can also be installed and configured. This runs on port 636.

To facilitate connections to remote computers and allow full remote control, Microsoft uses the Remote Desktop Connection program, which is based off the Remote Desktop Protocol (RDP). This works in three ways. First, users can be given limited access to a remote computer's applications (such as Word or Excel). Second, administrators can be given full access to a computer so that they can troubleshoot problems from another location. Third, another part of the program known as Remote Assistance allows users to invite a technician to view their desktops in the hopes that the technician can fix any encountered problems. These invitations can be made via e-mail. The RDP port, 3389, is also used by Remote Desktop Services/Microsoft Terminal Services, which is the server-based companion of Remote Desktop. Figure 5.2 shows the results of a netstat command that was run on a Windows Server that was upgraded to a domain controller. You can see that inbound port 389 is open—indicating LDAP is running and that it is indeed a domain controller—as well as port 3389, which allows for remote control of the server, which is exactly what I am doing in the figure.

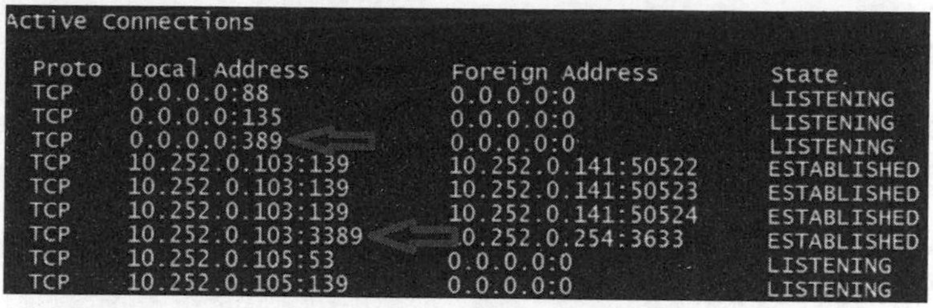

```
Active Connections

  Proto  Local Address          Foreign Address         State
  TCP    0.0.0.0:88             0.0.0.0:0               LISTENING
  TCP    0.0.0.0:135            0.0.0.0:0               LISTENING
  TCP    0.0.0.0:389       ←    0.0.0.0:0               LISTENING
  TCP    10.252.0.103:139       10.252.0.141:50522      ESTABLISHED
  TCP    10.252.0.103:139       10.252.0.141:50523      ESTABLISHED
  TCP    10.252.0.103:139       10.252.0.141:50524      ESTABLISHED
  TCP    10.252.0.103:3389 ←    10.252.0.254:3633       ESTABLISHED
  TCP    10.252.0.105:53        0.0.0.0:0               LISTENING
  TCP    10.252.0.105:139       0.0.0.0:0               LISTENING
```

FIGURE 5.2   **LDAP and RDP ports on a Windows Server**

More Protocols and Ports

There are a few more protocols that you should know for the exam, including
SMB/CIFS, NetBIOS/NetBT, AFP, SNMP, and SLP.

▶ **SMB:** The Server Message Block protocol provides access to shared
items such as files and printers. These are actual packets that authenticate
remote computers through what are known as interprocess communication (IPC) mechanisms. They can communicate directly over TCP using
port 445 or by working with the NetBIOS/NetBT protocol using a port
between 137 and 139. In the past, SMB was also referred to as the
Common Internet File System (CIFS) protocol.

▶ **AFP:** Apple Filing Protocol offers file services for Mac computers running macOS and OS X, allowing for the transfer of files across the network. It uses port 548 for establishing the communication between two
systems. Mac computers can also make use of SMB (and other protocols)
for making connections to other systems.

▶ **SNMP:** Simple Network Management Protocol is used as the standard
for managing and monitoring devices on your network. It manages routers, switches, UPS devices, and computers and is often incorporated in
software known as a network management system (NMS). The NMS is
the main software that controls everything SNMP-based; it is installed on
a computer known as a manager. The devices to be monitored are known
as managed devices. The NMS installs a small piece of software known
as an agent that allows the NMS to monitor those managed devices and
alert the SNMP manager software—and ultimately the administrator.
If there is an alert to be sent to an administrator, it is known as a trap.
SNMP by default uses port 161, and SNMP traps use port 162.

▶ **SLP:** The Service Location Protocol is a service discovery protocol that allows computers and other devices to find services in a local area network without prior configuration. It uses port 427 by default as its listening port.

Wow, that was a mouthful of acronyms. Study them and their port numbers! Use Table 5.3 to help. You will note that there are secure versions of some of the protocols and that each uses a different port number than the insecure version. You will also find whether a protocol rides on TCP, or UDP, or both. I listed the protocol name in the first column, but the table is sorted by port number for easier reference.

TABLE 5.3 **Protocol and Port Listing**

Protocol	Original Port	Secure Port	TCP/UDP Usage
FTP	21	989/990	TCP
SSH	22	22	TCP or UDP
Telnet	23	Not considered a secure protocol	TCP or UDP
SMTP	25	587 or 465	TCP
DNS	53		TCP or UDP
DHCP	67 (server) 68 (client)		TCP or UDP
HTTP	80	443 (HTTPS)	TCP
POP3	110	995	TCP
NetBIOS/NetBT	137–139		TCP or UDP
IMAP	143	993	TCP
SNMP	161		UDP
SNMPTRAP	162		TCP or UDP
LDAP	389	636	TCP or UDP
SLP	427		TCP or UDP
SMB	445		TCP
AFP	548		TCP
RDP	3389		TCP or UDP

ExamAlert

Know your protocols and their functions for the exam! Write 'em down or make flash cards to commit them to memory.

Note

There are 65,536 ports, but you only need to know a handful of them for the exam. If you want to find out about more of them, check out the complete list provided by the Internet Assigned Numbers Authority (IANA): https://www.iana.org/assignments/service-names-port-numbers/service-names-port-numbers.xml.

Cram Quiz

Answer these questions. The answers follow the last question. If you cannot answer these questions correctly, consider reading this section again until you can.

1. Which protocol uses port 22?
   - ○ **A.** FTP
   - ○ **B.** Telnet
   - ○ **C.** SSH
   - ○ **D.** HTTPS

2. Which of these would be used for streaming media?
   - ○ **A.** TCP
   - ○ **B.** RDP
   - ○ **C.** UDP
   - ○ **D.** DHCP

3. Which ports are used by the IMAP protocol?
   - ○ **A.** 53 and 68
   - ○ **B.** 80 and 443
   - ○ **C.** 110 and 995
   - ○ **D.** 143 and 993

4. A user can receive e-mail but cannot send any. Which protocol is not configured properly?

   ○ **A.** POP3

   ○ **B.** FTP

   ○ **C.** SMTP

   ○ **D.** SNMP

Cram Quiz Answers

1. **C.** SSH (Secure Shell) uses port 22. FTP uses port 21, Telnet uses port 23, and HTTPS uses port 443.

2. **C.** User Datagram Protocol (UDP) is used for streaming media. It is connection-less, whereas TCP is connection-oriented and not a good choice for streaming media. RDP is the Remote Desktop Protocol used to make connections to other computers. DHCP is the Dynamic Host Configuration Protocol used to assign IP addresses to clients automatically.

3. **D.** The Internet Message Access Protocol (IMAP) uses port 143 by default and port 993 as a secure default. DNS uses port 53. DHCP uses port 68. HTTP uses port 80. HTTPS uses port 443. POP3 uses port 110 and 995 as a secure default. Know those ports!

4. **C.** The Simple Mail Transfer Protocol (SMTP) is probably not configured properly. It deals with sending mail. POP3 receives mail. FTP sends files to remote computers. SNMP is used to manage networks.

2.2 – Compare and contrast common networking hardware devices

In this section we'll discuss the most common network hardware devices you'll be dealing with, including routers, switches, wireless access points, and many more.

As a computer technician you will be required to be able to connect to and configure network hardware. To allow communication between computers, we need to put some other devices in place. For example, switches, and access points connect computers on the LAN. Routers and firewalls enable connectivity to other networks and protect those connection points. The A+ Core 1 (220-1001) exam covers only the basics about networking, but it is still a lot of material to cover, so let's get to it!

Switches

A *switch* is a central connecting device that all computers connect to in a wired fashion (a design known as a star topology). A switch sends the signal (frames of data) to the correct computer instead of broadcasting it out to every port (the way an older hub would). It does this by identifying the media access control (MAC) address of each computer. The MAC address is the physical address that is programmed into the network adapter; for example 00-0C-29-C6-XX-XX. (In Windows, run a quick **ipconfig /all** to find out your MAC address.) By identifying each computer's MAC address, the switch can effectively make every port on the switch an individual entity. To further accomplish this, switches employ a matrix of copper wiring—everything is interconnected between the ports.

Switches are intelligent, and they use this intelligence to pass information to the correct port. This means that each computer has its own bandwidth (for example, 1000 Mbps). In today's networks, the switch is commonly found in 1000-Mbps (1-Gbps) and 10-Gbps networks. You might also see older 100-Mbps connections, though those should usually be upgraded to take advantage of today's hardware and software.

Switches work within the Ethernet standard, which is the most common networking standard used today; it was ratified by the IEEE and is documented in the 802.3 set of standards. For example, a typical Ethernet network running at 1000 Mbps and using twisted-pair cable is classified as 802.3ab. 10-Gbps Ethernet over twisted-pair cable is 802.3an.

Understand the difference between a managed switch and an unmanaged switch. Managed switches can be configured when accessed from a browser or SSH or similar configuration tool. For example, you can change the device's IP address, turn on Spanning Tree Protocol (STP) to avoid network looping, enable system logging (syslog), and monitor the switch and other devices with SNMP. On the other hand, unmanaged switches don't have these capabilities; they simply connect devices and computers together for transmission of data over the Ethernet network. Unmanaged switches are an inexpensive method of adding computers to your network.

A switch connects computers together in a wired fashion. From a design standpoint this is known as a *star topology*, with the switch in the "center" of it all. It is also the basis for a local area network (LAN). But what if you want to connect two LANs together? For example, two LANs that are in different cities? Enter the router.

Routers

A *router* is used to connect two or more networks to form an internetwork. Routers are used in LANs and WANs and on the Internet. This device routes data from one location to another, usually by way of IP address and IP network numbers. Routers are intelligent and even have their own operating systems. The router enables connections with individual high-speed interconnection points. A common example would be an all-in-one device or multifunction network device that might be used in a home or small office. These devices route signals for all the computers on the LAN out to the Internet. Larger organizations use more advanced routers that can make connections to multiple various networks as well as the Internet.

Wireless Access Points

A *wireless access point (WAP)*—or simply access point—enables data communications over the air when your computer is equipped with a wireless networking adapter. The WAP and the wireless networking adapter transmit data over radio waves either on the 2.4-GHz or 5-GHz frequencies. Wireless access points are everywhere you look: hotels, restaurants, shopping centers, you name it. This all-presence of WAPs brings mobility to a new level.

WAPs are also included in most multifunction network devices, known as SOHO routers or simply routers. This enables wireless computers to not only communicate with each other but also access the Internet. Although hubs and switches deal with wired networks, the WAP deals with wireless connections. It is also based on Ethernet, but now we are talking about the IEEE 802.11 group of standards that defines wireless LANs (WLANs), simply referred to as Wi-Fi. Wireless access points act as a central connecting point for Wi-Fi–equipped computers. Like the switch, a WAP identifies each computer by its MAC address.

Firewalls

A *firewall* is any hardware appliance or software application that protects a computer from unwanted intrusion. In the networking world, we are more concerned with hardware-based devices that protect an entire group of computers (such as a LAN). When it comes to small offices and home offices, firewall functionality is usually built into the router. In larger organizations, it is a separate device. Or it could be part of a more complex, all-in-one solution. The firewall stops unwanted connections from the outside and can block basic networking attacks. We'll discuss firewalls more in Chapter 31, "Physical and Logical Security," and Chapter 35, "Data Destruction and SOHO Security."

Network Interface Cards

A network interface card (NIC, pronounced like "*nick*"), also known as a network adapter, is a physical device that can be added to a computer or networking device that has an open and compatible slot. For example, a computer with an open PCI Express slot (×1 or ×4) can be used with a NIC. This allows for connectivity to a computer network. Most PCs and laptops have these built into the motherboard—these are known as *integrated NICs*. However, workstations and servers often require a more powerful, and separate network interface card, or more than one. Quite often, a server will use special network cards that have two, four, or more RJ45 ports to allow for increased data throughput as well as higher availability. We'll discuss the NIC more in Chapter 11, "Motherboards and Add-on Cards."

> **ExamAlert**
>
> For the exam and for the IT field, the last five items we discussed are probably the most important of this section: switches, routers, access points, firewalls, and network interface cards.

Cloud-based Network Controllers

A *network controller* is software (or a device and software) that provides for centralized management, configuration, and monitoring of a computer network—be it physical or virtual. It is often programmable and can automate its tasks to help you to manage your network infrastructure. A cloud-based network controller is simply one that you access over the Internet at your cloud provider: Microsoft, Amazon, Google, IBM, and so on. Or, it's one that is jointly managed by your organization and the cloud provider. That will all depend on the type of service you are paying for and have contracted for.

Repeaters

A *repeater* or extender is a device used to lengthen the signal farther than it was designed to go originally. For example, a standard wired LAN connection from a switch can transmit data 328 feet (100 meters), but a repeater could increase that distance by as much as two times. There are repeaters for wireless access points as well that can increase the range of your overall wireless network.

Hubs

The *hub* is the original connecting device for computers on the LAN. It creates a simple shared physical connection that all computers use to send data. It's a basic device that has multiple ports, usually in intervals of four. Internally, the hub actually has only one main circuit that all the ports connect to (as opposed to a switch that has a matrix of circuits). It regenerates and passes on the electrical signals initiated by computers. This device broadcasts data out to all computers. The computer that it is meant for accepts the data; the rest drop the information. Because of this broadcasting and sharing, this device allows only two computers to communicate with each other at any given time. In the days of 10-Mbps and 100-Mbps networks, it was common to have a hub. It's still listed on the A+ objectives, but in most instances today, the hub has given way to the switch.

> **Note**
>
> One thing you have to watch out for with a switch is something known as a *flood attack*. This type of attack can consume all the memory in the switch and cause it to fail-open, which means that it will fail to work as a switch, but will still work as a hub. This reduces the network throughput down to 10 percent or less and can also be a security concern. Update your switches and monitor them!

Cable/DSL Modems

Essentially, a cable or DSL modem is a device that allows a computer (or SOHO network) to access the Internet. Cable Internet and digital subscriber line (DSL) Internet connections use separate devices to connect. For example, a person with a cable Internet connection will use a device that has an RG-6 port for the provider's incoming coaxial cable. A DSL modem, on the other hand, will have an RJ11 port that makes use of a person's telephone line. Both, however, use an RJ45 port that connects to the consumer's computer or SOHO router by way of a twisted-pair patch cable.

> **Note**
>
> The term *modem* is a combination of the words *modulate* and *demodulate*. It originated with the dial-up modem that uses a standard telephone phone line. We'll discuss dial-up more in Chapter 8, "Network Types and Networking Tools." While it is arguable whether cable and DSL Internet devices are actually "modems," the plain truth is that the term is commonly used—even by manufacturers.

Bridges

The *bridge* is a device that can either connect two LANs together or separate them into two sections. There are wired bridges and wireless bridges; today they are used to increase the size of networks.

Patch Panels

A *patch panel* is a physical hardware device that acts as a termination point for all of the network cables in a building. It is often located in a wiring closet, server room, or data center, depending on the size of the organization. It consists of multiple RJ45 ports on the front that connect to switches by way of twisted-pair patch cables, and 110 IDC termination points on the back for connecting all of the individual wires in twisted-pair cables. Those cables lead out to the various computer ports in the building. While it isn't necessary to have a patch panel, it makes for easier patching of ports and is more reliable. A typical physical data path from a user to a server is: Computer > RJ45 jack > twisted-pair cable > patch panel > switch(s) > server.

Power over Ethernet

Power over Ethernet (PoE) is an Ethernet standard that allows for the passing of electrical power in addition to data over Ethernet cabling. It is described in the IEEE 802.3af-2003, 802.3at-2009, and 802.3bt standards. PoE can deliver between 15.4 and 100 watts maximum to a variety of devices, as long as the sending and receiving devices are both PoE compliant. The exact amount of wattage will depend on the standard, but 15 to 30 watts is common.

PoE is an excellent solution for devices that require specific placement but where no electrical connection can be made (for example, outdoor video cameras or WAPs that need to be mounted to the ceiling). In these cases, all that needs to be run is a twisted-pair network cable, which takes care of power *and* data. No electrical connection is necessary.

The technology is broken down into the two devices:

▶ The power sourcing equipment (PSE), which could be a switch or other similar device

▶ The powered device (PD), which, as mentioned, could be an IP-based camera (or WAP) and also an IP phone, IPTV device, router, mini network switch, industrial device, lighting controller, and more

For organizations with a group of remote devices, a 24- or 48-port PoE-enabled switch is the way to go. For a smaller organization that only has one or two remote devices that need to be powered, the *PoE injector* is a decent, cheaper PSE solution. This device is installed where the main network switch is and plugs into one of the switch's ports. It is also powered normally from an AC outlet. But the injector has a second RJ45 port used to connect out to the remote device. This port sends Ethernet data as well as power over the Ethernet connection. This way, the organization can get power and data to a PoE-compliant access point, IP camera, or other device that needs to be located in an area where it would be difficult (not to mention expensive) to add an electrical outlet. However, the correct type of cabling must be used that can handle the amperage required. Generally, this is Category 5 twisted-pair cabling and higher.

Ethernet over Power

Crossing the lines again, here we have Ethernet over power, which is effectively the converse of what we just discussed with PoE. In this case we are sending data over electrical lines. This is one variant of a concept known as power-line communication (PLC), which includes options for Ethernet, broadband, tele-communications, and more. In the home or office, it is usually implemented over standard 120-V AC electrical lines. To do this we add a modulated carrier signal to the wiring system. A power-line network uses power adapters for the AC outlets and Ethernet patch cables that connect from the adapters to what-ever is needed (for example, a compliant router). This technology can be a good solution where it is very difficult to run twisted-pair cables but 120-V AC elec-trical lines already exist.

> **ExamAlert**
>
> Know your network devices and try to imagine actual ways that you might incorpo-rate them into your home or office.

Cram Quiz

Answer these questions. The answers follow the last question. If you cannot answer those questions correctly, consider reading this section again until you can.

1. Which of the following is most often used to connect a group of computers in a LAN? (Select all that apply.)
   - ○ **A.** Router
   - ○ **B.** Switch
   - ○ **C.** Bridge
   - ○ **D.** WAP

2. What device protects a network from unwanted intrusion?
   - ○ **A.** Switch
   - ○ **B.** Router
   - ○ **C.** Access point
   - ○ **D.** Firewall

3. Which of the following network devices moves frames of data between a source and destination based on their MAC addresses?

   O **A.** Hub

   O **B.** Switch

   O **C.** Router

   O **D.** Modem

4. Which of the following network devices allows a remote device to obtain Ethernet data as well as electrical power?

   O **A.** PD

   O **B.** PoE injector

   O **C.** Repeater

   O **D.** Router

5. Which of the following devices can be configured when accessed from a browser or SSH or similar configuration tool?

   O **A.** Managed switch

   O **B.** Unmanaged switch

   O **C.** Patch panel

   O **D.** Network interface card

Cram Quiz Answers

1. **B and D.** Computers in a LAN are connected by a central connecting device; the most common of which are the switch and the wireless access point (WAP). Hubs can also be used, but those are deprecated devices; they are the predecessor of the switch. A router is designed to connect two networks together. Now, you might say, "Wait! My router at home has four ports on the back for computers to talk to each other." Well, that is actually the switch portion of a SOHO "router." The actual *router* functionality is in the connection between the two networks—the switched LAN and the Internet. A bridge is used to connect two LANs or separate a single LAN into two sections.

2. **D.** A firewall is a hardware appliance or software application that protects one or more computers from unwanted intrusion. A switch is a device that connects multiple computers together on a LAN. A router is used to connect two or more networks. An access point (or wireless access point) allows Wi-Fi–enabled computers and devices to communicate on the LAN wirelessly.

3. **B.** A switch sends frames of data between computers by identifying the systems by their MAC addresses. A hub broadcasts data out to all computers. The computer that it is meant for accepts the data; the rest drop the information. Routers enable connections with individual high-speed interconnection points and route signals for all the computers on the LAN out to the Internet. A modem is a device that allows a computer to access the Internet by changing the digital signals of the computer to analog signals used by a typical land-based phone line.

4. **B.** A Power over Ethernet (PoE) injector sends Ethernet data and power over a single twisted-pair cable to a remote device. PD stands for "powered device," the PoE-compliant remote device that is receiving the power. A repeater extends the distance of a network connection. While a PoE injector can act as a repeater, not all repeaters are PoE injectors. A router makes connections from one network to another or from the LAN to the Internet.

5. **A.** Managed switches can be configured when accessed from a browser or SSH or similar configuration tool. For example, you can change the device's IP address, configure ports, and monitor the switch and other devices with SNMP. On the other hand, unmanaged switches don't have these capabilities; they simply connect devices and computers together for transmission of data over the Ethernet network. A patch panel is a physical hardware device that acts as a termination point for all of the network cables in a building. A network interface card (NIC) allows for connectivity to a computer network. It is a physical device that can be added to a computer or networking device that has an open and compatible slot.

Another chapter done! Memorize those protocols and port numbers, take a quick breather, and move on!

CHAPTER 6

SOHO Networks and Wireless Protocols

This chapter covers the following A+ 220-1001 exam objectives:

▶ **2.3** – Given a scenario, install and configure a basic wired/wireless SOHO network.

▶ **2.4** – Compare and contrast wireless networking protocols.

This chapter focuses in on small office/home office (SOHO) networks. I'm talking about networks of less than 20 computers typically. These are driven by what we call a SOHO router—a combo device that includes a switch for wired connections, a connection to the Internet, a firewall, and wireless connectivity. Sometimes you will wire computers to the network, and perhaps more often, you will use wireless. Wireless takes the cable out of the mix, and allows for mobility and ease of use. But I caution you—the air is shared! So, when planning your wireless technologies, especially Wi-Fi, you have to take into account such things as frequencies, desired data transfer rates, distance between devices, and much more. We'll cover it all, but first, we need to configure that main point of access—the SOHO router.

2.3 – Given a scenario, install and configure a basic wired/wireless SOHO network

ExamAlert

Objective 2.3 concentrates on the following concepts: router/switch functionality, access point settings, IP addressing, NIC configuration, end-user device configuration, IoT device configuration, cable/DSL modem configuration, firewall settings, QoS, and wireless settings.

To prepare you for this objective we'll discuss how to set up a SOHO network including a SOHO router, wired connections, and wireless connections. In many cases, SOHO networking is easy, and automated—it was designed that way. However, sometimes you need to manually configure information. That's what makes a good tech. Let's go!

Router Setup and Wireless

Okay! Let's talk about the setup and configuration of our SOHO router. These devices have been called a plethora of different names—router, switch, firewall, access point, or multifunction network device—because they usually incorporate all of those functions into one device. Again, for simplicity, we'll refer to this as a *router*.

SOHO Router Setup

First, the router needs to be physically connected, which is very easy. It requires power from an AC outlet and a connection to the Internet, which is done with a twisted-pair patch cable using RJ45 plugs on each end; one end connects to the Internet (or WAN) port of the router, and the other end connects to the cable modem or other network interface device.

Most SOHO routers are set up to be plug-and-play, meaning that computers can be plugged in to the device's switch ports (often four of them) and they can communicate with each other and access the Internet right out of the box. But a word of caution: Watch out for the default settings that the manufacturer gives you; they might be insecure. So, the first thing we want to do is to log in to the router so that we can make some changes. (We'll assume that your computers are already cabled to the router.) To do this, open a browser window and type the IP address of the router. For example, different manufacturers use different default IP addresses (such as 192.168.0.1 or 192.168.1.1) or they allow a connection via a URL (such as http://routername). Check your documentation to find out what the address or link is. Sometimes the login information is very basic (for example, "admin" is the username) and there is no password or there is a very basic password (possibly the same as the username). That will depend on the age and manufacturer of the router. Newer routers usually offer more security. Again, the documentation that came with the router will tell you the defaults.

Once you have gained access to the router, the first thing you want to do is change the password to something more complex—in fact, you might be required to do it. Consider changing the username also, if possible. Next, update the firmware so that it gets the latest functionality, options, and security available. Now that the device has some basic security and is updated, it is ready to be configured.

SOHO routers normally obtain an IP address from the Internet service provider (ISP); it is dynamically assigned and is known as the *WAN address*. It is a public address that is visible on the Internet. The router also has a LAN address, which is a private address visible only to the computers on your network. That is the address you used to log in to the router (192.168.0.1 or 192.168.1.1, and so on) and also acts as the gateway address for the clients on your network. Figure 6.1 shows the LAN and WAN settings on a typical SOHO router.

LAN	
MAC Address:	30-B5-C2-B2-59-E6
IP Address:	192.168.0.1
Subnet Mask:	255.255.255.0

WAN	
MAC Address:	30-B5-C2-B2-59-E7
IP Address:	64.121.138.225
Subnet Mask:	255.255.240.0
Default Gateway:	64.121.128.1
DNS Server:	208.59.247.45 , 208.59.247.46

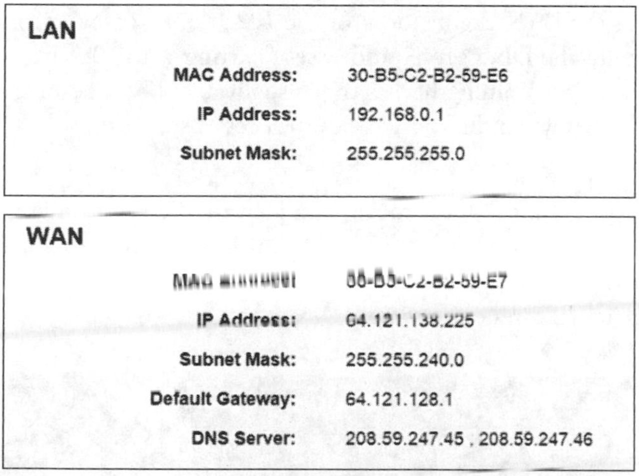

FIGURE 6.1   LAN and WAN connections on a typical SOHO router

As you can see from the figure, the router's LAN address is 192.168.0.1. This device makes use of DHCP, which can be turned on or off. When on, it automatically assigns IP addresses to most of the clients on this network starting with 192.168.0.100 and ascending from there—192.168.0.101, 192.168.0.102, and so on. The router and all of the clients are on the same local area network number (192.168.0.0) using the same subnet mask (255.255.255.0), so they can all communicate with each other. We'll discuss IP addressing in more depth within Chapter 7, "Networked Hosts and Network Configuration."

> **Note**
>
> Most people are wireless crazy nowadays, but don't forget that these SOHO routers have a built-in switch: they normally come with four wired LAN ports typically rated for 1000BASE-T. That means that it can transmit data at 1000 Mbps (1 Gbps). The BASE applies to any speed, and it is short for baseband, meaning every computer on the network shares the same channel or frequency. The T is short for twisted pair. By default, unshielded twisted-pair cables can send data 328 feet (100 meters) before the electronic signal attenuates to such a point where it is useless.

In Figure 6.1, the WAN address is 64.121.138.225. This was obtained automatically from the ISP and allows connectivity to the ISP's network infrastructure and out to the Internet. The subnet mask (255.255.240.0) is not a default subnet mask, so we know that subnetting (the subdividing of an IP network) has been implemented. The default gateway (64.121.128.1) is the address that our router looks for to get into (and beyond) the ISP network and out to the Internet, just as the LAN clients look for the 192.168.0.1 gateway to go beyond the LAN. Finally, the DNS server addresses (starting with 208) are on a completely different network altogether, as they usually are. These resolve domain names to IP addresses when the router tries to access a server on the Internet.

If you have one, take a look at your SOHO router and identify the LAN and WAN addresses. The numbers will often be different, but the concepts remain the same. If you don't have a SOHO router, you can easily find an emulator of a router online—many manufacturers offer them.

> **ExamAlert**
>
> Understand the concept of the LAN and WAN addresses of a SOHO router. It is the basis for all routing!

In some cases, you need to use a static IP address for your WAN connection, or perhaps you need to configure a secure connection to the Internet with Point-to-Point Tunneling Protocol (PPTP) or Layer 2 Tunneling Protocol (L2TP). If that is the case, you would have to input the correct information, including IP address, subnet mask, gateway, and DNS servers (and possibly a username). This information should be provided to you by the ISP you connect to.

Access Point Settings

Let's take a look at the actual wireless settings of a typical router. Examine Figure 6.2.

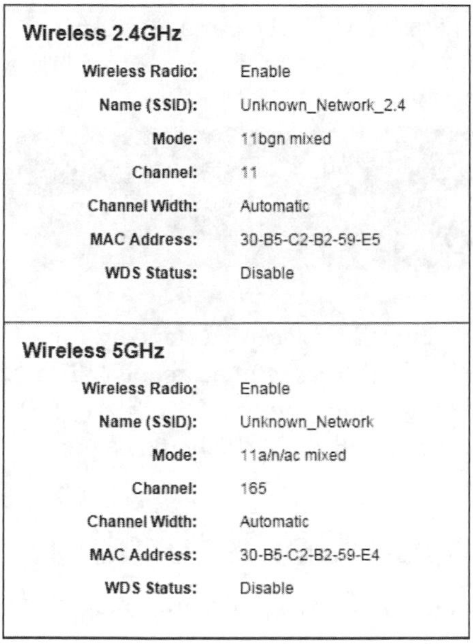

Wireless 2.4GHz

Wireless Radio:	Enable
Name (SSID):	Unknown_Network_2.4
Mode:	11bgn mixed
Channel:	11
Channel Width:	Automatic
MAC Address:	30-B5-C2-B2-59-E5
WDS Status:	Disable

Wireless 5GHz

Wireless Radio:	Enable
Name (SSID):	Unknown_Network
Mode:	11a/n/ac mixed
Channel:	165
Channel Width:	Automatic
MAC Address:	30-B5-C2-B2-59-E4
WDS Status:	Disable

FIGURE 6.2   Wireless configuration on a typical SOHO router

We can see that this device is running two wireless networks: one on the 2.4-GHz frequency and one on 5 GHz. Each has its own network name, also known as a Service Set Identifier (SSID). For example, the 5-GHz network's SSID is "Unknown_Network." (A bit of a quirky name, but you'll find that peculiar names are somewhat common when it comes to SSIDs.) That's the name that users would need to know in order to make a wireless connection to the LAN. It's currently running on channel 165. If using the 5-GHz frequency range in the United States, a wireless access point can be set up on several channels between 48 and 165. Other countries may have slightly different ranges. The wireless network shown in Figure 6.2 is currently configured to run in mixed mode, meaning that it can accept connections from wireless clients running the 802.11a, 802.11n, or 802.11ac protocols. This allows for greater compatibility. However, some organizations will require only a single type of connection for all clients (for example, 802.11ac). This can result in greater WAP efficiency and, of course, greater speed for all clients involved—but at greater expense.

The other wireless network on the 2.4-GHz frequency is set to channel 11. In the United States, the 2.4-GHz frequency range consists of channels 1 through 11. (Again, other countries may differ slightly.) For noninterference with other wireless networks, space your frequency selection apart wisely (more on that later in the "802.11 Wireless" section). This network is also running in mixed mode; it allows connections from 802.11b, 802.11g, and 802.11n (2.4 GHz) wireless clients.

> **ExamAlert**
>
> Know the difference between the wireless frequencies 5 GHz and 2.4 GHz and the channel ranges for each.

It's important to encrypt the wireless connection. The accepted standard for SOHO networks (as of the writing of this book) is to use the protocols Wi-Fi Protected Access Version 2 (WPA2) and Advanced Encryption Standard (AES). We'll discuss these protocols more as we progress through the book.

NIC and End-user Device Configuration

When configuring and analyzing the NIC, we can use several status indicators; some are hardware-based and some are software-oriented.

> **Note**
>
> Technicians use several terms when referring to a network card: network adapter, network interface controller (NIC), network interface card, Ethernet card, and so on. Be ready for different terminology on the exam and in the field. For this chapter, I usually refer to it as network adapter because it won't always be in "card" format.

The first types of indicators are physical; they show up as LED lights on the network adapter itself. Different network adapters have different LED lights, but typically you have a connectivity LED and an activity LED. The connectivity LED tells you if you have a good connection to a router or switch by displaying a solid color (for example, solid green), which would mean connectivity at 1000 Mbps. However, if the connectivity LED is blinking, then you know there is an intermittent connection that should be troubleshot. The activity LED blinks when data is passing through the network adapter. The functionality of both might be combined into one LED on some network adapters.

The second group of indicators is logical and shows up in the operating system. In Windows, these indicators normally manifest themselves in the Notification Area and can be put there by Windows or by the manufacturer of the network adapter, depending on whether you let Windows install the card or you used the additional software that came with the network adapter. However, you can add a shortcut to network adapters and place them on the desktop or on the taskbar.

Let's check out the status of a wired network connection and a wireless network connection. On a Windows system, right-click the Network icon in the Notification Area and select **Open Network and Sharing Center**. If wireless is your primary method of connecting to the network, you will see a wireless icon; if your primary connection is wired, you will see a little icon displaying a monitor and network cable.

In the Network and Sharing Center window, click the **Change adapter settings** link. This opens the Network Connections window. Double-click the desired connection to bring up its status window. This is named "Wi-Fi" for the wireless adapter or "Ethernet" ("Local Area Connection" in Windows 7) for the wired adapter. Figure 6.3 shows both types of connections.

> **Note**
>
> You can change the name of the network connection. Know the different names and the default settings.

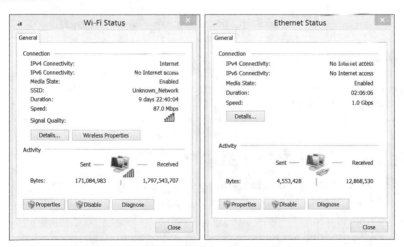

FIGURE 6.3 **Wireless and wired network adapter status**

From here, we can see what our "speed" is, how long we have been connected, and how many bytes have been sent and received. For example, the Wi-Fi connection is connected at 87 Mbps, even though it is a strong signal on an 802.11ac network (you can imagine the data that flies through my airwaves). On less frequently used wireless networks—or scenarios where the computer is in close proximity to the WAP—you might see connections of up to 300 Mbps, 600 Mbps, or even 1 Gbps. As you can see, the speed indicator can be very telling about a wireless connection. If you suspect a slow wireless speed, make sure that the latest driver is installed, verify placement of the wireless antennas, check for interference, and even check for unauthorized usage of the wireless network. Consider using a Wi-Fi analyzer to investigate your wireless network and the wireless networks around you. You might find that there is some frequency and channel overlap.

In the second window in Figure 6.3, we see that the Ethernet connection has a 1-Gbps connection. Remember that these connection speeds are the maximum at which the network adapter will transfer data. In addition, to get this speed, every link in the networking chain must operate at 1 Gbps (1000 Mbps), including the network adapter, patch cables, and the SOHO router itself. If any one of those links runs at less than 1000 Mbps, the entire connection would be brought down to that lesser number.

Data Networking Terms

In the computer networking world, "speed" is also referred to as "bandwidth," though both terms might not be quite accurate technically. If you purchase a gigabit network adapter for your computer, its maximum data transfer rate will be 1 Gbps. However, the *actual* data transferred is known as *data throughput*, which will usually be less than 1 Gbps.

Going further, most network adapters can send and receive data simultaneously, which is called *full-duplex*. This means that they can actually send 1 Gbps and receive 1 Gbps at the same time. Conversely, half-duplex means that the network adapter can send and receive data, but only one at a time.

IoT Device Configuration

We've mentioned the Internet of Things in this book already and said that just about anything that can be connected to the Internet could be considered part of the Internet of Things. More strictly speaking, technicians (and many consumers) look at the Internet of Things as a group of technology goodies found in home automation, within appliances, and as voice-activated digital assistants—devices that go beyond desktops, laptops, smartphones, and tablets.

The key is that they connect to the SOHO network and ultimately to the Internet to receive updates and so that they can be controlled from a mobile device or other computing system.

IoT devices include thermostats, light switches, security cameras, door locks, refrigerators (and other appliances), and smart speakers. They connect to the Internet, and collect and exchange data. Configuration of these is usually intuitive. The important part is how they are connected to the SOHO network and how they are secured. That's because they all connect out to the Internet, and the apps that control them may or may not have the most brilliant programming, and then—security vulnerabilities abound!

A great method for configuring and securing these devices is to do the following:

1. Update the firmware on the SOHO router.

2. Create a separate network.

   One good method is to use the guest network. Place the IoT devices on that network. Configure strong encryption; for example, WPA2 and AES, with a separate passcode from the main wireless networks.

3. Disable UPnP.

   Universal Plug and Play can make a user's life easier as far as discovery, but can create security vulnerabilities if it is running.

4. Update the firmware on the IoT devices.

5. Use strong passwords.

   Different passwords should be used for the main login to the SOHO router, the guest wireless network, and the IoT devices themselves. If the IoT device only has the option for a PIN, use it. While there are only 10,000 possible combinations in a four-digit PIN, it's still better than nothing.

6. Update the operating system.

   Update the OS on the mobile device or other computer that will be used to configure and control the IoT devices.

7. Update the app used to control the IoT devices.

8. Use only what you need.

   Use only the devices that are absolutely necessary and disconnect or turn them off when not needed.

9. Carefully select and monitor cloud-based connections.

   If your device relies on the cloud for control, then be very careful with the manufacturer you select, and the information that you give, as well as the actual connectivity made to the device. Every connection into your network increases the attack surface and creates new vulnerabilities.

Cable/DSL Modem Configuration

When it comes to cable and DSL modems, configuration is usually performed by the ISP. They can remotely connect to your modem and reconfigure and/or reset it. However, as a consumer there are a couple of things you should know. The first is how to connect the devices physically.

Cable modems have two important ports: a coaxial port and a twisted-pair port. The coaxial port is the same that is used for CATV—it accepts an RG-6 coaxial cable with a screw-on F-connector on the end. The other end of that coaxial patch cable connects to the wall jack (or similar device) and ultimately goes to your ISP. The twisted-pair port accepts an Ethernet patch cable with an RJ45 plug on the end. The other end of that connects to your router. There are also all-in-one devices that act as a cable modem and a router and have a four-port switch incorporated into the device. For configuration of those included router options, see the earlier sections of this chapter.

A DSL modem has the same twisted-pair port for connectivity to a router, but some also have an RJ11 port for use with a land-based phone line.

Firewall Settings and Additional Configurations

Most SOHO routers have a built-in firewall with some basic security functionality. Let's discuss a few of the common features you might find.

▶ **NAT:** Network address translation is the process of modifying IP addresses as information crosses a router. It hides an entire IP address space on the LAN (for example, 192.168.0.1 through 192.168.0.255). Whenever an IP address on the LAN wants to communicate with the Internet, the IP is converted to the public IP of the router (for example, 68.54.127.95) but it will be whatever IP address was assigned to the router by the ISP. This way, it looks like the router is the only device making the connection to remote computers on the Internet, providing a modicum of safety for the computers on the LAN. NAT also allows a single IP to do the work for many IP addresses in the LAN.

▶ **Port forwarding:** This forwards an external network port to an internal IP address and port. This enables you to have a web server, FTP server, and other servers, but you need to have only one port for each open on the WAN side of the router. It can be any port you like; of course, you would need to tell people which port they need to connect to if it is not a standard one. Some devices use what are called virtual servers, making the process a lot more user-friendly. So, for example, you might have an FTP server running internally on your LAN; its IP address and port might be 192.168.0.100:21 (notice how the colon separates the IP address from the port), but you would have users on the Internet connect to your router's WAN address (for example, 65.43.18.1) and any port you want. The router takes care of the rest, and the forwarding won't be noticed by the typical user. Port forwarding is also referred to as destination NAT (DNAT).

▶ **DMZ:** A demilitarized zone is an area that is not quite on the Internet and not quite part of your LAN. It's a sort of middle ground that is for the most part protected by a firewall, but particular traffic will be let through. It's a good place for web servers, e-mail servers, and FTP servers because these are services required by users on the Internet. The beauty of this is that the users will not have access to your LAN—if it is configured correctly, of course. Quite often, the DMZ is set up as the third leg of a firewall. The first leg connects to the LAN, the second leg connects to the Internet, and the third connects to the DMZ. You need to know the ports that your servers will use and create rules within the firewall (or an all-in-one device, such as a SOHO router) to allow only the required traffic into the DMZ.

▶ **UPnP:** Universal Plug and Play is a group of networking protocols that allows computers, printers, and other Internet-ready devices to discover each other on the network. It is a consumer-level technology designed to make networking easier for the user. For example, if you wanted easier accessibility and connectivity of a PC, a smartphone, and a printer that were all connected to the SOHO router, UPnP can provide that. However, it is often recommended to disable this function if you are concerned about security.

▶ **MAC filtering:** MAC filtering is the screening of computers that are allowed access to a device or network. Every computer, wired or wireless, gets a unique MAC address. It is difficult to change or mask, so it makes for a good address to screen out unwanted connections. And because the switch portion of a SOHO router sees the MAC addresses of the computers connected to it, it's the perfect place to incorporate filtering. Generally, MAC filtering—which might also be referred to as Access Control or something similar—is disabled by default, but if you were to enable it, you would have two options. First, you could specify a list of computers with allowed MAC addresses, also known as a whitelist. Second, you could specify the computers that are denied access, also known as a blacklist. Whatever you choose, it's the MAC address that is used to determine connectivity and access control. For ease of use, SOHO routers will often display the computers that are currently connected, including information such as the device name, connection type (wired or wireless), IP address, and of course, the MAC address.

Note

To find out the MAC address of a system, go to the command line and run the appropriate command, which, for example, is **ipconfig /all** in Windows.

ExamAlert

Understand that MAC filtering is also known as Access Control on some SOHO routers, and that filtering is broken down into accepted MAC addresses (whitelisting) and denied MAC addresses (blacklisting).

▶ **QoS:** Quality of service is a feature that attempts to prioritize data for specific computers or for specific programs. It could be that you want to prioritize certain types of data, such as Remote Desktop Protocol (RDP) traffic, streaming media, Voice over IP (VoIP) phone calls, gaming, or audio or video playback. Or, perhaps a user wants a gaming PC or a smartphone to have a higher priority in general. QoS allows a user to do both of these things. Figure 6.4 shows an example of QoS configured on a basic SOHO router. One computer has been given high-priority access to the router. Also, an application (FTP) has been given low priority for all systems connected. Most SOHO routers have a QoS database that can be updated to include newer types of applications. However, if the application is not listed, then there is usually an option to add a custom application by using its port number.

QoS Rule List		
High Priority:60%	Middle Priority:30%	Low Priority:10%
AV-EDITOR > 🗑		FTP 🗑

FIGURE 6.4 **Example QoS configuration**

Configuring Wireless Encryption

SOHO routers (as well as most operating systems) support wireless networking protocols such as WPA2 and encryption methods such as AES to provide data confidentiality. Figure 6.5 displays a common secure wireless encryption technique on a typical router. Table 6.1 shows the characteristics of the various wireless protocols and encryption methods.

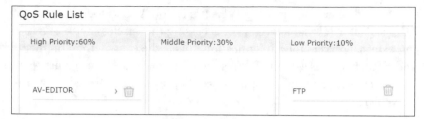

WPA

Use **WPA or WPA2** mode to achieve a balance of strong security and best compatibility. This mode uses WPA for legacy clients while maintaining higher security with stations that are WPA2 capable. Also the strongest cipher that the client supports will be used. For best security, use **WPA2 Only** mode. This mode uses AES(CCMP) cipher and legacy stations are not allowed access with WPA security. For maximum compatibility, use **WPA Only**. This mode uses TKIP cipher. Some gaming and legacy devices work only in this mode.

To achieve better wireless performance use **WPA2 Only** security mode (or in other words AES cipher).

WPA Mode : [WPA2 Only ▾]
Cipher Type : [AES ▾]
Group Key Update Interval : [3600] (seconds)

PRE-SHARED KEY

Enter an 8- to 63-character alphanumeric pass-phrase. For good security it should be of ample length and should not be a commonly known phrase.

Pre-Shared Key : [••••••••••••••••••••••••]

FIGURE 6.5 **Wireless network settings on a common router**

TABLE 6.1 **Wireless Encryption Methods**

Wireless Protocol	Description	Encryption Level
WEP	Wired Equivalent Privacy Deprecated and vulnerable to attacks	64-bit
WPA	Wi-Fi Protected Access	128-bit
WPA2	Wi-Fi Protected Access Version 2	256-bit
TKIP	Temporal Key Integrity Protocol Deprecated encryption protocol used with WEP or WPA	128-bit
AES	Advanced Encryption Standard Encryption protocol used with WPA/WPA2 Strongest encryption method in this table	128-, 192-, and 256-bit

Figure 6.5 shows a router that is using WPA2 only and AES as the encryption protocol. It also has a 16-character key for accessing the wireless network. Aside from using external servers for authentication, this is the best method on this router (and similar routers as well). This is the best line of defense against war drivers—attackers who attempt to gain access to unprotected wireless networks from their vehicles.

> **ExamAlert**
>
> As of the writing of this book, the best SOHO wireless encryption is WPA2 and AES. But be on the lookout for new and better versions and protocols!

WEP is the weakest type of encryption; WPA is stronger, and WPA2 is the strongest of the three. However, it is better to have WEP as opposed to nothing. If this is the case, use encryption keys that are difficult to guess and consider changing those keys often. Some devices can be updated to support WPA, whether it is through a firmware upgrade or through the use of a software add-on.

Final Word

When all configuration is complete, we need to place our SOHO router. It is important to keep the device away from any electrical sources (such as outlets, uninterruptible power supplies, or microwaves) and any large amounts of metal to avoid electromagnetic interference (EMI). The basement is probably not the best place for a router due to the thick walls, copper pipes, and electrical panels causing wireless interference. The device should be placed in the physical center of the office or the home for best reception. The more centralized the router is, the better the wireless access your computers will get. The antennas should be either at a 90-degree angle from each other or pointing toward where the computers are. And that pretty much wraps up the basic configuration of a SOHO router.

Cram Quiz

Answer these questions. The answers follow the last question. If you cannot answer these questions correctly, consider reading this section again until you can.

1. Which of the following allows for network throttling of individual computers or applications?

    ○ **A.** QoS

    ○ **B.** Port forwarding

    ○ **C.** DMZ

    ○ **D.** DHCP

2. Which of the following forwards an external network port to an internal IP address/port on a computer on the LAN?

   ○ **A.** NAT

   ○ **B.** Port forwarding

   ○ **C.** DMZ

   ○ **D.** DHCP

3. Which of the following is described as the simultaneous sending and receiving of network data?

   ○ **A.** Half-duplex

   ○ **B.** Latency

   ○ **C.** PoE

   ○ **D.** Full-duplex

Cram Quiz Answers

1. **A.** Quality of service (QoS) is a technology used in SOHO routers that can throttle bandwidth and give higher priority to individual computers or applications. Port forwarding is used to forward outside network ports to internal IP addresses. A demilitarized zone (DMZ) is a protected area between the LAN and the Internet—often inhabited by company servers. The Dynamic Host Configuration Protocol (DHCP) is the protocol in charge of automatically handing out IP address information to clients

2. **B.** Port forwarding is used to forward external network ports to an internal IP and port. This is done so a person can host services such as FTP internally. Network address translation (NAT) is used by most routers to convert the internal network of IP addresses to the single public IP address used by the router. The demilitarized zone (DMZ) is an area that is protected by the firewall but separate from the LAN. Servers are often placed here. DHCP is the protocol that governs the automatic assignment of IP addresses to clients by a server.

3. **D.** Full-duplex is when a network adapter (or other device) can send and receive information at the same time. Half-duplex is when only sending or receiving can be done at one time. Latency is the delay it takes for data to reach a computer from a remote location. PoE is Power over Ethernet, a technology that allows devices to receive data and power over an Ethernet network cable.

2.4 – Compare and contrast wireless networking protocols

In this section we'll discuss the IEEE 802.11 wireless protocols, and some other wireless standards available for cellular connections and for home automation. Bluetooth, NFC, and cellular protocols are also listed in the CompTIA objective, but we covered them previously in Chapters 3 and 4—make sure you know them. Let's go!

802.11 Wireless

To standardize *wireless LAN (WLAN)* communications—also known as Wi-Fi— the Institute of Electrical and Electronics Engineers (IEEE) developed the 802.11 series of protocols. These define the various speeds, frequencies, and protocols used to transmit data over radio waves in small geographic areas using unlicensed spectrums.

There are several different 802.11 derivatives you need to know for the exam: 802.11a, 802.11b, 802.11g, 802.11n, and 802.11ac. Table 6.2 shows these technologies and the characteristics that differentiate them.

TABLE 6.2 **802.11 Standards**

802.11 Version	Maximum Data Rate	Frequency
802.11a	54 Mbps	5 GHz
802.11b	11 Mbps	2.4 GHz
802.11g	54 Mbps	2.4 GHz
802.11n	300/600 Mbps	5 and/or 2.4 GHz
802.11ac	1.7 Gbps	5 GHz

One thing I left out of the table is coverage or distance. It is difficult to put an exact number on the maximum wireless transmission distances for each standard because it depends on the signal strength of the WAP's antenna, the use of additional features, and environmental factors such as obstructions and interference. But generally, the wireless range from WAP to client increases with each standard listed in the table, with 802.11n and 802.11ac providing similar ranges.

Note

New technologies are being developed as of the writing of this book that use higher frequency ranges and can transmit much more data per second. For example, 802.11ad runs at 60 GHz and can transfer multiple gigabits of data per second. Always be on the alert for emerging networking technologies!

The data transfer rates of newer wireless network technologies are increased using a concept known as *multipath propagation*. This is when an antenna (or antennas) receives radio signals on two or more paths. A common example of this is multiple-input and multiple-output (MIMO) technology, which is incorporated into 802.11n and 802.11ac wireless networks (as well as 4G LTE). As of the writing of this book, typical 802.11ac wireless devices use three or four antennas; the 802.11ac standard complies with multiuser MIMO (or MU-MIMO), which can have four simultaneous downlinks.

Depending on the frequency used, there are different channels that can be utilized by the average home or company. We touched on these previously, but let's summarize them in Table 6.3, and then expand on the concept.

TABLE 6.3 **2.4 GHz and 5 GHz Channels**

Frequency	Typical Channels	Example
2.4 GHz	1 through 11	802.11g
5 GHz	36, 40, 44, 48, 149, 153, 157, 161, 165	802.11ac

Let's take it to the next level. More accurately, 2.4 GHz and 5 GHz are frequency *ranges*. The exact range for these will vary from one country to the next. For example, the range for 2.4-GHz Wi-Fi in the United States is between 2.412 GHz and 2.462 GHz, broken up as channels 1 through 11—each is spaced 5 MHz apart from the next. When you set up a 2.4-GHz Wi-Fi network, it will have a *channel width* associated with it. By default, this is often 20 MHz—an amount that spans multiple channels. That's why I usually recommend placing wireless networks (and access points) on separate channels that are distant from each other. In the United States, the 2.4-GHz non-overlapping channels are 1, 6, and 11. For example, one Wi-Fi network could be on Channel 1 (2.412 GHz) and the next could be on Channel 6 (2.437 GHz), which allows for 25 MHz of space—more than enough in most cases to avoid interference.

However, to increase data rates, you can increase the channel width on many routers to 40 MHz for 2.4-GHz networks, and up to 80 MHz for 5-GHz networks. This is known as *channel bonding*. As you can guess, the chance for interference increases as well, so this notion can be risky. If we used 40-MHz channel bonding with our previous example, we would have interference from one Wi-Fi network to the next. Channel 6 is too close to channel 1 in this case. We would need to go to at least channel 9 (2.452 GHz) to avoid overlapping of the two Wi-Fi networks. The same goes for 5-GHz Wi-Fi networks. For example, channel 36's center frequency is actually 5.180 GHz. Channel 40 is 5.200 GHz. That is 20 MHz of channel width. If we wanted a separate Wi-Fi network on each of those channels, it would work fine by default, but if we wanted to perform channel bonding, then we would have to select another channel, such as channel 149 (5.755 GHz), which would allow for 40- or 80-MHz channel bonding, and possibly, higher data rates.

But air is free, right? So, we should perform a wireless site survey, and identify other companies' and homes' Wi-Fi networks that are nearby. They could be using channels that are too close, and cause interference. A *Wi-Fi analyzer* program is the best way to go when it comes to seeing who is using which frequencies, and then selecting frequencies that we can use (even with channel bonding) without causing overlap and interference. There are vendors that develop these programs for Windows, Android, and iOS. A Wi-Fi analyzer makes it easier for a person to discern where Wi-Fi networks exist in a given frequency range by showing the information in a graphical format, a chart, or something similar. It will also show the strength of the signal of each network. All of this can help you to decide on the right channel to use when you are performing your wireless site survey.

ExamAlert

Don't stand so close to me! Seriously, make sure your selected Wi-Fi channel is in its own "space" by investigating the airwaves with a Wi-Fi analyzer.

RFID

Radio-frequency identification (RFID) is a wireless technology used to read information that is stored on "tags." These tags can be attached to, or embedded in, just about anything. They are used in many industries and have many uses such as access control, commerce, advertising, manufacturing, agriculture, and so on.

For example, RFID tags can be used in a retail store. They can help with the tracking of inventory, and protection from theft. Tags are attached to clothing or other items, and are read by an RFID reader as part of the checkout process. After a customer pays for the item, the RFID reader deactivates that tag. In the case that a customer fails to pay for the item, an RFID detector can be placed at the entrance/exit. This will read the tag and send an alert. These readers and detectors must be nearby, but not necessarily within line-of-sight, which improves upon a basic barcode system. Plus, the RFID tag can hold a lot more information and can be programmed if necessary. For readers that can track items over larger distances, beyond close proximity, an active RFID system would be necessary, where the reader is AC powered.

When it comes to computers, networks, and authentication, RFID plays a vital role. For instance, as part of an access control solution, RFID tags are used as ID badges— proximity cards, dongles, and so forth—which can take the place of older and less secure magnetic stripe cards. Entrances to the building, specific offices, server rooms, data centers, and so on, can be equipped with an RFID reader. Simply placing the RFID badge on or near the reader will activate the reader and verify the ID of the employee. Of course, badges can be stolen; that's why a second factor of authentication is common, such as a passcode, which we will discuss in the security chapters. RFID is also present in smartphones and some other computing devices. Many smartphones are furnished with NFC, which is actually a subset of RFID. These readers are often locked down so that they can only read tags from a certain manufacturer, or for a specific purpose. Refer to Chapter 3, "Smartphones, Tablets, and Other Mobile Devices, Part 1," if you need a refresher on NFC.

Zigbee and Z-Wave

Zigbee and Z-Wave are two wireless protocols used primarily with home automation products, appliances, and voice-activated assistants. They each allow for communication between hundreds of different devices from different manufacturers. Generally, the two are incompatible, but there are hubs that can be used that will support both protocols. Smartphone apps are available to control the various Zigbee and Z-Wave devices and hubs that connect them together.

Zigbee is standardized as IEEE 802.15-4. It is a low-power wireless technology that is similar to Bluetooth as far as frequency, transmission power, and distance. For example, it runs on 2.4 GHz as well as 915 MHz for Zigbee Pro and typically has a communications distance of 10 to 20 meters maximum. However, it is designed and manufactured in such a way that Zigbee products can be cheaper than Bluetooth and Wi-Fi equivalents. Also, it has a unified data communications methodology that BT and Wi-Fi do not, allowing for more configurability, greater control, and better communications between devices. Zigbee-based devices have low power consumption, which increases their battery life tremendously compared to Wi-Fi and BT devices. You might find Zigbee modules in sensors that can control lighting, temperature, window blinds, and much more, including home entertainment control, industrial control, medical data collection, smoke and fire alarms, and safety and security in general.

Z-Wave is a protocol that is standardized by the Z-Wave Alliance and works within the 800- and 900-MHz frequencies. As with Zigbee, you might find Z-Wave modules in security systems, lighting control devices, thermostats, and so on. As of the writing of this book, Z-Wave has a longer transmission distance than Zigbee and is very common in the realm of home automation. However, protocol choice also depends on the manufacturer of the device, the exact purpose for the device, and cost. Some homes and offices use both Zigbee and Z-Wave because many devices only use one or the other. To control either Z-Wave or Zigbee devices, a smart hub is required that has support for one or both of the protocols. As with any wireless devices, security is a concern. Devices that use Zigbee or Z-Wave utilize 128-bit encrypting technologies—check and make sure that this is enabled. Also, make use of any PINs or passcodes available on devices.

> **ExamAlert**
>
> Remember that Zigbee and Z-Wave technologies transmit data on different frequencies.

> **Note**
>
> Chapter 4 discusses cellular (or WWAN) connections such as 3G, 4G, LTE, and 5G.

And that closes out this section on the electromagnetic spectrum. Transmission of data over radio waves can be done in so many ways. Be sure to know the basics of each technology we discussed in this chapter.

Cram Quiz

Answer these questions. The answers follow the last question. If you cannot answer
these questions correctly, consider reading this section again until you can.

1. Which of the following would a company most likely use for authentication to a
server room?

   ○ **A.** 802.11ac

   ○ **B.** 802.15-4

   ○ **C.** RFID

   ○ **D.** Z-Wave

   ○ **E.** MIMO

2. Which standard can attain a data transfer rate of 1 Gbps over a wireless
connection?

   ○ **A.** 802.11a

   ○ **B.** 802.11b

   ○ **C.** 802.11g

   ○ **D.** 802.11ac

   ○ **E.** 802.3ab

3. Which of the following is often broken down into groups of channels including
1-5, 6–10, and 11?

   ○ **A.** 802.11ac

   ○ **B.** 2.4 GHz

   ○ **C.** 5 GHz

   ○ **D.** 802.11a

Cram Quiz Answers

1. **C.** RFID (radio-frequency identification) is commonly used for access to areas of
a building such as a server room. It is often implemented as a proximity-based ID
card or badge. The other options are not usually associated with authentication.
802.11ac is a WLAN (Wi-Fi) standard that runs on 5 GHz and can provide 1 Gbps
of data transfer. 802.15-4 is the IEEE standard for Zigbee. Z-Wave, like Zigbee, is
a home automation and wireless sensor control technology. MIMO (multiple-input
and multiple-output) is a multiple propagation technology used to increase data
transfer in 802.11n and 802.11ac wireless networks.

2. **D.** 802.11ac can attain speeds in excess of 1 Gbps over wireless. 802.11a and g have a typical maximum of 54 Mbps. 802.11b (rarely used today) has a maximum of 11 Mbps. 802.3ab is the IEEE specification for 1-Gbps transfer over twisted-pair cables—it is wired, not wireless. By the way, this is also known as 1000BASE-T.

3. **B.** In the United States, the 2.4-GHz frequency range is broken down into three categories: Channel 1–5, 6–10, and 11. By placing separate wireless networks on separate distant channels (such as 1 and 11), you can avoid overlapping and interference. 802.11ac and 802.11a are standards, not frequencies. 5 GHz uses channels such as 36, 40, 149, 153, and so on.

You are doing fantastic! Great job with the chapter. Keep going, there's lots more!

CHAPTER 7

Networked Hosts and Network Configuration

This chapter covers the following A+ 220-1001 exam objectives:

▶ **2.5** – Summarize the properties and purposes of services provided by networked hosts.

▶ **2.6** – Explain common network configuration concepts.

Let's get a little bit deeper into networking. In this chapter we'll dig into the services provided by computer servers. I'm referring not only to commonly known servers such as web servers, file servers, and e-mail servers, but also servers that provide less-known underlying services, such as DHCP servers and authentication servers. In the second portion we'll discuss the foundation for these services, especially TCP/IP configurations: IP addressing, dynamic IP assignment, name to IP address resolution, and networking technologies such as VPNs and VLANs.

2.5 – Summarize the properties and purposes of services provided by networked hosts

ExamAlert

Objective 2.5 concentrates on the following concepts: server roles (web, file, print, DHCP, DNS, proxy, mail, authentication, syslog), Internet appliances, and legacy/embedded systems.

If the data we need is not stored locally, then we look to servers to provide it. In this section we'll discuss the various server roles that you should know for the exam: web servers that provide websites and e-commerce; file servers that provide access to data files of all kinds; e-mail servers that provide for a central administration and storage point for e-mail messages; and print servers that provide the ability to print to remote printers. Getting a bit more technical, we'll cover some of the essential servers on a mid-sized to large computer network, including DHCP, DNS, proxy, syslog, and authentication servers. At the end, we'll briefly discuss Internet appliances and legacy/embedded systems.

Server Roles

Servers take care of centralizing data, allowing access to the network, making connections to printers, controlling the flow of e-mail, and much more. Whatever the role, the concept of the server is to do this in a centralized fashion, reducing the burden on client computers. Regardless of whether the server is in the organization's LAN or in the cloud, it will have the same purpose.

File Servers

File servers store, transfer, migrate, synchronize, and archive files. Any computer can act as a file server of sorts. All you need to do is create a share on your local system and point remote computers to that share, either by browsing or through a mapped network drive. On a typical Windows client computer, however, those shares will be limited in the number of simultaneous connections allowed (usually 20 maximum). So, for larger network environments, we need a real server of some sort. Examples of actual server software include Microsoft Windows Server, macOS Server, and the various types of Linux server versions (for example, Red Hat or CentOS), not to mention Unix. As with most servers, the file server can be a physical box or a virtual machine, and can be located within your LAN or on the cloud.

> **Note**
>
> You could also build a network-attached storage (NAS) server. That's a basic box that often contains two or more hard drives and connects directly to the network. It will usually run some variant of Linux. We'll discuss NAS more in Chapter 10, "RAM and Storage."

Web Servers

The *web server* is the one that houses the website of an organization. Examples of web servers include Microsoft's Internet Information Services (IIS), which is part of Windows Server, Apache HTTP Server (Linux), and lighttpd (FreeBSD). Small and mid-sized companies will often host their websites with an external provider. Larger companies might choose to host their websites on web servers physically located in their data center, though many also choose to use the cloud. An organization's choice is usually dictated by the amount of resources and manpower that they possess.

Print Servers

Print servers are basic servers that take control of multiple printers on the network. All caching of information, spooling, printer pooling, sharing, and permissions is controlled centrally by the print server. While a Windows client computer (or other client) could act as a print server, and you can also purchase a basic print server device that plugs into your network, enterprise-level print servers will run software such as Windows Server, so that they can handle lots of simultaneous print requests from client computers.

Mail Servers

Mail servers (or *e-mail servers*) are part of the message server family. When we refer to a message server, we mean any server that deals with e-mail, faxing, texting, chatting, and so on. But for the purposes of the A+ exams, we concentrate strictly on the e-mail server. The most common of these is Microsoft Exchange. An Exchange Server might run POP3, SMTP, and IMAP, and allow for Outlook connections via a web browser. That's a lot of protocols running. So, it's not surprising to hear some Exchange admins confess that running an e-mail server can be difficult at times. For the A+ exams you should know how to connect a client to an e-mail server such as Microsoft Exchange. This is done by using appropriate e-mail client software (such as Outlook) and knowing the server name, the protocols and ports used, the username and password, and whether there is additional security involved. For more about e-mail client configuration, see Chapter 4, "Smartphones, Tablets, and Other Mobile Devices, Part 2."

Proxy Servers

A *proxy server* is used primarily as a go-between for the client and the website accessed. It is commonly used to cache information so that another user accessing the same web page won't have to get it from the Internet, because it already exists on the proxy server, which increases general performance and efficiency. For a client computer to use a proxy server, the web browser needs to be configured properly. (We'll examine this in Chapter 29, "Windows Networking and Application Installation.") In addition, the proxy server can analyze data as it passes through and filter it accordingly—this is referred to as content filtering. You can also have proxies for FTP, SMTP, and other protocols. There are also proxies that reside on the Internet, designed to hide users' IP addresses, allowing users to browse the web anonymously. Quite often, organizations will block these types of connections.

To protect a web server, an organization might implement a *reverse proxy*. This device is placed within the area of the network where the web server resides. Requests from clients on the Internet are forwarded by the reverse proxy to the web server so that the clients will be unaware of the identity of the web server. Reverse proxies can also be used for encryption of web sessions, and for load balancing, where client requests can be distributed to multiple web servers.

Authentication Servers

An *authentication server* acts as a central repository of user accounts and computer accounts on the network. All users log on to this server. The most common example of this would be a Windows Server system that has been promoted to a domain controller (meaning it runs Active Directory). This type of server validates the users that attempt to log on. Authentication servers utilize some kind of authentication protocol such as the Lightweight Directory Access Protocol (LDAP), or Kerberos, or both. The Windows domain controller is an example of an authentication server that uses LDAP.

DHCP Servers

Some servers do have less-tangible duties—but not any less important. For example, the *DHCP server* is in charge of handing out IP addresses to clients. But don't underestimate this function; if an organization has a couple thousand computers that rely on obtaining IP addresses from a DHCP server, it becomes one of the most important servers on the network. If it fails, computers will have great difficulty doing anything on the network. DHCP server functionality is built into Windows and Linux servers, SOHO routers, and many other devices. Whenever a device or computer obtains an IP address automatically, chances are that a DHCP server was involved.

DNS Servers

A *domain name system (DNS) server* takes care of resolving domain names to IP addresses. For example:

```
davidlprowse.com = 216.97.236.245
```

Try running the ping command in the Command Prompt and ping a domain name of your choice. For example:

```
ping example.com
```

The results should display the IP address of that domain—this is a basic example of DNS being performed. DNS servers also take care of reverse DNS, when IP addresses are resolved to domain name.

In smaller networks, this server is at the ISP. However, larger networks might decide to run a DNS server internally. In fact, it becomes a necessity if the company has a domain controller, because the domain relies on DNS name resolutions for just about everything that needs to be accessed. DNS functionality is built into most server operating systems such as Windows Server.

Syslog Servers

Syslog is a protocol that can take logged event information from a router or other network device and send that to a logging server—also known as a *Syslog server*. The Syslog server uses special software to store these logs in real time and is designed in a way that is easy for administrators to read, analyze, and save the information, which might consist of status, events, diagnostics, entry attempts, and so on. Best of all, the administrator can do all this from his or her workstation, without having to log in to each network device separately. Examples of Syslog software include Kiwi Syslog Server, PRTG, and Syslog Watcher.

> **ExamAlert**
>
> Know the differences between file servers, web servers, print servers, e-mail servers, proxy servers, authentication servers, DHCP servers, DNS servers, and Syslog servers. You might also want to tie in these concepts to the ports that the servers use, which can be found in Chapter 5, "Ports, Protocols, and Network Devices."

So, there's a little primer on servers. The server is the home of the systems administrator/network administrator. A lot of you reading this are probably very interested in servers. The Core 1 (220-1001) A+ exam focuses more on the client side of things, but you should attempt to learn as much as you can about the various servers we just discussed. Ultimately, you will be working on them!

Internet Appliances

There are a variety of security devices that can be used to block unauthorized access, including firewalls, UTMs, IDS and IPS solutions, and endpoint management servers. These are all examples of Internet appliances—or, more accurately, Internet *security* appliances.

The *network firewall* is first and foremost; almost every organization has one protecting its network. These are usually rack-mountable devices that connect to the LAN on one side and to the Internet on the other (and possibly to a DMZ or other secondary network using a third connection). Their primary function is to close ports (such as HTTP port 80) so that unwanted intrusion can be prevented. A typical firewall implementation closes all inbound ports so that external users are blocked from access to the LAN of an organization. However, in some cases, you will find that a port on a firewall was opened previously to allow communication by a service or application that is no longer in use. If that happens, you need to disable (or close) that port or delete the rule that was created for that type of communication. These rules are also known as access control lists (ACLs).

A firewall can be part of a *unified threat management (UTM)* gateway solution as well. UTM is the evolution of the firewall, incorporating the features of the firewall along with antivirus, antispam, content filtering, and intrusion prevention for the entire network. It might also incorporate data loss prevention (DLP) by way of content inspection. The idea behind UTM is that it can take the place of several units doing separate tasks and consolidate them into one easily administered system. The drawback to this is that it can act as a single point of failure. So, many organizations will consider secondary UTM units or fallback firewalls.

> **Note**
>
> You might not hear the term UTM used as often today, but it's still on the A+ objectives, so know it!

The A+ objectives also require that you understand two other terms, IDS and IPS, and that you know the difference between them. An *intrusion detection system (IDS)* can determine whether an unauthorized person has attempted to access the network and then alert the systems administrator of its findings. In this case, an admin is alerted to the problem, but the unauthorized user might actually gain access to the network; the damage might be done before the admin has a chance to rectify the situation. Building on this concept, an *intrusion prevention system (IPS)* will not only detect unauthorized access to the network, but attempt to thwart it, making the admin's job somewhat easier. IDS and IPS solutions are available as security appliances for the entire network and, in this case, are also referred to as network-based IDS (NIDS) and network-based IPS (NIPS), respectively. They are often incorporated into UTM devices, most commonly NIPS. However, IDS and IPS solutions are also available for individual hosts. In this case, they are referred to as host-based IDS (HIDS) and host-based IPS (HIPS).

Finally, know the term *endpoint management server*. That type of server is one element of an endpoint management solution. Endpoint management (or endpoint security management) is a policy-based approach to network security. It requires endpoint devices (meaning PCs, laptops, mobile devices, etc.) to meet particular criteria before they can be granted access to network resources. Endpoint management servers are servers that centrally control the discovery of endpoint devices, and the deployment and updating of those devices' security software and features. Companies such as Check Point and Sophos offer endpoint management solutions. Among other tasks, the endpoint management server can handle the updating of endpoint protection platforms. These platforms should also be installed to all endpoints, and should be updated across the board in a synchronous fashion. Examples of endpoint protection platforms are McAfee, Norton (Symantec), and Kaspersky. These are generally all-in-one solutions that have antivirus, anti-spyware, personal firewalls, spam protection, and so on. They might simply be referred to as anti-malware suites.

> **ExamAlert**
>
> Know the differences between the following: firewall, UTM, IDS, IPS, and endpoint management server.

Embedded/Legacy Systems

Embedded systems are devices that have an integrated CPU and RAM and can process information internally without the need for a controlling system. They are commonly found in home appliances, office automation, thin clients, security systems, telecommunications, automotive, medical, assembly systems, and much more.

One place where you will find embedded systems is in heating, ventilation, and air conditioning (HVAC). Taking it to the next level, larger infrastructures will often use a Supervisory Control and Data Acquisition (SCADA) system. These are found in electrical power grids, water treatment plants, gas/oil pipelines, hydroelectric systems, sewage systems, traffic systems, building controls, and so on. Compared to typical home offices and small offices, SCADA solutions must be heavily secured because they are often used in protected environments and infrastructures. Teams of engineers are employed to design and secure these SCADA solutions.

Some buildings might require *legacy systems* to control their older HVAC, plumbing, and other technologies. Some of these legacy systems might be single-board computers such as the PC/104 embedded system, which will typically run at 33 MHz and have 16 to 32 MB of RAM. Note that the last sentence read MHz and MB—instead of GHz and GB—that should help to define the term *legacy*! These boards can go bad over time and have to be replaced. Or, a particular technology might be controlled by a legacy thin client computer with an embedded operating system—and no hard drive. These are also generally single-board designs where a failure means a total board or unit replacement. If you are in charge of this type of technology, be ready to scour the Internet and locate quality distributors so that you can get quality replacements at a decent price.

Cram Quiz

Answer these questions. The answers follow the last question. If you cannot answer these questions correctly, consider reading this section again until you can.

1. While looking at the details of a server in your provider's control panel, you notice that it says "Apache" in the HTTP summary. What kind of server is this?

   O **A.** File server

   O **B.** Web server

   O **C.** E-mail server

   O **D.** Authentication server

2. Which type of server acts as a go-between for clients and websites?

   O **A.** Proxy server

   O **B.** Print server

   O **C.** Syslog server

   O **D.** DHCP server

3. Which type of server runs Microsoft Exchange?

   O **A.** File server

   O **B.** Authentication server

   O **C.** E-mail server

   O **D.** Web server

   O **E.** SCADA

Cram Quiz Answers

1. **B.** Apache is a type of web server that runs on Linux. It is also known as Apache HTTP Server. File servers are used to store and transfer files but not websites. E-mail servers deal with the sending and receiving of electronic mail via POP3, IMAP, and SMTP. Authentication servers verify the identity of users logging in and computers on the network.

2. **A.** A proxy server is a caching server used to store commonly accessed websites by clients. It can be incorporated into a web server but often it runs as a standalone server. A print server manages network printers and their spooling of print jobs, priorities, and so on. A Syslog server gathers logging data from network devices and allows for the easy analysis of those logs from a client workstation. A DHCP server hands out IP addresses (and other TCP/IP information) to client computers.

3. **C.** Microsoft Exchange is a type of e-mail server software. While you could run multiple services on a single server—for example, you could run the web server and e-mail server on the same machine—it isn't recommended. Unless you have a small office, all servers (such as file servers, authentication servers, e-mail servers, DHCP servers, and so on) should be separate entities. SCADA is not a server—it stands for Supervisory Control and Data Acquisition, a type of system used to control larger organizations' infrastructures such as heating/cooling, electricity, and so on.

2.6 – Explain common network configuration concepts

ExamAlert

Objective 2.6 focuses on the following concepts: IP addressing (static, dynamic, APIPA, link local), DNS, DHCP, IPv4, IPv6, subnet mask, gateway, VPN, VLAN, and NAT.

Here we'll discuss the core of networking for most computers: IP addressing. Without IP addresses our computers can't communicate—so it's vital that you know IP addressing frontward and backward. We'll also touch on some network configurations that use IP but in a more secure way, such as VPNs and VLANs. This could be considered one of the most important sections in the book, and it's packed with information. It's time to network!

Configuring IPv4

Configuring IP works the same way in most versions of Windows. First, we navigate to the Internet Protocol (TCP/IP) Properties window, which I will often refer to as the IP Properties dialog box. To do this, go to **Control Panel > Network and Internet > Network and Sharing Center**, and then select the **Change adapter settings** link. Then right-click the Ethernet icon (or Local Area Connection icon) and select **Properties**. Finally, highlight **Internet Protocol Version 4** and then click the **Properties** button.

Note

Navigation may differ slightly depending on the version of Windows and the way it is configured. Be ready for alterations over time, and be ready to use the search tool to simplify the process (or the Run prompt whenever possible!).

The first item to be configured is the IP address, which is the unique assigned number of your computer on the network. IPv4 IP addresses consist of four octets, with each octet's value ranging between 0 and 255. Each number is separated by a dot (for example, 192.168.0.100). The binary equivalent of 0–255 would be 00000000 through 11111111. For example, 192 is equal to 11000000 in binary. Because each octet contains 8 bits and there are four octets, the IP address collectively is a 32-bit number but is normally expressed in dotted-decimal notation.

There are two main types of addresses: dynamic and static. Dynamically assigned addresses are more common for a client computer; this is when the computer seeks out a DHCP server so that it can get its IP information automatically. Figure 7.1 shows a radio button labeled **Obtain an IP address automatically**. When you select this, the rest of the information becomes grayed out and the computer attempts to get that IP information from a DHCP server (such as a SOHO router or Windows Server). That DHCP server will have a range of IP addresses that was configured by an administrator—also known as a DHCP scope. The administrator might also configure DHCP reservations, which are IP addresses within the DHCP scope that are permanently reserved for special computers that need to use DHCP but don't want the IP address to change over time (which can happen periodically in DHCP environments).

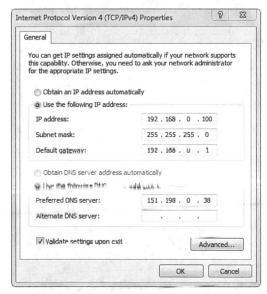

FIGURE 7.1   Internet Protocol Version 4 Properties dialog box in Windows

For client computers, DHCP is common; in fact, it's the default configuration for Windows. On the other hand, static addresses are generated when we configure the IP information manually. Figure 7.1 shows an example of statically configured IP settings. The computer is configured to use the address 192.168.0.100, but the IP address differs from machine to machine depending on several factors. Remember that the address should be unique for each computer on the network.

IP addresses can also be self-assigned by the computer. In Windows, this is known as *Automatic Private IP Addressing (APIPA)*, and it occurs when a computer cannot contact a DHCP server to obtain an IP address. When APIPA self-assigns an address, it will be on the 169.254.0.0 network. Addresses on this network are also known as *link-local* addresses.

IP addresses are divided into two sections: the network portion, which is the number of the network the computer is on, and the host portion, which is the individual number of the computer. The subnet mask defines which portion of the IP address is the network number and which portion is the individual host number. In this case, the subnet mask is 255.255.255.0. The 255s indicate the network portion of the IP address. So, 192.168.0 is the network this computer is a member of. The zeros (in this case, there is only one of them) indicate the host number, so 100 is the individual number of this computer. Quite often the subnet mask will be configured automatically by Windows after you type the IP address.

The gateway address is the IP address of the host that enables access to the Internet or to other networks. The IP address of the gateway should always be on the same network as the computer(s) connecting to it. In Figure 7.1, we know it is because the first three octets are 192.168.0. If a computer is not configured with a default gateway address, it cannot connect to the Internet.

The DNS server address is the IP address of the host that takes care of domain name translation to IP. When you use your browser to connect to a website, you might type something like www.davidlprowse.com. What you need to remember, however, is that computers actually communicate by IP address, not by name. So, the DNS server takes care of translating the name davidlprowse.com to its corresponding IP address and forwarding that information back to your computer. When your computer knows the IP address of the website, it can start a session with the website and transmit and receive files. Notice in Figure 7.1 that the DNS server address is on a completely different network from my computer. This is typical; in this case, the DNS server is run by the Internet service provider (ISP) that provides me with my Internet connection.

However, DNS servers can also be run internally by a company; this happens more often with larger companies.

You will also note a checkbox labeled **Validate settings upon exit**. If you set up a static IP address on a computer, you should select this checkbox. This way, Windows will check whether the configuration works properly and will let you know when any basic errors arise. Who knows, the IP configuration might have an incorrect DNS server, gateway address, or IP network number.

ExamAlert

Know where and how to configure client-side DNS and DHCP settings.

If your IP Properties dialog box is set to **Obtain an IP address automatically**, you will see the Alternate Configuration tab. This allows you to have a secondary IP configuration. Let's say there is a scenario in which you use a laptop at work and get your IP address from a DHCP server, but you also go on the road as part of your job. The alternate configuration would kick in automatically when you are away from the office and allow you access to the Internet or to virtual private networks, depending on how you configure it. The alternate configuration can be on a wholly different IP network from the main configuration.

Speaking of secondary IP addresses, every computer running TCP/IP has an additional address known as a *loopback* address. By default, this is 127.0.0.1 and can be used to test TCP/IP on the local machine regardless of whether the system is plugged into the network. Try running a **ping 127.0.0.1** or a **ping loopback -4** in the Command Prompt to test your system internally. Remember—replies are good!

Classful Versus Classless IP Addresses

The IPv4 system of IP addresses is divided into classes: A, B, and C, where specific subnet masks correspond to each class. For example, class C addresses use subnet mask 255.255.255.0—this is known as classful IP addressing. While those classes can still be used, most companies opt for a network that is classless—using something known as CIDR (Classless Inter-Domain Routing)—pronounced as *cider*. This way, any subnet mask can be used for any IP network. The important part to understand is that the 255s of a subnet mask relate to the network portion, and the 0s correspond to the host portion of the IP address. For example, if the IP address 10.252.0.101 uses the subnet mask 255.255.0.0, then the network portion is 10.252. The IP address and subnet mask can be written out together in the following manner: 10.252.0.101/16. For more about classful and classless IP addresses, see this post on my website: https://dprocomputer.com/blog/?p=2907.

Configuring IPv6

Though acceptance has been slow over the years, IPv6 is the next generation of IP addressing. Used on the Internet and on some LANs and WANs,
IPv6 is designed to meet the inadequacies of IPv4. One of the main reasons
for the development of IPv6 was the rapidly approaching global shortage of
IPv4 addresses. Where IPv4 (a 32-bit system) can have approximately 4 billion
total theoretical addresses, IPv6 (128-bit) can have a total of 340 *undecillion*
theoretical addresses—a far greater total. Various limitations of the system
will drastically reduce that number, but the remaining result is still orders of
magnitude above and beyond the IPv4 system. However, IPv6 is also known
for security. One feature of IPv6 security is IPsec, which authenticates and
encrypts data packets that are sent over IP networks. IPsec is a fundamental
piece of the IPv6 puzzle and, if used properly, can offer much more secure
communications than IPv4. IPv6 also supports larger packet sizes, which are
known as jumbograms. Table 7.1 summarizes some of the differences between
IPv4 and IPv6.

TABLE 7.1 IPv4 Versus IPv6

IPv4	IPv6
32-bit	128-bit
4 billion addresses	340 undecillion addresses
Less secure	More secure; uses IPsec
65,536 byte packet size max	4 billion bytes max

IPv6 addresses are 128-bit hexadecimal numbers that are divided into eight
groups of four numbers each. The most commonly used type is the unicast
address, which defines a single IP address on a single interface (such as a
network adapter). Windows auto-configures a unicast address when IPv6 is
installed. The address will start with FE80, FE90, FEA0, or FEB0. Collectively,
this range is shown as FE80::/10 and it comprises all of the link-local addresses
for IPv6. These link-local addresses are often based on the MAC address of the
network adapter. Every Windows computer with IPv6 installed also receives
a loopback address that is ::1. The IPv6 address ::1 is the equivalent to IPv4's
loopback address of 127.0.0.1. To test it, type **ping ::1** or **ping loopback -6** in
the Command Prompt.

> **ExamAlert**
>
> Know the loopback addresses for IPv6 and IPv4.

Here's an example of an IPv6 address:

```
2001:7120:0000:8001:0000:0000:0000:1F10
```

IPv6 addresses are broken down into three sections: the global routing prefix (in this case, 2001:7120:0000); a subnet that is 8001; and the individual interface ID, shown as 0000:0000:0000:1F10.

This is the full address, but you will more commonly see truncated addresses. There are two ways to truncate, or shorten, an IPv6 address. The first is to remove leading zeros. Any group of four zeros can be truncated to a single zero; basically zero is always zero, so the additional zeros are not necessary. Also, one consecutive group of zeros can be truncated as a double colon (::). The example shows 12 consecutive zeros that can be truncated simply to a double colon. (A double colon can be used only once in an address.) The following is the end result of both of these abbreviations:

```
2001:7120:0:8001::1F10
```

ExamAlert

Understand how IPv6 addresses can be truncated.

Though it is not common, IPv6 addresses can be assigned virtually as well, this can be done within the Internet Protocol Version 6 Properties dialog box, which can be accessed from Local Area Connection Properties (IPv6 is listed near to IPv4).

Note

You can find coverage of network address translation (NAT) in Chapter 6.

VLANs

A virtual LAN (VLAN) is implemented primarily to segment the network. But it can also be used to reduce data collisions, organize the network, potentially boost performance, and, possibly, increase security. A device such as a switch will often control the VLAN. A VLAN compartmentalizes the network and can isolate traffic. VLANs can be set up in a physical manner; an example of this would be the port-based VLAN, where switch ports are grouped and configured to act as individual VLANs. To do this you would need a *managed* switch—one that you can log in to and configure for VLAN use.

There are also logical types of VLANs, such as protocol-based VLANs. A VLAN can be set up in such a way that each VLAN is on a different IP network number: for example, 192.168.0.0, 192.168.1.0, 192.168.2.0, and so on. Or, you could take it to the next level and incorporate a separate technology called IP subnetting. This is when you divide the network into two or more subnetworks by changing the subnet mask that is used: for example, from 255.255.0.0 to 255.255.240.0. Some administrators prefer IP subnetting over VLANs, and some use them together: for example, a group of physical port-based VLANs, each of which is on a different IP subnetwork.

> **Note**
>
> VLANs and subnetting go a bit beyond what a typical A+ technician will be asked to perform, but you should know the basic definitions for these. To learn more about subnetting, see my blog post here: https://dprocomputer.com/blog/?p=1185.

VPNs

Let's say you want to connect to your network, but you are at a remote location. Enter the VPN. Virtual private networks (VPNs) were developed so that telecommuters, salespeople, and others could connect to the office from a remote location. If set up properly, the remote logon connection is seamless and appears as if you are actually at the LAN in the office. You log on just as you would if you were at your desk at headquarters. VPNs give the user access to all the resources that they get when logging on locally. VPNs take advantage of the infrastructure of the Internet and fast connections (such as cable, fiber, DSL, and so on). A VPN connection can be identified by an additional network connection in the Notification Area, as an additional network connection when using the **ipconfig** command, or as a pop-up window that comes up during the logon process. Connections to VPNs can be initiated by navigating to the Network and Sharing Center and selecting the **Set up a new connection or network** link. From there, you would opt for **Connect to a workplace** and then select **VPN**. There are also third-party offerings from companies such as Cisco, Check Point, and so on. Either way, you would need to know the IP address or name of the VPN server you are connecting to as well as a username and password to get in. Alternate IP configurations are sometimes used with VPN connections, so that the main IP configuration is not disturbed, especially if it is configured statically.

Cram Quiz

Answer these questions. The answers follow the last question. If you cannot answer
these questions correctly, consider reading this section again until you can.

1. Which of these addresses needs to be configured to enable a computer access to
   the Internet or to other networks?

   ○ **A.** Subnet mask

   ○ **B.** Gateway address

   ○ **C.** DNS address

   ○ **D.** MAC address

2. Which technology assigns addresses on the 169.254.0.0 network number?

   ○ **A.** DHCP

   ○ **B.** Static IP

   ○ **C.** APIPA

   ○ **D.** Class B

3. You want to test the local loopback IPv6 address. Which address would you use?

   ○ **A.** 127.0.0.1

   ○ **B.** ::1

   ○ **C.** FE80::/10

   ○ **D.** ::0

4. You have been tasked with compartmentalizing the network. Which of the
   following technologies should you use?

   ○ **A.** APIPA

   ○ **B.** VPN

   ○ **C.** VLAN

   ○ **D.** IPv6

Cram Quiz Answers

1. **B.** The gateway address must be configured to enable a computer access to
   the Internet through the gateway device. By default, the subnet mask defines
   the IP address's network and host portions. The DNS server takes care of name
   resolution. The MAC address is the address that is burned into the network
   adapter; it is configured at the manufacturer.

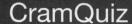

2. **C.** If you see an address with 169.254 as the first two octets, then it is Automatic Private IP Addressing (APIPA). This is also the link-local range for IPv4. The Dynamic Host Configuration Protocol (DHCP) assigns IP addresses automatically to clients but by default does not use the 169.254 network number. Static IP addresses are configured manually by the user in the IP Properties window. Class B is a range of IP networks from 128 through 191.

3. **B.** You would use the ::1 address. That is the local loopback address for IPv6. 127.0.0.1 is the local loopback for IPv4. FE80::/10 is the range of unicast auto-configured addresses. ::0 is not valid but looks similar to how multiple zeros can be truncated with a double colon.

4. **C.** You would create a virtual LAN (VLAN). Another valid option would be to implement IP subnetting. APIPA (also known as link-local) is an IP technology that auto-assigns addresses on the 169.254 network. A virtual private network (VPN) allows remote clients to connect to a network over the Internet using a secure tunnel. IPv6 in of itself does not compartmentalize the network. However, an IPv6 network that has been *subnetted* would be acceptable.

CHAPTER 8

Network Types and Networking Tools

This chapter covers the following A+ 220-1001 exam objectives:

▶ **2.7** – Compare and contrast Internet connection types, network types, and their features.

▶ **2.8** – Given a scenario, use appropriate networking tools.

Let's wrap up the computer networking section of this book with a shorter chapter on the types of networks you will see and some of the tools used to make network connectivity a reality. Of course, you will be using your networking knowledge as we progress through the book—especially as we get to the operating systems chapters—and as you advance in the IT field. One of the goals of this book is to help you retain knowledge over the long term. Remember to take notes and quiz yourself often. At the end of each domain (such as this, Domain 2.0: Networking), review what you have learned in the entire section. This will help you to transition to other areas of the book.

2.7 – Compare and contrast Internet connection types, network types, and their features

ExamAlert

Objective 2.7 concentrates on the following concepts: Internet connection types (cable, DSL, dial-up, fiber, satellite, ISDN, cellular, line-of-sight wireless), and network types (LAN, WAN, PAN, MAN, WMN).

In this section we discuss the types of Internet connections available to the typical home office and small office (SOHO) user, as well as the basics for enterprise Internet connectivity. But first we'll cover computer network *types*—such as local area networks and wide area networks. There are a lot of acronyms when it comes to network types, so let's get that out of the way first.

Network Types

It's important to know how networks are classified. The two most common terms are local area network (LAN) and wide area network (WAN). But you should also know what a MAN, PAN, and WMN are. Let's begin with LAN and WAN.

A *LAN* is a group of computers and other devices usually located in a small area: a house, a small office, or a single building. The computers all connect to one or more switches, and a router allows the computers access to the Internet. Generally, there are no other routers internally. Technicians often use phrases such as "Connect the computer to the LAN" or "How many computers are on your LAN?" The LAN is usually based on a network design called the star topology, where all hosts connect to a central connecting device such as a switch, access point, or SOHO router. Figure 8.1 shows an example of a typical LAN configured as a star.

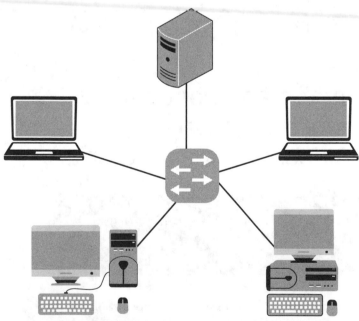

FIGURE 8.1 **A typical LAN and star topology**

A *WAN* is a group of one or more LANs over a large geographic area. Let's say a company has two LANs: one in New York and one in Los Angeles. Connecting the two would result in a WAN. However, to do this, the company would require the help of an Internet service provider (ISP) or telecommunications company. This provider would create the high-speed connection required for the two LANs to communicate quickly. Each LAN would require a router to connect to each other. The network administrator or network engineer or facilities department would be in charge of selecting an Internet service for the link between the offices. We'll discuss some of those Internet service options later in the chapter.

There is a smaller version of a WAN known as a metropolitan area network (*MAN*), also known as a municipal area network. This is when a company has two offices in the same city and wants to make a high-speed connection between them. It's different from a WAN in that it is not a large geographic area, but it is similar to a WAN in that an ISP is needed for the high-speed link.

Another network type is the wireless mesh network (WMN). Generally, a mesh means that wireless access points (or nodes) have multiple connections to each other in a mesh, or matrix pattern. Implementing a mesh can be very helpful with redundancy and availability. In a *WMN*, multiple wireless access points are used on the same channel. This allows for greater coverage in larger environments. As mobile devices move around the building or buildings, they quickly transition from one access point to another. In a WMN, the APs do not have to be physically cabled to a wired port like a traditional AP or wireless extender. However, the APs must have built-in mesh capability, which will often mean increased cost. This technology can provide a more efficient solution than the traditional wireless extender, as well as centralized management. This type of network can be used in larger infrastructures, and also in simpler SOHO environments (where it might be referred to as mesh Wi-Fi, Wi-Fi ad hoc, or a similar name).

On a slightly different note, a personal area network (*PAN*) is a smaller computer network used for communication by small computing devices. Take this to the next level by adding wireless standards such as Bluetooth, wireless USB, Zigbee, or Z-Wave, and you get a wireless PAN (WPAN). These networks are sometimes ad hoc, meaning there is no single controlling device, server, or access point. However, they might be controlled by a hub and gain access to the Internet from that device.

ExamAlert

Be able to define, compare, and contrast LAN, WAN, MAN, WMN, and PAN.

Internet Connection Types

There are a lot of different options for connecting to the Internet, including fiber-based systems, DSL, cable Internet, the venerable dial-up, and more. The type of Internet connection dictates download speeds to the clients on a SOHO network. Let's discuss some of the options available, starting with the slowest—dial-up.

Dial-Up

Strange as it might seem, dial-up Internet is still used by many people around the world, and in some areas of the United States, it is the only Internet connectivity available. Dial-up connections are inexpensive but at the cost of slow data throughput and dropped connections. To connect to a dial-up service, a user needs four things: a working phone line (with an RJ11 connection), an account with an ISP, a modem to dial-up to the ISP's networks, and some type of software to control the dial-up connection (for example, dial-up networking).

The modem sends and receives data in a serial fashion, meaning one bit at a time. Today, the dial-up modem is usually a USB-based device, but on older laptops it could be integrated, and on older desktops it could act as an internal adapter card or an external device that connects to a DE-9 serial port that utilizes the RS-232 data transmission standard. The modem uses a universal asynchronous receiver transmitter (UART)—this converts the serial information coming in from the phone line into parallel data to be sent to the processor. The UART is commonly integrated into a microcontroller either within the computer's motherboard or within the modem itself.

> **Note**
>
> We'll be discussing cables and ports in Chapter 9, "Cables and Connectors."

The Dial-up Modem

The term *modem* is a combination of the words *mo*dulate and *dem*odulate. It originated with dial-up modems that use a standard telephone phone line. To send data, they actually modulate from digital signals (inside the PC) to analog signals (used on the phone line). To receive data, they do the reverse—demodulate analog signals to digital. Dial-up modems are uncommon in the United States, but they are still used in rural areas, as backup Internet connections, and sometimes for direct administrative connections to networking devices.

Dial-up utilizes the plain old telephone service/public switched telephone network (POTS/PSTN). POTS is that simple landline that comes into a home, allowing a person to make phone calls. PSTN is the entire set of hardware and technologies at a telephone company's central office that controls POTS connections. Be careful when connecting a phone line to a computer. Make sure that it is connected to a modem (RJ11) and not to the network card (RJ45). The phone company sends a strong voltage through the line, which can damage a network adapter.

> **Note**
>
> Because dial-up connections are typically limited to 56 kbps, they should be avoided unless there is absolutely no other option for connecting to the Internet.

ISDN

Integrated Services Digital Network (ISDN) is a digital technology developed to combat the limitations of PSTN. Users can send data, talk on the phone, fax—and all from one line. It is broken down into two types of services:

▶ **BRI: Basic Rate ISDN:** 128 kbps. Two equal B channels at 64 kbps each for data and one separate 16-kbps D channel for timing.

▶ **PRI: Primary Rate ISDN:** 1.536 Mbps, runs on a T-1 circuit; 23 equal 64-kbps B channels for data and one 64-kbps D channel for timing.

ISDN is not used as often as cable Internet or fiber optic services, but some companies still use ISDN for video conferencing or as a fault-tolerant secondary Internet access connection. Data commuters use this if DSL or cable is not available.

DSL

Digital subscriber line (DSL) builds on dial-up by providing full digital data transmissions over phone lines but at high speeds. DSL modems connect to the phone line and to the PC's network adapter or to a SOHO router to enable sharing among multiple computers. One of the benefits of DSL is that you can talk on the phone line and transmit data at the same time. There are several derivatives of DSL, for example:

▶ **ADSL (Asymmetrical Digital Subscriber Line):** ADSL enables transmission over copper wires that is faster than dial-up. It is generally geared toward the consumer that requires more downstream bandwidth than upstream. Because the downloading and uploading speeds are different, it is known as an asymmetric technology. There is a group of ADSL technologies offering data transfer rates of anywhere from 8 Mbps download/1 Mbps upload to 52 Mbps download/16 Mbps upload, with newer, faster technologies being developed as of the writing of this book. ADSL is often offered to consumers who cannot get cable Internet.

▶ **SDSL (Symmetrical Digital Subscriber Line):** SDSL is installed (usually to companies) as a separate line and is usually more expensive. Unlike ADSL, SDSL upload and download speeds are the same, or symmetrical. Maximum data transfer rates for typical versions of SDSL are 1.5 Mbps and 5 Mbps (depending on the version).

Cable Internet

Broadband cable, used for cable Internet and cable TV, has download transfer rates from 5 Mbps to 150 Mbps or more (depending on the ISP). Upload speed is almost always slower, a fraction of the download speed. Like most Internet connectivity options, cable Internet is shared by the customer base. The more users who are on the Internet, the slower it becomes for everyone. Cable Internet is a common option for home use and for SOHO networks that use a router to allow multiple computers access to the Internet via a cable. An RG-6 cable is run into the office and connected to the cable modem by way of a screw-on F-connector. The cable modem also has an RJ45 connection for patching to the router or to an individual computer's network adapter.

> **ExamAlert**
>
> Understand how cable Internet connections are made.

Fiber

Instead of using a copper connection to the home or business the way dial-up, DSL, or cable Internet do, some companies offer fiber optic connections direct to the customer. This is known as fiber to the premises (FTTP)—it is the installation and use of optical fiber from a central point directly to individual buildings, such as residences, apartment buildings, and businesses.

Most FTTP services run over a fiber optic line to a network interface device in the home or office (specifically an optical network terminal); from there, it changes over to copper, which then makes the connection to the customer's

SOHO router or individual computer. This copper connection could be a twisted-pair patch cable (for example, a Cat 6 cable) or a coaxial cable using the Multimedia over Coax Alliance (MoCA) protocol. Examples of companies that offer FTTP include Verizon (Fios) and Google (Google Fiber).

However, there are other varieties of fiber available to the customer, and these varieties are defined by the point where the fiber ends and the copper begins. Collectively, these are referred to as "fiber to the x," where x equals the endpoint for the fiber run. For example, FTTN is fiber to the neighborhood, where the fiber is terminated/connected at a street enclosure that could be up to miles away from the customer's premises. Another example is FTTC, fiber to the cabinet, which generally means that the wiring cabinet is within 1000 feet of the premises. FTTdp (fiber to the distribution point) brings the connection within meters of the customer's premises.

Again, the service mentioned first, FTTP, is the most common and it's broken down into FTTB (fiber to the building or business) and FTTH (fiber to the home). But it's possible to get the fiber optic connection even closer to the individual user by acquiring the FTTD (fiber to the desktop) service. This could terminate at a fiber media converter near the user's computer or even connect directly to a fiber optic network adapter in the computer. However, a service such as FTTD is much more expensive and therefore is used much less frequently—that is, if the service is even available in your area.

Fiber optic cables can run at much higher data transfer rates than copper-based cables. Home-based fiber optic Internet connections can typically download data at 100 Mbps or 1000 Mbps. Upload speeds are typically less, as they are in most Internet services.

Satellite

Satellite connectivity uses a parabolic antenna (satellite dish) to connect via line of sight to a satellite; it is used in places where standard landline Internet access is not available. The satellite is in geosynchronous orbit, at 22,000 miles (35,406 km) above the Earth. This is the farthest distance of any Internet technology. The "dish" connects to coax cable that runs to a switching/channeling device for your computers. Today's satellite connections offer speeds close to traditional broadband access (similar to cable Internet access). One of the issues with satellite is electrical and natural interference. Another problem is latency. Due to the distance (44,000 miles total) of the data transfer, there can be a delay of .5 seconds to 5 seconds. That's the highest latency of any Internet technology. Latency goes hand-in-hand with distance. In the past, satellite-based Internet connections offered high-speed downloads, but uploads were slow due to the fact the service would use a dial-up line to upload information.

Newer satellite Internet technologies allow for the upload of data to the satellite as well, and while this is often still slower than the download speed, it is much faster than uploading via dial-up.

Line-of-Sight Wireless Internet Service

Line-of-sight, or *fixed*, wireless Internet service requires the customer's reception device to face the access point at the tower or ground station of the provider—without obstruction. This can be done over various frequencies, but to avoid congestion and interference, high-frequency microwave bands can be used. This type of service can be used in a point-to-point fashion, where two buildings communicate with each other; or it could be a point-to-multipoint setup, where multiple residences direct their antennas at the provider's access point. Because it is fixed, the potential data transfer rates are high, rivaling fiber optic speeds. Fixed wireless Internet broadband services are found more commonly in rural areas or in areas where there are large bodies of water. Fixed wireless is not a satellite service, but it can use parabolic antennas, which are essentially what satellite Internet services use—the difference is where the antenna points to. Remember, this type of service requires a clear line of sight, with no obstructions.

> **Note**
>
> WiMAX (Worldwide Interoperability for Microwave Access) can operate as line of sight (LOS) or non-line of sight (NLOS). WiMAX is an IEEE 802.16 wireless technology that offers high-speed connections over large distances. As of the writing of this book, it has been all but overtaken by 4G LTE and is only used in specific niche markets.

> **Note**
>
> For more information on cellular technologies such as tethering and mobile hotspot, see Chapter 4, "Smartphones, Tablets, and Other Mobile Devices, Part 2."

Cram Quiz

Answer these questions. The answers follow the last question. If you cannot answer these questions correctly, consider reading this section again until you can.

1. Which of the following is a group of Windows desktop computers located in a small area?

   ○ **A.** LAN

   ○ **B.** WAN

○ **C.** PAN

○ **D.** MAN

2. Which Internet service makes use of PSTN?

○ **A.** Dial-up

○ **B.** ISDN

○ **C.** DSL

○ **D.** Cable Internet

3. You have been tasked with setting up a small office with the fastest Internet service possible. There is no fiber optic availability in the area because of the rocky, hilly terrain. Which Internet service will typically offer the best data transfer rates?

○ **A.** WMN

○ **B.** FTTP

○ **C.** DSL

○ **D.** Cable Internet

○ **E.** Fixed wireless

Cram Quiz Answers

1. **A.** A local area network (LAN) is a group of computers, such as a SOHO network located in a small area. A wide area network (WAN) is a group of one or more LANs spread over a larger geographic area. A personal area network (PAN) is a smaller computer network used by smartphones and other small computing devices. A metropolitan area network (MAN) is a group of LANs in a smaller geographic area of a city.

2. **A.** Dial-up Internet connections make use of the public switched telephone network (PSTN) and POTS phone lines. ISDN was developed to meet the limitations of PSTN. DSL provides faster data transmissions over phone lines (or separate data lines). Cable Internet is a broadband service that offers higher speeds than DSL; it is provided by cable TV companies.

3. **D.** The Internet service with the best data transfer rates will typically be cable Internet. Cable Internet service is generally "faster" than DSL. WMN stands for wireless mesh network, a type of network that uses multiple access points—but it is not an Internet service. FTTP stands for fiber to the premises, which is not available in the scenario. Fixed wireless (or line-of-sight wireless Internet service) can offer very high data transfer rates, but it requires an unobstructed view of the provider's tower. This is probably not an option due to the rocky, hilly area where the customer's office resides.

2.8 – Given a scenario, use appropriate networking tools

For this objective you should know some of the cabling and networking tools that can help you to create, modify, and troubleshoot network patch cables and longer network cables that terminate at patch panels and RJ45 jacks. We'll also briefly talk about Wi-Fi analyzers that can be used to identify wireless networks.

Network Cabling Tools

If you plan to build a physical network, you will need to stock up on some key networking tools. These tools will aid you when running, terminating, and testing cable. For this short section, let's imagine a scenario where you are the network installer and are required to install a wired network for 12 computers.

To start, you should check with your local municipality for any rules and regulations for running networking cable. Some municipalities require an installer to have an electrician's license. But most require only an exemption of some sort that anyone can apply for at the town or county seat. Due to the low-voltage nature of network wiring (for most applications), some municipalities have no rules regarding this. But in urban areas, you will need to apply for a permit and have at least one inspection done when you are done with the installation. Permits and regulations aside, let's say that in this scenario you have been cleared to install 12 wired connections to computers (known as drops) and have diagrammed where the cables will be run and where they will terminate. All cables will come out of a wiring closet, where you will terminate them to a small patch panel. On the other end, they will terminate at in-wall RJ45 jacks near each of the computers. Let's discuss each of the tools that you will use to complete this job.

▶ **Cable cutter:** The first tool you should have is a good, sharp cutting tool. You will need to make a clean cut on the end of the network cable; scissors will not do. Either cut pliers or other cable cutting tools will be necessary.

▶ **Cable stripper:** The second tool is a cable stripper (or wire stripper). This tool is used to strip a portion of the plastic jacket off the cable, exposing the individual wires. At this point, you can separate the wires and get ready to terminate them with a punchdown tool.

▶ **Punchdown tool:** The third tool is a punchdown tool. This device punches the individual wires down into the 110 IDC clips of an RJ45 jack and the patch panel. This "punching down" of the wires is the actual termination.

▶ **Cable testers:** The last tool necessary for the job is a cable testing tool. There are a few options here:

▶ The best option is a proper network cable tester, also known as a continuity tester or cable certifier. This device will have a LAN testing unit that you can plug into a port on the patch panel and a terminator that you plug into the other end of the cable in the corresponding RJ45 jack (or vice versa). This tool will test for continuity and will test each wire in the cable, making sure each one is wired properly.

▶ Another option is the tone generator and probe kit (also known as a fox and hound). This kit consists of two parts: a tone-generating device, which connects to one end of the network cable and, when turned on, sends a tone along the length of the cable; and a probing device, also known as an inductive amplifier which can detect the tone anywhere along the cable length and at the termination point. This tool is not as good as a proper network cable tester because it tests only one of the pairs of the wires. However, it is an excellent tool for finding individual phone lines and is more commonly used for that. You can also use a multimeter to do various tests of individual lines, but it is usually not necessary if you own the other tools mentioned. The cable tester mentioned previously can usually create tone as well.

At this point, the cables have been run, terminated on both ends, and tested. The only other thing you need is patch cables. The patch cables connect the various ports of the patch panel to a switch, and the RJ45 jacks to the computers.

▶ **RJ45 crimper:** Usually, you would buy patch cables for $2 or $3 each and be done with it. However, you can make them, too. You would have to purchase cable as well as RJ45 plugs. The plugs are attached to the cable ends with an RJ45 crimping tool. This tool can come in especially handy when you need to make a crossover patch cable, which can be used to connect a computer to another computer directly. There are other types of crimpers for coaxial cable as well.

▶ **Patch tester:** Before connecting the patch cables, you should test them with a patch tester. This device has two RJ45 jacks; you plug each end of the patch cable into the tester, and then press the button to make sure each wire makes a proper connection and has continuity.

> **Note**
>
> You could also test continuity of a patch cable (or just about any cable or wire) with a *multimeter*. To do this, you would set the multimeter to Ohms (with audible beep) and place the leads on the corresponding wires of both RJ45 plugs. However, this requires very thin probes, which you would have to either purchase separately or rig yourself with sewing needles or something similar. Bottom line—use the right tool for the job, in this case a proper patch tester.

▶ **Loopback plug:** Another tool every PC tech should have is a loopback plug. It simulates a network connection and has two main functions. First, it can help find what port on a switch an RJ45 jack is wired to. You plug it into an RJ45 jack on the wall and it bounces the signal back down the cable to the switch, lighting up the port that the cable is ultimately connected to. This tells you which port on the switch a particular cable is connected to in case it wasn't labeled previously. You can also accomplish this by connecting it to the end of a patch cable because the device usually has a male and a female RJ45 connection. Second, you can test the network adapter on a PC and find out if TCP/IP is functioning properly. An easy way to do this is to plug the loopback adapter into the RJ45 port of the PC, open the command line, and then ping the IP address of the local system. The loopback plug is essentially a really short crossover connection—the appropriate pins are crossed within the device, looping the signal and data back to where it came from.

> **Note**
>
> You could even make your own loopback plug if you really wanted to! It's essentially a crossover connection, so you could connect an individual wire on an RJ45 plug to pins 1 and 3 and a second wire to pins 2 and 6. Tedious stuff, but great to know if you are in a tight spot and only have twisted-pair wire and RJ45 plugs on you (and a crimper).

Figure 8.2 identifies some of the tools described in this section.

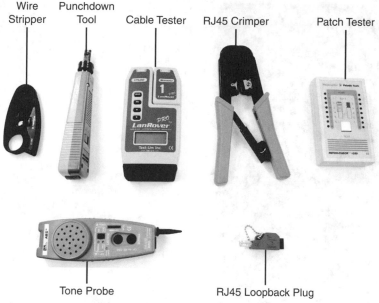

FIGURE 8.2   **Twisted-pair cabling tools**

Wi-Fi Analyzers

A *Wi-Fi analyzer* is a tool that can identify wireless networks on 2.4-GHz and 5-GHz frequencies. The tool shows things such as the channels used by neighboring wireless networks, any overlapping that might be occurring between those networks and yours, and the signal strength of access points. Wi-Fi analyzers come in two types: handheld, all-in-one devices with a built-in Wi-Fi antenna and incorporated analysis programs (these are much more expensive); and then there are various apps for Windows, Android, and iOS. Whatever device you run the app on has to have a properly set up wireless network adapter. Figure 8.3 shows an example of a basic Wi-Fi analyzer app. It is displaying the 2.4-GHz Wi-Fi networks in the general vicinity. As you can see, the lower channels (1–5) are being used much more than the upper channels. This type of data should play into your decision-making process when setting up a new Wi-Fi network or when selecting an access point to connect a client to—if there is more than one.

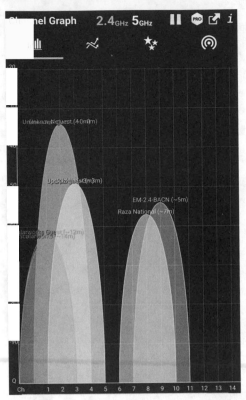

FIGURE 8.3   Wi-Fi analyzer viewing the 2.4-GHz range

Cram Quiz

Answer these questions. The answers follow the last question. If you cannot answer these questions correctly, consider reading this section again until you can.

1. Which tool is used to test a network adapter not connected to the network?

   ○ **A.** Punchdown tool

   ○ **B.** Cable tester

   ○ **C.** Loopback plug

   ○ **D.** Tone generator and probe

2. Your boss is concerned with overlapping wireless networks from neighboring companies using 802.11ac. Which tool should you use to analyze the problem, and which frequency should you display for analysis?

   ○ **A.** Wi-Fi analyzer; 5 GHz

   ○ **B.** Cable certifier; 5 GHz

   ○ **C.** Loopback plug; 2.4 GHz

   ○ **D.** Wi-Fi analyzer; 2.4 GHz

3. What would be required to attach RJ45 plugs to the ends of a single patch cable?

   ○ **A.** Tone and probe kit

   ○ **B.** Multimeter

   ○ **C.** Cable stripper

   ○ **D.** Crimper

Cram Quiz Answers

1. **C.** To test a network adapter without a network connection, you would use a loopback plug. This simulates a network connection. It can also be used to test a switch port. Punchdown tools are used to punch individual wires to a patch panel. Cable testers such as continuity testers test the entire length of a terminated cable. A tone generator and probe kit can also test a cable's length, but only tests one pair of wires at a time.

2. **A.** To analyze the problem, use a Wi-Fi analyzer! Because your boss is concerned about wireless networks using 802.11ac, you would display the results for 5-GHz networks, not 2.4 GHz. Cable certifiers are used to check long-distance *wired* connections, for example, from a patch panel to an RJ45 jack. The loopback plug is used to simulate a network connection, which can help with identifying switch ports, and testing a PC's network connection.

3. **D.** RJ45 plugs are attached to the cable ends with a tool called a crimper. A tone generator and probe kit is used to trace hard-to-find telecommunication and data communication cables/wires. A multimeter can be used to test continuity of a patch cable. A cable stripper is used to strip a portion of the plastic jacket off the cable, exposing the individual wires.

CORE 1 (220-1001)

Domain 3.0: Hardware

CHAPTER 9

Cables and Connectors

This chapter covers the following A+ 220-1001 exam objectives:

▶ **3.1** – Explain basic cable types, features, and their purposes.

▶ **3.2** – Identify common connector types.

Welcome to Domain 3: Hardware. This domain is listed as having the highest percentage of content within the 220-1001 exam (sharing first place with Domain 5: Hardware and Network Troubleshooting). Every chapter covering this domain is chock-full of hardware information you need to know. Treat them accordingly!

Cabling! Even with the massive amount of wireless technologies and wireless usage, the good old cable is still necessary, and used in many applications. This chapter gets you familiar with all the cables and connectors you need to network systems together, add peripherals, and adapt or convert from one technology to another. Everything can be linked together!

Because they are so interconnected, the 3.1 and 3.2 objectives are covered as one section in this chapter.

3.1 – Explain basic cable types, features, and their purposes

ExamAlert

Objective 3.1 concentrates on the following concepts: network cables, video cables, multipurpose cables, peripheral cables, hard drive cables, and adapters.

3.2 – Identify common connector types

> **ExamAlert**
>
> **Objective 3.2** focuses on the following connector types: RJ11, RJ45, RS-232, BNC, RG-59, RG-6, USB, Micro-USB, Mini-USB, USB-C, DB-9, Lightning, SCSI, eSATA, and Molex.

Network Cables

Cable types are broken down into two categories: cables that use electricity and cables that use light. Twisted-pair and coaxial cables use copper wires as their transmission media and send electricity over those wires. Fiber optic, on the other hand, uses glass or plastic as the transmission medium and sends light (photons) over those.

Twisted Pair

The most common type of cable used in today's networks is *twisted pair*. It is referred to as twisted pair because the copper wires inside of the cable are twisted together into pairs throughout the entire length of the cable. Regularly, admins use UTP cable, short for unshielded twisted pair. Typical versions of twisted pair include *Category 6* and *Category 5e* (often abbreviated to just Cat 6 or Cat 5e). Table 9.1 shows the various categories of twisted pair you should know for the exam and the networks they are rated for.

TABLE 9.1 **UTP Categories and Speeds**

Category UTP	Rated For
Category 5	100 Mbps networks (100 MHz)
Category 5e	100 Mbps and 1 Gbps networks (100 MHz/350 MHz)
Category 6/6a	1000 Mbps and 10 Gbps networks (250 MHz/500 MHz)
Category 7/7a	1000 Mbps and 10 Gbps networks (600 MHz/1000 MHz)

Data transfer rate (also known as *speed* or *bandwidth*) is normally measured in bits because networks usually transfer data serially, or one bit at a time. 100 Mbps is 100 megabits per second. 1 Gbps is equal to 1 gigabit per second (known as a gigabit network), or 1000 Mbps. 10 Gbps is equal to 10 gigabits per second. Now, a cable might be rated for 10-Gbps networks (such as Cat 6), but you probably won't attain that speed over the cable. Typically, the actual speed (known as throughput) might be 250 Mbps, 500 Mbps, 1 Gbps, and possibly more. That depends on many factors, including the frequency of the cable (for example, Cat 6 is 250 MHz and Cat 6a is 500 MHz), the technology used to send data, the encoding rate, whether duplexing is involved, the length of the cable, the quality of the installation, and so on. So, it's difficult to put a specific number to each category of cable—just remember what network speeds each category of cable is rated for.

ExamAlert

Know what network speeds Cat 5, 5e, 6, and 7 are rated for.

Note

As of the writing of this book, Category 8 is under development, with potential frequencies between 1600 and 2000 MHz and capable of supporting 25 or 40 Gbps over copper wire!

The Telecommunications Industry Association (TIA) defines standards for cabling and wiring, such as the 568A and 568B standards. Generally speaking, the most common standard you see is the 568B standard. Table 9.2 shows the color sequence for each of the eight wires (or pins) for the 568B and 568A standards. Figure 9.1 shows a close-up of the wires organized for a 568B connection.

TABLE 9.2 **568B and 568A Wiring Standards**

Pinouts	568B	Pinouts	568A
Pin 1	White/Orange	Pin 1	White/Green
Pin 2	Orange	Pin 2	Green
Pin 3	White/Green	Pin 3	White/Orange
Pin 4	Blue	Pin 4	Blue
Pin 5	White/Blue	Pin 5	White/Blue
Pin 6	Green	Pin 6	Orange
Pin 7	White/Brown	Pin 7	White/Brown
Pin 8	Brown	Pin 8	Brown

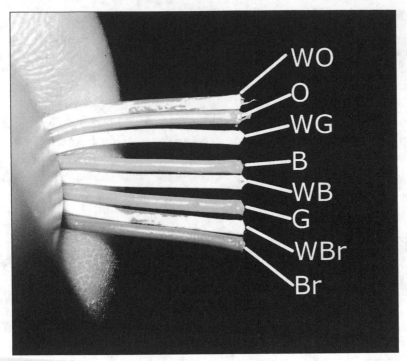

WO
O
WG
B
WB
G
WBr
Br

FIGURE 9.1 Wires organized for the 568B standard

Any physical cabling equipment used in the network must comply with this standard. This includes cables, patch panels, jacks, and even connectors. The connector used with twisted-pair networks is known colloquially as the RJ45 (more specifically, the 8P8C connector). RJ45 plugs connect to each end of the cable, and these cables connect to RJ45 sockets within network adapters and on network switches.

> **ExamAlert**
>
> If a computer cannot connect to the network, check the network cable first. Make sure the RJ45 plug has a solid connection.

As you can see in Figure 9.2, RJ45 plugs look a lot like the plugs that connect your telephone (known as RJ11). However, the RJ45 plug is larger and contains eight wires, whereas the RJ11 plug holds only a maximum of six wires (and normally only uses four).

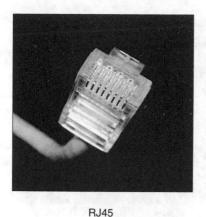 

RJ45   RJ11

FIGURE 9.2   **RJ45 and RJ11 plugs**

A standard twisted-pair patch cable that you would use to connect a computer
to a switch or RJ45 jack is wired for 568B on each end. That makes it a *straight-
through cable*. However, if you wanted to connect a computer directly to another
computer, you would need to use a *crossover cable*. This type of cable is wired for
568B on one end and 568A on the other. You can see in Table 9.2 that certain
pins are "crossed" to each other from 568B to 568A. Pin 1 on 568B crosses
to pin 3 on 568A, and pin 2 crosses to 6. You can also use a crossover cable to
connect one switch to another; though this is usually not necessary nowadays
because most switches will auto-sense the type of cable you plug into them.

Note

The way that a crossover cable's pins are wired is the basis for a loopback—a connection made to test the local computer or system (for example, an RJ45 loopback
plug).

UTP has a few disadvantages:

▶ It can be run only 100 meters (328 feet) before *signal attenuation* occurs,
   which is the weakening or degrading of signal.

▶ Its outer jacket is made of plastic and it has no shielding, making it susceptible to electromagnetic interference (EMI) and vulnerable to unauthorized network access in the form of wiretapping.

Because the UTP cable jacket is made of PVCs (plastics) that can be harmful to
humans when they catch on fire, most municipalities require that plenum-rated

cable be installed in any area that cannot be reached by a sprinkler system. A *plenum* is an enclosed space used for airflow. For example, if cables are run above a drop ceiling, building code requires that they are plenum-rated. This means that the cable has a special Teflon coating or is a special low-smoke variant of twisted pair, reducing the amount of PVC chemicals that are released into the air in the case of fire.

> **ExamAlert**
>
> To meet fire code, use plenum-rated cable above drop ceilings and anywhere else necessary.

Because UTP is susceptible to EMI, a variant was developed known as STP or shielded twisted pair. This includes metal shielding over each pair of wires, reducing external EMI and the possibility of unauthorized network access. A couple of disadvantages of STP include higher cost of product and installation and the fact that the shielding needs to be grounded to work effectively. Keep in mind that all server room and wiring closet equipment—such as patch panels, punch blocks, and wiring racks—should be permanently grounded before use.

> **ExamAlert**
>
> STP cable is resistant to EMI.

Coaxial

Coaxial cable is another way to transfer data over a network. This cable has a single conductor surrounded by insulating material, which is then surrounded by a copper screen and, finally, an outer plastic sheath. Some networking technologies still use coaxial cable; for example, cable Internet connections use RG-6 coaxial cable (and possibly the older RG-59 cable). This cable screws on to the terminal of a cable modem using an F-connector. It is the same cable and connector used with cable TV set-top boxes (STB) and DVRs.

Generally, RG-6 cable can be run as far as 500 to 1000 feet. The maximum distance varies because several factors play into how far the data can travel before attenuation (for example, the frequency used, protocol used, and so on). Its speed also varies depending on what type of transmission is sent over it. A typical RG-6 cable has a minimum bandwidth of 1 GHz, which can loosely translate to 1 Gbps, but the data throughput will most likely be capped at some number below that. For example, cable Internet providers will often cap that at 30 Mbps to 50 Mbps, and some fiber optic providers (who change the cable type from fiber optic to coaxial at the house or business) might cap it at anywhere between 100 Mbps and 500 Mbps. This all varies according to the provider and how many services are being transmitted over the same line.

There are two derivatives of RG-6 that you should know: RG-6/U, which is double-shielded, and the more common RG-6/UQ, which is quadruple-shielded and is often referred to as "quad shield." It is a better option if you are running RG-6 in ceilings or near any electrical appliances.

> **Note**
>
> Long ago, local area networks were built using RG-58 coaxial cable and BNC screw-on connectors. It is unlikely that you will see these because of their slow speeds, but you might still see the BNC connector used in other applications (such as older video switching devices). BNC is listed in the CompTIA objectives, but because it is rare, it is unlikely you will see a question on it.

> **ExamAlert**
>
> Make sure you know cable terminology such as RJ11, RJ45, and RG-6 for the exam.

Fiber Optic

Fiber optic is fast and, when dealing with EMI, it's a better option than copper-based cables. Because fiber optic cables transmit data by way of light instead of electricity, they can send signals much faster and further than copper wires, and EMI doesn't even play into the equation. Plus, fiber optic cables are difficult to splice into, unlike copper-based cables. Due to these reasons, fiber optic cable is the most secure type of cable.

You might encounter single-mode and multimode fiber; for the most part, single-mode fiber is used over longer distances, but both types are easily capable of supporting 1000-Mbps and 10-Gbps networks and can be run farther than twisted-pair cable. A couple types of connectors used with fiber include ST and SC, as shown in Figure 9.3. Another connector is LC, which looks quite similar to SC.

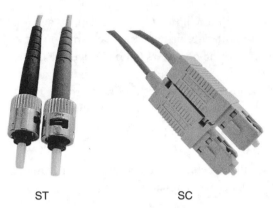

ST   SC

FIGURE 9.3   **ST and SC connectors**

Multimode cables have a larger core diameter than single-mode cables. It is the more commonly used fiber optic cable in server rooms and when making network backbone connections between buildings in a campus. It transmits data approximately 600 meters. Single-mode, on the other hand, is used for longer distance runs, perhaps from one city to the next (as far as thousands of kilometers). At shorter distances, single-mode cable can go beyond 10 Gbps.

> **ExamAlert**
>
> Know the differences between multimode and single-mode, as well as the approximate speed and distance limitations.

Video Cables and Connectors

Your choice of video card will probably dictate the cable and connector that you will use. Most of today's PCIe video cards come with either DVI, HDMI, or DisplayPort outputs. Some monitors also have VGA connections for legacy compatibility. Table 9.3 details some of the common connectors you will see in the field. Figure 9.4 shows some of the typical video ports you will use.

TABLE 9.3 **Video Card Connectors**

Connector Type	Full Name	Description
DVI	Digital Visual Interface	High-quality connections used with LCD displays. Carries uncompressed digital video; is partially compatible with HDMI. Types include: ▶ **DVI-D:** Digital-only connections. ▶ **DVI-I:** Digital and analog connections. ▶ **DVI-A:** Analog-only connections. Dual-link connections are available for DVI-D and DVI-I. Non-dual-link versions have a gap in the center of the pins, using 1/3 less pins total.
HDMI	High-Definition (HD) Multimedia Interface	Used mainly for high-definition television. Can carry video and audio signals Version 2.1 (released 2017) is the latest as of the writing of this book. ▶ **Type A:** Supports all HD modes, compatible with DVI-D connectors. ▶ **Type B:** Double-video bandwidth, supports higher resolutions. Also known as dual-link; uncommon. ▶ **Type C:** Mini-HDMI, used in portable devices. ▶ **Type D:** Micro-HDMI; smallest connector, also used in portable devices. ▶ **Type E:** Used in automobiles; has a locking tab.
DisplayPort	DisplayPort	▶ Royalty-free interface similar to HDMI; designed to be the replacement for HDMI and DVI. ▶ Often has a locking tab. ▶ Uses packet transmission similar to Ethernet. ▶ Mini version developed by Apple. ▶ Version 1.4 (released 2016) is the latest as of the writing of this book.
VGA (also known as SVGA)	Video Graphics Array	▶ 15-pin, usually blue, known as DE15 (also sold as DB15 or HD15). Used for older monitors that display VGA, SVGA, and XGA resolutions. Signal quality degrades over shorter distances than HDMI, DVI, and DisplayPort.

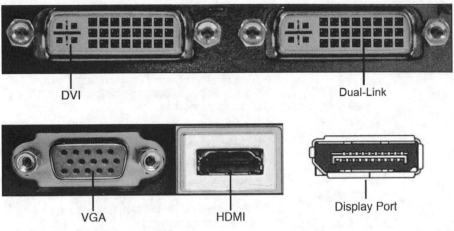

FIGURE 9.4 **Typical video ports**

> **ExamAlert**
>
> Be able to identify VGA, HDMI, Mini-HDMI, DisplayPort, and DVI video connectors and ports.

There are adapters, splitters, and signal boosters available for just about every type of video connection: HDMI to DVI, DVI to VGA, and so on. In some cases, a passive adapter or splitter works fine. In other cases, an active (AC-powered) connection is required. This is common with DVI and HDMI, especially if you want a clean, quality signal over any length beyond 1 meter.

Multipurpose Cables and Connectors

This is sort of the catch-all category for several types of cables: USB, Apple device cables, and serial cables.

USB

USB ports are used by many devices, including keyboards, mice, printers, flash drives, and much more. The USB port enables data transfer between the device and the computer and usually powers the device as well. The speed of a USB device's data transfer depends on the version of the USB port, as shown in Table 9.4.

TABLE 9.4   **Comparison of USB Versions**

USB Version	Name	Data Transfer Rate
USB 2.0	High-Speed	480 Mbps
USB 3.0	SuperSpeed	5 Gbps
USB 3.1	SuperSpeed+	10 Gbps
USB 3.2 (USB-C)	SuperSpeed+	10/20 Gbps

Note

You might also see USB data transfer rates written as Mbit/s and Gbit/s.

Note

USB 1.0 (1.5 Mbps) and 1.1 (12 Mbps) are deprecated. If you encounter an older computer that has only these ports, consider installing a USB adapter card that adheres to a higher version of USB.

ExamAlert

Memorize the specifications for USB 2.0 through 3.2.

There are various plugs used for the different types of USB connections. Figure 9.5 displays an illustration of these connectors.

Type A and Type B connectors are commonly used for printers and other larger devices. Mini- and micro-connectors are often used for handheld computers, smartphones, mice, digital cameras, portable music players, and cell phones. USB-C is used for newer smartphones and other devices developed after 2017. However, some companies create proprietary cables and connectors for their devices based off of the USB specifications. These devices will not connect properly to Type A, Type B, and mini- or micro-connectors.

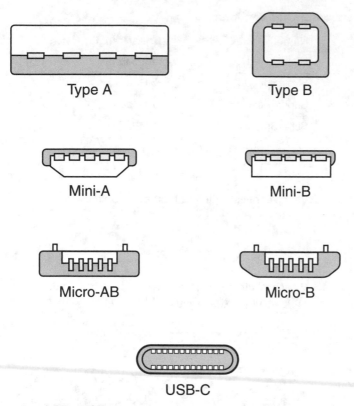

Type A

Type B

Mini-A

Mini-B

Micro-AB

Micro-B

USB-C

FIGURE 9.5 **USB connectors**

Lightning and Thunderbolt

Lightning is a proprietary port built into Apple devices such as the iPad and iPhone. It's an 8-pin connector that replaced the 30-pin dock predecessor. As with USB-C, the Lightning connector can be inserted face up or face down. It supports USB 3.0 speeds.

Thunderbolt is a high-speed hardware interface developed by Intel. As of the writing of this book, this is used primarily by Apple computers. It combines elements of PCI Express and DisplayPort technologies. Versions 1 and 2 use the Mini DisplayPort connector and version 3 uses the USB Type-C connector. Thunderbolt 2 gives access to 4K monitors. Because Thunderbolt is based on DisplayPort technology, it provides native support for the Apple Thunderbolt Display and Mini DisplayPort displays.

Thunderbolt can be used to transfer data at high rates to external storage devices or to displays (or both; up to six devices can be daisy-chained, meaning wired together in sequence). If you look at the ports of the computer and see the thunderbolt icon next to the Mini DisplayPort port, then it is meant to be used for data transfer to peripherals. If you see a display icon, then it can be used with a monitor. While you can physically connect a Thunderbolt device to a Mac with DisplayPort, the device will not work, but if you connect a DisplayPort device to a Mac with Thunderbolt, the device will work. Table 9.5 describes the different versions of Thunderbolt.

TABLE 9.5 **Comparison of Thunderbolt Versions**

Thunderbolt Version	Data Transfer Rate	Connector Type	PCI Express Version Required
Version 1	10 Gbps	DisplayPort	Version 2.0
Version 2	20 Gbps	DisplayPort	Version 2.0
Version 3	40 Gbps	USB Type-C	Version 3.0

ExamAlert

Know the Thunderbolt versions, speeds, and connection types.

Serial

The term *serial* is used with many technologies: USB, Serial-attached SCSI, bit streams over network cables, and so on; but generally, if a person refers to serial connections for peripheral devices, that person is talking about the Recommended Standard 232 (RS-232) data transmission standard. Though it is an old technology, it is still used in many environments. For example, the RS-232 standard describes how DTEs (computers) and DCEs (dial-up modems) communicate using serial ports.

RS-232 communicates via serial cables that have either 9 wires (DE-9, also known as DB-9) or 25 wires (DB-25). RS-232 has been used for many years, and that will most likely continue. That is because of its simple design, and the vast array of devices out there that use RS-232 interfaces such as handheld and mountable terminals, networking equipment, industrial machines, and analytical instruments. Because of this, you can still find motherboards with a built-in RS-232 port—usually a DE-9. If a computer does not have one, and you need to access RS-232-based equipment, there are PCIe add-on cards. And for laptops and other mobile devices, there are USB to RS-232 converters. RS-232 and other Recommended Standards (such as RS-422 and RS-485) are published by the TIA, the same organization that publishes the standard for 568B.

Hard Drive Cables and Connectors

The three types of hard drive cables listed in the objective are as follows:

▶ **Serial ATA (SATA):** A very common connection for internal hard drives (SATA) and external HDs (eSATA). It uses a 7-pin data connector and a 15-pin power connector.

▶ **Integrated Drive Electronics (IDE):** A much older type of connection that runs in parallel (8 bits at a time) instead of serial (1 bit at a time). It uses a 40-pin ribbon cable for data and a 4-pin Molex connector for power.

▶ **Small Computer System Interface (SCSI):** Around since the 1980s, SCSI at first was designed as a parallel technology that could run faster than IDE and other connections. Today, a common type of SCSI is Serial Attached SCSI (SAS), which can transfer data as fast as 22.5 Gbps (SAS version 4).

We'll be discussing some of these drives and connections more in Chapter 10, "RAM and Storage."

Adapters

You can't put a square peg in a round hole (normally). Sometimes you need to make a connection, but the devices and/or cables don't match up, so you'll need an adapter—and there are adapters for virtually everything you might want to do. Let's say you need to make a connection to a USB Type B connector from a USB Type A connector, or you need to connect from USB to RJ45, or you need to connect from a USB to the older PS/2 connector—well, there are adapters for all of those situations and more.

Video can be especially troublesome. For example, what if your laptop has an HDMI output but the monitor you want to connect to only has DVI and VGA? An HDMI to DVI output would be necessary. But remember, DVI does not normally carry audio signal the way that HDMI does, so you might also need to run an audio cable from the 3.5-mm audio output of the laptop to a set of speakers. You might need to switch from DVI to VGA, or from DVI to HDMI. Be ready to use adapters and research whether the length of your connection, and/or the quality of signal, requires an active AC-powered adapter.

A common adapter today is the USB to Ethernet adapter. These allow you to take just about any USB port and send data from the computer (or device) over an Ethernet network. There are adapters that go from USB (Type A) to RJ45, USB-C to RJ45, and so on. USB-C is preferred for many devices because it can handle higher data throughputs with less latency.

Most PC technicians will carry a variety of adapters with them just in case the need arises. Something to think about for your PC toolkit.

Cram Quiz

Answer these questions. The answers follow the last question. If you cannot answer these questions correctly, consider reading this chapter again until you can.

1. Which of the following would be suitable for 1000-Mbps networks? (Select all that apply.)
   - ○ **A.** Category 3
   - ○ **B.** Category 5
   - ○ **C.** Category 5e
   - ○ **D.** Category 6

2. Which type of cable would you use if you were concerned about EMI?
   - ○ **A.** Plenum-rated
   - ○ **B.** UTP
   - ○ **C.** STP
   - ○ **D.** Coaxial

3. You have been tasked with connecting a newer Android-based smartphone to an external TV so that you can display the CEO's smartphone screen during a meeting. Which of the following adapters would be the best solution typically?
   - ○ **A.** Micro-USB to HDMI
   - ○ **B.** Micro-USB to DVI
   - ○ **C.** USB-C to DVI
   - ○ **D.** USB-C to Ethernet
   - ○ **E.** USB-C to HDMI

4. Which type of cable can connect a computer to another computer directly?
   - ○ **A.** Straight-through
   - ○ **B.** Crossover
   - ○ **C.** 568A
   - ○ **D.** SATA
   - ○ **E.** 568B

5. Which connector is used for cable Internet?

- ○ **A.** LC
- ○ **B.** F-connector
- ○ **C.** BNC
- ○ **D.** RJ45
- ○ **E.** DE-9

6. Which cable type would be suitable for longer distances such as connecting two cities?

- ○ **A.** Coaxial
- ○ **B.** Twisted pair
- ○ **C.** Multimode fiber
- ○ **D.** Single-mode fiber

Cram Quiz Answers

1. **C and D.** Category 5e and Category 6 are suitable for 1000-Mbps networks (and Cat 6 is also suitable for 10-Gbps networks). Category 3 is suitable for 10-Mbps networks only. It is outdated and you most likely won't see it. Category 5 is suitable for 100-Mbps networks. In general, Cat 3 and Cat 5 networks should be upgraded.

2. **C.** STP (shielded twisted pair) is the only cable listed here that can reduce electromagnetic interference. However, fiber optic cable is another good solution, though it will be more expensive, and more difficult to install. Plenum-rated cable is used where fire code requires it; it doesn't burn as fast, releasing fewer PVC chemicals into the air.

3. **E.** Typically, you would use USB-C to HDMI. If it is a newer Android-based smartphone, then chances are that it will have a USB-C port. If you are attempting to connect it to a TV, then HDMI is the most likely port to use. Micro-USB is used with many mobile devices, but newer devices (especially Android-based devices) have switched to, or are moving toward, USB-C. You wouldn't want USB-C to DVI because TVs normally don't have DVI inputs. USB to Ethernet helps to convert from a computer or mobile device to the Ethernet network. These devices can ultimately allow a device or computer with a USB port to access the Internet. This wired connection might be favored over wireless for its speed, quality connection, and low latency.

4. **B.** A crossover cable is used to connect like devices: computer to computer or switch to switch. Straight-through cables (the more common patch cable) do not connect like devices (for example, they connect from a computer to a switch). 568B is the typical wiring standard you will see in twisted-pair cables; 568A is the less common standard. A crossover cable uses the 568B wiring standard on one end and 568A on the other end. (By the way, sometimes you will see these written as T568A and T568B.) SATA is used to connect hard drives internally to a desktop or laptop computer.

5. **B.** Cable Internet connections use RG-6 coaxial cable (usually) with an F-connector on the end. LC is a type of fiber optic connector. BNC is an older connector type used by coaxial networks. RJ45 is the connector used on twisted-pair patch cables. DE-9 (or DB-9) is a serial connector used with RS-232 connections.

6. **D.** Single-mode fiber is used for longer distance runs, perhaps from one city to the next (as far as thousands of kilometers). Coaxial is common for connections between utility poles and houses/buildings. Twisted pair is common in LANs. Multimode cables have a larger core diameter than single-mode cables. It is the more commonly used fiber optic cable in server rooms and when making network backbone connections between buildings in a campus.

CHAPTER 10
RAM and Storage

This chapter covers the following A+ 220-1001 exam objectives:

▶ **3.3** – Given a scenario, install RAM types.

▶ **3.4** – Given a scenario, select, install and configure storage devices.

This chapter is all about how data is accessed and stored—over the short term, and the long term. We use random access memory (RAM) for the short term, and storage drives, such as hard drives and optical drives, over the long term. There are different levels of performance for the different types of RAM and hard drives available. A weak component can act as a bottleneck when it comes to processing data, opening and running programs, and saving and rendering information. This ultimately can lead to decreased performance of the entire system. So, pay careful attention to the selection of RAM and hard drives when building or upgrading computers. This is a big chapter, so be sure to take breaks as you go!

3.3 – Given a scenario, install RAM types

ExamAlert

Objective 3.3 concentrates on the following concepts: RAM types (DDR2, DDR3, DDR4, SODIMM), single channel, dual channel, triple channel, error correcting, parity vs. non-parity.

When people talk about the RAM in their computer, they are almost always referring to the "sticks" of memory that are installed into the motherboard. This is known as *dynamic random access memory (DRAM)*, or main memory, and often comes in capacities of 4, 8, 16, or 32 GB, or more. This type of RAM has its own speed and must be compatible with the motherboard's RAM slots. It's not the only type of RAM, but it's the one you should be most concerned with for the exam. For all practical purposes, the terms stick, DIMM, and memory module mean the same thing; they refer to the RAM installed into a motherboard's RAM slots.

The most important concept in this chapter is *compatibility*. There are a lot of RAM technologies to know, but the bottom line is, "Will it be compatible with my motherboard?" The best way to find out is to go to the RAM manufacturer's website and search for your motherboard. They usually list the matching RAM. Let's discuss the types of RAM you should know.

RAM Types

There are many types of RAM, but for the exam you need to know about two types: *desktop RAM* and *laptop RAM*. Generally, desktops use dual-inline memory modules (DIMMs), and laptops use small-outline DIMMs (SODIMMs). They both use RAM that is based on Double Data Rate (DDR) technology. The original DDR got its name because it doubles the data per cycle as compared to older types of RAM. A typical data transfer rate for DDR version 1 was 1600 MB/s. This is not nearly enough for today's computers, so let's move on to DDR2, DDR3, and the more common DDR4.

DDR2

DDR2 builds on the original DDR specification by decreasing voltage (to 1.8 V) and by increasing speed. It increases speed through faster signaling, which requires additional pins. Standard DDR2 DIMMs have 240 pins and cannot be used in other DDR memory slots.

> **ExamAlert**
> Know the number of pins in the various DDR memory modules.

A typical stick of DDR2 RAM is called DDR2-800 (also known as PC2-6400). This can perform *800* million transfers per second, amounting to *6400* MB/s. All the numbers you need to know are in the names!

> **Note**
> Millions of transfers per second is usually expressed as megatransfers per second or MT/s.

DDR3

DDR3 was designed for lower power consumption and higher reliability while enabling higher levels of performance. 240-pin DDR3 DIMMs are similar to DDR2 DIMMs but are *not* backward compatible. Compared to DDR2, DDR3 has the capability to transfer twice as much data, use less voltage (1.2 to 1.5 V), and ultimately work faster and more efficiently.

Figure 10.1 shows a typical DDR3-1333 memory module. It is also known as PC3-10600. That means that it can do 1333 MT/s and has a total data transfer rate of 10,600 MB/s.

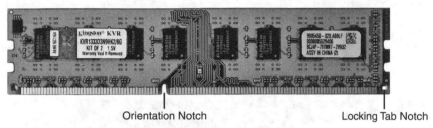

Orientation Notch   Locking Tab Notch

FIGURE 10.1   **A 240-pin PC3-10600 4-GB DIMM (DDR3-1333)**

The DDR3 module in Figure 10.1 has a sticker on the left that shows an identification code. You might not be able to read it, but it says KVR1333D3N9HK2/8G and Kit of 2, 1.5 V. The 1333 and D3 in the code tell you that this is DDR3-1333 RAM. The 8G tells you the capacity (8 GB) but only when installed as a kit of two memory modules—as the label goes on to say. Finally, it tells you that the memory runs at 1.5 volts. Leave the sticker on the memory module. This way, the warranty will not be voided, and you can find out important characteristics of the RAM later. Often you will come across sticks of RAM just lying about and you might not remember what they are— the code on the sticker tells you everything you need to know.

DDR4

At 1.2 to 1.35 V, DDR4 has a lower voltage range than most DDR3. It also has a higher module density and a higher data transfer rate. Of course, like previous versions of DDR, it is not backward compatible—this type of RAM has 288 pins and has a different physical configuration. Table 10.1 compares some typical DDR4 types, and Figure 10.2 shows an example of DDR4.

TABLE 10.1   **Comparison of DDR4 Types**

DDR4 Standard	Transfers per Second	Maximum Transfer Rate	Module Name
DDR4-2133	2133 MT/s	17,066 MB/s	PC4-17000
DDR4-2400	2400 MT/s	19,200 MB/s	PC4-19200
DDR4-2666	2666 MT/s	21,333 MB/s	PC4-21333
DDR4-3200	3200 MT/s	25,600 MB/s	PC4-25600

> **Note**
>
> The standards listed in Table 10.1 are based on the JEDEC standards (www.jedec.org). JEDEC develops various open standards for the microelectronics industry.

FIGURE 10.2   **A 288-pin PC4-17000 4-GB DIMM (DDR4-2133)**

As you have probably guessed, the RAM in Figure 10.2 can perform 2133 MT/s and has a maximum data transfer rate of 17,066 MB/s. I actually used the memory module in Figure 10.2 within my *AV-Editor* computer. Or more accurately, I used four of them in a quad-channel configuration that we will speak of more later. Note how both connectors are slightly angled. This, and the number of pins (among other things), make it incompatible with DDR3 slots.

As of the writing of this book, DDR4 is the fastest type of RAM module you can get for your motherboard, but DDR5 is fast on its heels. Technology is constantly changing—be ready.

> **Note**
>
> We discuss SODIMM types and installation in Chapter 1, "Laptops, Part 1."

Installing RAM

Installing DRAM is fun and easy. Simply stated, it can be broken down into these steps:

1. Orient the RAM properly.

2. Insert the RAM into the slot.

3. Press down with both thumbs until the ears lock.

4. Test.

Easy! But let's take it a little further. Remember that some people refer to memory modules as DIMMs, DRAM, RAM sticks, or just plain RAM, and you could encounter any of these terms on the exam as well. Once you have selected the correct memory module for your motherboard, and employed ESD prevention (antistatic strap), you can install the RAM.

Be careful with the RAM and the RAM slot! They are delicate! Hold the RAM by the edges and do not touch any pins or other circuitry on the memory module. If you need to put it down, put it down on an antistatic mat or in the container it shipped in.

Take a look at the slot; there should be a break in the slot somewhere near the middle (but not the exact middle). This is where the notch in the memory module will go. Gently place the memory module in the slot, pins down. If the notch does not line up with the break in the slot, you might need to turn the module around. When it appears that the RAM is oriented correctly, press down with both thumbs on the top of the memory module. Keep your thumbs as close to the edge as you can so that you can distribute even pressure to the memory module. Press down with both thumbs at the same time until the tab(s) on the edge of the RAM slot close and lock on to the memory module. (The tabs are also called "ears"; for DDR4, look for a single ear.) You might hear a click or two when it is done. You might need a bit of force to fully insert the RAM, but don't go overboard! If the motherboard is bending excessively, you are using too much force. If this is the case, make sure that the RAM is oriented correctly; the notches should match up and the RAM should be straight within the slot. Figure 10.3 shows a bank of DDR4 memory modules installed into the gray DIMM slots in a quad-channel configuration. Each of these is 4 GB, giving us a total of 16 GB of RAM.

Channel A, DIMM A1   Channel B, DIMM B1

Channel D, DIMM D1   Channel C, DIMM C1

FIGURE 10.3   Installed bank of DDR4 memory modules

Now, the most important thing to do with any installation is to *test*. With the case still open, boot the computer, access the UEFI/BIOS, and make sure that the system recognizes the new RAM as the right type and speed. The amount is often on the main page, but you might need to look deeper for the exact configuration, depending on the motherboard. Next, access the operating system (after it is installed) and make sure it boots correctly. Complete several full cycles and warm boots. Also, at some point, you should view the RAM within the operating system. For example, in Windows use the System Window or the Task Manager to verify that the operating system sees the correct capacity of RAM:

▶ **System Window:** Go to **Control Panel > All Control Panel Items > System**. The total RAM should be listed within this window.

▶ **Task Manager:** You can view the Task Manager by right-clicking the taskbar and selecting **Task Manager**. There are several other ways to open this; I like this one: Press **Windows+R** to bring up the Run prompt and type **taskmgr**. When it is open, go to the **Performance** tab and view the **Memory** section. It should show the total physical memory as well as the memory that is in use. Figure 10.4 shows my AV Editor computer running Windows 10 Pro, displaying 32 GB of RAM in the Task Manager, or more accurately, 31.9 GB, as circled toward the upper left of the figure. The in-use amount is 6.1 GB.

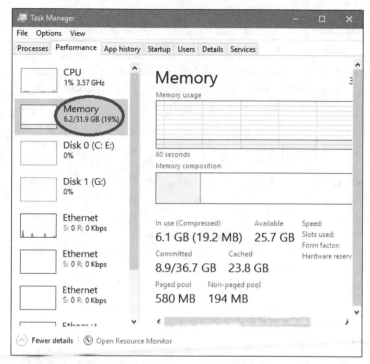

FIGURE 10.4   Task Manager showing 32 GB of RAM

Another good test of RAM is to make sure that you can open several applications at once without any issues or delays. Finally, if everything looks okay, close up the case, and if all went well, congratulate yourself on another job well done!

ExamAlert

Know how to select, install, and verify RAM.

There are a couple of other important things to mention here.

First, if you were for some reason to install two different speeds of RAM, then generally the system would run at the lower of the two speeds. This is an example of *underclocking*, and you won't get the most out of the computer. However, this could also cause the system to fail, because some motherboards insist that the modules be identical.

Second, if you install the very latest type of RAM that is supposed to be compatible with a motherboard, be prepared to update the UEFI/BIOS so that the system can recognize the new RAM. The firmware update (also known as a "flash") is one of the most important jobs a PC technician will perform.

RAM Technologies

Once you have chosen the type of RAM to use, you must then decide on more technical details; for example, the configuration of channels, which will be dictated in part by the motherboard. Your particular solution might also require the use of parity and/or error-correcting RAM, which is uncommon for desktop PCs and laptops, but might be necessary for more customized computers. Let's begin with memory channels.

Single-Channel Versus Multichannel Architectures

Single-channel is the original RAM architecture. It means that there is a 64-bit address bus (or data channel) between the memory and the memory controller (usually within the CPU). One or more sticks of RAM can be installed into the motherboard, but they share the same channel.

Dual-channel is a technology that essentially doubles the data throughput. Two separate 64-bit channels are employed together, resulting in a 128-bit bus. To incorporate this, the proper motherboard will have color-coded matching banks divided into Channel A and Channel B. Triple-channel architecture accesses three memory modules at the same time, in effect a 192-bit bus.

Quadruple-channel (or simply quad-channel) architecture takes this idea to the next level. It works only when four identical memory modules are placed in the correct slots. Quad-channel is common in computers that use DDR4. Now we have four 64-bit-wide buses working together, but for it to work properly, a module of RAM must be installed to each of the four banks. If only three modules are installed (thus only three banks used), the architecture downgrades to triple-channel automatically. Likewise, if only two are used, the motherboard scales back to dual-channel architecture. However, in some cases, the reduction in performance will be negligible.

Figure 10.5 shows an example of a motherboard's RAM slots making use of quad-channel technology. As you can see in the figure, there are four banks, each with two slots (one of which is black and one of which is gray). By installing a memory module into each of the gray slots (known as A1, B1, C1, and D1), we can harness the collective power of the quad-channel technology.

Channel B, DIMM B1 and B2

Channel A, DIMM A1 and A2

Channel C, DIMM C2 and C1

Channel D, DIMM D2 and D1

FIGURE 10.5   **A motherboard with quad-channel capable RAM slots**

This is the configuration used in AV Editor computers, which we'll discuss more as we progress throughout the book. Of course, we have the ability to add another four memory modules if we wish (those would be added to the black slots). The ASUS X99-A motherboard used in this computer can handle 64 GB of RAM total.

ExamAlert

Know the difference between single-, dual-, triple-, and quad-channel for the exam.

Parity Versus Non-parity

There are several types of parity in computing; RAM parity is when memory stores an extra bit (known as a parity bit) used for error *detection*. This means that the memory module can store 9 bits instead of 8 bits for every byte of data. So, parity RAM includes this extra bit and the more common non-parity RAM does not. Parity RAM might be required when data integrity is a necessity; for example, with servers or special workstations.

ECC Versus Non-ECC

Error correction code (ECC) in RAM can detect *and* correct errors. Real-time applications might use ECC RAM. Like parity RAM, additional information needs to be stored, and more resources are used in general. This RAM is the slowest and most expensive of RAM types. DDR ECC modules are identified with either the letter E or as ECC (for example, PC3-10600E).

One Final Word About RAM

The main thing to "remember" when working with RAM is that it needs to be compatible with the motherboard. Check your motherboard's documentation regarding capacity per slot (or channel), channel/slot configuration, maximum capacity, and speed. The best thing to do is to run a search on your particular motherboard at the RAM manufacturer's website to obtain a complete list of compatible RAM, and then cross-reference that with your motherboard's manual.

Cram Quiz

Answer these questions. The answers follow the last question. If you cannot answer these questions correctly, consider reading this section again until you can.

1. What is the transfer rate of DDR4-2133?

- ○ **A.** 17,066 MB/s
- ○ **B.** 19,200 MB/s
- ○ **C.** 21,333 MB/s
- ○ **D.** 25,600 MB/s

2. How many pins are on a DDR3 memory module?

- ○ **A.** 288
- ○ **B.** 184
- ○ **C.** 240
- ○ **D.** 200

3. Which of the following allows for a 256-bit-wide bus?

- ○ **A.** ECC
- ○ **B.** Quad-channel
- ○ **C.** Parity
- ○ **D.** DDR2

Cram Quiz Answers

1. **A.** The transfer rate of DDR4-2133 is 17,066 MB/s. It is also known as PC4-17000. 19,200 MB/s is the speed of DDR4 2400 (PC4-19200). 21,333 MB/s is the speed of DDR4-2666 (PC4-21333). 25,600 MB/s is the speed of DDR4-3200 (PC4-25600).

2. **C.** DDR3 is a 240-pin architecture. 288-pin is DDR4, 184-pin is the first version of DDR (DDR1), and you can find 200-pin architectures in laptops; they are known as SODIMMs. To review, Table 10.2 shows the pin configurations for PC-based DDR1 through DDR4.

TABLE 10.2 **Comparison of DDR Pinouts**

DDR Standard	Number of Pins
DDR1	184 pins
DDR2	240 pins
DDR3	240 pins
DDR4	288 pins

3. **B.** The quad-channel memory architecture can allow for a 256-bit-wide bus (64-bit per channel). However, this will only be the case if all four channels have memory installed to them. ECC stands for error correction code, which can detect and correct errors in RAM. Parity is when the RAM stores an extra bit used for error detection. DDR2 is a type of DRAM that, for the most part, was used in either single-channel or dual-channel environments.

3.4 – Given a scenario, select, install and configure storage devices

> **ExamAlert**
>
> **Objective 3.4** focuses on the following: optical drives, solid-state drives, magnetic hard drives, hybrid drives, flash drives, and configurations such as RAID 0, 1, 5, and 10.

Everyone needs a place to store data. Whether it's business documents, audio/video files, or data backups, users must decide on the right storage medium. This can be magnetic media, solid-state media, or optical media. Devices include hard drives, DVD/CD-ROM drives, and flash-based drives, among others. It all depends on what is stored and how often and where it is needed. This section concentrates on those three categories of media and how to identify, install, and troubleshoot them. We begin with the most typical storage place—the hard drive.

The hard drive is where the operating system is normally stored. Users also store frequently accessed data on the hard drive as well, such as Word documents, music, pictures, and so on. The two main types of hard drives are solid-state (which contains no disk) and magnetic (the hard disk drive). We'll discuss both of these, but first, let's take a look at a common standard for hard drive storage—SATA.

SATA

Serial AT Attachment (also known as Serial ATA, or just SATA) is a serial bus used to move data to and from hard drives and optical drives. To transmit that data, the drive has a 7-pin data port, as shown in Figure 10.6. Use an SATA cable to connect that to the motherboard or SATA adapter card of the computer.

For power, the SATA drive utilizes a 15-pin power connector, as shown in Figure 10.6. The hard drive's connectors have vertical tabs in the center, making for easier orientation when connecting the cables. Power supplies send 3.3 V, 5 V, and 12 V to the SATA drive.

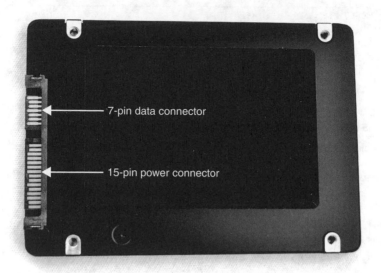

FIGURE 10.6   **SATA data and power connectors on a 2.5-inch SSD**

SATA technology is used by magnetic hard drives and solid-state drives. What has been described so far is SATA Revision 3.0. However, there is also SATA Revision 3.2. It is less common than 3.0 and requires either an SATA Express port or an M.2 slot to operate. SATA Express ports are like triple-connectors with 18 pins (7 pins + 7 pins + 4 pins). SATA Express isn't very common. Many people and technicians prefer other technologies over it, such as NVMe-based M.2 cards, which we'll discuss in a little bit. Table 10.3 shows these two SATA revisions.

TABLE 10.3   **Comparison of SATA 3.0 and 3.2**

Standard	Maximum Data	Transfer Rate
SATA Revision 3.0	6 Gb/s	600 MB/s
SATA Revision 3.2	16 Gb/s	1969 MB/s

> **ExamAlert**
>
> Know the maximum data transfer rates for SATA Revisions 3 and 3.2.

> **Note**
>
> You might also see some organizations refer to SATA measurements as Gbit/s or Gbps, instead of Gb/s, but they mean the same thing.

Data Transfer Discrepancy

If you were dividing by 8 for Rev 3.0, the actual data written to the drive is less than you would expect. This is due to overhead in the form of encoding. That brings Rev 3.0 down from 6.0 to 4.8 Gb/s (which equates to 600 MB/s). SATA 3.2 is not affected by this.

SATA 3.0 was released in 2009. However, if you come across older systems with older versions of SATA, these can be easily upgraded to a newer hard drive technology with the use of a PCI Express adapter card. If the system is so old that it does not have a PCI Express slot, then it might be wise to upgrade the entire system!

Magnetic Hard Drives

Magnetic hard drives, or *hard disk drives (HDDs)*, are the most common form of magnetic media. A hard disk drive contains one or more platters with a magnetic surface. As the platters rotate at high speed, read/write heads store and read information to and from the disk.

HDDs come in two main widths: 3.5 inch and 2.5 inch. The 3.5-inch drive is used in desktop computers, network-attached storage (NAS), and other larger devices. The 2.5-inch drive is used in laptops and other smaller devices. Generally, HDDs use SATA, though less commonly you will find SCSI and IDE versions. They are typically sold with data storage capacities of 500 GB, 1 TB, 2 TB, 4 TB, and beyond.

> **Note**
>
> A typical operating system such as Windows will display a 500-GB drive as 476 GB (or 465 GB or a similar number). This is due to a difference in numbering systems used to measure the drive. A hard drive manufacturer will use the base-10 system, whereas Windows will use the base-2 system, resulting in a slightly lower number. No actual space was lost during the conversion!
>
> I describe this phenomenon further at my website: https://dprocomputer.com/blog/?p=1239.

HDDs are very common because they have been available for a long time and are generally cheaper than solid-state drives. However, there are a couple of things that set them apart, such as these specifications:

▶ **Rotational speed:** The platters in an HDD rotate at a certain speed. For example, 7200 revolutions per minute (RPM) is common; other typical speeds for hard drives include 5,400 RPM (slower access time) and 10,000 RPM and 15,000 RPM (faster access time).

▶ **Latency:** After a track has been reached by the read head, latency is the delay in time before a particular sector on the platter can be read. It is directly related to rotational speed and is usually half the time it takes for the disk to rotate once. For example, a 7200-RPM drive has an average latency of 4.2 ms (milliseconds), but a 10,000-RPM drive has an average latency of 3.0 ms.

Solid-State Drives

A *solid-state drive (SSD)* is used to store operating systems and files, similar to a magnetic hard disk drive. However, SSDs don't use spinning disks or read/write heads; they instead write data to non-volatile microchips. Because of this, they are silent, more resistant to physical shock, and have lower access time and less latency than magnetic hard drives. Because there are no moving parts, you are not concerned with rotation speed.

SATA based SSDs normally measure 2.5 inches in width. Installation requires either a 2.5-inch internal bay, special screw holes drilled directly into the computer case, or an adapter kit to install it to a 3.5-inch internal bay.

However, there are other types of SSDs; for example, the M.2-based SSD. These are small form factor cards that are installed directly into a motherboard or to an adapter card if the motherboard doesn't have an M.2 slot. Either way, the M.2 card is installed at a slight angle, then pressed flat against the board and screwed in. There are a variety of different M.2 card sizes. A common example is 2280, which means it is 22 mm wide by 80 mm long. M.2 cards are known to offer as much as six times the data transfer rate of a typical 2.5-inch SATA 3.0 SSD. While the M.2 slot can be used with different types of technologies, the most common and fastest (as of the writing of this book) is Non-Volatile Memory Express (NVMe), which is a specification for accessing storage while using PCI Express. Essentially, the M.2 slot on a motherboard taps into the PCI Express bus (x4) and uses a portion of the total bandwidth associated with that bus. This usually results in the loss of one PCI Express version 3 slot, and depending on the type of CPU and motherboard, it could also mean a battle for bandwidth between the video card and the M.2 card (and possibly other devices). In addition, NVMe-based M.2 cards tend to run hot. So, careful planning is required before installing an M.2 card.

> **Note**
>
> I have an in-depth video/article on my website that demonstrates the installation of an NVMe M.2 SSD drive: https://dprocomputer.com/blog/?p=2112.

> **Note**
>
> SSD technology can be combined with magnetic disk technology—this is known as a hybrid drive. This could be accomplished in a drive that incorporates NAND flash memory (for caching of data and speed) and a magnetic disk (for increased capacity). There are also M.2-based caching cards that can be used in combination with a magnetic disk to increase performance.

RAID

Redundant Array of Independent Disks (RAID) technologies are designed to increase the speed of reading and writing data, to create one of several types of fault-tolerant volumes, or both. Fault tolerance is the capability of the hard drive system to continue working after there is a problem with one of the drives.

To create a RAID array, you need two or more hard drives. Then, you need to set up the array through either software or hardware. Some operating systems support the software option, but it is not usually recommended. Generally, in the field we utilize hardware-based RAID, which means one of three things: either we use the motherboard's built-in RAID support if present, or we use a RAID adapter card, or we use an external device such as network-attached storage (NAS) that has RAID capability.

The exam requires you to know RAID levels 0, 1, 5, and 10. Table 10.4 describes each of these.

TABLE 10.4 **RAID 0, 1, 5, and 10 Descriptions**

RAID Level	Description	Fault Tolerant?	Minimum Number of Disks
RAID 0	Striping. Data is striped across multiple disks in an effort to increase performance.	No	2
RAID 1	Mirroring. Data is copied to two identical disks. If one disk fails, the other continues to operate. When each disk is connected to a separate controller, this is known as disk duplexing. See Figure 10.7 for an illustration.	Yes	2 (and 2 only)
RAID 5	Striping with parity. Data is striped across multiple disks; fault-tolerant parity data is also written to each disk. If one disk fails, the array can reconstruct the data from the parity information. See Figure 10.8 for an illustration.	Yes	3
RAID 10	Combines the advantages of RAID 1 and RAID 0. Requires a minimum of two disks but will usually have four or more. The system contains at least two mirrored disks that are then striped.	Yes	4

Figure 10.7 shows an illustration of RAID 1—mirroring. You can see that data is written to both disks and that both disks collectively are known as the M: drive or M: volume. So, even though we have two 2-TB drives, this volume only has a total capacity of 2 TB.

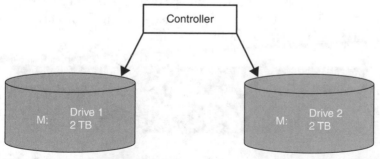

FIGURE 10.7 **RAID 1 illustration**

Figure 10.8 displays an illustration of RAID 5—striping with parity. In a RAID 5 array, blocks of data are distributed to the disks (A1 and A2 are a block, B1 and B2 are a block, and so on) and parity information is written for each block of data. This is written to each disk in an alternating fashion (Ap, Bp, and such) so that the parity is also distributed. If one disk fails, the parity information from the other disks will reconstruct the data. Some organizations prefer RAID 6, which requires four drives minimum, and writes two sets of parity. This can work well for larger arrays—meaning ones with more hard drives. In larger environments, *hot-swappable* capability is a must—this is when drives can be removed and inserted while the system is on.

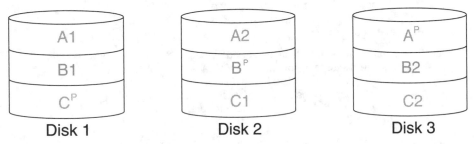

FIGURE 10.8 RAID 5 illustration

Remember that hard drive arrays should be built using identical drives. That means using a group of the same magnetic disk drives or a group of the same solid-state drives. Deviate from this suggestion at your own risk!

I mentioned that RAID can be a type of fault tolerance. It is important to make the distinction between fault tolerance and backup. *Fault tolerance* means that the hard drives can continue to function (with little or no downtime) even if there is a problem with one of the drives; for example, RAID 1 or RAID 5. *Backup* means that you are copying the data (and possibly compressing it) to another location for archival in the event of a disaster. An example of a disaster would be if two drives in a RAID 5 array were to fail.

Flash

Flash memory is used in all kinds of solid-state technologies. Most of these technologies use NAND-based flash memory. For this section we'll focus on USB flash drives and Secure Digital cards.

USB Flash Drives

The USB flash drive is probably the most familiar of all flash media. Also known as USB thumb drives, they are often retractable and can be carried on a keychain.

When you plug in a USB flash drive on a Windows system, the drive shows up as a volume within File Explorer (or Windows Explorer). Connecting the drive is easy; just find an open USB port. But remember that you should eject the flash drive in the operating system before disconnecting the drive physically. If you don't, it can cause electrical irregularities that can damage the data on the drive. In Windows, right-click the **Safely Remove Hardware and Eject Media** icon in the Notification Area, and then click **Eject** to shut down power to the selected USB device. Then you can safely remove it from the physical USB port. The icon appears as a USB cable with a check mark. If your USB device has a light, make sure that light is off before physically removing the device. You can also "eject" optical drives and virtual drives in this manner.

> **ExamAlert**
>
> Remember to *safely remove* USB flash drives in the operating system before physically disconnecting them.

> **Tip**
>
> Sometimes a USB or other flash-based, solid-state device can't be removed with the Safely Remove Hardware option in Windows. If this happens, consider shutting down the computer before physically disconnecting the device to avoid data corruption or loss.

The advantages of a USB flash drive are obvious. Quick and efficient moving of data—and a lot of data at that. However, it is not meant for long-term storage in the way that a magnetic or solid-state hard drive is—it is meant for transfer of data from one system to another. It can also be used to boot systems for installation purposes or for troubleshooting.

Let's talk about the type of memory used in this solid-state device: NAND flash memory is the core of a USB flash drive. This memory is divided into blocks that are generally between 16 KB and 512 KB. Know that a USB flash drive's blocks can be written to only so many times before failures occur. With some flash drives, manufacturers estimate this limit is 1 million write/erase cycles or

10 years of use. However, just like hard drives will never attain their maximum data transfer rate, it is doubtful that a flash drive will ever attain that maximum number of write/erase cycles. In addition, the number of years is subjective; it all depends on how often a user works with the flash drive. Basically, if you take the number given by the manufacturer and cut it in half, you should be in good shape, unless you are an extreme power user. Now back to NAND flash failures: Because this type of memory incurs a small number of faults over time (as opposed to NOR flash, which should remain free of faults), a method known as Bad Block Management is implemented. Bad Block Management maintains a table of the faulty blocks within the USB flash device, making sure not to save data to those blocks. Blocks are divided into pages, which can be between 512 bytes and 4 KB. Each page has error detection and correction information associated with it. All this is done to prolong the lifespan of devices that use NAND memory.

Normally, USB flash drives are shipped in a formatted state, for example FAT32. This enables the drive to be accessed by just about any computer on the market and makes for easy repair of corrupted files with Windows utilities. If the user so chooses, these drives can also be formatted as NTFS or other file systems, which may be necessary to interface with certain systems or perform particular installations. Sometimes NAND flash devices (such as USB flash drives) act up intermittently. Unless the device has failed completely, a quick reformat usually cures the flash drive of its woes. Just be sure to back up your data first! This method applies to other forms of solid-state, NAND-based media. After reformatting, test the drive by moving files to it and then opening them. Of course, after a certain point, the drive will fail and will need to be replaced. Periodically check USB flash drives for stability.

Some USB flash drives are preloaded with software that can restore data and possibly secure transferred data.

One problem with USB flash drives is that although they are small, they can't fit inside most digital cameras, smartphones, and other handheld devices. For that, you need something even smaller: Enter the SD card.

Secure Digital Cards

SD cards, for the most part, are technically the same type of device as a USB flash drive. They are solid-state, they use NAND memory, and they have most of the same pros and cons as a USB flash drive. However, SD technology can write and transfer data much faster. The other main difference is the form factor of the SD device; because of this, SDs are used differently.

Instead of connecting an SD card to a USB port of a computer, it slides into a memory card reader. There are specialized readers for SD cards only and other readers that can read multiple formats of cards. Like USB flash drives, be sure to use the **Safely Remove Hardware** icon in Windows before physically removing the SD card. There are three sizes of SD cards, each smaller than the last: standard (32 mm × 24 mm), miniSD (21.5 mm × 20 mm), and microSD (15 mm × 11 mm). You can still find many standard-sized SD cards used in cameras and some other devices, but note that most cell phones and smartphones use microSD cards for additional memory. Figure 10.9 shows a full-size SD card and a microSD card.

FIGURE 10.9   A typical microSD card (left) and a standard SD card (right)

> **Note**
>
> You might run across an xD-Picture Card. This is a flash memory technology similar to SD that is used in some older digital cameras.

Standard SD cards have capacities up to 4 GB. High-capacity (SDHC) cards range up to 32 GB. eXtended Capacity (SDXC) has a maximum capacity of 2 TB and supports up to 90 MB/s. Secure Digital Ultra Capacity (SDUC) supports up to 128 TB and 985 MB/s data transfer over the SD Express bus.

When it comes to data transfer rate, SD cards are divided into a variety of classes: SD Class 2, 4, 6, and 10 as well as UHS 1 through 3, and SD Express bus, each with a different range of speeds. For example, Class 10, required for Full HD video recording (1080p), has a minimum data writing speed of 10 MB/s. To record 4K video, you would need at least UHS 3, which has a minimum data writing speed of 30 MB/s. To simplify things a bit, SD cards are labeled with a video speed class rating. For example, V30 means that the card can write 30 MB/s minimum, but today's SD cards will often display their maximum transfer rate as well.

> **ExamAlert**
>
> Know the different capacities of standard SD, SDHC, SDXC, and SDUC.

> **Note**
>
> CompactFlash (CF) is another kind of solid-state memory categorized as either Type I cards (3.3 mm thick) or Type II cards (5 mm). These cards are larger than SD cards and are used in older devices, high-end cameras (Type I), and microdrives (Type II). Their maximum capacity is generally 32 GB with a typical data transfer rate of 133 MB/s.

Optical Drives

The three main types of optical media in use today are compact discs (CDs), digital versatile discs (DVDs), and Blu-ray discs. These discs have a variety of functions, including audio, video, application, data, and so on. Some discs can be read from and some can also be written to. Finally, some discs can be rewritten to as well. It all depends on which media you use. Now there are a lot of different versions of optical media; let's try to organize them so that they will be easier to remember. We start with the most familiar: the compact disc.

> **ExamAlert**
>
> You've probably noticed by now that most magnetic media is known as "disk" and optical media is known as "disc." Keep this in mind for the exam.

Compact Disc (CD)

A CD is a flat, round, optical disc used to store music, sounds, or other data. It can be read from a compact disc player. For example, audio CDs can be played on a compact disc player that is part of a stereo or a computer. However, data CDs can be read only from CD-ROM drives that are part of, or externally connected to, a computer. The A+ exam focuses on data CDs, so let's talk about some of the different data CD technologies.

The most common acronym that comes to mind is the compact disc-read-only memory (CD-ROM). Data is written to a CD-ROM in a similar way that audio is written to a music CD; a laser shines on the reflective surface of the CD and stores data as a plethora of microscopic indentations known as lands and pits. These are the types of CDs you get when you purchase a computer program or game. They can be read from but not written to and can be read only from a compatible CD-ROM drive. CD-ROM drives are rated in read speeds (for example, 48x). The x equals 150 KB/s. So, to calculate a CD-ROM drive's maximum read speed, you multiply the number preceding the x by 150 KB. In this example, this would be 48 × 150 KB = 7.2 MB/s. A typical CD can hold up to 700 MB of data. Table 10.5 describes the two most common recordable technologies.

TABLE 10.5 **Comparison of CD Recording Technologies**

Technology	Full Name	Typical Maximum Recording Speed
CD-R	Compact Disc-Recordable	48x (7.2 MB/s) or 52x (7.8 MB/s)
CD-RW	Compact Disc-ReWritable	24x (3.6 MB/s) or 32x (4.8 MB/s)

Most optical drives that you can purchase for a computer today have all three compact disc functions. They can read from CD-ROMs, write to CD-Rs, and write/rewrite to CD-RWs. Usually, the read speed and CD-R speed are the same.

ExamAlert

Know the difference between CD-ROM, CD-R, and CD-RW.

CD-ROM discs are known as removable media; however, the drive is normally fixed in the computer. It installs much like an SATA hard drive. One notable exception is that most CD-ROM drives are 5.25 inches wide (instead of 3.5 or 2.5 inches). So, they must be installed to one of the larger bays in a case that has an opening on the front; this way, the drive tray is accessible. The same goes for all optical drives. Most CD-ROM drives can also play audio CDs and they have a volume knob on the front. In addition, many drives have a pinhole near the volume knob. This small hole is for when a CD (or the tray) gets jammed. Insert a paper clip into the hole to attempt to free the tray and CD. Most other optical drives have this feature as well.

> **ExamAlert**
>
> The paper clip should be added to your toolkit; it dislodges jammed optical trays. A mobile device tray pin also works.

Digital Versatile Disc (DVD)

For data, Digital Versatile Discs, also known as Digital Video Discs, are the successor to CDs for a variety of reasons. First, they can be used to play and record video. Second, they have a much greater capacity than CDs. This is because the pits etched into the surface of the DVD are smaller than CD pits (.74 micrometers compared to 1.6 micrometers). Also, DVDs can be written to faster than CDs. There are read-only DVDs and writable DVDs; however, there are a lot more variations of DVDs than there are CDs. Table 10.6 describes some of the DVD-ROM (Digital Versatile Disc-Read-Only Memory) versions, specifications, and differences, starting with the common DVD-5 version.

TABLE 10.6 **Comparison of DVD Technologies**

DVD-ROM Technology	Sides	Total Layers	Capacity
DVD-5	1	1	4.7 GB
DVD-9	1	2	8.5 GB
DVD-10	2	2	9.4 GB
DVD-14	2	3	13.2 GB
DVD-18	2	4	17 GB

The most common DVD is currently the single-sided, single-layer (SS, SL) DVD-5 technology that can store 4.7 GB of data. But some DVDs can be written to two sides (known as dual-sided or DS); simply flip the DVD to access the information on the other side. Layers, however, work differently. A DVD with two layers (known as dual layer or DL) incorporates both layers onto a single side of the disc. The second layer is actually underneath the first one; the DVD laser reads this second layer by shining through the first semi-transparent layer. By combining dual-sided and dual-layer technologies, you end up with a DVD that can store up to 17 GB of data (known as DVD-18) at 8.5 GB per side.

> **ExamAlert**
>
> Know the capacity of common DVD technologies such as DVD-5 and DVD-18.

Once again, for DVD-ROMs and recordable DVDs (DVDR), the most common is DVD-5. Typically, a DVD drive reads these discs at 16x. However, the x in DVD speeds is different than the x in CD-ROM speeds. For DVDs, the x means approximately 1.32 MB/s or about nine times the core CD speed. So a typical 16x DVD is equal to 21 MB/s. Typically, a DVD drive reads at 16x, records once at 22x or 24x, and rewrites at 6x or 8x. Table 10.7 provides a description of the different types of recordable DVDs.

TABLE 10.7 **Comparison of DVD Recordable Technologies**

DVD Recordable Technology	Capacity	Typical Write Speed*
DVD-R SL	4.707 GB	22x or 24x
DVD+R SL	4.700 GB	22x or 24x
DVD-R DL	8.544 GB	12x
DVD+R DL	8.548 GB	16x
DVD-RW SL or DL	4.707 or 8.544 GB	6x
DVD+RW SL or DL	4.700 or 8.548 GB	8x

* The write speeds vary from drive to drive. The stated typical speeds are the write speeds of a Samsung combo drive (DVD/CD) used for this book.

Blu-ray

Currently, Blu-ray is *the* standard for high-definition video. It is used by high-def movies, console games, and for storing data (up to 50 GB per disc, 10 times the amount of a typical DVD-5 disc). The standard disc is 12 cm (the same size as a standard DVD or CD) and the mini-disc is 8 cm. Table 10.8 shows some of the Blu-ray specs.

TABLE 10.8 **Comparison of Blu-ray Specifications**

Blu-ray Type	Layers	Capacity
Standard disc, single-layer	1	25 GB
Standard disc, dual-layer	2	50 GB
Standard disc, XL 3 layer	3	100 GB
Standard disc, XL 4 layer	4	128 GB
Mini-disc, single-layer	1	7.8 GB
Mini-disc, dual-layer	2	15.6 GB

Note

Triple- and quadruple-layer discs can be accessed by BD-XL drives.

Drive speeds range from 1x to 16x (with more undoubtedly on the way). 1x is equal to 36 Mb/s or 4.5 MB/s. A 16x would be 16 times that core amount, which is 576 Mb/s or 72 MB/s, which is superior to DVD write speeds. Single-layer discs, though their capacity is half, can be written to in half the time of dual-layer discs.

Want to record to Blu-ray discs? There are two methods of "burning" Blu-ray discs: Blu-ray Disc Recordable (BD-R), which can write to a disc once, and Blu-ray Disc Recordable Erasable (BD-RE), which can be erased and re-recorded multiple times. Burning speed depends on the drive, but as of the writing of this book, there are some that can go as high as 16x. To burn discs in Blu-ray format, you must either install the drivers and software that came with the drive or utilize a third-party program. Generally, you will see a typical maximum of 50 MB/s when writing data to Blu-ray.

ExamAlert

Know the differences between BD-R and BD-RE.

Cram Quiz

Answer these questions. The answers follow the last question. If you cannot answer these questions correctly, consider reading this section again until you can.

1. How much data can an SATA Revision 3.0 drive transfer per second?
   - ○ **A.** 50 MB/s
   - ○ **B.** 90 MB/s
   - ○ **C.** 1969 MB/s
   - ○ **D.** 6 Gb/s
   - ○ **E.** 16 Gb/s

2. Which level of RAID stripes data and parity across three or more disks?
   - ○ **A.** RAID 0
   - ○ **B.** RAID 1
   - ○ **C.** RAID 5
   - ○ **D.** Striping
   - ○ **E.** RAID 10

3. Which of the following has the largest potential for storage capacity?
   - ○ **A.** OD-R
   - ○ **B.** CD-RW
   - ○ **C.** DVD-RW
   - ○ **D.** Blu-ray

4. A customer complains that an important disc is stuck in the computer's DVD-ROM drive. What should you recommend to the customer?
   - ○ **A.** To get a screwdriver and disassemble the drive
   - ○ **B.** To format the disc
   - ○ **C.** To use a paper clip to eject the tray
   - ○ **D.** To dispose of the drive and replace the media

5. Which of the following best describes a specification for accessing storage while using PCI Express?
   - ○ **A.** NVMe
   - ○ **B.** 7200 RPM
   - ○ **C.** Hot-swappable
   - ○ **D.** 3.5-inch and 2.5-inch

Cram Quiz Answers

1. **D.** SATA Revision 3.0 drives can transfer 6 Gb/s, which after encoding amounts to 600 MB/s. SATA Revision 3.2 is 16 Gb/s (1969 MB/s) but requires SATA Express or M.2. 50 MB/s is a typical write speed for Blu-ray discs and some flash media. 90 MB/s is a typical write speed for an SD card.

2. **C.** RAID 5 stripes data and parity across three or more disks. RAID 0 does not stripe parity; it stripes data only and can use two disks or more. RAID 1 uses two disks only. Striping is another name for RAID 0. RAID 10 contains two sets of mirrored disks that are then striped.

3. **D.** Blu-ray, at a typical maximum of 50 GB, has the largest storage capacity. CDs top out just under 1 GB. DVDs have a maximum of 17 GB.

4. **C.** Tell the customer to use a paper clip to eject the DVD-ROM tray. Disassembling the drive is not necessary; the customer shouldn't be told to do this. If the disc is rewritable, formatting it would erase the contents, even if you could format in this scenario. Never tell a customer to dispose of a DVD-ROM drive; they rarely fail.

5. **A.** Non-Volatile Memory Express (NVMe) is a specification for accessing storage while using PCI Express. Essentially, the M.2 slot on a motherboard taps into the PCI Express bus (×4) and uses a portion of the total bandwidth associated with that bus. The platters in a hard disk drive (HDD) rotate at a certain speed. For example, 7200 RPM is common; other typical speeds include 5400 RPM and 10,000 RPM. Hot-swappable capability is when drives can be removed and inserted while the system is on. SATA-based hard drives come in two main widths: 3.5-inch and 2.5-inch. The 3.5-inch drive is used in desktop computers, network-attached storage, and other larger devices. The 2.5-inch drive is used in laptops and other smaller devices.

CHAPTER 11

Motherboards and Add-on Cards

This chapter covers a portion of the following A+ 220-1001 exam objective:

▶ **3.5** – Given a scenario, install and configure motherboards, CPUs, and add-on cards.

Without a doubt, the motherboard is the foundation of the computer. Everything connects to the motherboard and all data is transferred through this matrix of circuitry.

Over the years I have found that if a student is going to lack knowledge in one area, it's quite often going to be the motherboard. This is one of the key elements in a computer system. It's the starting point for a quick and efficient computer. Because it connects to everything in the computer system, you need to know many concepts concerning it. Let's get right into it.

> **Note**
>
> Objective 3.5 covers a *lot*. That's why I broke it up into two chapters. This chapter covers motherboards and add-on cards. The next chapter will cover CPUs.

3.5 – Given a scenario, install and configure motherboards, CPUs, and add-on cards

> **ExamAlert**
>
> This portion of **Objective 3.5** concentrates on the following concepts: motherboard form factors and connector types; BIOS/UEFI settings; CMOS battery; and expansion cards.

Motherboard Form Factors and Connectors

A computer form factor specifies the physical dimensions of some of the components of a computer system. It pertains mainly to the motherboard but also specifies compatibility with the computer case and power supply. The form factor defines the size and layout of components on the motherboard. It also specifies the power outputs from the power supply to the motherboard. The most common form factors—and the ones you need to know for the exam—are ATX, microATX, and Mini-ITX. Let's discuss these a little further now.

ATX

Advanced Technology Extended (ATX) was originally designed by Intel in the mid-'90s to overcome the limitations of the now-deprecated AT form factor. It has been the standard ever since. The motherboard shown in Figure 11.1 is ATX. This is the board used in the *AV-Editor* computer, which is my main workstation. Full-size ATX motherboards measure 12 inches × 9.6 inches (305 mm × 244 mm). ATX motherboards have an integrated port cluster and normally ship with an I/O plate that snaps into the back of the case, filling the gaps between ports and keeping airflow to a minimum

FIGURE 11.1   **ATX motherboard and its components**

One identifying characteristic of ATX is that the RAM slots and expansion bus slots are perpendicular to each other. The ATX specification calls for the power supply to produce +3.3 V, +5 V, +12 V, and –12 V outputs and a 5 V standby output. These are known as "rails" (for example, the +12 V rail). The original ATX specification calls for a 20-pin power connector (often referred to as P1); the newer (and much more common) ATX12V Version 2.x specification calls for a 24-pin power connector. You can test these voltages with a power supply tester, which typically comes with a 24-pin input as well as other inputs for SATA power, PCI Express 6-pin and 8-pin, and Molex.

> **ExamAlert**
>
> Know the voltages supplied to an ATX motherboard by a power supply: +3.3 V, +5 V, +12 V, and –12 V outputs and +5 V standby output.

An ATX motherboard is attached to the computer case with several screws. Before you screw it in though, attach the I/O plate to the back of the case, and dry fit the motherboard to see where the screws will attach to the case. Apply rubber standoffs if required. Then, attach the accepting screws to the case wall according to where the motherboard screws will be placed; be sure that the motherboard will be properly supported. Angle the motherboard slightly so that the port cluster fits into the I/O plate. Then line up the screw holes and attach the screws. Finally, connect the CPU, RAM, power connections, adapter cards, fans, and anything else necessary!

microATX

microATX (or mATX) was introduced as a smaller version of ATX; these motherboards can be a maximum size of 9.6 inches × 9.6 inches (244 mm × 244 mm) but can be as small as 6.75 inches × 6.75 inches (171.45 mm × 171.45 mm). In comparison, microATX boards are usually square, whereas full-size ATX boards are rectangular. microATX is backward compatible with ATX, meaning that most microATX boards can be installed within an ATX form-factor case and they use the same power connectors as ATX. Often, they have the same chipsets as ATX as well. microATX works well for desktop cases, small rackmount servers, and home theater PCs (HTPCs).

Mini-ITX

ITX is a group of form factors developed by VIA Technologies, Inc. between 2001 and now for use in small, low-power motherboards. The ITX group includes Mini-ITX, Nano-ITX, Pico-ITX, and Mobile-ITX, but Mini-ITX (mITX) is what is covered in the A+ objectives.

Originally designed in 2001, Mini-ITX is a 6.7 × 6.7-inch (17 × 17 cm) motherboard that is a bit smaller than microATX and is screw-compatible, enabling it to be used in microATX and ATX cases if so desired. The original version used passive cooling to keep it quiet and to conserve power, making it ideal for HTPCs; newer versions use active cooling due to the more powerful processors involved. The first version of these boards came with one expansion slot: PCI. The second version comes with a single PCIe ×16 slot.

Table 11.1 compares the ATX, microATX, and Mini-ITX form factors, supplying the sizes of these motherboards and some of the characteristics that set them apart.

TABLE 11.1 **Comparison of Motherboard Form Factors**

Form Factor	Width	Depth	Identifying Characteristic
ATX	12 inches (305 mm)	9.6 inches (244 mm)	RAM slots and expansion slots are perpendicular to each other (90-degree angle).
microATX	9.6 inches (244 mm)	9.6 inches (244 mm)	Smaller than ATX but backward compatible to it.
Mini-ITX	6.7 inches (17 cm)	6.7 inches (17 cm)	Designed for HTPCs and other small-footprint systems.

ExamAlert

Know the basics of ATX, microATX, ITX, and Mini-ITX for the exam.

Expansion Buses

There are two main expansion buses and their corresponding adapter card slots that you need to know for the exam. They include PCI Express and PCI:

▶ **PCI Express (PCIe):** Currently the king of expansion buses, PCIe is the high-speed serial replacement of the older parallel PCI standard and the deprecated AGP standard. The most powerful PCIe slots—such as ×16—connect directly to the processor (or northbridge). The lesser PCIe slots—such as ×1—connect to the chipset. The PCIe expansion bus sends and receives data within *lanes*. These lanes are full-duplex, meaning they can send and receive data simultaneously. There are several versions of PCIe—their data rates are shown in Table 11.2. Commonly, PCIe video cards are ×16 (pronounced "by 16"), which means they use 16 lanes, and usually require version 3 minimum. They can typically transfer 16 GB/s—in each direction. Most other PCIe adapter cards are ×1, but you might find some ×4 cards as well. Of course, compatibility is key. A ×1 card can go in a ×1 slot or larger, but a ×16 card will fit only in a ×16 slot, nothing smaller. Figure 11.2 displays three ×16 slots and one ×1 slot.

TABLE 11.2 **Comparison of PCIe Versions and Data Transfer Rates**

PCIe Version	Frequency	Max. Data Rate
Version 1	2.5 GHz*	2 Gb/s (250 MB/s) per lane
Version 2	5 GHz	4 Gb/s (500 MB/s) per lane
Version 3	8 GHz	8 Gb/s** (1 GB/s) per lane
Version 4	16 GHz	16 Gb/s** (2 GB/s) per lane

* This is also measured in transfers per second, referring to the number of operations that send and receive data per second. It is often closely related to frequency. For example, PCIe v1 is 2.5 gigatransfers per second (2.5 GT/s) and PCIe v4 is 16 GT/s.

** These numbers are approximate.

> **Note**
>
> Maximum data transfer rates are never attained, even in a lab environment. You can expect actual throughput to be substantially lower, but professionals use the maximum data rate as a point of reference and as a way of comparison.

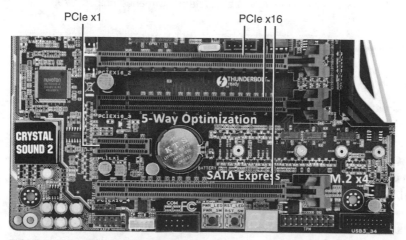

FIGURE 11.2 **PCIe ×16 and PCIe ×1**

> **ExamAlert**
>
> Identify the PCIe ×16 and ×1 expansion slots for the exam.

▶ **PCI:** The Peripheral Component Interconnect bus was developed in the '90s by Intel as a faster, more compatible alternative to the deprecated ISA bus. It allows for connections to modems and to video, sound, and network adapters. This uncommon bus connects exclusively to the chipset (or southbridge). Because of this, other high-speed video alternatives were developed that could connect directly to the processor (or northbridge). PCI version 2.1 cards are rated at 66 MHz, and their corresponding PCI bus is 32-bit wide, allowing for a maximum data transfer rate of 266 MB/s. Derivatives of PCI include PCI-X, which was designed for servers using a 64-bit bus and rated for 133 MHz/266 MHz, and Mini PCI, which is used by laptops. PCI slots are seldom found on today's motherboards. For the most part, they have been overtaken by PCIe technology.

> **Note**
>
> I've mentioned the *chipset* several times. The chipset connects all of the motherboard's secondary device interfaces together, such as USB, SATA 3.0, the network card, and more. The chipset then connects to the CPU, which has connections to the primary devices (RAM and video card). The motherboard displayed in Figure 11.1 uses the X99 chipset. To see a diagram of this chipset, and all of its connections, use the following link or search the Internet for "Intel X99 chipset diagram."
>
> https://www.intel.com/content/www/us/en/chipsets/performance-chipsets/x99-chipset-diagram.html

Expansion Cards

If a motherboard does not have a necessary integrated component, you will have to add an expansion card to a PCIe slot. During the planning stage you should make sure one is available, and then determine the requirements of the card: version of PCIe, bus width, and so on. There are plenty of different expansion cards that you might add, but the most common is probably the video card. Some computers come with integrated video cards (also known as on-board). In some cases, these utilize powerful processing that is built into the board (some AMD systems have this), but many times the integrated video card is designed for basic computing and does not perform well enough for any high-end computing. So, an actual video card is often necessary.

Installing Video Cards

Today's video cards are like little self-contained computers! They have a processor, known as a graphics processing unit (GPU), and a substantial amount of RAM. When choosing a video card, there are several things to consider, including the expansion bus that the card connects to, the card's GPU speed and amount of memory, the connectors it offers, whether there is an expansion slot available for it on the motherboard, whether the video card can fit in the case, and whether the case has adequate power and cooling capabilities for the card.

Video cards, like other adapter cards, are inserted into an expansion bus slot and then screwed into the chassis of the case to keep them in place. However, PCI Express cards require the installer to do a few more things. And keep in mind that some newer PCIe cards are *big*. When deciding on a video card, make sure it fits in the computer case first and doesn't cover any important ports! The following steps describe how to install a PCIe video card:

Step 1. Check if the card is compatible: Verify that there is an open, compatible slot on the motherboard. Also, make sure that the card is compatible with the operating system.

Step 2. Ready the computer: Make sure that the computer is turned off and unplugged. Then implement ESD prevention measures (antistatic mat, antistatic wrist strap, and so on).

Step 3. Ready the video card: Remove the card from the package and keep it in the antistatic bag until it is ready to be inserted. (Make sure the card is sealed when first opening it.)

Step 4. Document: If the computer had a video card already, document how and where it was connected, either by taking a photo or by drawing a diagram. Otherwise, review the documentation that came with the motherboard and video card. Plan where to install the card and what cables need to be connected to the card, and how they should be routed through the case.

Step 5. Prepare the slot: Use a Phillips-head screwdriver to remove the slot cover (or covers) where the card will be installed. Bigger PCIe cards inhabit the space used by two slot covers. On most PCIe slots there will be a thumb lever. Open this gently. When the card is inserted, the lever locks the card into place.

Step 6. Install the card to the slot: Insert the card using both thumbs, applying equal pressure straight down into the slot. Try not to wiggle the card in any direction. Press down until the card snaps into place and you can't see any of the gold edge connectors. If it doesn't seem to be going in, don't force it. There might be something in the way (for example, one of the slot covers hasn't been removed or the thumb lever isn't in the correct position).

Step 7. Connect cables: PCIe cards need their own power connection (or two). These are 6- or 8-pin PCIe power connectors. Most cases come with PCIe power connectors, but if yours does not, you can use a PCIe to Molex adapter (or two), which will work with older cases and power supplies. Next, make any Scalable Link Interface (SLI) connections necessary, in case you have two or three video cards (which is less common but popular in high-end gaming systems). Then connect optional cables (for example, connect an S/PDIF header cable to the motherboard) and any other ancillary cables. When complete, it should look similar to Figure 11.3.

FIGURE 11.3 **An installed PCIe video card**

Step 8. Test: Testing is simple: plug in the monitor to the video card's port and boot the computer. If you don't get anything on the display, it's time to troubleshoot. Make sure that the monitor is connected securely to the correct port. Then (after shutting down the PC) make sure that the card is seated properly and that the power connections and any other connections are connected firmly. Listen for any beep codes that might be issued by the BIOS/UEFI POST. Check if the computer is booting without video; this can be done by watching the LED lights on the front of the case and listening for the power supply fan and hard drive activity.

Step 9. Install the driver: When the system boots properly, install the driver from the manufacturer's disc. If no disc was supplied with the device or it is missing, or if you don't have an optical drive on the computer in question, go to the manufacturer's website and download the latest version of the driver for the exact model of the video card.

Step 10. Test again: Now that the driver is installed, test again. Verify whether the card is shown as the correct make and model in Device Manager (**Run > devmgmt.msc**). Then make sure the display can output the desired resolution. Keep in mind that some video cards can output a higher resolution than a monitor can support. If the computer is used for graphics or gaming, open the appropriate application and verify that it works as expected. For example, check for fluidity, quick response, frame rate, and so on.

> **ExamAlert**
>
> Know how to install and test a video card.

> **Note**
>
> Check out this video of a step-by-step video card install/upgrade on my website:
> https://dprocomputer.com/blog/?p=1699.

Sound Cards

The sound card is responsible for generating sound from the data sent to it by the operating system. Audio devices can be integrated into the motherboard, installed to PCIe slots, and can be connected to USB. However, the typical audio device known as the sound card is installed to a PCIe slot on the motherboard.

Sound cards are not used as often as they once were. With the advent of USB 3.0 and beyond, many manufacturers choose to design their speakers and headphones with USB-only connectivity—or they are wireless. However, some still utilize connections that require a traditional sound card. And some audiophiles are concerned with the potential for USB latency, or wireless interference, and prefer the direct connectivity—and ports—that a sound card offers. Generally, the connections are 1/8 inch (3.5 mm).

Most sound cards are color-coded. This color scheme was originally defined by the *PC System Design Guide*, version PC 99 (which was finalized as version PC 2001—and the colors have stuck even today). It specifies the following colors for the TRS 1/8 inch (3.5 mm) mini-jacks like the ones shown in Figure 11.4:

▶ **Light blue:** Line input. Sometimes this seconds as a microphone input.

▶ **Pink:** Microphone input.

▶ **Lime green:** Main output for stereo speakers or headphones. Can also act as a line out.

▶ **Black:** Output for surround sound speakers (rear speakers).

▶ **Silver/Brown:** Output for additional two speakers in a 7.1 system (middle surround speakers).

▶ **Orange:** Output for center speaker and subwoofer.

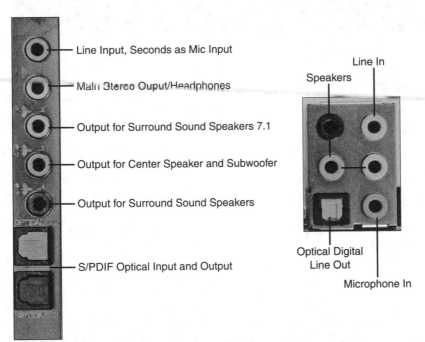

FIGURE 11.4   **A typical sound card's ports and integrated audio ports on a motherboard**

On the sound card shown in Figure 11.4, note an optical input and output. This is known as a Sony/Phillips Digital Interconnect Format (S/PDIF) port. This particular version of S/PDIF is called TOSLINK. It delivers high-quality digital sound over fiber optic cable. It is also known as a *digital optical port*.

Some users prefer to use an external audio interface that connects via USB, but provides plenty of different connectivity options that are easily accessible on top of a person's desk. They usually offer high-fidelity sound (for example, 24-bit/192 kHz). These normally require USB 2.0 or higher, but for greater productivity and less latency, USB 3.0 is often recommended.

Other Expansion Cards

There are expansion cards for just about anything you can think of. Many motherboards come with integrated network cards, USB ports, and so on. But sometimes a user simply needs a more powerful solution or more ports.

Motherboards usually have one RJ45 port for a wired Ethernet connection. However, a user might require more. Network interface cards are available that have one or more RJ45 ports that can be used for connections to other networks, or can be "teamed" together to provide link aggregation (combining the bandwidth of each port), and to offer redundancy in case one port fails.

Most motherboards have plenty of USB ports, but if not, then USB hubs can be connected to a USB port in order to add devices. But what if the motherboard doesn't have the right *version* of USB? For example, if your motherboard has USB 3.0 SuperSpeed ports, but you want to make use of a device that can run USB 3.2 SuperSpeed+ at 20 Gbps, then you would need to add a USB 3.2 expansion card.

There are also external SATA-based devices (eSATA). A few motherboards come with these ports, but if you need to connect to external hard drives that use eSATA, then you might need an adapter card.

All of these cards are installed in a similar way to the video card, but they are simplified. Simply unscrew the slot cover, and insert the expansion card straight down into the slot. Try not to wiggle the card, and only hold the card from the edges to avoid ESD or other damage. Then, screw the card in. Check the card in the Device Manager (or similar tool in other OSes) to make sure it is seen properly, and if not, download the driver from the manufacturer and install it. Test the card to make sure it works properly, and then checkmark another tech job that's been well done!

ExamAlert

Know how to install, configure, and test sound, network, USB, and eSATA expansion cards.

More Ports and Connectors

The main type of drive technology on motherboards is Serial ATA (SATA). SATA supports the connection of hard drives and optical drives. So, most motherboards come equipped with several 7-pin SATA connectors, and possibly one or more 18-pin SATA Express connectors. The A+ objectives also make mention of IDE, but it is rare that you will see it. We talk more about hard drive technologies in Chapter 10, "RAM and Storage."

You will find other ports as well, such as: integrated audio ports, for use with an optical drive or sound card; internal USB ports, for the front panel USB connections; and a variety of power connections that we will discuss further in Chapter 13, "Peripherals and Power."

Then there's the case connector group, which is usually on the edge of the motherboard and allows connectivity for the front panel connectors. These wires start at the inside front of the case and have thin 2-, 3-, or 4-pin plugs on the other end. They are labeled with names such as POWER LED, POWER SW (for power switch), HDD LED, and so on. These plugs connect to items such as the Power button, reset button, and LED lights.

Computers with limited motherboard space might come with a *riser card*. The riser card can provide for additional expansion slots such as PCIe (and PCI). It generally plugs into one of the expansion slots and allows for an additional two slots typically. This allows a person to take advantage of three-dimensional space, but it could decrease airflow leading to increase heat. Riser cards are more common in small proprietary designs and with small form factor motherboards.

BIOS/UEFI Settings

Historically, the Basic Input/Output System (BIOS) has been the firmware loaded on most desktop and laptop computers. However, since 2005 the Unified Extensible Firmware Interface (UEFI) has gained in popularity to the point where in 2014 it became the predominant type of firmware shipped with motherboards. But many technicians (and even some manufacturers) will still just refer to it as "BIOS" or possibly as "UEFI/BIOS." For simplicity during the course of the book, I often refer to a motherboard's firmware simply as BIOS.

UEFI communicates more effectively with the operating system, allows for a mouse-driven firmware-based setup program (instead of the menu-based BIOS setup program) and includes advanced system diagnosis (except for the worst of errors, such as the CPU failing). It also has a built-in secure boot mode, which prevents digitally unsigned drivers from being loaded and helps prevent root-kits from manifesting themselves. It has faster startup times than the BIOS. It also allows for the hard drive usage of the GUID Partition Table (GPT), which supports more partitions (128) and larger drive sizes than the older master boot record (MBR) option. We will discuss GPT and MBR further in the 220-1002 portion of the book.

The firmware is loaded onto a chip on the motherboard and can (and should) be updated, or "flashed," periodically to take advantage of the latest functionality and security updates. There are several ways to update the firmware, but generally you would do it either from within Windows or by using some kind of bootable media (USB flash drive or optical drive) to boot the system and rewrite the firmware—also known as "flashing the BIOS."

This firmware stays resident in the computer after restarts. However, time and the individual settings that you select are stored elsewhere; for example, in a complimentary metal-oxide semiconductor (CMOS). This chip is *volatile*, meaning that the settings could be lost if the computer is restarted. That's why the motherboard comes with a lithium battery (also known as a *CMOS battery*). That battery retains the individual settings and keeps time while the computer is shut down. The most common battery used on today's motherboards is the CR2032, a nickel-sized battery that snaps into the motherboard and has a shelf life of anywhere from 2 to 10 years, depending on usage. The more you leave the computer on, the longer the battery lasts.

The BIOS is where you go to set a password, change boot options, configure time and date, configure devices, overclock the computer, and much more. Accessing the BIOS must be done before the operating system boots. This can be accomplished by pressing a key on the keyboard (for example, F2 or Delete). Different manufacturers will use different keys. Here are a couple of examples of settings you might modify in the BIOS:

▶ **Boot options:** Also known as BIOS boot order or device priority, this setting enables you to select which media will be booted: hard drive, USB, optical drive, over-the-network, and so on. Usually, this should be set to hard drive first. But if you install an operating system (OS) from removable media, you would want to configure that removable media as first on the boot options list. For a secure and trouble-free system, it is recommended that you set this to hard drive first, as shown in Figure 11.5. If the system is set to optical drive first, and there is a disc in the drive, it could cause Windows to fail to load properly and could pose a security risk. You'll note that the first boot device in the figure says Windows Boot Manager, P1, and the name of the device—a 250-GB Samsung solid-state drive. Windows Boot Manager is the primary boot file in Windows and it is the first file on the hard drive that the BIOS looks for when it starts up. P1 means the first physical SATA port connection.

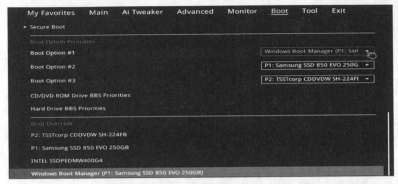

FIGURE 11.5 **Configuring the BIOS boot order**

ExamAlert

Know how to set the BIOS boot options! Also, if you boot a PC and see a black screen with a white blinking underscore on the top left, the issue could be the boot order.

▶ **Passwords:** Two passwords are available on most BIOS: user and administrator. The user password authenticates a user before it enables the operating system to boot. The administrator password authenticates a user to the BIOS Setup Utility itself. For a secure system, enter a strong administrator password. By strong, I'm talking about length and complexity, my friend!

▶ **More security settings:** *Secure boot* is an option on UEFI-equipped systems. If enabled, it blocks rootkits and other malware from launching boot loaders that have been tampered with. Newer versions of Windows make use of a certificate stored in the UEFI that will check the boot loader for authenticity—meaning whether it has been digitally signed by Microsoft. If the hard drive's boot loader is not authentic, then the computer will not boot to that hard drive. To allow for hard drive encryption, some motherboards come with a *Trusted Platform Module (TPM)*, a chip that stores encryption keys—it can be enabled in the BIOS. We'll discuss computer security in more depth within the 220-1002 portion of the book.

ExamAlert

Secure UEFI-equipped systems with secure boot and a TPM.

▶ **Virtualization support:** To support virtual computing, the BIOS must be configured properly. This setting is often buried within the BIOS in a CPU submenu. For Intel CPUs, the Intel Virtualization Technology (Intel VT) option should be enabled. For AMD CPUs, enable AMD-V. We'll talk more about virtualization in upcoming chapters.

The POST

The power-on self-test (POST) is essentially a piece of code that the UEFI/BIOS runs to find out which type of processor is on the motherboard and verifies the amount of RAM. It also identifies buses on the motherboard (and other devices) as well as which devices are available for booting.

The BIOS indicates any system problems that the POST finds by either on-screen display codes, beep codes, or an integrated error code readout on the motherboard itself. The exact code(s) will depend on the type of BIOS used. Your motherboard should come with documentation about any possible BIOS error codes. If not, the documentation can usually be downloaded from the manufacturer's website; you just need to know the model number of the board. In the case of a proprietary computer (Dell, HP, and such), you need the model number of the computer to download any necessary documentation from its website. We'll be discussing more computer troubleshooting when we get to the chapters within Domain 5: Hardware and Network Troubleshooting.

> **ExamAlert**
>
> The POST is a built-in troubleshooting tool provided by the motherboard. Use it!

Cram Quiz

Answer these questions. The answers follow the last question. If you cannot answer these questions correctly, consider reading this chapter again until you can.

1. Which motherboard form factor measures 12 inches × 9.6 inches (305 mm × 244 mm)?

   ○ **A.** microATX

   ○ **B.** SATA

   ○ **C.** ATX

   ○ **D.** mITX

2. Which component supplies power to the CMOS when the computer is off?

   - ○ **A.** Lithium battery
   - ○ **B.** POST
   - ○ **C.** Power supply
   - ○ **D.** BIOS

3. To implement a secure boot process, which device should be listed first in the Boot Device Priority screen?

   - ○ **A.** Network
   - ○ **B.** CD-ROM
   - ○ **C.** USB
   - ○ **D.** Hard drive

4. Which of the following connectors would you use to power a video card?

   - ○ **A.** 24-pin power
   - ○ **B.** 6-pin PCIe
   - ○ **C.** Molex
   - ○ **D.** 3.5-mm TRS

5. Which of the following is a chip that stores encryption keys?

   - ○ **A.** Intel VT
   - ○ **B.** Secure boot
   - ○ **C.** Firmware
   - ○ **D.** TPM

Cram Quiz Answers

1. **C.** ATX boards measure 12 inches × 9.6 inches (305 mm × 244 mm). microATX boards are square and measure 9.6 × 9.6 inches (244 mm × 244 mm). SATA is a type of hard drive technology and the port used to connect hard drives to the motherboard. mITX (or Mini-ITX), also square, measures 6.7 × 6.7 inches (17 cm × 17 cm).

2. **A.** The lithium battery (or CMOS battery) supplies power to the CMOS when the computer is off. This is because the CMOS is volatile and would otherwise lose the stored settings when the computer is turned off.

3. **D.** To ensure that other users cannot boot the computer from removable media, set the first device in the Boot Device Priority screen to hard drive.

4. **B.** A video card is normally powered by a 6-pin or 8-pin PCIe connector. Lesser cards are simply powered by the PCIe bus. The 24-pin power connector is the main connector that leads from the power supply to the motherboard. Molex is used for fans, older IDE drives, and other secondary devices. 3.5 mm (or 1/8 inch) TRS is an audio connection.

5. **D.** To perform hard drive encryption, some motherboards come with a Trusted Platform Module (TPM), a chip that stores encryption keys—it can be enabled in the BIOS. Intel Virtualization Technology (VT) is part of the firmware that supports the use of virtualization software such as Hyper-V and VMware. Secure boot can block rootkits and other malware from launching boot loaders that have been tampered with. Firmware (such as a motherboard's BIOS) should be updated or "flashed," periodically to take advantage of the latest functionality and security updates.

CHAPTER 12

CPUs

This chapter covers a portion of the following A+ 220-1001 exam objective:

▶ **3.5** – Given a scenario, install and configure motherboards, CPUs, and add-on cards.

Here it is, the core of the desktop computer: the CPU. This is part two of our coverage of Objective 3.5. During this chapter I often refer to the *AV-Editor* computer, which has a motherboard with an X99 chipset and a Core i7-5820K CPU. Refer back to Chapter 11, Figure 11.1 and the supporting text, for more information about the motherboard. Lots to do!—let's not waste any time.

3.5 – Given a scenario, install and configure motherboards, CPUs, and add-on cards

ExamAlert

This portion of **Objective 3.5** concentrates on the following concepts: CPU features, compatibility, and cooling mechanisms.

CPU Features

The central processing unit (CPU) is quite often referred to as the "brain" of the computer. While that terminology may be debatable, the CPU is most definitely at the core of the computer—and it is fast. A typical CPU today runs between 2 and 4 GHz or higher. That CPU frequency is known as speed, or more accurately—clock rate.

Clock Rate

The *clock rate* is the frequency (or speed) of a component. It is rated in cycles per second and measured in hertz (Hz). For all practical purposes, the term clock rate is the same as the more commonly used term: *clock speed*.

Components are sold to consumers with a *maximum* clock rate, but they don't always run at that maximum number. To explain, let me use a car analogy. The CPU is often called the "engine" of the computer, like a car engine. Well, your car's speedometer might go up to 120 MPH, but you'll probably never drive at that maximum—for a variety of reasons! When it comes to CPUs, the stated clock rate is the *maximum* clock rate, and the CPU usually runs at a speed less than that. In fact, it can run at any speed below the maximum, but there are only a few plateaus that it will usually hover around.

Now, we're all familiar with speeds such as 2.4 GHz, 3.0 GHz, or 3.5 GHz. But what is the basis of these speeds? Speed can be divided into two categories that are interrelated:

▶ **Motherboard bus speed:** This is the base clock of the motherboard and is often referred to simply as "bus speed." This is generated by a quartz oscillating crystal soldered directly to the motherboard. For example, the base clock of the motherboard in Chapter 11, Figure 11.1 is 100 MHz.

▶ **Internal clock speed:** This is the internal frequency of the CPU and is the well-known number that CPUs are associated with. For example, the Intel Core i7-5820K—which I use with the motherboard in Chapter 11, Figure 11.1—is rated at 3.3 GHz. The CPU uses an internal multiplier based off the motherboard base clock. The maximum multiplier for this particular CPU is 33. The math is as follows: base clock × multiplier = internal clock speed. In our example, that would be 100 MHz × 33 = 3.3 GHz. However, as mentioned, the CPU can (and often does) run slower. Fewer open programs means a lower speed (for example, 1.2 GHz). As more programs are opened and more CPU power is required, the CPU throttles up; for example, to 2.4 GHz, and ultimately 3.3 GHz. This motherboard can support faster and slower CPUs from a variety of CPU families, but the math works in the same way. To see the specifications for the i7-5820k CPU, or any Intel CPU, check out the Intel ARK: https://ark.intel.com/.

> **ExamAlert**
>
> For today's CPUs, two of the most commonly used terms are *bus speed* (the base clock of the motherboard) and *clock speed* (the frequency of the CPU). They might not be completely accurate, technically, but you will see and hear them often and you could see them on the exam as well.

Overclocking

Many motherboards allow for *overclocking*, which enables the user to increase the base clock within the BIOS, thereby increasing the clock speed of the CPU. For example, the Core i7-5820K CPU that I am using has a normal top speed of 3300 MHz (3.3 GHz). On this motherboard, increasing the base clock (BCLK) from 100 to 125 MHz results in an increase of the CPU top speed from 3300 MHz to 4000 MHz. You can also overclock RAM and some video cards, independently of the CPU.

As you can guess, overclocking is risky—it increases the voltage, creates more heat, and could possibly cause system instability, or even damage to the system—analogous to blowing the engine of a car when attempting to run a 10-second quarter mile. So, approach overclocking with extreme caution! Generally, if you find a system in the workplace that has been overclocked, it should be disabled in the BIOS.

Hyperthreading and Multicore

Intel's Hyper-Threading (HT) enables a single CPU to accept and calculate two independent sets of instructions simultaneously, thereby simulating two CPUs. The technology was designed so that single CPUs can compete better with true multi-CPU systems but without the cost involved. In an HT environment, only one CPU is present, but the operating system sees two virtual CPUs and divides the workload, or threads, between the two.

Whereas HT technology simulates multiple CPUs, *multicore* CPUs physically contain two or more actual processor cores in one CPU package acting as a single entity. This enables more-efficient processing of data and less generated heat.

A typical CPU will combine Hyper-Threading and multicore technologies. For example, the Core i7-5820K CPU we mentioned has 6 cores, each of which can handle two threads at the same time, for a total of 12 threads. The total amount of threads can be viewed within the Device Manager under Processors.

ExamAlert

Know the differences between Hyper-Threading and multicore technologies. Hyper-Threading enables a single-core CPU to calculate two instruction sets simultaneously, whereas multicore CPUs calculate two or more instruction sets simultaneously—one instruction set per core.

Cache Memory

Several types of cache are used in computers, but CPU cache is a special high-speed memory that reduces the time the CPU takes to access data. By using high-speed static RAM (SRAM) and because the cache is often located directly on—or even in—the CPU, CPU cache can be faster than accessing information from dynamic RAM (DRAM) modules. However, it will be limited in storage capacity when compared to DRAM. Cache is typically divided into three levels, which are accessed by the CPU sequentially: L1 (built into the CPU) and L2 and L3 (built onto the CPU). L1 and L2 cache are distributed to each core of the CPU, but L3 cache is shared by all of the CPU's cores. Generally, the more cache, the better. The less the CPU needs to access DRAM, the faster it can calculate data.

CPU Compatibility

CPU compatibility boils down to the socket available to you, and the manufacturer you decide to use. Though there are others, Intel and AMD dominate the desktop and laptop market.

Intel and AMD

CPU manufacturers use the make/model system. For example, the Intel (make) Core i7-5820K (model); or the AMD (make) Ryzen 7 1800X (model). There are dozens of models of Intel and AMD CPUs. The A+ exam does not require you to know all of the individual models, but you should have a working knowledge of some of the basic makes and models available. Periodically visit the Intel and AMD websites for the latest and greatest CPUs.

Some CPUs come with a built-in graphics processing unit (GPU). This means that with a compatible motherboard, no separate video card is necessary, and the monitor can be plugged directly into the video port on the motherboard. Both Intel and AMD have many CPUs with an *integrated GPU*. AMD refers to this as the Accelerated Processing Unit (APU). Integrated GPUs have come a long way, but for power users (gamers, graphics designers, and so on), a separate video card is usually required for best functionality.

Intel and AMD are both good companies that make quality products, which leads to great competition. Which is better? In all honestly, it varies and depends on how you use the CPU. You can find advocates for both (albeit subjective advocates), and the scales are constantly tipping back and forth. On any given day, a specific Intel CPU might outperform AMD; three months later, a different AMD CPU can outperform an Intel. It's been that way for many years now. Whichever CPU you choose, make sure that you get a compatible motherboard. A couple of things to watch for are compatibility with the chipset and the socket type.

The chipset will either be Intel-based or AMD-based, depending on what type of motherboard you are using. It will only be compatible with a certain group of CPUs. For example, the motherboard in Chapter 11, Figure 11.1 uses the Intel X99 chipset. For Intel, the chipset is also known as a Platform Controller Hub (PCH). This chipset can work with Core i7 CPUs and Intel Xeon E5 CPUs. (Xeon CPUs are primarily used in servers.) Verify that the CPU make and model will be compatible with the chipset, and therefore the motherboard. So, for instance, the motherboard shown in Figure 11.1 is an ASUS X99-A, and it accepts the Core i7-5820K, among others. The motherboard's socket type will also dictate compatibility, as we discuss in the next section.

Sockets

The *socket* is the electrical interface between the CPU and the motherboard. It attaches directly to the motherboard and houses the CPU. It also physically supports the CPU and heat sink and enables easy replacement of the CPU.

The socket is made of either plastic or metal and uses metal contacts for connectivity to each of the pins/lands of the CPU. One or more metal levers (retaining arms) lock the CPU in place. Figure 12.1 shows an example of an unlocked Land Grid Array (LGA) socket from the X99-A motherboard.

FIGURE 12.1 **An unlocked LGA 2011 socket**

Historically, the socket has been considered a ZIF, short for zero insertion force. This means that the CPU should connect easily into the socket, with no pressure or force involved during the installation. The socket will have many pin inserts, or lands, for the CPU to connect to. Pin 1 can be found in one of the corners and can be identified by either a white corner drawn on the motherboard or one or more missing pins or pinholes. This helps you to orient the CPU, which also has the arrow, or missing pin(s), in the corresponding corner. Here are two types of sockets you should know for the exam:

▶ **PGA:** Pin Grid Array sockets accept CPUs that have pins covering the majority of their underside. The pins on the CPU are placed in the pinholes of the socket and the CPU is locked into place by a retaining arm. Many AMD CPUs use PGA sockets.

▶ **LGA:** Land Grid Array sockets use lands that protrude out and touch the CPU's contact points. This newer type of socket (also known as Socket T) offers better power distribution and less chance to damage the CPU compared to PGA. LGA is commonly used today on Intel motherboards.

The CPU and socket must be compatible. For example, the X99-A motherboard used in the *AV-Editor* computer has an LGA 2011 socket, which is common but not the only socket that Intel uses on its motherboards. The Core i7-5820K CPU used on that motherboard is designed to fit into the LGA 2011 socket, and several other CPUs—but not all CPUs—can fit into this socket as well. Table 12.1 shows some typical Intel and AMD sockets and the CPUs that can be installed to them. Keep in mind this is not a finite list; there are lots of other sockets, both older and newer.

TABLE 12.1 Intel and AMD Sockets and Corresponding CPUs

Intel Sockets	Intel CPUs	AMD Sockets	AMD CPUs
LGA 1155	Core i7, i5, i3, Xeon	AM3+	FX, Phenom II, Athlon II, Sempron
LGA 2011	Core i7, Xeon	FM2+	A8/A10 series
LGA 2066	Core i9, i7, i5	AM4	Ryzen 7, 5, 3

ExamAlert

Compatibility is key! Find the correlation between sockets, chipsets, and CPUs by analyzing the motherboard and CPU documentation.

Power Consumption

Power consumption of CPUs is normally rated in watts. For example, the Core i7-5820K is rated as a 140 watt-hour CPU. This rating is known as *thermal design power (TDP)* and it signifies the amount of heat generated by the CPU, which the cooling system is required to dissipate when operating with a complex workload. This number is usually displayed as the maximum; it could be less, depending on CPU usage, and does not take into account overclocking. The measurement should play into your decision when planning which power supply to use and which kind of cooling system. For more information on power supplies, see Chapter 13, "Peripherals and Power." 100 to 150 watts (or thereabouts) is a common TDP rating for multicore CPUs. That's more than a typical incandescent light bulb.

Because we are talking electricity, another important factor is voltage. CPUs are associated with a voltage range; for example, the Core i7-5820K runs at about 1 V by default. However, a CPU's voltage can increase as applications demand more processing power. It is important to monitor the voltage that is received by the CPU; you can do this in the UEFI/BIOS or, better yet, with applications within Windows. If the CPU goes beyond the specified voltage range for any extended length of time, it *will* damage the CPU. This becomes especially important for overclockers.

Cooling Mechanisms

Now that you know a CPU can effectively use as much electricity as a light bulb, you can understand why it gets so hot. Hundreds of millions of transistors are hammering away in these powerhouses, so you need to keep it and other devices in the computer cool. This is done in a few ways, as outlined in this section.

Heat Sinks

The *heat sink* is a block of metal made to sit right on top of the CPU, with metal fins stretching away from the CPU. It uses conduction to direct heat away from the CPU and out through the fins. With a passive heat sink, that's all there is to it; it dissipates heat and requires no moving parts—it is "fanless." But with an active heat sink, a fan is attached to the top of, or on the side of, the heat sink. The fan plugs into the motherboard for power. If installed on top, the fan blows air into the heat sink and toward the CPU, helping to dissipate heat through the heat sink fins. If installed on the side of a larger heat sink, it blows air sideways through the heat sink toward the case's exhaust fan. More powerful aftermarket CPU heat sinks/fans can be installed as well; just make sure that your power supply can handle the increased power requirements and that you have the space needed, because some CPU heat sinks and fans are *big*.

In PC-based motherboards, the chipset usually has a passive heat sink, but all new CPUs come with active heat sinks. Traditionally, heat sinks have been made of aluminum, but now you also see copper heat sinks used due to their superior conductivity. An important point about heat sinks: If they come loose, they could adversely affect the performance of the CPU or cause overheating, which could lead to random reboots. Make double sure that the heat sink is attached securely.

Thermal Compound

The CPU cap and the bottom of the heat sink have slight imperfections in the metal. Surface area is key; the best heat dissipation from CPU to heat sink would occur if the metal faces on each were completely and perfectly straight and flat, but...we live in the real world. So, to fill the tiny gaps and imperfections, thermal compound is used. (This is also known as *thermal paste* or thermal interface material.) One example of thermal compound is Arctic Silver, available online and at various electronics stores.

Now, if this is a new installation, thermal compound might not be needed. Some new CPUs' heat sinks have factory-applied thermal compound that spreads and fills the gaps automatically after you install the heat sink and boot the computer. However, if you need to remove the heat sink for any reason (for example, to clean it, or when upgrading, or if the CPU did not come with a heat sink), then thermal compound should be applied to the CPU cap before installing or upgrading the heat sink.

To do this, first clean any old thermal compound off of the CPU cap and the heat sink with thermal compound remover. Then apply new thermal compound to the CPU cap. The application method will vary depending on the CPU used, but it could require the traditional surface spread method (have an old, clean credit card handy for spreading), the middle dot method, or the increasingly common vertical line method (no credit card required!). There are other methods as well; review your CPU's documentation to find out which method is recommended. Another great resource is www.arcticsilver.com, where you will find a variety of application methods and in-depth, step-by-step guides for a host of CPU families. Finally, install the heat sink. Try to do so in one shot, without jostling the heat sink excessively.

Fans

Case fans are also needed to get the heat out of the case. The power supply has a built-in fan that is adequate for lesser systems. However, more powerful systems should have at least one extra exhaust fan mounted to the back of the case, and many cases today come with one for this purpose. An additional fan on the front of the case can be used as an intake of cool air. If you aren't sure which way the fan blows, connect its power cable to the computer but don't mount it; then hold a piece of paper against the fan. The side that pulls the paper toward it should be the side facing the front of the computer when it is mounted. Some cases come with fans that are mounted to the top, which is also ingenious because heat rises.

Another thing to consider is where the heat goes after it leaves the case. If the computer is in an enclosed area, the heat has a hard time escaping and might end up back in the computer. Make sure there is an area for air flow around the computer case. I have seen some people point the front of their computer toward an AC vent in the summer and even use special exhaust fans (such as bathroom fans) that butt up against the power supply or secondary exhaust fan on the case and lead hot air directly out of the house, but I digress.

Of course, three or four fans can make a decent amount of noise, and they still might not be enough for the most powerful computers, especially the overclocked ones, which leads us to our next option.

Liquid Cooling Systems

Although this method is not as common as the typical CPU/heat sink/fan combination, liquid-cooled systems are looked at as more of a viable option than they would have been 10 years ago. And newer water-cooling kits can be used to not only cool the CPU, but cool the chipset, hard drives, video cards, and more. A kit might come with a CPU water block, pump, radiator/fan, PVC tubing, and, of course, coolant; although there are more simplified versions of liquid cooling systems as well. The advantages are improved heat dissipation (if installed properly), potential for higher overclocking rates, and support for the latest, hottest CPUs. Some of the disadvantages include the risk of a leak that can damage components; pumps becoming faulty over time; air being trapped in the lines, which can cause the system to overheat; and the need for maintenance in the form of inspecting the lines and replacing the coolant every few years. Due to the fact that most computers do not need this level of heat dissipation, and because of the complexity of some of these systems, liquid cooling is usually employed by enthusiasts (such as gamers). But you might see it in other CPU-intensive systems, such as virtualization computers, CAD/CAM systems, audio/video editing systems, and possibly server systems. Regardless of cost, installation complexity, and maintenance, liquid cooling systems can help dissipate heat the most efficiently.

> **ExamAlert**
>
> Of all PC cooling methods, liquid cooling systems can dissipate heat the most efficiently, but they are usually only necessary for the most powerful PCs.

Installing CPUs

As with most computer components, installing a CPU is easy. But you must be careful because it can be easily damaged. Take it slow and employ proper safety measures. Let's break it down into some simple steps:

Step 1. Select a CPU: If you build a new computer, the CPU needs to be compatible with the motherboard; consider the type of CPU, speed, and socket type. If you upgrade a CPU, be sure that it is on the motherboard's compatibility list (which can be found at the manufacturer's website).

Power down the PC, disconnect the power cable (or turn off the kill switch), open the PC, and get your boxes of components ready!

Step 2. Employ ESD prevention methods: Use an antistatic strap and mat. Remove the CPU and heat sink from the package, inspect them, and then place the CPU back in its plastic holder, or inside an antistatic bag, until you are ready to install it. (An antistatic bag usually comes with the motherboard, but you should have extra ones handy.) To prevent damage, make sure that the CPU's lands or pins are facing up, if it is in an antistatic bag. Never touch the lands or pins of a CPU. Before touching any components, place both hands on an unpainted portion of the case chassis. For more information on ESD preventative measures, see Chapter 40, "Safety Procedures and Environmental Controls."

Step 3. Ready the motherboard: Some technicians prefer to install the CPU into the motherboard and then install the motherboard into the case. If you do so, place the motherboard on the antistatic mat. (The mat should be on a hard, flat surface.) If you install the CPU directly into an already installed motherboard, clear away any cables or other equipment that might get in the way or could possibly damage the CPU, heat sink, or fan.

Step 4. Install the CPU: Be careful with the CPU! It is extremely delicate! Always touch the case chassis before picking up the CPU. Hold it by the edges and do not touch any pins, lands, or other circuitry on the CPU. Most of the time, a CPU will be installed to either an LGA socket or a PGA socket. The following two bullets show how to install a CPU into each type of socket. Be sure to refer to the installation guide that comes with your particular CPU and motherboard.

> ► If you install to an LGA socket, unlock the socket by releasing the retaining arm(s) and swinging it open as far as it can go. Open the socket hatch, unhook it if necessary, and remove any plastic cover. Next, place the CPU into the socket. One corner of the CPU has an arrow that should be oriented with either a white corner or other similar marking on the motherboard or the socket's missing pin(s); both of these corresponding corners indicate pin 1, as shown in Figure 12.2. Carefully place the CPU into the socket. If it is oriented correctly, the lands on the CPU match up with the lands on the socket. Make sure it is flush and flat within the socket. Close the cap and secure the retaining arm underneath the tab that is connected to the socket, thus securing the CPU. Install thermal compound if necessary. Next, install the heat sink/fan assembly. (If the heat sink came with the CPU, it might have thermal compound applied already.) LGA sockets usually have four plastic snap-in anchors. Carefully press each of these into and through the corresponding motherboard holes. Don't use too much force! Then turn each of them to lock the heat sink in place. Make sure that the heat sink is installed flush with the CPU by inspecting the assembly from the side. You want to be positive of this before turning on the computer because the thermal compound will begin to expand and fill the imperfections right away. Plug the fan into the appropriate motherboard power connector. (These are usually labeled directly on the motherboard; if not, see your motherboard documentation for details on where to plug in the fan.) Install the entire motherboard assembly into the case (if that is your method of choice).

FIGURE 12.2   Orientation markings on a CPU and LGA socket

▶ If you install to a PGA socket, unlock the socket by moving the retaining arm(s) out and upward until it is open as far as it will go, without forcing it. Then gently place the CPU into the ZIF socket. There will be an arrow on one corner of the CPU that should correspond to a missing pin (or arrow) on the socket. Don't use force; slide the CPU around until it slips into the socket. Look at the CPU from the side and make sure it is flush with the socket. Lock down the retaining arm to keep the CPU in place. Then attach the heat sink/fan assembly to the metal clips that are on the sides of the socket. Make sure that the heat sink is installed flush with the CPU by inspecting the assembly from the side. You want to be positive of this before turning on the computer because the thermal compound will begin to expand and fill the imperfections right away. Attach the fan's power cable to the motherboard. (See your motherboard documentation for details on where to plug in the fan.) Install the entire motherboard assembly into the case (if that is your method of choice).

Step 5. **Test the installation:** With the case still open, boot the computer to make sure that the UEFI/BIOS POST recognizes the CPU as the right type and speed. Enter the BIOS and view the CPU information to verify this. If the BIOS doesn't recognize the CPU properly, check if a BIOS upgrade is necessary for the motherboard. Also make sure that the CPU fan is functional. Then view the details of the CPU within the BIOS. Be sure that the voltage reported by the BIOS is within tolerance. Then access the operating system (after it is installed) and make sure it boots correctly. Complete several full cycles and warm boots. Finally, view the CPU(s) within Windows and/or third-party tools (such as CPU-Z).

For example, check in the Device Manager to make sure that the CPU is identified correctly. This can be accessed within the Control Panel, within Computer Management, or by pressing **Windows+R** to open the Run prompt and typing **devmgmt.msc** and pressing **Enter**. Once opened, you should see a category named Processors; expand it and the CPU that is installed should be listed. Remember, it will show up as multiple *logical* processors, equal to the number of threads that the CPU can simultaneously run.

> **Note**
>
> You can view basic CPU information in Windows at the System Information window, which can be accessed by opening the Run prompt and typing **msinfo32**.

Step 6. Close the case and monitor the system: Finally, if everything looks okay, close the case and consider monitoring the clock rate, voltage, and heat during the first few hours of operation. Voltage and heat can usually be monitored within the BIOS. All three can be monitored within Windows and by using third-party applications, or by using monitoring utilities that accompany the motherboard. If all went well, congratulate yourself on a job well done!

Cram Quiz

Answer these questions. The answers follow the last question. If you cannot answer these questions correctly, consider reading this chapter again until you can.

1. What does Hyper-Threading do?
   - ○ **A.** It gives you multiple cores within the CPU.
   - ○ **B.** It enables four simultaneous threads to be processed by one CPU core.
   - ○ **C.** It enables two simultaneous threads to be processed by one CPU core.
   - ○ **D.** It provides a high-speed connection from the CPU to RAM.

2. What seals the tiny gaps between the CPU cap and the heat sink?

  ○ **A.** Grape jelly

  ○ **B.** Plumber's putty

  ○ **C.** 3-in-1 house oil

  ○ **D.** Thermal compound

  ○ **E.** TDP

3. Which of the following can be defined as the amount of heat generated by the CPU, which the cooling system is required to dissipate?

  ○ **A.** GPU

  ○ **B.** TDP

  ○ **C.** PSU

  ○ **D.** 140 watts

4. When deciding on a CPU for use with a specific motherboard, what does it need to be compatible with?

  ○ **A.** Case

  ○ **B.** Socket

  ○ **C.** Wattage range

  ○ **D.** PCIe slots

5. Which kind of socket incorporates "lands" to ensure connectivity to a CPU?

  ○ **A.** PGA

  ○ **B.** Chipset

  ○ **C.** LGA

  ○ **D.** Copper

  ○ **E.** AM4

6. Which of the following enables the user to increase the base clock within the BIOS, thereby increasing the clock speed of the CPU?

  ○ **A.** Overclocking

  ○ **B.** L3 cache

  ○ **C.** Integrated GPU

  ○ **D.** Heat sink

Cram Quiz Answers

1. **C.** Hyper-Threading allows for an operating system to send two simultaneous threads to be processed by a single CPU core. The OS views the CPU core as two virtual processors. Multiple cores would imply multicore technology, which means there are two physical processing cores within the CPU package. Hyper-Transport is a high-speed connection used by AMD from the CPU to RAM.

2. **D.** Thermal compound/thermal paste is used to seal the small gaps between the CPU and heat sink. It is sometimes referred to as thermal gel or jelly (among a variety of other names), but not *grape* jelly. (Did I ever tell you about the time I found grape jelly inside a customer's computer? Fun times.) Note: Never use petroleum-based products (such as 3-in-1 oil or WD-40) inside a computer; the oils can damage the components over time. TDP stands for thermal design power.

3. **B.** TDP (thermal design power) is the amount of power required to cool a computer and is linked directly to the amount of heat a CPU creates. Some CPUs come with a built-in graphics processing unit (GPU). This means that with a compatible motherboard, no separate video card is necessary. PSU stands for power supply unit. 140 watts is a potential TDP rating but does not define what TDP is.

4. **B.** The CPU needs to be compatible with the socket of the motherboard. The case doesn't actually make much of a difference when it comes to the CPU. (Just make sure it's large enough!) There is no wattage range, but you should be concerned with the voltage range of the CPU. PCI Express (PCIe) slots don't actually play into this at all because there is no direct connectivity between the two.

5. **C.** LGA (Land Grid Array) is the type of socket that uses "lands" to connect the socket to the CPU. PGA (Pin Grid Array) sockets have pinholes that make for connectivity to the CPU's copper pins. AM4 is a PGA socket that accepts AMD CPUs such as the Ryzen 7.

6. **A.** Overclocking enables the user to increase the clock speed of the CPU within the BIOS. Level 3 (L3) cache comes in the largest capacities of the three types of cache and has the most latency; therefore, it is the slowest. If the CPU can't find what it needs in L1, it moves to L2 and finally to L3. An integrated GPU is a video adapter that is built into the motherboard. The heat sink helps to dissipate heat from the CPU and is usually aided by a fan or liquid cooling system.

CHAPTER 13

Peripherals and Power

This chapter covers the following A+ 220-1001 exam objectives:

▶ **3.6** – Explain the purposes and uses of various peripheral types.

▶ **3.7** – Summarize power supply types and features.

Don't be fooled—a computer is just a hunk of metal and circuits without user intervention; however, people and computers are not naturally compatible. We need to be able to manipulate computers; and we need ways to understand the information held within them. That's where peripherals—input and output devices—come in. They allow us to take control of the computer, and enable us to see and hear the results in a way that we can comprehend.

The third piece of the puzzle is power. Without power, a computer won't function at all. Without clean and stable power, a computer cannot work efficiently. The power supply unit is at the core of the power structure within the computer—that will be the focus of the second half of this chapter. But first…peripherals.

3.6 – Explain the purposes and uses of various peripheral types

ExamAlert

Objective 3.6 concentrates on the following concepts: printer, ADF/flatbed scanner, barcode scanner/QR scanner, monitors, VR headset, optical drive types, mouse, keyboard, touchpad, signature pad, game controllers, camera/webcam, microphone, speakers, headset, projector, external storage drives, KVM, magnetic reader/chip reader, NFC/tap pay device, and smart card reader.

> **Note**
>
> As you can see, this objective has a *long* list of input and output devices. But, you are only required to know their purpose or usage, not necessarily the configuration of each and every device.

To take advantage of a computer, we input information with devices such as keyboards and mice, and the computer outputs information with devices such as monitors, speakers, and printers. The appropriate input/output devices and peripherals must be connected to the proper input/output (I/O) ports. This section briefly describes some of those input and output devices, their uses, and the ports they connect to.

Input Devices

Input devices are devices you use to input information into the computer. The category of input devices contains many different peripherals including keyboards, mice, touchpads, writing tablets, and microphones. Let's begin with the most common, keyboards and mice.

Keyboards and Mice

Computer keyboards are used to type text and numbers into a word processor or other application. We use them all the time. They can also be used to manipulate the operating system. Aside from straight typing, a keyboard can also be used for shortcuts through the operating system or the application using combination shortcut keys. For example, **Ctrl+S** saves a document; **Alt+F4** closes an application; and **Ctrl+Shift+Esc** brings up the Task Manager.

> **Note**
>
> Here's a comprehensive list of Windows keyboard shortcuts:
>
> https://support.microsoft.com/en-us/help/12445/windows-keyboard-shortcuts

The 104-key keyboard is the standard U.S. layout, though there are versions that have more or fewer keys. We have been using the 104-key design for several decades. Figure 13.1 shows an example of a 104-key keyboard. If you haven't familiarized yourself with a standard layout keyboard yet—do it. Strong typing ability is an important skill for a tech. Practice by typing out your A+ notes and by using free online typing programs. Ten minutes of practice a day will yield amazing results in just a month or two.

FIGURE 13.1 **A standard 104-key keyboard**

The keyboard in Figure 13.1 is a QWERTY design—those letters are in order on the third row. This is the most common design, though there are others. Some applications require completely different keyboards, which have their own learning curve.

Keyboards currently come in one of three main types: membrane (quiet), mechanical (very clicky), and a combination of the two, sometimes referred to as mecha-membrane. I am currently writing this book with a mecha-membrane keyboard. Membrane-based keyboards are inexpensive but don't normally last as long as the other two types. If there is damage or failure to a membrane keyboard, then the entire keyboard usually needs to be replaced. The beauty of mechanical keyboards is that individual keycaps can be replaced if they wear out or are damaged. Because of this—and because they are stronger in general—mechanical keyboards usually last longer, but they cost more money.

Wired keyboards normally connect via USB, while much older ones connect via a Personal System/2 (PS/2) connector. I only mention PS/2 because the acronym is listed in the A+ objectives acronyms list. Rarely will you will see a PS/2 connector, but just in case, you should have a PS/2 to USB adapter in your toolkit! Wireless keyboards often use Bluetooth or another similar protocol that runs on 2.4 GHz. Whether it is wired or wireless, it must be configured appropriately. Usually, keyboards are detected automatically by Windows, but specialized keyboards will require a driver installation. If a driver does not come with the keyboard, then you will have to download it from the manufacturer's website. Either way, make sure that the device—known as a human interface device (HID)—is recognized in the Device Manager, without any question marks or exclamation points, as shown in Figure 13.2.

FIGURE 13.2   Windows 10 Device Manager displaying the keyboards and mice

> **Note**
>
> One question I commonly get is this: "How do I tell the slash key from the backslash key?" My answer: "Usually, the *back*slash key is near the *Back*space key." Look at Figure 13.1 and your own keyboard to see what I mean.

Mice are used to control the graphical user interface (GUI) in Windows and other operating systems and applications. They work in two dimensions and can have two or more buttons and a scroll wheel to manipulate the OS. The Buttons tab in **Control Panel > All Control Panel Items > Mouse Properties** is used to change which buttons act as the primary and alternative click buttons, but by default the primary is left-click (or simply, click) and the alternate is right-click. You can also change the type of pointer, the speed of the pointer, and more in the Mouse Properties dialog box.

Mice connect with the same wired and wireless methods as keyboards and show up in the Device Manager as displayed in Figure 13.2. Some mice have the ability to change the optical resolution, which is measured in dots per inch (DPI). This is also known as *sensitivity*. A common basic resolution is 800 DPI, but more advanced mice can go into the 10,000s, where the slightest move of the mouse will result in a lot of movement on the screen. Higher resolution mice are used in gaming and in some design environments. These types of mice often require the installation of a specialized control program, and a specific type of surface to operate on. Many higher-end mice require a wired USB connection.

Other Input Devices

There are tons of other input devices. Tons. This is a huge part of the computer aftermarket. As a trainer, I use five different input devices at my main workstation. Table 13.1 gives some examples.

TABLE 13.1 **Description of Various Input Devices and Peripherals**

Device	Description	Types and Connections
Touchpad	▶ Device used on a laptop to control the cursor on the screen. ▶ There are also external USB touchpads for PCs.	Often integrated to the laptop but can also be connected externally via USB or Wi-Fi.
Gamepad	▶ Specialized one-hand keyboard with extra buttons. ▶ Game controller similar to gaming console controller.	Connects via USB or wireless.
Writing tablet	▶ Device used for art, graphics, presentation, notes, etc. ▶ Used with a stylus. ▶ Wacom is a common brand.	Connects via USB.
Web camera (webcam)	Enables a user to monitor other areas of a home or building, communicate via video telephony and take still images.	Can connect to a PC via USB, to a LAN via RJ45, or via Wi-Fi.
Scanner	▶ Used to optically scan images and other objects and convert them into digital images to be stored on the computer. ▶ Automatic document feeder (ADF) types pull the paper/image from the top and return it at the bottom. ▶ Flatbed scanner requires the user to place the document flat on a glass surface manually.	Can connect via USB or via Wi-Fi.
Microphone	Enables users to record their voices or other sounds to the computer. Common usages are webcasts, podcasts, for voice-overs while screen capturing, and for gaming.	Can connect to a PC via 1/8 inch (3.5 mm) mini-jack (sound card) or via USB.
Biometric device	Provides access to systems based on a particular physical characteristic of a user. Used for authentication purposes (for example, a fingerprint reader).	Can be integrated to the PC or can be connected via USB, Wi-Fi, or connected to the network.

Device	Description	Types and Connections
Barcode scanner/ QR scanner	▶ Scans codes; for example, linear barcodes, 2D barcodes, Post Office barcodes, and Quick Response (QR) codes. ▶ After physical installation, sometimes needs to be programmed to understand these codes.	Connects to the PC via USB or 2.4-GHz Wi-Fi, or might be integrated into handheld computers and smartphones.
Smart card reader	Device that accepts smart cards used for authentication and data storage.	Can be integrated as a slot (for, example to a laptop). Also available in USB versions.
Magnetic reader/ chip reader	Device that reads credit cards (stripe or chip), or identification smart cards.	Can connect via USB, Bluetooth, or Wi-Fi.
NFC/tap pay device	Contactless payment using near field communication (NFC) or proprietary technology.	Built-in NFC in mobile devices.
Signature pad	Pressure-sensitive electronic pad used for customer signatures.	Connects via USB.
Musical Instrument Digital Interface (MIDI) device	Enables computers, music keyboards, synthesizers, digital recorders, samplers, and so on to control each other and exchange data.	Uses a 5-pin DIN connector.
Motion sensor	Device used with PCs, Macs, and gaming consoles to allow a user to control the computer by swiping, grabbing, pinching, and so on in mid-air.	Often connected via USB or Wi-Fi, these are controlled with infrared technology or voice activated.

That's not a complete list, of course. There are plenty more input devices available, and more to come undoubtedly. One thing to keep in mind is that many specialized input devices will require specific software installations. Another thing to remember is that devices will have to be connected to the system in one way or another Often that means Wi-Fi, USB, or Bluetooth. We discuss each of these elsewhere in the book, but let's touch on USB and Bluetooth a little more.

USB Connectivity

USB devices connect to what is known as a root hub, regardless of whether they are USB version 1.1, 2.0, 3.0, or higher devices. The USB devices, root hub, and host controllers can be viewed from within Windows in a couple ways:

▶ **Device Manager:** Within the Device Manager, click **Universal Serial Bus Controllers** to expand it. The root hub and controllers are listed within. Individual devices will be listed under such categories as Human Interface Devices.

▶ **System Information:** Open System Information by opening the Run prompt and typing **msinfo32**. Expand Components, and then select **USB**.

When removing USB devices from a computer, remember to disable them in the Notification Area before disconnecting them. Do this by right-clicking the **Safely Remove Hardware and Eject Media** icon and selecting **Eject**. This will avoid damage to a USB device (for example, corruption to the USB flash drive). If you cannot disable it in the system, power down the computer and then disconnect it. For more information about USB, visit https://usb.org/.

Bluetooth Connectivity

Bluetooth is a short-range, low-speed wireless network primarily designed to operate in peer-to-peer mode (known as ad hoc) between PCs and devices such as printers, projectors, smartphones, mice, keyboards, and so on. It can be used with gaming consoles and by connecting a smartphone to a car's technology system or to a smart TV.

Bluetooth runs in virtually the same 2.4-GHz frequency used by IEEE 802.11b, g, and n wireless networks, but it uses a spread-spectrum frequency-hopping signaling method to help minimize interference. Bluetooth version 1.2 offers a data transfer rate of 1 Mbps. Version 2 is rated at 3 Mbps. The more common Version 3 (and higher) has theoretical speeds of up to 24 Mbps, but it achieves them by combining with 802.11 technology. Bluetooth is divided into classes, each of which has a different range. Table 13.2 shows these classes, their ranges, and the amount of power their corresponding antennae use to generate signal. Class 2 devices are the most common when it comes to computer peripherals.

TABLE 13.2 **Bluetooth Classes**

Class	mW	Range
Class 1	100 mW	100 meters (328 ft.)
Class 2	2.5 mW	10 meters (33 ft.)
Class 3	1 mW	1 meter (3 ft.)
Class 4	.5 mW	.5 meter (1.5 ft.)

> **Note**
>
> Some manufacturers have their own proprietary 2.4-GHz wireless technologies that are very similar to Bluetooth, but may not be compatible with Bluetooth devices.

Output Devices

It's true, we need to *see* and *hear* things that are outputted from the computer. (Smell and feel, not so much.) Monitors, projectors, speakers, headsets, printers, and the list goes on. Let's start with the types of monitors you will find in the field.

We talked about some of the different monitor types in Chapter 2, "Laptops, Part 2." Let's review those now and continue on with projectors, speakers, and AR/VR headsets.

LCD

A liquid-crystal display (LCD) is an active-matrix, flat-panel display that consists of two sheets of polarizing material surrounding a layer of liquid-crystal solution. LCD displays use a cold cathode fluorescent lamp (CCFL) as the lighting source, and an inverter to change power from DC to the required AC for the lamp.

Here are two types of active-matrix LCD technologies you should know for the exam:

- ▶ **Twisted nematic (TN):** This technology uses liquid crystals that actually twist and untwist at varying angles, letting certain amounts of light through. Less expensive LCD monitors will often use TN technology, but it is not commonly found in computer monitors.

- ▶ **In-plane switching (IPS):** This technology aligns the liquid crystals on a plane that is parallel to the glass. Because of this, an additional transistor is required for each picture element (pixel). This means that an IPS-based LCD uses more power than a TN-based LCD. However, IPS allows for better color reproduction and wider viewing angles. All this comes at a higher cost, of course. These are much more common than TN when it comes to computer displays.

Many of the displays we use are LCDs, but as of 2015 or so, there has been a shift in the lighting used. Instead of a lamp, most of today's displays use LEDs; for example, the LED-LCD.

LED

LED monitors utilize light-emitting diodes to display images. LED monitors are essentially LCD monitors with a different backlight. You may see the acronym "WLED," which stands for white LED. This is simply a common implementation of standard LED.

OLED

Organic light-emitting diode (OLED) displays use organic semiconductor substances as the lighting material. In the beginning of 2018, OLED TVs were common, but were just making inroads into the PC monitor market. OLED technology is also common in smartphones and tablets.

> **Note**
>
> QLED is another acronym bandied about by techies. Essentially, when it comes to TVs, OLED and QLED are designed by competing manufacturers. The specific differences are not very important to the average technician or for the A+ exams.

Projectors

Video projectors can be plugged into a computer's external video port to project the computer's video display to a projection screen. An extremely bright bulb is necessary to project this image to the screen. The light output is measured in *lumens*. A typical high-def projector might output 2000 to 3000 lumens—never allow a person to look into the projector's lamp! Increased lumens are necessary for locations with a higher amount of ambient light (existing light in the room). Projectors are used for presentations and for teaching and are common in conference rooms and training centers; however, some schools and companies opt to use large, flat-screen TVs instead of projectors, even though projectors can usually project a larger image. Projectors are available in LCD, LED, and Digital Light Processing (DLP) versions. The LCD type works in a similar fashion to the monitor technology of the same name, whereas DLP uses light valves with rotating color wheels. Common high-definition display resolutions used by projectors include 1080p and 4K; the price of the projector increases with the resolution standard and with other characteristics, such as the brightness, contrast, and noise. A video projector can be used with a laptop by utilizing the display toggle button, or it can be used with a computer that has a video card with dual outputs.

Speakers

Back in the day, a pair of speakers would be connected to the sound card and you were done. But nowadays, you might be using a 5.1 or 7.1 system and, if so, you need to color coordinate! 5.1 surround sound means that the system uses five regular speakers (left, right, center, back left, and back right) and one speaker for low frequencies, which is usually a subwoofer. 7.1 builds upon this by adding two additional surround speakers. Normally, the lime-green output is for the first two speakers (or headphones), which gives standard stereo 2.1 output (two speakers + sub). The black output is for two rear speakers and the orange output is for the center channel and the subwoofer; an AC outlet will be necessary to power the subwoofer. A gray, brown, or other dark port is used for two additional speakers (middle surround) in a 7.1 system. Another option is to use the digital fiber optical output or digital coaxial output. There are a lot of options, so read the manual on the sound card and the speakers when trying to hook everything together, and pay attention to the little icons that are engraved into the back of the sound card next to the ports.

There is a multitude of wireless speakers as well. Many people choose to control them from a mobile device via a Bluetooth connection. If you choose to control a wireless speaker from a laptop or computer, that system will need to have a Bluetooth antenna installed. Many laptops do, but most desktops do not. The solution is as small as a thumbnail—the Bluetooth "dongle"—which really is just a tiny USB adapter.

AR/VR Headsets

Previously in the book I mentioned virtual reality and augmented reality. (Is this the Matrix? Nope, just more A+ objectives.) I said that virtual reality meant a completely new "reality" created from a computer program. VR headsets immerse a person into the video and audio of that program. However, augmented reality (or mixed reality) is when a person can see the real world (or a close facsimile) and images and holograms are overlaid on top of reality—augmenting the world. There are wired options, but as of the writing of this book, the AR/VR market is mostly wireless to allow freedom of movement for the user. AR/VR headsets incorporate powerful video cards that enable high-end game playing, and various types of training simulations, and can be used independently or in conjunction with other input and output devices.

> **Note**
>
> Of course, printers are a very important when it comes to output devices. That's why I dedicate Chapter 15, "Printers and Multifunction Devices," to those.

Hybrid I/O Devices and Others

Hybrid peripherals can output information and have information inputted to them. The best example of this is the touchscreen. Touchscreens can be found just about everywhere. They allow user input by hand or stylus, and output video to the screen. Previously I mentioned the writing tablet, which is an input device, but there are also writing tablets that incorporate video screens. These are used by artists, graphic designers, and content creators to easily interact with a desktop computer.

Another example of a hybrid device is a KVM (keyboard-video-mouse) switch. This is a device used to switch between two or more computers that share a keyboard and mouse input and a video output, as demonstrated in Figure 13.3. This particular KVM switch has four inputs for computers using HDMI for video and USB for keyboard and mouse (the last of which is shown on the right). Then, there is an output on the left for HDMI video and USB.

FIGURE 13.3   **The ports on the back of a KVM switch**

KVM switches are great for the person that needs to consistently work at two or more computers but doesn't want clutter in the form of extra monitors, keyboards, and mice. KVM switches work well with server farms also, allowing a systems administrator to quickly access many servers at once. However, with the advent of headless motherboards, the KVM switch isn't quite as necessary. Many server motherboards come with headless technology known as Intelligent Platform Management Interface (IPMI), which allows an admin to connect to and monitor the system remotely—often from a browser—without the need for a hardwired video connection.

There are plenty of other examples of hybrid I/O devices. Computer headsets are hybrid devices because they have headphones that output music and a microphone that can input the user's voice. Some AR/VR headsets fall into this category as well. And then there are multifunction printers (when used for copying documents), smart TVs, voice-activated assistants…the list goes on, and you can expect the number of peripherals to continue to grow and become more complex over time.

Cram Quiz

Answer these questions. The answers follow the last question. If you cannot answer these questions correctly, consider reading this section again until you can.

1. What does a KVM do?

   ○ **A.** Connects a computer to Bluetooth-enabled devices

   ○ **B.** Allows multiple users to share a single computer

   ○ **C.** Networks multiple computers together

   ○ **D.** Connects multiple computers to save resources

2. Which of the following are considered both input and output devices?

   ○ **A.** Keyboard, mouse, touchpad

   ○ **B.** Smart card reader, motion sensor, biometric device

   ○ **C.** Printer, speakers

   ○ **D.** Smart TV, touchscreen, KVM, headsets

3. Which of the following devices can be used to perform combination shortcuts?

   ○ **A.** Keyboard

   ○ **B.** Mouse

   ○ **C.** Printer

   ○ **D.** KVM

4. Which of the following incorporate the concept of resolution? (Select all that apply.)

   ○ **A.** Keyboard

   ○ **B.** Mouse

   ○ **C.** Printer

   ○ **D.** Signature reader

   ○ **E.** LED display

   ○ **F.** Speakers

5. Which of the following terms describes how the light output from a video projector is measured?

   ○ **A.** IPS

   ○ **B.** CCFL

   ○ **C.** Lumens

   ○ **D.** OLED

Cram Quiz Answers

220-1001 Answers

1. **D.** A KVM connects multiple computers to a single keyboard, mouse, and monitor. This way, fewer resources in the way of peripherals (input/output devices) are necessary to use the computers.

2. **D.** Smart TVs, touchscreens, KVMs, and headsets are considered both input and output devices. Keyboards, mice, touchpads, smart card readers, motion sensors, and biometric devices are considered input devices. Printers and speakers are considered output devices.

3. **A.** A keyboard can be used to perform combination shortcuts. An example of a shortcut key is Ctrl+P, which initiates a print job within an application. While a KVM will have a keyboard connected to it, it's at the keyboard that you perform the shortcut operation.

4. **B, C, and E.** The mouse, printer, and LED display all deal with resolution. A mouse's sensitivity is rated in DPI; for example, 800 DPI is a low resolution for mice. A printer will commonly print out documents at the resolution 600 DPI (more on that in Chapter 15). A monitor will commonly have a resolution of 1920 × 1080 (or greater!).

5. **C.** A video projector's light output is measured in lumens. In-plane switching (IPS) technology allows for a wider viewing angle. Some LCDs use a cold cathode fluorescent lamp (CCFL) as the lighting source instead of LEDs. OLED stands for organic light-emitting diode—that's the lighting material used in the display.

3.7 – Summarize power supply types and features

ExamAlert

Objective 3.7 focuses on the following: input 115 V vs. 220 V, output 5 V vs. 12 V, 24-pin motherboard adapter, wattage rating, and number of devices/types of devices to be powered.

Everything relies on power. Clean, well-planned power is imperative in a computer system. Power requirements should always be in the back of your mind when designing a computer. After the components of a computer have been selected—especially the CPU and GPU—the power supply needs to be chosen carefully. Not enough power and the system might become unstable, or not work at all. Too much power and it becomes expensive and wasteful. I can't tell you how much power plays into my decision-making process, and how many power-related issues I have troubleshot in the past.

The power supply unit (PSU) in a PC is in charge of converting the alternating current (AC) drawn from the wall outlet into direct current (DC) to be used internally by the computer. The power supply makes use of a transformer and a rectifier, working together to convert AC over to DC. The power supply feeds the motherboard, hard drives, optical drives, and any other devices inside of the computer. Talk about a single point of failure! That is why many higher-end workstations and servers have redundant power supplies.

Planning Which Power Supply to Use

It is important to use a reliable brand of power supply that is approved for use by organizations such as the International Electrotechnical Commission (IEC), Federal Communications Commission (FCC), UL, and so on, and meets directives such as the Restriction of Hazardous Substances (RoHS). Accordance with the appropriate standards reduces the risk of fire, and allows for safer products in general.

You also must consider the following factors when planning which power supply to use in your computer:

▶ Type of power supply and compatibility

▶ Wattage and capacity requirements

▶ Number and type of connectors

Types of Power Supplies and Compatibility

The most common form factor used in PCs today is Advanced Technology Extended (ATX). Depending on the type of ATX, the main power connector to the motherboard will usually have 24 pins (or 20+4 pins), or 20 pins for much older ATX power supplies. Generally, today's systems use power supplies that adhere to one of the ATX 12V 2.x standards. The key is compatibility. If a computer were *proprietary*, you could go to the computer manufacturer's website to find out the exact form factor and possibly a replacement power supply for that model computer. Some third-party power supply manufacturers also offer replacement power supplies for proprietary systems. However, if a computer were custom built, you would need to find out the form factor used by the motherboard and/or case, and you should open the computer to take a look at all the necessary power connections. Then you need to find a compatible power supply (according to those specifications) from a power supply manufacturer.

Most of today's motherboards have an additional 4-pin or 8-pin 12 V power port for the CPU (referred to as EATX12V). A typical power supply offers one or two 4-pin connectors or one 8-pin connector for this extra power. If the motherboard and power supply don't match up, there are 4- to 8-pin adapters available. Figure 13.4 shows an example of a 24-pin ATX connector and an example of an 8-pin CPU connector.

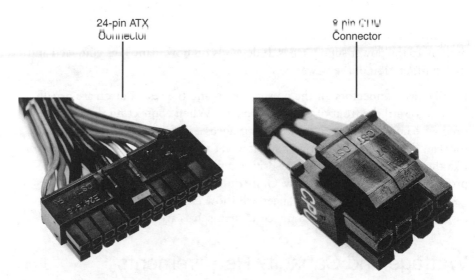

24-pin ATX
Connector

8-pin CPU
Connector

FIGURE 13.4 **24-pin ATX and EATX12V 8-pin CPU connectors**

> **ExamAlert**
>
> Be able to identify the main 24-pin power port/connector, and the CPU's EATX12V 8-pin port/connector.

A quick word about rails. Remember, the ATX specification requires the power supply to produce +3.3 V, +5 V, +12 V, and –12 V outputs as well as a 5 V standby output. These are known as "rails" (for example, the +12 V rail). You might have heard of dual-rail or multi-rail power supplies, for example multiple 12 V rails. This technology is important in systems that draw a lot of power. It is a way of monitoring power circuits individually instead of collectively (single-rail) and helps to prevent overheating and possible fire by shutting down the PSU if a certain point is reached (for example, more than 18 amps on a single 12 V wire). If you plan to run a CPU-intensive system, such as a gaming system or multimedia system, you should look into a multi-rail PSU.

> **ExamAlert**
>
> The purpose of "dual-rail" PSUs is to separate and limit the current through each wire to avoid overheating.

Also, remember about case fans. If they have 4-pin connectors, they can connect directly to the motherboard. However, additional case fans may connect directly to the power supply feeds. It depends on how many fans you need and the configuration of the power connections.

Finally, case connectors for the power button and the reset button are usually located toward the front of the motherboard. When connecting these, the colored wire normally goes to positive (+) if necessary. Some of the case connectors can be connected either way and it won't make a difference. But connectors like the power LED and the hard-drive activity LED need to be connected properly for the LEDs to display. Quite often the motherboard will be color-coded; the fold-out instruction sheet will show exactly where to plug in each case connector, and the case connectors themselves are normally labeled.

Wattage and Capacity Requirements

Power supplies are usually rated in watts. They are rated at a maximum amount that they can draw from the wall outlet and pass on to the computer's devices. Remember that the computer will not always use all that power the way in which a light bulb does. And the amount of power used depends on how many devices work and how much number-crunching your processor does! In addition, when computers sleep or suspend, they use less electricity. What you need to be concerned with is the maximum amount of power all the devices need collectively. Most power-supply manufacturers today offer models that range from 300 watts all the way up to 1500 watts. Devices use a certain amount of power defined in amps and/or watts. By adding all the devices' power consumption together, you can get a clearer picture of how powerful a power supply you need. Consult the manufacturer's web page of the device for exact requirements. Then consider using a power supply calculator on the Internet to find out how many watts you might need. Many desktop and tower computers can typically get away with using a 600 watt power supply. But if you decide to add devices—especially video cards—you might find that the current power supply will not meet your needs anymore, and an upgrade will be necessary. So, plan for the future as well. (Apparently, technicians need to be prescient!)

Number and Type of Power Connectors

It is important to know how many of each type of power connector you need when planning which power supply to use. You must be familiar with each type of power connector for the A+ exams. Be prepared to identify them by name and by sight. Table 13.3 defines the usage and voltages for some typical power connectors. Figure 13.5 shows these connectors.

TABLE 13.3 **Power Connectors**

Power Connector	Usage	Pins and Voltages
SATA	Serial ATA hard drives and optical drives	15-pin, 3.3 V, 5 V, and 12 V
Molex	Case fans, IDE hard drives, and optical drives	4-pin, 5 V (red), 12 V (yellow), two ground wires
PCIe	PCI Express video cards	6-pin, 12 V (ATX12V version 2.1) 8-pin, 12 V (ATX12V version 2.2 and higher)

SATA Power Connector   Molex Power Connector   PCIe Power Connector

FIGURE 13.5 **SATA, Molex, and PCIe power connectors**

Note

Don't confuse 8-pin PCIe power connectors with 8-pin CPU connectors! To tell the difference, look for the label! Also, the PCIe video connector will usually separate two of the pins so that you can use it in 6-pin or 8-pin scenarios.

Note

Many PSUs still come with a Berg connector for backward compatibility. It's a smaller 4-pin connector used with the venerable 3.5-inch floppy drive.

Installing the Power Supply

When the power supply arrives, you can install it. But first take a look at the back of the power supply to identify the components you see, as shown in Figure 13.6.

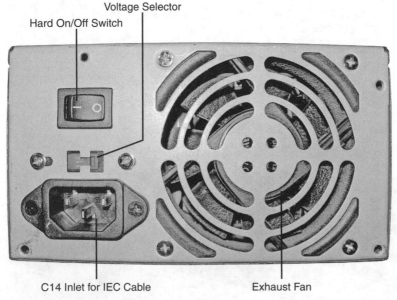

FIGURE 13.6 **Rear view of power supply**

On the top-left portion of Figure 13.6, you see a hard on/off switch, sometimes referred to as a kill switch. This is a helpful feature when troubleshooting PCs. Instead of disconnecting the power cable, you can shut off this switch. It works effectively in emergencies as well. Below that, you see a (red) voltage selector switch. This indicates that this is a dual-voltage power supply. This should be set to 115 V in the United States. It also has a 230 V option to be used in other countries. (An additional adapter might be necessary for the different wall outlets you might encounter.) Always shut down the computer and disconnect the power cable before changing the voltage selector switch. Be sure to check this setting before initially using the power supply. This selector switch indicates an older, or atypical, power supply. Most newer power supplies are equipped with a universal input, enabling you to connect the power supply to any AC outlet between 100 V and 240 V without having to set a voltage switch—the power supply "auto-detects" the voltage. To determine if a PSU without a voltage switch is truly dual-voltage, look for the phrase: "100-240 V input" or something similar.

Back to Figure 13.6, below the voltage selector, you see the power cable inlet; this is known as a C14 inlet and is where you attach your power cord to the power supply. These inlets and the cables that connect to them are defined by the IEC 60320 specification and, because of this, some techs refer to the power cord as an "IEC cable." This cord actually has a standard three-prong connector suitable for an AC outlet on one end and a C13 line socket on the other to connect to the power supply. To the right, you see the power supply fan that is of great importance when troubleshooting power supplies. We'll discuss troubleshooting in Chapters 17 through 22.

Back to our power supply installation! For new computer builds, I usually install the power supply at the end. This may or may not be possible depending on your configuration, but it is a good rule of thumb. If this is a repair or upgrade, and there is a power supply currently connected to the computer, turn off the computer and unplug the power supply. ATX motherboards are always receiving 5 volts even when they are off (if the computer is plugged in). Be sure that you use antistatic methods. Remove the old power supply and prepare to install the new one.

You might want to test the new power supply before installing it. This can be done by connecting a power supply tester, plugging in the power supply to the AC outlet, and turning on the hard on/off switch. (I'll show this in Chapter 18, "Troubleshooting Motherboards, CPUs, RAM, and Power.") Or you can test the power supply after it is installed by simply turning the computer on.

The power supply is placed inside the case and is often mounted with four standard screws that are screwed in from the back of the case. Make sure that there are no gaps between the power supply and the power supply opening in the case. Next, connect the main ATX 24-pin power connector to the motherboard. It can only be plugged in one way: a locking tab prevents a wrong connection and keeps the plug in place. Then, connect the 8-pin CPU power connector—again, tabbed for easy orientation. After that, attach the SATA and PCIe connectors as necessary to their corresponding devices. You might also have Molex connections to make for additional fans, monitoring devices, lights, or legacy devices. Most connectors are molded in such a way as to make it difficult to connect them backward or upside down. If you need a lot of strength to plug in the connector, make sure that it is oriented correctly. Don't force the connection. Afterward, remove any antistatic protection and, finally, plug in the power supply to the AC outlet, turn on the hard on/off switch (if the power supply has one), and turn on the computer. Check to see if the fan in the power supply is working and if the computer boots correctly. Do a final check of the CPU fan, case fans, internal/external indicator lights, and POST code readout—if the motherboard has one. If all systems are go, then close up the case, and chalk up one more successful install!

Cram Quiz

Answer these questions. The answers follow the last question. If you cannot answer these questions correctly, consider reading this section again until you can.

1. Which power connector should be used to power an SATA hard drive?
   - ○ **A.** Molex
   - ○ **B.** 6-pin
   - ○ **C.** 24-pin
   - ○ **D.** 15-pin

2. Which voltages are supplied by a Molex power connector?
   - ○ **A.** 12 V and 5 V
   - ○ **B.** 5 V and 3.3 V
   - ○ **C.** 3.3 V and 1.5 V
   - ○ **D.** 24 V and 12 V

3. A company salesperson just returned to the United States after three months in Europe. Now the salesperson tells you that her PC, which worked fine in Europe, won't turn on. What is the best solution?

○ **A.** Install a new power supply.

○ **B.** The computer will not work in the United States due to European licensing.

○ **C.** Install a power inverter to the power supply.

○ **D.** Change the voltage from 230 to 115.

4. Which of the following can have 8 pins? (Select all that apply.)

○ **A.** PCIe

○ **B.** SATA

○ **C.** ATX main power

○ **D.** CPU

○ **E.** Molex

Cram Quiz Answers

1. D. 15-pin connectors power SATA hard drives and other SATA devices (such as optical drives). Molex connectors power fans, older IDE devices, and other secondary devices. 6-pin power connectors are used for video cards (as are 8-pin connectors). 24-pin refers to the main power connection for the motherboard.

2. A. Molex connectors provide 12 volts and 5 volts. There are four wires: it color-coded, yellow is 12 V, red is 5 V, and the two blacks are grounds.

3. D. Most likely, the voltage selector was set to 230 V so that it could function properly in Europe (for example, in the UK). It needs to be changed to 115 V so that the power supply can work properly in the United States. Make sure to do this while the computer is off and unplugged.

4. A and D. PCIe power can be 8-pin or 6-pin. CPU power (EATX12V) can be 8-pin or 4-pin. SATA power is 15-pin (and data is 7-pin). ATX main power is typically 24-pin. Molex is a 4-wire connector; it is sometimes also referred to as "peripheral."

CHAPTER 14

Custom PCs and Common Devices

This chapter covers the following A+ 220-1001 exam objectives:

▶ **3.8** – Given a scenario, select and configure appropriate components for a custom PC configuration to meet customer specifications or needs.

▶ **3.9** – Given a scenario, install and configure common devices.

Let's customize! This chapter is all about purpose; the reasons people use computers, and how people use them. In short, custom computers. We'll also briefly discuss the basics of first time computer usage. Let's go!

3.8 – Given a scenario, select and configure appropriate components for a custom PC configuration to meet customer specifications or needs

ExamAlert

Objective 3.8 concentrates on the following concepts: graphics/CAD/CAM design workstation, audio/video editing workstation, virtualization workstation, gaming PC, network attached storage device, standard thick client, and thin client.

There are several custom configurations that you might encounter in the IT field. You should be able to describe what each type of computer is and the hardware that is required for these custom computers to function properly.

Graphic/CAD/CAM Design Workstation

Graphic workstations are computers that illustrators, graphic designers, artists, and photographers work at (among other professions). Often, these graphic workstations will be Mac desktops, but can be PCs as well; it depends on the preference of the user. Professionals will use software tools such as Adobe Illustrator, Photoshop, and Fireworks, as well as CorelDRAW, GIMP, and so on.

Computer-aided design (CAD) and computer-aided manufacturing (CAM) workstations are common in electrical engineering, architecture, drafting, and many other engineering arenas. They run software such as AutoCAD.

Both types of software are GPU- and CPU-intensive and the images require a lot of space on the screen. 3-D design and rendering of drawings and illustrations can be very taxing on a computer. So, hardware-wise, these workstations need a high-end video card, perhaps a workstation-class video card—which is much more expensive. They also require as much RAM as possible. If a program has a recommended RAM requirement of 4 GB of RAM, you should consider quadrupling that amount; plus, the faster the RAM, the better—just make sure your motherboard (and CPU) can support it. Next, a solid-state drive can be very helpful when opening large files, saving them, and especially, rendering them into final deliverable files. That means a minimum SATA Rev. 3.0 solid-state hard drive is good, but something NVMe would be better—either M.2 or PCI Express-slot based, or possibly something more advanced than that. Finally, going beyond the computer itself, a large display is often required; one that has the correct input based on the video card. For example, a 27-inch LED-LCD with excellent contrast ratio and black levels, and the ability to connect with DisplayPort, DVI, or HDMI—whichever the professional favors.

ExamAlert

Don't forget, graphic/CAD/CAM design workstations need powerful high-end video cards, solid-state drives (SATA and/or M.2), and as much RAM as possible.

Audio/Video Editing Workstation

Multimedia editing, processing, and rendering require a fast computer with high-capacity storage and big displays (usually more than one). Examples of audio/video workstations include

► **Video recording/editing PCs:** These run software such as Adobe Premiere Pro or Apple Final Cut Pro X.

273

3.8 – Given a scenario, select and configure appropriate components for a custom PC configuration to meet customer specifications or needs

▶ **Music recording PCs:** These run software such as Apple Logic Pro X or Avid Pro Tools.

Note

Identify the software programs listed above and understand exactly what they are used for.

Adobe Premiere Pro: https://www.adobe.com/products/premiere.html

Apple Final Cut Pro X: https://www.apple.com/final-cut-pro/

Apple Logic Pro X: https://www.apple.com/logic-pro/

Avid Pro Tools: https://www.avid.com/en/pro-tools

This just scratches the surface, but you get the idea. These computers need to be designed to easily manipulate video files and music files. So, from a hardware standpoint, they need a specialized video or audio card, the fastest hard drive available with a lot of storage space (definitely SSD and perhaps NVMe-based, or SATA Express), and multiple monitors (to view all of the editing windows). Keep in mind that the video cards and specialized storage drives are going to be expensive devices; be sure to employ all antistatic measures before working with those cards.

Some video editing workstations might require a secondary video card or external device for the capturing of video or for other video usage. Likewise, many audio editing workstations will require a secondary audio device, and will often rely on external audio processors and other audio equipment to "shape" the sound before it enters the computer via USB or otherwise.

ExamAlert

Remember that audio/video workstations need specialized A/V cards; large, fast hard drives; and multiple monitors.

Note

Most specialized, custom computers should have powerful multicore CPUs.

Virtualization Workstation

A virtualization workstation is a computer that runs one or more virtual operating systems (also known as virtual machines or VMs). Did you ever wish that you had another two or three extra computers lying around so that you could test multiple versions of Windows, Linux, and possibly a Windows Server OS all at the same time? Well, with virtual software, you can do this by creating virtual machines for each OS. But if you run those at the same time on your main computer, you are probably going to bring that PC to a standstill. However, if you build a workstation specializing in virtualization, you can run whatever operating systems on it that you need. The virtualization workstation uses what is known as a hypervisor, which allows multiple virtual operating systems (guests) to run at the same time on a single computer. It is also known as a virtual machine manager (VMM). But there are two different kinds:

▶ **Type 1: Native:** This means that the hypervisor runs directly on the host computer's hardware. Because of this, it is also known as *bare metal*. Examples of this include VMware vSphere and Microsoft Hyper-V (for Windows Server).

▶ **Type 2: Hosted:** This means that the hypervisor runs within (or "on top of") the operating system. Guest operating systems run within the hypervisor. Compared to Type 1, guests are one level removed from the hardware and therefore run less efficiently. Examples of this include VirtualBox, VMware Workstation, and Hyper-V for Windows 10. Figure 14.1 shows an example of VMware Workstation running. You will note that it has a variety of virtual machines inside, such as Windows 10 Pro (running), Windows Server, and Ubuntu Linux.

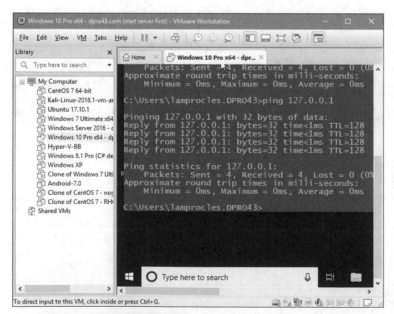

FIGURE 14.1 **VMware Workstation**

275

3.8 – Given a scenario, select and configure appropriate components for a custom PC configuration to meet customer specifications or needs

Generally, Type 1 is a much faster and efficient solution than Type 2. Because of this, Type 1 hypervisors are the kind used for virtual servers by web-hosting companies and by companies that offer cloud-computing solutions. It makes sense, too. If you have ever run a powerful operating system within a Type 2 hypervisor, you know that a ton of resources are used, and those resources are taken from the hosting operating system. It is not nearly as efficient as running the hosted OS within a Type 1 environment. However, keep in mind that the hardware/software requirements for a Type 1 hypervisor are more stringent and costlier.

For virtualization programs to function, the appropriate virtualization extensions need to be turned on in the UEFI/BIOS. Intel CPUs that support x86 virtualization use the VT-x virtualization extension. Intel chipsets use the VT-d and VT-c extensions for input-output memory management and network virtualization, respectively. AMD CPUs that support x86 virtualization use the AMD-V extension. AMD chipsets use the AMD-Vi extension. After virtualization has been enabled in the UEFI/BIOS, some programs, such as Microsoft Hyper-V, need to be turned on in Windows. This can be done in **Control Panel > All Control Panel Items > Programs and Features**, and click the **Turn Windows features on or off** link. Then checkmark **Hyper-V**. Windows will disallow it if virtualization has not been enabled in the UEFI/ BIOS, or in the uncommon case that the CPU doesn't support virtualization.

Any computer designed to run a hypervisor often has a powerful CPU (or multiple CPUs) with multiple cores and as much RAM as can fit in the system. This means a powerful, compatible motherboard as well. So in essence, the guts—the core of the system—need to be robust. Keep in mind that the motherboard UEFI/BIOS and the CPU should have virtualization support.

ExamAlert

Remember that virtualization systems depend on the CPU and RAM heavily. These systems require maximum RAM and CPU cores.

Gaming PC

Now we get to the core of it: Custom computing is taken to extremes when it comes to gaming. Gaming PCs require almost all the resources mentioned previously: a powerful, multicore CPU; lots of fast RAM; one or more SSDs (SATA Express or PCI Express); advanced cooling methods (liquid cooling if you want to be serious); a high-definition sound card; plus a fast network adapter and strong Internet connection.

But without a doubt, the most important component is the video card. Typical end-user video cards cannot handle today's PC games. So, a high-end video card with a specialized GPU is the key. Also, a big monitor that supports high resolutions and refresh rates couldn't hurt. (And let's not forget about *mad* skills.)

All of this establishes a computer that is expensive and requires care and maintenance to keep it running in perfect form. For the person who is not satisfied with gaming consoles, this is the path to take.

> **ExamAlert**
>
> A gaming PC requires a high-end video with specialized GPU, a high-definition sound card, an SSD, and high-end cooling.

Games are some of the most powerful applications available. If even just one of the mentioned elements is missing from a gaming system, it could easily ruin the experience. You might think you could do without an SSD; however, SSDs provide faster load times of games and levels, but don't do too much after that. However, when you look at the mammoth size of some of today's games, that's enough reason to install one. As of the writing of this book (2019), many gamers rely on M.2 drives.

Don't forget, the video card is the number one component of this equation. Gamers are always looking to push the envelope for video performance by increasing the number of frames per second (frames/s or fps) that the video card sends to the monitor. One of the ways to improve the video subsystem is to employ multiple video cards. It's possible to take video to the next level by incorporating NVIDIA's Scalable Link Interface (SLI) or AMD's Cross-Fire (CF). A computer that uses one of these technologies has two (or more) identical video cards that work together for greater performance and higher resolution. The compatible cards are bridged together to essentially work as one unit. It is important to have a compatible motherboard and ample cooling when attempting this type of configuration. Currently, this is done with two or more PCI Express video cards (×16/version 3 or higher) and is most commonly found in gaming rigs, but you might find it in other PCs as well (such as video editing or CAD/CAM workstations). Because some motherboards come with only one PCIe ×16 slot for video, a gaming system needs a more advanced motherboard: one with at least two PCIe ×16 slots to accomplish SLI. It is costly being a gamer!

277

3.8 – Given a scenario, select and configure appropriate components for a custom PC configuration to meet customer specifications or needs

Network-Attached Storage Device

Network-attached storage (NAS) is when one or more hard drives are installed into a device known as a NAS box or NAS server that connects directly to the network. The device can then be accessed via browsing or as a mapped network drive from any computer on the network. For example, a typical two-bay NAS box can hold two SATA drives to be used together as one large capacity or in a RAID 1 mirrored configuration for fault tolerance. Remember, RAID 1 mirroring means that two drives are used in unison and all data is written to both drives, giving you a mirror or extra copy of the data if one drive fails. Larger NAS boxes can have four drives or more, and can incorporate RAID 5 (striping with parity), RAID 6 (striping with double parity), or RAID 10 (stripe of mirrors).

You could also build your own custom PC that acts as a NAS box. This would require two or more identical drives, preferably with trays on the front of the case for easy accessibility. Then, run FreeNAS or other similar software to take just about any system with the right hard drives and turn it into a network attached storage box. With the right hardware you can end up with a faster NAS box than a lot of the devices on the market today.

These devices connect to the network by way of an RJ45 port (often a gigabit NIC running at 1000 Mbps, or even 10 Gbps). Of course, there are much more advanced versions of NAS boxes that would be used by larger companies. These often have hot swappable drives that can be removed and replaced while the device is on. Usually, they are mounted to a plastic enclosure or tray that is slid into the NAS device. But watch out: Not every hard drive in a plastic hard drive enclosure is hot-swappable. The cheaper versions are usually not; they can be swapped in and out but not while the computer is on. These devices might work in conjunction with cloud storage or, in some cases, act as cloud storage themselves. It all depends on their design and their desired usage.

The ultimate goal of the NAS box is to allow file sharing to multiple users in one or more locations. To do this, the administrator of the NAS box first sets up the RAID array (if the device is to use one). Then the admin formats the drives to a particular file system; for instance, ext4 or BTRFS (for typical Linux-based NAS devices) or perhaps ZFS (for PC-based free NAS solutions). Next, the admin sets up services; for example, SMB for Windows and Mac connectivity. To connect to the NAS box from a system over the network, the path would be *nasbox* (for Windows) or smb://*nasbox* (for Mac). Replace *nasbox* with whatever name the device uses. The admin might also choose to make use of AFP or NFS for connectivity. See Chapter 5, "Ports, Protocols, and Network Devices," for more information about these protocols. All of this is configured in the included software that is loaded into a separate volume from the data to be stored by the users. Generally, an admin makes configurations in the NAS box with an Internet browser, using either the IP address or the name of the device to connect.

Some of these NAS devices go beyond simple file sharing. For example, they might also incorporate media streaming of videos, an FTP server, and a web server. Some provide many other services, but beware, any of these can be taxing on the CPU, and can lead to potential security vulnerabilities. Use only what you need!

> **Note**
>
> The following link leads to a video/article demonstrating a NAS device installation: https://dprocomputer.com/blog/?p=2006

> **ExamAlert**
>
> Network-attached storage (NAS) devices usually require a RAID array, gigabit NIC, file sharing, and the capability for media sharing.

Thin Client

A thin client (also known as a slim, lean, or cloud client) is a computer that has few resources compared to a typical PC. Usually, it depends heavily on a server. It is often a small device integrated directly into the display or could be a stand-alone device using an ultra-small form factor (about the size of a cable modem or gaming console). Some thin clients are also known as diskless workstations because they have no hard drive or optical discs. They do have a CPU, RAM, and ports for the display, keyboard, mouse, and network; they can connect wirelessly as well. They are also known simply as computer terminals which might provide only a basic GUI and possibly a web browser.

Other examples of thin clients include point-of-sale (POS) systems such as the self-checkout systems used at stores or touchscreen menus used at restaurants. They serve a single purpose and require minimum hardware resources and minimum OS requirements.

When a typical thin client is turned on, it loads the OS and applications from an image stored (embedded) on flash memory or from a server. The OS and apps are loaded into RAM; when the thin client is turned off, all memory is cleared.

ExamAlert

Viruses have a hard time sticking around a thin client because the RAM is completely cleared every time it is turned off.

So, the thin client is dependent on the server for a lot of resources. Thin clients can connect to an in-house server that runs specially configured software or they can connect to a cloud infrastructure to obtain their applications (and possibly their entire operating system).

Note

Back in the day, this was how a mainframe system worked; however, back then, the terminal did virtually *no* processing, had no CPU, and was therefore referred to as a "dumb" terminal. This is an example of *centralized computing*, where the server does the bulk of the processing. Today, we still have mainframes (super-computers), but the terminal (thin client) incorporates a CPU.

The whole idea behind thin clients is to transfer a lot of the responsibilities and resources to the server. With thin-client computing, an organization purchases more powerful and expensive servers but possibly saves money overall by spending less on each thin client (for example, Lenovo thin clients) while benefitting from a secure design. The typical thin client might have one of several operating systems embedded into the flash memory, depending on the model purchased. This method of centralizing resources, data, and user profiles is considered to be a more organized and secure solution than the typical PC-based, client/server network, but it isn't nearly as common.

ExamAlert

A thin client runs basic, single-purpose applications, meets the minimum manufacturer's requirements for the selected operating system, and requires network connectivity to reach a server or host system where some, or even the majority, of the processing takes place.

CramQuiz

3.8 – Given a scenario, select and configure appropriate components for a custom PC configuration to meet customer specifications or needs

Standard Thick Client

A standard thick client is effectively a PC. It is much more common in the workplace than the thin client. Unlike a thin client, a thick client performs the bulk of data processing operations by itself and uses a drive to store the OS, files, user profile, and so on. In comparison to thin clients and the somewhat centralized computing, with a thick client, a typical local area network of PCs would be known as *distributed computing*, where the processing load is dispersed more evenly among all the computers. There are still servers, of course, but the thick client has more power and capabilities compared to the thin client. Distributed computing is by far the more common method today. When using a thick client, it's important to verify that the thick client meets the recommended requirements for the selected OS.

An example of a standard thick client is a desktop computer running Windows 10 and Microsoft Office, and offers web browsing and the ability to easily install software. This standard thick client should meet (or exceed) the minimum requirements for Windows 10, including a 1-GHz 64-bit CPU, 2 GB of RAM, and 20 GB of free hard drive space.

> **Note**
>
> Personally, I always recommend exceeding the minimum requirements as much as possible; and an SSD can't hurt either.

> **ExamAlert**
>
> A standard thick client runs desktop applications such as Microsoft Office and meets the manufacturer's recommended requirements for the selected operating system. The majority of processing takes place on the thick client itself.

Cram Quiz

Answer these questions. The answers follow the last question. If you cannot answer these questions correctly, consider reading this section again until you can.

1. Which of the following is the best type of custom computer for use with Pro Tools?

   ○ **A.** Graphic/CAD/CAM design workstation

   ○ **B.** Audio/video editing workstation

   ○ **C.** Gaming PC

   ○ **D.** Virtualization workstation

3.8 – Given a scenario, select and configure appropriate components for a custom PC configuration to meet customer specifications or needs

CramQuiz

2. Which of the following would include a gigabit NIC and a RAID array?

   ○ **A.** Gaming PC

   ○ **B.** Audio/video editing workstation

   ○ **C.** Thin client

   ○ **D.** NAS

3. Your organization needs to run Windows in a virtual environment. The OS is expected to require a huge amount of resources for a powerful application it will run. What should you install Windows to?

   ○ **A.** Type 2 hypervisor

   ○ **B.** Gaming PC

   ○ **C.** Type 1 hypervisor

   ○ **D.** Thin client

Cram Quiz Answers

1. **B.** The audio/video editing workstation is the type of custom computer that would use Pro Tools, Logic Pro X, and other music and video editing programs.

2. **D.** A NAS (network attached storage) device will allow users to access files and stream media; it normally has a gigabit NIC and a RAID array. The rest of the answers will most likely include a gigabit network connection, but not a RAID array.

3. **C.** If the virtual operating system needs a lot of resources, the best bet is a "bare metal" Type 1 hypervisor. Type 2 hypervisors run on top of an operating system and therefore are not as efficient with resources. Gaming PCs have lots of resources but are not meant to run virtual environments. Thin clients have the least amount of resources.

3.9 – Given a scenario, install and configure common devices

This section is about doing basic configurations of desktops and mobile devices. A lot of what is covered in this section is fairly basic and may have been covered elsewhere in the book. Also, a good deal of it probably is well-known to a lot of you readers. So, I've decided to keep it brief and explain things with a "train the trainer" mindset. As a technician, you will often be called upon to explain to users how to use a computer, connect peripherals, and configure basic settings. Allow me to share some of my training knowledge with you to make the process more efficient and pleasant for everyone involved.

Desktop Devices and Settings

The setups of thin and thick clients can differ from a hardware and connectivity standpoint. The main difference is that the thick client has a hard drive (and additional hardware). But generally, they use the same types of ports and peripherals, such as keyboards, mice, monitors, and wired and wireless network connections.

Thin and thick clients might even run the same operating system. The real difference is how the operating system is "installed" and how it runs. For example, a typical thick client has its operating system installed locally, to a hard drive that is internal to the computer. But a thin client doesn't use a hard drive. Instead, it either gets its OS from a server (over the network or from the cloud) or uses an embedded OS image stored in flash memory. In the more common case of a server, the concept is that the thin client requires limited resources, but this means the server must have a greater amount of resources to support the thin client's needs: OS, apps, and data. Quite often this means virtualization and the use of backend products from Citrix, Microsoft, AWS, and others.

Regardless of whether we use thin or thick clients, the basic settings and account setup is going to be very similar. Once everything has been connected and the operating systems have been set up, the user needs to perform an initial login. The user will usually be required to enter a username and password, and possibly use other authentication methods such as biometric data. If the computer is a member of a domain (for example, a Windows 10 client connecting to a Windows Server 2016), then the user will have to select the domain to log on to. This is normally listed directly below the username and password.

For initial logins, the user will often be prompted to go through account setup. Typical setup questions include: "What country are you from?"; "What language would you like to use?"; and "What time zone are you located in?" Then, there may be additional configuration questions based on video, the Internet connection the user would like to use, and so on. All of this information is stored in a user profile, so that the user doesn't have to reconfigure everything after each login. This setup is virtually the same irrespective of the OS you use: Windows, macOS, or Linux.

One of the things I like to tell users is to select a strong password and commit it to memory right away before first logging in. It's also a good idea to write a setup guide—a short document that explains step-by-step how the user can first start using their computer. This type of documentation might be required if your organization is compliant with certain regulations or standards.

Laptop Configurations and Settings

Laptops and Chromebooks have some added features such as the touchpad and touchscreen. These are configured for the average user by default, but in some cases, a device might automatically attempt to calibrate itself based on the user during the initial login, potentially asking the user to tap, drag, and perform other motions. If not, then these devices can be configured in the Control Panel (in Windows), and **Settings > Device** (in Chrome OS). For example, Figure 14.2 displays the Mouse Properties window in Windows 10. It shows a Synaptics touchpad device being used by a laptop. Configuration of these is similar to the configuration of a mouse—which is why Windows usually places it in the Mouse Properties—but you might have additional configurations for touch sensitivity and the types of two-finger or multi-finger gestures. Often, a touchpad can be disabled from one of the tabs in the Mouse Properties window as well.

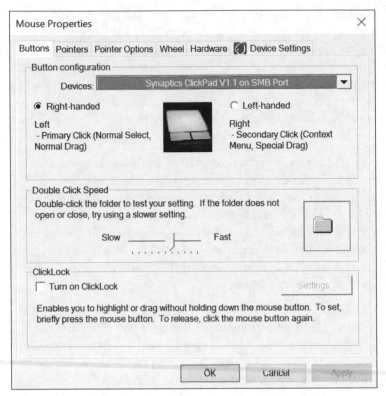

FIGURE 14.2   **Typical touchpad Mouse Properties in Windows**

When working with users, teach them about the primary click and the secondary click (also known as alternate click). For the right-handed user, the primary click is the left-click; for the left-handed user, the primary click is the right-click. As shown in Figure 14.2, a touchpad's buttons are usually on the bottom, as opposed to a mouse, which normally has them at the top. Teach users that they can usually tap and drag on today's touchpads in the same way that they would with a touchscreen (which almost everyone knows how to do).

Speaking of touchscreens, there are some that can have the touch sensitivity increased or decreased, but many (as of the writing of this book) have a set pressure sensitivity configuration that either cannot be changed or is hidden deep within the OS. However, the touchscreen orientation can be modified for landscape or portrait mode (and locked into place), and some touchscreens can be configured to work better with a stylus instead of a finger. Once again, teach users how to tap, drag, pinch, expand, and perform two-finger scrolls and other multi-finger gestures.

A user should also be trained on how to install applications (if he/she has the ability to do so!), synchronize data, perform initial account setup, and connect to wireless networks. Most of these things we discuss elsewhere in the book. The basic steps for these are virtually the same whether a user account is Apple, Microsoft, or Google based. But there are several things to remember:

▶ When a user first logs on to a computer, that user will need to know the username (which could be an e-mail address or common name) and the password. Complex and lengthy passwords can be difficult for some users to remember and often result in help desk and tech support calls. Train the user to memorize a password when it is first selected by going over it again and again in his or her mind.

▶ To access the Internet, a user might be required to connect to a wireless network. Make it easy for the user to remember the wireless network name (SSID) and the password (pre-shared key or PSK). If the password is in some way delivered to the user, make sure that the password becomes deleted or unavailable after 24 hours. If any passwords are written down, make sure that they are shredded after memorization.

▶ Apps can be downloaded from a variety of locations: the Google Play Store, the Apple App Store, the Microsoft Store, and so on—it all depends on what OS is being used. Train the user to be very careful when selecting an app, and consider locking mechanisms that disallow users from installing apps at all; that is, if they aren't part of the OS design by default.

▶ Know that many operating systems and their associated apps will by default save files that are created to the cloud. Train the user as to how this works and that this type of file save happens automatically (auto-save). However, a user can opt to save documents locally (if storage is available). Teach them to find the "save as" icon or use F12 on the keyboard, or Ctrl+S.

▶ Most companies and their OSes set up new accounts to synchronize to the cloud automatically. That means that settings and data can be transferred from one device to another. Teach users how this works and—for older users—how this is a departure from the way user profiles had been approached for decades. If the account can follow the user, then the settings and data can follow as well, because they are all stored on the cloud. But a user can go further, for example, synchronizing across different systems and programs: for example, Microsoft Outlook with Gmail, or Thunderbird with Gmail, or going from Apple to Google. This is where it can get a bit more difficult for the user and the tech because tech organizations like to keep everything in house. Just remember, there's always a way to connect systems, synchronize across platforms, and use one provider's account with another provider's OS and apps.

Cram Quiz

Answer these questions. The answers follow the last question. If you cannot answer
these questions correctly, consider reading this section again until you can.

1. You have set up a user to work at a thin client. They will be accessing the OS
   image and data from a Windows Server 2016 as well as data from the Google
   Cloud. Which of the following does this configuration *not* require? (Select the two
   best answers.)

   - A. Network connection
   - B. CPU
   - C. M.2
   - D. Virtualization
   - E. SSD

2. A customer has a brand new Chromebook and needs help configuring it. Which of
   the following should you help the user with? (Select the three best answers.)

   - A. Touchpad
   - B. Initial account setup
   - C. Registry
   - D. Touchscreen
   - E. App Store applications
   - F. Task Manager

Cram Quiz Answers

1. **C and E.** This configuration will not need a hard drive, be it M.2 or other SSD.
   Thin clients are meant to either use an OS that is embedded in RAM (or other
   similar memory) or, more often, grab an image from a server, often as a virtual
   machine. To do so, the thin client will need a network connection (wired or
   wireless), and every computer needs a CPU.

2. **A, B, and D.** You should show the user how to configure the touchpad and
   touchscreen, and guide the user through the initial account setup. Chrome OS
   is a fairly simple system compared to Windows and other operating systems. To
   configure devices, simply go to the "Home" or app launcher button, then Settings,
   then Devices. The registry is a Windows configuration tool—even if this was a
   Windows computer, the typical user has no place in the registry. The App Store is
   Apple's application download site. Google uses the Play Store. The Task Manager
   is another Windows utility. Consider writing a short user guide in Word document
   format if you have multiple users accessing the same type of system for the first
   time. Write it once, and train many!

CHAPTER 15

Printers and Multifunction Devices

This chapter covers the following A+ 220-1001 exam objectives:

▶ **3.10** — Given a scenario, configure SOHO multifunction devices/ printers and settings.

▶ **3.11** — Given a scenario, install and maintain various print technologies.

Printers are the number two output device, behind video displays. Their main purpose is to output paper versions of what you see on the computer screen. Many printers connect via USB, but you will also encounter printers that connect directly to the network (be it wired or wirelessly)— and on the rare occasion, you might encounter printers that connect via infrared or to serial or parallel ports. Some printers also act as fax machines, copiers, and scanners; these are known as multifunction devices or multifunction printers.

Generally, the different versions of Windows behave the same when it comes to printing. So whenever one operating system is mentioned in this chapter, the same applies to the other operating systems, unless otherwise stated.

While there is a worldwide initiative to reduce the usage of paper, printers are still an important part of the business world. Be ready to install and troubleshoot them.

3.10 – Given a scenario, configure SOHO multifunction devices/printers and settings

ExamAlert

Objective 3.10 concentrates on the following concepts: use appropriate drivers for a given operating system (configuration settings such as duplex, collate, orientation and quality); device sharing; and public/shared devices.

The small office/home office (SOHO) multifunction device is usually a printer that can do other things such as scan and save documents, copy documents, fax information, and more. However, the more important concept of the two for the A+ exam is printing, so we will focus mainly on that throughout this objective.

Printer Configuration Settings

Configuration of printers can be done in one of three places:

- ▶ The first is the small display that might be included on a printer; these displays are more common on laser printers. These menu-driven displays are usually user-friendly and intuitive.

- ▶ The second is within a printer's web interface (if it is a network printer); this is often accessed through a web browser.

- ▶ The third—and the one that I'd like to focus on in this section—is within Windows, specifically by double-clicking the printer icon within the Devices and Printers window and by accessing the appropriate properties or preferences page of the printer.

To open a printer in Windows, simply double-click it. To manage its properties and preferences, right-click the printer in question and select **Printer properties** or select **Printing preferences** (or another similar name). If you work with printers often, consider placing a shortcut to the printer or printers on the desktop, Quick Launch, or pin it to the taskbar. Several items can be configured by double-clicking the printer and by using the Printer properties window, including managing print jobs, setting the priority of the printer, configuring the print spooler, and managing permissions.

Basic Printer Configuration Settings

A typical print job is simple—one printed page, printed on one side, on 8 1/2 by 11-inch paper in portrait mode, and at the standard 600 DPI resolution. For example, you might print a typical document (such as a resume) this way. However, there are many occasions where the typical settings are not enough. There are four basic printer configuration settings you should know for the exams: duplexing, collating, orientation, and print quality. They are generally found in the Printing preferences or Printer properties section. Let's briefly describe each one now.

First is *duplexing*. This means printing on both sides of the paper. Some organizations require this (for most print jobs), establishing policies in their efforts to reduce paper consumption; however, most printers are not set to duplex by default. In Windows, this needs to be configured in the Printer properties window. This might simply be called "print on both sides." Once enabled, you might also see this on the main print screen when you go to perform a print job—it might be called "manual duplex."

Next is *collating*. If you print a single job, collating is not an issue. But it's when you print multiple copies of the same job that collating might become necessary. Historically, multiple copies of the same print job would print out all of page 1, then all of page 2, then all of page 3, and so on. It was up to the user to manually arrange, or collate, these pages. However, as printers became more sophisticated, they were equipped with the processing power to collate the jobs, sorting them as page 1, page 2, page 3, and so on, and then moving on to the next copy of the entire job. This, of course, saves a lot of time for the user. Some printers are set this way by default. Others have to be configured to do so. An example of this configuration is shown in Figure 15.1. This setting is often found in the advanced section of the printing preferences. The figure shows Copy Count set to 5 and that collating is enabled. Once it is enabled, you can also select it from the main print screen when you go to print a document.

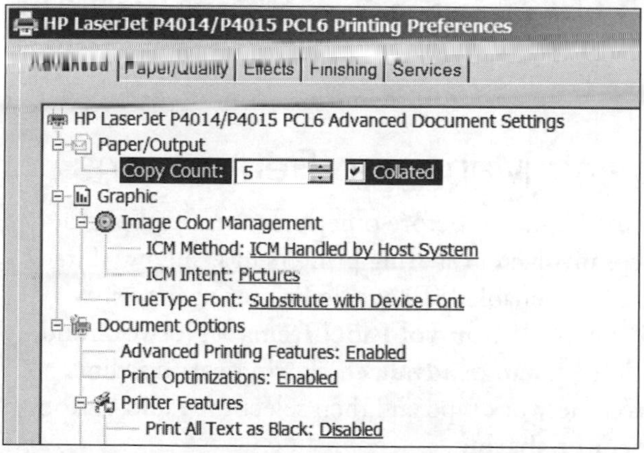

FIGURE 15.1 **Collating on a typical printer**

Then we have *orientation*. This is the method of positioning a printed page and is based on whether the page is going to be viewed vertically (portrait) or horizontally (landscape). This can be set permanently from the printer preferences page, but it can also be set manually when you go to print a single document. Often, it will be found in the "layout" section. Most documents are printed in portrait mode (such as a report or a resume done in a word proces-sor), but sometimes you need to print a spreadsheet or a slide presentation, which is best done in landscape mode.

Finally, we have print *quality*. This is the print resolution, as measured in DPI. 600 DPI or higher is considered to be letter quality and acceptable as a professional document. But you might want an even better quality (1200 or 2400 DPI), especially if your document includes graphics. This can usually be configured for a default number of DPI within the advanced section of the Printing preferences, but it can also be configured from the print window, often using more generic terms (such as draft, normal, and best).

Take a look at your Printing preferences, Printer properties pages, and the main print screen (when you go to print a document) and view the four configuration settings we just discussed. Even if you don't have a printer, you can set up a false printer on your system by adding the printer in the Devices and Printers window in the Control Panel. Typically, I suggest selecting any one of the newer HP laser printers from the list as a fake printer. You can then access its printer properties just like you would on a printer that is actually installed to the computer or network.

> **ExamAlert**
>
> Know the four printer configuration settings: duplex, collate, orientation, and quality.

Sharing Printers and Managing Permissions

A networked printer must first be shared before other users can send print jobs to it. There are two steps involved in sharing printers in Windows. First, printer sharing in general must be enabled. To enable Printer Sharing in Windows, go to **Control Panel > All Control Panel Items > Network and Sharing Center**. Then click the **Change advanced sharing settings** link. Click the down arrow for your network type and then select the radio button labeled **Turn on file and printer sharing**.

> **Note**
>
> You can also make a computer's devices visible when Windows is first installed. We'll discuss this and network discovery in the Windows networking section of this book.

Next, the individual printer needs to be shared. This can be done in the Sharing tab of the Printer properties window. Check the **Share This Printer** checkbox and give the printer a share name. Note that the share name does not need to be the same as the printer name. Click OK, and the printer should show up as shared within the Printers window.

Permissions can be set for a printer in the Security tab of the Printer properties window. Users and groups can be added in this window, and the appropriate permission can be assigned, including Print, Manage Printers, and Manage Documents. Standard users normally are assigned the Print permission, whereas administrators get all permissions, enabling them to pause the printer or cancel all documents (Manage Printers) and pause, cancel, and restart individual documents. For more information on permissions, see Chapter 33, "Windows Security Settings and Best Practices."

Local Versus Network Printers

A local printer is one that connects directly to a computer, normally by USB, or on rare occasions, by RS-232 serial (DB9M) or parallel (DB25F) connections. When a user works at a computer, that computer is considered to be the local computer. So, when a printer is connected to that computer, it is known as the local printer.

A network printer is one that connects directly to the network (usually Ethernet) or to a print server device. Network printers are shared by more than one user on the computer network. Usually, network printers are given an IP address and become yet another *host* on the network. If the printer connects directly to the network, it is usually by way of a built-in RJ45 port on the printer, just as a computer's network card connects to the network. A print server could be a computer or smaller black box device. Many SOHO routers offer integrated print server capabilities. In this case, the printer connects via USB to the print server/router and a special piece of software is installed on any client computers that want to print to that printer.

Network printing can also be accomplished wirelessly on most of today's printers. This can be done via Wi-Fi (802.11 a, b, g, n, and ac) or by Bluetooth. The former is more common in a wireless LAN, where everything connects to a wireless access point—this is referred to as infrastructure mode. The latter is more common with mobile devices and, in this case, no wireless access point exists—also known as ad hoc mode. Remember that Wi-Fi will typically have greater range than Bluetooth.

Then there is cloud-based printing. It is altogether possible today to harness the power of the cloud to print remotely. You might have a document you need printed to a printer in a network in another city. If your organization has implemented a cloud-based solution, you can do this simply by selecting the printer in a drop-down menu. We'll discuss cloud-based technologies more in Chapter 16, "Cloud Computing and Client-side Virtualization."

If a network printer is being controlled by Windows, we generally rely on direct TCP/IP connections. However, printers that are controlled by macOS might also make use of the networking service Bonjour, and use AirPrint to automatically locate and download drivers for printers. Bonjour, also known as zero-configuration networking, enables automatic discovery of devices and services on a local network using industry-standard IP protocols. AirPrint is an Apple technology that helps you create full-quality printed output without the need to download or install drivers.

Regardless of how the printer is connected, and how the user connects to the printer, data privacy concerns should be addressed. An insecure printer can retain copies of information that could be accessible to anyone with a little know-how. The printer might cache information to memory, or to a print server's hard drive. This caching should be cleared at least every day, perhaps more often depending on the policy of your organization. As an administrator, you can also consider implementing user authentication for the printer or print server, ultimately requiring a person to present credentials of some kind, which could range from a basic PIN to a username/password and biometric combination. We'll discuss this concept more in Chapter 31, "Physical and Logical Security." For now, remember that personal and confidential data can be stored in many places, and that those locations should be organized and secured accordingly.

Cram Quiz

Answer these questions. The answers follow the last question. If you cannot answer these questions correctly, consider reading this section again until you can.

1. Where would you go in Windows to enable printer sharing?
   - ○ **A.** Network Connections
   - ○ **B.** Network and Sharing Center
   - ○ **C.** The printer's OSD
   - ○ **D.** Bonjour

2. Your printer supports printing to both sides of paper. What should you enable in the Printing preferences?

   ○ **A.** Collate

   ○ **B.** Orientation

   ○ **C.** Duplex

   ○ **D.** Quality

3. Which of the following address printer data privacy concerns? (Select the two best answers.)

   ○ **A.** Implementing user authentication on the device

   ○ **B.** Ad hoc mode

   ○ **C.** AirPrint

   ○ **D.** Clearing the cache

Cram Quiz Answers

1. **B.** The Network and Sharing Center in Windows is where printer sharing is enabled. Network Connections is the window that shows the Ethernet and Wi-Fi connections a PC has to the network. Windows sharing has to be done in Windows; it can't be done from the printer's on-screen display (OSD). Bonjour is a macOS service that enables automatic discovery of devices on the LAN; it can also be run on Windows.

2. **C.** Duplexing (as it relates to printers) means to print to both sides. Collating means printing multiple copies of a document's pages in sequence, instead of printing all of the copies of one page at a time. Orientation is how the print job is displayed on the paper; it could be portrait (vertically—the default) or landscape (horizontal). Quality refers to the clarity of the print job, usually measured in dots per inch (DPI)—the higher the DPI the better.

3. **A and D.** Implementing user authentication for the printer or print server (PIN or password) and clearing the cache on the printer both address printer data privacy concerns. Bluetooth ad hoc mode network printing can be used by mobile devices where no wireless access point exists. AirPrint is an Apple technology for macOS and iOS used to automatically locate and download drivers for printers.

3.11 – Given a scenario, install and maintain various print technologies

ExamAlert

Objective 3.11 focuses on the following: laser printers, inkjet printers, thermal printers, impact printers, virtual printing, and 3D printers.

Businesses utilize several types of printers. The most common business-oriented printer is the laser printer. However, inkjet printers are more prevalent in the home due to their lower cost and their capability to print in color with excellent resolution. A technician might also encounter thermal, impact, and 3D printers. This section describes those five types of printers and how they function. We'll also discuss virtual printing and the basic installation of printers.

Types of Printers

Each type of printer has its own characteristics that affect how a technician installs, configures, and troubleshoots it. The most common type of printer used at a business is the laser printer; this type of printer also happens to be the most complicated and difficult to troubleshoot. We'll discuss troubleshooting later in the book, but to be a good troubleshooter, you should know the technology well. Let's examine this technology now.

Laser Printers

Laser printers can produce high-quality text and graphics on cut sheets of paper; printers that print to individual pieces of paper are known as *page printers*. The bulk of laser printers print in black, but there are also color laser printers (which, of course, are more expensive). They are called laser printers because inside the printer is a laser beam that projects an image of the item to be printed onto an electrically charged drum; this image is later transferred to the paper. Text and images that are shown on paper are created from electrically charged toner, which is a type of powder stored in a replaceable toner cartridge. The type of toner used can vary from one brand to the next, but they all work essentially the same way.

Known also as a photoelectric or photosensitive drum, the laser printer drum is at the center of the whole laser printing process, but there are a couple of other important components, including the primary corona wire, transfer corona wire, fuser assembly, and of course, the laser itself. Figure 15.2 shows these components.

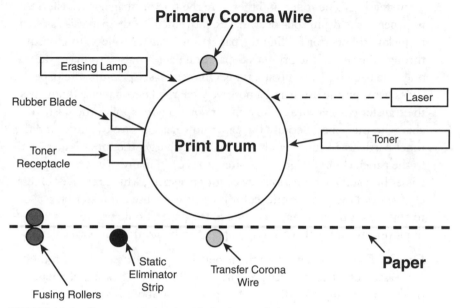

FIGURE 15.2   **Components involved in the laser printing process**

The laser printing process that a laser printer goes through is sometimes referred to as an imaging process (including in Objective 3.11). Knowledge of this process can help you when it comes time to troubleshoot and/or maintain a laser printer.

The following list describes the typical laser printing process:

1. **Processing:** The text or image to be printed is sent to the printer, where a processor recalculates it and stores it in RAM while the printer readies itself for the ordeal of laser printing! Note that additional processing may be done at the local computer that initiated the printing.

2. **Charging:** Also known as conditioning, a negative charge is applied to the drum by the primary corona wire, which is powered by a high-voltage power supply within the printer.

3. **Exposing:** Also known as writing, the laser is activated and "writes" to the drum as it spins. Where the laser hits the drum, it dissipates the negative charge toward the center of the drum that is grounded. The "exposed" areas of the drum now have a lesser negative charge. (By the way, the drum is also known as an imaging drum.)

4. **Developing:** The surface of the drum that was previously exposed to the laser is now applied with negatively charged toner. This toner has a higher charge than the areas of the drum that were written to.

5. **Transferring:** The toner, and therefore the text or image, is transferred to paper as the drum rolls over it. The movement of the paper is assisted by pickup rollers (for feeding the paper) and transfer rollers (to move it through the rest of the printer). Separation pads are used to make sure only one page is picked up at a time. On many laser printers, the paper slides between the drum and a positively charged corona wire (known as the transfer corona wire). The transfer corona wire applies the positive charge to the paper. Because the paper now has a positive charge, and the toner particles on the drum have a negative charge, the toner is attracted to the paper. (For voltages, opposites attract.) In many printers the paper passes by a static elimination device (often a strip), which removes excess charge from the paper. Some color laser printers use a transfer belt to apply the various layers of colors to the paper. Some printers use a duplexing assembly that allows the paper to be printed on both sides.

6. **Fusing:** The toner is fused to the paper. The paper passes through the fuser assembly that includes pressurized rollers and a heating element that can reach approximately 400 degrees F (or about 200 degrees C).

7. **Cleaning:** A rubber blade removes excess toner from the drum as it spins. An erasing lamp removes any leftover charge on the drum, bringing it to zero volts. The printer is now ready for another print job.

> **ExamAlert**
>
> Know the steps of the laser printing process (also known as the imaging process).

> **ExamAlert**
>
> Know that laser printer components include the imaging drum, fuser assembly, transfer belt, transfer roller, pickup rollers, separation pads, and duplexing assembly.

In some laser printers, the drum, laser, and primary corona wire are contained within the toner cartridge. Issues that are caused by these components can usually be fixed just by replacing the toner cartridge.

> **Note**
>
> Toner cartridges are replaceable; they are known as *consumables*. Whatever material it is that actually prints onto paper is usually considered a consumable, regardless of the type of printer.

Laser printers have some advantages over other printers:

▶ **Speed:** A laser printer can print anywhere from 10 to 100 pages per minute (ppm), depending on the model and whether it is a color or black-and-white laser printer.

▶ **Print quality:** The laser printer commonly prints at 600 dots per inch (DPI), which is considered letter quality, but 1200 DPI and 2400 DPI resolution printers are also available.

> **ExamAlert**
>
> Of all printer types, the laser printer is considered to have the lowest cost per page, making it an excellent long-term printer choice for businesses.

Maintenance of laser printers is vital. You should periodically inspect the laser printer, and replace the toner cartridge if necessary. Many laser printers have a counter that can be set to notify you when the printer has printed out X number of pages; for example, 50,000. Once the printer gets to that point, you should perform maintenance or, at the very least, carefully inspect the internals of the printer. Most laser printer manufacturers offer maintenance kits that include a variety of components, which we will discuss more in Chapter 21, "Troubleshooting Printers." If you do use the maintenance kit, reset the counter when you are finished. You will find that this is similar to the maintenance counter of a vehicle.

Another Automotive Parallel

You will find that a manufacturer will often set a relatively low number for the laser printer's counter, similar to how an automobile manufacturer will set the mileage maintenance counter to a number on the low end of the maintenance range. To put it nicely, the manufacturer is assuming the worst conditions for your printer. While this might be suitable for dirty environments, the average office printer can often last longer than the manufacturer's recommended time without using a maintenance kit. The beauty of this is that you can set the counter to a higher number if you think it is appropriate, which ultimately can save time and money for your organization. To be sure, keep a log of when printers were maintained, and when failures occur. If failures occur earlier than expected on the whole, consider decreasing the counter once again.

During your maintenance of the printer, you should clean it up, including the outside cover, the trays, the bin where the cartridge sits, and possibly the rollers. After maintenance is complete, be sure to calibrate the printer. This is usually a subroutine that is built into the printer's firmware; you might also be able to initiate it from Windows. Calibration allows you to set the horizontal and vertical printing coordinates and margins so that text and images appear clear and straight.

Inkjet Printers

Inkjet printers are common in small offices, home offices, and for personal use. They can print documents but more commonly print photographs and graphical information in color; most of the time, they connect to the computer by way of USB or Wi-Fi.

The inkjet printer works by propelling ink onto various sizes of paper. Many inkjets store ink in multiple ink cartridges that are consumable; they have to be replaced when empty. Some inkjet printers stop operating if just one of the ink cartridges is empty. Two common types of inkjet printers are the thermal inkjet and the piezoelectric inkjet:

▶ **Thermal inkjets:** These account for the bulk of consumer inkjets and are the more recognizable type of inkjet printer. To move the ink to the paper, heat is sent through the ink cartridge, forming a bubble (known as the thermal bubble) that pushes the ink onto the paper; immediately afterward, another charge of ink is readied. The reservoir of ink is within the ink cartridge; this is where the heat transfer occurs. HP and Canon develop many models of thermal inkjet printers. Don't confuse thermal inkjets with thermal printers.

▶ **Piezoelectric inkjets:** These account for the bulk of commercial inkjets. The printing processes within a piezoelectric inkjet and a thermal inkjet are similar; however, the piezo inkjet applies current to the ink material, causing it to change shape and size, forcing the ink onto the paper. The reservoir of ink is in another area outside of where the current is applied. This process enables longer print head life as compared to thermal inkjets. Epson develops many models of piezoelectric inkjet printers. Piezoelectric inkjets can also be found in manufacturing assembly lines.

The inkjet print process is fairly simple:

1. The paper or other media is pulled or moved into position by a roller and feeder mechanism or it's moved into position by an assembly line's conveyor belt (as with some piezoelectric inkjets).

2. The print head, located on a mechanical arm, moves across the paper, assisted by a carriage and belt system. The print head delivers black and colored ink from the ink cartridges as directed by the print driver.

3. At the end of the line, the paper or media is advanced and the print head either reverses direction and continues to print (often referred to as Hi-Speed mode) or returns to the left margin before printing continues. In printers that allow for duplexing, a duplexing assembly refeeds the paper into the printer for printing on the other side.

4. After the page is completed, the paper or other media is ejected.

> **ExamAlert**
>
> Know that inkjet printer components include ink cartridge, print head, roller, feeder, duplexing assembly, carriage, and belt.

Maintenance of an inkjet printer is often much simpler than with a laser printer. Check the ink cartridges periodically by using the printer's on-screen display (OSD), or within Windows (if possible), or physically inspect them if necessary. If one or more cartridges are low, be prepared to replace them. If there is a buildup of residue on the print cartridge, clean it with a manufacturer-supplied solution, or consider using a 50/50 mix of isopropyl alcohol and water. (A box of cotton swabs is handy in your toolkit!) Inkjet printers should be periodically calibrated so that horizontal and vertical imagery lines up properly, and so colors are blended appropriately. This should always be done when cartridges are removed and replaced. While inspecting and maintaining an inkjet printer, look for any bits of paper that might have been caught up in the rollers or feeder and remove them, clearing any paper jams that might have occurred.

Thermal Printers

Thermal printers produce text and images by heating specially coated thermal paper. It is typical to see thermal printers used in point-of-sale (POS) systems, gas station pumps, and so on. Thermal printers consist of the following parts:

▶ **Thermal head:** This generates the heat and takes care of printing to the paper.

▶ **Platen:** This is the rubber roller that feeds the paper past the print head.

▶ **Spring:** This applies pressure to the print head, which brings the print head into contact with the paper.

▶ **Circuit board:** This controls the mechanism that moves the print head.

To print, special thermal paper is inserted between the thermal head and the platen. The printer sends current to the thermal head, which, in turn, generates heat. The heat activates the thermo-sensitive coloring layer of the thermal paper, which becomes the image.

Maintenance of a thermal printer includes inspecting the paper tray and replacing the paper, cleaning the heating element, and removing any debris that can be left behind by the thermal printing process.

Impact Printers

Impact printers use force to transfer ink to paper (for example, a print head striking a ribbon with paper directly behind it—similar to a typewriter). This type of printer is somewhat deprecated although certain environments might still use it: auto repair centers, warehouses, accounting departments, and so on.

One type of impact printer, the daisy wheel, utilizes a wheel with many petals, each of which has a letter form (an actual letter) at the tip of the petal. These strike against the ribbon, impressing ink upon the paper that is situated behind the ribbon. But by far the most common type of impact printer is the dot matrix.

Dot-matrix printers are also known as line printers because they print text one line at a time and can keep printing over a long roll of paper, as opposed to page printers that print to cut sheets of paper. The paper is fed into the printer using a tractor-feed mechanism—many dot-matrix printers use paper that has an extra perforated space with holes on each side that allow the paper to be fed into the printer. Dot-matrix printers use a matrix of pins that work together to create characters, instead of using a form letter. The print head that contains these pins strikes the ribbon that, in turn, places the ink on the paper. Print heads come with either 9 pins or 24 pins; the 24-pin version offers better quality, known as *near letter quality (NLQ)*. Dot-matrix printers are loud and slow but are cheap to maintain.

> **ExamAlert**
>
> Know that impact printer components include print head, ribbon, and tractor feed. Also know that impact paper is used.

Maintenance of an impact printer includes replacing the ribbon, replacing the print head, replacing the paper, and checking for bits of the perforated paper along the tractor feed mechanism and elsewhere in the printer.

3D Printers

3D printing is when various materials—often plastic—are joined together to build a three-dimensional object. It is done by designing the object on the computer (with CAD and slicing software) and, ultimately, exporting the appropriate files to the correct 3D printer. The technology is often used to create prototypes of products to be later manufactured in bulk. However, it can be used to actually create commercial products as well.

> **ExamAlert**
>
> Know that 3D printers use a special plastic filament.

3D printing can be accomplished by implementing one of a few processes, namely fused deposition modeling (FDM) or laser sintering. FDM is an additive process where materials are fed into an extruder, superheated, and then applied on top of a substrate, layer by layer, to create 3D shapes which harden immediately. Laser sintering uses a laser that compacts a piece of material—such as nylon—using heat and/or pressure, and binds the materials to create the structure.

> **Note**
>
> 3D "printing" is not considered an accurate name by some, but it is used widely. You will also see the name *additive manufacturing*, among others.

3D printers are made by several manufacturers. Some use proprietary processes and file types, while others use standardized processes and files. Either way, the device is usually of cuboid shape with one or more glass walls allowing the user to view the manufacturing process. The center of the device contains a platform (or build plate) with open space above it for the item to be built, and an extruder moves about that area in three dimensions (X, Y, and Z axes).

What's really important for the A+ tech is how to install, maintain, and troubleshoot printers. Let's discuss installation and maintenance briefly; we will get to printer troubleshooting in Chapter 21.

Many 3D printers can connect via USB, Wi-Fi, and Ethernet. These printers are controlled by a computer running an operating system such as Windows 7 and higher or OS X 10.9 and higher. The computer itself should meet the recommended requirements for the various design software—such as CAD software and slicing software. Some manufacturers of 3D printers make their own software, while others use third-party programs. Be ready to install the different programs necessary, and to even work with design templates, many of which are freely available on the Internet.

When first installing a 3D printer, and periodically afterward, be sure to update the firmware for the device. Next, periodically make sure the build plate is level; this is usually done via the LCD panel. Then, lubricate, tighten, and re-align the rods and pulleys periodically. Finally, clean the device including the extruder's drive gear, the build plate, and so on. Users *should* clean up after themselves when completing a 3D print job, but you and I know that this is a utopian concept, especially given the fast pace of engineering and prototyping work, so be ready to clean up excess plastic filament from the device.

Virtual Printing

Let's go beyond the physical printer and briefly discuss virtual printing. Virtual printing is when a document, image, or web page is "printed" to a file format and stored on the computer instead of being printed on paper at a printer. There are several reasons to do this, including accessibility, compatibility, storage of documents to be printed later, and so on. There are four types of virtual printing you should know for the exam: print to file, print to XPS, print to PDF, and print to image. Let's begin with the oldest type and a great fallback solution: print to file.

Print to File

Let's say that you finish creating a document at your home office on a PC but you don't have a printer to print the document to and you *do* want to print the document so you can submit it to someone at work. Let's also imagine that your organization's main office has a couple of printers but none of the computers have the application you use, and purchasing another license for that application is too expensive. One possible solution is to print to file, which stores the document as a printable file that can then be transported by flash drive or other means to a computer at the main workplace and printed from there.

Let's say this is a Microsoft Word document. You could select Print, as you normally would, and then instead of selecting a particular printer, you could select the Print to file checkbox. This then saves the file as a .prn file to be stored as you wish and can be printed from later. When you arrive at your workplace, you can print the file from the Command Prompt using the following sample syntax:

```
copy x:\filename.prn \\computername\printersharename
```

What does that mean? Well, you need to know several bits of information. First, you need to know the drive letter of the flash drive (or other storage medium) where the file is stored. I used "x:" as a variable, but it could be any letter. We'll say it's a flash drive that is using the F: drive letter. Next, you need to know the filename—we'll say it's "printjob1." Then you need the name of the computer that the printer is connected to (or controlled by). We'll say the printer is connected to a computer named "workstation3." Finally, you need to know the share name of the printer. (See the previous section on printer sharing.) Let's say the share name is "printer1." Now we have all the information we need and the syntax in this scenario would be

```
copy f:\printjob1.prn \\workstation3\printer1
```

> **Note**
>
> If the printer is connected directly to the network, you can forgo the computer-name\ printersharename and connect directly to the printer name or, better yet, its IP address (for example, \\192.168.1.150).

That "copies" the print job to the printer and prints it out to the best of its ability. And I say "best" because you might encounter several issues with print to file technology, including print failures, incorrect printing, ASCII printing, and so on. The technology is not without its quirks. That's why other, newer tech might be more often selected, such as printing to PDF and printing to XPS.

Print to XPS

Windows incorporates the XML Paper Specification (XPS) print path. The XPS spooler is meant to replace the standard Enhanced Metafile print spooler that Windows has used for years. XPS provides improved color and graphics support, support for the CMYK colorspace, and reduces the need for colorspace conversion.

This is implemented as the Microsoft XPS Document Writer that can be found in **Control Panel > Devices and Printers**. A document created within any application in Windows can be saved as an .xps file to be later viewed on any computer that supports XPS. It can also be printed from any computer that supports XPS but prints with proper fidelity only when the computer has an XPS-compliant printer. If you do not have an XPS printer, the functionality might need to be turned on within the Windows Features utility (a link that can be found in **Control Panel > All Control Panel Items > Programs and Features**).

In most cases, this solution will replace "print to file," but it is good to have print to file as a backup in case XPS fails or is not running on the computer in question.

Print to PDF

To make a document universally readable, you have several options. One of the most common is to convert it into Portable Document Format (PDF), also known as "print to PDF." The most common PDF-making software is Adobe Acrobat (which is a paid program), and Adobe also makes the most common PDF reader software (Adobe Acrobat Reader, which is free). However, there are other versions of PDF-making and PDF-reading software freely available on the Internet.

They all work in the same manner: as a virtual printer. If you want to convert a document into a PDF, there are several ways to do it. For example, in Microsoft Word you could go to **Save As** and then select **.PDF** from the list of file types, or you could go to **Print** and select **Microsoft Print to PDF** from the Printers list (and those are just a couple of available options that are built into Word). That then creates a file with a .pdf extension that can be distributed how you wish. As long as the target user has a PDF-reading program, he will be able to view the document without any need for the original program that the document was written on.

Print to Image

It is also possible to capture a document, web page, or even a window (or region) of the operating system as an image file. A simple example of this print-to-image technology can be found on any Windows computer simply by using the Print Screen button on the keyboard. The entire screen capture can then be pasted into the appropriate program. Going beyond this, screen capturing programs such as the Snipping Tool (included in Windows 7 and higher) and Snagit can be used to capture the entire screen, an individual window, a region of the screen, or even a scrolling web page as an image file. Programs such as this enable you to save the file as a .jpg, .gif, .tif, .png, and so on—just about any one of the commonly used graphic file extensions. These screen captures are also often referred to as screenshots. Most of the Windows screen captures you see in this book were produced with Snagit (a free trial version is available on the TechSmith website). So, it works great for instructional purposes and for documentation. However, you might also need to capture a particular set of data and send that final captured image to engineers, designers, marketers, and so on—anyone who does not have the program that you use installed on their computer.

Printer Installation and Drivers

When installing printers, focus on several things:

▶ **Compatibility:** Make sure that the printer is compatible with the version of Windows that runs on the computer that controls the printer. Check the Windows compatibility lists to verify this. If the printer is to connect to the network, make sure that it has the right type of compatible network adapter to do so.

▶ **Installing printer drivers:** Generally, the proper procedure is to install the printer driver to Windows before physically connecting the printer. However, if the driver already exists on the computer, the printer can simply be connected. Usually, the best bet is to use the driver that came on the disc with the printer or download the latest driver from the manufacturer's website. Verify whether the driver to be installed is the right one based on the version and edition of the operating system (for example, 32-bit or 64-bit versions of Windows, and Windows 10 versus Windows 7). Printer drivers are installed in a similar fashion to other drivers described in this book; it is performed in the Devices and Printers section of the Control Panel. Any current printers should be listed. From there, right-click anywhere in the work area and select "Add..." (the text will vary according to the version of Windows you are using).

▶ **Connecting the device:** In general, devices connecting via USB can be connected without turning the computer off. (That is, they are hot-swappable.) However, devices that connect to older parallel ports or serial ports require the computer to be shut down first. Plug the USB or other connector cable into the computer first, and then connect the printer to an AC outlet. (It's recommended to use a surge protector for printers, but it is *not* recommended to use a UPS for a laser printer due to the high draw of the laser printer.) Verify that the device turns on.

▶ **Calibrating the printer:** Color laser printers, inkjet printers, and multifunction printers might need to be calibrated before use. This involves aligning the printing mechanism to the paper and verifying color output. Usually the software that accompanies the printer guides a user through this process. In some cases, these calibration tests can be done via the small display on the printer.

▶ **Testing the printer:** First, test the printer by printing a test page in Windows. This is also done from the Devices and Printers window. Right-click the printer, select Printer properties, and then click the Print Test Page button on the General tab. The resulting page should show the operating system the local computer runs and various other configuration and driver information. If the page can be read properly and the Windows logo is using the correct colors, the test passed. Some printers offer a test page option on the display of the printer as well. After a test page has been printed, it might be wise to try printing within the most used applications as well, just to make sure they work properly. Some applications might behave differently, and some configurations of printers in Windows might cause a particular application to have print failures. I say it all the time: "Always remember to test! Your reputation depends on it!"

Cram Quiz

Answer these questions. The answers follow the last question. If you cannot answer these questions correctly, consider reading this section again until you can.

1. During which step of the laser printing/imaging process is the transfer corona wire involved?

   ○ **A.** Developing

   ○ **B.** Transferring

   ○ **C.** Fusing

   ○ **D.** Cleaning

2. Which stage of the laser printing/imaging process involves extreme heat?

   ○ **A.** Fusing

   ○ **B.** Transferring

   ○ **C.** Exposing

   ○ **D.** Writing

3. Which represents the proper order of the laser printing/imaging process?

○ **A.** Processing, charging, developing, exposing, fusing, transferring, cleaning

○ **B.** Developing, processing, charging, exposing, transferring, fusing, cleaning

○ **C.** Charging, exposing, developing, processing, transferring, fusing, cleaning

○ **D.** Processing, charging, exposing, developing, transferring, fusing, cleaning

4. Which of the following sets of parts is associated with inkjet printers?

○ **A.** Imaging drum, fuser assembly, transfer belt, transfer roller, pickup rollers, separation pads, duplexing assembly

○ **B.** Ink cartridge, print head, roller, feeder, duplexing assembly, carriage, and belt

○ **C.** Feed assembly, thermal heating unit, thermal paper

○ **D.** Print head, ribbon, tractor feed, impact paper

5. When finished installing a new printer and print drivers, what should you do? (Select all that apply.)

○ **A.** Calibrate the printer.

○ **B.** Install the print drivers.

○ **C.** Check for compatibility.

○ **D.** Print a test page.

Cram Quiz Answers

1. **B.** The transfer corona wire gets involved in the laser printing/imaging process during the transferring step.

2. **A.** The fusing step uses heat (up to 400 degrees Fahrenheit/200 degrees Celsius) and pressure to fuse the toner permanently to the paper.

3. **D.** The proper order of the laser printing/imaging process is processing, charging, exposing, developing, transferring, fusing, cleaning.

4. **B.** Inkjet printer components include ink cartridge, print head, roller, feeder, duplexing assembly, carriage, and belt. Imaging drum, fuser assembly, transfer belt, transfer roller, pickup rollers, separation pads, and duplexing assembly are associated with laser printers. Feed assembly, thermal heating unit, and thermal paper are associated with thermal printers. Print head, ribbon, tractor feed, and impact paper are associated with impact printers.

5. **A and D.** After the printer is installed (meaning it has been connected and the drivers have been installed), you should calibrate the printer (if necessary) and print a test page. You should also consider updating the firmware for the printer. Before starting the installation, you should check for compatibility with operating systems, applications, and so on.

Domain 4.0: Virtualization and Cloud Computing

CHAPTER 16 Cloud Computing and Client-side Virtualization

CHAPTER 16

Cloud Computing and Client-side Virtualization

This chapter covers the following A+ 220-1001 exam objectives:

▶ 4.1 – Compare and contrast cloud computing concepts.

▶ 4.2 – Given a scenario, set up and configure client-side virtualization.

Cloud computing and virtualization in general have grown by leaps and bounds for many years. These technologies have become so popular for businesses, organizations, and home users that they are now commonplace. You can't spend one day without connecting to some kind of cloud-based service or virtualized system.

The cloud can be defined as the suite of hardware and software— managed by a service provider or an organization—that provides data, applications, and other resources to users, often via the Internet. Virtualization is when a simulation of something is created that behaves in the same manner as the real thing. An example is a virtual machine (VM), which looks and behaves like a real computer and operating system. The difference? It exists virtually, meaning within another operating system. Virtualization is used extensively in today's networks and in the cloud. It is used to create virtual instances of servers and clients. In this chapter we'll focus on client-side virtualization.

One chapter is not nearly enough to even scratch the surface when it comes to the cloud and virtualization. However, for the A+ exams, you need only know the basics. Let's begin with cloud computing.

4.1 – Compare and contrast cloud computing concepts

> **ExamAlert**
>
> **Objective 4.1** concentrates on the following concepts: common cloud models, shared resources, rapid elasticity, on-demand, resource pooling, measured service, metered, off-site e-mail applications, cloud file storage services, virtual application streaming/cloud-based applications, and virtual desktop.

Cloud computing can be defined as a way of offering on-demand services that extend the capabilities of a person's computer or an organization's network. These might be free services, such as browser-based e-mail from providers such as Yahoo! and Gmail, and personal storage from providers such as Microsoft (OneDrive); they might also be offered on a pay-per-use basis, such as services that offer data access, data storage, infrastructure, and online gaming. A network connection of some sort is required to make the connection to the "cloud" and gain access to these services in real time.

Some of the benefits cloud-based services provide for organizations include lowered costs, less administration and maintenance, more reliability, increased scalability, and possible increased performance. A basic example of a cloud-based service would be browser-based e-mail. A small business with few employees definitely needs e-mail, but it can't afford the costs of an e-mail server and perhaps does not want to have its own hosted domain and the costs and work that go along with that. By connecting to a free browser-based service, the small business can benefit from nearly unlimited e-mail, contacts, and calendar solutions. However, with cloud computing, you lose administrative control, and there are some security concerns as well.

Common Cloud Models

Cloud computing services are generally broken down into a few categories of services, for instance:

> ▶ **Software as a service (SaaS):** The most commonly used and recognized of the three categories, SaaS is when users access applications over the Internet that are provided by a third party. The applications need not be installed on the local computer. In many cases, these applications are run within a web browser; in other cases, the user connects with screen-sharing programs or remote desktop programs. A common example of

this is webmail such as Gmail. Other examples include Dropbox and Microsoft Office 365. SaaS can potentially offer lower hardware, software, and maintenance costs because the provider houses the hardware and software.

▶ **Infrastructure as a service (IaaS):** IaaS is a service that offers computer networking, storage, load balancing, routing, and VM hosting. The cloud provider hosts the network infrastructure hardware components that are normally present in a traditional on-premises data center. Through a subscription service, you access hardware only when you need it. The potential benefits include scalability, minimized hardware maintenance and support, and reduced downtime. Common examples of IaaS include Amazon Web Services (AWS) and Microsoft Azure. More and more organizations are seeing the benefits of offloading some of their networking infrastructure to the cloud.

▶ **Platform as a service (PaaS):** PaaS is a service that provides various software solutions to organizations, especially the ability to develop and test applications in a virtual environment without the cost or administration of a physical platform. It is also used on a subscription basis in an attempt to reduce costs and increase collaboration. PaaS is used for easy-to-configure operating systems and on-demand computing. Often, this utilizes IaaS as well for an underlying infrastructure to the platform. Cloud-based virtual desktop environments are often considered to be part of this type of service, but they can be part of IaaS as well. The virtual desktop can act as part of a user's computing system, or it can be the only place where the user performs his or her work. It can be as simple as a browser window with a single application inside of it, or it could include everything from a virtual OS to virtual hardware such as a virtual network interface card (virtual NIC), and on down to all the required individual virtual applications.

ExamAlert

Know what SaaS, IaaS, and PaaS are.

Note

Other types of cloud services in the CompTIA A+ acronyms list include: data as a service (DaaS), database as a service (DBaaS), and network as a service (NaaS). Be aware of them.

There are different types of clouds used by organizations: public, private, hybrid, and community. Let's discuss each briefly.

▶ **Public cloud:** When a service provider offers applications and storage space to the general public over the Internet. A couple of examples of this include free, web-based e-mail services and pay-as-you-go business-class services. The main benefits of this include low (or zero) cost and scalability. Providers of public cloud space include Google, Microsoft, Rackspace, and Amazon.

▶ **Private cloud:** As opposed to the public cloud, the private cloud is designed with the needs of the individual organization in mind. The security administrator has more control over the data and infrastructure. There are a limited number of people who have access to the cloud, and they are usually located behind a firewall of some sort in order to gain access to the private cloud. Resources might be provided by a third party or could come from the security administrator's server room or data center. Some companies incorporate broad network access—meaning that resources are available to a wide range of devices including PCs, Macs, laptops, tablets, smartphones, and so on. While a private cloud creates increased availability for clients, it also intensifies the level of security concerns.

▶ **Hybrid cloud:** A mixture of public and private clouds. Dedicated servers located within the organization and cloud servers from a third party are used together to form the collective network. In these hybrid scenarios, confidential data is usually kept in-house.

▶ **Community cloud:** Another mix of public and private, but one where multiple organizations can share the public portion. Community clouds appeal to organizations that usually share a common form of computing and way of storing data.

> **ExamAlert**
>
> Know what public, private, hybrid, and community clouds are.

Cloud Computing Concerns

Cloud computing is all about shared resources—data, devices, and network resources that can be accessed from a remote location. Generally, if the resources are stored internally within the organization, users will get faster and more efficient access to them; but not always. Sometimes, externally stored resources can be just as effective, especially if they have a small footprint, and don't use much in the way of networking and processing power. One example of this is off-site e-mail and e-mail applications. E-mail in and of itself has been so streamlined over the years that it can be accessed from almost any device from just about anywhere. Even the e-mail application itself can be run in a way so as to tax the client less and the server more; such as web-based e-mail clients, or e-mail clients that run virtually—a form of *virtual application streaming*. Or, perhaps the entire desktop, including the e-mail application, is virtual, running either within a browser or from a thin client. So, in this case, having externally shared resources is a viable option, though it might not integrate well with an organization's security policy. Also, for the enterprise environment, e-mail technologies are often simply too immense and complex to be stored anywhere but privately.

Another consideration is the type of applications that will be run from the cloud, what type of devices will use them, and how they will synchronize. Basic e-mail applications from major providers have one version for desktops/laptops and another version for mobile devices such as smartphones and tablets. Complex applications will be more difficult to port to more than one type of device, but we don't want to have a PC version of an application running on a mobile device such as a smartphone; that would put additional strain on the end user. However, the more versions of software we offer, and the more types of end-point devices that connect to them, the greater the need for more resources within the cloud.

So, ultimately, the type of cloud an organization uses will be dictated by the organization's budget, the amount and type of resources to be supplied to users, the level of security the organization requires, and the amount of manpower (or lack thereof) it has to administer its resources. While a private cloud can be very appealing, it is often beyond the ability of an organization, forcing that organization to seek the public or community-based cloud. Whatever an organization chooses, the provider will measure the services supplied. *Measured services* is when the provider monitors the services rendered so that the provider can properly bill the customer and make sure that the customer's use of services is being handled in the most efficient way. This can work in conjunction with a pay service called *metered services*—where an organization has access to virtually unlimited resources, but pays only for the resources that are used. This should be measured carefully, and the details of the resources should be stated clearly every month.

There are some other cloud-based terms you should be familiar with for the A+ 220-1001 exam. For example, *rapid elasticity*, which is the ability to build or extend your cloud-based network quickly and efficiently. Choosing a provider that can provide you with a scalable model is important for an organization's growth. You also want to have *on-demand* service. The cloud should be available in real time and whenever you need it (24/7). In a community cloud scenario, the provider usually implements *resource pooling*, which is the grouping of servers and infrastructure for use by multiple customers but in a way that is on-demand and scalable.

All of this cloud technology might seem a bit beyond what an A+ technician will be routinely called upon to do. However, you should have a basic knowledge of cloud types, cloud technologies, and cloud terminology, so that you can better facilitate users in your role as a help desk specialist or other tech support position. Later, if you decide to specialize in one of the big cloud/virtualization providers, you will find that it really is a technology specialty all its own, with a lot of competition in the market, and certifications to prove your worth.

Cram Quiz

Answer these questions. The answers follow the last question. If you cannot answer these questions correctly, consider reading this section again until you can.

1. Which of the following types of cloud services offers e-mail through a web browser?

   ○ **A.** SaaS

   ○ **B.** IaaS

   ○ **C.** PaaS

   ○ **D.** Community cloud

2. Your organization requires more control over its data and infrastructure. Money is apparently not an issue. There are only two admins and about 30 users that will have access to the data on the cloud. Which of the following types of clouds is the best option?

   ○ **A.** Public

   ○ **B.** Private

   ○ **C.** Hybrid

   ○ **D.** Community

3. You require the ability to add on to your cloud-based network whenever necessary, quickly and efficiently. What is this referring to?

   ○ **A.** Measured services

   ○ **B.** Metered services

   ○ **C.** Rapid elasticity

   ○ **D.** On-demand service

Cram Quiz Answers

1. **A.** Software as a service (SaaS) is the most commonly recognized cloud service; it allows users to use applications to access data that is stored on the Internet by a third party. Infrastructure as a service (IaaS) is a service that offers computer networking, storage, load balancing, routing, and VM hosting. Platform as a service (PaaS) is used for easy to configure operating systems and on-demand computing. A community cloud is a mix of public and private clouds, but one where multiple organizations can share the public portion.

2. **B.** The best option listed is a private cloud. This gives the most control over data and resources in an environment where there are limited users (and a healthy budget). These resources could be entirely internal, or a portion of them could also be provided by a third party. Public cloud technology is used for the general public to access applications over the Internet. Hybrid is a mixture of the two, but not necessary in this situation because of the healthy budget and the limited number of users. Community cloud is similar to hybrid but is meant for multiple organizations that share data, which is not necessary in this scenario.

3. **C.** Rapid elasticity is the ability to build your cloud-based network, or extend upon an existing one, quickly and efficiently. Measured services is when a provider monitors a customer's services used so that the customer can be properly billed. Metered services is when the customer can access as many resources as needed but only be billed for what was accessed. On-demand service means that the cloud service is available at all times. The leaders of a successful organization don't care what it takes; they simply want high-speed, secure access to services 24/7.

4.2 – Given a scenario, set up and configure client-side virtualization

ExamAlert

Objective 4.2 focuses on the following: purpose of virtual machines, VM requirements (resources, emulator, security, network), and hypervisor.

Virtualization is the creation of a virtual entity, as opposed to a true or actual entity. The most common type of entity created through virtualization is the virtual machine—usually housing an operating system. We talked about virtualization a little bit in Chapter 14, "Custom PCs and Common Devices," but let's take it a bit further and discuss types of virtualization, identify their purposes, and define their requirements. We'll also review the types of hypervisors you should know for the exam. However, we will focus on client-side virtualization in this book.

Purpose of Virtual Machines

Many types of virtualization exist, from network and storage to hardware and software. The CompTIA A+ exam focuses mostly on virtual machine software. The VMs created by this software run operating systems or individual applications. The virtual operating system—also known as a guest—is designed to run inside a real OS. So, the beauty behind this is that you can run multiple various operating systems simultaneously from just one computer. This has great advantages for programmers, developers, and systems administrators, and can facilitate a great testing environment. Nowadays, many VMs are also used in live production environments as servers and as clients, or as individual applications.

Know this: anything can be run virtually—from individual apps and browser windows to operating systems—and in some cases it can be hard to tell what's virtual and what's not. Nowadays, anything that runs an OS virtually is generally referred to as a virtual machine, and that's what we will be discussing in the rest of this chapter.

Virtualization Versus Emulation

The terms *virtualization* and *emulation* are often used interchangeably, but they are not quite the same. There are a couple of main differences between a virtual machine and an emulator. First, a VM is designed to create an isolated environment, whereas an emulator is designed to reproduce the behavior of some type of hardware and/or firmware. Secondly, VMs make use of a CPU's built-in virtualization capabilities, but emulators will imitate hardware without relying on the CPU; they can even be coded to mimic an entire processor that is wholly different from the one in the programmer's computer. An example of an emulator is a SOHO router's firmware that you can access online for testing purposes. It doesn't really control a SOHO router, and it has no connectivity to anything. Another example is an emulated UEFI/BIOS that some motherboard manufacturers offer on their websites for testing purposes. An example of a VM is a virtualized Windows operating system that runs within your computer's main operating system, makes use of the hardware of that computer, and can connect to other systems internally or externally. Developing an emulator would usually require a programmer, whereas any tech can create a VM. Another way to differentiate between the two is that an emulator does not use a hypervisor, but a VM does.

Hypervisors

Chapter 14 mentioned that there are two main types of hypervisors. Table 16.1 reviews these. Remember that Type 1 will be faster, but it requires a proper server, requires more knowledgeable administration, and is costlier. The A+ exams focus mainly on Type 2 hypervisors and the virtualization software that utilizes that technology. These can be run on typical client operating systems such as Windows 10, Windows 7, and so on.

TABLE 16.1 **Review of Hypervisors**

Hypervisor	Description	Examples
Type 1	AKA: Native or bare metal. The hypervisor runs directly on the host computer's hardware.	VMware vSphere, Microsoft Hyper-V (Windows Server)
Type 2	AKA: Hosted. The hypervisor runs within the operating system. Guest VMs are one step removed from the hardware.	VMware Workstation, VirtualBox, Hyper-V for Windows clients

ExamAlert

Know the difference between Type 1 and Type 2 hypervisors!

Examples of Virtual Machine Software

Let's look at a couple of examples of virtualization software that make use of the Type 2 hypervisor on a typical Windows 10 computer. First on the list is Microsoft Hyper-V. For this to work, virtualization must be enabled in the UEFI/BIOS. Then, Hyper-V needs to be turned on in Windows Features as shown in Figure 16.1. You can get to Windows Features by navigating to **Control Panel > All Control Panel Items > Programs and Features** and clicking the **Turn Windows features on or off** link. Enabling Hyper-V requires a restart. If you are not sure whether Hyper-V will be compatible with your system, you can open the Command Prompt or the PowerShell and type **systeminfo**. At the bottom of the results you will see the Hyper-V Requirements section and details.

FIGURE 16.1   **Hyper-V enabled in Windows Features on a Windows 10 system**

> **Note**
>
> Hyper-V works only on certain editions of Windows. For example, it works on Windows 10 Pro, Enterprise, and Education, but not Home, Mobile, or Mobile Enterprise. Similar restrictions apply for other versions of Windows.

Once you have performed those actions, you can then create VMs in Hyper-V Manager. During the creation process you will be prompted to create a virtual hard drive and install an operating system—which you will need to obtain in .iso format, or in a virtual format. The virtual hardware for the VM can be configured in the Settings section. The networking connections can be configured in the Virtual Switch Manager. Figure 16.2 shows an example of a VM that was installed to Hyper-V Manager.

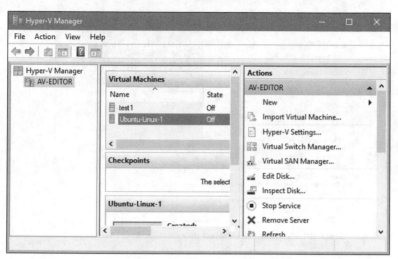

FIGURE 16.2   **An Ubuntu Linux virtual machine created in Hyper-V Manager**

Another popular example of a Type 2 hypervisor is VMware Workstation. For an example of that, see Chapter 11, Figure 11.1. The concept is essentially the same, but of course navigation and names will be slightly different. One difference is the type of file extensions used. For example, VMware uses the .vmdk file extension for the virtual hard disk of a virtual machine, whereas Hyper-V uses the .vhdx extension. The two types of VMs are not compatible by default, meaning you can't take a VM from VMware and run it in Hyper-V, or vice versa.

A third well-liked offering is Oracle VirtualBox. This is a free and easy way to test operating systems. Admins have been using it for years and years. Figure 16.3 shows an example of a VM that was created in VirtualBox. The default virtual storage file extension for VirtualBox VMs is .vdi; however, you can also use .vmdk, for compatibility with VMware. That is the extension that was chosen for the VM shown in Figure 16.3.

FIGURE 16.3 A Kali Linux virtual machine created in VirtualBox

If at all possible, try out the different types of virtualization software so that you can learn more about them.

One more thing: I can't stress this enough—Be sure to update your virtualization software! Vulnerabilities are always being found in all the major vendors' software, so updates are frequently available. Get in the habit of checking for updates!

Virtual Machine Requirements

There are a couple of requirements that we have to consider: virtualization hosting software requirements, and virtual machine requirements. Generally, most computers built over the previous 5 years can run the latest version of virtualization software—as long as the UEFI/BIOS can support virtualization—but the VMs themselves can be very power hungry; especially newer operating systems. For example, to install Windows 10 Pro as a virtual machine, you will need to assign virtual resources—CPU, RAM, network connection, hard drive, and so on.

The Windows 10 VM might run okay with one virtual processor and a single core (the default), but multiple cores are often recommended. Commonly, the

VM will require 2 GB of RAM, but again, more is suggested. The setting you select will depend on the physical hardware of the host. If you have a computer that is 5 years old with limited cores and RAM, then assigning more virtual CPU and RAM power to the VM will simply bog down the main host system even more. The beauty of the VM is that you can change the virtual resources at any time, as long as you shut down the VM first. This way, you can test, tweak, and find the right balance.

Then there is the network connection. Generally, you have three to four options. The following example is based on VMware:

► **Bridged networking:** This gives the VM (also known as the guest) direct access to the hosting computer's network connection. It allows external access, but in this case, the VM must have its own IP address on the external IP network. Because of the direct connectivity to the external network, this can be a security concern. In most cases, some type of NAT is preferred.

► **Network address translation (NAT):** Often the default, this gives the guest access to the external network, but by using NAT the guest gets a separate IP address on a private network.

► **Host-only networking:** This creates a private virtual network for the guests, and they can communicate with each other but not with the external network.

► **No networking:** This option disables networking for the VM altogether, which might be required for users that are working on confidential systems, testbeds, applications, and so on.

ExamAlert

Know the virtualization network connection options.

Networking is usually required for VMs. Just remember that any network connection (mapped network drive, browsing connection, and so on) can be a security concern. If there is a connection from the VM to the hosting OS—and the VM has a vulnerability that is exploited—then the exploit could carry over to the host. Be ready to monitor for, and disable, any unused or unnecessary network connections between VMs and between the VMs and the host. Conversely, the host should be updated and secured vigilantly. If the hosting OS fails, then all guest VMs will go offline immediately.

ExamAlert

Because VM network connections can be security vulnerabilities, you will need to monitor and disable them as necessary, and in some cases you will have to disable networking altogether.

Different providers use different names for the types of networking connections, but they will be similar; for example, Hyper-V uses external, internal, and private. You have the ability to create and configure virtual switches for the various VMs, and allow or disallow connectivity between them (and between the VMs and the host) as you see fit. It can get pretty complex, so it is wise to create network documentation that diagrams the various virtual machines and switches using software such as Microsoft Visio.

You can select different virtual hard drive connections such as SCSI, SATA, and IDE that emulate those technologies. Then you choose the size of virtual drive (for instance, 60 GB). Know that a VM will not use all of this space on the physical drive. Instead, it uses only what it needs, and it is dynamic—the size of the virtual drive can grow as needed, up to the maximum that was selected.

Note

To find out the minimum requirements of virtualization software, go to the manufacturers' websites:

▶ VMware Workstation: https://docs.vmware.com

▶ Windows 10 Hyper-V: https://docs.microsoft.com/virtualization

Note

I built a Xeon-based virtualization server to house my VMs. It runs VMware ESXi server. Check out the build here: https://dprocomputer.com/blog/?p=2938

Cram Quiz

Answer these questions. The answers follow the last question. If you cannot answer these questions correctly, consider reading this section again until you can.

1. Of the following listed technologies, which one should you select if you want to run an instance of Ubuntu Linux within your Windows 10 Pro workstation?

   ○ **A.** Type 1

   ○ **B.** Type 2

   ○ **C.** Bare metal

   ○ **D.** Emulator

2. Which of the following is the greatest risk of a virtual computer?

   ○ **A.** If a virtual computer fails, all other virtual computers immediately go offline.

   ○ **B.** If a virtual computer fails, the physical server goes offline.

   ○ **C.** If the physical server fails, all other physical servers immediately go offline.

   ○ **D.** If the physical server fails, all the virtual computers immediately go offline.

3. Which of the following file extensions Is used by VMware?

   ○ **A.** .vmdk

   ○ **B.** .vdi

   ○ **C.** .vhdx

   ○ **D.** VT-x

4. Which of the following network connection types should be used to allow for connectivity to the external network but keep the VMs on a separate IP network?

   ○ **A.** Bridged

   ○ **B.** NAT

   ○ **C.** Private

   ○ **D.** No networking

5. A customer running Windows 10 Pro wishes to install a Linux VM in Hyper-V Manager. Which of the following requirements must be met in order for this to happen? (Select all that apply.)

   ○ **A.** Update and secure the host system.

   ○ **B.** Virtualization must be enabled in the UEFI/BIOS.

   ○ **C.** Hyper-V needs to be turned on in Windows Features.

   ○ **D.** Restart the system.

Cram Quiz Answers

1. **B.** You would need to run virtualization software that includes a Type 2 hypervisor such as Windows 10 Hyper-V, VMware Workstation, or VirtualBox. Type 1 hypervisors are used on servers; they are also known as bare metal because they allow virtual machines to access the computer hardware directly. Examples include VMware vSphere and Windows Server–based Hyper-V. An emulator is something that imitates hardware and firmware, such as an emulated BIOS. Emulators do not use hypervisors.

2. **D.** The biggest risk of running a virtual computer is that it will go offline immediately if the server that it is housed on fails. All other virtual computers on that particular server will also go offline immediately.

3. **A.** VMware uses the .vmdk file extension for the virtual hard drive file. VirtualBox uses .vdi by default (though it can use others). Hyper-V uses .vhdx. VT-x is the Intel virtualization extension that is incorporated into Intel-based systems and must be enabled in the UEFI/BIOS for virtualization software to work.

4. **B.** Network address translation (NAT)-based network connections are the most common default. This allows the VMs to have their own IP network but still connect to the external network and make use of the Internet. This is the same principle behind NAT used in a SOHO network. Bridged means that the VMs have access to the external network, but they must use IP addresses from that external network. Private means that multiple VMs within a host can communicate with each other, but not beyond the host. The no networking option disables any type of networking connectivity for the VM in question.

5. **B, C, and D.** Virtualization must be enabled in the UEFI/BIOS. Then, Hyper-V needs to be turned on in Windows Features. Finally, the system needs to be restarted. Updating and securing the host system is recommended, but is not a requirement.

CORE 1 (220-1001)

Domain 5.0: Hardware and Network Troubleshooting

CHAPTER 17

Computer Troubleshooting 101

This chapter covers the following A+ 220-1001 exam objective:

▶ **5.1** – Given a scenario, use the best practice methodology to resolve problems.

Excellent troubleshooting ability is vital; it's probably the most important skill for a computer technician to possess. It's what we do—troubleshoot and repair problems! So, it makes sense that an ever-increasing number of questions about this subject are on the A+ exams. To be a good technician, and to pass the exams, you need to know how to troubleshoot hardware, software, and network-related issues. The key is to do it methodically. One way to do that is to use a troubleshooting methodology or process. In this chapter we will focus on the CompTIA A+ six-step troubleshooting methodology.

5.1 – Given a scenario, use the best practice methodology to resolve problems

ExamAlert

Objective 5.1 concentrates on the CompTIA A+ six-step troubleshooting methodology.

It is necessary to approach computer problems from a logical standpoint, and to best do this, we use a troubleshooting process. Several different troubleshooting methodologies are out there; this book focuses on the CompTIA A+ six-step troubleshooting methodology.

This six-step methodology included within the A+ objectives is designed to increase the computer technician's problem-solving ability. CompTIA expects the technician to take an organized, methodical route to a solution by memorizing and implementing these steps. Incorporate this six-step methodology into your line of thinking as you read through this book and whenever you troubleshoot a desktop computer, mobile device, or networking issue.

Step 1. Identify the problem.

Step 2. Establish a theory of probable cause (question the obvious).

Step 3. Test the theory to determine cause.

Step 4. Establish a plan of action to resolve the problem and implement the solution.

Step 5. Verify full system functionality and, if applicable, implement preventive measures.

Step 6. Document findings, actions, and outcomes.

> **ExamAlert**
>
> Before you *do* anything, always consider organizational and corporate policies, procedures, and impacts before implementing any changes.

Let's talk about each of these six steps in a little more depth.

Step 1: Identify the Problem

In this first step, you already know that there is a problem; now you have to identify exactly what it is. This means gathering information. You do this in several ways:

▶ **Question the user.** Ask the person who reported the problem detailed questions about the issue. You want to find out about symptoms, unusual behavior, or anything that the user might have done of late that could have inadvertently or directly caused the problem. Of course, do this without accusing the user. If the user cannot properly explain a computer's problem, ask simple questions to further identify the issue.

▶ **Identify any changes made to the computer.** Look at the computer. See if any new hardware has been installed or plugged in. Look around for anything that might seem out of place. Listen to the computer—even smell it! For example, a hard drive might make a peculiar noise, or a power supply might smell like something is burning. Use all your senses to help identify what the problem is. Define if any new software has been installed or if any system settings have been changed. In some cases, you might need to inspect the environment around the computer. Perhaps something has changed outside the computer that is related to the problem.

▶ **Review log files.** Review any and all log files that you have access to that can tell you more information about the problem. For example, in Windows use the Event Viewer to analyze the System and Application logs, and perhaps the Security log. Figure 17.1 shows an example of the System log within the Event Viewer.

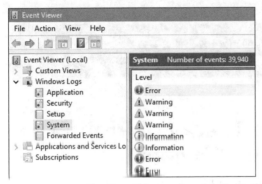

FIGURE 17.1   **The Event Viewer showing the System log in Windows**

▶ **Inquire as to any environmental or infrastructural changes.** Perhaps there was a change on the computer network, or a new authentication scheme is in place. Maybe the environment has changed in some way: higher temperatures, more or less humidity, or a user now works in a dustier/dirtier location. Perhaps there have been recent changes to the HVAC system or the electrical system. Changes such as these will often affect more than one computer, so be ready to extend your troubleshooting across multiple systems.

▶ **Review documentation.** Your company might have electronic or written documentation that logs past problems and solutions. Perhaps the issue at hand has happened before. Or perhaps other related issues can aid you in your pursuit to find out what is wrong. Maybe another technician listed in the documentation can be of assistance if he or she has seen the problem before. Perhaps the user has documentation about a specific process or has a manual concerning the computer, individual component, software, or other device that has failed. Documentation is so important; the more technology there is, the more documentation that is created to support it. A good technician knows some details by heart, but a technician doesn't need to know every single specification—those can be looked up. A great technician needs to understand how to locate the right documentation, how to read it, and how to update it as necessary.

Keep in mind that you're not taking any direct action at this point to solve the problem. Instead, you are gleaning as much information as you can to help in your analysis. However, in this stage it is important to back up any critical data before you do make any changes in the following steps.

> **ExamAlert**
>
> Perform backups before making changes!

Step 2: Establish a Theory of Probable Cause (Question the Obvious)

In Step 2, you theorize as to what the most likely cause of the problem is. Start with the most probable or obvious cause. For example, if a computer won't turn on, your theory of probable cause would be that the computer is not plugged in! This step differs from other troubleshooting processes in that you are not making a list of causes but instead are choosing one probable cause as a starting point. In this step, you also need to define whether it is a hardware- or software-related issue.

If necessary, conduct external or internal research based on symptoms. This means that you might need to consult your organization's documentation (or your own personal documentation), research technical websites, and make calls to various tech support lines—all depending on the severity of the situation. It also means that you might inspect the inside of a computer or the software of the computer more thoroughly than in the previous step.

The ultimate goal is to come up with a logical theory explaining the root of the problem.

Step 3: Test the Theory to Determine Cause

In Step 3, test your theory from Step 2. Back to the example, go ahead and plug in the computer. If the computer starts, you know that your theory has been confirmed. At that point move on to Step 4. But what if the computer *is* plugged in? Or what if you plug in the computer and it still doesn't start? An experienced troubleshooter can often figure out the problem on the first theory but not always. If the first theory fails during testing, go back to Step 2 to establish a new theory and continue until you have a theory that tests positive. If you can't figure out what the problem is from any of your theories, it's time to escalate. Bring the problem to your supervisor so that additional theories can be established.

Step 4: Establish a Plan of Action to Resolve the Problem and Implement the Solution

Step 4 might at first seem a bit redundant, but delve in a little further. When a theory has been tested and works, you can establish a plan of action. In the previous scenario, it's simple: plug in the computer. However, in other situations the plan of action will be more complicated; you might need to repair other issues that occurred due to the first issue. In other cases, an issue might affect multiple computers, and the plan of action would include repairing all those systems. Whatever the plan of action, after it is established, have the appropriate people sign off on it (if necessary), and then immediately implement it.

Step 5: Verify Full System Functionality and, If Applicable, Implement Preventive Measures

At this point, verify whether the computer works properly. This might require a restart or two, opening applications, accessing the Internet, or actually using a hardware device, thus proving it works. As part of Step 5, you want to prevent the problem from happening again if possible. Yes, of course, you plugged in the computer and it worked. But why was the computer unplugged? The computer being unplugged (or whatever the particular issue) could be the result of a bigger problem that you would want to prevent in the future. Whatever your preventive measures, make sure they won't affect any other systems or policies; if they do, get permission for those measures first.

> **ExamAlert**
>
> Make sure it works! Always remember to verify full system functionality.

Step 6: Document Findings, Actions, and Outcomes

In this last step, document what happened. Depending on the company you work for, you might have been documenting the entire time (for example, by using a trouble-ticketing system). In this step, finalize the documentation, including the issue, cause, solution, preventive measures, and any other steps taken.

Documentation is extremely important and helps in two ways. First, it provides you and the user with closure to the problem; it solidifies the problem and the solution, making you a better troubleshooter in the future. Second, if you or anyone on your team encounters a similar issue in the future, the history of the issue will be at your fingertips. Most technicians don't remember specific solutions to problems that happened several months ago or more. Plus, having a written account of what transpired can help to protect all parties involved in case there is an investigation and/or legal proceeding.

So that's the six-step A+ troubleshooting methodology. Try to incorporate this methodology into your thinking when covering the chapters in this book. In the upcoming chapters, apply it to hardware, software, and network-related issues.

> **Note**
>
> I also have a video on my website that discusses this six-step process:
> https://dprocomputer.com/blog/?p=2941

Cram Quiz

Answer these questions. The answers follow the last question. If you cannot answer
these questions correctly, consider reading this chapter again until you can.

1. What is the second step of the A+ troubleshooting methodology?
   - ○ **A.** Identify the problem.
   - ○ **B.** Establish a theory of probable cause.
   - ○ **C.** Test the theory.
   - ○ **D.** Document.

2. When you run out of possible theories for the cause of a problem, what should
   you do?
   - ○ **A.** Escalate the problem.
   - ○ **B.** Document your actions so far.
   - ○ **C.** Establish a plan of action.
   - ○ **D.** Question the user.

3. What should you do before making any changes to the computer? (Select the
   best answer.)
   - ○ **A.** Identify the problem.
   - ○ **B.** Establish a plan of action.
   - ○ **C.** Perform a backup.
   - ○ **D.** Escalate the problem.

4. Which of the following is part of Step 5 in the six-step troubleshooting process?
   - ○ **A.** Identify the problem.
   - ○ **B.** Document findings.
   - ○ **C.** Establish a new theory.
   - ○ **D.** Implement preventive measures.

5. What should you do next after testing the theory to determine cause?
   - ○ **A.** Establish a plan of action to resolve the problem.
   - ○ **B.** Verify full system functionality.
   - ○ **C.** Document findings, actions, and outcomes.
   - ○ **D.** Implement the solution.

6. There is a problem with the power supplied to a group of computers and you do not know how to fix the problem. What should you do first?

   ○ **A.** Establish a theory of why you can't figure out the problem.

   ○ **B.** Contact the building supervisor or your manager.

   ○ **C.** Test the theory to determine cause.

   ○ **D.** Document findings, actions, and outcomes.

Cram Quiz Answers

1. **B.** The second step is to establish a theory of probable cause. You need to look for the obvious or most probable cause for the problem.

2. **A.** If you can't figure out why a problem occurred, it's time to get someone else involved. Escalate the problem to your supervisor.

3. **C.** Always perform a backup of critical data before making any changes to the computer.

4. **D.** Implement preventive measures as part of Step 5 to ensure that the problem will not happen again.

5. **A.** After testing the theory to determine cause (Step 3), you should establish a plan of action to resolve the problem and implement the solution (Step 4). Memorize the six-step troubleshooting methodology! You will use it often.

6. **B.** If you can't figure out a cause to a problem and have exhausted all possible theories, escalate the problem to the appropriate persons. It happens—no one of us knows everything; and sometimes, we have to ask for help!

CHAPTER 18

Troubleshooting Motherboards, CPUs, RAM, and Power

This chapter covers the following A+ 220-1001 exam objective:

▶ 5.2 – Given a scenario, troubleshoot problems related to motherboards, RAM, CPUs, and power.

Let's continue on our troubleshooting quest. This chapter gets into the guts of the PC. Sometimes it can be a bit difficult to figure out which component is causing the problem. In this chapter I'll give some tips to help you identify whether the problem comes from the motherboard, the CPU, or the RAM, or if it is a power issue.

Always refer back to the six-step CompTIA A+ troubleshooting methodology that we discussed in Chapter 17, "Computer Troubleshooting 101." This best practice methodology will help you to think logically and clearly as you troubleshoot computer problems. If you are new to computers, I suggest reviewing the corresponding hardware chapters for all of that in Chapters 10 through 13.

This chapter only refers to one exam objective, but it is a pretty massive one. We're basically talking about the entire core of a PC—we could fill a book on this subject. Alas, our time and space are limited. So, I've condensed as much as possible. Consider acquiring and breaking down older systems to help develop your troubleshooting skills.

5.2 – Given a scenario, troubleshoot problems related to motherboards, RAM, CPUs, and power

ExamAlert

Objective 5.2 concentrates on troubleshooting common symptoms related to motherboards, RAM, CPUs, and power, such as unexpected shutdowns; blank screen on bootup; no power; proprietary crash screens; and using log entries and error messages.

Troubleshooting Motherboards

It is uncommon to see a motherboard fail, but if it does, it can be because of a few different things. Let's discuss several of these now.

First and probably the most common of these rarities are UEFI/BIOS firmware issues. I'll refer to this as "BIOS" for simplicity. Remember that you might need to flash the motherboard's BIOS to the latest version. For example, a new CPU or RAM might not be recognized at the correct clock speeds. An adapter card might not be seen properly. Or perhaps Windows isn't working as it should be with the hardware in the system. Updating the BIOS can fix many of these issues. On a separate note, you might encounter a PC that instead of booting normally accesses the BIOS. A drained or faulty CMOS battery could be the culprit. Change out the battery and the system should boot normally. Usually, this is a CR2032 lithium battery. If you are not sure whether the battery is discharged, it can be tested with a multimeter. CR2032 batteries normally have an output of 3 volts. The CR2032 is only usable down to 2 V, so if it measures 2.5 V or less, then it should be replaced. Also, if the battery is discharged, then the time and date will revert to a default (such as January 1, 2012). Also, any other settings you configured will be lost. After a new battery is installed, the time/date and any other required settings will have to be reconfigured, or imported from backup.

> **ExamAlert**
>
> If the time and date have reset on a system, there is a good chance that the rest of the settings have also reset to defaults. You should always review the BIOS configuration settings, compare them with your organization's documentation, and make any modifications necessary. Always remember to save your work!

If the system attempts to boot to an incorrect device, then it could be because the intended boot device is new, and again, a BIOS flash could fix the problem. Of course, it could also be due to configuration error. You should know how to change the BIOS boot order and many other settings in the BIOS. You should also know where to go in the BIOS to view log entries and error messages. The BIOS log can help to describe various system problems (though it might require a bit of translation with the aid of the motherboard manual). We discuss the BIOS more in Chapter 11, "Motherboards and Add-on Cards."

Second are electrostatic discharge (ESD) and other electrical issues. These might present themselves intermittently. If you find some intermittent issues (for example, the computer reboots out of nowhere) or you receive random stop errors, also known as Blue Screens of Death (BSODs), ESD could be the culprit. Or a power surge could cause the problem. A particular wire, circuit, or capacitor on the motherboard could have been damaged. Document when failures occur. Swap out the motherboard with a known good one to see if the issue happens again when running through the same processes. If the issue doesn't recur, chances are the original motherboard is headed for the bit bucket. There are lots of circuits on a motherboard; electrical damage to any one circuit could cause the system to behave "irrationally" at best, triggering intermittent device failure. Beyond this, electrical damage can go right through the power supply to the motherboard, disabling it permanently. Be sure to use a surge suppressor or uninterruptible power supply (UPS) to protect your equipment and, of course, implement antistatic measures whenever you work inside a system.

> **Note**
>
> Antistatic measures such as an antistatic wrist strap and mat are crucial when working on systems. I cover this concept in more depth within Chapter 40, "Safety Procedures and Environmental Controls."

Third are component failures. It is possible that a single component of the motherboard (for example, the SATA controller) can fail, but the rest of the motherboard works fine. This can also be verified by doing a power-on self-test (POST) analysis. The POST process starts when the computer first boots. It can result in visible codes or audible beeps. The visible codes could be on the screen, or could be part of a two-digit digital readout that is incorporated into the motherboard. Either way, the visible codes or the beep codes can be deciphered by using the motherboard manual. To fix a problem such as an SATA controller failure, a separate PCIe SATA controller card can be purchased. Then you can connect the hard drives to the new controller and disable the original integrated SATA controller in the BIOS. A good bench or lab will have extra controller cards of all kinds so that you can test these types of problems. In some cases, a failed controller can be symptomatic of a bigger problem, where the entire motherboard might need to be replaced. Some component failures can cause system lockups, where the OS freezes and the keyboard and mouse become non-functional. This could be due to a controller issue, chipset issue, or a faulty hard drive. Check all connections, and consider flashing the BIOS. Worst-case scenario: replace the motherboard. We'll discuss hard drive troubleshooting in Chapter 19, "Troubleshooting Hard Drives and RAID Arrays."

And last are manufacturing defects and failed motherboard components. Printed circuit boards (PCBs), such as motherboards, are mass-produced at high speeds. Problems might be found immediately when receiving a motherboard. In general, defects are uncommon but can occur due to mechanical problems in the machinery or due to an engineering error. If you suspect a manufacturing defect, you should return the motherboard. Motherboard component failure can also manifest itself over time, such as in the form of distended capacitors. This is when a capacitor becomes swollen and possibly leaks electrolytic material; this bulging can cause the system to unexpectedly restart or shut down, cause a BSOD, or cause other errors. If possible, the affected capacitor(s) should be replaced right away. If that does not work, the motherboard should be replaced. In the early 2000s, swollen caps were somewhat prevalent due to raw material issues—the problem was even dubbed the "capacitor plague." However, the problem is much less common today. In fact, motherboards that are received in a DOA (dead-on-arrival) state are uncommon with reputable manufacturers. To give you an idea of just how uncommon they are, I have built over 1000 systems and have only had to return one motherboard—and I'm fairly sure that the board failure was due to poor shipping and handling.

Troubleshooting CPUs

The most common issue with a CPU is when it isn't installed properly or securely. This could possibly cause a complete failure when trying to turn on the system. This failure might be accompanied by a series of beeps from the POST. If this happens, always check the power first, just in case—the main power connections and the 8- or 4-pin CPU power connection. Another possibility is that the system will turn on and power will be supplied to the system, but nothing else will happen: no POST, no display (blank screen), and no hard drive activity. In any of these situations, after checking power, make sure of the following:

▶ **Fan is connected and functional:** Some motherboards have a safeguard that disables booting if the fan is defective or not plugged in. Or you might get a message on the screen or other type of warning depending on the motherboard. Be sure that the fan is plugged into the correct power connector on the motherboard (or elsewhere), and verify whether it turns when the computer is on. If the fan has failed, replacement fans can be purchased; just make sure that the new fan is compatible with the heat sink and motherboard.

▶ **Check other major components:** Remember that the CPU is a part of a bigger system; one in which other components are more likely to be the cause of many problems. These components include the video card, RAM, and motherboard. Be sure to check these other components for simple connectivity problems, which could be the actual culprit here. Always check connections first before taking the CPU assembly apart.

▶ **Heat sink is connected properly:** Make sure that the heat sink is flush with the CPU cap and that it is securely fastened to the motherboard (or socket housing).

▶ **CPU is installed properly:** Make sure it was installed flush into the socket and that it was oriented correctly. Of course, this means removing the heat sink. If you do so, you should clean off excess thermal compound and reapply thermal compound to the CPU cap before reinstalling the heat sink.

ExamAlert

When troubleshooting the CPU, be sure to first check all connections and then make sure the fan, heat sink, and CPU are secure and installed properly.

Following are a few more possible symptoms of a failing CPU:

▶ Unexplained crashes (shutdowns) during bootup or during use.

▶ The system locks after only a short time of use.

▶ Voltage is near, at, or above the top end of the allowable range.

Sometimes, the CPU is just plain defective. It could have been received this way, or maybe it overheated. Perhaps there was a surge that damaged it, or maybe someone overclocked it too far and it was the victim of overvoltage (and subsequent overheating). Regardless of which of these reasons is the culprit, the CPU needs to be replaced. Now, by default, CPUs come with a heat sink and fan; if that is the case, install the CPU as you normally would. But in some cases, you can save money by purchasing only the CPU and using the existing heat sink. In this case, remember to clean excess thermal compound and then reapply thermal compound; but reapply to the CPU cap, not to the heat sink. If the CPU were installed properly, users don't usually have many problems with it (aside from the overclockers). Keep this in mind when troubleshooting the CPU or when troubleshooting an issue that *might* appear to be a CPU issue but is actually something else altogether.

On a lighter note, sometimes you might get reports from customers about strange noises coming from inside a PC, almost a buzzing of sorts. The noise could be caused by a wire or cable that is brushing up against the CPU fan (or other case fan). Be sure to reroute cables inside the computer so that they are clear of the CPU and any other devices. This will also aid with airflow within the PC, keeping the PC cooler. The CPU fan might also make noise due to it being clogged with dust, especially in dirtier environmental conditions. If the fan is still functional, you can use compressed air to clean it out. But be careful, because too much air movement could cause a static discharge. For example, if the CPU fan (or case fans) is moved from the air flow of a compressor, it could cause ESD. Use a piece of foam or other plastic stopper to keep the fan(s) in place while you use compressed air. Keep a computer vacuum handy to clean up the mess if necessary; I've seen computers that had so much dust and dirt inside, it could fill a garden! But be careful with computer vacuums and air compressors. Use a plastic nozzle or tip (never metal) and don't actually touch any of the components.

Troubleshooting RAM

It's not common, but RAM modules can cause intermittent issues, or they can fail altogether. Always make sure that the RAM is fully seated within the RAM slot and that the plastic ears are locking the RAM into place. An unstable system can be caused by several components including RAM. Remember to check other components in the system as well: video card, motherboard, and CPU.

A lot of the issues you see are because a user has purchased and installed a memory stick that is not compatible, or is semi-compatible, with the motherboard: wrong speed, incorrect capacity, improper configuration, and so on. Be ready for this; check the RAM compatibility against the motherboard, even if the user swears it has been checked already. Remember, a good technician has documentation available, has access to the Internet, and knows how to use both.

> **ExamAlert**
> Verify compatibility of RAM with the motherboard when troubleshooting!

Perhaps there was some kind of surge inside the computer; maybe the computer is not protected by a surge suppressor/protector or UPS. Another possibility is that the RAM was damaged by ESD, and this damage manifests itself as intermittent problems. There are expensive hardware-based RAM testers that can tell you if the RAM is electrically sound and if it can process data correctly.

If your company owns one, or if you can get your hands on one for a short time, you might narrow the problem. However, from personal experience, I have rarely needed to use these.

Here are some possible symptoms of a RAM issue and corresponding trouble-shooting techniques:

▶ **Computer will not boot/intermittently shuts down:** If there is no RAM in the computer, or if the RAM is damaged or not installed securely, it can prevent the computer from doing anything at all (aside from draining electricity from your AC outlet). For example, the power supply fan turns but nothing else—no beeps and no displays. First, if the RAM were just installed, make sure that the RAM is compatible. Next, and in general, try reseating the RAM before you attempt to troubleshoot a CPU or motherboard. Add RAM if none exists. (Sounds silly but I've seen it!) If you suspect faulty RAM, corroded contacts, or a faulty RAM slot, you can try taking the RAM out, cleaning the RAM and RAM slot if necessary, and putting the RAM back in, being sure to seat the memory module properly. (For cleaning, use contact cleaner on the RAM contacts and use compressed air on the slot.) Next, try moving memory modules to different slots—check your motherboard documentation for proper orientation. As mentioned, a POST analysis can be helpful in these situations as well. If necessary, replace the memory module with an identical one (if you have an extra one handy), or at worst, purchase a new one if you have identified the memory module as the source of the problem. In some cases, RAM can overheat and cause intermittent shutdowns. Heat sinks can be purchased for RAM. These are made of aluminum or copper, just like CPU heat sinks, and are sometimes referred to as heat spreaders. RAM can also be purchased with heat sinks preinstalled. This type of RAM might be necessary for high-end systems, such as virtualization systems, computer-aided design (CAD) workstations, and gaming systems.

▶ **BIOS indicates a memory error:** The BIOS can indicate a memory error through a gray message on the screen and a flashing cursor or by beeping. If it beeps, you need to reference your motherboard documentation for the specific beep codes. Sometimes a BIOS setting can be incorrect. If the computer has a saved version of the BIOS settings, you can try reverting to them, or you can try loading the BIOS defaults; I can't tell you how many times this has worked for me! Sometimes the BIOS indicates the wrong amount of RAM. If this is the case, check the RAM as explained in the first bullet. Finally, a BIOS update can be the cure; perhaps the BIOS just doesn't have the programming necessary to identify the latest type of RAM that was installed.

▶ **Stop error, aka BSOD or Blue Screen of Death:** This is a critical system error that causes the operating system to shut down. Most of the time, these are due to device driver errors (poor code), but they can be associated with a physical fault in memory. One example of this would be a non-maskable interrupt (NMI). An NMI can interrupt the processor to gain its attention regarding nonrecoverable hardware errors, resulting in a BSOD. The BSOD usually dumps the contents of memory to a file (for later analysis) and restarts the computer. If you don't encounter another BSOD, it's probably not much to worry about. But if the BSOD happens repeatedly, you want to write down the information you see on the screen and cross-reference it to the Microsoft Support website at https://support.microsoft.com. Again, if you suspect faulty RAM, try the trouble-shooting methods in the first bullet ("Computer will not boot").

> **Note**
>
> BSODs are covered in more depth in Chapter 36, "Troubleshooting Microsoft Windows."

Chances are you won't need them often, but memory testing programs such as MemTest86 (https://www.memtest86.com/) are available online. In fact, there is a whole slew of testing and benchmarking software that is freely available to you. Search around! Plus, you can use the Windows Memory Diagnostics Tool, which can be accessed by typing **mdsched.exe** in the Run prompt or from the Windows Recovery Environment (more on that in Chapter 36). These can help diagnose whether a memory module needs to be replaced. But in general, trust in your senses; look at and listen to the computer to help diagnose any RAM issues that might occur.

Troubleshooting Power Supply Issues

There are many types of power problems that can happen. We discuss more about power in general within Chapter 13, "Peripherals and Power," and Chapter 40, "Safety Procedures and Environmental Controls," but for now we will focus on power issues that occur related to the power supply within the computer.

Many issues that occur with power supplies are intermittent, making the troubleshooting process a little tougher. Your best friends when troubleshooting power supplies are going to be a power supply tester and your eyes and ears.

Of course, always make sure that the power supply cable connects from the power supply itself to a properly wired AC outlet properly before troubleshooting further! Next, check all of the internal power connections. Make sure they are connected firmly. To test these connections, use a power supply tester.

The power supply tester (or PSU tester) is a tool every computer tech should have in their toolkit. Figure 18.1 shows an example of a PSU tester. These testing devices normally test for 12 V, 5 V, and 3.3 V, for most of the connections within the computer including the main 24-pin ATX power connector, 8- and 4-pin CPU connector, PCI Express 8-pin and 6-pin connectors, SATA power connector, and Molex power connector. If there are error readings, error lights, no lights, or missing lights for specific voltages on the tester, you should consider replacing the power supply; or if it is modular, replace that particular power cable. If all the lights and indicators are normal, then the issue resides somewhere else.

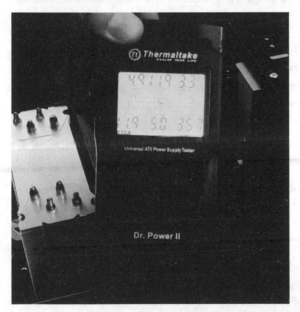

FIGURE 18.1   **PSU tester testing the 24-pin ATX power connector**

Here are several of the issues you might encounter with power supplies:

▶ Fan failure

▶ Fuse failure

▶ Quick death

▶ Slow death

Fan failure can be due to the fact that the power supply is old, the fan is extremely clogged with dirt, or the fan was of a cheaper design (without ball bearings). However, for the A+ exam, it doesn't make a difference. As far as the A+ exam is concerned, if the fan fails, the power supply needs to be replaced (and that strategy makes sense). Chances are, if the fan has failed, other components of the power supply are on their way out also. It is more cost-effective to a company to simply replace the power supply than to have a technician spend the time opening it and trying to repair it. More important, although it is possible to remove and replace the fan by opening the power supply, this can be a dangerous venture because the power supply holds an electric charge. So, the A+ rule is to never open the power supply.

> **ExamAlert**
>
> Do not open a power supply! If it has failed, replace it with a working unit.

Fan failure can sometimes cause a loud noise to emanate from the power supply; it might even sound like it is coming from inside the computer. Any fan in the computer (power supply fan, case fan, or CPU fan) can make some strange noises over time. If a customer reports a loud noise coming from the inside of a PC, consider the power supply fan.

On the other hand, sometimes the fans spin but no other devices receive power and the computer doesn't boot. This could be due to improper installation (or failure) of the motherboard, CPU, or RAM.

Fuse failure can occur due to an overload or due to the power supply malfunctioning. Either way, the proper course of action is to replace the power supply. Do not attempt to replace the fuse. Chances are that the power supply is faulty if the fuse is blown.

If the power supply dies a quick death and provides no power, it might be because of several reasons, ranging from an electrical spike to hardware malfunction. First, make sure that the IEC power cable is connected properly to the power supply and to the AC outlet. Sometimes it can be difficult to tell whether the power supply has failed or if it's something else inside or outside the computer system. You should check the AC outlet with your trusty receptacle tester, make sure that a circuit hasn't tripped, and verify that any surge protectors and/or UPS devices work properly. Depending on what you sense about the problem, you might decide to just swap out the power supply with a known good one.

If the power supply is dying a slow death and is causing intermittent errors or frequent failure of hard drives and other devices, it could be tough to troubleshoot. If you suspect intermittent issues, first make sure that the power cord is connected securely and then try swapping out the power supply with a known good one. Boot the computer and watch it for a while to see if the same errors occur.

> **Note**
>
> If a system were recently upgraded, the power supply could cause the system to reboot intermittently because the new components are causing too much of a power drain. When upgrading components, be sure to check if you need to upgrade the power supply as well!

Remember that connections sometimes can be jarred loose inside and outside the computer. Check the IEC cord on both ends and all power connections inside the computer. This includes the main motherboard connector as well as the CPU, Molex, SATA, and PCIe connectors. Any single loose connector can have "interesting" results on your computer!

Heating and Cooling

Another thing to watch for is system overheating. This can happen for several reasons:

- ▶ Power supply fan failure
- ▶ Auxiliary case fan failure
- ▶ Inadequate number of fans
- ▶ Missing or open slot covers
- ▶ Case isn't tightly closed and screwed in
- ▶ Location of computer

Air flow is important on today's personal computers because their processors can often operate at hundreds of billions of instructions per second or more (referred to as 100 giga-instructions per second [GIPS]). They typically use 100 to 150 watts of power. That creates a lot of heat! Add to that the video card and other cards that have their own on-board processors and you quickly realize it can get *hot* inside the computer case. Plus, environmental factors and higher temperature areas (such as warehouses and cafeterias) can cause heat to be trapped in the case, producing intermittent shutdowns. Circulation is the key word here. Air should flow in the case from the front and be exhausted out the back. Any openings in the case or missing slot covers can cause circulation to diminish. If you have a computer that has a lot of devices, does a lot of processing, or runs hot for any other reason, your best bet is to install a case fan in the front of the case (which pulls air into the case) and a second case fan in the back of the case (which, with the power supply fan, helps to exhaust hot air out the back). Standard sizes for case fans are 80 and 120 mm. Also, try to keep the computer in a relatively cool area and leave space for the computer to expel its hot air! Of course, there are other special considerations and options, such as liquid cooling and special processor cooling methods such as oversized tower heat sinks.

You should also train your nose for smells and watch for smoke. If a power supply starts to emit a burning smell, or you see any smoke emanating from it, you should turn off the computer and disconnect the power right away. The power supply is probably about to fail, and it could short out, trip the circuit, or, worse yet, start a fire. Be sure to replace it. In some cases, a power supply has a burn-in period of 24 to 48 hours, during which time you might smell some oils burning off, but it's best to be safe and check/test the power supply if you smell something that seems wrong.

Troubleshooting Questions in the A+ Exams

Hardware and software troubleshooting make up at least a quarter of the A+ exam objectives. For bench techs, help desk people, and other tech support personnel, it makes up a much larger percentage of work. When it really comes down to it, we as technicians are here to solve problems, and troubleshooting is a key component in the world of problem solving. So, I have included a lot more cram quiz questions for these troubleshooting chapters as compared to previous chapters. It seemed the proper way…

Cram Quiz

Answer these questions. The answers follow the last question. If you cannot answer these questions correctly, consider reading this chapter again until you can.

1. What is the best way to tell if a CR2032 lithium battery has been discharged?

- ○ **A.** Use a power supply tester.
- ○ **B.** Check within Windows.
- ○ **C.** Use a multimeter.
- ○ **D.** Plug it into another motherboard.

2. A PC reboots without any warning. You ruled out any chance of viruses. When you look at the motherboard, you see that some of the capacitors appear distended and out of shape. What should you do?

   ○ **A.** Replace the motherboard.

   ○ **B.** Replace the hard drive.

   ○ **C.** Remove and replace the capacitors.

   ○ **D.** Reconfigure the BIOS.

3. A computer you are troubleshooting won't boot properly. When you power on the computer, the video display is blank and you hear a series of beeps. What should you do?

   ○ **A.** Check power supply connections.

   ○ **B.** Consult the vendor documentation for the motherboard.

   ○ **C.** Remove all memory and replace it.

   ○ **D.** Unplug the speakers because they are causing a conflict.

4. You are troubleshooting a CPU and have already cut power, disconnected the power cable, opened the case, and put on your antistatic strap. What should you do next?

   ○ **A.** Check the BIOS.

   ○ **B.** Check connections.

   ○ **C.** Remove the CPU.

   ○ **D.** Test the Motherboard with a multimeter.

5. What is a possible symptom of a failing CPU?

   ○ **A.** CPU is beyond the recommended voltage range.

   ○ **B.** Computer won't boot.

   ○ **C.** BIOS reports low temperatures within the case.

   ○ **D.** Spyware is installed into the browser.

6. You are repairing a computer that has been used in a warehouse for several years. You suspect a problem with a memory module. What should you do first?

   ○ **A.** Replace the module with a new one.

   ○ **B.** Install more RAM.

   ○ **C.** Clean the RAM slot.

   ○ **D.** Install RAM heat sinks.

7. You just investigated a computer that is suffering from intermittent shutdowns. You note that the RAM modules are overheating. What is the best solution?

   ○ **A.** Install a heat sink on the memory controller.

   ○ **B.** Install more CPU fans.

   ○ **C.** Install heat sinks on the RAM modules.

   ○ **D.** Install a heat sink on the chipset.

8. You just installed new, compatible RAM into a motherboard, but when you boot the computer, it does not recognize the memory. What should you do?

   ○ **A.** Flash the BIOS.

   ○ **B.** Replace the RAM.

   ○ **C.** Upgrade the CPU.

   ○ **D.** Add more RAM.

9. You are troubleshooting a computer that won't power on. You have already checked the AC outlet and the power cord, which appear to be functioning properly. What should you do next?

   ○ **A.** Test the computer with a PSU tester.

   ○ **B.** Plug the computer into a different outlet.

   ○ **C.** Check that the RAM is seated correctly.

   ○ **D.** Install a UPS.

10. A computer you are troubleshooting shuts down without warning. After a few minutes, it boots back up fine, but after running for a short time, it shuts down again. Which of the following components could be the cause? (Select the two best answers.)

    ○ **A.** Power supply

    ○ **B.** SATA hard drive

    ○ **C.** RAM

    ○ **D.** CPU fan

    ○ **E.** Video card

Cram Quiz Answers

1. **C.** Although there might be a Windows application that monitors the battery, the surefire way is to test the voltage of the lithium battery with a multimeter. A CR2032 lithium battery is designed to run at 3 volts. Some UEFI/BIOS programs can also monitor the voltage of the battery.

2. **A.** You should replace the motherboard if it is damaged. It would be much too time-consuming to even attempt replacing the capacitors and probably not cost-effective for your company.

3. **B.** You should check the BIOS version and consult the documentation that accompanies the motherboard. You might need to go online for this information. You can also try performing a POST analysis to discern the problem. The issue could be video-based, or RAM-based, but the beep code should help to identify the problem.

4. **B.** Check connections first; it is quick, easy, and a common culprit.

5. **A.** If the CPU is running beyond the recommended voltage range for extended periods of time, it can be a sign of a failing CPU. If the computer won't boot at all, another problem might have occurred, or the CPU might have already failed. Low case temperatures are a good thing (if they aren't below freezing!). Spyware is unrelated, but we talk about it plenty in the security chapters.

6. **C.** Because the computer is being used in a warehouse (which is often a fairly dirty environment), you should use compressed air on the RAM slot and clean the memory module with contact cleaner. Clean out all of the dust bunnies within the entire computer. Using MemTest86 or another memory diagnostic tool is another good answer.

7. **C.** The best thing to do in this situation is to install heat sinks on the RAM modules. On older computers, the memory controller in a northbridge doesn't usually overheat because it already has a heat sink; on newer computers, it is within the CPU. A CPU can have only one fan. You can't install more (although an additional case fan might help). The chipset also usually has a heat sink.

8. **A.** If you are sure that the RAM is compatible and the system doesn't recognize it during POST, try flashing the UEFI/BIOS. It could be that the RAM is so new that the motherboard doesn't have the required firmware to identify the new RAM.

9. **A.** You should test the computer with a PSU tester. This can tell you whether the power supply functions properly. You already know that the AC outlet is functional, so there is no reason to use another outlet. The computer would still turn on if the RAM wasn't seated properly. A UPS won't help the situation because it is part of the power flow before the power supply.

10. **A and D.** The two components that could cause the system to shut down are the power supply and the CPU fan. Check the CPU fan settings and temperature in the BIOS first before opening the computer. If those are fine, you most likely need to replace the power supply. The RAM, video card, and hard drive should not cause the system to suddenly shut down.

CHAPTER 19

Troubleshooting Hard Drives and RAID Arrays

This chapter covers the following A+ 220-1001 exam objective:

▶ **5.3** – Given a scenario, troubleshoot hard drives and RAID arrays.

Hard drives contain the data that we need. So, we depend on our hard drives and RAID arrays to run efficiently every day. For this to happen, the drives need to be healthy. We can keep our drives healthy by carrying out a variety of precautionary measures. But sometimes, our systems can be affected by powers outside of our control, and beyond our planning. Then, they can potentially fail—and then, we have to troubleshoot.

5.3 – Given a scenario, troubleshoot hard drives and RAID arrays

ExamAlert

Objective 5.3 focuses on troubleshooting common symptoms of hard drives and RAID arrays, such as read/write failure, slow performance, loud clicking noise, failure to boot, drive not recognized, OS not found; RAID not found, RAID stops working, proprietary crash screens (BSOD/pin wheel), and S.M.A.R.T. errors.

Troubleshooting Hard Drives

Hard drives will fail. It's not a matter of if; it's a matter of when, especially when it comes to mechanical drives. The moving parts are bound to fail at some point. Hard drives have an average warranty of 3 years, as is the case with the SATA drives used in the examples in this book. It is interesting to note that most drives last around 3 years before failing. But remember, an ounce of prevention is worth a pound of cure, or for those of you using the metric system, 29 grams and .45 kg—but that just doesn't seem to roll off the tongue quite so well! Either way, by implementing good practices, you can extend the lifespan of a hard drive. So, before we get into troubleshooting hard drives, let's give some examples of prevention:

▶ **Turn the computer off when not in use:** This can help the lifespan of a magnetic-based drive. By doing this, the hard disk drive is told by the operating system to spin down and enter a "parked" state. It's kind of like parking a car or placing a record player's arm on its holder. Turning the computer off when not in use increases the lifespan of just about all its devices (except for the lithium battery). You can also set the computer to hibernate or standby, or simply set your operating system's power scheme to turn off hard disks after a certain amount of inactivity, such as 5 minutes. The less the drive is in motion, the longer lifespan it will have. Of course, if you want to take the moving parts out of the equation, you could opt for a solid-state drive, as discussed later in this chapter.

▶ **Clean up the disk:** Use a hard drive cleanup program to remove temporary files, clean out the Recycle Bin, and so on. Microsoft includes the Disk Cleanup program in Windows. And there are free cleanup programs available on the Internet (just be careful what you download). By removing the "junk" from the hard drive, there is less data that the drive must sift through, which makes it easier on the drive when it is time to defragment.

▶ **Defragment the drive:** Defragmenting, also known as *defragging*, rearranges the data on a partition or volume so that it is laid out in a contiguous, orderly fashion. You should attempt to defragment the disk every month, maybe more often if you are a power user. Don't worry: the operating system tells you if defragging is not necessary during the analysis stage. Over time, data is written to the drive and subsequently erased, over and over again, leaving gaps in the drive space. New data will sometimes be written to multiple areas of the drive, in a broken or fragmented fashion, filling in any blank areas it can find. When this happens, the hard drive has to work much harder to find the data it needs. Logically, data access time is increased. Physically, the drive will be spinning more, starting and stopping more—in general, more mechanical movement. It's kind of like changing gears excessively with the automatic transmission in your car. The more the drive has to access this fragmented data, the shorter its lifespan becomes due to mechanical wear and tear. But before the drive fails altogether, fragmentation can cause intermittent read/write failures. Defragmenting the drive can be done with Microsoft's Disk Defragmenter, with the command-line **defrag**, or with other third-party programs. If using the Disk Defragmenter program, you need 15 percent free space on the volume you want to defrag. If you have less than that, you need to use the command-line option **defrag -f**. To summarize, the more contiguous the data, the less the hard drive has to work to access that data, thus decreasing the data access time and increasing the lifespan of the drive. While defragmenting works best on magnetic drives, it can also help with solid-state drives, but not to the same extent, or in the same way because of the design differences between the two.

> **Note**
>
> Be careful with defragging; it can wear out a drive if it is done too much, especially when performed on SSDs.

> **ExamAlert**
>
> Know how to troubleshoot failures such as read/write errors using tools; for instance, Optimize Drives/Disk Defragmenter and the **defrag** command.

▶ **Leave at least 10 percent of the drive free:** If you use up all the space of a drive, its performance and lifespan will decrease greatly. Consider leaving between 10 and 25 percent of the space on the drive free of data. Some manufacturers add a 10 percent buffer by design, and some companies have a policy that states drives should never go past 50 or 60 percent of capacity. This preventive measure applies to HDDs and SSDs.

▶ **Make sure that high-performance drives have good airflow:** NVMe drives (such as M.2 and PCIe-based), as well as RAID arrays, can generate a lot of heat. Be sure to have good airflow and adequate cooling, and if at all possible, don't cramp the drives too much.

▶ **Scan the drive with anti-malware:** Make sure the computer has an anti-malware program installed. Also known as an endpoint protection platform, it should include antivirus and anti-spyware at the very least. Verify that the software is scheduled to scan the drive at least twice a week. (Manufacturers' default is usually every day.) The quicker the software finds and quarantines threats, the less chance of physical damage to the hard drive.

It's the preventive techniques that will save you time, save your users some heartache, and save your organization money.

Now, let's get into some of the problems you might encounter concerning hard drives:

▶ **BIOS does not "see" the drive:** If the BIOS doesn't recognize the drive you have installed, you can check a few things. First, make sure the power cable is firmly connected and oriented properly. Next, make sure SATA data cables are fully seated in the ports, and weren't accidentally installed upside down; if you find one that was, consider replacing it because it might be damaged due to incorrect installation. An OS Not Found error message, or other boot failure, could also be caused by improperly connected drives, or an erroneous BIOS boot order. Finally, check if there is a motherboard BIOS update to see the drive; sometimes newer drives require new BIOS code to access the drive.

▶ **Windows does not "see" a second drive:** There are several reasons why Windows might not see a second drive. Maybe a driver needs to be installed for the drive or for its controller. This is more common with newer hard drive technologies. Perhaps the secondary drive needs to be initialized within Disk Management. Or it could be that the drive was not partitioned or formatted. Also try the methods listed in the first bullet.

▶ **Slow reaction time:** If the system runs slow, it can be because the drive has become fragmented or has been infected with a virus or spyware. Analyze and defragment the drive. If it is heavily fragmented, the drive can take longer to access the data needed, resulting in slow reaction time. You might be amazed at the difference in performance! If you think the drive might be infected, scan the disk with your anti-malware program to quarantine any possible threats. It's wise to schedule deep scans of the drive at least twice a week. You will learn more about viruses and spyware in Chapter 32, "Wireless Security, Malware, and Social Engineering."

In extreme cases, you might want to move all the data from the affected drive to another drive, being sure to verify the data that was moved. Then format the affected drive and, finally, move the data back. This is common in audio/video environments and when dealing with data drives, but it should not be done to a system drive (meaning a drive that contains the operating system).

▶ **Missing files at startup:** If you get a message such as BOOTMGR Is Missing, the file needs to be written back to the hard drive. For more on how to do this, see Chapter 36, "Troubleshooting Microsoft Windows." In severe cases, this can mean that the drive is physically damaged and needs to be replaced. If this happens, the drive needs to be removed from the computer and slaved off to another drive on another system. Then the data must be copied from the damaged drive to a known good drive (which might require a third-party program), and a new drive must be installed to the affected computer. Afterward, the recovered data can be copied on the new drive.

▶ **Other missing/corrupted files:** Missing or corrupted files could be the result of hard drive failure, operating system failure, malware infection, user error, and so on. If this happens more than once, be sure to back up the rest of the data on the drive, and then use the preventive methods mentioned previously, especially defragmenting and scanning for malware. You can also analyze the drive's S.M.A.R.T data. S.M.A.R.T. stands for Self-Monitoring, Analysis, and Reporting Technology—it is a monitoring system included with almost all hard drives that creates reporting data which, when enabled in the BIOS, can be accessed within the operating system. You can easily view some basic S.M.A.R.T.-based information in the Windows Command Prompt by using the command **wmic diskdrive get status**. Each drive (if S.M.A.R.T.-enabled) will be analyzed: a message of **OK** means that Windows didn't find any issues. A message of Bad, Unknown, or Caution should convince you to initiate more analysis. There are also plenty of third-party tools available that can be downloaded from the Internet and are very easy to use. The problem with S.M.A.R.T. data is that it can be unreliable at times due to lack of hardware and driver support within the third-party S.M.A.R.T. application, lack of common interpretation, and incorrectly diagnosed data. Also, a hard drive might be diagnosed as a failing drive when in reality the problem is power surges or another issue.

> **Note**
>
> If a file is written during a power surge (whether originating internally or externally), that file will most likely be placed on the drive in a corrupted fashion—the associated sector being affected by the power surge. In this case, you should find out two things: 1, if the power supply has the right capacity for the equipment in the computer, and 2, if the proper power suppressing/conditioning equipment is being used. If a drive is making clicking sounds or other strange noises, analysis with S.M.A.R.T. data is not recommended. See the following bullet for more information.

▶ **Noisy drive/lockups:** If your SATA magnetic disk drive starts getting noisy, it's a sure sign of impending drive failure. You might also hear a scratching or grating sound, akin to scratching a record with the record player's needle. Or the drive might intermittently just stop or lock up with one or more loud audible clicks. You can't wait in these situations; you need to connect the drive to another computer immediately and copy the data to a good drive. Even then, it might be too late. However, there are some third-party programs available on the Internet that might help recover the data.

> **Note**
>
> Hard drive issues can also result in proprietary crash screens: either a Windows "Blue Screen of Death" (BSOD) or a macOS "spinning pinwheel." Fixing these issues often requires using recovery environment tools and/or restoring the system to an earlier point in time. If these issues happen often and hard drive repair methods do not work, then consider either a new installation of Windows or a new hard drive. We cover how to troubleshoot these problems further in the Core 2 (220-1002) portion of the book.

As I mentioned, hard drives *will* fail, so it is important to make backups of your data. The backup media of choice will vary depending on the organization. It could be the cloud, a secondary system, DVD-ROM discs, even USB flash drives. It differs based on the scenario. In some cases, an organization might decide to back up to tape. Remember that RAID arrays are not considered to be backups. They are fault-tolerant ways of storing data. Backup and archiving goes beyond the RAID array, and usually incorporates some kind of off-site storage system.

Troubleshooting RAID Arrays

Sometimes, hardware RAID arrays will fail. They might stop working or the OS could have trouble finding them. If you see an issue like this, check whether the hard drives are securely connected to the controller and that the controller (if an adapter card) is securely connected to the motherboard. Also, if you use a RAID adapter card or external enclosure, and the motherboard also has built-in RAID functionality of its own, make sure you disable the motherboard RAID within the BIOS—it could cause a conflict. Verify that the driver for the RAID device is installed and updated. Finally, check if any of the hard drives or the RAID controller has failed. If a RAID controller built into a motherboard fails, you will have to purchase a RAID adapter card.

Intel-based RAID setups are common as part of server and workstation motherboards, and as separate RAID adapter cards. To configure Intel RAID, a technician needs to press Ctrl+I when the system first boots up, perhaps even before the BIOS on some systems. From there, the RAID array can be configured as shown in Figure 19.1.

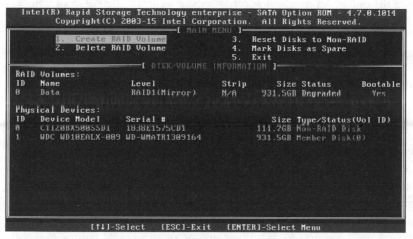

FIGURE 19.1 **Intel RAID configuration screen**

In Figure 19.1 you will see that there is a RAID 1 Mirror, but that the status is "Degraded." That means that the array has failed, or has been deconstructed in some way. The listed drive is part of a RAID 1 volume called Data, but the second drive of the mirror is missing, so the mirror is broken. (That's because I removed it from the system to show this very error.) Look in the listed physical devices for the drive that is 931.5 GB; you will see that it is listed as a

Member Disk, meaning that it is part of an array. A degraded RAID 0, 1, 5, or 10 array will result in either a loss of access to data or—if the OS is installed to the array—failure of the OS to boot. Either way, the array would have to be repaired or the data would have to be recovered from backup and placed on a new array. Repairing a RAID array could be as simple as reconnecting the physical drives, but it could also mean reconfiguring the array within the RAID utility. Some organizations have a rule: if a RAID array fails—and it is older than 3 years—then, downgrade the array, create a new array with new drives, and recover the data from backup.

Now, let's say that our RAID functionality is indeed built into our motherboard as it is on the system shown in Figure 19.1. In order to configure a RAID array, we first have to enable RAID in the BIOS. Quite often, that is done by accessing the SATA configuration screen and changing from AHCI to RAID. If you don't, then you won't be able to access the RAID utility at bootup. Take it to the next level. If someone was to reset the BIOS to defaults, then that SATA setting would revert to AHCI, rendering the RAID array useless and non-bootable—ultimately leading to various error messages. This could also happen after a BIOS flash update. Yet another reason to know the BIOS of your systems!

> **Note**
>
> AHCI stands for Advanced Host Configuration Interface, the default setting for SATA drives in many BIOS programs.

One way to check the status of a RAID array is to use S.M.A.R.T. For example, in Figure 19.2 you can see the S.M.A.R.T. information screen for one of the disks in a RAID 1 mirror of a network-attached storage (NAS) device. This screen gives some meaningful data that requires some analysis, but for quick peace of mind, just check the Status column. OKs are good—anything else requires further attention, and could be a precursor to a RAID failure. You will also note in the figure a S.M.A.R.T. Test page where you can do additional testing of the drive, drives, or array. Just be sure to run tests of this nature off-hours!

Health Info - Disk 1

Overview | S.M.A.R.T. Test | **S.M.A.R.T. Info** | History

The information shown here is directly obtained from the hard drive, and should be consulted alongside with S.M.A.R.T. test results to ensure that the hard drive is healthy.

ID	Attribute	Value	Worst	Threshold	Status	Raw data
1	Raw_Read_Error_Rate	200	200	051	OK	0
3	Spin_Up_Time	163	163	021	OK	6808
4	Start_Stop_Count	098	098	000	OK	2789
5	Reallocated_Sector_Ct	200	200	140	OK	0
7	Seek_Error_Rate	200	200	000	OK	0
9	Power_On_Hours	098	098	000	OK	1865
10	Spin_Retry_Count	100	100	000	OK	0
11	Calibration_Retry_Count	100	100	000	OK	0
12	Power_Cycle_Count	098	098	000	OK	2661
192	Power-Off_Retract_Cou...	200	200	000	OK	2
193	Load_Cycle_Count	200	200	000	OK	2788
194	Temperature_Celsius	120	112	000	OK	30
196	Reallocated_Event_Co...	200	200	000	OK	0

Close

FIGURE 19.2 **S.M.A.R.T. information and status of a NAS hard drive**

RAID Is Not Backup!

Remember, in the workplace, RAID is generally used for fault tolerance; it is not a backup of data, even if you are using RAID 1, mirroring. A RAID array's data should be properly backed up to a *separate* system, according to your organization's procedures. The backup should be tested thoroughly and documented.

Cram Quiz

Answer these questions. The answers follow the last question. If you cannot answer these questions correctly, consider reading this chapter again until you can.

1. What should you do first to repair a drive that is acting sluggish?

   ❍ **A.** Remove the drive and recover the data.

   ❍ **B.** Run Disk Cleanup.

   ❍ **C.** Run Disk Defragmenter.

   ❍ **D.** Scan for viruses.

2. Which of the following are possible symptoms of hard drive failure? (Select the two best answers.)

   ○ **A.** System lockup

   ○ **B.** Antivirus alerts

   ○ **C.** Failing bootup files

   ○ **D.** Network drive errors

   ○ **E.** BIOS doesn't recognize the drive

3. You just replaced an SATA hard drive that you suspected had failed. You also replaced the data cable between the hard drive and the motherboard. When you reboot the computer, you notice that the SATA drive is not recognized by the BIOS. What most likely happened to cause this?

   ○ **A.** The drive has not been formatted yet.

   ○ **B.** The BIOS does not support SATA.

   ○ **C.** The SATA port is faulty.

   ○ **D.** The drive is not jumpered properly.

4. You are troubleshooting an SATA hard drive that doesn't function on a PC. When you try it on another computer, it works fine. You suspect a power issue and decide to take voltage readings from the SATA power connector coming from the power supply. Which of the following readings should you find?

   ○ **A.** 5 V and 12 V

   ○ **B.** 5 V, 12 V, and 24 V

   ○ **C.** 3.3 V, 5 V, and 12 V

   ○ **D.** 3.3 V and 12 V

5. You are troubleshooting a Windows Server that normally boots from an SATA-based RAID 0 array. The message you receive is "missing operating system." As it turns out, another technician has been updating the BIOS on several of the servers in your organization, including this one. What configured setting needs to be changed? (Select the best answer.)

   ○ **A.** RAID 1

   ○ **B.** AHCI

   ○ **C.** S.M.A.R.T.

   ○ **D.** NVMe

6. What should you do *first* if your SATA magnetic disk begins to make loud clicking noises? (Select the best answer.)

   ○ **A.** Copy the data to another drive.

   ○ **B.** Replace with a new SATA drive.

   ○ **C.** Update the UEFI/BIOS.

   ○ **D.** Replace the SATA power cable.

Cram Quiz Answers

1. **C.** Attempt to defragment the disk. If it is not necessary, Windows lets you know. Then you can move to other options, such as scanning the drive for viruses.

2. **A and C.** System lockups and failing bootup files or other failing file operations are possible symptoms of hard drive failure. Antivirus alerts tell you that the operating system has been compromised, viruses should be quarantined, and a full scan should be initiated. Sometimes hard drives can fail due to heavy virus activity, but usually if the malware is caught quickly enough, the hard drive should survive. Network drives are separate from the local hard drive; inability to connect to a network drive suggests a network configuration issue. If the BIOS doesn't recognize the drive, consider a BIOS update.

3. **C.** Most likely, the SATA port is faulty. It might have been damaged during the upgrade. To test the theory, you would plug the SATA data cable into another port on the motherboard. You can't format the drive until it has been recognized by the BIOS, which, by the way, should recognize SATA drives if the motherboard has SATA ports! SATA drives don't use jumpers unless they need to coexist with older IDE drives. Most of today's drives do not come with jumpers.

4. **C.** If you test an SATA power cable, you should find 3.3 V (orange wire), 5 V (red wire), and 12 V (yellow wire). If any of these doesn't test properly, try another SATA power connector.

5. **B.** When the BIOS was updated, the SATA setting in the BIOS probably reverted to AHCI. That caused the RAID 0 array to be ignored, and so the OS would not boot, because it is stored on that array. The setting should be changed from AHCI to RAID (or similar name). Now, if this was a RAID 1 mirror, then a copy of the OS would be on each drive, and it might still boot (though you will will probably receive a message as to the state of the mirror being degraded or broken). But with RAID 0, the OS is *striped* across two or more drives—all drives need to be present and accessed via RAID in order for the OS to boot. That's one of the reasons why the golden rule for many years was to "mirror the OS, and stripe the data." Phew! Anyways, on to the incorrect answers. RAID 1 is incorrect because there would be no option to set this; in the scenario, we are using RAID 0. S.M.A.R.T. is the monitoring system included in HDDs and SSDs. NVMe (Non-Volatile Memory Express) is the specification for non-volatile storage used by M.2 drives, PCIe card–based drives, and so on. Remember to back up any and all BIOS configurations!

6. **A.** Don't hesitate! Copy the data to another drive. Afterward, update the UEFI/BIOS, replace the drive with a new one, and consider a new SATA cable while you are at it.

CHAPTER 20

Troubleshooting Video Issues and Mobile Devices

This chapter covers the following A+ 220-1001 exam objectives:

▶ **5.4** – Given a scenario, troubleshoot video, projector, and display issues.

▶ **5.5** – Given a scenario, troubleshoot common mobile device issues while adhering to the appropriate procedures.

Video is another one of those technologies that you will troubleshoot often. Video issues could be hardware-based or software-based. There are so many types of video connectors, standards, and different output devices; and so, there is plenty of work for us techs. Be sure to refer back to Chapter 9, "Cables and Connectors," and Chapter 10, "Peripherals and Power," for more information on video.

There are a lot of potential video issues with mobile devices as well, so that makes for a good place to transition over to mobile device troubleshooting. We'll also discuss batteries, overheating, and proper disassembly techniques. Be ready to refer back to Chapter 3, "Smartphones, Tablets, and Other Mobile Devices, Part 1," and Chapter 4, "Smartphones, Tablets, and Other Mobile Devices, Part 2," for more information on mobile devices.

5.4 – Given a scenario, troubleshoot video, projector, and display issues

> **ExamAlert**
>
> **Objective 5.4** concentrates on troubleshooting common symptoms of video issues, such as VGA mode, no image on screen, overheat shutdown, dead pixels, artifacts, incorrect color patterns, dim image, flickering image, distorted image, distorted geometry, burn-in, and oversized images and icons.

There are several parts that make up a video system, both hardware and software: GPUs, monitors, cables and connections, video drivers, video settings, and so on. So, there is plenty to troubleshoot when it comes to video. I like to look at it as a system within the computer system, and follow the path of video when troubleshooting; for example, from the software > to the operating system and driver > to the video card itself > through the cables and connectors > out to the display (or displays, whatever they might be). And let's not forget power—many video cards require a power connection, and the monitor does as well. Also remember your types of video connections: HDMI, DVI, DisplayPort, and so on. Keep all these things in the back of your mind as you are troubleshooting video—and remember to write it out. Document and write down (or type) as much as possible: include pictures and illustrations to help in the troubleshooting process.

Video Troubleshooting

When troubleshooting video issues, there are a number of things to check, including the following:

- ▶ **Connections:** If nothing is showing up on the display, first make sure that the monitor is plugged into the video card properly (and to the correct video port), and then verify whether the monitor is connected to the AC outlet and is powered on. Check which video port the monitor is configured to use by accessing the on-screen display (OSD) with the appropriate button on the monitor. If necessary, try removing the video card and reseating it carefully. Poor connectivity of cables or the video card can also cause screen flicker.

- ▶ **Power cycle the computer, display, and any power protection equipment:** Power cycling the equipment can fix all kinds of problems and is an easy solution to implement. Problems such as video memory (image retention) and stuck pixels might be easily repaired by a power cycle of the display, the computer, and any surge suppressor that the equipment is plugged into. You might also need to leave a display off for a couple of hours to fix a video memory problem—for example, the video memory/image retention issue, which is sometimes referred to as burn-in. But burn-in is actually a *symptom* of the problem that occurs in the older (but still used) cathode ray tube (CRT) type of monitor. While image retention and flickering image issues are more common with CRTs, you might still see them with flat-panel monitors as well. If you use a KVM switch, power cycle that as well. Many KVMs need to be turned on first (and left on for 10 seconds or so) before a connecting computer can be turned on; otherwise that computer won't display through the KVM properly.

▶ **Check for an onboard video setting in the UEFI/BIOS:** If you install a new video card to a computer that previously used onboard video, always check that the onboard video setting is disabled in the UEFI or BIOS. It can conflict with the new video card. And, of course, be sure to plug the monitor into the new video card—not the old onboard connection.

▶ **Resolution and refresh settings:** If the resolution was set too high or was set to a resolution not supported by the monitor, you might get a distorted image or no image at all. Boot into low-resolution VGA mode or Safe Mode. This starts the computer with a resolution of 640×480. Then modify the resolution setting in the Screen Resolution window. Lower resolutions will result in oversized icons and images that might be preferable to some but will make it difficult for the typical user to view all the information required on one screen (for example, within a spreadsheet or A/V editing program). Simply increase the resolution to "resolve" the problem! For CRT monitors, an incorrect resolution setting could cause distorted geometry—where the image doesn't fit the display properly—though this might also be caused by poor horizontal or vertical settings on the monitor itself. The refresh rate can also cause issues if it is not set correctly; for example, screen flicker, or no display at all. The refresh rate is the number of times that the screen image is refreshed per second; a common number is 60 Hz. The number it is set to should coincide with the monitor's capability. More on resolution and refresh rate later in Chapter 28, "Windows Control Panel Utilities."

▶ **Check the driver:** Maybe the driver failed, or perhaps the wrong driver was installed during installation, or maybe an update is necessary. If there is nothing on the display, or if the image is distorted, or if the monitor only displays a lower resolution, boot into low-res mode or Safe Mode and update the driver from within Device Manager, or consider "rolling back" the driver, which reverts to the older driver that installed previously. Driver failures could also be the cause of Blue Screens of Death (BSODs).

▶ **Check the version of DirectX:** DirectX is a Windows technology that includes video, animation, and sound components. It helps a computer get more performance out of multimedia, games, and movies. The DirectX Diagnostic Tool (DxDiag) helps to troubleshoot DirectX-related issues. This tool gives information about the installed version of DirectX and whether it is operating correctly, among other things. The DirectX Diagnostic Tool can be started by opening the Run prompt and typing **dxdiag**. By default, Windows 7 and 8 use DirectX 11, and Windows 10 uses DirectX 12. However, these systems can be updated to newer versions of DirectX if necessary.

▶ **Check the temperature threshold of the video card:** High-end video cards are intensely used by gamers and designers, and they can be the hottest component in a computer. If the temperature surpasses the safeguards in place, it might cause the card to throttle back the GPU speed. Or, it might cause an overheat shutdown, where the video card might stop working altogether, causing the current application to close or, at worst, the display to go blank. If this happens more than once or twice, consider additional cooling fans or a liquid cooling system.

▶ **Use software to check and repair stuck or dead pixels:** When a single pixel fails, it can be irritating. But there are third-party software programs that can be used to identify stuck pixels and possible dead pixels and attempt to fix them (search "LCD repair," "dead pixel repair," or similar terms). Always try power-cycling the device as well. If you can't repair the stuck or dead pixel, you might have to send the display to the manufacturer or authorized repair center for repair or for replacement, or if it is a laptop, replace it yourself!

▶ **Calibrate the monitor:** If you see artifacts (image distortions) or you notice incorrect color patterns, or the display just doesn't seem to look quite as good as it used to, try calibrating the monitor either by resetting it with the OSD or by adjusting the contrast, brightness, and color levels. Also try adjusting the color depth in Windows, and check the screen resolution. You can also try using the built-in Windows 10 Display Color Calibration tool, which can be accessed by going to Search and typing **color calibration** or by going to Run and typing **dccw**. Try to limit reflections on the screen. If using an older CRT monitor and the artifacts still appear, consider upgrading to an LCD display! Dim images could also be caused by misconfiguring the brightness and contrast. Always configure the brightness first, and once the optimal brightness level has been found, then configure the contrast.

▶ **Use a filter on the monitor:** Sometimes a user will complain of eye strain. This might not be a video issue at all; it could be due to glare. Consider using an antiglare filter. Companies make these filters specifically for individual models of monitors. They help to reduce glare from fluorescent lights, sunlight, and so on. In a more secure environment, consider also using privacy filters. These reduce the viewing angle of the screen—only the person sitting directly in front of the screen can read it, helping to reduce the chance of shoulder surfing. Privacy filters often reduce glare as well.

▶ **Check for newly installed applications:** New applications could cause the display to malfunction or stop working altogether. Check the application manufacturer's website for any known hardware compatibility issues.

▶ **Check inside the computer:** I usually leave this for last because it is time-consuming to open the system, unless I have a sneaky suspicion that one of the connections inside the computer is loose. Check whether the video card is seated properly. In areas in which the temperature and humidity change quickly, the card could be unseated due to thermal expansion and contraction. (Some refer to this as chip creep or card creep.) Also, if the computer was moved recently, it could cause the card to come out of the slot slightly. Verify that the power connections and other cables are not loose. Check all other connections inside the PC to make sure it isn't a video problem. For example, if the system makes use of an onboard video controller and you start seeing garbled images, strange colors, or cursor trails, you might have defective RAM (or maybe you have been working on computers too long). Remember that onboard video controllers rely on the sticks of RAM in the motherboard, as opposed to individual video cards that have their own RAM.

ExamAlert

The previous 12 bullets are all very important troubleshooting techniques that you should know for the 220-1001 exam. Study them carefully!

Again, verify that it is actually a video problem. Don't forget about the other major components of a computer system. When you can't see anything on the display and you know the computer is receiving power, you can narrow it down to video, RAM, processor, and the motherboard (what I sometimes refer to as the "big four"). But if the system appears to boot, and you can see hard drive activity from the LED light on the front of the case, and/or hear the hard drive accessing data, then it is most likely a video problem. Go back to the basics: Check power and connections. Try substituting a known good monitor in place of the current one. When it comes to video, the simple answers are the most common.

Cram Quiz

Answer these questions. The answers follow the last question. If you cannot answer these questions correctly, consider reading this section again until you can.

1. A user set the resolution in Windows too high, resulting in a scrambled, distorted display. What should you do to fix the problem? (Select the best answer.)
   - ○ **A.** Upgrade the video driver.
   - ○ **B.** Boot into low-resolution mode.
   - ○ **C.** Press the monitor toggle key.
   - ○ **D.** Check the video connections.

2. You are troubleshooting a video issue. Which utility should you use?
   - ○ **A.** Regedit
   - ○ **B.** Msconfig
   - ○ **C.** DxDiag
   - ○ **D.** Task Manager

3. You receive a very basic computer that has a broken on-board DVI connector. What should you attempt first?
   - ○ **A.** Replace the motherboard.
   - ○ **B.** Replace the DVI connector.
   - ○ **C.** Install a video card.
   - ○ **D.** Use an adapter.

4. You just replaced a video card in a PC with another card from a different manufacturer. However, the driver installation does not complete. What should you do first?
   - ○ **A.** Install the driver again.
   - ○ **B.** Locate the latest version of the driver.
   - ○ **C.** Roll back the driver.
   - ○ **D.** Install the original video card.

Cram Quiz Answers

1. **B.** Boot into a low-resolution mode. In Windows, this is called Enable Low-Resolution Video. Safe Mode is another valid option, but keep in mind that Safe Mode loads Windows with a minimal set of drivers and you can't access the Internet. Depending on the display configuration, pressing the monitor toggle key might actually fix the problem temporarily by displaying the screen on a secondary monitor, but it doesn't solve the root cause of the problem.

2. **C.** You should use DxDiag to troubleshoot video issues. The other three answers are not used to troubleshoot video. Regedit is used to perform advanced configurations in the registry. Msconfig is used to change how the system boots and enable/disable services. The Task Manager is used to see the performance of the computer and view applications and processes that are running. We'll discuss the rest of those tools in more depth in the Windows portion of this book.

3. **C.** Try installing a video card first to see if the system will still work. Unless it is a specialized system, the video card should be less expensive than the motherboard. (Not to mention it will take a lot less time to install.) As PC techs, we usually do not replace connectors; it is a possibility, but it should be further down your troubleshooting list. An adapter cannot help if the DVI port is broken.

4. **C.** If the driver installation doesn't complete, you should roll back the driver. It could be that you have attempted to install the incorrect driver. After you roll back the faulty installation, find the correct latest version of the video driver from the manufacturer's website. Installing the driver again can most likely have the same result. Only reinstall the original video card temporarily if you cannot find a proper solution right away.

5.5 – Given a scenario, troubleshoot common mobile device issues while adhering to the appropriate procedures

> **ExamAlert**
>
> **Objective 5.5** focuses on troubleshooting common symptoms of mobile device issues, such as battery not charging, no power, no wireless connectivity, touchscreen non-responsive, short battery life, frozen system, and overheating. It also covers disassembling processes for proper reassembly.

Time to think portable and mobile. Fixing mobile devices could be a life-long career. Just look at the abundance of mobile device repair shops—there seems to be no end to cracked screens, missing displays, overheated devices, and battery issues to sustain all these shops. And most mobile devices can be difficult to open and work on because of their small size.

There is some overlap between this objective and 220-1002 Objective 3.4. Some of the content (mostly hardware-based) I cover here, while the rest (mostly software-based) I cover in Chapter 38, "Troubleshooting Mobile Operating Systems."

> **Note**
>
> Laptop troubleshooting was covered in Chapters 1 and 2. Some of the bullets listed in Objective 5.5 are covered there.

Mobile Device Display Troubleshooting

The display is the cause of many a user's headache. Lots of things can go wrong with it; sometimes they are a failure of the device, but more often than not, they are due to user error or, more accurately, user ignorance.

For example, the display might look dim. This could be because the brightness level is too low in the display settings. Or it could be that automatic brightness was enabled and perhaps it doesn't react well in highly lit areas. Or perhaps auto-brightness isn't calibrated properly; perhaps it was initially enabled in a very bright (or very dark) environment. To recalibrate the device's light sensor, turn off auto-brightness and then go to an unlit room and set the brightness to the lowest setting. Finally, turn auto-brightness back on and leave the unlit room. The device should now make better use of its light sensors, and auto-brightness should function better.

You might also encounter a situation in which there is no display whatsoever or what appears to be no display. This could simply be that the device is in sleep mode (or off). Always check the simple solutions first; as a tech, you'll find they work more often than you would expect! But it could also be that the brightness (once again) is at the lowest setting and the user is working in a bright area. When taking the device out of sleep mode, the user can't tell that the display is working (though it may be barely visible). Take the device to a dark area to fix it or hold it under a desk or table to be able to see the screen until it is fixed. The brightness might have been turned down by accident, the user might have turned it down the night before (because it was dark out), or a virus could affect the slider that controls the brightness. Brightness is definitely a common culprit— let's just thank our lucky stars that there is no contrast setting on the bulk of mobile devices! However, no display or a nonresponsive display could also mean that the device is indeed off or that the battery has been discharged. Finally, it could be that the display connection is loose, or the display is damaged. In these last two scenarios, the device will have to be opened to repair/replace the display. If your organization uses an authorized repair center to perform these duties, document what the problem is and pack it securely to be shipped out right away.

Mobile Device Overheating

How many times have you heard a user say that a mobile device is running hot? How many times has your own device run hot? It's common. Overheating can be caused by a number of things: poorly written applications, excessive use of applications, excessive browsing, old batteries, damaged batteries, and, of course, the simple fact that the device is very small and that there is an inherent lack of ventilation.

Some applications use a lot of power (CPU-wise and battery-wise). It's these applications that tend to slow down the mobile device, eat up battery reserves, cause a power drain, and make the device run hot. Certain GPS programs, games, and streaming media apps are among the top contenders for this, but just about any app could cause this. And then you have the aging effect; newer apps don't run so well on older devices because of the lack of resources, and as a result, they can overheat the device. Unfortunately, there isn't too much the user can do about this other than self-policing, removing apps suspected to be the cause of the problem, and disabling unnecessary functionality on the device. Does the user need that live wallpaper? Has that user collected enough "coins" in that game? You know what I mean. Let's not forget about mobile OS updates; they can make the device feel like it was in an oven. This is normal, and the device should be plugged in and placed in a cool area while the update proceeds.

But the battery can get hot simply because it is old (or damaged). Battery manufacturers use the term "charging cycle." That is when you take a mobile device that is completely discharged and charge it up to 100 percent. Most battery manufacturers say that a typical battery can handle several hundred charge cycles maximum. That essentially means that a typical smartphone battery has a shelf life of about two to three years, because most people charge them every day. Tablets usually last much longer because of the greater battery capacity and the fact that they aren't charged as often. So, it's the mobile phone that we are most concerned with. A user can do the following to increase the lifespan of their battery:

▶ **Avoid draining the battery:** Charge the device often, before it gets too low. The more the battery is discharged below 50 percent, and especially below 10 percent, the less shelf life it will have in general.

▶ **Conserve power:** Set sleep mode to 1 minute or less. Decrease brightness. Disable or remove unnecessary functions and apps. Restart the phone at least once a day to stop any running apps (this is a big power saver). Consider putting the device into airplane mode at night.

▶ **Keep the device away from heat sources:** For example, if the device is mounted near a vehicle's air vent during the dead of winter, it's bound to run hot. Sarcasm aside, this can actually cause battery wear and damage over time. Keep it out of direct sunlight, too, if at all possible.

▶ **Turn off the mobile device when not in use:** Some people simply cannot do this, but I thought I'd mention it anyway!

▶ **Don't bang or throw the device:** Sounds crazy that I would have to say this, but it's good advice. Not only can a user break the device completely, but dropping, throwing, or banging the device can damage the battery, which can cause it to overheat, reduce the lifespan of the battery, and, in the worst-case scenario, cause a battery leak, which is a toxic mess that you don't want to be a part of.

▶ **Select protective cases carefully:** A protective case is a very good idea (especially if you are prone to actions in the previous bullet), but make sure it has good airflow. Sometimes these cases can envelop the battery, causing it to overheat.

ExamAlert

Know how to increase the lifespan of a mobile device's battery.

More Mobile Device Troubleshooting

When it comes to mobile devices, batteries—and power in general—tend to account for a lot of troubleshooting. No power, or if a battery won't charge, could be a sign that the battery needs to be replaced, either because it is simply too old and won't hold a charge anymore, or because it is damaged. Battery damage can manifest itself internally (which can't be seen with the naked eye), or it could show up as a swollen battery. As mentioned previously in the book, watch out for swollen batteries; they could be caused by damaging, overcharging, overvoltage, or a manufacturing problem. These should be removed (if possible); use great care if you are the one handling the battery, and make sure it is stored in a cool dark place until it can be recycled.

Be sure to clean your device. Every month or so, turn off the device, take it out of the case, and clean it (and the inside of the case) with a mix that is half isopropyl alcohol and half water (applied to a dry, lint-free cloth). Take extra care when cleaning the charging port—use a cotton swab and/or toothpick. This really works. Use that solution sparingly though; a little goes a long way.

A battery issue could also cause a system to "freeze" or lock up, rendering it useless; though a frozen system could also be caused by faulty applications or a problem with the mobile OS or a driver. If the system does freeze up, it might require you to force stop an application, or perform a battery pull (if possible), or more likely a soft reset (again, if possible). Worst-case scenario is to initiate a hard reset, which we normally want to avoid if we can because it will wipe the system. We'll discuss force stops and resets in Chapter 38.

Sometimes the touchscreen of a mobile device may become nonresponsive. There are several potential reasons for this:

▶ An application or the OS has failed.

▶ The system froze up.

▶ The display connection is loose.

▶ The display needs to be replaced.

▶ User error.

This last one should always be on your mind. A person might be wearing gloves that prohibit proper touchscreen response. Or, perhaps the person is using the wrong type of stylus, or the touchscreen doesn't accept stylus input. Perhaps the touchscreen needs to be calibrated; it's less common with today's devices, but possible. Be ready for a variety of issues!

No sound from the speaker? Start with the easy stuff—is the volume muted or turned down? But this is not always easy for some users because of the built-in mixer in most of today's smartphones: there are separate volumes for voice calls, media, notifications, and so on. So even though one volume might be up, another might be down. Going further, perhaps the speaker has been blocked by a protective case that doesn't quite fit right. Or maybe an app simply isn't registering sound correctly or has its own volume or mute option. It's unlikely, but another possibility is that the speaker connection is loose—or the speaker has failed. Once again, this will require a tech to open the device or send it out for repair.

Keep an open mind. When you are dealing with technology that can potentially fail often, combined with users that might not have been trained to use devices properly, you end up with *lots* of troubleshooting.

Disassembling Processes for Proper Reassembly

That heading was a mouthful, wouldn't you agree? What it means is that you should try to disassemble mobile devices in a logical manner, so that when it comes time to put them back together, you will not be confused, and can reduce the chance of a mistake.

The first and best way to do this is to document. Just like with bigger computers such as PCs, write as much down as you can. Take notes and make little illustrations—even if your artwork is a bunch of chicken scratch like mine! Organize any parts that have been removed. Document and label wires and cables and where they are supposed to connect to. Record what type of screws go where and store them temporarily in an organized manner. Some people put them all in a bowl or can. My preference is to use a large weekly pill box (many healthcare organizations give these away for free). In your documentation, mark which screws are where; for example, Monday has the #6-32 thumbscrews, and Tuesday has the T4 Torx screws, and so on. Chances are that you won't see both on the same device; the first is for PCs, and the second is for phones and similar devices. Take photos with your smartphone or other digital camera during the disassembly process. Those are just examples! Remember, good documentation aids in efficient planning, proper testing, and insightful troubleshooting.

Make use of manufacturer resources, such as: tech support via phone or website, help forums, downloadable manuals in PDF format, information on disc… the list goes on.

ExamAlert

Use manufacturer-supplied resources such as manuals, tech support, and forums.

Use appropriate hand tools when working with mobile devices. Of course, first make sure you are protecting against ESD—that means the use of proper antistatic equipment. Then, have your tools at the ready: miniature screwdrivers, shims, spudgers, magnifying glass, mini-flashlight, multimeter and other testing gear, SD and microSD card reader, and various USB, Lightning, and other cables and adapters ready to hook up the mobile device to a testing PC or laptop. Take a look at Figure 20.1 for an example of some of the hand tools I use on mobile devices. The list goes on, and there are several manufacturers of mobile device toolkits that can help you on your way toward mobile device repair. Make sure that you are not using magnetically charged tools, and again, implement your ESD prevention methods before you start working.

FIGURE 20.1 **Mobile device hand tools**

Cram Quiz

Answer these questions. The answers follow the last question. If you cannot answer these questions correctly, consider reading this section again until you can.

1. A user's mobile device is overheating. Which of the following could be the problem? (Select the two best answers.)

   ○ **A.** A damaged battery.

   ○ **B.** The brightness setting is too low.

   ○ **C.** Excessive gaming.

   ○ **D.** The device is not in a case.

   ○ **E.** The charging cable is defective.

2. You are troubleshooting a user's smartphone. The user informs you that he can't see anything on the screen. Of the following, what should you do first?

   ○ **A.** Disassemble the device for proper reassembly.

   ○ **B.** Check the volume mixer sliders.

   ○ **C.** Verify the brightness setting.

   ○ **D.** Calibrate the screen.

   ○ **E.** Restart the phone.

3. When disassembling a mobile device, what should you *not* do?

   ○ **A.** Document everything you see.

   ○ **B.** Store screws in a logical manner.

   ○ **C.** Make use of manuals.

   ○ **D.** Implement antistatic procedures.

   ○ **E.** Use magnetic-tip screwdrivers.

   ○ **F.** Label cables.

Cram Quiz Answers

1. **A and C.** The best answers listed are a damaged battery and excessive gaming. If the brightness setting is low, the device should use less power and run cooler. If the device is not in a case, it should not overheat; however, a poorly manufactured case could cause it to overheat. A defective charging cable will usually not cause the device to overheat; if it is defective, it likely is not even charging the device.

2. **C.** Check the brightness slider first! Chances are that the brightness is turned all the way down—in a bright environment, it might appear that nothing is on the screen. Or, the device might simply need to be woken up—use the side button, home button, or double-tap the screen to wake the device up. If these are not successful, restart the device. Screen calibration has nothing to do with brightness, but on some more rare mobile devices it might be necessary. The volume sliders are not part of the problem. Don't open the device until you have exhausted every other known option—and only if you are qualified to work on that device; otherwise, send it to an authorized repair center.

3. **E.** Stay away from magnetically charged tools such as screwdrivers and bits. These can potentially damage circuitry and components. All of the other answers are valid procedures; things you *should* do when working on mobile devices, and computers in general.

CHAPTER 21

Troubleshooting Printers

This chapter covers the following A+ 220-1001 exam objective:

▶ **5.6** – Given a scenario, troubleshoot printers.

This chapter delves into a variety of common printer issues that you will face. They can happen in large organizations and small offices alike. A printer is a mechanical device. However, it is controlled by embedded firmware and by computers that manage it. Be ready to get your hands dirty (perhaps literally) as you fix printer problems, but be ready to work within the operating system as well.

5.6 – Given a scenario, troubleshoot printers

ExamAlert

Objective 5.6 focuses on troubleshooting common symptoms of printers, such as streaks, ghost images, toner not fused to paper, paper not feeding, paper jams, garbled characters on paper, low memory errors, error codes, and multiple failed jobs in logs.

Troubleshooting Printers

If a printer will not print or prints incorrectly, it has to be fixed. Sometimes companies hire paid consultants to manage all their printers and copiers, and sometimes the care of these devices is the job of the in-house IT technician. Either way, it is a good idea to know some of the basic issues that can occur with printers and how to troubleshoot them. Table 21.1 describes some of these issues and possible solutions. Some of these problems (for example, paper jams and resulting error codes) might be displayed on a printer's LCD.

TABLE 21.1 **Printer Problems and Solutions**

Printer Issue	Possible Solutions
Paper jams or creased paper	1. Turn the printer on and off in the hopes that the printer will clear the jam. This is known as power-cycling the printer. If that doesn't work, open the printer. Turn the printer off and unplug it before doing so.
	2. Remove paper trays and inspect them for crumpled papers that can be removed by grabbing both ends of the paper firmly and pulling or rotating the rollers to remove it. In general, clear the paper path.
	3. Verify that the right paper type is in the printer. If the paper is too thin or thick, it might cause a paper jam. Also, watch for paper that has been exposed to humidity.
	4. Check for dirty or cracked rollers. A temporary fix for dirty rubber rollers is to clean them using isopropyl alcohol. A permanent fix is to replace the rollers.
	5. Check whether the fusing assembly has overheated. Sometimes the printer just needs time to cool, or perhaps the printer is not in a well enough ventilated area. In uncommon cases, the fuser might have to be replaced. Be sure to unplug the printer and let the printer sit for an hour or so before doing so, due to the high temperatures of the fuser. The fusing assembly can usually be removed by removing a few screws.
	6. Finally, check the entire paper path. Duplexing printers (ones that print on both sides of the paper) will have more complicated and longer paper paths, providing more chances for paper to get jammed.
Printing blank pages	1. The toner cartridge is empty or has failed. Install a new one. Toner cartridge failures could be associated with the developing and transferring stages of the laser printing process, with the developing stage being more common.
	2. The toner cartridge was installed without the sealing tape removed.
	3. The transfer corona wire has failed. If the transfer corona wire fails, there will be no positive (opposite) voltage to pull the toner to the paper. Replace the wire.

Printer Issue	Possible Solutions
Paper not feeding	Check the type and condition of the paper. Check the rollers (raise humidity if possible). Clean the rollers. Reset the printer. Consider a maintenance kit.
Multiple pages are fed in at once	Check whether the separation pad is getting enough traction; it might need to be cleaned. Also check whether the paper is too thin; 20 lb. or heavier paper is usually recommended.
Error codes	If a specific error is shown on the printer's LCD, read it. It might tell you exactly what the error is and how to fix it (or at least what the error is). On some printers, it displays an error number. Check your printer's documentation to find out what the error means.
Out of memory error or low memory error message	Check whether the user's computer is spooling documents. The setting with the least chance of this error is the Start Printing Immediately spool setting. You might also need to restart the Print Spooling service. If a user tries to print a large image, he might need to change settings in the application in which the image was made. In some cases, the printer's RAM might need to be upgraded. Whenever installing RAM to a printer, take all the same precautions you would when working on a PC.
No image on printer display	Check whether the printer is in sleep mode (or off altogether). Verify that the printer is plugged in. In rare cases, the internal connector that powers the display might bo loose.
Vertical lines on page, streaks, smearing, toner not fused to paper	Black lines or streaks (and sometimes faded print) can be caused by a scratch in the laser printer drum or a dirty primary corona wire. Usually, the toner cartridge needs to be replaced. White lines could be caused by a dirty transfer corona wire; this can be cleaned or replaced. Wide white vertical lines can occur when something is stuck to the drum. Smearing can occur if the fusing assembly has failed; in this case, you might also notice toner coming off of the paper easily. If it is an inkjet, one or more ink cartridges might need to be replaced or the printer might need to be calibrated.
Faded prints	Replace ink or toner. Clean ink cartridge head. Also, check the fuser, and increase humidity if necessary.
Garbage printout or garbled characters on paper	This can occur due to an incorrect driver. Some technicians like to try "close" drivers. This is not a good idea. Use the exact driver for the exact model of the printer that corresponds to the appropriate version of the operating system. A bad formatter board or printer interface can also be the cause of a garbage printout. These can usually be replaced easily by removing two screws and a cover.
Ghosted image	Ghosted images or blurry marks can be a sign that the drum has some kind of imperfection or is dirty, especially if the image reappears at equal intervals. Replace the drum (or toner cartridge). Another possibility is that the fuser assembly has been damaged and needs to be replaced.

Printer Issue	Possible Solutions
No connectivity	If there is no connectivity, check the following: ▶ The printer is plugged into an AC outlet and is "online." ▶ The printer is securely connected to the local computer or to the network. ▶ The computer has the correct print driver installed. ▶ The printer is shared to the network. ▶ The printer has a properly configured IP address. (This can be checked on the LCD of most networkable laser printers.) ▶ Remote computers have a proper connection over the network to the printer. ▶ The printer is set up as the default printer if necessary.
Access denied	If an Access Denied message appears on the screen while attempting to print, the user doesn't have permission to use the printer. You (or the network administrator) will have to give the user account permissions for that particular printer. This message might also be displayed when a person attempts to install a printer without the proper administrative rights.
Backed-up print queue	If your printer window shows several documents listed in the queue, but is not currently printing anything, then a document might have stalled and needs to be restarted. Also, the print spooler might need to be restarted within the Services console window, Task Manager, or in the Command Prompt.
Color printouts are different (wrong) color from the screen	The printout will always be *slightly* different from the screen. But if the difference is more noticeable, check the ink or toner cartridges and make sure none of the colors are empty. Verify that the printer is a PostScript-capable printer that can do raster image processing (RIP). If this functionality is not built into the printer, then it might be available as a separate software solution.
Multiple failed jobs in logs	Reset the printer, analyze the controlling operating system or print server, clear the print queue, and reconfigure the spooler.
Unable to install printer	Check whether the printer is physically connected to the computer or network properly. Check whether it is getting an IP address. In Windows, start the Print Spooler service, and update the driver. (Advanced: Define new printer keys in the registry.) More on the spooler and how to start it appears later in this chapter.

In general, when working with printers, keep them clean and use printer maintenance kits. Like changing the oil in a car, printers need maintenance also. HP and other manufacturers offer maintenance kits that include items such as fusers, rollers, separation pads, and instructions on how to replace all these items. Manufacturers recommend that this maintenance be done every once in a while (for example, every 200,000 pages printed). When you finish installing a maintenance kit, be sure to reset the maintenance count. You should also have a toner vacuum available for toner spills. A can of compressed air can be helpful when you need to clean out toner from the inside of a laser printer; remember to do this outside. Vacuum any leftover residue. Printer maintenance can be broken down into the following basic categories:

- ▶ **Laser:** Replace toner, apply maintenance kit, calibrate, clean.

- ▶ **Inkjet:** Clean heads, replace cartridges, calibrate, clear jams.

- ▶ **Thermal:** Replace paper, clean heating element, remove debris.

- ▶ **Impact:** Replace ribbon, replace print head, replace paper.

- ▶ **3D printer:** Clean the filament nozzle and platform, check if fans are working, check axis and gear movement.

When troubleshooting printers, don't forget to RTM (Read The Manual)! Most printers come with manuals, and these manuals often provide trouble-shooting sections toward the end of them. In some cases, the manual will be in PDF format on the disc that accompanied the printer. Regardless of whether a manual accompanied the printer or can't be found, the manufacturer will usu-ally have the manual on its website, in addition to a support system for their cus-tomers. Use it!

Keep in mind that many products come with a warranty or the customer might have purchased an extended warranty. I remember one time I was troubleshoot-ing two color-laser printers. They were only two weeks old when they failed. When I described to the manufacturer the error code that was flashing on the printers' displays, the representative didn't need to hear anything else and sim-ply sent out a tech the next day because the devices were under warranty. To sum up, let the manufacturer help you. If it doesn't cost the company anything, it can save you a lot of time and aggravation.

Print Jobs and the Print Spooler

Of course, it can also help to know how to work with printers in Windows, which is common in the workplace. To this end, you should know how to man-age printers and print jobs, and be able to configure the print spooler. Let's talk about those two concepts now.

Managing Printers and Print Jobs

To manage a printer or an individual print job in Windows, just double-click the printer to which the job was sent. This might result in a proprietary screen designed by the printer manufacturer, or a Microsoft window similar to Figure 21.1.

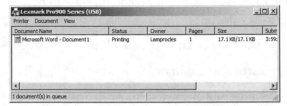

FIGURE 21.1   A typical printer window showing one print job

Figure 21.1 shows that one print job, called Document1, is listed. The job went to the printer properly; you can tell because it says Printing under the Status column. Any other message would mean that the job was either spooled, queued, stopped, or failed altogether. These jobs can be paused, restarted, or stopped completely if they are not printing properly. This can be done by right-clicking on the job in the window or by clicking the Document menu. Keep in mind that larger documents might take longer to spool before they start printing. (We'll discuss that topic in a little bit.) In addition to this, all documents can be paused or canceled or the entire printer can be taken offline from the Printer menu. Use these tools to help troubleshoot printing issues.

The Windows Print Spooler

Spooling is the page-by-page processing done at the local system before the print job goes to the printer.

Whenever a job goes to print, there are three options:

▶ **Print directly to the printer:** This means that the print job goes right to the printer without any delays. This relies solely on the amount of memory in the printer (which can be increased, just like with computers). Of course, if the print job is larger than the amount of RAM in the printer, the job will probably fail. Usually a better solution is to spool the document.

▶ **Start printing immediately:** This is the first of two spooling options. When this setting is selected, one page at a time of the document will be *spooled* to the hard drive. When an entire page has been spooled, it is sent to the printer for printing. This repeats until all the pages of the document have been spooled and ultimately printed. This is the default setting in Windows and is usually the best option because it prints faster than other spooling options. Figure 21.2 shows an example of this.

▶ **Start printing after last page is spooled:** This means that the entire document will be spooled to the hard drive and then pages are sent to the printer for printing. This is usually slower than the Start printing immediately option but might have fewer issues, such as stalls or other printing failures.

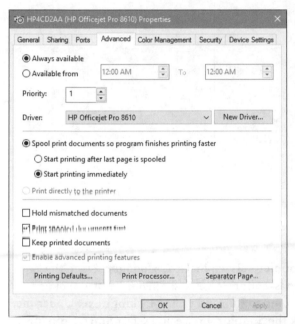

FIGURE 21.2   **Printer spooling options in Windows**

The print spooler is controlled by the Print Spooler service. This service processes print requests and sends them to the printer. Not only can you experience issues in which print jobs or printers stop working, the Print Spooler service also can fail. This service can be started, stopped, and restarted from the GUI and from the Command Prompt:

▶ **Adjusting the Print Spooler service in Computer Management:** Open the Computer Management console window, click the **>** sign to expand Services and Applications, and then click **Services**. Scroll until you find the Print Spooler service. To start a stopped service, right-click it and click **Start**. Alternatively, you can click the Start button or other buttons on the toolbar. Also, you can double-click the Print Spooler service to see its properties, where you can start and stop the service and make more configurations. An example of this is shown in Figure 21.3. By the way, you can get to the Services window directly by accessing the Run prompt and typing **services.msc**.

FIGURE 21.3   The Print Spooler service Properties window

▶ **Adjusting the Print Spooler service in Task Manager:** Open the Task Manager from the taskbar or Power User menu, or by pressing **Ctrl+Shift+Esc**, or by going to Run and typing **taskmgr.exe**. Under the **Services** tab, right-click the **Spooler** service and select **Start, Stop, or Restart service**.

▶ **Adjusting the Print Spooler service in the Command Prompt:** When the Command Prompt is open (in elevated mode), you can start the Print Spooler service by typing **net start spooler**. Typing **net stop spooler** stops the service.

ExamAlert

Know how to configure spooling and how to start and stop the Print Spooler service within Computer Management, the Task Manager, and in the Command Prompt.

Cram Quiz

Answer these questions. The answers follow the last question. If you cannot answer these questions correctly, consider reading this chapter again until you can.

1. How can a paper jam be resolved? (Select all that apply.)

   ○ **A.** Clear the paper path.

   ○ **B.** Use the right type of paper.

   ○ **C.** Check for damaged rollers.

   ○ **D.** Check for a damaged primary corona wire.

2. What is a possible reason for having blank pages come out of a laser printer?

   ○ **A.** Failed transfer corona wire

   ○ **B.** Failed primary corona wire

   ○ **C.** Failed fusing assembly

   ○ **D.** Damaged roller

3. What is a possible reason for having black lines on printouts?

   ○ **A.** Scratch on the laser printer drum

   ○ **B.** Damaged roller

   ○ **C.** Damaged transfer corona wire

   ○ **D.** Scratch on the fusing assembly

4. Which of the following are usually included in a laser printer maintenance kit? (Select the two best answers.)

   ○ **A.** Rollers

   ○ **B.** Image drum

   ○ **C.** Toner

   ○ **D.** Duplexer

   ○ **E.** Fuser

5. One of your customers is connected to a standalone printer. The customer says there is an "out of memory error" when printing large graphic files. What should you do?

   ○ **A.** Upgrade the hard drive on the computer.

   ○ **B.** Upgrade RAM on the printer.

   ○ **C.** Upgrade RAM on the computer.

   ○ **D.** Reinstall the printer drivers.

6. What should you do first when removing a paper jam?

   ○ **A.** Take the printer offline.

   ○ **B.** Clear the print queue.

   ○ **C.** Open all the doors of the printer.

   ○ **D.** Turn off the printer.

7. You have been called to a customer site to perform maintenance on an impact printer. Which should you consider?

   ○ **A.** Replacing paper, cleaning heating element, removing debris

   ○ **B.** Replacing toner, applying maintenance kit, calibrating, cleaning

   ○ **C.** Replacing ribbon, replacing print head, replacing paper

   ○ **D.** Cleaning heads, replacing cartridges, calibrating, clearing jams

8. Which is the faster option for spooling documents?

   ○ **A.** Print directly to the printer

   ○ **B.** Start printing immediately

   ○ **C.** Start printing after last page is spooled

   ○ **D.** Start printing after the separator page

9. How can you immediately stop the Print Spooler service? (Select the three best answers.)

   ○ **A.** Start printing immediately.

   ○ **B.** Type **sc config spooler start= disabled** in the Command Prompt.

   ○ **C.** Print directly to the printer.

   ○ **D.** Type **net stop spooler** in the Command Prompt.

   ○ **E.** Open the Services console window, right-click **Print Spooler**, and select **Stop**.

   ○ **F.** Open the Task Manager, click the **Services** tab, right-click **Spooler**, and select **Stop**.

Cram Quiz Answers

1. **A, B, and C.** There are several possible reasons why a paper jam might occur. The paper could be stuck somewhere in the paper path, the paper could be too thick, or the rollers could be damaged.

2. **A.** If the transfer corona wire has failed, there is no way for the toner to be "attracted" to the paper, resulting in blank sheets coming out of the printer. It is also possible for the toner cartridge to fail, causing blank pages to print. This

would mean that blank pages could be caused by failures during the developing and transferring stages of the laser printing process, with failures during the developing stage being more common.

3. **A.** A scratch on the laser printer drum can account for black lines showing up on printouts. Another culprit can be a dirty primary corona wire.

4. **A and E.** Maintenance kits usually include things like paper pickup rollers, transfer rollers, and a fuser. The duplexer, image drum, and toner are parts of the printer and/or toner cartridges. Toner cartridges are not included in maintenance kits.

5. **B.** You should upgrade the RAM on the printer. Large graphic files need a lot of memory to work with (both on the PC and the printer). But if the PC can send the file to the printer, it has enough RAM and hard drive space. Printer drivers will not cause an out of memory error to display on the printer.

6. **D.** Turn off the printer before you start working inside of the printer. You want to make sure it is off (and unplugged) before you put your hands inside of it. Taking it offline is not enough in this case.

7. **C.** Impact printer maintenance procedures include replacing ribbon, replacing the print head, and replacing paper. Laser printer maintenance includes replacing toner, applying maintenance kit, calibrating, and cleaning. Thermal printer maintenance includes replacing paper, cleaning heating element, and removing debris. Inkjet printer maintenance includes cleaning heads, replacing cartridges, calibrating, and clearing jams.

8. **B.** The Start printing immediately option is faster than the Start printing after last page is spooled option when spooling documents. The Print directly to the printer option doesn't use the spooling feature. There is no option named Start printing after the separator page.

9. **C, E, and F.** To immediately stop (or turn off) the Print Spooler service, we have several options. We can stop it in the Command Prompt with the **net stop spooler** command or the **sc stop spooler** command. We can also do it in the Services console window or in the Task Manager. By the way, the answers listed are based on Windows 10 Pro. Note that in Services we look for "Print Spooler" and in the Task Manager we look for "Spooler." The answers Start printing immediately and Print directly to the printer are options for how (or if) documents will be spooled. While printing directly to the printer does not use the spooler, it doesn't turn it off either. Finally, **sc config spooler start= disabled** will *disable* the service, but it won't turn it off—immediately, that is. However, it won't start the next time the computer is restarted. Try that command and then the **net stop spooler** command to see what I mean. Then, to set everything back to run as normal, type the following:

```
sc config spooler start= auto
net start spooler
```

Yes, we went there. Chapter over.

CHAPTER 22

Troubleshooting Wired and Wireless Network Problems

This chapter covers the following A+ 220-1001 exam objective:

▶ **5.7** – Given a scenario, troubleshoot common wired and wireless network problems.

Here we have the last of the 220-1001 troubleshooting chapters. In this chapter we'll discuss troubleshooting network connectivity issues. Because you will have users that connect in a wired fashion and other users that connect in a wireless fashion—and some connecting both ways—you have to be ready to support a variety of network connectivity. The goal of this chapter is to explain some basic troubleshooting techniques in a more generic sense—meaning, less step-by-step procedures and more of the troubleshooting mindset that you should maintain. To perform their work, users need access to resources, and network connectivity enables this. So, a faulty network connection means little to no available resources; and consequently, little to no work getting done. This should help to stress the importance of network connectivity.

5.7 – Given a scenario, troubleshoot common wired and wireless network problems

ExamAlert

Objective 5.7 concentrates on troubleshooting common symptoms of wired and wireless network problems, such as limited connectivity, intermittent connectivity, no connectivity, unavailable resources, APIPA/link local addresses, IP conflicts, slow transfer speeds, low RF signal, and SSID not found.

Troubleshooting Common Symptoms

Network troubleshooting? Oh yes, it could be one of the best ways to learn how networks operate. First, I recommend reviewing the CompTIA troubleshooting methodology in Chapter 17, "Computer Troubleshooting 101." Second, for successful troubleshooting, remember to check the simple and obvious first. Power connections, network connections, and so on are common culprits for network problems.

When we think about network troubleshooting, we should consider access to resources. If a resource—be it a data share or printer, or whatever—is unavailable, then the user won't be able to get his or her work done. Efficiency decreases, and the organization loses money. Resources can be broken down into two types: local resources—meaning ones on the LAN; and remote resources—ones that are beyond the LAN, possibly on the Internet or another external network.

▶ **Local resources:** You might find that a user can't browse the network or map network drives to network shares, or connect to network printers, or access an e-mail server on the LAN. There are lots of examples, but the bottom line is this: if a user can't access local resources, then you need to troubleshoot the network connection. That's the bulk of what we discuss in this chapter. If multiple users can't access resources, then it could be a more centralized problem. For example, a server is down; perhaps a DHCP server is not properly handing out IP addresses to clients, or a domain controller has failed, and users cannot be authenticated to resources. As a technician with the A+ certification, this might go beyond the scope of your work, so be prepared to escalate the problem if necessary.

▶ **Internet-based resources:** If remote resources are not available to a user—for example, websites, VPN connections, and streaming media services—then it could be that the IP configuration (especially the gateway and DNS settings) needs to be inspected and possibly reconfigured. If multiple users are having connectivity problems, then it could be the gateway itself or the DNS server that needs to be fixed (among other things). Again, escalate the problem if necessary.

All of the following bullet points list symptoms you might encounter that can lead to unavailable resources, either locally or on the Internet. Let's discuss these symptoms and how to troubleshoot the underlying problems.

▶ **No connectivity:** If a user complains of a problem connecting to the network and you verify that there is indeed a problem, check that patch cable first and verify there is a link light. Make sure the user's computer is actually connected to the network. If it appears to be a cable issue, use a patch cable tester or cable certifier to test the cable. If it isn't a cable problem, make sure the network adapter is enabled. If it's a laptop and the user has wireless, check the Wi-Fi switch or button. Next, run an **ipconfig /all** and check the settings. Afterward, ping the local computer to see if TCP/IP works. If you haven't resolved the problem by now (and you probably will), access the Network and Sharing Center in Windows and view the graphical connections to see if there is a red x anywhere denoting a problem. Use the network troubleshooter if necessary. You can also right-click the Network icon in the Notification Area and select Troubleshoot problems. This brings up the Windows Network Diagnostics program; follow the steps for a possible resolution. Check for the latest drivers for the network adapter. You can also try rebooting the computer to find out if any programs were recently installed or updated. Sometimes antivirus software or firewall updates can cause connectivity issues. Some switches and routers have the capability to enable/disable specific ports; make sure the port in question is enabled in the firmware.

If it's a network-wide problem, power down the network equipment (SOHO routers, cable modems, and so on); then disconnect the network and power cables and wait 10 seconds. Finally, reboot the network equipment. If users cannot find the wireless network that they need to connect to using Windows or the wireless adapter's software, there are third-party Wi-Fi locator programs that you can download for free. These will locate all wireless networks in the vicinity and display SSID, signal quality, distance, and channel used (as long as the wireless network adapter is functional). If an SSID does not show up in Windows *or* in third-party software, you should enter the SSID manually.

▶ **Limited and intermittent connectivity:** If the problem is limited connectivity, attempt some pings. First, ping the localhost to see if TCP/IP is functioning. If that works, ping the router or another system on the network. If that fails, then the user only has local connectivity. Run an **ipconfig /all** and check the rest of the IP settings. If pinging the router *did* work, try pinging a website by domain name. If that fails, then the DNS server address is probably not configured properly. Check it with an **ipconfig /all** and modify in the IP Properties dialog box if necessary. Run an **ipconfig /release** and **/renew** if you suspect an issue with obtaining an address from a DHCP server. Intermittent connectivity could be caused by a faulty patch cable, wireless network adapter that is too far away from the WAP, or a router that needs to be reset. In a larger environment, if a person can access some networks but not others, you might want to try a **tracert** to inaccessible networks to see where the problem lies. This type of network troubleshooting gets a bit more in depth, but the **tracert** program will basically show which router between you and the final destination has failed.

▶ **Slow transfer speeds:** The type of Internet connection is going to be the biggest contributor to this. If a user has dial-up and complains about slow transfer speeds, it's time to upgrade! Even though dial-up can be tweaked for speed, it's simply easier to move up to DSL, cable, or fiber-based services. Slow transfer speeds could also be caused by the network equipment, patch cables, and network adapter. The newer and faster the equipment and cables, the better the data transfer rate. Of course, slow speeds could also be caused by network congestion. Run a **netstat -a** to see which types of connections the local computer has to the Internet currently. If you see dozens of connections, the computer might be compromised by malware or be part of a botnet. Or perhaps the user runs torrent software or just goes to a lot of websites for various reasons. Check the router as well. See what kind of traffic is passing through it. Update everything, clear all cache, power cycle all equipment, and you just might see an improvement.

▶ **Low RF signal:** A low radio frequency signal spells doom for wireless users. The first thing to check is the distance of the computer from the WAP. Make sure the computer is within the appropriate range. If the WAP uses 802.11ac and the wireless adapter is 802.11g, consider upgrading to an 802.11ac adapter. Update the software on the wireless adapter and WAP as well. Placement of the router is important; it should be central to all users and away from sources of EMI. Try different antenna placement on the router and the wireless adapter. Normally, the 90-degree angle is best, but a little tweaking can go a long way. Also, some routers can boost their wireless signals. Check for this setting in the firmware.

▶ **IP conflict:** An IP conflict message will pop up on the displays of both Windows computers that are causing the conflict. Usually, the first computer that used the IP address will continue to function, whereas the second computer will not be able to access the network. The second computer will have to be reconfigured to a different IP address and rebooted. Reboot the first computer for good measure. IP conflicts usually happen only when static IP addresses are being used. If this is the case, consider using DHCP for all client computers.

▶ **Link-local/APIPA address:** If a computer is showing an IPv4 link-local address such as 169.254.49.26 when you type **ipconfig /all**, it generally means that the computer is attempting to obtain an IP address from a

4. A user moves a laptop from one office to another. The patch cable and the network adapter do not appear to be working properly at the new office. The cable is plugged in correctly and tests okay when checked with a patch tester. Which of the following should be done first?

   ○ **A.** Check whether the port on the switch is enabled.

   ○ **B.** Update the network adapter driver.

   ○ **C.** Replace the patch cable with a crossover cable.

   ○ **D.** Make sure the network adapter is compatible with the OS.

Cram Quiz Answers

1. **C.** Check the super-obvious first. Make sure the computer has a physical cabled connection to the network. Then attempt things such as **ipconfig**, **ping**, and network driver updates.

2. **D.** Use a patch cable tester to check the patch cable and possibly use a continuity tester to test longer network cable runs. Multimeters are great for testing wires inside the computer or AC outlets, but they are not used for network troubleshooting. A PSU tester tests power supplies. The loopback plug will verify whether the local computer's network adapter is functional.

3. **B.** This is the concept of pinging outward. Start by pinging the localhost, then a computer, and then the router on the network. Then ping a domain name or website. If you can ping the website but the browser cannot get through, the browser might have been compromised. If you cannot ping the website, you should check the IP configuration; the DNS server address might be incorrectly configured. Updating the OS and AV software should be done right away if you suspect that the browser has been compromised.

4. **A.** Some routers and switches can disable physical ports (a smart security measure). Check that first. Later, you can check whether the network adapter is compatible with the OS and update it if necessary. Do not replace the cable with a crossover; those are used to connect one computer to another.

220-1001 Wrap-up

This is the end of the 220-1001 chapters of this book. Following, you will find a practice exam that is designed to test your knowledge of the 220-1001 objectives. Good luck!

If you are planning on taking the actual CompTIA A+ 220-1001 exam, be sure to go through the 220-1001 checklist. It can be found in "Introduction to Core 1 (220-1001)," just before Chapter 1. However, keep in mind that I recommend going through this *entire* book before attempting either of the A+ exams.

DHCP server but is failing to do so. IPv4 link-local addresses always start with 169.254. Microsoft also uses the name Automatic Private IP Addressing (APIPA). Usually, a link-local address is assigned internally, so the real problem could be that the computer is not getting connectivity to the network. Check everything in the first bullet point. Also, consider using **ipconfig /release** and **/renew**. Finally, if these do not work, check the DHCP server to make sure it is functional and available.

ExamAlert

Double-study your troubleshooting techniques! It's all about troubleshooting!

Cram Quiz

Answer these questions. The answers follow the last question. If you cannot answer these questions correctly, consider reading this chapter again until you can.

1. A user complains that the computer is not connecting to the network. Which of the following should be done first?

   ○ **A.** Use **ipconfig /all**.

   ○ **B.** Ping the router.

   ○ **C.** Check the patch cable.

   ○ **D.** Check the network drivers.

2. One computer loses connectivity. All connectors and settings appear to be correct. Which tool should be used to fix the problem?

   ○ **A.** Multimeter

   ○ **B.** PSU tester

   ○ **C.** Loopback plug

   ○ **D.** Cable tester

3. One of your customers no longer has access to a frequently accessed website. You ping another computer and the router on the network successfully. Which of the following should be done next?

   ○ **A.** Check the IP configuration.

   ○ **B.** Ping the website.

   ○ **C.** Update the OS.

   ○ **D.** Update the AV software.

A+ Core 1 (220-1001) Practice Exam

The 80 multiple-choice questions provided here help you to determine how prepared you are for the actual exam and which topics you need to review further. Write down your answers on a separate sheet of paper so that you can take this exam again if necessary. Compare your answers against the answer key that follows this exam. Read through the explanations and also the incorrect answers very carefully. If there are any concepts that you don't understand, go back and study them more.

Exam Questions

1. Which of the following components can be considered the "brains" of a computer?

    ○ **A.** RAM

    ○ **B.** Hard drive

    ○ **C.** CPU

    ○ **D.** Motherboard

2. You are attempting to load an operating system from a USB flash drive at computer startup. Which of the following settings should you modify in the BIOS?

    ○ **A.** Enable a BIOS password

    ○ **B.** Boot sequence

    ○ **C.** Enable TPM

    ○ **D.** Disable TPM

3. Which of the following is the most common type of networking connector?

    ○ **A.** RJ11

    ○ **B.** F-connector

    ○ **C.** BNC

    ○ **D.** RJ45

4. Which of the following is the module format used by a laptop's DDR4 SODIMMs?

    ○ **A.** 200-pin

    ○ **B.** 204-pin

    ○ **C.** 240-pin

    ○ **D.** 260-pin

5. Which of the following should be reset during normal printer maintenance?

    ○ **A.** Page count

    ○ **B.** Job queue

    ○ **C.** Print job cache

    ○ **D.** Tray settings

Okay, those were some easy ones. Now, let's get on with some more difficult questions!

6. You are a technician for an accounting company. You have submitted a request for a new wireless access point. You receive and set up the new device and power it on, but the company router doesn't appear to recognize it. Which of the following statements best describes how to fix the problem? (Select the best answer.)

   ○ **A.** You should perform an apt-get update.

   ○ **B.** You should run Windows Update.

   ○ **C.** You should perform an RPM update.

   ○ **D.** You should install the firmware update.

7. A laptop's battery fails to charge. Which of the following should be checked first?

   ○ **A.** DC-in jack

   ○ **B.** AC-in jack

   ○ **C.** CMOS battery

   ○ **D.** AC circuit breaker

8. One of your co-workers has opened a trouble ticket concerning paper jams on a laser printer. The paper jams have become more frequent of late. You decide to attempt to re-create the problem and then check the printer log for more information. Which of the following are the most likely solutions to the problem? (Select the two best answers.)

   ☐ **A.** Clean and inspect the entire paper path

   ☐ **B.** Clean the fuser roller and verify fuser operation.

   ☐ **C.** Clean and replace the paper out sensor.

   ☐ **D.** Use a printer maintenance kit to replace parts.

   ☐ **E.** Replace the paper exit assembly switch.

   ☐ **F.** Clean and inspect the print drum.

9. A user boots a computer and a message is displayed that reads "Alert! Cover previously removed." Which of the following was configured in the UEFI/BIOS to cause this alert?

   ○ **A.** Date and time settings

   ○ **B.** Boot sequence

   ○ **C.** Intrusion detection

   ○ **D.** Virtualization support

10. The power supply fan and case fans spin, but there is no power to other devices. Which of the following is the most likely cause of this?

   ○ **A.** Failed hard drive

   ○ **B.** Improper connectivity

   ○ **C.** Drive not recognized

   ○ **D.** Failed RAM

11. One of the desktop computers at a customer site is randomly rebooting several times per day. You have checked for overheating issues, but everything seems okay with the case fans, CPU fan, and power supply. What should you check for next?

   ○ **A.** The integrated network adapter has the latest drivers.

   ○ **B.** The hard drive is defragmented.

   ○ **C.** The motherboard for signs of swollen capacitors.

   ○ **D.** The RAM to confirm it is of the right type.

12. Which of the following should be used when building a high-end graphics workstation for CAD applications? (Select the two best answers.)

   ☐ **A.** An IDE drive

   ☐ **B.** More than four accessible USB 3.0 ports

   ☐ **C.** Main memory of 16 GB or more

   ☐ **D.** A 32-bit OS for the large amount of expected drive I/O

   ☐ **E.** A PCIe video card with a large amount of memory

13. Which of the following is an example of a MAC address?

   ○ **A.** 10.1.1.255

   ○ **B.** 4410:FF11:AAB3::0012

   ○ **C.** https://dprocomputer.com

   ○ **D.** 00-1C-C0-A1-55-21

14. You are installing an IP-based camera system that connects directly to the network. To access the system remotely, which capability most likely requires configuration?

   ○ **A.** QoS

   ○ **B.** Port forwarding

   ○ **C.** Static IPs

   ○ **D.** VPN passthrough

15. Which of the following best describes the most likely reason for connecting a tone generator to an RJ45 cable drop?

   ○ **A.** To confirm continuity of the conductors

   ○ **B.** To locate the position of the cable on a patch panel

   ○ **C.** To test the transmission quality of the connection

   ○ **D.** To validate proper wiring of the network jack

16. When placing a mobile device into airplane mode, which of the following features are typically disabled? (Select the two best answers.)

   ☐ **A.** Wireless

   ☐ **B.** Cellular data

   ☐ **C.** Multitouch capability

   ☐ **D.** Data encryption

   ☐ **E.** Camera

17. One of your co-workers has asked for a cable for an Apple mobile device that can charge it and transfer data to and from it. Which of the following connection types would meet the customer's requirements?

   ○ **A.** Lightning

   ○ **B.** Micro-USB

   ○ **C.** Molex

   ○ **D.** Mini-USB

18. You have been tasked with resolving a shadowy image that is being printed from a network printer. What should you do?

   ○ **A.** Replace the drum.

   ○ **B.** Replace the fuser.

   ○ **C.** Run a calibration.

   ○ **D.** Replace the network cable.

19. A desktop computer (named workstation22) can't connect to the network. A network card was purchased without documentation or driver discs. Which of the following is the best way to install the network card driver?

   ○ **A.** Purchase the disc online and install.

   ○ **B.** Run Windows Update to install the drivers.

   ○ **C.** From the desktop computer (workstation22), download and install the drivers.

   ○ **D.** Copy the driver to a flash drive and install.

20. You are working in a command line and see the following results:

`dprocomputer.com = 216.97.236.245`

Which of the following server types has most likely helped supply this information to you?

○ **A.** DHCP server

○ **B.** DNS server

○ **C.** Authentication server

○ **D.** Syslog server

○ **E.** Print server

21. Which of the following computer components connect directly to the CPU or northbridge?

○ **A.** Video card

○ **B.** Hard drive

○ **C.** Audio

○ **D.** Fan

○ **E.** RAM

22. A customer of yours is opening an Internet café and wants to offer computers for the patrons to access the Internet. Which type of computer system should you recommend?

○ **A.** Thin client

○ **B.** Standard thick client

○ **C.** Audio/video workstation

○ **D.** Gaming PC

○ **E.** HTPC

23. You are part of a team that has decided to make use of a cloud provider for some of your organization's technology needs. Your top priority is to offload some of your networking, storage, and VM hosting to the cloud. Which of the following services best suits your needs?

○ **A.** SaaS

○ **B.** IaaS

○ **C.** PaaS

○ **D.** DBaaS

24. Your guest virtual machines get direct access to the hosting computer's network connection. What is another name for this?

   ○ **A.** NAT

   ○ **B.** Private virtual network

   ○ **C.** Host-only networking

   ○ **D.** Bridged networking

25. Your office printer was working earlier in the day but is no longer printing any documents. Preexisting workstations are manually configured to print to the printer directly over the network. You begin troubleshooting the problem and determine that the printer is still visible when browsing the network directory. You also verify, at the physical printer, that the printer can print test pages successfully. Which of the following is the most likely cause of the problem?

   ○ **A.** The print spooler was restarted.

   ○ **B.** Two users sent print jobs at the same time, which caused a collision.

   ○ **C.** The printer's IP address has changed.

   ○ **D.** The message "perform printer maintenance" is displayed on the printer's display panel.

26. Which of the following is an advantage of UDP over TCP?

   ○ **A.** It uses flow control.

   ○ **B.** It transfers packets faster.

   ○ **C.** It uses connection handshakes.

   ○ **D.** It is connection based.

27. John is a PC technician for an organization that has a computer network with 12 computers. Each contains vital information, so each uses static IP addresses (on the 192.168.50.0 network). John just finished troubleshooting a Windows computer that could not access the network. He ascertained (correctly) that the computer needed a new network card. He purchased a plug-and-play card and physically installed the card. He then turned on the computer, noting that the network card's LED link was lit and that there was activity. He then rebooted the computer to Windows and then documented the whole process. Later, his boss tells him that the user is complaining that she cannot access the Internet. Which step of the A+ troubleshooting methodology did John forget to perform?

   ○ **A.** Identify the problem.

   ○ **B.** Establish a theory of probable cause.

   ○ **C.** Test the theory to determine cause.

   ○ **D.** Establish a plan of action to resolve the problem.

   ○ **E.** Verify full system functionality.

   ○ **F.** Document findings, actions and outcomes.

28. On your server, two drives of a RAID 5 array have failed. What should you do?

   ○ **A.** Replace one of the drives and run RAID repair.

   ○ **B.** Replace the failed drives and format the RAID array using the quick option.

   ○ **C.** Replace one of the failed drives and repair the RAID array using system utilities.

   ○ **D.** Replace the failed drives and restore the data from tape backup to the repaired RAID array.

29. A user working at a PC is experiencing screen flicker. Of the following, what should you reconfigure? (Select the best answer.)

   ○ **A.** CCFL

   ○ **B.** Refresh rate

   ○ **C.** Resolution

   ○ **D.** Switch from HDMI to DVI

30. Which of the following types of printers requires a maintenance kit that contains a fuser, transfer roller, and pickup rollers?

   ○ **A.** Thermal

   ○ **B.** Laser

   ○ **C.** Inkjet

   ○ **D.** Impact

31. You are tasked with fixing a laptop that is not booting. You have analyzed the system and can't see any system lights or display, and you can't hear any sounds when the Power button is pressed. Which of the following should be attempted first when troubleshooting the problem?

   ○ **A.** Boot the system from a boot CD.

   ○ **B.** Disconnect the AC and the battery and press and hold the Power button for several seconds.

   ○ **C.** Remove hard drives and optical drives, RAM, and USB devices from the laptop.

   ○ **D.** Connect an external monitor to the laptop to determine if the LCD has failed.

32. You are planning to build a computer that will be used at trade shows on several different continents. Part of your planning includes specifications such as maximum RAM and a typical video card, CPU, and storage drive. Which of the following specifications is the most important for you to consider when you select a power supply unit?

    ○ **A.** Efficiency

    ○ **B.** 12 V rail amperage

    ○ **C.** Input voltage

    ○ **D.** Number of SATA connectors

33. Which of the following devices should a technician calibrate as part of an installation?

    ○ **A.** Touchscreen

    ○ **B.** Mouse

    ○ **C.** Keyboard

    ○ **D.** Video card

34. A monitor's on-screen display (OSD) indicates that the proper video source has been selected, yet no image is displayed. Which of the following are the most likely causes? (Select the two best answers.)

    ☐ **A.** The monitor's brightness setting is too low.

    ☐ **B.** The monitor's backlight has failed.

    ☐ **C.** There is no device sending video.

    ☐ **D.** The source cable has been disconnected.

    ☐ **E.** The monitor's contrast setting is too high.

35. A computer you are working on randomly reboots. Which of the following should be checked first when troubleshooting the computer? (Select the two best answers.)

    ☐ **A.** Memory integrity

    ☐ **B.** Video card integrity

    ☐ **C.** CMOS battery

    ☐ **D.** PSU integrity

    ☐ **E.** Optical drive integrity

36. One of your customers has signed up for a mobile pay service to be used on a first-generation smartphone. However, the smartphone does not work at any location that supports mobile pay service. Which of the following is missing from the customer's smartphone?

- ○ **A.** IMSI
- ○ **B.** NFC
- ○ **C.** RFID
- ○ **D.** Bluetooth

37. You are setting up a network for a small office with 30 computers and one server. The server will be used as a file sharing device, a print server, and will act as the domain controller. What kind of addresses should you assign to the server? (Select the two best answers.)

- ☐ **A.** DHCP
- ☐ **B.** MAC
- ☐ **C.** Static IP
- ☐ **D.** Dynamic IP
- ☐ **E.** Subnet mask
- ☐ **F.** FTP

38. Which protocol is relied upon most by Active Directory? (Select the best answer.)

- ○ **A.** SMB
- ○ **B.** HTTP
- ○ **C.** LDAP
- ○ **D.** WINS

39. You are building a new PC and you notice that the motherboard has eight DIMM sockets that are labeled 0 through 7. Four of them are gray, and the other four are a darker shade of gray. Which of the following should be performed first?

- ○ **A.** Install the memory into the gray slots.
- ○ **B.** Install the memory into the dark-gray slots.
- ○ **C.** Install the memory into slots 0 through 3.
- ○ **D.** Fill all the slots with memory.
- ○ **E.** Consult the motherboard documentation.

40. Which of the following printer technologies uses piezoelectric pressure pads to produce small bubbles that are moved to the paper?

- ○ **A.** Laser
- ○ **B.** Inkjet
- ○ **C.** Thermal
- ○ **D.** Impact

41. You need to describe RAID to a nontechnical customer. Which of the following represents the best way describe RAID?

- ○ **A.** RAID stands for Redundant Array of Independent Disks.
- ○ **B.** RAID utilizes multiple disks to increase performance and/or enable protection from data loss.
- ○ **C.** RAID is a dynamic disk management system.
- ○ **D.** RAID uses striping to reduce the amount of hard drive write time and utilizes parity bits to reconstruct the data from a failed hard drive.

42. You just completed a CPU installation. However, when you turn on the computer, the POST sounds a series of beeps and the system won't boot. What is the most likely cause?

- ○ **A.** The mouse is not plugged in.
- ○ **B.** The operating system is corrupted.
- ○ **C.** The CPU is not properly seated.
- ○ **D.** The fan is running too fast

43. Which of the following devices should be configured to block specific ports on the network?

- ○ **A.** Firewall
- ○ **B.** Gateway
- ○ **C.** Router
- ○ **D.** Bridge
- ○ **E.** Access point

44. Which connector is necessary to supply power to a graphics expansion card? (Select the best answer.)

- ○ **A.** 8-pin EATX12V
- ○ **B.** PCIe 6-pin
- ○ **C.** 24-pin ATX
- ○ **D.** SATA 15-pin

45. Which of the following monitor types provide for the widest viewing angle along with rich colors and consistent backlighting? (Select the two best answers.)

☐ **A.** Plasma

☐ **B.** TN

☐ **C.** IPS

☐ **D.** LED

☐ **E.** CCFL

46. You replaced a bad internal WLAN card in a Windows laptop. You completed the installation and verified that the new WLAN card is listed in the Device Manager as enabled. What should you do next to actually use the card?

○ **A.** Type the security passphrase.

○ **B.** Update the firmware of the WLAN card.

○ **C.** Configure encryption on the router.

○ **D.** Add the SSID of the network to the connection.

47. You need to connect external peripherals to a typical PC. Which of the following connector types will allow you to do this? (Select the two best answers.)

☐ **A.** SATA

☐ **B.** SAS

☐ **C.** EIDE

☐ **D.** eSATA

☐ **E.** USB 3.0

48. Look at the following list of wires. What wiring standard is being used here?

1. White/orange, 2. Orange, 3. White/green, 4. Blue,

5. White/blue, 6. Green, 7. White/brown, 8. Brown

○ **A.** RJ45

○ **B.** T568B

○ **C.** T568A

○ **D.** TIA

49. You need to make a patch cable to connect a computer to an RJ45 wall jack. Which of the following tools should be used to attach the RJ45 plugs to the patch cable?

○ **A.** Crimper

○ **B.** Punchdown tool

○ **C.** Loopback plug

○ **D.** Cable tester

50. There are four people who share a connection to a SOHO router that connects to the Internet. When a single user starts streaming media over the Internet, browsing slows down for the rest of the users. Which setting should be configured to alleviate the problem?

- ○ **A.** QoS
- ○ **B.** DSL
- ○ **C.** WAN
- ○ **D.** VPN

51. A user with an inkjet printer states that all color printouts are missing red ink. The printer has cartridges for each of the CMYK colors and the user has recently replaced the magenta cartridge. Which of the following steps should be performed next?

- ○ **A.** Verify that the printer cables are connected.
- ○ **B.** Perform printer head cleaning.
- ○ **C.** Purchase a maintenance kit.
- ○ **D.** Use different weighted paper.

52. A user calls you and tells you that his computer won't boot and that there is a faint smell of something burning. Which tool should be used to identify the problem?

- ○ **A.** Loopback plug
- ○ **B.** Cable tester
- ○ **C.** PSU tester
- ○ **D.** ESD strap

53. Which of the following describes the function of a switch in a network?

- ○ **A.** Converts a packet for transmission from one network to another network
- ○ **B.** Transmits packets it receives to specific connections
- ○ **C.** Broadcasts packets it receives to all connections
- ○ **D.** Determines whether a packet belongs on an internal or an external network

54. Of the following, which components are the most important in a virtualization server? (Select the two best answers.)

- ☐ **A.** Maximum memory
- ☐ **B.** High-end sound card
- ☐ **C.** High-end video card
- ☐ **D.** Dual-rail 1000w PSU
- ☐ **E.** Quad-core CPU

55. Which of the following cables is prone to EMI?

    ◯ **A.** Fiber optic

    ◯ **B.** STP

    ◯ **C.** UTP

    ◯ **D.** Multimode

56. You just installed a barcode reader. Which of the following should you do to configure the reader?

    ◯ **A.** Use the Device Manager to enable the IR port.

    ◯ **B.** Adjust jumper switches.

    ◯ **C.** Enable the reader in the BIOS.

    ◯ **D.** Scan in program codes.

57. A workgroup of five PCs uses a shared printer. A customer says she cannot print to the printer but can access shares on another PC used for common files. The printer appears to be powered on. Which of the following would be the most likely cause?

    ◯ **A.** The PC is off the network.

    ◯ **B.** The printer needs to be restarted.

    ◯ **C.** The printer is low on toner.

    ◯ **D.** Device drivers are corrupted.

58. Which of the following is a possible symptom of a damaged video display?

    ◯ **A.** Disconnected punchdown

    ◯ **B.** Low RF signal

    ◯ **C.** Dead pixel

    ◯ **D.** Computer repeatedly boots to Safe Mode

59. You just set up a printer in the company training room. The trainer wants to be able to print multiple copies of the training documentation for class. Which feature should be enabled on the printer?

    ◯ **A.** Duplexing

    ◯ **B.** Faxing

    ◯ **C.** Collating

    ◯ **D.** Scanning

    ◯ **E.** Print to PDF

60. Which of the following voltages are normally supplied by a PSU's rails? (Select the two best answers.)

☐ **A.** 1.5 V

☐ **B.** 3.3 V

☐ **C.** 5 V

☐ **D.** 9 V

61. You are troubleshooting a printer. Which of the following are common symptoms of printer failure or other printer issues? (Select the two best answers.)

☐ **A.** Vertical lines on the page

☐ **B.** Num Lock indicator lights are on

☐ **C.** Unable to install the printer to the OS

☐ **D.** Failure to document cable and screw locations

☐ **E.** Failure to organize parts

62. Which of the following cable types would most likely experience degraded video signal quality over long distances?

○ **A.** VGA

○ **B.** HDMI

○ **C.** DVI

○ **D.** DisplayPort

63. Which of the following is the best option for storing 6153 MB of data on one disc?

○ **A.** DVD-9 DL

○ **B.** CD-R 48x

○ **C.** DVD-5 SL

○ **D.** RAID 5

64. You are tasked with fixing a client's PC that hasn't booted after the latest test of the building's backup generator. As you analyze the computer, you notice that once it is powered on there is no display or beep codes. After 15 seconds, the fans inside the computer start spinning faster and making more noise. The computer was working fine before the test, and you verify that no one has opened the computer. Which of the following is most likely the problem?

○ **A.** The RAM was damaged by ESD.

○ **B.** The motherboard was damaged by the power test.

○ **C.** The hard drive was erased due to the power test.

○ **D.** The power supply was damaged and is nonfunctional.

65. Which of the following memory technologies enables protection against random inconsistencies when storing data?

- ○ **A.** Quad-channel
- ○ **B.** Parity
- ○ **C.** Dual-channel
- ○ **D.** ECC
- ○ **E.** RAID 5

66. A PC's network adapter has a link light that is lit, but the PC can't access internal network resources. Which of the following is the most likely cause of the issue?

- ○ **A.** IP address conflict
- ○ **B.** Incorrect gateway
- ○ **C.** Packet collisions
- ○ **D.** Slow transfer speed

67. A workstation fails to boot. The POST found an error, and the computer beeps twice. This happens again and again. Which of the following is the most likely issue?

- ○ **A.** Power supply failure
- ○ **B.** Video adapter failure
- ○ **C.** Memory failure
- ○ **D.** CPU failure

68. You are attempting to install Hyper-V on a Windows computer. However, you receive an error that the software cannot be installed. Which of the following CPU characteristics should be checked?

- ○ **A.** Number of cores
- ○ **B.** Virtualization support
- ○ **C.** Hyper-Threading
- ○ **D.** Cache size

69. Which of the following best describes why you might hear a loud clicking noise coming from a faulty hard drive?

- ○ **A.** The hard drive has a bad spindle motor bearing.
- ○ **B.** The solid-state read/write head is scratching the platter surface.
- ○ **C.** The coil reversing the polarity is in an endless loop.
- ○ **D.** The noise is created by the repeated motion of the read/write head arm located parallel to the platter.

70. You are troubleshooting a laptop that has a problem with the cursor. When working on Word documents, the cursor jumps around the display. Which of the following is the most likely cause?

  ○ **A.** Improper screen calibration

  ○ **B.** Faulty software

  ○ **C.** Touchpad settings

  ○ **D.** Unsigned device drivers

71. Which of the following ports can be used for audio, video, and storage?

  ○ **A.** Thunderbolt

  ○ **B.** DisplayPort

  ○ **C.** HDMI

  ○ **D.** DVI

72. You are responding to a server issue reported to you by the accounting department. A particular mapped network drive has high latency. When you go to the server room, you identify the problem as one of the drives in a RAID array. Which of the following best describes how to fix the problem?

  ○ **A.** You should reseat the faulty drive.

  ○ **B.** You should replace the faulty drive.

  ○ **C.** You should reinstall the RAID driver.

  ○ **D.** You should replace the RAID controller.

73. Which of the following protocols is used to perform file sharing between Apple computers running macOS and PCs running Windows on a LAN?

  ○ **A.** RDP

  ○ **B.** SSH

  ○ **C.** POP3

  ○ **D.** SMB

74. You have been tasked with installing Microsoft Office on a customer's computer. As you attempt to do so, you are told that Office cannot be installed directly to that computer. Which of the following types of computers are you working on?

  ○ **A.** Thin client

  ○ **B.** MacBook

  ○ **C.** Tablet

  ○ **D.** Thick client

75. You replace a failed hard drive with a new one. You then boot to a special pre-installation environment disc so that you can install a custom operating system build that is meant for deployment to the network. The hard drive is recognized in the UEFI/BIOS, but once you have booted to the preinstallation environment, the hard drive is not recognized, the process fails, and the drive can't be imaged. Which of the following statements best describes the most likely problem?

   ○ **A.** The PC's power supply cannot provide enough power for the new drive.

   ○ **B.** The boot media has failed and needs to be replaced.

   ○ **C.** The hard drive has not been partitioned correctly.

   ○ **D.** The hard drive must be configured in the UEFI/BIOS.

76. Which of the following LAN hosts would most likely provide the services needed to allow multiple clients access to cached Internet web pages?

   ○ **A.** File server

   ○ **B.** Proxy server

   ○ **C.** Web server

   ○ **D.** DNS server

77. Your organization subscribed to a cloud service and is paying monthly for a group of services. The organization is then billed incrementally when it exceeds the monthly amount. Which of the following cloud concepts does this represent?

   ○ **A.** Rapid elasticity

   ○ **B.** On-demand

   ○ **C.** Measured services

   ○ **D.** Resource pooling

78. You are tasked with building a high-end gaming PC and need to select the right power supply. Which features should you be looking for? (Select the three best answers.)

   ☐ **A.** Large number of connectors

   ☐ **B.** 20-pin power connector

   ☐ **C.** 24-pin power connector

   ☐ **D.** Mini-ITX form factor

   ☐ **E.** Dual 12 V rails

   ☐ **F.** 400 watts

79. You are planning a secure DMZ that will incorporate several servers, including a web server, an FTP server, and a mail server. Which inbound ports will need to be opened at the firewall so that the servers can securely communicate with users on the Internet? (Select the four best answers.)

☐ **A.** 21

☐ **B.** 22

☐ **C.** 23

☐ **D.** 53

☐ **E.** 80

☐ **F.** 110

☐ **G.** 143

☐ **H.** 443

☐ **I.** 587

☐ **J.** 995

☐ **K.** 3389

80. You need to run a diagnostic disc on a laptop running Windows. You modify the boot order in the UEFI/BIOS and set it to DVD first. However, the laptop still boots into Windows. What do you need to adjust to boot to the DVD?

○ **A.** Secure Boot

○ **B.** TPM

○ **C.** UEFI/BIOS password

○ **D.** Virtualization

Answers at a Glance

1. C	**28.** D	**55.** C
2. B	**29.** B	**56.** D
3. D	**30.** B	**57.** A
4. D	**31.** B	**58.** C
5. A	**32.** C	**59.** C
6. D	**33.** A	**60.** B, C
7. A	**34.** C, D	**61.** A, C
8. A, D	**35.** A, D	**62.** A
9. C	**36.** B	**63.** A
10. B	**37.** C, E	**64.** B
11. C	**38.** C	**65.** D
12. C, E	**39.** E	**66.** A
13. D	**40.** B	**67.** C
14. B	**41.** B	**68.** B
15. B	**42.** C	**69.** D
16. A, B	**43.** A	**70.** C
17. A	**44.** B	**71.** A
18. A	**45.** C, D	**72.** B
19. D	**46.** D	**73.** D
20. B	**47.** D, E	**74.** A
21. A, E	**48.** B	**75.** C
22. A	**49.** A	**76.** B
23. B	**50.** A	**77.** C
24. D	**51.** B	**78.** A, C, E
25. C	**52.** C	**79.** B, H, I, J
26. B	**53.** B	**80.** A
27. E	**54.** A, E	

Answer Explanations

1. Answer: **C**. The central processing unit (CPU), otherwise known as the processor, is often considered to be the "brains" of the computer because it performs the bulk of the calculations for the system. See Chapter 12, "CPUs," for more information.

   Incorrect answers: Random access memory (RAM) stores calculated data over the short term—it is often called volatile memory because its contents are lost when the computer is shut down. A hard drive stores data over the long term—it is often called nonvolatile memory, or simply "storage," because it retains data when the computer is shut down. The motherboard is the central connecting point for all components and connections within the computer, including the CPU, RAM, and hard drive.

2. Answer: **B**. Most of the time a computer's BIOS (or UEFI) will be configured to boot to the hard drive first. To boot from a USB flash drive, or optical disc, or other removable media, you might need to change the boot sequence, otherwise known as the boot order or boot priority, and place the removable media first. However, if the drive is brand new and blank, you might be able to still boot from the removable media, even if it is not first on the list. This will depend on the system, but essentially, the BIOS will see that the drive is blank and move on to the next boot media on the list. Keep in mind that you might boot to removable media with an operating system for other reasons than installing the OS (for example, recovering an existing system). See Chapter 11, "Motherboards and Add-on Cards," for more information.

   Incorrect answers: Enabling a password is not necessary, but there should be a password. If there is, you will need to know it in order to access the BIOS. If not, you should create one while you are there. TPM (Trusted Platform Module) deals with the encryption of data on the hard drive and should be enabled or disabled before an operating system is installed; it won't have any bearing on the boot sequence.

3. Answer: **D**. The RJ45 connector is the most common type of networking connector. It is used in twisted-pair networks. See Chapter 9, "Cables and Connectors," for more information.

   Incorrect answers: RJ11 is the connector used by landline-based phones (POTS connections) and DSL connections in households. The F-connector is a type of coaxial connector used for cable TV and cable Internet connections. BNC is another type of coaxial connector used in some video applications and in older networks.

4. Answer: **D**. DDR4 SODIMMs use the 260-pin module format. See Chapter 1, "Laptops, Part 1," for more information.

   Incorrect answers: As far as SODIMM technology goes, DDR1 and DDR2 use the 200-pin module format and DDR3 is 204-pin. 240-pin is used by full-size desktop DDR3.

5. Answer: **A**. The page count should be reset whenever you perform normal, scheduled printer maintenance. For example, a laser printer can print about 200,000 pages before it needs a scheduled maintenance. By resetting the page count after a successful maintenance, you will know when the next maintenance should occur. This is reset on the printer itself. See Chapter 15, "Printers and Multifunction Devices," for more information.

Incorrect answers: The job queue and cache should reset automatically; this is because you would normally turn the printer off before maintaining it. Any print queue located on a computer is not reset automatically, but jobs in the queue will probably have to be resent. The tray settings do not have to be reset.

6. Answer: **D**. Always check if there is a new firmware update available for your wireless access point or other networking device before configuring it and making it available for use. In the scenario, a protocol is probably not the correct version, so the router cannot see the wireless access point. In this case, updating the firmware is the right move. But always check your company policies before doing so. See Chapter 6, "SOHO Networks and Wireless Protocols," for more information.

Incorrect answers: The apt-get command is used to install and update applications in Linux operating systems. Windows Update is the program used to update and patch Windows operating systems. A Red Hat Package Manager (RPM) update, now simply known as RPM Package Manager, is used to install software on Linux systems.

> **Note**
>
> Yes, be ready for questions that might traverse the 220-1001 *and* 220-1002 objectives. That's why I suggest going through this entire book before attempting either of the exams. Read it all, then revisit the concepts and objectives for each exam—taking one exam at a time.

7. Answer: **A**. Of the listed answers, you should check the DC-in jack on the laptop. The very first thing you should do is check the basics; see if the power brick is connected to the AC outlet and to the DC-in jack and verify that the battery is connected properly. See Chapter 2, "Laptops, Part 2," for more information.

Incorrect answers: Laptops don't have an AC-in jack—the power adapter takes care of converting AC power to DC power for the laptop to use. Of course, you should always check the laptop battery first, in the event that it is missing or not connected properly. Next, make sure the power adapter is plugged into the DC-in jack and that the jack is not damaged. A damaged DC-in jack can also cause the laptop to occasionally shut off. Users often damage the DC-in jack because they leave the power adapter plugged in while they are in transit. On most laptops, a new one has to be soldered on to the board. The CMOS battery is inside the laptop. It retains UEFI/BIOS settings and has nothing to do with charging the main laptop battery. The AC circuit breaker might have tripped, but is less likely than the previously listed reasons. Also, a good indication of a failed AC circuit is that all of the devices on that circuit would stop working.

8. Answers: **A** and **D**. You should clean and inspect the entire paper path first. This costs nothing; plus, by clearing out any papers within the path, you will often solve the problem, at least temporarily, if not permanently. Also, use the corresponding printer maintenance kit to replace worn parts. The parts from these kits should be installed every 100,000 to 200,000 pages printed (depending on the printer). Older worn parts can often lead to paper jamming, and is the most likely answer, especially if the problem has been getting worse of late. See Chapter 21, "Troubleshooting Printers," for more information.

   Incorrect answers: Paper jams don't usually occur in the fusing assembly, but it is a possibility. Of course, you should wait 10 to 15 minutes for the fuser to cool before cleaning or replacing it. (Don't forget to make sure the printer is turned off and unplugged.) Replacing other components such as sensors and switches (if they exist) is less common. It is also uncommon to clean and inspect the print drum; instead, you would simply replace the toner cartridge. However, this concerns problems such as streaking, marks, and ghosting more than it does paper jams.

9. Answer: **C**. If the intrusion detection setting is enabled in the UEFI/BIOS, and the computer was opened, the system will display a message and log what happened. This is a security feature on most of today's motherboards. See Chapter 11, "Motherboards and Add-on Cards," for more information.

   Incorrect answers: Configuring the date and time settings would not result in a message. The boot sequence deals with the list of drives that the system will attempt to boot from in order. Virtualization support allows the system to use CPUs that take advantage of Intel and AMD virtualization extensions.

10. Answer: **B**. If the power supply fan and the case fans are spinning but there is no power to other devices, the chances are that the main 24-pin power connection was not made from the power supply to the motherboard. In this scenario, the case fans would have been connected by way of Molex power connectors directly to the power supply. Although it's usually better to connect case fans to the motherboard, if they were connected to the motherboard, they would not spin, because the motherboard is not receiving power. If this scenario was to occur, no other devices would get power, including the CPU, RAM, motherboard, hard drives, optical drives, and so on. See Chapter 13, "Peripherals and Power," for more information.

   Incorrect answers: If the hard drive fails, the operating system will fail to boot up. If the hard drive cannot be repaired, it will have to be removed (often with a Phillips-head screwdriver) and replaced. If the drive is not recognized, again, the OS will not boot. It would have to be reconnected properly, configured in the UEFI/BIOS, or partitioned and formatted properly in Windows, depending on the specific situation. Failed RAM could cause a boot failure and will definitely be registered by the POST, but it doesn't necessarily mean that the RAM (or any other device) is not receiving power.

11. Answer: **C**. The best answer listed is to check the motherboard for swollen capacitors. A swollen (or distended) capacitor could cause the system to reboot intermittently. The capacitor (or entire motherboard) needs to be replaced. See Chapter 18, "Troubleshooting Motherboards, CPUs, RAM, and Power," for more information.

Incorrect answers: It is unlikely that the network adapter or fragmented hard drive would cause the system to sporadically reboot, but you should check for the latest drivers and firmware for the network adapter anyway and analyze whether the hard drive has been defragmented of late (especially for magnetic disks). RAM could cause the system to periodically reboot, mainly if the RAM is overheating. (RAM heat sinks could fix that.) But the wrong type of RAM will usually result in a POST failure instead.

12. Answers: **C** and **E**. The most important components in a CAD workstation are maximized RAM, high-end video, and an SSD (as well as a good multicore CPU). See Chapter 14, "Custom PCs and Common Devices," for more information.

    Incorrect answers: IDE drives are not seen much anymore, because they are an older technology that is not nearly as fast as SATA. It is more likely that the system will use internal SATA 3.0 drives, or NVMe-based drives (or perhaps SATA Express drives). The USB ports are not as important on a CAD workstation. More likely, the system will run a 64-bit OS, not 32-bit.

13. Answer: **D**. The only answer listed that is an example of a MAC address is 00-1C-C0-A1-55-21. The MAC address is the address burned into the ROM chip of a network adapter that uniquely identifies it. This address is composed of six hexadecimal numbers, each between 00 and FF. The decimal equivalent of this is 0 through 255. The first three numbers are the OUI (organizationally unique identifier); 00-1C-C0 is an Intel OUI. The last three numbers are the individual address of the particular network adapter. You might also encounter MAC addresses separated by colons instead of hyphens. See Chapter 5, "Ports, Protocols, and Network Devices," for more information.

    Incorrect answers: 10.1.1.255 is an IPv4 address. 4410:FF11:AAB3::0012 is a truncated IPv6 address. https://dprocomputer.com is a web address. It includes the protocol used (HTTPS) and the domain name (dprocomputer.com).

14. Answer: **B**. Port forwarding is the best answer. For a person to remotely access the network and gain access to the system, you should forward a specific port from the router over to the system. This happens after the remote user has made a virtual private networking (VPN) connection to the network. See Chapter 6, "SOHO Networks and Wireless Protocols," for more information.

    Incorrect answers: QoS stands for quality of service, which can be configured to grant more connection performance to particular services, such as streaming media and Voice over Internet Protocol (VoIP). Static IP addresses are used when you need to have a permanent identification for a server (or the entire network) that can be accessed by hosts on the Internet. Although this might be used in the scenario, it isn't necessary and doesn't need to be configured to access the camera system.

    VPN passthrough means that VPN traffic is allowed on routers that utilize network address translation (NAT). NAT is the technology that allows multiple clients on the LAN to share the router to access the Internet.

15. Answer: **B**. A tone generator (part of a tone and probe kit) is often used to locate cables, especially if there are a bunch of them in a small area. In the scenario, the technician is connecting the tone generator to an RJ45 port, perhaps near a person's desk. Then the technician uses the probe (an inductive amplifier) to

locate the other end of that cable at the patch panel either in a wiring closet or in the server room. See Chapter 8, "Network Types and Networking Tools," for more information.

Incorrect answers: The other answers require a cable certifier. Although a cable certifier can often act as a tone generator, a tone generator is not a cable certifier—it can only generate a tone across the cable. Cable certifiers are used to confirm continuity, validate proper wiring, and test the transmission quality of a given connection.

16. Answers: **A** and **B**. Cellular connections are disabled when a mobile device enters airplane mode, and any other wireless connections as well, such as Wi-Fi, Bluetooth, GPS, and NFC. However, on some devices, some of these other wireless technologies can be turned on individually after the device has been placed in airplane mode. See Chapter 4, "Smartphones, Tablets, and Other Mobile Devices, Part 2," for more information.

Incorrect answers: The display's multitouch capabilities will work as normal, but web browsers, e-mail programs, and other apps that require Internet access will appear not to function properly when tapped on and navigated through—because, indeed, they are not functioning at all due to airplane mode. Data encryption will still function, though you won't be able to send that encrypted data anywhere. The camera will work, but posting images and video to a remote source will not function.

17. Answer: **A**. The Lightning connector is a proprietary connector used by Apple mobile devices. It is the successor to the 30-pin connector. However, keep in mind that some Apple devices use USB-C. See Chapter 3, "Smartphones, Tablets, and Other Mobile Devices, Part 1," for more information.

Incorrect answers: Apple devices do not use Micro-USB or Mini-USB, although adapters may be available depending on the device used. Micro-USB is common on Android-based devices. Molex is a power connection found inside PCs.

18. Answer: **A**. Try replacing the drum. If this is within the toner cartridge (which it often is), then replace that as well. See Chapter 21, "Troubleshooting Printers," for more information.

Incorrect answers: If the fuser needs replacing, you will probably see smeared text and images. If images or text are not straight or are colored incorrectly, you might need to calibrate the printer. If the network cable fails, the printer should not print at all from networked computers; however, a test page run locally at the printer should print just fine.

19. Answer: **D**. You will need to go to another computer, download the driver from the manufacturer's website, copy that to a flash drive, and bring it back to the affected computer. See Chapter 22, "Troubleshooting Wired and Wireless Network Problems," for more information.

Incorrect answers: If you have access to another computer, it would be silly to wait for a disc from the manufacturer. And any manufacturer that charges for drivers (or a driver disc) should be ashamed, as should the user who actually purchases the disc! You can't run Windows Update or download drivers from the computer in question because the computer has no network connection; and remember, Windows Update is used to download Microsoft drivers, not other vendors' drivers.

20. Answer: **B**. The Domain Name System (DNS) server is the server that is in charge of resolving domain names (such as davidlprowse.com) to their corresponding IP addresses (such as 216.97.236.245). So, in other words, it provides mapping of user-friendly names to network resources. The DNS server can supply this information to you when you make use of various commands in the command-line such as **ping, tracert, nslookup**, and **dig**. See Chapter 7, "Networked Hosts and Network Configuration," for more information.

Incorrect answers: A DHCP server takes care of handing out IP addresses to client computers automatically. An authentication server—such as a domain controller running LDAP—is in charge of verifying the identity of users who attempt to log in. A Syslog server is used to gather the logs from network devices and present the information in a manageable way to an admin's workstation. Though you could probably find out the name resolution within the log details, it wouldn't be done in the command line and it wouldn't be presented in the manner that it was in the question. A print server is a computer that is in charge of one or more printers on the network.

21. Answers: **A** and **E**. The video card and RAM are situated in such a way so that they can connect quickly to the CPU or to the northbridge. On newer Intel systems, the northbridge is actually part of the CPU. The video card connects by way of PCI Express ×16 or ×4 slots. The RAM connects via the address bus. See Chapter 10, "RAM and Storage," and Chapter 11, "Motherboards and Add-on Cards," for more information.

Incorrect answers: The hard drive and audio connect to the southbridge; in newer Intel systems, they connect directly to the single chip within the chipset (which is still referred to as a southbridge.) Fans are physically connected to the motherboard; any functionality is controlled by the UEFI/BIOS.

22. Answer: **A**. The best answer listed is thin client. A thin client is used for basic applications, and it meets the minimum requirements for a selected OS. It is usually a diskless workstation with limited CPU power. It gets its operating system from flash-based memory or from a server and doesn't have a hard drive. In addition, it resets itself every time it is restarted. This helps to protect against malware and decreases the chances of hardware failure. See Chapter 14, "Custom PCs and Common Devices," for more information.

Incorrect answers: A standard thick client is generally a PC. Internet cafes do not need the power of a thick client, an audio/video workstation, a gaming PC, or an HTPC. By the way, HTPC stands for home theater PC—a kind of computer used to connect to television stations, play DVDs and Blu-rays, connect to streaming services, as well as work like a regular computer. The acronym is not in the CompTIA A+ bulleted objectives, but it is listed in the CompTIA A+ Acronyms list at the end of the objectives.

23. Answer: **B**. The best answer listed is infrastructure as a service (IaaS). This allows for networking services (also known as NaaS), storage, load balancing, routing, VM hosting, and more. See Chapter 16, "Cloud Computing and Client-side Virtualization," for more information.

Incorrect answers: Software as a service (SaaS) provides common applications to clients over the Internet. Platform as a service (PaaS) provides software solutions such as the ability to develop and test applications within the cloud. Database as a service (DBaaS)—or cloud database—is where the creator of the database does not have to install or support the database software or server; instead, it is provided by a cloud service. The acronym DBaaS is not in the CompTIA A+ bulleted objectives, but it is listed in the CompTIA A+ Acronym list, where you will also find data as a service (DaaS) and network as a service (NaaS).

24. Answer: **D**. Bridged networking is when virtual machines can get *direct* access to the hosting computer's network connection and access other systems on the LAN and the Internet. You might also see this referred to as "external" or "public." See Chapter 16, "Cloud Computing and Client-side Virtualization," for more information.

    Incorrect answers: Network address translation (NAT) is when the guest can access the external network, but not directly. Instead, the guests using NAT get IP addresses on a separate private IP network. Host-only networking creates a private virtual network for the guests, and they can communicate with each other, but not out to the external network or Internet.

25. Answer: **C**. In this scenario, it is possible that the printer's IP address has been changed, and it is the best choice of the listed answers. The workstations were manually configured (most likely via IP address), which means that an IP address change on the printer would cause any print jobs from those workstations to fail. The IP address could have been configured manually by another tech, or if it was set to DHCP, the printer might have received a new address from the DHCP server. Because of this exact scenario, it is always a good idea to configure a static IP address at the printer itself (within the LCD display). Remember, in the scenario the printer can be seen in the network directory, which usually searches by printer *name* as opposed to printer IP address. Also, test pages are printing successfully. All these are clues that point to a potential IP problem. See Chapter 21, "Troubleshooting Printers," for more information.

    Incorrect answers. Restarting the print spooler service is a troubleshooting technique used when the spooler service is hung up for some reason. It generally doesn't cause problems but can fix a lot of spooling issues. Two print jobs can't be sent at the same time—collisions are a concept related to networking. It is possible that packets or frames can collide, but not the print jobs. The print jobs are placed into a queue either at the printer or at the print server. The need to perform printer maintenance doesn't usually cause print failures, but if you see that message, you should attend to it right away.

26. Answer: **B**. The main advantage of UDP (User Datagram Protocol) over TCP (Transmission Control Protocol) is that it can transfer data packets faster. Because it is a connectionless protocol, it doesn't require the synchronization or sequencing that TCP does. This makes it a faster option for streaming services, VoIP, and so on. See Chapter 5, "Ports, Protocols, and Network Devices," for more information.

    Incorrect answers: UDP does not have an option for flow control. Also, it does not use a handshaking process. (TCP uses the three-way handshake: SYN, SYN-ACK, ACK.) As mentioned, UDP is connectionless, whereas TCP is connection based. However, even though UDP can transmit packets faster, you will find that TCP is used for most services and applications you will deal with.

27. Answer: **E**. John forgot to verify full system functionality. As I've said many times during the course of the book, always *test*! And by "test" I mean verify functionality—make sure it works—not "test the theory." With a default installation of a plug-and-play network card, the card will, by default, be set to obtain an IP address automatically. If the computers need to be configured for static IP addresses, this will most likely cause a problem. There might not even be a device or server that is handing out IP addresses on the network. If that is the case, the Windows computer would attempt to self-assign an IP address (an APIPA address starting with 169.254). If that happens, the computer will most definitely not be able to communicate with the gateway—or the Internet, for that matter. And even if there is a DHCP server on the network, the chances are very slim that it is handing out addresses on the 192.168.50.0 network. Most SOHO routers will hand out addresses on the 192.168.0.0 or 192.168.1.0 networks, and that is only if DHCP is enabled.

John should have logged in to Windows, ran a ping test, tried to connect to websites with one or more browsers, and so on. Verifying full functionality is very important. Always remember to test every repair thoroughly. See Chapter 17, "Computer Troubleshooting 101," for more information.

Incorrect answers: All the steps of the A+ troubleshooting methodology are listed in the answers. John performed each step except for verifying full system functionality.

ExamAlert

Know the A+ troubleshooting methodology like the back of your hand for both exams!

---

28. Answer: **D**. You will need to replace both failed drives (which causes a total RAID 5 array failure, by the way) and restore the entire set of data from tape backup. See Chapter 19, "Troubleshooting Hard Drives and RAID Arrays," for more information.

Incorrect answers: In a RAID 5 array, one drive can fail and you can still recover from the issue without tape backup (using the RAID parity information), but no more than one can fail. If more than one fails—as in the question's scenario—then you need to restore all data from a previous backup. However, in RAID 6, two drives can fail and it can still recover. Formatting the RAID array is a good idea if you have to recover from backup but not a good idea otherwise because it will make the current data inaccessible. However, the term "quick option" is a Windows term, implying that the RAID array was created in Windows, and is therefore a software-based array. It is recommended that you create hardware-based arrays that connect to a RAID adapter card (or RAID-enabled motherboard). In a hardware-based system such as this, you could repair the array with the system utilities, but again, in this scenario (RAID 5) only if one drive has failed.

29. Answer: **B**. If the PC's display is experiencing screen flicker then it could be due to an improperly configured refresh rate. Usually, monitors and operating systems will auto-configure a setting such as this, but not always—for example, if you are using a less common operating system or a more advanced applica- tion. The refresh rate is the number of times the display is drawn on the screen per second. A common amount is 60 Hz, but perhaps the user is working with an editing program or game that requires a higher refresh rate, and the monitor supports it, but it is not configured properly, either in the OS or in the application. Or perhaps it is an older system that is more prone to refresh rate issues. As you can see, there are a lot of possibilities when it comes to video. See Chapter 20, "Troubleshooting Video Issues and Mobile Devices," for more information.

Incorrect answers: The cold-cathode fluorescent bulb (CCFL) is the backlight for LCD screens. You wouldn't reconfigure it, but you might have to replace it if the display starts blinking or shuts off completely. Keep in mind that many displays are LED based today and do not use a CCFL. A different resolution shouldn't cause screen flicker on a flat-panel display—it would either show the different resolution, no resolution, or possibly a distorted image. Resolution issues are more common with CRT monitors. Screen flicker could be caused by a loose connection, regardless of the connection used. But switching from one video port type to another probably won't help fix the actual problem.

30. Answer: **B**. The laser printer is the one that is most associated with maintenance kits. Common components of a laser printer maintenance kit include a fuser, transfer roller, and pickup rollers. See Chapter 21, "Troubleshooting Printers," for more information.

Incorrect answers: Common components of a thermal printer include the feed assembly and heating element. The inkjet printer normally includes the ink car- tridge, print head, roller, feeder, duplexing assembly, carriage, and belt. An impact printer's components include the print head, ribbon, and tractor feed.

01. Answer. **B**. Although you could try several things, the best of the listed answers is to disconnect the AC connection and the battery and press and hold the Power button for several seconds. This effectively discharges the laptop (capaci- tors and such) and may also clear the BIOS, either one of which can fix the prob- lem. Exactly what happens will depend on the model of laptop, and the length of time you will need to hold down the Power button will vary. Afterward, reconnect the battery and AC connection and continue troubleshooting from there if neces- sary. The key in this question is that you cannot hear or see anything happening. In most cases, something will happen, but in this case, the laptop may have had a voltage overload or other similar problem. Discharging it in this fashion can fix the problem, but you might have to reconfigure your BIOS. See Chapter 1, "Laptops, Part 1," for more information.

Incorrect answers: Booting the system to a disc will probably result in nothing. If you can't see or hear anything, you need to take stronger measures than that. Sometimes, removing drives and USB devices can help when troubleshooting, but again, in this scenario where you can see and hear nothing, it probably won't help. Connecting an external monitor is a good idea if you can see LED lights blinking when you press the Power button but get no main display. In this case, the result will probably be no image on both displays.

32. Answer: **C**. One of your most important considerations should be the input voltage. For example, in the United States (and some other countries) this is

120 volts. However, in many other countries it is 240 volts. (These are also represented as 115 V and 230 V.) It's better to avoid voltage converters if at all possible, so you will need a power supply unit (PSU) that can handle both. That means one of two things: 1. An auto-selecting PSU, or 2. A PSU with a voltage switch. The former is preferable, so that the person setting up the computer at trade shows does not need to remember to check the switch. However, keep in mind that you might still need an adapter for the actual three-prong connection used in other countries. See Chapter 13, "Peripherals and Power," for more information.

Incorrect answers: The efficiency rating tells you how effectively the PSU uses energy. For example, the 80 Plus program promotes energy efficiency of more than 80 percent. While this is important for most computers—because we all want to conserve energy, right?—it is not as important for this particular system, because the PC will be relying on power that is provided by the trade show venues. Rail amperage is important for resource-intensive computers such as gaming PCs, design systems, and so on, where an individual rail (such as the 12 V) can overheat if driven too hard. Of course, we don't want our devices (such as GPUs) to draw too much current from the PSU (which generally can max out at about 30 amps or so); however, the system is using typical components, so current should not be a factor. As long as the PSU meets the wattage requirements, it should be okay. Maximizing the RAM shouldn't cause the computer to go beyond the maximum current or wattage (as long as we don't overclock it! And even then it is unlikely.) Almost all PSUs come with several SATA power connectors, and we are only using one hard drive, so that should not be a factor either.

33. Answer: **A**. Some touchscreens require calibration to respond to input properly. See Chapter 3, "Smartphones, Tablets, and Other Mobile Devices, Part 1" for more information.

Incorrect answers: Keyboards and mice do not require this. Video cards are not calibrated, but monitors can be (in a variety of ways). Printers can be calibrated as well.

34. Answers: **C** and **D**. The most likely answers here are that there is no device sending video (such as a video card) or that the source cable has been disconnected (for example, from the computer's video card to the monitor). Always check the connections on both ends, and make sure that the computer (the video source) is on and booting properly. See Chapter 20, "Troubleshooting Video Issues and Mobile Devices," for more information.

Incorrect answers: The brightness and contrast settings are not likely to cause a no-image issue. On most monitors you can reduce the brightness to zero but still see the image on the screen. Likewise, you can increase the contrast to 100 (or whatever maximum number is used) and still see the image on the screen. It is not possible for the monitor's backlight to have failed because you can see in the OSD that the proper video source has been selected. The OSD would not be visible (or would only be barely visible with a flashlight) if the backlight had failed. Again, it is much more likely that there is a connectivity or source video problem. Always check the connections first!

35. Answers: **A** and **D**. Check the memory and the power supply unit (PSU) first. Both of these can fail intermittently, causing random reboots. Try reseating and cleaning RAM (and replacing if necessary). Test the PSU with a PSU

tester or multimeter and replace if necessary. The PSU can also cause the computer to quickly shut down immediately after it was started. See Chapter 18, "Troubleshooting Motherboards, CPUs, RAM, and Power," for more information.

Incorrect answers: If the video card fails, the computer simply won't display to the monitor. If the CMOS battery fails (or discharges), the time and date will reset to an earlier date (for example, to January 1, 20XX.) Other settings in the BIOS will be lost as well. If the optical drive fails, you won't be able to read CDs and DVDs, but the optical drive should not cause the computer to reboot.

36. Answer: **B**. Near field communication (NFC) is missing from the smartphone. Older (first generation) smartphones do not have NFC. Always check the minimum requirements of any software or service that you are planning to use with a smartphone, tablet, or other computer. Make sure that the mobile device in question meets the minimum requirements. See Chapter 3, "Smartphones, Tablets, and Other Mobile Devices, Part 1" for more information.

Incorrect answers: IMSI stands for International Mobile Subscriber Identity and is a unique 64-bit field used to identify the user of a cellular network. By the way, don't confuse IMSI with IMEI. IMEI stands for International Mobile Station Equipment Identity, which identifies the phone. RFID stands for radio-frequency identification, a technology that uses tags and radio-frequency scanning to identify those tags. Bluetooth is a technology primarily used to allow for peripherals' access to a computer, such as using a Bluetooth headset with a smartphone.

37. Answers: **C** and **E**. Unless a company has a lot of servers, then the servers will usually be assigned static IP addresses, as opposed to being dynamically assigned those IP addresses by a DHCP server. When you manually configure the TCP/IP properties of a computer you are required to enter the IP address and a subnet mask; for example, IP: 192.168.1.100 and subnet mask: 255.255.255.0. Often times, you will also configure a gateway address and a DNS server address, though they might not be required. The great thing about the static IP address is that you know what it is because you assigned it; you can enter it into your network documentation knowing that it will not change. DHCP-assigned addressed can change from time to time, depending on how the DHCP scope was configured. See Chapter 7, "Networked Hosts and Network Configuration," for more information.

Note

There is one glaring issue in this question's scenario. Ever heard of the phrase "putting too many eggs in one basket"? That's exactly what is happening here. The server is doing everything: it's a domain controller, a file server, a print server, and who know what else. While small companies sometimes have to make do with the resources at hand, it would be wise to separate one or more of these services and place them on a second server.

Incorrect answers: Dynamic Host Configuration Protocol (DHCP)—as a rule of thumb—is not used for servers in a small company. Dynamic IPs are handed out by the DHCP server to client computers. The MAC address is the hexadecimal address that is programmed into the firmware of the network adapter at the manufacturing plant; it is not (normally) set by the administrator. A File Transfer Protocol (FTP) address is rather vague—does that mean an IP address or a name? Either way, the scenario didn't mention anything about FTP.

38. Answer: **C**. Of the listed answers, the Lightweight Directory Access Protocol (LDAP) is relied upon most by Active Directory. LDAP deals with directory lists (such as the users within a Microsoft Active Directory domain) or the users' e-mail addresses listed within a Microsoft Exchange server. See Chapter 5, "Ports, Protocols, and Network Devices," for more information.

   Incorrect answers: Server Message Block (SMB) is a protocol that allows shared access to files; it is important to any computer running Windows, not just computers that are in charge of, or connect to, a Microsoft Active Directory domain. SMB is also known as the Common Internet File System (CIFS.) HTTP stands for Hypertext Transfer Protocol, used to transfer data from a web server to a client computer's web browser. WINS stands for Windows Internet Naming Service, a name resolution technology that converts NetBIOS names to IP addresses. It is somewhat deprecated and is not commonly used; its successor is the Domain Name System (DNS.)

39. Answer: **E**. Always check the motherboard documentation before you begin installing components. You need to know what type of memory you should be using, what type of channel configuration (most likely dual- or quad-channel), and where the sticks of RAM should be installed depending on what configuration you will use. The motherboard documentation will have a table or matrix explaining all the different possibilities. A single motherboard might allow one stick of RAM, plus configurations for dual-channel, tri-channel, and quad-channel. You need to know what is allowed and plan for the right type of RAM before you purchase it. In this scenario there are eight slots in total (0–7). If you install the memory into all the gray slots, then you are probably setting the system up for a multichannel configuration, but you must get the correct RAM. Note that the colors of the slots can be different depending on the manufacturer; for example, they might be blue and black, and the first slots you should use are the blue ones. It all depends—always check documentation first! See Chapter 10, "RAM and Storage," for more information.

   Incorrect answers: Installing the memory to the dark-gray slots might work, but it might not if those are the secondary slots for each channel. Going by the first four numbers might not be correct either, depending on the motherboard. In fact, a motherboard will often use the numbering system A1, A2, B1, B2, C1, C2, D1, D2, with each letter corresponding to a different channel. Filling all the slots might work, perhaps if you get quad-channel-compliant memory (and a lot of it), but it is not the recommended choice because it can be expensive and probably is not necessary. The main lesson here is that there are a lot of possibilities, depending on the motherboard, and depending on what you as the user wish to accomplish. So always RTM (read the manual) and plan your purchases wisely.

40. Answer: **B**. The inkjet printer uses piezoelectric pressure pads to produce small bubbles that are moved to the paper. See Chapter 15, "Printers and Multifunction Devices," for more information.

Incorrect answers: The laser printer applies toner to the paper in the electrophotographic imaging process. A thermal printer uses heat to create text and images on specially coated paper. Impact printers use a print head to hammer the letters through a ribbon and on to the paper.

41. Answer: **B**. The best answer is "RAID utilizes multiple disks to increase performance and/or enable protection from data loss." RAID 0 and 5 can be used to increase read performance, while RAID 1, 5, and 10 can be used to enable protection from data loss. See Chapter 10, "RAM and Storage," for more information.

Incorrect answers: Telling a customer that RAID stands for Redundant Array of Independent (or Inexpensive) Disks is technical jargon that you should try to avoid. RAID is not a dynamic disk management system. However, in Microsoft operating systems, you need to set disks to dynamic in the Disk Management utility if you wish to add them to RAID arrays. Regardless, this is more information that the customer does not need to know. Finally, the statement "RAID uses striping to reduce the amount of hard drive write time and utilizes parity bits to reconstruct the data from a failed hard drive" is not altogether correct. RAID can also be mirroring. In addition, not all versions of RAID can use parity bits to reconstruct data from a failed hard drive. RAID 0, 1, and 10 do not. However, RAID 5 and 6 do. Remember that the customer needs to know how the technology will make their business more efficient; he or she does not need to know the technical details or jargon.

42. Answer: **C**. Of the listed answers, the most likely cause is that the CPU needs to be reseated. This will result in a series of beeps from the power-on self-test (POST) as the BIOS searches for the CPU and can't find it. If a computer was being built in this scenario, then it's also possible that the RAM was not seated properly, or there is some RAM compatibility issue. See Chapter 18, "Troubleshooting Motherboards, CPUs, RAM, and Power," for more information.

Incorrect answers: No other answer choice would cause the POST to issue a series of beeps. The mouse would not, but a lack of a keyboard would result in beeps. (Always make sure the keyboard is securely connected!) Also, the POST doesn't look for operating system corruption; it is relegated to hardware only. But it can display messages such as "no operating system found" or a similar message if the hard drive is missing, not formatted, or not in the correct location in the BIOS boot order. "The fan is running too fast" is subjective; regardless, its maximum speed is usually governed by the BIOS, and shouldn't affect how the system boots.

43. Answer: **A**. The firewall is the device that prevents outside intrusion by blocking ports and protocols. In many networks it is the first line of defense. See Chapter 5, "Ports, Protocols, and Network Devices," for more information.

Incorrect answers: A gateway is a device (usually a router) that allows multiple clients on one network access to another (for example, computers on the LAN that want to gain access to the Internet). A router connects two networks together. A bridge separates a LAN into two distinct network sections. An access point allows wireless connectivity to the network for Wi-Fi-enabled computers.

44. Answer: **B**. PCIe 6-pin is the best answer. 8-pin PCIe power connectors are also common, but don't confuse them with 8-pin CPU power connectors. See Chapter 13, "Peripherals and Power," for more information.

Incorrect answers: Though there are 8-pin 12 V connectors for PCIe, the EATX12V 8-pin connector is used for CPUs. 24-pin ATX refers to the main power connection from the PSU to the motherboard. SATA power connectors are 15-pin and are used for hard drives and optical drives.

45. Answers: **C** and **D**. IPS (in-plane switching) monitor technology offers the widest viewing angle, and LED (light-emitting diode) monitors offer rich colors and consistent backlighting. See Chapter 13, "Peripherals and Power," for more information.

Incorrect answers: Plasma screens do not perform as well in these respects. TN (twisted-nematic) monitors are less expensive monitors that do not have as good of a viewing angle as IPS. CCFL stands for cold-cathode fluorescent lamp, which is the backlight used in standard LCD monitors. LED is superior to plain LCD when it comes to backlighting and rich colors. Note: LED also performs the best (compared to the others listed) when it comes to use in an area with a lot of natural light.

46. Answer: **D**. The next thing you need to do is connect to a wireless network, the first step of which will be to scan for network names (SSIDs) or to add them manually. See Chapter 6, "SOHO Networks and Wireless Protocols," for more information.

Incorrect answers: You won't type the security passphrase until you connect to a wireless network. Updating the firmware and/or drivers for the WLAN card (Wi-Fi adapter) should be done as part of the installation of that card. If the router is set up to accept wireless connections, encryption should have already been configured on that router as well.

47. Answers: **D** and **E**. External SATA (eSATA) is an SATA port that is meant for use with external devices. It is sometimes found as a port on the back of a PC or can be added with an adapter card. Of course, USB (3.0, 2.0, and so on) is another external port that is used to connect to audio and video equipment as well as external hard drives. See Chapter 10, "RAM and Storage," for more information.

Incorrect answers: Normally, SATA (without the e preceding it) is used for internal devices, not external. Serial Attached SCSI (SAS) is a type of hard drive technology, which is used more in servers and power workstations, not typical PCs. Enhanced IDE (EIDE, also known as Parallel ATA) is an older hard drive standard that you won't see often—unless you are recovering data!—and it is internal by default.

48. Answer: **B**. White/orange, orange, white/green, blue, white/blue, green, white/brown, brown is the correct wiring sequence for the T568B wiring standard. You might also see this shown as: WO, O, WG, B, WB, G, WBr, Br. It's the same thing, just abbreviated. See Chapter 9, "Cables and Connectors," for more information.

Incorrect answers: The T568A standard, which switches the orange and green pins, is the older standard that was replaced by T568B. But to stay within electrical code and municipal guidelines, use the wiring scheme defined by the

T568B standard on each end for straight-through cables. To create a crossover cable, use T568B on one end and T568A on the other. RJ45 is a type of plug (or jack) that network cards, switches, and network jacks use. TIA stands for Telecommunications Industry Association—they developed the T568 standards, and other wiring standards.

49. Answer: **A**. Use an RJ45 crimper to crimp those RJ45 plugs on the ends of a patch cable. See Chapter 8, "Network Types and Networking Tools," for more information.

    Incorrect answers: Use a punchdown tool to terminate individual wires to the RJ45 wall jack and to patch panels. Use a loopback plug to test a network adapter by plugging it into the card's RJ45 port. Use a cable tester to test patch cables or longer LAN cable connections.

50. Answer: **A**. Quality of service (QoS) is the performance of user connections over the network, particularly connections to the Internet. On some small office/home office (SOHO) routers, this can be configured to allow for equal data transfers among all users, or it can be used to configure special traffic (such as streaming media) to transfer faster. See Chapter 6, "SOHO Networks and Wireless Protocols," for more information.

    Incorrect answers: DSL stands for Digital Subscriber Line, which is a family of technologies used to transfer data over the Internet. WAN stands for wide area network—a network that spans a large geographic area and connects two or more LANs. VPN stands for virtual private network, which allows for secure (tunneled) connections over the Internet.

51. Answer: **B**. You should clean the print head! Most printers come with an on screen utility that will do this or you can manually clean the print head (delicately!). Similar to this, printers might need to be calibrated if colors are slightly off. See Chapter 11, "Troubleshooting Printers," and Chapter 15, "Printers and Multifunction Devices," for more information.

    Incorrect answers: If the printer cables weren't connected, the printer wouldn't print anything at all. Maintenance kits are used more often for laser printers and are unnecessary in this case. The weight of the paper will not affect what colors are printed by an inkjet printer.

52. Answer: **C**. Use a power supply unit (PSU) tester to check if the power supply is malfunctioning. If you ever smell something burning, even if it is a faint smell, turn off the power to any associated computers or devices and disconnect them from the AC outlet. Then test the affected PSU. Sometimes there is a burn-in period when it comes to new PSUs, and there might be a very faint smell for the first 24 to 48 hours. This is possible if the PSU was newly installed, but you should still test and monitor the PSU until the smell goes away. However, if the computer was working previously and suddenly doesn't work anymore, and you smell something burning, then you should most likely replace the PSU after testing it. Only test the PSU in your lab, and make sure you have all the necessary fire prevention tools and technologies available to you. See Chapter 18, "Troubleshooting Motherboards, CPUs, RAM, and Power," for more information.

    Incorrect answers: A loopback plug is used to test a switch port or the RJ45 port on a computer. There are many cable testers, but the term is often associated with network cabling, such as cable certifiers for Category 6 (Cat 6) cable.

The ESD strap, or more accurately antistatic strap, is used to protect components from electrostatic discharge (ESD).

53. Answer: **B**. A switch can be described as a network device that transmits packets it receives to specific connections. It does this by mapping systems' MAC addresses to physical ports on the switch. See Chapter 5, "Ports, Protocols, and Network Devices," for more information.

Incorrect answers: A router would convert a packet for transmission from one network to another network. It also determines whether a packet belongs on an internal or an external network, though this process can be augmented by other devices. A hub broadcasts packets it receives to all connections.

54. Answers: **A** and **E**. A virtualization computer (especially a virtualization server) requires memory and a powerful multicore CPU above all else. Because virtual machines require a lot of raw resources, maximum memory and maximum-core CPUs are the most important items for virtualization workstations. See Chapter 14, "Custom PCs and Common Devices," for more information.

Incorrect answers: High-end sound cards and video cards are typical in gaming computers and audio/video editing workstations. High-end video cards are also common in CAD/CAM computers (which, by the way, also require a lot of RAM and CPU power.) A dual-rail PSU is one that has two amperage outputs instead of just one; this is common in today's PSUs. 1000 watts is quite a high amount and is required by computers with a lot of powerful components, such as gaming computers.

55. Answer: **C**. Unshielded twisted-pair (UTP) cable is prone to electromagnetic interference (EMI). See Chapter 9, "Cables and Connectors," for more information.

Incorrect answers: Fiber optic cable is not prone to EMI because it uses light as the medium instead of electricity. Multimode cable is a type of fiber optic. STP stands for shielded twisted pair, and as the name indicates, it incorporates an aluminum shield around the wires in order to prevent EMI.

56. Answer: **D**. After installing a barcode reader, you should start scanning various test barcodes in order to calibrate and configure the reader. Many reader devices will come with a physical book that has printed test codes used to calibrate the device. See Chapter 13, "Peripherals and Power," for more information.

Incorrect answers: The infrared (IR) port should work automatically on a barcode reader; there is no reason to enable it. Barcode readers do not usually have jumper switches. Also, these are usually plug-and-play devices that do not need to be enabled in the BIOS.

57. Answer: **A**. The most likely listed cause is that the PC to which the printer is connected is currently off of the network. It would appear from this scenario that the printer is connected to a PC by way of USB and is shared at the PC itself, which is offline. If the customer can connect to other shares on other PCs, you know that that particular computer is functional on the network. See Chapter 15, "Printers and Multifunction Devices," for more information.

> **Note**
>
> In this scenario, the user is accessing shared files from another PC. Remember that this is a *shared printer*. That means that the printer is connected to another PC on the network, not directly to the network. The answer "PC is off the network" means the PC that has the printer connected to it.
>
> The key here is that the customer can access shares on other PCs, indicating an issue with the computer that has the printer connected to it.

Incorrect answers: The printer is on, and restarting a printer can fix some issues, but it will most likely return the printer to the same state it was in previously. The printer being low on toner should have no effect on whether it can be accessed. But a message would probably appear on one of the computer's screens stating that the toner cartridge should be changed soon. If device drivers are corrupted, the printer should still be accessible and might print, but it will probably print garbled information.

58. Answer: **C**. A dead pixel on a video display is a possible symptom of a damaged monitor screen. Sometimes dead pixels can be repaired with third-party software programs, but more often than not, the dead pixel indicates a damaged display. Another common display issue is when artifacts show up on the screen. This could be due to a damaged display or an incorrect video setting (such as resolution). See Chapter 20, "Troubleshooting Video Issues and Mobile Devices," for more information.

    Incorrect answers: A disconnected punchdown at a punchblock, patch panel, or RJ45 jack can cause a disruption in wired network data transfer, just as a low radio frequency (RF) signal can cause a loss in wireless network data transfer, but these will not affect the video display. If there is a problem with a wired connection, a punchdown tool will be required to rewire the network connection. Generally, the best method is to remove the cable's individual wires, cut it, strip the plastic jacket with a wire stripped, and re-terminate the individual wires. If a computer repeatedly boots into Safe Mode, there might be a driver issue, malware issue, or other OS problem, and though the system will boot in VGA resolution (640×480), that doesn't mean there is damage to the video display.

59. Answer: **C**. The functionality that the trainer desires is collating. This prints the documentation as entire jobs (for example, page 1 through 10, then repeat) instead of printing all the required copies of page 1 before moving to page 2. This makes it easier on the trainer when it comes time to hand out documentation to students. Collating is usually enabled on today's printers, but if not, you would enable it in the printer properties in Windows or on the display of the printer. To test if it works, simply print out a document that has two or more pages and select 2 for the number of copies. See Chapter 15, "Printers and Multifunction Devices," for more information.

    Incorrect answers: Duplexing means that the printer will print to both sides of the paper. Faxing and scanning are options found commonly on multifunction printers, but they don't have anything to do with collating. There are several ways to print to a file, such as printing to PDF, which takes a document such as one created in Microsoft Word and converts it into a PDF. The physical printer isn't actually involved with this at all.

60. Answers: **B** and **C**. The voltages a power supply unit (PSU) typically supplies include 3.3 V, 5 V, and 12 V (as well as their negatives) to components in the computer. See the section titled "Power Supplies" in Chapter 13, "Peripherals and Power," for more information.

Incorrect answers: 1.5 is a common voltage for DDR3 RAM and for AA and AAA batteries. 9 V is usually associated with batteries used by handheld devices such as power supply testers and multimeters. PSU's do not supply a 9 V rail or 1.5 V rail.

61. Answers: **A** and **C**. Some common symptoms of printer trouble include vertical lines on the page, which would indicate a print drum issue, likely fixed by a toner cartridge replacement or inkjet cartridge calibration. Also, problems installing the printer to an operating system are a symptom of printer trouble. If the printer has failed, the OS will have difficulty seeing it and the printer will have to be repaired before the printer and print driver can be installed to the client computer's OS. See Chapter 21, "Troubleshooting Printers."

Incorrect answers: Num Lock (Number Lock) indicator lights are displayed on laptop and PC keyboards. If a laptop's Num Lock indicator light is on, it will probably be difficult for a user to log in to the system. Instead of the user typing the regular password, a mixture of unwanted letters and numbers will be typed, causing the login to fail. Of course, this is not a common symptom of printer failure but could be the cause for a failed login. Failure to document cable and screw locations and the failure to organize parts could make reassembly of a printer or laptop difficult. These failures could possibly even be reasons why the printer or laptop fails, but they wouldn't be symptoms of the problem. When troubleshooting, be sure to understand the difference between a symptom of a problem and a cause of a problem. And of course, think carefully about the best solution to the problem!

62. Answer: **A**. VGA is an older standard that outputs analog signals to a monitor. Of the listed answers, it is the most susceptible to signal degradation. See Chapter 9, "Cables and Connectors," for more information.

Incorrect answers: HDMI, DVI, and DisplayPort are designed to work best sending digital signals and can send them over longer distances than analog cables (such as VGA). Digital is inherently better as far as distance and signal quality goes.

63. Answer: **A**. DVD-9 DL is the best answer when it comes to saving 6153 MB (6 GB) of data. DL stands for dual-layer. DVD-9 has one side and two layers by default, allowing it to save up to 8.5 GB of data maximum. See Chapter 10, "RAM and Storage," for more information.

Incorrect answers: CD-R discs can only save 700 MB or so; the 48x simply tells you the write speed. DVD-5 SL discs are standard single-sided, single-layer DVDs that can save up to 4.7 GB. A RAID 5 array would definitely be able to hold the data, but it is not a "disc"; in fact, it is three or more drives—if those drives were magnetic-based, then it would be "disks." Either way, a lot of work is required to build that array, plus the question did not mention that fault tolerance was required.

64. Answer: **B**. The most likely answer (of the listed answers) is that the motherboard was damaged by the power test. This causes a failure to power-on self-test (POST) and causes the fans to function improperly. There was probably some kind of surge or spike of electricity, which could have overloaded the mother-board in a variety of ways. Perhaps a capacitor burst, or maybe one of the circuits burned out. You might be able to repair it, but chances are you will need to replace the motherboard. You should notify your manager or your building facilities about the issue. Also, to protect systems from this kind of problem in the future, consider upgrading the surge suppressor, installing a new one, or using a line conditioner or uninterruptible power supply, or UPS (depending on the type of system). See Chapter 18, "Troubleshooting Motherboards, CPUs, RAM, and Power," for more information.

Incorrect answers: If no one opened the computer, then it is unlikely that the RAM was damaged by electrostatic discharge (ESD). Internal components are usually only affected by ESD when someone handles them improperly. You don't know yet, but the hard drive could have data corruption or become erased due to a power surge. But that isn't the cause of the problem in the scenario; it is simply another potential result. It's another reason to have good protective power equipment to plug the computer into. If the power supply was damaged and was nonfunctional, then the fans wouldn't spin at all. However, the power supply might also be partially damaged. You will need to do a lot of testing of the computer to make sure it is fully functional before putting it back into its normal work environment.

65. Answer: **D**. ECC stands for error correcting code. ECC memory can detect and correct common types of data corruption. It is often used in servers. It is not typically installed to desktops but might be used if data corruption cannot be tolerated. It provides for error correction, and therefore protection while storing data in RAM. See Chapter 10, "RAM and Storage," for more information.

Incorrect answers: Quad-channel means that the RAM can send data over four 64-bit channels at the same time—four sticks of RAM are required to take advantage of that. Parity support in RAM means that the memory can *detect* errors, but not correct them the way ECC does. Dual-channel RAM uses two 64-bit data channels at the same. RAID 5 is not a memory technology; rather it is a redundant hard drive array technology. While RAID 5 does use parity, it is not the same type of parity that RAM might use.

Note

You may have heard of unbuffered and buffered memory. While these terms are not in the A+ objectives, as a tech, you should know what they mean: Unbuffered memory is standard RAM that you would install to a typical PC. Buffered memory (also known as registered memory) places less electrical load on the memory controller, making a system that has a lot of sticks of RAM more stable. It is sometimes found in servers.

66. Answer: **A**. An IP address conflict is a possible cause for the problem. This happens when two computers are assigned the same IP address (usually when at least one was configured statically). When this happens, the link light on the network adapter will still work as usual because the system has a physical link to a central connecting device such as a switch, and bits (and frames) of data are still being sent back and forth between that computer and that switch. It's the IP layer that is nonfunctional due to the IP conflict. See Chapter 22, "Troubleshooting Wired and Wireless Network Problems," for more information.

Incorrect answers: The answer "incorrect gateway" is not correct because the scenario states that the PC cannot access *internal* network resources. A gateway deals with external network resources. Packet collisions only occur if the system has a valid IP connection. Slow transfer speed doesn't mean *no* transfer of data. Although slow transfer speeds could cause the system to take a while to connect, it should still connect at some point to internal network resources. You can tell if the system has sent or received data in the current session by going to the network icon in the Notification Area or by running a **netstat -e** command in the Command Prompt (in Windows); these will show packets that were transceived (transmitted and received).

67. Answer: **C**. The most likely cause is a memory failure. Two beeps often means a problem with memory. Of course, this will depend on the type of BIOS or UEFI. For example, two beeps in some Dell systems means that no memory has been detected, causing a RAM failure. Two short beeps in AMI BIOS systems means a memory parity error. See Chapter 18, "Troubleshooting Motherboards, CPUs, RAM, and Power," for more information.

Incorrect answers: If the power supply were to fail, the system wouldn't even POST because the motherboard didn't receive power. If the video adapter failed, you would get a different set of beeps. For example, in Award BIOS systems, one long and two short beeps (or three short beeps) means some kind of video error. In some Dell systems, six beeps means a video card failure. Read the motherboard documentation to find out what the beep codes mean exactly. If the CPU fails, the system will not boot or power-on self-test (POST).

68. Answer: **B**. You need to check whether the CPU has virtualization support enabled in the BIOS/UEFI. If this is not enabled, Windows will not allow the installation of Hyper-V to continue. You may receive an error message, or Windows will simply have a grayed-out area where you want to select Hyper-V in Programs and Features. See Chapter 11, "Motherboards and Add-on Cards," for more information.

Incorrect answers: The number of cores, Hyper-Threading, and cache size will not cause an error in Windows. However, you should make sure that your system meets the minimum requirements to run Hyper-V. In most cases, if the system can run Windows, then it *should* be able to run Hyper-V.

69. Answer: **D**. The loud clicking noise coming from a faulty hard drive is usually due to repeated motion of the read/write head parallel to the platter. It could be that the armature (arm) or its corresponding actuator is faulty and is not moving correctly. See Chapter 19, "Troubleshooting Hard Drives and RAID Arrays," for more information.

Incorrect answers: Remember that this is a problem associated with hard *disk* drives, meaning magnetic-based drives. It does not affect solid-sate drives (SSDs) because they do not use read/write heads. If a bearing in the motor was causing problems, then the arm might not move at all. If the coil was in an endless loop, there would be no activity or data would keep getting written to the same place; either way, you probably wouldn't hear anything.

70. Answer: **C**. The problem is most likely due to the touchpad settings (or calibration). The sensitivity might be too high, causing the cursor to jump quickly across the display. Another possibility is that the user's sleeve (or part of their arm or hand) is dragging across the touchpad. As a quick fix, you can disable the touchpad, often from a function key on the keyboard of the laptop (or in the Device Manager), until it is configured to the user's liking. See Chapter 1, "Laptops, Part 1," for more information.

Incorrect answers: Touchpad calibration is separate from screen calibration, which should not cause a problem with the cursor. Faulty software is a pretty vague answer. It's possible that third-party software that is used to configure the touchpad is where the issue lies, but more accurately, this would still be the touchpad settings. You don't know if the laptop uses Windows to configure the sensitivity of the touchpad, so the answer is not accurate enough. If a driver is unsigned, then Windows will ask for an administrator's permission to go ahead with the installation. If you can't provide the admin username and password (or you are not logged in as an admin), then the installation will fail. So, the driver either installs or it doesn't, but that has no bearing on the settings or calibration of the touchpad.

71. Answer: **A**. Thunderbolt is the only answer listed that can be used for audio, video, and storage. See Chapter 9, "Cables and Connectors," for more information.

Incorrect answers: DisplayPort and HDMI can transfer audio and video data but are not used for storage. DVI is used for video only.

72. Answer: **B**. You should replace the faulty drive. If one of the drives is performing below expectations due to high latency, then it might be because the drive is about to fail. You should back up the data, replace the drive, and restore the data (either from mirror, parity, or tape backup, as the case may be) to the array as soon as possible. See Chapter 19, "Troubleshooting Hard Drives and RAID Arrays," for more information.

Incorrect answers: Reseating the drive probably won't fix the problem. You might reseat a drive immediately after installation if it isn't responding properly. But if it has been working properly for a time, then this isn't a valid solution. Reinstalling the RAID driver would require that you take the entire array down (which might be necessary anyway) but is not something to try first due to the fact that it will require a lot of time and configuration (not to mention the downtime associated with the task). Replacing the RAID controller should be far down the troubleshooting list. If only one drive has failed (or is causing latency in this case), then it probably isn't the controller. Remember, hard drives will fail. It's just a matter of time, and it will normally happen before a controller fails.

73. Answer: **D**. SMB (Server Message Block) can be used to facilitate file sharing between Windows computers and computers running macOS. It is sometimes referred to as its older name CIFS (Common Internet File System). If SMB is for some reason unavailable on the Mac-based systems, then they will attempt to use the Apple File Protocol (AFP). See Chapter 5, "Ports, Protocols, and Network Devices," for more information.

Incorrect answers: RDP is the Remote Desktop Protocol, used to view or take control of remote computers from a central workstation. SSH is Secure Shell, a protocol used to make secure connections to other systems; it replaces protocols such as Telnet. POP3 is the Post Office Protocol (version 3) used with downloading e-mail.

74. Answer: **A**. A thin client is the best answer. That is typically a computer that has an embedded operating system (one that is stored on flash memory); it cannot have additional programs installed to it. Any programs that the thin client makes use of quite often come from a server. This isn't always the case (because there are varying levels of thin clients), but it is common. See Chapter 14, "Custom PCs and Common Devices," for more information.

Incorrect answers: Microsoft Office could be installed to any of the other computing systems listed in the answers. There is a version for macOS (for MacBooks), there is a version for some tablets, especially ones that run Microsoft OSes, and thick clients are essentially PCs, so Office can usually be installed to those as well.

75. Answer: **C**. Of the listed answers, the most likely problem is that the hard drive has not been partitioned correctly. In this scenario, the point of the preinstallation environment (PE)—which is often located on removable media such as a USB flash drive or boot disc—is to boot the system and partition the hard drive, readying it for the image to be obtained over the network. If the drive is not partitioned properly, the process will fail because the image will expect to be installed to a specific partition. See Chapter 19, "Troubleshooting Hard Drives and RAID Arrays," for more information.

> **Note**
>
> In some scenarios, a drive can be fully unpartitioned, and you can have the image install properly. This depends on several factors, including the local system hardware, what type of network installation is being done, and what software is being used for the imaging process.

Incorrect answers: Hard drives don't vary much from one to the next in regard to power, so the power supply should provide plenty of power. If it didn't, then you wouldn't see the drive in the UEFI/BIOS. The boot media has not failed; in the scenario it says that you have accessed the preinstallation environment. That is only possible if the PE boot media was booted to successfully. Today, it is uncommon for the drive to be configured in the BIOS or UEFI (unless it is part of a RAID array, which is controlled by the motherboard). Normally, the drive is either seen or not. If not, you might need to perform a flash of the BIOS or UEFI.

76. Answer: **B**. A proxy server provides the services needed for multiple clients to access Internet web pages. It is a server that is normally located on the LAN, or the internal computer network, and as such is known as a LAN host or a network host. See Chapter 7, "Networked Hosts and Network Configuration," for more information.

Incorrect answers: A web server provides web pages, yes, but the web server is not normally on the LAN. Web servers normally exist on the Internet, or on an intranet, or in a DMZ, so they cannot be considered network hosts or LAN hosts. File servers simply store files for multiple clients to access; Word documents and Excel spreadsheets are examples. A DNS server is used to resolve hosts' domain names to their corresponding IP addresses. They are very common on the Internet, though they can exist on the LAN as well. However, they don't deal with *cached* web pages the way that a proxy server will.

77. Answer: **C**. Measured services is when the provider monitors services rendered; this allows the provider (and the customer) to analyze the rate of resource usage. See Chapter 16, "Cloud Computing and Client-side Virtualization," for more information.

Incorrect answers: Rapid elasticity is when a provider offers a scalable cloud-based network that can grow as the organization needs it to. On-demand is the ability for customers to gain access to resources 24 hours a day, 7 days a week. Resource pooling is when servers and infrastructure are grouped together for multiple customers to share.

78. Answers: **A**, **C**, and **E**. You should be looking for a high number of connectors because gaming PCs will often have multiple video cards, hard drives, and so on. You should also look for a 24-pin main power connector as opposed to a 20-pin. Finally, look for a multirail system. This distributes the power used (and gaming PCs use a lot of power) and avoids overheating on the rails. See Chapter 13, "Peripherals and Power," for more information.

Incorrect answers: The 20-pin main power connector is the older ATX style that is not often used today. Mini-ITX is good for smaller computing systems, but the form factor simply doesn't allow for the space necessary for most gaming PCs. 400 watts is not nearly enough power for a high-end gaming PC; the number will be double that or more.

79. Answers: **B**, **H**, **I**, and **J**. In the scenario, the secure DMZ needs to have several inbound ports open to the servers. To do this in a secure way, one possibility would be to use SFTP on port 22, HTTPS on port 443, SMTP on port 587 (for outbound mail), and POP3 on port 995 (for inbound mail). That meets the requirements for our secure FTP server, web server, and mail server. Besides SFTP—which rides on Secure Shell (SSH)—the rest of the secure solutions use SSL/TLS by default. See Chapter 5, "Ports, Protocols, and Network Devices," for more information.

Incorrect answers: While you can use any port and secure it with the appropriate protocols, there are default security port numbers that you will usually work with. For example, when configuring FTP you would use SFTP (port 22) or FTPS (ports 989/990), but not port 21, which is used with standard FTP. As for the rest of the incorrect answers: Port 23 is used with Telnet (considered insecure). Port 53 is used by DNS, which can be secured in a variety of ways, but the scenario does not require a DNS server. Port 80 is HTTP (which is rarely seen today). Port 110 is POP3 without security. Port 143 is IMAP without security. Port 3389 is used by Remote Desktop Protocol (RDP). By the way, you probably won't get a question with 11 possible answers—I'm just trying to stress that you should know your ports and protocols!

80. Answer: **A**. You need to adjust the Secure Boot setting. Secure Boot uses encryption in conjunction with operating systems such as Windows to make sure that only that particular operating system will boot. In this scenario, to boot off of the DVD, you not only need to change the UEFI/BIOS boot order, but you most likely also need to disable Secure Boot. See Chapter 11, "Motherboards and Add-on Cards," for more information.

Incorrect answers: TPM stands for Trusted Platform Module (located on the motherboard), which is used to encrypt the entire hard drive. The UEFI/BIOS password most likely refers to the administrator password of the UEFI/BIOS. You already knew this password; otherwise, you would not have been able to modify the boot order. Virtualization refers to the ability for the CPU to work with virtual machine software (such as Windows Hyper-V). It has to be enabled for Hyper-V and other virtualization managers to work properly.

A Final Word About the 220-1001 Exam

After taking this practice exam, if you are unsure or unconfident in any way, then I urge you to step back, and continue studying the 220-1001 objectives before attempting the real exam.

Be ready for anything! I can't tell you *exactly* what will be on the exam, because that would violate the CompTIA NDA, and more importantly, the questions can change at any time! But the bottom line is this: if you know the concepts, you can pass any test. Use the official CompTIA A+ objectives as your guide. Review this book thoroughly. Finally, I challenge you to study in a hands-on manner on real computers, and investigate all the concepts to the best of your ability. This will help you not only for the exam, but also for the real world!

PART II

Introduction to Core 2 (220-1002)

Welcome to the Core 2 (220-1002) section of this book. This portion of the CompTIA A+ certification focuses on operating systems, computer and network security, software troubleshooting, and operational procedures. Sound like a lot? It is—but you can do it. Study hard, stay confident, and you will prevail.

The Core 2 content of this book comprises Chapters 23 through 42. For the most part, I've written the content to match the order of the objectives. This way, you can follow along with the official CompTIA A+ objectives and mark them up as you wish while you progress through the book. After Chapter 42 you will find a practice exam that is designed to test your knowledge of the 220-1002 objectives.

Core 2 (220-1002) Domains

The CompTIA A+ Core 2 exam objectives are broken down into four domains:

- ▶ 1.0—Operating Systems
- ▶ 2.0—Security
- ▶ 3.0—Software Troubleshooting
- ▶ 4.0—Operational Procedures

After this introduction, we'll go through these in order, starting with Chapter 23, "Operating System Types and Windows Versions." Be sure to study each of the domains! To do so effectively, I always recommend studying in a hands-on manner. If at all possible, get your hands on some operating systems such as Windows (preferably Windows 10), macOS, Linux (for example, Ubuntu), Android, and iOS. Work with as many of these systems as possible so that you can learn how the software really works. Then apply that knowledge to the objectives and the content in this book.

Core 2 (220-1002) Checklist

You must be fully prepared for the exam, so I created a checklist that you can use to make sure you are covering all the bases as you study. Take a look at the table below and make sure you check off each item before attempting the 220-1002 exam. Historically, my readers and students have benefited greatly from this type of checklist. Use the table as a guide for ordering your studies. I suggest you bookmark this page, and refer back to it as you complete each item.

EXAM PREPARATION CHECKLIST

Step	Item	Details	220-1002 Status
1.	Read the Core 2 (220-1002) content.	Thoroughly read through Chapters 23 through 42.	
2.	Review the Exam Alerts.	The little boxes with Exam Alerts are interspersed throughout the book. Review these and make sure you understand every one.	
3.	Review the Cram Quizzes.	Cram Quizzes are categorized by exam. You can review them in the text or on the companion website.	
4.	Complete the practice exam in the book.	Directly after Chapter 42 is a 220-1002 practice exam. Your goal should be to get at least 90 percent correct on the exam on the first try. (100 percent would be preferable!) If you score less than 90 percent, go back and study more!	
5.	Study the Core 2 Real-World Scenarios.	These can be found on the companion website. Complete these by reading and answering the scenarios and questions within the PDFs, and accessing the corresponding videos and simulations.	
6.	Create your own cheat sheet.	Although there is a Cram Sheet in the beginning of this book, you should also create your own. The act of writing down important details helps commit them to memory. Keep in mind that you will not be allowed to take this or the Cram Sheet into the actual testing room.	

Step	Item	Details	220-1002 Status
7.	Register for the exam.	Do not register until you have completed the previous steps; you shouldn't register until you are fully prepared. When you are ready, schedule the exam to commence within a couple days so that you won't forget what you learned! Registration can be done online. Register at Pearson Vue (https://home.pearsonvue.com/). It accepts payment by major credit cards for the exam fee. You need to create an account to sign up for exams.	
8.	Read the test-taking tips.	These can be found in the last chapter of the book and on the companion website.	
9.	Study the Cram Sheet and cheat sheet.	The Cram Sheet is a fold-out in the beginning of this book. It is also on the disc. Study from the Core 2 portion of this and your cheat sheet during the last 24 hours before the exam. (If your exam is delayed for any reason, go back to step 3 and retake the Cram Quizzes and practice exam 24 hours prior to your test date.)	
10.	Take the exam!	When you pass, place that final check mark in the box! Good luck!	

[1] Some electronic editions do not have access to the practice test software,

ExamAlert

Do not register for the exam until you are thoroughly prepared. Meticulously complete items 1 through 6 in the table before you register.

CORE 2 (220-1002)

Domain 1.0: Operating Systems

CHAPTER 23

Operating System Types and Windows Versions

This chapter covers the following A+ 220-1002 exam objectives:

▶ **1.1** – Compare and contrast common operating system types and their purposes.

▶ **1.2** – Compare and contrast features of Microsoft Windows versions.

Welcome to the first chapter of the 220-1002 section of this book. Until now, we have been talking about hardware for the most part. But without software, the hardware is fairly useless. So now we'll be digging into the software side of things.

In this chapter we'll discuss the most common operating systems used by PCs and mobile devices, including Windows, macOS, Linux, Android, iOS, and Chrome OS. Then, we'll cover the different versions and editions of Windows. Let's go!

1.1 – Compare and contrast common operating system types and their purposes

ExamAlert

Objective 1.1 concentrates on 32-bit vs. 64-bit, workstation operating systems, smartphone/tablet operating systems, vendor-specific limitations, and compatibility concerns between operating systems.

> **Note**
>
> Don't forget, a complete list of the Core 2 (220-1002) objectives can be found on the companion website of this book (see the introduction for details) and on CompTIA's website: https://certification.comptia.org/certifications/a

What type of operating system do you run at home? What do you run at work? What do other people you know use? Think about those questions for a moment. The answers will usually be dependent on the type of computer a person has: desktop, laptop, handheld, and so on. It will also depend on a person's preference, or a company's preference. However, it's usually based on *need*. Always ask yourself: What kind of work does the user need to perform? This will help to dictate what type of operating system—and ultimately the type of computer—that the user will require. Let's discuss the most common operating systems now.

Workstation Operating Systems

Workstation OSes include Microsoft Windows, Apple macOS, and Linux. By "workstation," we mean a desktop or laptop computer that a user sits at to perform work. So, we are not including servers in this section.

By far, the most common workstation OS in the workplace is Microsoft Windows, and that will be the main focus of the rest of this book. For the exam, you need to be able to work with Windows 7, 8, 8.1, and 10. However, in order of importance, I would list it as Windows 10, 7, 8.1, and then 8. Regardless, the good thing about all these Windows versions is that they are quite similar architecturally and from a user standpoint. Most of the built-in programs work in the same manner, though the names and navigation might be slightly different. Also, the Command Prompt hasn't changed too much in the past 10 years. So, most of the questions you will come upon, and most of the Windows problems you will face, can be approached in the same manner, irrespective of the *version* of Windows.

Next on the list is macOS, previously known as OS X. It is the proprietary operating system used by Apple for its Macintosh desktop computers and MacBook Pro and Air laptop computers. This operating system (and the Mac computer in general) has been a favorite of multimedia designers, graphic artists, and musicians since the 1990s. macOS has used version numbers since its inception. For example, as of the writing of this book (early 2019), the latest version is macOS 10.14 (codenamed Mojave). Apple used the name "OS X" through version 10.11 (El Capitan), but changed to the name macOS from version 10.12 (Sierra) and onward.

Although Macintosh computers have Intel processors, they are not PCs. Likewise, macOS is not compatible with PC hardware. Conversely, PC-based operating systems, such as Windows and Linux, do not normally run on Macintosh computers—though it can be done in the case of Windows (for example, with Boot Camp, which is described in Chapter 30, "Linux and macOS Tools").

Linux is an ever-expanding group of operating systems that are designed to run on PCs, gaming consoles, DVRs, mobile phones, IoT devices, and many other devices. Originally, Linux was designed as an alternative operating system to Windows; however, it has been estimated that no more than 3 percent of the U.S. market uses Linux on PCs. Linux does, however, have a much larger market share when it comes to servers, penetration-testing laptops, and other computer devices, and in those markets, the percentage is growing rapidly. Linux was originally written by Linus Torvalds (thus the name) and can be freely downloaded by anyone. Several companies emerged, developing this free code (or a variant of the free code) into their own versions of Linux, which are referred to as *distributions* (often abbreviated as *distros*). Some examples of these distributions include Ubuntu, CentOS, Red Hat, and Kali, each of which use their own version number schemes. Although Linux is free to download, it is licensed under a General Public License (GPL). This states that derived works can be distributed only under the same license terms as the software itself.

As we progress through the book we will look at examples of each of these OSes.

> **Note**
>
> If you have access to Windows, macOS, and Linux operating systems, I recommend that you attempt to locate the following for each: the Control Panel (or Settings or System Preferences, and so on), the command-line, and the built-in Internet browser. This will get you started on your way to becoming familiar with each interface.

32-Bit Versus 64-Bit

Almost all of today's PC-based CPUs are 64-bit; it's a type of CPU architecture that incorporates registers that are 64 bits wide. These registers, or temporary storage areas, allow the CPU to work with and process 64-bit data types and provide support for address space in the terabytes. 64-bit CPUs have been available for PCs since 2003.

A little history: The predecessor to the 64-bit CPU was the 32-bit CPU. Intel started developing well-known 32-bit CPUs as early as 1985 with the 386DX

CPU (which ran at a whopping 33 MHz!) and AMD did likewise in 1991 with the Am386. A 32-bit CPU can't support nearly as much address space as a 64-bit CPU; 32-bit is limited to 4 GB. Most editions of Windows are available in both 32-bit and 64-bit versions.

You still see 32-bit CPU technologies in the field; however, due to applications' ever-increasing need for resources, these older CPUs continue to diminish, whereas 64-bit technologies have become more prevalent. In addition, you will find that some applications are still written for the 32-bit platform. 32-bit technologies are still common in the mobile device market, but 64-bit technologies are also available.

You might hear of the terms x86 and x64. x86 refers to older CPU names that ended in an 86—for example, the 80386 (shortened to just 386), 486, 586, and so on. Generally, when people use the term x86, they refer to 32-bit CPUs that enable 4 GB of address space. On the other hand, x64 (or x86-64) refers to newer, 64-bit CPUs that are a superset of the x86 architecture. This technology has a wider data path to handle program execution; it can run 64-bit software and 32-bit software and can address a default maximum of 256 terabytes (TB) of RAM. This can optionally be extended to 4 petabytes (PB), but that extension isn't currently used on PCs. As of the writing of this book, only a true supercomputer would need more than 256 TB of RAM. The real limitation right now is the operating system. For example, some Windows 7 64-bit editions can go as high as 192 GB, Windows 8.1 Pro 64-bit can handle 512 GB, and Windows 10 Pro and Enterprise 64-bit can use up to 2 TB. To put this into perspective, the motherboard of the *AV-Editor* computer—which I discuss earlier in the book—supports a maximum of only 64 GB of RAM. This is far less than Windows 7, 8, or 10 can handle, which in itself is just a tiny slice of what a 64-bit CPU can address.

ExamAlert

Know the differences between 32-bit and 64-bit architectures. For example, remember that 32-bit CPUs can only address a maximum of 4 GB of RAM, but 64-bit CPUs can address many TBs of RAM.

Windows comes in 64-bit (x64) and 32-bit (x86) versions so that users from both generations of computers can run the software efficiently. Not only that, but 64-bit versions of Windows are also backward compatible—meaning that they can run 32-bit Windows applications as well as 64-bit. The 64-bit system files and apps are stored in C:\Windows\System32, and the 32-bit system files and apps are stored in C:\Windows\SysWOW64.

> **Note**
>
> Yes, the path names are sort of backward from what you would expect, but that is due to how Windows developed over time and how it progressed from a 32-bit system to a 64-bit system.

There are two locations for programs as well. 64-bit programs are stored in C:\Program Files and 32-bit programs are stored in C:\Program Files (x86).

> **ExamAlert**
>
> Know the locations for 64-bit and 32-bit system files and program files in Windows.

Smartphone and Tablet Operating Systems

The world of mobile device OSes can be boiled down into four main players: iOS, Android, Chrome OS, and Windows. While Windows has a definite presence in the mobile device market, we'll omit that from this section. In the past Microsoft had different OSes for its mobile devices, but for the most part (and for the A+ exam), Microsoft uses Windows 10—mostly Home edition. Other than hardware connections, Windows is Windows, regardless of whether you use it on a PC, laptop, Surface device, or other device.

> **Note**
>
> Microsoft previously installed Windows RT to some of their mobile devices, which is similar to Windows 8; however, Microsoft stopped using it in 2015. In the unlikely event you come across RT, you will probably need to update it to Windows 10 (if the device is at all updateable).

Mobile device software comes in one of two forms: open source, which is effectively free to download and modify; and closed source, otherwise known as commercial or vendor-specific, which cannot be modified without express permission and licensing. There are benefits and drawbacks to each type of system. Because you will see both in the field, you should know each one equally. Let's give examples of these using Android and iOS.

Android

Android is an example of open-source software. It is a Linux-based operating system used mostly on smartphones and tablet computers and is developed by the Open Handset Alliance, a group directed by Google. Google releases Android code as open source, allowing developers to modify it and freely create applications for it. Google also commissioned the Android Open-Source Project (AOSP); its mission is to maintain and further develop Android. You'll know when you are dealing with the Android open-source OS and related applications when you see the little robot caricature, usually in green.

Android versions are referred to by such sweet names as: Lollipop, Marshmallow, Nougat, Oreo, and Pie (versions 5 through 9 respectively), and the list continues. To find out the version you are currently running, start at the Home screen; this is the main screen that boots up by default. Access the Settings screen (often by swiping down from the top). Locate the About section and then tap it. The version should be listed there. For example, Figure 23.1 shows a smartphone using Android version 8.0.0 (Oreo).

FIGURE 23.1   Typical smartphone using Android version 8.0.0

Suppose a company wanted to create a custom version of Android for a handheld computer that it was developing. According to the license, the company would be allowed to do this and customize the OS to its specific hardware and applications. This is exactly what companies such as Samsung, HTC, and a host of others do, and it's what differentiates those devices' software packages from each other. These companies will all design their own type of launcher software.

The launcher is the part of the graphical user interface (GUI) in Android where a user can customize the Home screen.

Manufacturers of Android-based devices (as well as the general public) can create their own applications for Android as well. To do this, a developer would download the Android application package (APK), which is a package file format used by the Android for distribution and installation of application software and middleware.

iOS

Apple's iOS is an example of closed-source software. It is found on iPhones and iPads. To find out the version of iOS you are running, go to the Home screen and then tap Settings. Tap General and then tap About. You'll see the Version number. For example, Figure 23.2 shows an iPad running Version 11.3.1 (15E302). 15E302 is the build number, 11 is the version, and .3.1 is the point release.

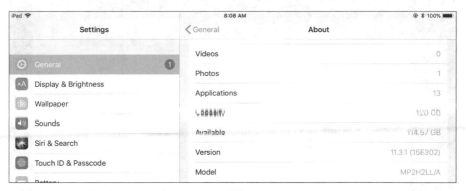

FIGURE 23.2 **iPad using version 11.3.1 of iOS**

Unlike Android, iOS is not open source and is not available for download to developers. Only Apple hardware uses this operating system. This is an example of vendor-specific software. However, if developers want to create an application for iOS, they can download the iOS software development kit (SDK). Apple license fees are required when a developer is ready to go live with the application.

> **ExamAlert**
>
> Understand the difference between open source and closed source.

Chrome OS

The Chrome operating system is designed by Google to act as a workstation that uses mostly web-based applications. Chrome OS can run on a variety of devices but is best known for being loaded on Chromebooks, which are a favorite among grade schools and some home users. While Chrome OS is based on Android, and ultimately based on Linux, and can access many apps from the Google Play Store, it is still considered to be a separate operating system, because it has been so heavily modified to work with Chromebook hardware. However, Chrome OS is designed in such a way where a user could accomplish everything he or she needs to do from within the Chrome browser. To find out the version of Chrome OS that you are running, go to About Chrome OS. For example, go to the Launcher, then Settings, access the menu, and click About Chrome OS. Figure 23.3 shows an example of a Chromebook running version 71.0.3578.127 of Chrome OS.

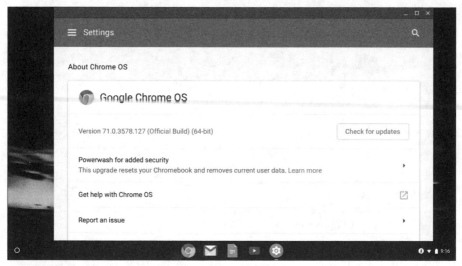

FIGURE 23.3   **Chromebook using Version 71**

> **Note**
>
> We don't cover the basic usage of Android, iOS, or Chrome OS in this book. It is considered prerequisite knowledge to the CompTIA A+ exams. We do cover mobile OS troubleshooting later in the book, but if you are new to Android or iOS, consider getting your hands on a device or two and practicing with the OS!

Vendor-Specific Limitations

Nowadays, most computing devices and their operating systems have limited lifespans. Some manufacturers of hardware and software decide on an end-of-life date as part of the original design of the system. This can mean a couple of things, including the discontinuing of updates and the ending of support for software/hardware. It's all part of the lifecycle policy. Table 23.1 gives some examples of support end dates (as of the writing of this book). While these are not set in stone, manufacturers usually adhere to them once they have published an end date. I sorted these examples chronologically for easy reference. The listed Windows dates are "end of *extended* support" dates, which is the important one to know. Depending on when you are reading this book, you will note that Windows 7 end-of-support is right around the corner, or has already happened!

TABLE 23.1   **End-of-Life/End-of-Support**

Product	Ending Date
Windows 7	January 2020
Chromebook 13 (7310)	September 2020
Windows 10 (1809)	Home/Pro: May 2020
	Edu/Ent: May 2021
Windows 8.1	January 2023
Chromebook (3400)	June 2025

What does this all mean? You need to be cognizant of the fact that all hardware and software has a limited lifespan. When that end-of-support date comes, then no more updates—most importantly, security updates—will be available. That is a risk that most companies are not willing to take. So, in many cases, a company needs to upgrade hardware and/or software every couple of years; more often if the company uses several different platforms.

While Windows 7, 8, 8.1, and 10 are all considered different *versions*, Windows 10 takes a bit of a different approach compared to previous Windows platforms. With Windows 10, we now have different "versions" of Windows, such as Windows 10—version 1607, and Windows 10—1809. Windows 10 uses this numbering convention instead of the commonly used *point release* numbering convention, but it is similar conceptually. While the published end of extended support for 1809 is May of 2021, chances are that the system will attempt to auto-update to the next version; for example, if you run Windows 10 Home or Pro, and if not configured properly, the update could happen at an inopportune time! Companies that run Windows 10 Enterprise (and other select editions) often disable auto-update and/or defer updates until they can be tested. In addition, the Windows 10 Enterprise LTSC extended support end date is pushed out much further. To find out the version of Windows you are running, go to the Run prompt and type **winver**.

> **Note**
>
> For more about the Windows lifecycle and extended support end dates, see this web page:
>
> https://support.microsoft.com/en-us/help/13853/windows-lifecycle-fact-sheet

> **ExamAlert**
>
> Remember that software versions will have an end-of-support date, also known as an end-of-life date. Be ready to have an upgrade plan well before that date!

Some companies don't publish end-of-support dates—that is until they stop supporting them! But you can take a good guess as to when this will happen based on historical data. For example, Android 6.0—released in late 2015—was discontinued in late 2018, and Google stopped updating security patches for it: a three-year span. Another example: at the time of writing, Apple only supports MacBooks that were built in 2014 or after—essentially five years' worth. What it boils down to is this: you can expect a device to be supported for *x* amount of time before security patches stop. Plan for it!

Compatibility Concerns Between Operating Systems

In a computer network that has multiple platforms, there is definite concern for how the different operating systems will work with each other. That's why some organizations opt to become single-shop houses—meaning they only use one manufacturer, such as Microsoft. But that isn't always possible (or preferable), so operating systems often have to interoperate. That means file sharing compatibility, and the process of different systems logging into each other; for example, a Linux computer connecting to a Microsoft domain, or an Apple Mac system interacting with Chrome OS. As we progress through the book we'll be discussing different ways to approach compatibility between different systems.

Furthermore, even if two systems *are* compatible, it doesn't mean that every *version* of each of those systems is compatible. An older version of Android might have no chance of connecting to a newer Windows domain controller. Or an older version of Windows (such as Vista or XP) won't be able to interact properly with a newer version of a Linux server—not to mention that those Windows versions are not supported anymore, and are security risks. As I mentioned, we'll get into compatibility issues more as we progress through the book.

The bottom line is this: the more platforms and systems you introduce to your infrastructure, the more complex things get, and the more you need to think about how these systems will all interact from networking, security, and usability standpoints.

Cram Quiz

Answer these questions. The answers follow the last question. If you cannot answer these questions correctly, consider reading this section again until you can.

1. Which of the following operating systems is a free download with no evaluation period limitations?

   ○ **A.** Windows 10 Home

   ○ **B.** Ubuntu 18.04

   ○ **C.** macOS

   ○ **D.** iOS

2. What is the name of the folder where Windows 10 stores 64-bit system files?

   ○ **A.** Systemroot

   ○ **B.** System32

   ○ **C.** SysWOW64

   ○ **D.** Program Files (x86)

3. Which of the following is used on iPads?

   ○ **A.** Chrome OS

   ○ **B.** Windows 10

   ○ **C.** iOS

   ○ **D.** Android

4. Scenario: It's the summer of 2023. Your company has many types of technologies running—many of which interact with each other. Of the following OSes and devices that are used in your company's infrastructure, which are security concerns? (Select the best answers.)

   ○ **A.** Windows 7

   ○ **B.** Windows 10

   ○ **C.** MacBook Pro 2012

   ○ **D.** Android 6.0

   ○ **E.** Windows 8.1

5. Which of the following statements is true?

- ○ **A.** Android is an example of closed-source software.
- ○ **B.** 32-bit CPUs can only address a maximum of 256 GB of RAM.
- ○ **C.** Chrome OS is designed by Apple to use mostly desktop applications.
- ○ **D.** 64-bit versions of Windows can run 32-bit apps as well as 64-bit apps.

Cram Quiz Answers

1. **B.** Ubuntu (regardless of the version) is a free download. While you can download some versions of Windows, they are only for evaluation periods of time. Apple-based operating systems, such as macOS and iOS, are not free downloads.

2. **B.** System32 is the folder used by Windows to store 64-bit system files. Systemroot is a variable used for the main Windows folder. More accurately, it is written as %systemroot%. It usually equals C:\Windows. SysWOW64 is actually the location of 32-bit system files. Program Files (x86) is where 32-bit versions of programs are stored.

3. **C.** iOS is the operating system used on iPads and iPhones. Chrome OS is used on a group of devices, most notably Chromebooks. Windows 10 is used on PCs, laptops, and Microsoft Surface devices. Android is used by several manufacturers of smartphones and tablets—it is the main competitor of iOS.

4. **A, B, C, D, and E.** Trick question. All of them are! Every OS and device on your network should be a security concern, regardless of their age. The only one on the list that is potentially not a *major* security concern is Windows 10. But as of the writing of this book (2019) we can't know that for sure. Every year, possibly more often, systems administrators should review the security posture of their IT environment. That said, Windows 7 will not be supported beyond early 2020; and Windows 8.1 will not be supported beyond early 2023. The MacBook Pro 2012 and Android 6.0 already are not supported as of the writing of this book. Remember, the more platforms you have running, the more complex the security gets, and the more you have to keep track of security updates, and when end-of-support for devices and software is going to occur.

5. **D.** The only true statement is 64-bit versions of Windows can run 32-bit apps as well as 64-bit apps. 32-bit CPUs enable 4 GB of address space (RAM) maximum. On the other hand, 64-bit CPUs have a wider data path and can address a default maximum of 256 terabytes (TB) of RAM. For the A+ exam, remember that Android and Linux are examples of open-source software while Windows, macOS, and iOS are examples of closed-source commercial software. Chrome OS is designed by Google to act as a workstation that uses mostly web-based applications.

1.2 – Compare and contrast features of Microsoft Windows versions

No doubt about it, Windows still dominates the marketplace when it comes to employee workstations. As such, Windows takes up a large percentage of the rest of this book, and of course, you will be supporting it in the field.

There are several versions of Windows that you need to know for the A+ exams: Windows 7, Windows 8, Windows 8.1, and Windows 10. Plus, each of these is broken up into various *editions*, which are different implementations of the operating system; for example, editions used for work, for home, for the enterprise, and so on. The needs of a home user will be vastly different than the needs of a business user. So, be ready to support different editions, based on the role of the person that will be working at that system.

You will note that many features are listed throughout this chapter. We'll be covering those features in more depth as we progress through the chapters of this book. Let's discuss the different versions and editions of Windows now.

Note

As I mentioned previously, consider getting your hands on at least one version of Windows to practice with. Windows 10 is probably your best bet because it is the newest one on the A+ exams. I suggest looking into virtual machines and/or older cheap laptops to start your studies with Windows. I don't recommend using your main home or work system, but instead something separate that won't cause a problem if there is any data loss.

Windows 7

Windows 7 is a line of Microsoft operating systems designed for desktop PCs and laptops. Within the Windows 7 group are the following *editions*: Starter, Home Basic, Home Premium, Professional, Ultimate, and Enterprise. Starter is only available through original equipment manufacturers (OEMs) and was common among laptops. In addition, Starter is only available in a 32-bit version. However, the other editions are all available in 64-bit and 32-bit versions. In Table 23.2, the check marks indicate some of the components that are included in these various editions of "Win7." Hyphens indicate that those components are not available in those editions.

TABLE 23.2 **Comparison of Windows 7 Editions**

Component	Starter	Home Basic	Home Premium	Professional	Ultimate	Enterprise*
Internet Explorer 8	✓	✓	✓	✓	✓	✓
Create Home Group	—	✓ but join only	✓	✓	✓	✓
Windows Media Center (WMC)	—	—	✓	✓	✓	✓
Domain access	—	—	—	✓	✓	✓
Windows XP Mode	—	—	—	✓	✓	✓
Backup to home or business network	—	—		✓	✓	✓
BitLocker Encryption	—	—	—	—	✓	✓

* Windows Enterprise editions are not sold through retail or OEM channels.

ExamAlert

Know the differences between the various editions of Windows 7.

Windows 8 and 8.1

Windows 8 is a group of Microsoft operating systems designed for desktop PCs, laptops, and tablet computers. The editions include Windows 8 (known as "Core"), Windows 8 Pro, Windows 8 Enterprise, and Windows 8 RT. While

Windows 8 has the core features necessary to the average user, Windows 8 Pro includes more features, such as encryption and virtualization, and optional features, such as Windows Media Center. The Enterprise edition has almost everything from the Pro edition plus additional network services for large-scale IT infrastructures. As previously mentioned, Windows RT was phased out, but was designed for tablet PCs that use 32-bit ARM-based CPUs. The rest of the Windows editions are available for 32-bit and 64-bit architectures—x86 (also known as IA-32) and x64 platforms, respectively. In Table 23.3, the check marks indicate some of the components that are included in these various editions of Windows 8.

> **Note**
>
> When I refer to Windows 8, I generally mean Windows 8.1 because that is the secure update for Windows 8. Any system that is running Windows 8 should be checked and updated to 8.1 or to Windows 10.

TABLE 23.3 **Comparison of Windows 8 Editions**

Component	Windows 8	Windows 8 Pro	Windows 8 Enterprise
Internet Explorer 10	✓	✓	✓
Remote Desktop	✓ but client only	✓	✓
Domain Join	—	✓	✓
BitLocker Encryption and EFS	—	✓	✓
Hyper-V	—	✓ but 64-bit edition only	✓ but 64-bit edition only
Windows To Go	—	—	✓
Windows Media Center (WMC) (Discontinued in 2015)	—	✓	—

> **ExamAlert**
>
> Know the differences between the various editions of Windows 8.

Windows 10

Windows 10 is a group of OS editions including Home, Pro, Education, and Enterprise. There are more derivatives of Windows 10, but for the purposes of simplicity, we'll focus on those four. Take a look at Table 23.4 for a basic comparison of the editions.

TABLE 23.4 **Comparison of Windows 10 Editions**

Component	Windows 10 Home	Windows 10 Pro	Windows 10 Education	Windows 10 Enterprise
Edge	✓	✓	✓	✓
Cortana	✓	✓	✓	✓
Remote Desktop	✓ but client only	✓	✓	✓
Domain Join	—	✓	✓	✓
EFS and BitLocker	—	✓	✓	✓
Hyper-V	—	✓ but 64-bit edition only	✓ but 64-bit edition only	✓ but 64-bit edition only
Windows To Go	—	✓	✓	✓
Credential Guard	—	—	✓	✓
AppLocker	—	—	✓	✓
BranchCache	—	—	✓	✓

ExamAlert

Know the differences between the various editions of Windows 10.

You will note that the Home edition has far fewer features than the Enterprise edition. For example, a home user will normally not need to connect to and log on to a domain, or use virtual machines, so those features are omitted from that edition. But Enterprise users will be more sophisticated when it comes to features. Their needs might include domain access, BranchCache (for the distribution of cached data to remote sites), and encryption of data—either single file (using Encrypting File System [EFS]), or the entire hard drive (using BitLocker).

As of 2017, Windows 10 has become more of a morphing operating system. Features and newer versions of included programs are incorporated as the

OS goes through its updates. This sets it aside from Windows 7 and 8 for the most part. So, features that are not available in one edition today could be available tomorrow, and vice versa; features that are available could be removed at any time. It's unlikely, but be prepared for changes to built-in programs and features.

> **Note**
>
> Always remember to check the minimum requirements for the version of Windows you are going to install. Most PCs and laptops can easily meet the minimum—for example, Windows 10 requires a 1-GHz CPU, 2 GB of RAM, and 32 GB of hard drive space (for 64-bit systems). However, other devices or older systems and especially virtual machines should be checked and/or configured appropriately to work with the OS efficiently.

Windows User Interfaces and Components

The essence of Windows is the graphical user interface (GUI), which is what Windows employs to interact with the user. Normally, a keyboard, a mouse, a touchpad, or a touchscreen are used to input information to the operating system's GUI, and that input is shown on the screen. Basically, everything you see on the display (including windows, icons, menus, and other visual indicators) is part of the GUI, but remember that the GUI also governs how the user interacts with the OS.

The Windows GUI has many parts, including the desktop with all its pieces, the Start screen, applications such as File Explorer/Windows Explorer and the Control Panel, and Administrative Tools such as Computer Management and the Device Manager. To master Windows, you need to learn how to navigate quickly through the GUI to the application or tool that you need. The GUI can be customized for a particular user, or it can be customized to optimize the system. What do you see when you start Windows? Some of the components that make up Windows include:

▶ **Desktop:** In Windows, the desktop environment is basically what you see on the screen—essentially, it *is* Windows, from a cosmetic standpoint. An example of the Windows 10 desktop is shown in Figure 23.4; it displays the Start menu in the open position. The desktop is a key component of the GUI; it includes icons, wallpapers, windows, toolbars, and so on. It is meant to take the place of a person's physical desktop, at least to a certain extent, replacing calculators, calendars, and so on.

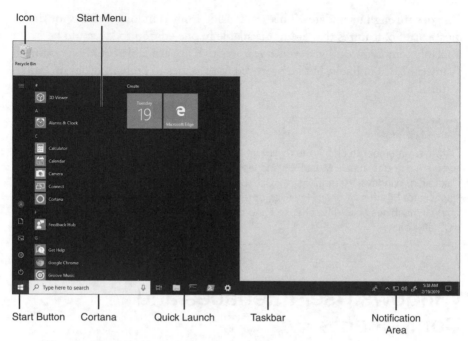

FIGURE 23.4   **Windows 10 desktop**

▶ **Start screen:** In Windows 8, the Start screen is displayed by default. This
is the initial environment that a user can work in. It includes clickable
(or tappable) elements, known as "tiles," which link to applications. It
also contains *live* tiles, which can display real-time updated information.
This interface is also referred to by some technicians as "Metro," though
Microsoft doesn't use that term in its documentation. You can search the
system and access tools within the Control Panel as well as perform other
functions by navigating to the Charms toolbar (also known as the Charms
bar), which is a vertical toolbar that appears when you point the mouse at
the right corner or when you swipe from the right edge of a touchscreen
or touchpad. The desktop is also accessible in Windows 8 by clicking the
Desktop tile on the Start screen; by clicking the Start button on the Start
screen, Charms bar, and elsewhere; or by pressing Windows+D on the
keyboard. If the desktop was started previously, you can also point the
mouse to the top-left corner of the Start screen to reveal an icon of it.

> **Note**
>
> Windows 10 and Windows 7 do not use the Start screen.

Let's refer to Figure 23.4 and talk about the various elements of the desktop:

▶ **Icons:** Icons are the little, clickable pictures you see on the desktop. They can be entire programs that run directly from the desktop, files that are stored directly on the desktop, or *shortcuts* that redirect to a program or file that is stored elsewhere in Windows. You can often tell if it's a shortcut by the little arrow in the lower-left corner of the icon. Shortcuts are small, usually around 1 KB to 4 KB in size, which store well on the desktop. However, storing actual files and programs on the desktop is not recommended because it can adversely affect the performance of the computer—and can quickly get really unorganized!

▶ **Start menu:** This is the main menu that is launched from the Start button. It contains a listing of all the tools within Windows and any Microsoft or third-party applications. From here, you can search for files and access the Control Panel—you can get anywhere in Windows from the Start menu. It shows who is currently logged on to the system and also enables you to log off, restart, shut down, or place the computer in sleep mode. (Windows 8 does away with this Start menu, but in Windows 8.1, you can right-click the Start button to bring up many Windows utilities.)

▶ **Taskbar:** This is the bar that spans the bottom of the desktop. It houses the Start button, Quick Launch, any open applications, and the Notification Area (where applicable). It can be moved to the top or to any sides of the desktop and can be resized to fill as much as 40 percent of the screen. The taskbar and Start menu can be customized to just about any user's liking. To make modifications to these, right-click the taskbar and select Taskbar Settings (or Properties). From here, you can unlock/lock the taskbar, auto-hide it, and so on.

▶ **Cortana:** This is Windows 10's built-in virtual assistant search tool, which you can communicate with by typing or by voice.

▶ **Quick Launch:** The Quick Launch is directly to the right of the Start button. It contains shortcuts to applications or files. The beauty of the Quick Launch is that, by default, it is always visible, whereas shortcuts on the desktop background are covered up by open applications.

▶ **Notification Area:** To the far right of the taskbar is the Notification Area. This houses the clock, volume control, network icon, battery power indicator, and so on. Also, if you click the show hidden icons symbol (^), it shows the icons of applications that are running in the background. The more icons you see in the Notification Area, the more resources are used (in the form of memory and CPU power), possibly making the computer less responsive. In Windows 8, this presents itself in the desktop environment but not in the Start screen. You can modify the Notification Area in the Taskbar settings or by right-clicking the clock.

To actually do anything in Windows you will have to open a program or a configuration window. There are two main elements you will work in: application windows and dialog boxes.

Application windows are the windows that are opened by programs such as Microsoft WordPad, as shown in Figure 23.5. The window consists primarily of a Title bar (which says Document – WordPad), a Menu bar (with the File, Edit, and other menus), a toolbar (with icons for opening, saving, and printing documents), and a work area. This program runs as an actual process known as wordpad.exe.

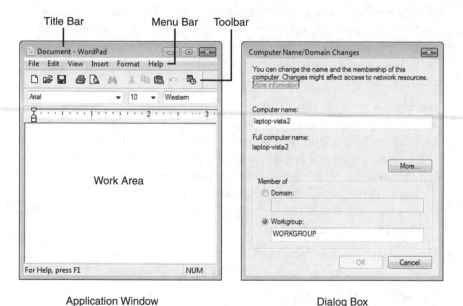

FIGURE 23.5 **An application window and a dialog box**

Dialog boxes are windows that open from within another window, usually an application window. For example, Figure 23.5 shows the Computer Name/ Domain Changes dialog box, which was opened from System Properties. System Properties (not shown) runs as a process, but the Computer Name dialog box is just part of that overall process. The dialog box prompts a user for information (in this case, for the name of the computer) and the name of the network the computer is a member of.

ExamAlert

Be able to identify the various Windows components by name.

Today's versions of Windows can run side by side apps with the use of Snap technology. This means that you can drag an application to an edge of the screen, and it will snap in place, inhabiting that half of the display. A second application can be dragged in the same manner to the other side of the screen. It's an easy way to run two apps on the same screen without having to resize them manually. This becomes a bit more complex when you have multiple monitors, but, essentially, only the outer edges of the collective group of monitors can be used with Snap.

Now, we just covered a lot of stuff in just a few pages. I highly recommend you practice navigating through Windows and become accustomed to the GUI.

Cram Quiz

Answer these questions. The answers follow the last question. If you cannot answer these questions correctly, consider reading this section again until you can.

1. Which editions of Windows 10 offer Hyper-V? (Select the three best answers.)

   ○ **A.** Windows 10 Home

   ○ **B.** Windows 10 Pro

   ○ **C.** Windows 10 Education

   ○ **D.** Windows 10 Enterprise

2. What is the minimum hard drive requirement for Windows 10 64-bit?

   ○ **A.** 2 GB of RAM

   ○ **B.** 2 GHz

   ○ **C.** 32 GB of hard drive space

   ○ **D.** 32 GB of RAM

   ○ **E.** 200 GB of hard drive space

3. Where should you go to find out what applications are running in the background of Windows 10?

   ○ **A.** Taskbar

   ○ **B.** Start menu

   ○ **C.** Quick Launch

   ○ **D.** Notification Area

   ○ **E.** Cortana

Cram Quiz Answers

1. **B, C, and D.** Of the listed answers, Windows 10 Pro, Education, and Enterprise offer Hyper-V virtualization functionality. Windows 10 Home does not. Remember that just because Hyper-V is included as a feature doesn't mean it will work. The motherboard of the computer has to support virtualization (and be enabled), and Hyper-V has to be enabled within Programs and Features.

2. **C.** Windows 10 64-bit requires 32 GB of hard drive space. This is usually not an issue with today's computers, but it can be an issue if you are installing to a virtual machine or to a USB flash drive, because your space might be limited in those scenarios. Make sure that the target for the installation—whatever it is—has the appropriate amount of space (and then some!). Windows 10 (64-bit) requires a 1-GHz CPU and 2 GB of RAM.

3. **D.** Go to the Notification Area to find out what applications are running in the background. (Another way is to use the Task Manager.) In Windows 10, click the arrow that points up to show hidden icons. In other versions of Windows, the applications might actually show in the Notification Area itself.

CHAPTER 24

Operating System Installation

This chapter covers the following A+ 220-1002 exam objective:

▶ **1.3** – Summarize general OS installation considerations and upgrade methods.

A technician may be called upon to install or re-install an operating system to a new computer, an older computer, or to a virtual machine. The smart technician will know the various ways to boot from an installation source, whether it is removable media, a source that is internal to the computer, or a source that is stored on the network. Professional technicians will ask questions such as: What type of installation is it? How will we partition and format the drive? Are there any special considerations during setup? Always ask these questions beforehand as part of your planning.

When working in a small environment, clean installs are typical; but when working in a larger environment, network installs, unattended installations, imaging, and repairs become much more common. This chapter covers the gamut when it comes to operating system considerations. When you are done here, you should understand how to install any OS (Windows, Linux, macOS, and so on) from any source, and to any destination drive. Let us begin.

1.3 – Summarize general OS installation considerations and upgrade methods

ExamAlert

Objective 1.3 focuses on boot methods, type of installations, partitioning, file system types/formatting, and additional considerations concerning the initial setup of the OS.

Boot Methods

To install an operating system to a computer, we first have to boot the system to the installation media. There are several types of boot methods you should know for the exam:

▶ **Local installation from an external drive/flash drive:** The most common of these is the USB flash drive. To do this, download the operating system .ISO file (or similar file type) from the OS developer's website. Make the USB flash drive bootable, and extract the contents of the .ISO file to the drive. There are free programs available that can speed up the process by making the drive bootable, formatting it, and extracting the .ISO all at once; for instance, Rufus, Yumi, and the Windows USB/DVD Download Tool. Once the flash drive is set up, insert the flash drive to the target system, boot the computer, change the BIOS boot order to USB flash drive first, and get installing! Often this will be quick and painless. Less commonly, you might install from an eSATA hard drive.

> **Note**
>
> Try downloading an .ISO image of Linux or Windows (evaluation), and extract the contents to a USB flash drive. Then, install the OS to a physical computer so that you can see the installation process. You can also run through the install process with virtual machines by accessing the .ISO file directly.

▶ **Local installation from optical disc:** This means that you insert the disc into the optical drive of the computer you are sitting at, known as the local computer. Generally, this will be from DVD-ROM, but it is not used often because it is a slow process, and there are other faster methods. By the way, when you sit at the computer and answer all the questions it asks you, step-by-step, it is known as an *attended* installation; you are attending to the computer as the install progresses.

▶ **Network boot (PXE) installation:** You can install an OS to a client by booting to the network and using a Windows Server and the Windows Deployment Services (WDS) and/or System Center Configuration Manager (SCCM), or by accessing any Windows or Linux server acting as a repository of the Windows installation files. (Those servers will also operate as DHCP and TFTP servers.) If you do need to perform an over-the-network installation, be sure that the target computer has a Preboot Execution Environment (PXE)-compliant network adapter. This allows the computer to boot to the network and locate the DHCP server and ultimately perform the installation (as long as the server is configured properly). We'll discuss a couple of those options in an upcoming section.

▶ **Internal drive installation:** Finally, you can install from fixed media inside the computer. However, usually the source of the media should not be stored in the same location as the target area for the OS. What does that mean? There are two options here: install from a separate partition of a hard drive; or install from a separate hard drive altogether. And I use the term "hard drive" loosely. It could be a magnetic-based disk, an SSD, an NVMe-based drive, or even a USB flash drive if the motherboard has an internal USB port (with a USB drive inserted). Some power workstations and server motherboards come with these, for installation purposes, or even to run the OS! Either way, the installation media will have to have the .ISO or another image of the operating system to be installed.

> **ExamAlert**
>
> Know these boot methods for OS installation and upgrades: optical disc, external/flash drive, network boot (PXE), and internal drive.

Whatever method you choose, be sure to select that method as the first boot option in the BIOS/UEFI of the computer. Other configurations might also be necessary. When you are finished, reset the BIOS boot priority to hard drive first, and if necessary, disable any removable media options in the BIOS.

Types of Installations

Along with the boot method, you should be prepared for the type of installation you require. There are several types of OS installation, including:

▶ **Clean install:** Simply put, a clean installation means that the OS is installed to a blank partition. It could be a new hard drive, or a drive or individual partition that was wiped clean of data. Generally, the clean install is attended to by the technician, who interacts step-by-step with the OS as it is installing.

▶ **Upgrade:** An upgrade install is when the target hard drive (or partition) already has an operating system installed and is upgraded to a newer version of that operating system; for example, from Windows 8.1 to Windows 10. Going further, another example is the in-place upgrade (often used for repairs). This is when the OS is effectively reinstalled, but without losing files or applications. The repair in-place upgrade and other similar repair-based installations are usually a last resort to fix an individual system. Remember that upgrades may or *may not* save a user's data. Regardless of the type, you should always back up the data, and possibly the user profile, before initiating an upgrade.

▶ **Unattended installation:** This type of installation requires an answer file that has been created in advance. Also, it normally requires a specific service. For instance, to automate the process of installing Windows, you can use Windows Deployment Services. This server-based program works with the Windows System Image Manager program in Windows. This program can be used to create the answer file that is used during the unattended installation. The answer file provides the responses needed for the installation, with no user intervention necessary. In Windows, there is a single XML-based answer file called Unattend.xml.

> **Note**
>
> The Windows System Image Manager (SIM) is part of the Windows Assessment and Deployment Kit (ADK) for Windows 10 and Windows 8.1, and the Windows Automated Installation Kit (AIK) for Windows 7, which can both be downloaded from Microsoft's website.
>
> For more information about Windows 10 deployment with ADK, visit the following site:
>
> https://docs.microsoft.com/en-us/windows/deployment/windows-deployment-scenarios-and-tools

▶ **Image deployment:** Images can be made and deployed in a variety of ways; for example, cloning the entire drive image of another installation. This can be done by using programs such as Acronis True Image or Symantec Ghost. When cloning a drive image, both computers must be identical, or as close to identical as possible. The hard drive of the target for a cloned installation must be at least as large as the original system. To avoid Security Identifier (SID) conflicts, use the Sysprep utility. The Sysprep utility for Windows is installed with the operating system and can be found by navigating to C:\Windows\System32\Sysprep. Sysprep uses an answer file created with the SIM. It creates a unique SID and makes other changes as needed to the network configuration of the system. You can also "image" the computer with a *pre-made* OS image. Do this with the Microsoft Deployment Toolkit or with third-party tools such as Symantec Ghost. In addition, you can install from a recovery disc/drive that you created or that was supplied by the vendor of the computer.

▶ **Remote network installation:** Remote network installations can be initiated while the target computer is booted to a pre-existing OS, or by booting a PXE-compliant computer to the network and specifying the server (where the OS installation files are located) to access from the BIOS. Once again, Windows Deployment Services (WDS) and the

Microsoft Deployment Toolkit are key components if you are remotely deploying Windows.

▶ **Refresh/Reset/Restore:** These are three options for troubleshooting problems with a Windows PC. In Windows 8.1, there are two options: **Refresh your PC** and **Reset your PC**. Refreshing the PC means that Windows is reinstalled, and the personal files and settings are kept, and resetting the PC means a reinstall of Windows, but the files and settings are deleted. However, in Windows 10, the only option is **Reset your PC**, which gives the user the ability to clear everything, or keep personal files. Restoring the PC means that you undo recent changes that were made. Windows can also be installed from a previously made System Restore image. For more information on System Restore, and troubleshooting Microsoft Windows in general, see Chapter 36, "Troubleshooting Microsoft Windows."

▶ **Installing from a recovery partition or disc:** Computers with Windows preinstalled use a recovery disc, hidden partition, or both. This disc and/or partition contains a factory image of Windows. The purpose of this is to enable users to return their computers back to the state when they were first received. This means that the system partition (usually the C: drive) will be properly formatted and reimaged with Windows. This works well in a two-partition system, in which the operating system is on C: and data is stored on D: or another drive letter. In this scenario, when the operating system fails and cannot be repaired, the computer can be returned to its original "factory" state, but the data won't be compromised. Whenever buying a computer from a company such as HP, Dell, and so on, make sure that they offer some kind of factory recovery partition, recovery disc (or flash drive), or other recovery option.

> **ExamAlert**
>
> Know the difference between a local, network, drive image, and recovery disc installation.

Multiboots: Since the 1990s, technicians have been setting up two or more operating systems on the same hard drive; this is known as dual-booting, tri-booting, and so on. This is easier than it used to be back in the 1990s; nowadays you can usually get away with using built-in tools in Windows or Linux. For example, if you have Windows 10 installed, you can modify the partition structure with Disk Management, create an additional partition, and install another OS to that new partition. This requires a bit of planning, but if successful, both operating systems display in a menu when the computer is booted. The information pertaining to these operating systems is stored in the Boot Configuration Data (BCD) store in Windows, and the GNU GRUB (GRand Unified Bootloader) in Linux. If you attempt a dual-boot without previously configuring the system, then Windows or Linux (whichever is installed second) will attempt to create the dual boot for you. However, you might be better off with third-party tools such as GParted or KDE Partition Manager depending on the scenario and the partition structure that you currently have. More about partitioning in just a bit!

> **ExamAlert**
>
> Understand that multiboots allow two or more operating systems to inhabit one hard drive.

Partitioning

Partitioning is the act of dividing up the hard drive into sections. It's kind of like a floor plan for your hard drive, with "walls" that separate your formatted areas for data. You don't have to have any walls, so to speak; you can have a single partition, or more than one. The design is up to you. Let's talk about the basic partitioning terms you should know for the exam. We will revisit partitioning and drive management in general within Chapter 26, "Microsoft Operating System Features and Tools, Part 1."

Primary and Extended Partitions and Logical Drives

The first partition that the OS is installed to is called a primary partition. Many systems have a single primary partition, which is inhabited by the OS and also stores the data. It is usually known as the C: drive. However, it is a good practice when first partitioning the drive to create two partitions: one for the OS, and one for the data; perhaps C: and D:, or C: and F:. This keeps the data *safer* in the event of an OS crash, and subsequent repair or reinstall of the OS. In a typical Windows system, the hard drive is limited to four partitions. Those can be four primary partitions, or three primary partitions and one extended partition. The extended partition can be further broken up into logical drives, allowing a person to have as many sections as there are letters in the alphabet—which is usually enough!

Letter assignments (C:, F:, G:, and so on) are also referred to as volumes. A volume can be a single partition or logical drive, or it can span across different drives, even different systems. We'll discuss that concept more as we progress through the book.

Basic and Dynamic Drives

A typical installation of an OS such as Windows normally results in a basic drive. This is a hard drive that has finite-sized partitions and volumes. Those partitions cannot be resized unless you convert the drive to a dynamic drive. This is a process done in Windows with the Disk Management program, or in the Command Prompt with the diskpart utility. Once converted, partitions and volumes can be resized as the user sees fit—as long as there is space available on the drive. There is a risk to using this process, and data should be backed up prior to initiating the conversion. We'll describe this process and the techniques that can be used after conversion later in the book.

> **ExamAlert**
>
> Know the differences between basic and dynamic drives.

GPT Versus MBR

There are two partitioning schemes that you should know for the exam: GPT and MBR. These define the maximum amount of partitions that a drive can have as well as the maximum size of each partition. Which partitioning scheme will you use? You will usually make use of the GUID Partition Table (GPT) instead of the older Master Boot Record (MBR). GPT is a newer standard that has for the most part replaced MBR; it is not limited in the way that MBR is. With GPT, you can have up to 128 partitions and no extended partition is necessary. Also, you are not limited to the MBR's maximum partition size of 2 TB. In addition, the GPT is stored in multiple locations, so it is harder to corrupt the partition table data.

GPT is used heavily in Linux systems, and Windows has supported it since 2005. It forms a part of the UEFI standard, so your system needs to have a UEFI-compliant motherboard. It uses globally unique identifiers (secure 128-bit numbers) to reference each partition, making it virtually impossible for any two computers to have two partitions with the same ID.

In essence, GPT was designed to replace MBR, and it is strongly linked to how the UEFI is designed to replace (or augment) the BIOS. It's important to remember that you might need to select your method (GPT or MBR) when you first add a new drive or start an installation. You can, however, convert a drive from MBR to GPT, but the drive will be wiped. For more information on how to do this, visit https://technet.microsoft.com/en-us/library/dn336946.aspx.

> **ExamAlert**
>
> Know the differences between GPT and MBR!

File System Types and Formatting

Once you have chosen your partition scheme and created the partition, you then need to format the partition so that it will be ready to accept data. To do this, you must select a file system which enables the storing and reading of data to and from the drive.

Windows File System Basics

When formatting a hard drive in a Windows environment, you have the option to format it as NTFS (recommended), FAT32, or FAT. NTFS is a more secure and stable platform and can support larger volume sizes. It also supports encryption with the Encrypting File System (EFS) and works better with backups. FAT32 and FAT should be used only to interact with older versions of Windows and to format devices such as USB flash drives. Depending on the cluster size used, NTFS can support partitions up to 16 TB (4-KB clusters) or 256 TB (64-KB clusters), but some systems will be limited to 2 TB due to the limitations of partition tables on MBR-based drives. This hardware limitation applies to maximum FAT32 partition sizes of 2 TB as well (aside from the installation maximum of 32 GB). To go beyond this, a set of striped or spanned dynamic drives would have to be employed, creating a multidrive volume.

Another file system introduced by Microsoft is called the Extended File Allocation Table (exFAT), which is suited specifically for USB flash drives but addresses the needs of many other mobile storage solutions. The successor to FAT32, it can handle large file sizes and can format media that is larger than 32 GB with a single partition. In fact, exFAT (also known as FAT64) has a recommended maximum of 512 TB for partitions, with a theoretical maximum of 64 ZB (zettabytes). The file size limit when using exFAT is 16 EB (exabytes). This file system can be used in many versions of Windows. If NTFS is not a plausible solution and the partition size needed is larger than 32 GB, exFAT might be the best option.

As of the writing of this book, exFAT is not used for internal SATA hard drives; it is used for flash memory storage and other external storage devices. exFAT is considered to be a more efficient file system than NTFS when it comes to flash memory storage; it has less fragmentation, leading to more possible read/write cycles over the life of the flash memory device.

> **ExamAlert**
>
> Know the differences between NTFS, FAT32, and exFAT.

Regardless of the file system used, in Windows you can opt for a quick format or a full format (which is also known as a normal format). In Windows, a quick format removes *access* to files on the partition or drive; a full format writes zeros to the entire partition, and also scans the partition or drive for bad sectors, which altogether can be quite time consuming. Generally, the full format should be avoided by technicians. However, if the drive is brand new and has never been formatted, or if the drive has been acquired from another source and you are concerned with its integrity, then consider running a full format. But be careful with full formats, because they put a lot of stress on the hard drive, which can reduce its lifespan, especially in the case of magnetic-based drives. If you are concerned that a partition was "quick" formatted, and possibly has bad sectors, you can run the **chkdsk /r** command to find out for sure.

> **Note**
>
> Quick and full formats are *not* considered secure solutions for drives that will be repurposed or have been obtained from other parties. More secure solutions that do *multiple* passes (zeroing out the data) are required. We'll discuss this more in Chapter 35, "Data Destruction and SOHO Security."

CDFS

Another file system you should understand is the Compact Disc File System (CDFS). This is the ISO 9660 standard, which defines how information is written to optical discs and is used by Windows, macOS, and Linux. A CD-ROM consists of frames, which can each hold 24 bytes. Ninety-eight frames put together creates a sector. Those bytes are divided up; the majority of them are used for data and others are used for error detection and correction. How they are divided is determined by the mode used. CD-ROM Mode 1 and Mode 2 Form 1 are usually used for computer data. CD-ROM Mode 2 Form 2 is more tolerant of errors and is used by audio and video data.

Linux File System Basics

Linux supports many file systems, including the ext family, FAT32, and NTFS. It also supports the Network File System (NFS), a distributed file system that allows a client computer to access files over the network; it was designed especially for Linux and Unix systems, but other systems such as Windows can use it as well.

> **Note**
>
> In the following two paragraphs I'll be discussing commands that you can type in Linux. This is done in the Terminal, which is the command-line tool used in Linux and macOS. It is similar to the Command Prompt used in Windows. It can be opened by searching **terminal** or by pressing **Ctrl+Alt+T**.

However, the most common file systems used on the local system are ext3 and ext4. ext4 is the Fourth Extended file system, which can support volume sizes of up to 1 exabyte (EB). You can discern the type of file system used in Linux by typing the **df -T** command. On systems commonly used during the writing of this book (2019), the /dev/sda1 (or /dev/hda1) partition (where the Linux OS is installed) is usually ext4.

The /dev refers to the file system representation of devices. There can be more than one hard drive within the /dev path. Originally, "sd" stood for SCSI devices, but now also includes SATA drives. (You might also see "hd," which refers to older IDE drives and other drives that Linux sees.) Instead of calling each disk "disk 0," "disk 1," and so on (as Windows does), Linux refers to them as "a," "b," "c," and so on. The number at the end of the path is the number of the partition. Linux is normally installed to partition 1, the full path being either /dev/sda1 or /dev/hda1; this is known as the boot partition. The second partition listed is an extended partition, similar to the Windows extended partition in that it can be used to create additional partitions for data, such as /dev/sda3 or /dev/sda4 and beyond. Often /dev/sda5 is used by the OS as a swap file (paging file) between the memory and the hard drive. You can find a list of the partitions available on most Linux systems by opening the command line (Terminal) and typing one of the following commands. First is **parted /dev/sda print**. The GNU parted utility is the preferred method for accessing GPT and MBR partition schemes. The second is the **fdisk -l** command, but fdisk should only be used on MBR-based systems. Be ready to prefix those commands with **sudo** and type an administrator password.

> **Note**
>
> There are a variety of other file systems used by Linux, so be prepared for lots of different acronyms. For example, btrfs is another Linux-based file system used by some network-attached storage (NAS) devices.

Linux also makes use of a *swap partition*, also known as swap space. The swap partition acts as an overflow for RAM. If the RAM fills up, any subsequently opened applications will run inside of the swap partition on the hard drive until some RAM space is cleared up. This is somewhat similar to the Windows pagefile concept, but the Linux swap space exists on a separate partition, whereas the Windows pagefile exists on C:\ by default.

macOS File System Basics

As of the writing of this book, and since macOS version 10.13, Apple has used the Apple File System (APFS). It is the successor to Hierarchical File System Plus (HFS+). These work in a similar fashion to Linux-based file systems (it's all Unix-based), and can be analyzed in a similar way in the Terminal. For example, to see a list of the partitions, type **df -t** (lowercase letter), or use the macOS command **diskutil list**. You can also use parted and fdisk based on whether the partition scheme is GPT or MBR, respectively. However, be ready for slightly different parameters and syntax when using those commands as compared to Linux. macOS also uses a set of swap files in a similar manner to Linux. They are stored in /private/var/vm. They can be displayed with the Disk Utility program, or in the Terminal using the **ls -lh /private/var/vm/swapfile*** command.

More OS Installation Considerations

There are plenty of other considerations to make before, and during, an OS install. See the following list of A+ objectives for a quick description of them; we'll be covering them in more depth as we progress through the book.

► **Load alternate third-party drivers when necessary:** For example, if you are installing Windows to a newer and less common hard drive (SAS, or NVMe), then you might have to supply the manufacturer's drivers if Windows or Linux doesn't recognize the drive.

▶ **Workgroup vs. domain setup:** If a Windows computer will be standalone or used in a small office, chances are it will be set up to connect in workgroup mode. If it is a larger environment that is controlled by a Windows server, then you might have to select "domain." Before this, however, you will need to make sure that the network adapter is properly configured with the IP address of the DNS server on the network.

▶ **Time/date/region/language settings:** During the install you will be prompted to enter basic information such as the time, date, time zone (and/or region of the world), and the language you will be using. For the rest of this book we will focus on English as the main language (personal preference as well as a necessity)!

▶ **Driver installation, software, and Windows updates:** You might be prompted to load additional drivers, especially for network interface cards, so that the system can access the Internet. In a Windows installation, you'll also be asked about how you would like to have updates handled, meaning when and how. We'll discuss updates more in Chapter 26.

▶ **Properly formatted boot drive with the correct partitions/format:** If you install Windows and decide to customize the partitions, then you have to be sure to utilize the right formatting and build out at least one recovery partition. The unwritten rule is to use the NTFS file system for the main primary partition where the OS will be housed, and the written rule is to make it 32 GB or more (for Windows 10). The minimum size of the recovery partition will depend on the version of Windows, but, for example, Windows 10 will often use 450 MB and Windows 7 will use 100 MB—so you can see the progression over time. These recovery partitions are created automatically if you do a default installation of Windows (for example, Windows 10) and select the default partition layout. After the installation is complete, you can view the partitions in Disk Management, or with the diskpart utility in the Command Prompt. For example, type **diskpart** to enter the utility, then type **select disk 0** (where 0 is the first drive), and then type **list partition**. Figure 24.1 shows an example of this. Partition 4 is 145 GB. That is the C: drive and it is where I installed Windows 10. Then, I store the data separately on Partition 7, which is 86 GB. Also, there are three recovery partitions in this case, ranging between 300 and 450 MB. The Disk Management equivalent is shown in Figure 24.2, though this does not display Partition 3 "Reserved." Keep in mind that your default installation of Windows will probably have fewer partitions; for example, you might see a recovery partition, an EFI system partition, and the OS partition.

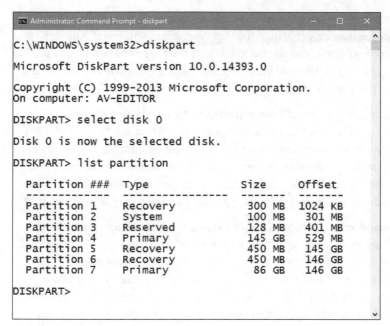

FIGURE 24.1   Diskpart utility showing the partitions of a Windows 10 boot drive

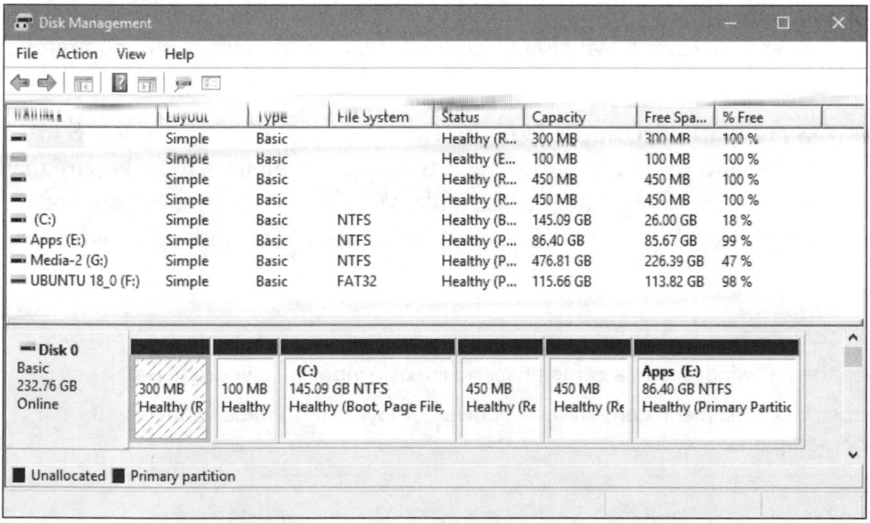

FIGURE 24.2   **Disk Management showing the partitions of the same Windows 10 boot drive**

ExamAlert

Know how to use the Disk Management and diskpart utilities!

▶ **Factory recovery partition:** If you buy a computer from a manufacturer, the software may be preloaded. In that case, there will usually be one or more recovery partitions on the hard drive that are separate from the system partition. These are generally less than 1 GB each and can be used to repair the system and recover from errors if they occur.

▶ **Prerequisites/hardware compatibility:** As I mentioned earlier, you have to make sure that your physical computer (or virtual machine) will meet the minimum requirements as set by Microsoft or another OS developer. Before installing, you should also check the hardware compatibility list for that particular OS and make sure that the motherboard, CPU, video card, audio card, network adapter, and hard drives will work with that OS.

▶ **Application compatibility:** This all stems from the original question: What are you going to use the computer for? If it's going to be used to run Logic (audio software), then you need a Mac computer. If you are running Pro Tools, then you need to decide whether you will use Windows or Mac. Or maybe you want to build a Hyper-V virtualization system using Windows 10. If so, then it will run on any edition except Windows 10 Home. Always know what you are doing with the computer before installing it, and know whether or not the applications will run on the computer's hardware, and within the version and edition of the OS you wish to install. We discuss some of the custom purposes of computers in Chapter 14, "Custom PCs and Common Devices."

▶ **OS compatibility/upgrade path:** If you are upgrading from one OS to another and wish to save the data/settings, then you have to make sure that the upgrade path is valid. For example, Window 7 Ultimate can only be upgraded to Windows 8.1 Pro or to Windows 10 Pro and higher editions.

> **Note**
>
> See the following link for a comprehensive list of Windows 10 upgrade paths:
>
> https://docs.microsoft.com/en-us/windows/deployment/upgrade/windows-10-upgrade-paths

Planning Is #1!

There is a lot to consider in this chapter, that's for sure. That's why I always say, *planning is key*. Clean and sharp planning helps you to avoid problems, and saves time in the long run. It is extremely important when dealing with all things technology. Commit it to memory.

Cram Quiz

Answer these questions. The answers follow the last question. If you cannot answer these questions correctly, consider reading this section again until you can.

1. Which of the following installation types would require PXE compliance?

   ○ **A.** Local

   ○ **B.** Network

   ○ **C.** Internal

   ○ **D.** USB flash drive

2. To avoid SID conflicts when drive imaging, which program should you use in Windows?

   ○ **A.** Sysprep

   ○ **B.** Diskpart

   ○ **C.** SIM

   ○ **D.** Windows Deployment Services

3. You are tasked with installing Windows with the standard configuration. The file system needs to be able to access an 8-TB partition. Which of the following should you configure the system to use?

   ○ **A.** GPT

   ○ **B.** NTFS

   ○ **C.** FAT32

   ○ **D.** MBR

   ○ **E.** ext4

4. Which of the following uses an answer file to provide responses with no user intervention required?

   ○ **A.** Factory recovery partition

   ○ **B.** Clean installation

   ○ **C.** Unattended installation

   ○ **D.** Reset your PC

Cram Quiz Answers

1. **B.** A network-based installation requires that the network card be PXE compliant, so that it can boot to the network and locate a DHCP server and deployment server. Local installations, such as using a USB flash drive or optical disc, do not need the network adapter. Internal installations, such as ones that are done from a secondary internal hard drive, also do not need a PXE-compliant network card.

2. **A.** Sysprep can modify unattended installations so that every computer gets a unique SID (and other unique information). Windows SIM creates the answer files for unattended installations. Diskpart is used to view and configure partitions from the Command Prompt in Windows. Windows Deployment Services is run on Windows Server and is used to deploy operating systems across the network.

3. **B.** Use NTFS. That file system is the default when installing Windows and in a typical installation (4-KB clusters) can support 16-TB partitions. You most likely will use GPT as well (instead of MBR), but that is a partitioning scheme, not a file system. FAT32 is an older file system that you could use, but would not support the 8-TB partition that is required. Ext4 is a Linux-based file system not used in Windows. Know your file systems for the exam!

4. **C.** An unattended installation uses an answer file that provides the responses needed for the installation. A factory recovery partition is preloaded by the computer manufacturer. A clean installation means that the OS is installed to a blank partition or new hard drive. "Reset your PC" is an option in Windows 10 that allows a user to repair a computer by reinstalling the OS with one of two options: wiping all data, or keeping user files. However, in Windows 8.1, it wipes all data only.

CHAPTER 25

Microsoft Command Line Tools

This chapter covers the following A+ 220-1002 exam objective:

▶ 1.4 – Given a scenario, use appropriate Microsoft command line tools.

The command line, that's where the real technicians live. Anything you can do in a GUI-based system can be done in the command line, sometimes more. Get to know it. For Microsoft Windows, you should become fluent in the Command Prompt and the PowerShell and know as many commands as you can.

This chapter covers one of the most important objectives in the A+, so I suggest you take breaks after each group of commands. We'll begin with how to navigate folders and files within the Command Prompt. By the way, when working in the command-line interface, the original name for folders was *directories*, so I will be using that term often. Next, we'll discuss some of the commands that can be used to analyze and configure the hard drive and file system. Then we'll move into some networking commands, and finally some advanced tools.

Once you get the hang of the command line, it's a blast. The great thing about the command line is that it hasn't changed much over time. Or at least, not nearly as much as the various GUI changes that Windows has undergone. Plus, many companies desire technicians that have good command line skills, which can ultimately translate to job security. Enough said.

1.4 – Given a scenario, use appropriate Microsoft command line tools

ExamAlert

Objective 1.4 focuses on Microsoft command line tools: dir, cd, ipconfig, ping, tracert, netstat, nslookup, shutdown, dism, sfc, chkdsk, diskpart, taskkill, gpupdate, gpresult, format, copy, xcopy, robocopy, net use, net user; help and /?; and commands available with standard vs. administrative privileges.

Command Prompt Basics

Microsoft's Command Prompt is its command-line interface (CLI). This is the text-based interface in which you can issue commands concerning files and folders, networking, services, and so on. You can open it in several ways, including the following:

▶ **For all versions of Windows:** Open the Search tool and type **CMD** (or search for a variety of words/phrases associated with the Command Prompt). Windows 10 displays the Search tool on the taskbar by default. The Search tool can be found on the Start screen or by bringing up the Charms bar in Windows 8. The Search tool can be found in Windows 7 by simply clicking **Start**.

▶ **For all versions of Windows:** Press **Windows+R** to open the Run prompt and type **CMD** (my personal favorite).

▶ **In Windows 10 and 8:** Right-click the **Start** button and select **Command Prompt**. Another great keyboard shortcut is **Windows+X**. This is the same as right-clicking the Start button.

▶ **In Windows 10:** Click **Start**, then on the programs list, scroll down to **Windows System > Command Prompt**.

▶ **In Windows 7:** Navigate to **Start > All Programs > Accessories > Command Prompt**.

In Windows, some commands need to be run as an administrator; to open the Command Prompt as an administrator, do one of the following:

- ▶ **In all versions of Windows:** Open the Search tool and type **CMD** in the Search field; instead of pressing Enter, press **Ctrl+Shift+Enter**. (Make sure it is highlighted.)

- ▶ **In Windows 10:** Go to the **Start > Windows System**, right-click **Command Prompt**, click **More**, then select **Run as administrator**.

- ▶ **In Windows 10 and 8:** Right-click the **Start** button and select **Command Prompt (Admin)**.

- ▶ **In Windows 7:** Click **Start > All Programs > Accessories**, then right-click **Command Prompt** and select **Run as Administrator**.

Running the Command Prompt as an administrator is also known as running it in *elevated mode*. You will be using it often.

ExamAlert

Know how to open programs from the Search tool, from the Start menu, and from the Run prompt.

An additional command line environment called the PowerShell is integrated into Windows. PowerShell is a combination of the Command Prompt and a scripting language. (It is the successor to the Windows Script Host.) It enables administrators to perform administrative tasks that integrate scripts and executables. This can be opened in the following ways:

- ▶ **In all versions of Windows:** Use the Search tool.

- ▶ **In all versions of Windows:** Go to the Run prompt and type **powershell.exe**.

- ▶ **In Windows 10:** Navigate to **Start > Windows PowerShell > Windows PowerShell**.

- ▶ **In Windows 7:** Navigate to **Start > All Programs > Accessories > Windows PowerShell**.

It should be noted that if you use PowerShell in place of the Command Prompt, you should remember to always use a space after a command; otherwise the shell will not recognize the command. For example, typing **ipconfig /all** is correct, whereas **ipconfig/all,** would not function. Remember: using a space after a command is the proper way.

For administrators who write scripts often, there is also the Windows Power-Shell ISE (Integrated Scripting Environment); this allows an admin to not only run commands, but also write, test, and debug scripts with the shell and the script running in a side-by-side manner. So, you can write a script in the text editor, and "run" it over and over again, making modifications as you go. You can open this from the Run prompt by typing **powershell_ise**.

Ask for Help!

If you are ever stumped about a particular command, read the help file associated with it. For example, for more information about the **ping** command, you can type **ping /?**. In some cases, you can also type **help** and then the command (for instance, **help dir**), but **/?** is the best all-around way to do it because that option encompasses all of the commands available. You can also find out more about Microsoft commands at this link:

https://docs.microsoft.com/en-us/windows-server/administration/windows-commands/windows-commands

---

Navigating and Working with Directories and Files in the Command Prompt

Have I mentioned yet that just about anything you can do in Windows can also be done in the Command Prompt? It's true. And sometimes the Command Prompt is faster than the GUI—if you can type quickly! There are three commands used to work with directories in the Command Prompt. As a reminder, *directory* is the original name for *folder*. Folders are more accurately called *directories* when working in any command line (such as the Windows Command Prompt) and *folders* when working in the GUI, but the two terms can be used interchangeably.

- ▶ **cd:** Change Directory. This command enables you to move from one directory to another. Actually, you can go from any one directory to any other using just one **cd** command. Two simple commands that you can issue are **cd..** and **cd**. The **cd..** command moves you up one directory; it takes you from the current directory to the parent directory. The **cd** command takes you directly to the root of the volume that you are working in.

- ▶ **md:** Make Directory. This command creates directories.

- ▶ **rd:** Remove Directory. This command enables you to remove directories. You can also remove directories that contain files by utilizing the **/S** switch.

All these commands can be used such that their functions affect any folder you choose within the directory structure (which used to be known as the DOS tree, but I digress). Figure 25.1 provides a sample directory structure.

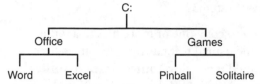

FIGURE 25.1 **A sample directory structure**

For example, let's say that your current position is C:\Office. From here or any other location, you can do anything to any folder in the entire directory tree. Let's consider a couple examples:

▶ Change the current position to the Pinball folder. To do this, the command would be either **cd c:\games\pinball** or just **cd \games\ pinball**.

▶ Make a directory called "documents" within Word. To do this, the command syntax would be **md c:\office\word\documents**.

▶ Delete the directory Excel. To do this, the command would be **rd c:\ office\excel**.

ExamAlert

Know how to navigate the Command Prompt with the **cd** command, **cd..** and **cd**.

Some other commands you might use when working with directories and files include **dir**, **tree**, **copy**, **xcopy**, **robocopy**, and **del**.

▶ **dir:** This is the directory command. When used alone, it displays the contents of the current directory. But it can be configured to show information in any other directory. For example, **dir \office\excel** will show the contents of the Excel directory regardless of what directory you are currently in. You can also use the **dir** command to customize how content is listed. For example, **/p** will show information by the page, **/w** is wide list format, and so on. To find out more about the **dir** command (or any other command, for that matter), type **dir /?**. The **/?** is the switch that tells the Command Prompt to display the help file for that command. It can be placed on the end of any valid Command Prompt command.

▶ **tree:** This command shows all the directories and subdirectories within your current position. Be careful where you run this because it could list information for quite a while and cause some stress on the hard drive. For example, stay away from big directories, such as the root, which is C:\, \Windows, and \Windows\System32.

▶ **copy:** This command allows you to copy one or more files to another location. If I wanted to copy a file named test.txt from the office directory to the Excel directory, I would type **copy \office\test.txt \office\ excel**. Now the original file is in \office and the copy is in \excel. There are more powerful versions of this command—known as **xcopy** and **robocopy**—that we talk about next.

▶ **xcopy:** The **xcopy** command is meant to copy large amounts of data from one location to another; it even makes exact copies of entire directory trees. One example of its usage would be to copy the contents of a Windows DVD-ROM over to a USB flash drive so that you can use the USB flash drive as installation media. The command for this would be **xcopy d:*.* /E/F e:**. This is assuming that D: is the DVD-ROM drive and E: is the USB flash drive. *.* means all files with all extensions within the D: drive. **/E** indicates that all folders and subfolders will be copied including empty ones. **/F** displays full source and destination files while copying. For more information about **xcopy**, type **xcopy /?**.

▶ **robocopy:** (Robust File Copy) is a directory replication tool. It is meant to copy directories that contain lots of data; it can even mirror complete directory trees from one computer to another. **robocopy** is the successor to **xcopy**. Some of the advantages of this tool are that it can tolerate network interruptions, skip past junctions (such as the \Documents and Settings to \Users junction), and preserve data attributes and time stamps. **robocopy** does not copy individual files; it copies only directories (for example, **robocopy c:\office c:\games**). This will copy all the information within the \office directory to the \games directory. It also gives in-depth results of its actions. You can also use **robocopy** to copy information to other computers by using the **\\computername\share**, which is Microsoft's Universal (or Uniform) Naming Convention (UNC).

▶ **del:** When you are done with a file and are ready to delete it, use **del**. For example, if you want to delete the test.txt file that you just copied to the Excel folder, type **del \office\excel\test.txt**.

> **Note**
>
> By the way, I created the test.txt text file within Notepad, which is available via the Search tool or by going to Run and typing **notepad**. Notepad is Windows' default graphical text editor that you can use for editing text and batch files. However, you might opt to use third-party text editors, especially if you plan to create batch files or do any coding (for example, in the PowerShell, HTML, or PHP).

> **ExamAlert**
>
> Understand how to use **dir**, **tree**, **copy**, **xcopy**, **robocopy**, and **del**.

Partitioning and File System-based Commands

There are a slew of commands that you can use to make changes to your hard drive's partitions and file systems, and check the hard drive and file system integrity. Some that you should know for the exam include: **diskpart**, **format**, **defrag**, and **convert**.

▶ **diskpart:** This utility is the command line counterpart of Windows' Disk Management program. This program needs to be run by typing **diskpart** before any of the **diskpart** actions can be implemented. This brings the user into the DISKPART> prompt. From here, you can create, delete, and extend volumes, assign drive letters, make a partition active, and so on. Essentially, everything that you can do in Disk Management can be done with **diskpart**. When you are in the DISKPART> prompt, enter a question mark (?) to learn about the various options within the Diskpart program. When you finish using **diskpart**, type **exit** to return back to the standard Command Prompt.

▶ **format:** A command used to format magnetic media such as hard drives and solid-state media (such as USB flash drives) to the FAT, FAT32, or NTFS file systems. An example of formatting a USB flash drive in the command line would be **format F:**. The type of file system that the media will be formatted to can be specified with the switch **/FS:*filesystem***, where *filesystem* will equal FAT32 or NTFS, and so on.

▶ **defrag:** The command line version of the Disk Defragmenter. To analyze a drive, type **defrag -a**. If a volume needs to be defragmented, but has less than 15 percent free space, use the **-f** parameter.

▶ **convert:** This command enables you to convert a volume that was previously formatted as FAT32 over to NTFS without losing any data. An example of the **convert** command would be **convert d: /FS:NTFS**, which would convert the hard drive volume D: to NTFS. Sometimes you might encounter older computers' hard drives (or flash media) that require being formatted as NTFS for compatibility with other devices and networked computers.

Chkdsk and SFC

A good technician uses commands to analyze and possibly repair a hard drive and its system files. Two commands that can aid in this endeavor include chkdsk and SFC.

Chkdsk

Chkdsk checks a drive, fixes basic issues like lost files, and displays a status report; it can also fix some errors on the drive by using the **/F** switch. Here's an example of the three stages of results when running the **chkdsk** command:

```
The type of the file system is NTFS.
Volume label is WinXPC.
WARNING! F parameter not specified.
Running CHKDSK in read-only mode.
CHKDSK is verifying files (stage 1 of 3)...
File verification completed.
CHKDSK is verifying indexes (stage 2 of 3)...
Index verification completed.
CHKDSK is recovering lost files.
Recovering orphaned file ~WRL3090.tmp (59880) into directory file
    28570.
Recovering orphaned file ~DFA188.tmp (59881) into directory file
    28138.
CHKDSK is verifying security descriptors (stage 3 of 3)...
Security descriptor verification completed.
Correcting errors in the master file table's (MFT) BITMAP attribute.
Correcting errors in the Volume Bitmap.
Windows found problems with the file system.
Run CHKDSK with the /F (fix) option to correct these.
 31471300 KB total disk space.
```

I shortened the results, but notice that the utility warned that the **/F** switch was not specified. Also notice that the orphaned files were recovered, although they are just .tmp files and most likely not necessary for the functionality of Windows. Finally, the program found issues with the file system; to repair these, you would have to use the **/F** option. Be sure that you actually need to run **chkdsk** with the **/F** parameter before doing so. For example, if the system seems to function properly, but the standard **chkdsk** command gave an error, it might not be absolutely necessary to run **chkdsk** with the **/F** parameter.

One issue that plagues users is the infamous Missing Operating System message. If you get this, it usually means that either the drive has a few small errors or the master boot record (MBR) on older systems has been damaged. But even though the system won't boot, you can still run **chkdsk** to find and fix problems on the drive. Boot to the repair environment (if possible) or to the Windows media, access Windows RE, and then open the Command Prompt. From there, run **chkdsk** with either the **/F** switch (which fixes errors on the drive) or the **/R** switch (which locates bad sectors and recovers data)—or run both. This procedure can also help with Invalid Boot Disk errors. (Of course, first check that the BIOS is booting to the correct drive in the boot priority menu.)

SFC

System File Checker (SFC) is a Windows utility that checks protected system files. It replaces incorrect versions or missing files with the correct files. SFC can be used to fix problems with Edge/Internet Explorer or other Windows applications. To run SFC, open the Command Prompt and type **SFC** with the appropriate switch. A typical option is **SFC /scannow**, which scans all protected files immediately and repairs files. During this procedure, SFC writes the details of each repair to a file called CBS.log located in %systemroot% \Logs\CBS, which can be used to further analyze the system and the integrity of files. Another is **SFC /verifyonly**, which scans the integrity of files but does not perform a repair. If SFC finds that some files are missing, you might be prompted to reinsert the original operating system disc so the files can be copied to the DLL cache.

> **Note**
>
> Remember that %systemroot% is the folder where Windows was installed; by default, it is C:\Windows.

> **ExamAlert**
>
> Know your basic switches for **chkdsk** and **SFC**, such as **chkdsk /F** and **sfc /scannow**.

Networking Commands

There are many command line tools that we can use in Windows to help us analyze and troubleshoot a computer's network connection; in this section, we delve into several of them. I recommend that you try all the variations of these on your computer. Some commands require that you open the Command Prompt as an administrator (elevated mode).

The most commonly used command for analyzing a computer's networking configuration is **ipconfig**. Let's start with that.

ipconfig

The Internet protocol configuration command, **ipconfig**, displays current TCP/IP network configuration values. This is one of the first tools you should use when troubleshooting network connectivity. When you type **ipconfig**, you get results similar to the following:

```
Windows IP Configuration
Ethernet adapter Local Area Connection:
Connection-specific DNS Suffix . :
Link-Local IPv6 Address. . . . . : fe80::404b:e781:b150:b91a%11
IPv4 Address. . . . . . . . . . . : 192.168.0.100
Subnet Mask . . . . . . . . . . . : 255.255.255.0
Default Gateway . . . . . . . . . : 192.168.0.1
```

Ipconfig combined with the **/all** switch shows more information, including whether or not DHCP is being used, the DNS server address, and the MAC address. The MAC address is the hexadecimal address that is burned into the ROM of the network adapter. This is a set of six hexadecimal numbers (for example, 00-03-FF-A0-55-16).

> **ExamAlert**
>
> To view additional IP configuration information, such as DNS servers and MAC addresses, use the **ipconfig /all** command.

This command can offer a lot of information about a problem. For example, if a user cannot connect to any Internet resources, it could be because the gateway address is improperly configured. Remember that the gateway address must be on the same network number as the IP address of the client computer. If a user can't connect to any websites but can connect to other computers on the LAN, it could be that the DNS server address is incorrectly configured. **Ipconfig** also tells you whether the client computer's IP address is obtained from a DHCP server or assigned via APIPA and whether it is a private or public address.

Ipconfig can also be used to release and renew IP addresses. Sometimes this needs to be done if a computer's IP address is not working properly and you want to obtain a new address from a DHCP server. To release the current IP address, type **ipconfig /release**; to renew, type **ipconfig /renew**.

Finally, if you are having DNS issues (for example, problems connecting to websites), you can erase the DNS cache by typing **ipconfig /flushdns**. Check out the various **ipconfig** switches by opening the Command Prompt and typing **ipconfig /?**. You should try this with every command in this section.

ping

Ping tests whether another host is available over the network. It's the easy way to see if another host is "alive." Let's say your gateway's IP address is 192.168.0.1. To ping that computer, you would type **ping 192.168.0.1** (as an example) and hopefully get the following output:

```
Pinging 192.168.0.1: with 32 bytes of data:
Reply from 192.168.0.1: bytes=32 time<1ms TTL=64
Reply from 192.168.0.1: bytes=32 time<1ms TTL=64
Reply from 192.168.0.1: bytes=32 time<1ms TTL=64
Reply from 192.168.0.1: bytes=32 time<1ms TTL=64
Ping statistics for 192.168.0.1:
Packets: Sent = 4, Received = 4, Lost = 0 (0% loss),
Approximate round trip times in milli-seconds:
Minimum = 0ms, Maximum = 0ms, Average = 0ms
```

The replies indicate that the host is alive and can be communicated with on the network. Any other message would indicate a problem (for example, the Request Timed Out or Destination Host Unreachable messages would require further troubleshooting). Keep in mind that if it's the local computer that is configured incorrectly, you might not be able to ping anything! Also watch for the amount of time the ping took to reply. A longer latency time could indicate network congestion.

> **Note**
>
> Latency is the time it takes for sent data packets to be received by a remote computer. Latency increases with distance, type of network connection used, and network congestion. For example, a ping to a computer on the LAN should have very low latency, perhaps less than 1 millisecond (ms). But a ping initiated from a computer in New York City to a computer in Los Angeles, over a cable Internet connection, might have a latency of 25 ms. This can be a very enlightening piece of the ping results.

You can also use **ping** to test whether a computer has TCP/IP installed properly, even if it isn't wired to the network! To do this, use the **ping 127.0.0.1** command for IPv4 and **ping ::1** for IPv6. These IP addresses are known as loopback addresses; they are used for testing and are available on every host that has TCP/IP installed. They differ from the IP addresses we talked about previously (for example, 192.168.0.100) in that they work internally. Loopback **ping** commands essentially enable you to ping yourself, meaning you can test the local computer's network connection without a valid IP configuration and without a physical connection to the network. Replies are simulated within the local computer; they prove if the network adapter and TCP/IP have been installed properly. However, it does not prove if TCP/IP has been *configured* properly for your particular network.

> **Note**
>
> You can also use the **ping loopback** and **ping localhost** commands, adding **-4** for IPv4 and **-6** for IPv6, but for testing, pinging the IP address is usually recommended.

> **ExamAlert**
>
> Know how to ping the local loopback IPv4 and IPv6 addresses.

You can also modify the way that **ping** works with switches. Six that you should know for the exam are **-t, -n, -l, -a, -4**, and **-6**:

▶ **ping -t:** This pings the host until the command is stopped. Remember, a host is any device or computer with an IP address. An example of this would be **ping -t 192.168.0.1**; the switch can go before or after the IP address. You will keep getting replies (or timeouts) until you stop the command by pressing **Ctrl+C** or by closing the Command Prompt. This is a great way to test cable connections. After running the command, you can plug and unplug cables and watch the screen to see which cables or ports are live. You can also use it to monitor a connection over a period of time, discerning whether there are many packet drops or whether the connection slows down at certain times.

▶ **ping -n:** This pings a host a specific number of times. For example, the syntax **ping -n 20 192.168.0.1** would ping that host 20 times and then display the results. This can be a good baselining tool if you run it every day against a router or server and compare the results. (You would probably want to do a higher quantity than 20.)

▶ **ping -l:** This pings the host but you can specify the number of bytes per packet to be sent. If you look at the previous ping results, you can see that the default number of bytes is 32, but this can be increased to simulate real data. For example, **ping -l 1500 192.168.0.1** would send four 1500-byte packets to the other host. This can also be beneficial when testing how a server, router, or other device reacts to larger packet sizes.

▶ **ping -a:** This resolves addresses to hostnames. When pinging an IP address with **-a**, you also see the hostname associated with the IP address.

▶ **ping -4:** This forces the use of IPv4 and results in IPv4-based data. For example, in Windows, if you are running both IPv4 and IPv6 and type a command such as **ping loopback**, your results will by default be IPv6-based and might result in a reply from ::1 (that is, if your system is working properly). But by adding the **-4** option, you force the use of IPv4, so the command **ping -4 loopback** can result in a reply from 127.0.0.1. Try it!

▶ **ping -6:** This forces the use of IPv6 and results in IPv6-based data. For example, a **ping -6 loopback** will result in a reply from ::1.

> **ExamAlert**
>
> Know how to use the **-t**, **-n**, **-l**, **-a**, **-4**, and **-6** switches with **ping**.

These switches can be combined as well, for example, ping -n 450 -l 1500 **192.168.0.1** would send 450 pings, each 1500 bytes in size. To create a baseline, you could do this at a specific time every month, store the results, and then compare them to find possible deficiencies in performance of a server, router, and so on.

arp

The Address Resolution Protocol (ARP) resolves between IP addresses and MAC addresses, so that data communications can flow from the operating system to the physical network adapter. Every computer that runs TCP/IP has an ARP table, which is a cache of information including the IP address and MAC address of every other computer that the local system has been in contact with. The arp command can be used to display or modify those ARP entries. If you were to type **arp -a**, you might get results similar to the following:

```
Interface: 192.168.41.202 --- 0x19
  Internet Address      Physical Address      Type
  192.168.41.1          30-b5-c2-b2-59-e6     dynamic
  192.168.41.103        e8-4e-06-69-1a-99     dynamic
```

```
192.168.41.104          00-e0-4c-68-00-e9       dynamic
192.168.41.201          38-60-77-59-68-58       dynamic
192.168.41.255          ff-ff-ff-ff-ff-ff       static
224.0.0.2               01-00-5e-00-00-02       static
```

The local system is 192.168.41.202. Every computer that it has connected to in the recent past is shown. For example, you can see that there has been a connection to 192.168.41.103; that computer's corresponding MAC address is displayed as well. It is shown as a dynamic connection, meaning that it will time out at a specific point, usually when the computer restarts. However, you can have static connections as well, which won't time out. Default broadcasts are set up this way automatically. Individual static connections can be added to the ARP table with the **-s** parameter. I personally use these for connections to servers, so as to reduce the amount of IP to MAC resolutions that are done from my system to the systems I administer the most.

> **Note**
>
> ARP is shown in the CompTIA A+ objectives acronym list. Know it!

tracert

Tracert, short for trace route, builds on **ping** in that it send packets to destinations beyond the local computer's network. It pings each router along the way between you and the final destination. Let's say we ran the command **tracert davidlprowse.com**. An example of the **tracert** output follows:

```
Tracing route to davidlprowse.com [216.97.236.245] over a maximum of
   30 hops:
1 6 ms 5 ms 5 ms bdl1.eas-ubr16.atweas.pa.cable.rcn.net [10.21.80.1]
2 10 ms 9 ms 9 ms vl4.aggr1.phdl.pa.rcn.net [208.59.252.1]
```

The **tracert** would continue for a dozen or more lines and end in the following:

```
18 86 ms 86 ms 86 ms unused-240-180-214.ixpres.com [216.240.180.214]
19 98 ms 96 ms 97 ms lwdc.dbo2.gi9-4.host1.23680.americanis.net
   [38.96.20.2]
20 97 ms 96 ms 96 ms zosma.lunarpages.com [216.97.236.245]
Trace complete.
```

Note that there are three pings per line item measured in milliseconds (ms). Also note that every line item contains a router name and IP address. It starts by sailing through the various routers in our ISP, RCN.net. It ends at a server named zosma.lunarpages.com that hosts davidlprowse.com (as of the writing of this book). If you saw any asterisks in the place of the millisecond amounts, you might question whether the router is functioning properly. If the **tracert** stops altogether before saying Trace Complete, you would want to check your network documentation to find out which router it stopped at and/or make sure that the router is troubleshot by the appropriate personnel. As with **ping**, the **-4** and the **-6** options will force IPv4 and IPv6, respectively.

The **tracert /d** command will not resolve IP addresses to hostnames. So instead of seeing zosma.lunarpages.com on the last line, you would see only the IP address 216.97.236.245. Running numerical versions of commands can be faster because there is no name resolution to get in the way. Connecting directly by IP will always be faster than connecting by name.

netstat

Moving on to another concept, **netstat** shows the network statistics for the local computer. The default command displays sessions to remote computers. In the following example, I connected to google.com and ran the **netstat** command. Output follows:

```
Active Connections
TCP Music-Box:1395 8.15.228.165:https ESTABLISHED
TCP Music-Box:1396 he-in-f101.google.com:https ESTABLISHED
```

This output shows that there are two established TCP sessions (they're actually both to the same website) to google.com. In the local address column, we see our computer (Music Box) and the outbound ports it uses to access the website (1395 and 1396). In the foreign address column, we see an IP address and the protocol used (https); in the second session, we see a hostname followed by the protocol (again https). The protocol used by google.com corresponds to port 443. This command can tell us a lot about our sessions (for example, whether a session times out or whether it closes completely). To see this information numerically, try using the **-n** switch. To see TCP and UDP sessions, use the **-a** switch. To see TCP *and* UDP in numeric format, use the **-an** switch. To include the executable name for each session shown, use the **-nab** switch.

> **Note**
>
> There are plenty of other **netstat** options; for example, **netstat -e** shows Ethernet statistics. For more information on **netstat**, see the following link:
>
> https://docs.microsoft.com/en-us/windows-server/administration/windows-commands/netstat

nbtstat

Nbtstat displays network protocol statistics that use NetBIOS over TCP/IP connections. **Nbtstat** can be used to show the services running on the local computer or a remote computer. It calls this the name table. For example, you could find out what services are running, what the computer's name is, and what network it is a part of by typing **nbtstat -A 192.168.0.100** (or whatever your local IP address is). The results would be similar to the following:

```
Computer1 <00> Unique Registered
Workgroup <00> Group Registered
Computer1 <20> Unique Registered
```

The computer and network names are easy to see: Computer1 and Workgroup. But also notice that there are numbers in alligators, such as <00> and <20>. These are the services mentioned previously. <00> is the workstation service, which is the service that allows your computer to redirect out to other systems to view shared resources. <20> is the server service that allows your computer to share resources with other systems.

The **-a** switch (lowercase *a*) shows the same name table but you invoke this information using the computer name instead of the IP address. **Nbtstat** has a variety of other switches that can display, purge, and reload name tables and sessions. Check out the other various switches by typing **nbtstat /?**.

nslookup

Nslookup queries DNS servers to discover DNS details, including the IP address of hosts. For example, to find the IP address of davidlprowse.com, I would type **nslookup davidlprowse.com**. The resulting output should look something like this:

```
Non-authoritative answer:
Name: davidlprowse.com
Address: 216.97.236.245
```

So, from the output, we now know the IP address that corresponds to the domain name davidlprowse.com. **Nslookup** means *name server lookup* and can aid in finding DNS servers and DNS records in a domain as well. If the command **nslookup** is typed by itself, it brings the user into the **nslookup** shell. From here, several commands can be utilized; to find out more about these, type **?** and press **Enter**. To exit the **nslookup** shell, type **exit**, press **Ctrl+C**, or press **Ctrl+Break**. The Linux equivalent of this is Dig, which can also be installed to Windows as part of the BIND tools: https://www.isc.org/downloads/.

net

The **net** command is actually a collection of commands. You can use the **net stop** command to stop a service and the **net start** command to start a service from the Command Prompt. In networking, you might use the **net view** command to see which computers are currently available on the network or the **net share** command to share folders for other users to view.

For the exam, you should know the types of **net** commands that enable you to view or create mapped network drives. To view any currently mapped network drives, simply type **net use**. To create a mapped network drive, use the following syntax:

```
net use x: \\computername\sharename
```

X: is the drive letter (in this case, *X* is a variable; you can use whatever drive letter you want, if it's available, including X!). *computername* is the name of the remote host you want to connect to, and *sharename* is the share that was created on that remote host.

There is a network share on another computer on my network called C$. The following syntax shows the command to connect to it and the resulting output:

```
net use f: \\Music-Box\c$
The command completed successfully.
```

In this example, we used F: as our drive letter; the computer we connected to is called Music-Box and the share is C$ (the default hidden share). For more information on the **net** command, type **net /?**. For more information on the **net use** command, type **net use /?**.

> **Note**
>
> See the following link for a video demonstrating how to use **net share** and **net use** between two systems:
>
> https://dprocomputer.com/blog/?p=864

Another **net** command listed in the A+ objectives is **net user**. When typed by itself, that command will list the user accounts on the local computer. You can also create accounts from here with the **net user /add %username%** command, where **%username%** is a variable. For example, to create the user account dadams, you would type **net user /add dadams**. That creates a standard user account. In addition, you can activate or deactivate user accounts with the **/active** switch or delete accounts with the **/delete** switch. There is lots more; check out the command with **/?** for more information.

Advanced Commands

Let's get into some advanced commands: **tasklist**, **taskkill**, **dism**, **shutdown**, **gpupdate**, and **gpresult**.

tasklist

Tasklist shows all the processes running, similar to the Processes tab of the Task Manager. Each process is assigned a Process Identification number, or PID. These are assigned dynamically and won't use the same number for an application twice. **Tasklist** also shows the memory usage of each process. An example of a process would be excel.exe (Microsoft Excel) or winword.exe (Microsoft Word).

taskkill

Just as you can shut processes down in the Task Manager, you can also use the command line tool **taskkill**. Perhaps you run into a situation where certain applications or processes are frozen and you cannot open the Task Manager. If you can get to the Command Prompt, you can end these processes without restarting the computer. For example, if Microsoft Excel has stopped responding, you can find out its process ID with **tasklist** (say it was 4548) and close it by either typing **taskkill /IM excel.exe or taskkill /PID 4548**. **Tasklist** and **taskkill** are not available in the Windows Recovery Environment (WinRE) Command Prompt in Windows 10/8/7.

DISM

The Deployment Image Servicing and Management (DISM) tool is used to scan and repair Windows operating system images, or prepare and service Windows operating system images for deployment.

First, let's talk about basic scanning and repair of an image. Sometimes technicians will use DISM if the System File Checker (SFC) is not working properly. When SFC does repairs, it takes files from a Windows image. If the image is damaged, then SFC won't function. So you can use the DISM utility to check the health of the image and potentially restore it to health if it is damaged. Before running DISM, it is a good idea to back up files and create a restore point. Here's an example of how you would check the health of the image:

```
dism /online /cleanup-image /checkhealth
```

This does a basic check to see if any corruption has occurred. For a more advanced analysis, replace **/checkhealth** with **/scanhealth** (which can take several minutes or more). If corruption exists, then you can attempt the same command but with the **/restorehealth** option. That will attempt to restore the image. If it cannot, you might need to provide a Windows image. (You can download Windows 10 from Microsoft's website.) Once you have an image, you'll need to mount it by double-clicking it (or right-clicking it) in File Explorer. Then, locate the actual image installation file. In Windows 10 that is *X*:\sources\install.esd, where *X*: is the mounted drive letter. Older versions of Windows use the install.wim file. Then run the same command as before, but point DISM to the image file; for example:

```
dism /online /cleanup-image /restorehealth /source:X:\sources\
install.esd
```

Nowadays, it's better to first try the WinRE options—Reset your PC or Refresh your PC (depending on the version of Windows) before using DISM. DISM is really designed to prepare and service images for deployment to other systems. You can configure, append and apply images, but before you do so, they have to be mounted. Here's an example of mounting an image for servicing:

```
dism.exe /Mount-Image /ImageFile:F:\images\install.esd  /MountDir:G:
\mounted-images\Win10-service
```

In this example, we're using the Windows 10 install.esd file, but you can use other file types as well, such as install.wim for older versions of Windows, or .vhd and .vhdx files for virtual images. The current image file (install.esd) is stored in F:\images, and its mount point will be G:\mounted-images\ Win10-service.

This tool comes in handy if you need to add or remove drivers or settings to or from the overall image, or to enable new Windows features. This way, you don't have to create an entirely new image of Windows just because some additional desired features become available. After mounting the image, we can service the image with the **DISM** command and using parameters such as **/Add-Driver /DriverName:"C:\drvlib\driver.inf"**. It gets pretty in depth, and really at this point, it is Microsoft Windows Certification level content. For the A+ exam, you should know what DISM is, and be able to spot DISM command usage.

Older versions of Windows will need an updated DISM tool, which is included as part of the Windows ADK download mentioned in Chapter 24, "Operating System Installation."

> **Note**
>
> For more about DISM, see this link:
>
> https://docs.microsoft.com/en-us/windows-hardware/manufacture/desktop/what-is-dism

shutdown

The **shutdown** command is used to turn off the computer, restart it, send it to hibernate mode, log a person off, and so on. For example, if you want to shut down the computer after a short delay, you can type **shutdown /s**. For an immediate shutdown, you can type **shutdown /p**. The command can also be used programmatically to shut down systems at specific times while providing a pop-up window explaining the reason for the shutdown.

gpupdate and gpresult

Windows uses a set of policies to define rules that users and computers are effectively forced to follow. These policies can be viewed within the Local Group Policy Editor (**Run > gpedit.msc**) and a subset of that, the Local Security Policy (**Run > secpol.msc**). To properly work with these policies and tools, you should be running Windows Pro edition or higher.

You can also use commands to view and analyze that information. For example, the **gpresult** command displays the Resultant Set of Policy (RSoP) information for a user and computer (it is designed for remote users/computers). **Gpresult /R** will display some basic information about the local computer, the user, and what policies are running. You can view this information for remote computers and users by using the **/S** switch and the name of the remote system; for example, **gpresult /S** *computername* **/R**, where *computername* is whatever the target system's name is. To save the reported information, use the **/x** (for XML) or **/h** (for HTML) parameters.

In many cases, policy changes that were made in the Local Group Policy Editor or Local Security Policy won't take effect until the admin logs off and logs back on. Enter the **gpupdate** command, which can be used by itself or by specifying a remote system. When run, it updates all policies that have been modified on the target computer, without having to log off and log back on.

These commands can be run on Windows workstations or servers. But be very careful when using these. You have to be sure your policy changes are allowed, and you should consider scheduling them to run after work hours.

> **Note**
>
> For more information on **gpresult** and **gpupdate**, see the following links:
>
> https://docs.microsoft.com/en-us/windows-server/administration/windows-commands/gpresult
>
> https://docs.microsoft.com/en-us/windows-server/administration/windows-commands/gpupdate

> **ExamAlert**
>
> I know I just hit you with over two dozen commands, but try to memorize as many of them as you can! Try them on your computer, and write them down to force those little gray cells into action.

Cram Quiz

Answer these questions. The answers follow the last question. If you cannot answer these questions correctly, consider reading this section again until you can.

   1. Which command can copy multiple files and entire directory trees?

      ○ **A. copy**

      ○ **B. cut**

      ○ **C. paste**

      ○ **D. robocopy**

2. Which command will determine if protected system files have been overwritten and replace those files with the original version?

   ○ **A. chkdsk**
   ○ **B. msconfig**
   ○ **C. SFC**
   ○ **D. xcopy**

3. Which command will show the path of routers between your computer and a web server?

   ○ **A. ping**
   ○ **B. ipconfig**
   ○ **C. tracert**
   ○ **D. nbtstat**

4. You need to map a network drive to a share named data1 on a computer named Jupiter-Server. You want to use the J: drive letter. Which syntax should you use if you were to do this in the Command Prompt?

   ○ **A. net use J: \\Jupiter-Server\data1**
   ○ **B. net use J \Jupiter-Server\data1**
   ○ **C. net use Jupiter-Server\J\data1**
   ○ **D. net use J: \Jupiter-Server\data1**

5. You have been tasked with bringing the policies of a Windows 10 computer up to date. You won't be able to log off and back on, and you must use the Command Prompt. Which of the following tools should you use?

   ○ **A. shutdown**
   ○ **B. DISM**
   ○ **C. gpupdate**
   ○ **D. Local Security Policy**
   ○ **E. nslookup**

6. A user's WINWORD.EXE application is completely frozen. How can you determine the application's process ID and then terminate the frozen application process? (Select the two best answers.)

   ○ **A.** Use the **net user** command to identify the current PID of the application.
   ○ **B.** Use the **net user /delete** command to terminate the frozen process ID.
   ○ **C.** Run **tasklist** and record the process ID (PID).
   ○ **D.** Run **taskkill /PID** *number*.

Cram Quiz Answers

1. **D. robocopy** can copy an entire drive of information with just one command (including switches). **Xcopy** could also do the job, but **robocopy** takes the place of that.

2. **C. SFC** determines whether system files have been overwritten and replaces those files with the original versions. **Chkdsk** can check for errors and fix some errors but not when it concerns system files. **msconfig** is used to boot the system in a selective way and disable services and applications. **Xcopy** is used to copy large amounts of data exactly to a new location.

3. **C. Tracert** is used to run a trace between the local system and a remote destination. It shows all routers along the way. **Ping** is used to test connectivity to another system directly. **Ipconfig** will display the Internet Protocol configuration of the local computer. **Nbtstat** shows the name table cache and services running on the system.

4. **A.** You should use this syntax: **net use J: \\Jupiter-Server\Data1**. All other answers are incorrect. The Universal Naming Convention (UNC) is \\computername\sharename.

5. **C.** You should use **gpupdate** to bring the Windows 10 policies up to date. It can do this without the need for logging off and on again. The **shutdown** command is used to turn off or restart a computer. **DISM** is used to mount and service Windows image files. The Local Security Policy is where you can go to modify many policy settings (such as the password policy), but it is graphical. To enforce the changes made in the Local Security Policy, use the **gpupdate** command. **Nslookup** is used to query DNS servers to find out more information about hosts or domains (for instance, the IP address of a host computer on the Internet).

6. **C and D. Tasklist** shows all the processes running and each process is assigned a process identification number (PID). Run **tasklist** and record the PID of the frozen WINWORD.EXE application first. (Quick tip: to sort the results alphabetically, type **tasklist | sort**; the pipe | symbol shares the backslash key.) Then run **taskkill /PID *number*** of the WINWORD.EXE application to terminate the frozen app. A and B are invalid options as worded in the answer choices. The **net user** command will list the user accounts on the computer and **net user** with the **/delete** switch will remove a user account. But, listing and removing user accounts will not help you terminate a running process or application.

CHAPTER 26

Microsoft Operating System Features and Tools, Part 1

This chapter covers a portion of the following A+ 220-1002 exam objective:

▶ **1.5** – Given a scenario, use Microsoft operating system features and tools.

Now let's move into the graphical side of things. The Windows GUI is popular because users are familiar with it, and for many people its usage is intuitive, meaning it comes naturally. However, there are a lot of utilities, tools, and features for an administrator to know. In fact, there are so many utilities that I split this objective into two chapters. In this chapter we'll be covering some Administrative Tools, the System Configuration utility (MSConfig), and the Task Manager. This is important stuff, so let's not waste any time.

1.5 – Given a scenario, use Microsoft operating system features and tools

ExamAlert

This portion of **Objective 1.5** concentrates on administrative tools (such as the Device Manager, Services, and the Event Viewer); MSConfig; and the Task Manager.

Administrative Tools

The administrator (that's you) of a computer or network can access Administrative Tools from the Control Panel in any version of Windows. Alternatively, in Windows 10 you can go to **Start > Windows Administrative Tools**, and in Windows 7 you can go to

Start > All Programs > Administrative Tools. Of course, you can also use the Search tool. In addition, to get to the Administrative Tools directly, go to **Run** and type **control admintools**. You will find that different versions of Windows have different navigation paths to the same program. That's why I recommend getting in the habit of using the Run prompt and typing the executable name of the program or tool you want to access. It works the same way across different Windows platforms, and in the long run will save you time.

> **Note**
>
> For a table of the Run commands that we cover in this book, see this link:
>
> https://dprocomputer.com/blog/?p=3010

Some of the administrative tools are covered very briefly here, but most of those will be covered in more depth as we progress through the book. Either way, there are a lot of tools, so this is a big section. Let's take them one at a time.

Computer Management

There are a lot of tools used to configure advanced options for the computer. One example is Computer Management, which you will use quite often. It has many utilities loaded into one nice, little console window. Figure 26.1 shows an example of Computer Management.

FIGURE 26.1   **The Computer Management window**

Note this is a three-pane window. The left pane has all the modules that you might work on, such as the Event Viewer, Device Manager, and Disk Management. The middle pane shows the details of whatever you click in the left pane. The right pane provides additional actions, which are also available on the Menu bar. There are a few other ways to open this window, including:

- ▶ **In all versions of Windows:** Access the **Run** prompt and type **compmgmt.msc**. The extension .msc defines the file type as a Microsoft Management Console Snap-in Control file, also known as Microsoft Console.

- ▶ **In Windows 10 and 8:** Right-click **Start** and then click **Computer Management**.

- ▶ **In Windows 7:** Click **Start**, right-click **Computer**, and then select **Manage**.

> **ExamAlert**
>
> Know how to access the Computer Management console window.

MMC

Computer Management and other console windows can be grouped into one master console window known as the Microsoft Management Console (MMC) window. The MMC acts as a shell for these other console windows. You can also use it to control remote computers in addition to the local computer. And you can control what particular users see by changing the Console Mode. Finally, part of the beauty of the MMC is that it saves everything you added and remembers the last place you worked. To create an MMC window, open the **Run** prompt and type **MMC**. By default, the MMC window is empty.

> **Note**
>
> You will learn quickly that administrative functions should be carried out only by users who have administrative privileges. Even if you have administrative privileges, a pop-up User Account Control (UAC) window displays every time you try to access tools such as the MMC. Simply click Yes or Continue to open the program. If users don't have administrative capabilities, they will be blocked altogether or when the UAC window pops up, they won't be able to continue.

To add consoles (known as snap-ins), do the following:

1. On the Menu bar, click **File** and then click **Add/Remove Snap-in**. The Add or Remove Snap-ins window should appear.

2. Select the components you want from the left by highlighting them one at a time and clicking the **Add** button. In some cases, you will need to

select the local computer or a remote computer. Click **OK** when finished. These snap-ins should now be shown inside of the Console Root. Figure 26.2 shows an example MMC.

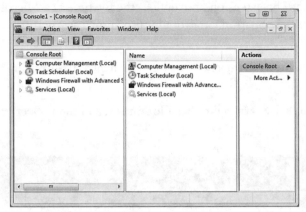

FIGURE 26.2   **The MMC**

3. Save the MMC. By default, this window prompts you to save to the Administrative Tools folder of the user who is currently logged on.

Device Manager

A computer probably has a dozen or more devices that all need love and attention. Taking care of a computer means managing these devices. The primary tool with which a technician does this is the Device Manager.

There are a few ways to open the Device Manager, for example:

▶ Open it from the Control Panel (in icons mode). You can get to the Device Manager from a lot of locations in the Control Panel, by the way.

▶ Open **Computer Management**, expand **System Tools**, and then select **Device Manager**. (Don't forget, you can also open Computer Management as a snap-in within an MMC.)

▶ Open the **Run** prompt and type **devmgmt.msc** (as always, my favorite).

When the Device Manager opens, as shown in Figure 26.3, you will notice that there are categories for each type of device. By expanding any one of these categories, you will see the specific devices that reside in your computer.

FIGURE 26.3 Device Manager

By right-clicking a specific device, you can update its driver; enable or disable it; uninstall it altogether; check for any hardware changes; or access additional properties, such as the driver details and resources used by the device. Figure 26.3 shows the resulting menu when right-clicking an Intel network adapter. These are the standard options, but your options might be more or less, depending on the device you have right-clicked.

> **ExamAlert**
>
> Know how to access the properties of a device, install drivers, and enable/disable devices in the Device Manager.

Some drivers are installed/updated through .exe files that are downloaded from the manufacturer's website. Others are installed from within the Device Manager; it can search for drivers automatically, or you can manually install a driver by browsing for the correct file (often, it's a file with an .inf extension). Windows attempts to install drivers automatically when it recognizes that a device has been added to the system. Usually, however, it is recommended that you use the driver disc that came with the device or that you download the latest version of the driver from the manufacturer's website, especially when dealing with video, audio, and hard drive controller drivers.

> **Note**
>
> Device Manager troubleshooting is covered in Chapter 36, "Troubleshooting Microsoft Windows."

Local Users and Groups

This utility can be accessed from the Administrative Tools list, and also from within **Computer Management > System Tools**. You can access it directly by going to **Run**, and typing **lusrmgr.msc**.

While you can add users within the Control Panel (or in Settings in Windows 10), Local Users and Groups is where you go if you want to take more control of user account management. From here, you can add users, change passwords, group those users together, or take advantage of the built-in Windows groups such as Backup Operators and Performance Monitor Users.

Local Security Policy

This is where you make the rules!—or configure the rules as put forth by your organization. You can access this from **Run** by typing **secpol.msc**. Here you can configure the policies for passwords, account lockout, encryption keys, software restriction, and much, much more. I usually add Local Security Policy as a snap-in to my MMC. The content within the LSP is a subset of the Local Group Policy Editor content, which you can access from **Run > gpedit.msc**. We'll be revisiting both of these in the security section of this book.

Performance Monitor

There are several tools you can use to track the performance of a Windows-based computer. The Performance Monitor is an extensive program that can track how much your devices are utilized; for example, what percentage of the processor is used or how much RAM is currently being accessed. It uses real-time ActiveX graphs to track usage, and can log the information for later viewing. It can be accessed from **Run > perfmon.exe**. Figure 26.4 shows an example.

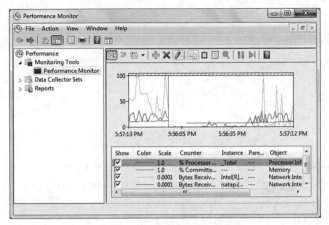

FIGURE 26.4 **Performance Monitor in Windows**

By working with Performance Monitor, you can track the usage of any device in the computer (known as objects) and you can track it using a variety of measurements (known as counters). By default, this screen tracks only the CPU. By clicking the + sign toward the top of the window, you can add devices to track—and in myriad ways. In Figure 26.4, I added the default counters for memory and the network adapter card. The highest spikes are from the network adapter; at the time of this monitor, it is sending and receiving a lot of data over the Internet. The second highest levels are from the processor, which in running several different applications simultaneously.

Information can be viewed in different formats, such as line charts and histograms, and can also be viewed and saved in Report view. They can be exported as well. However, any objects that are added in this program are not saved when you close the window. But you can configure the program so that it saves your additions; enter the MMC. From an MMC, a user in Windows can add the Performance Monitor. You can also use the System Monitor Control snap-in, which effectively *is* the Performance Monitor; it is one of the ActiveX controls that can be added to the MMC. In addition, you can add Performance Logs and Alerts to log your findings and alert you to any changes or tripped thresholds. The MMC saves its contents and remembers the last place you were working in, which works great if you will be analyzing the same things day in and day out.

The Performance Monitor (and similar Windows applications) can tell you a lot about the functionality of your computer. When troubleshooting why a certain piece of hardware isn't living up to its reputation, the Performance Monitor can be invaluable.

> **Note**
>
> Other tools that can be used to track resource usage include the Resource Monitor (**Run > resmon.exe**) and the Performance tab of the Task Manager, though these are not as thorough as the Performance Monitor, nor do they have the ability to save the tracked resource usage.

Services

The Services console window is where you go to start, stop, and restart services—such as the Print Spooler—as well as configure their startup type. For example, if the Windows Firewall service was interfering with another application, you could stop the service from here and see if that fixes the problem (at least temporarily). We'll be covering this more during the Windows troubleshooting section of the book. You can access it directly from **Run > services.msc**, and it is also available within Computer Management.

Task Scheduler

The Task Scheduler can run particular programs, send e-mails, or display messages at a scheduled time (or times) designated by the user. You can open it either from Administrative Tools, by going to **Run** and typing **taskschd.msc**, or by using the Search option and typing **schedule**. Aside from basic scheduling, you can specify certain conditions and triggers that cause a task to run, and you can tell the Task Scheduler which actions to take when the task starts. Plus, there are a slew of built-in preprogrammed tasks in the Task Scheduler Library—from memory diagnostics to registry backups. Instead of re-creating the wheel, consider using one of these tasks to help automate the process. Some of these built-in tasks are enabled by default. Try creating some tasks yourself, such as memory diagnostic, registry backup, and time synchronization.

Print Management

This utility allows you to install, configure, and troubleshoot multiple printers, drivers, ports, print servers, and more, all from a single window. It's a must for technicians that deal with company printers, and can be added to the MMC (for local and remote systems), and can be accessed directly from **Run > printmanagement.msc**.

Windows Memory Diagnostics

In Chapter 10, "RAM and Storage," we talked about several ways to troubleshoot RAM. One way is to use Windows Memory Diagnostics. You might need to check your memory while within Windows, or perhaps Windows won't boot, and you want to check the memory from bootup. Because of this, there are a couple of other ways to open this tool: by accessing **Run** and typing **mdsched**, or by booting to the Windows Recovery Environment (Windows RE), which we will cover in Chapter 36.

If you do this from within Windows, a pop-up window asks you if you want to restart the computer immediately and run the check or wait until the next time the computer is restarted. The Windows RE (Startup Settings) method starts the check immediately. The test checks if there are any physical issues with the RAM and attempts to identify which memory module is causing the problem. When done, it restarts the computer automatically. If an error is found, it displays after you log back on. You can also view errors in the System log of the Event Viewer. To find results quickly, right-click the **System** log, click **Find**, and enter **MemoryDiagnostics-Results**. If there are errors with a particular stick of memory, try removing it, cleaning it and the RAM slot, and reseating it. Run the test again; if you get the same results, replace the RAM.

Windows Defender Firewall with Advanced Security

The Windows Defender Firewall with Advanced Security is part of the built-in firewall designed to block intrusion to the operating system. The main difference between this and the basic Windows Defender Firewall within the Control Panel is the ability to create rules for incoming and outgoing traffic. You can open the basic firewall directly from **Run > firewall.cpl**, and the Windows Defender Firewall with Advanced Security directly from **Run > wf.msc**. We'll be discussing both in more depth in the security section of this book.

Event Viewer

Applications are a boon and a bane to mankind. They serve a purpose, but sometimes they are prone to failure. The operating system itself can cause you grief as well by underperforming, locking up, or causing other intermittent issues. One good tool for analyzing applications and the system is the Event Viewer.

The Event Viewer tells a technician a lot about the status of the operating system and programs. It notifies of any informational events or audits, warns about possible issues, and displays errors as they occur. Aside from being within Administrative Tools, it can be accessed from the System Tools node in the

Computer Management console window, or by typing **eventvwr.msc** in the Run or Search prompts. Try opening it on your system!

Information, auditing entries, warnings, and errors are stored in several log files within the Windows Logs folder. Of those, there are three main log files that you should know for the exam:

▶ **System:** The System log contains information, warnings, and errors about hardware, device drivers, system files, and so on. This log deals primarily with the operating system.

▶ **Application:** The Application log contains events about programs that are built into Windows, such as the Command Prompt and File Explorer/Windows Explorer, and might contain information about applications that have been loaded after the operating system was installed.

▶ **Security:** The Security log holds information that was gathered for auditing and security purposes; for example, it might log who logged on to the computer or who tried to gain access to a particular file.

An event listed in a log file can be viewed by double-clicking it. Events are organized into four categories:

▶ **Information:** Indicated by an "i" in a circle. This tells you basic information about a service starting or an application that ran successfully. The log files are usually chock-full of these as part of the normal operation of the system.

▶ **Warning:** Indicated by an exclamation point ("!") within a yellow triangle. This might be a message telling you an installation did not complete or a service timed out. You should check for these now and again and investigate them if nothing else is pressing.

▶ **Error:** Indicated by an "!" in a red circle. This means that something failed or has been corrupted, a service failed to start, and so on. Errors should be investigated right away.

▶ **Audit Success:** Indicated by a gold-colored key; these entries are located within the Security log file. They track what a user attempts to accomplish within the operating system. For example, if auditing was turned on for a specific folder and a person attempted to access that folder, a security event would be written to the log, especially if the person was denied access. Auditing entries are maintained by organizations so that they can trace what happened to deleted or modified data.

You can find more information about a specific error code by either typing the code number for the event or typing the description into Microsoft Help and Support: https://support.microsoft.com. Sometimes you can find out information about these types of services just by running a search, but it is best to go to the source: Microsoft. You never know when an error can occur, so the Event Viewer logs should be reviewed regularly. Entire logs can be erased by right-clicking the log file (for example, System) and selecting Clear Log. The system asks if you want to save the log for future viewing. By right-clicking a log and selecting Properties, you can modify the maximum size of the log and disable logging altogether.

> **ExamAlert**
>
> Be able to describe the System, Application, and Security log files as well as the information, warning, error, and audit success events.

Component Services

Component Services is a snap-in you can add to the MMC. It allows you to configure and administer three types of components: the Component Object Model (COM), COM+ Applications, and the Distributed Transaction Coordinator (DTC).

COM is a software interface used to allow interprocess communications and dynamic object creation by using different programming languages. The term COM includes the following technologies: ActiveX controls (such as the real-time charts found in the Task Manager), Object Linking and Embedding (OLE databases), COM+ (an extension to COM, providing better memory and processor management), and DCOM (programming as it relates to networked computers).

The Distributed Transaction Coordinator is a component of Windows that uses a transaction manager to coordinate information between databases, file systems, and other resources. It works in conjunction with COM and .NET architectures.

For more information on Component Services administration, visit http://technet.microsoft.com/en-us/library/cc731901.aspx.

If certain dynamic-link libraries (DLLs) or ActiveX controls need to be troubleshot (for example, ones that work with Internet Explorer), they can be registered or unregistered within the Windows registry by manipulating them with the **regsvr32** command. For example, to register a sample ActiveX control, you would open the Command Prompt (as an administrator) and type

regsvr32 sample.ocx. Unregistering requires the **/u** parameter. To register a .DLL file, you would type **regsvr32 msi.dll**, replacing **msi** with whatever DLL you wish to register or unregister.

> **Note**
>
> More information on regsvr32can be found at:
>
> https://support.microsoft.com/en-us/help/249873/how-to-use-the-regsvr32-tool-and-troubleshoot-regsvr32-error-messages

Data Sources (ODBC)

Open Database Connectivity (ODBC) is an interface used within the C programming language to access database management systems. It is primarily used by Microsoft for its SQL database systems but can also be utilized by Microsoft Access Databases, dBASE, or Excel files. Different applications within Windows and from third-party vendors might make use of one of these technologies and will, therefore, need ODBC. If you want to make configuration changes to ODBC, you can access it by going to Administrative Tools and then clicking **ODBC Data Sources**. That opens the ODBC Data Source Administrator. From here, you can add or remove Database Source Names (DSNs), which are data structures that describe a connection to a data source. DSNs include the name of the data source, the folder it is located in, the driver used to access the data source, and so on. For example, if you wanted to run a program in Windows 7 that was reliant on a SQL Server database, or if you just wanted to make a connection to a SQL database, you would need to add the Microsoft SQL Server data source to the User DSN list. The name of the SQL Server would be required to complete the connection. For more information on ODBC in Windows, visit https://technet.microsoft.com/en-US/library/ms187039(v=sql.105).aspx.

> **Note**
>
> COM, ODBC, and regsvr32 deal with in-depth system configuration and application developing within Windows, going a bit beyond what a PC technician will usually be required to perform. That's why I put them at the end of the "Administrative Tools" section. However, Component Services and Data Sources are listed on the CompTIA A+ objectives, so you should at least know what they are and how to access them in Windows.

System Configuration/MSConfig

MSConfig is the commonly used name for the System Configuration tool. It can help to analyze and troubleshoot various things, from operating system startup issues to application and service problems. To open MSConfig in Windows 10, go to **Start > Windows Administrative Tools** and click **System Configuration**, or you can open it in any version of Windows by opening the **Run** prompt and typing **msconfig.exe** (or simply **msconfig**). A program similar to Figure 26.5 should display.

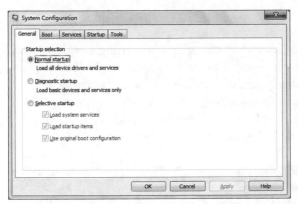

FIGURE 26.5 **System Configuration (MSConfig) application**

This is an excellent troubleshooting tool that has multiple tabs that enable you to do the following:

▶ **General:** You can configure the system for diagnostic or selective startup. This helps to troubleshoot devices or services that are failing.

▶ **Boot:** You can modify OS bootup settings, such as using Safe boot, logging the boot process, and booting without video. If you have multiple operating systems, you can change the order and choose which to set as default (instead of configuring the BCD file). Also, clicking the **Advanced options** button lets you choose things such as how much memory you want to use and what port to use if you need to output debugging information.

▶ **Services:** This tab lists the services and their current status. You can enable or disable them from here (it requires a computer restart). However, you can't start or stop them. To do that, you would need to go to the Services section of Computer Management or do it from within the Command Prompt. The beauty of this tab is the speed at which you can enable/disable services compared to using other options in Windows.

▶ **Startup:** In Windows 10 and 8, the Startup tab still exists but displays "To manage Startup items, use the Startup section of Task Manager" and it provides a link to open the Task Manager. In Windows 7 it displays the various applications that start when the computer boots up that can be disabled and enabled.

▶ **Tools:** This tab lists a lot of the common utilities you might use in Windows and allows you to launch them from there. As a launching point for programs we have used a lot (Computer Management, System Properties, Task Manager, Command Prompt, and so on), this tab can be a real time-saver.

Consider MSConfig as a time-saver when changing boot settings, working with services, and troubleshooting the system. One word of caution: Be sure to reset MSConfig to the regular settings when you finish using it. For example, if a user complains about a system booting to Safe Mode every time or other similar problems in which the user doesn't have full access to the system, MSConfig might need to be reconfigured to Normal startup on the General tab.

> **ExamAlert**
>
> Know the reasons to use MSConfig.

Task Manager

One simple, yet effective, tool to use when analyzing the computer is the Task Manager. There are several ways to open the Task Manager, including

▶ Right-click on the taskbar and select **Task Manager**.

▶ Press **Ctrl+Alt+Del** and select **Task Manager**.

▶ Open the **Run** prompt and type **taskmgr**.

▶ Press **Ctrl+Shift+Esc**.

The Task Manager gives you the ability to analyze your processor and memory performance in real time; this can be done from the Performance tab, as shown on the left in Figure 26.6, and the Processes tab, shown on the right. You can see on the Performance tab that the CPU usage fluctuates and is currently at 10 percent, but more importantly, the Processes tab shows that the Firefox and Chrome browsers are using the bulk of the memory on that system.

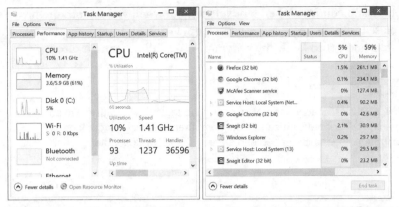

FIGURE 26.6   **Windows Task Manager showing the Performance and Processes tabs**

Optimizing the system can be as simple as shutting down programs. In Windows 10 and 8, apps are shut down in the Processes tab. In Windows 7, programs can be shut down in the Applications tab. But sometimes you need to shut down the underlying process. For example, the Processes tab in Figure 26.6 shows all the processes that are running and the amount of CPU and RAM resources they are using individually. A process that is hoarding resources can be stopped by right-clicking it and then selecting **End Task** in Windows 10/8, and **End Process** in Windows 7. (This can also be done in the Details tab of Windows 10/8.) Keep in mind that this shuts down only the process or application temporarily. If it is designated to do so, it will turn back on when the computer is rebooted.

> **ExamAlert**
>
> Understand how to open the Task Manager, how to read its Performance tab, and how to end processes and applications.

The Task Manager has several other tabs. For example, the Users tab shows the resources being used by each user. Normally, on a Windows client computer, this will only show the currently logged-in user. However, if another user is listed, and that account is using resources, then that user can be signed off from here (just right-click the username and select **Sign off**). This way, the resources are freed up. For example, if a remote user was connected previously, and chose to disconnect instead of logging off, then it will show that user as "Disconnected," but it might still be using memory resources because the user left some programs opened before disconnecting. This is common with Remote Desktop sessions. That's the difference between *disconnecting* and *logging off*—when you disconnect, the programs and resources are left open, allowing you to reconnect later and continue where you left off; but when you log off, the programs are closed, and the resources are freed up. Work with the Task Manager on your system and get to know the program—you will be using it often.

> **Note**
>
> The Windows 7 Task Manager has a Networking tab that shows statistics relating to each of the network adapters present in the computer, including percentage of network utilization and the link speed and state of the network adapter.

Cram Quiz

Answer these questions. The answers follow the last question. If you cannot answer these questions correctly, consider reading this chapter again until you can.

1. Which of the following should be typed in the Run prompt to open the Device Manager?

   ○ **A. MMC**

   ○ **B. secpol.msc**

   ○ **C. CMD**

   ○ **D. devmgmt.msc**

2. Which of the following would you use to track what percentage of resources are being used?

   ○ **A. devmgmt.msc**

   ○ **B. eventvwr.msc**

   ○ **C. systempropertiesadvanced.exe**

   ○ **D. perfmon.exe**

3. Where can a user go to start and stop services in Windows? (Select all that apply.)

   ○ **A.** MSConfig

   ○ **B.** Task Manager

   ○ **C.** Computer Management

   ○ **D.** Command Prompt

4. Which log file in the Event Viewer contains information concerning auditing?

   ○ **A.** System

   ○ **B.** Application

   ○ **C.** Local Users and Groups

   ○ **D.** Security

5. You are preparing to troubleshoot a system that is having some driver issues. Which of the following tools should you use to configure the system to boot safely?

- ○ **A.** Event Viewer
- ○ **B.** Performance Monitor
- ○ **C.** Local Users and Groups
- ○ **D.** System Configuration
- ○ **E.** MMC

6. Which tool can run particular programs at a time designated by the user?

- ○ **A.** Services
- ○ **B.** Task Scheduler
- ○ **C.** Event Viewer
- ○ **D.** Windows Memory Diagnostics

Cram Quiz Answers

1. **D. Devmgmt.msc** is the Microsoft console window known as Device Manager. **MMC** opens up a new blank Microsoft Management Console. **Secpol.msc** opens the Local Security Policy window. **CMD** opens the Command Prompt.

2. **D. Perfmon.exe** opens the Performance Monitor utility, which is used to graphically track the resources that are being used on a computer such as CPU, RAM, and so on. You could also use the Task Manager > Performance tab to track resource usage (but without the ability to save the data), as well as the Resource Monitor. **Devmgmt.msc** opens the Device Manager. **Eventvwr.msc** opens the Event Viewer. **Systempropertiesadvanced.exe** (if typed in the Run prompt or Command Prompt) opens the System Properties dialog box to the Advanced tab.

3. **B, C, and D.** You can start/stop services in the **Task Manager > Services** tab; **Computer Management > Services** section; and in the Command Prompt using the **net start**, **net stop**, **sc start**, and **sc stop** commands. MSConfig is not a correct answer because it lets you enable/disable services, but does not *start/ stop* them.

4. **D.** The Security log contains information about auditing and other security events. The System log contains information about the OS and system files. The Application log contains information about built-in Windows programs and some third-party programs. Local Users and Groups is the administrative tool used to add people and systems to the local computer.

5. **D.** Use the System Configuration utility (MSConfig) to configure the system to boot safely by going to the **Boot** tab and check marking the **Safe boot** option, as shown in Figure 26.7. In the figure it is configured as Minimal (the default), meaning that the system will boot with a minimal set of drivers and programs; but there are several other options listed there. Make sure you go through the Windows utilities and all the tabs—know what everything does!

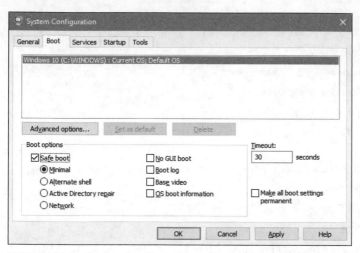

FIGURE 26.7   System Configuration utility displaying the Boot tab

6. **B.** The Task Scheduler can run particular programs at a scheduled time
(or times) designated by the user. The Services console window is where you go
to start, stop, and restart services. The Event Viewer is used to find out messages
about the system, applications, and security developments. Windows Memory
Diagnostics is used to analyze the computer's RAM for errors.

CHAPTER 27

Microsoft Operating System Features and Tools, Part 2

> **This chapter covers a portion of the following A+ 220-1002 exam objective:**
>
> ▶ **1.5** – Given a scenario, use Microsoft operating system features and tools.
>
> There is so much to discuss when it comes to Windows features and utilities. That's why I split this objective into two chapters. In this chapter we'll complete the objective by describing Disk Management, and then covering a slew of system utilities. Onward!

1.5 – Given a scenario, use Microsoft operating system features and tools

> **ExamAlert**
>
> This portion of **Objective 1.5** concentrates on Disk Management and system utilities (such as Explorer, System Restore, and Regedit).

Disk Management

The information in this section applies to working with new drives that are designated for operating system installation, as well as drives that have already been installed to. Either way, the concepts of partitioning and formatting remain the same. Regardless of what you are doing with the drive, the proper order for drive preparation is to partition the drive, format it, and then copy files to your heart's delight. However, sometimes you might also need to initialize additional drives within Windows; this would be done before partitioning. All of these things can be done within the Disk Management program.

The Disk Management Utility

The Disk Management utility within Computer Management is the GUI-based application for analyzing and configuring hard drives (**Run > diskmgmt.msc**). You can do a lot from here, including the following:

▶ **Initialize a new drive:** A secondary hard drive installed in a computer might not be seen by File Explorer/Windows Explorer immediately. To make it accessible, locate the drive (for example, it might be referred to as Disk 1), right-click where it says Disk 1, Disk 2, and such, and then select **Initialize Disk**. When you install an OS to the only drive in the system, it is initialized automatically.

▶ **Create volumes, partitions, and logical drives:** When creating these, Windows generally refers to them simply as volumes, but you will also see the terms *partition* and *logical drive*. Regardless, you must right-click the area with the black header (which identifies it as unallocated). Figure 27.1 shows an example of creating a new simple volume by right-clicking that area.

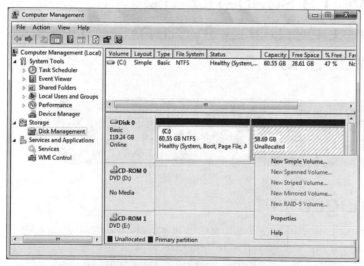

FIGURE 27.1   Creating a volume within unallocated disk space

▶ **Format volumes:** When formatting, select the file system (NTFS usually) and whether to do a quick format. Remember: quick formats are usually the way to go, but if you leave this option unchecked (for a full format), it will take much longer, and could reduce the lifespan of the drive. When you format the partition, you must select a drive letter, such as C: or E: or F:, and so on. You can change drive letters in the future, but it's a good idea to plan it out beforehand. You can use up to Z:, but you probably won't need to; regardless, keep a few open in the case that you need to map a network drive in the future.

> **Note**
>
> WARNING: ALL DATA WILL BE ERASED during the format procedure.

▶ **Make partitions active:** Partitions need to be set to active if you want to install an operating system to them.

▶ **Convert basic disks to dynamic:** Basic disks can have only simple volumes or regular partitions/logical drives. If you want to create a spanned, striped, mirrored, or RAID-5 volume, you need to convert the disk to dynamic. This is done by right-clicking the drive where it says Disk 0 or Disk 1, for example, and selecting **Convert to Dynamic Disk**. It's highly recommended that you back up your data before attempting this configuration.

▶ **Extend, shrink, and split volumes:** A volume can also be extended, shrunk, or split if you have converted it to a dynamic disk. Just about any volume can be shrunk or split, but to extend a volume, you need available unallocated space on the drive. By shrinking a volume that takes up the entire hard drive, you can also ultimately split that partition into two pieces, allowing you to better organize where the OS is stored and where the data files are stored.

You might ask: What is the difference between a partition and a volume? The partitions are physical (and logical) divisions of the drive. A volume is actually any space among one or more drives that receives a drive letter.

You can also see the drive at the top of the window shown in Figure 27.1 and its status. For example, the C: partition is healthy. You also see it is a System partition, which tells you that the OS is housed there. It also shows the capacity of the drive, free space, and percentage of the drive used. What's more, this section tells you if the drive is basic or dynamic or if it has failed. In some cases, you might see "foreign" status. This means that a dynamic disk has been moved from another computer (with another Windows operating system) to the local computer and it cannot be accessed properly. To fix this and access the drive, add the drive to your computer's system configuration. This is done by right-clicking the drive and then clicking **Import Foreign Disks**. Any existing volumes on the foreign drive become visible and accessible when you import the drive.

Mount Points and Mounting a Drive

You can also "mount" drives in Disk Management. A mounted drive is a drive that is mapped to an empty folder within a volume that has been formatted as NTFS. Instead of using drive letters, mounted drives use drive paths. This is a good solution for when you need to work with disc or OS images. It's also helpful in the uncommon case that you need more than 26 drives in your computer (because you are not limited to the letters in the alphabet). Mounted drives can also provide more space for temporary files and can allow you to move folders to different drives if space runs low on the current drive. To mount a drive:

1. Right-click the partition or volume you want to mount and select **Change Drive Letters and Paths**.

2. In the displayed window, click **Add**.

3. Then browse to the *empty* folder you want to mount the volume to, and click **OK** for both windows.

As shown in Figure 27.2, the DVD-ROM drive has been mounted within the Data folder on the F: volume on the hard drive. It shows that it is a mounted volume and shows the location of the folder (which is the mount point) and the target of the mount point, which is the DVD drive containing a Windows DVD. To remove the mount point, just go back to Disk Management, right-click the mounted volume, select **Change Drive Letters and Paths**, and then select Remove. Remember that the folder you want to use as a mount point must be empty, and it must be within an NTFS volume.

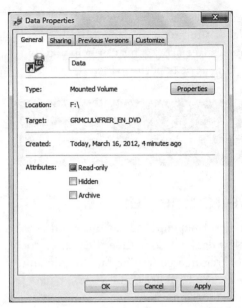

FIGURE 27.2 **An empty NTFS folder acting as a mount point**

Storage Spaces

Windows 8 and newer, as well as Windows Server 2012 and newer, incorporate a technology called Storage Spaces. This enables the Windows user to virtualize storage by grouping physical hard drives into storage pools and then creating virtual drives called storage spaces from the available capacity in the storage pools. The physical drives (or arrays of drives) need to be SATA or Serial Attached SCSI (SAS). The Storage Spaces tool can be accessed by typing **spaces** in the Search field or by going to **Control Panel > System and Security > Storage Spaces**. From here, multiple drives can be selected and used collectively as a "pool." From within that pool you can then create a storage space. There are four main types of storage spaces that can be selected:

▶ *Simple*, which is similar to RAID 0 and has no fault tolerance

▶ *Two-way mirror*, which is similar to RAID 1 mirroring

▶ *Three-way mirror*, which is similar to RAID 10

▶ *Parity*, which is similar to RAID 5

The concept is similar to RAID in that you either are looking to increase performance or, more likely, fault tolerance. But remember, a hardware-based RAID solution is usually the more effective option, but it will all depend on your environment. If you do use Storage Spaces, consider downloading the Diskspd Utility from Microsoft TechNet (or finding a similar tool), which can test the speed and efficiency of the storage space array. This can help you to verify quantitatively if your array is working at peak performance.

> **ExamAlert**
>
> Know that drives are grouped together into a storage pool. The storage capacity from that pool is then used to create storage spaces.

Optimize Drives/Disk Defragmenter

Over time, data is written to the drive and subsequently erased, over and over again, leaving gaps in the drive space. New data will sometimes be written to multiple areas of the drive in a broken or fragmented fashion by filling in any blank areas it can find. When this happens, the hard drive must work much harder to find the data it needs—spinning more and starting and stopping more (in general, more mechanical movement). The more the drive has to access this fragmented data, the shorter its lifespan becomes due to mechanical wear and tear. Also, the computer will run slower and continually get worse until the problem is fixed. A common indicator of this is when the hard drive LED constantly shows activity. When this happens, you need to rearrange the file sectors so that they are contiguous—you need to defragment!

Defragmenting the drive can be done with Microsoft's Optimize Drives utility (Disk Defragmenter in Windows 7), with the command line utility **defrag.exe**, or with third-party programs. The Optimize Drives utility is actually listed within the Administrative Tools in Windows 10 and 8 as Defragment and Optimize Drives, but when it opens, the title will simply say Optimize Drives. You can also search for the utility by typing **defragment** in the Search field, or open it directly via **Run > dfrgui.exe**. In Windows 7, navigate to **Start > All Programs > Accessories > System Tools > Disk Defragmenter**.

This program can be used to analyze your drives for fragmentation, remove fragmentation, and schedule periodic examinations. You can also access this utility by right-clicking a volume in Explorer, selecting **Properties**, then clicking the **Tools** tab, and finally clicking **Optimize** (or **Defragment now** in Windows 7). Either way, the ultimate goal is to make the data contiguous—moving and reorganizing it so that it is not fragmented, or at least, *as* fragmented.

If you are using the Disk Defragmenter program, you need 15 percent free space on the volume you want to defrag. If you have less than that, you need to force the operation by using the command-line option **defrag -f**.

ExamAlert

Know how to access the Optimize Drives/Disk Defragmenter utility in Windows, and know the **defrag** command in the Command Prompt.

If you do initiate a defrag, it could take a while, so it's best to do this off-hours. After it completes, a restart is recommended.

System Utilities

This CompTIA A+ objective covers a bit of a hodge-podge of system utilities, from basic utilities such as Notepad to advanced utilities such as the Registry Editor. We'll start with some basic ones, and progress through the section to the more advanced ones. As usual, take it slow, and try to digest them one at a time.

Notepad

This is Windows' built-in text editor. You can find it by typing **notepad** in the Search field or the Run prompt. It's also located in Windows 10 at **Start > Windows Accessories**. While you can format the text to a certain extent, this is the tool to use when you need to write, or copy, plain text with no formatting. It can also be helpful for creating scripts and batch files, or doing web developing, though I would recommend other tools for those jobs. (Feel free to contact me at my website to ask what tools I currently use.)

Note

In the old days of Windows, you could edit text within the command line with the **edit** command. That was when you could use the command line called command.com. However, that version of the command line was replaced by cmd.exe long ago, so the built-in command-line text editor is no longer. However, you can install third-party tools to edit text in the Command Prompt, or use the PowerShell.

Explorer

You probably use Explorer quite often; it is the default file browser in Windows. Windows 10 and 8 call it File Explorer, whereas Windows 7 and earlier call it Windows Explorer. To keep it simple, we'll just call it "Explorer" and that is how you can access it from the Run prompt (**Run > explorer.exe**). You can also get to it by pressing **Windows+E**. In Windows 7 you can navigate to it by going to **Start > All Programs > Accessories > Windows Explorer**. In Windows 10, navigate to **Start > Windows System > File Explorer**.

Most importantly, users work with Explorer to open, move, copy, and delete files and folders. These files and folders can be accessed within local drives and mapped network drives, and by browsing the network. Explorer includes a group of folders associated with each user account on the computer, including Desktop, Documents, Downloads, Music, Pictures, and Videos. These are displayed at the top of the left pane, but they are logically stored within C:\Users*%userprofile%*, where *%userprofile%* equals the name of the currently logged-in user. Under that you see all the volumes on the computer; for instance C:, D:, and E:, including local drives and mapped network drives. Then you see the Network section, which is used for browsing. (In some versions of Windows, you will see the HomeGroup option, though that has been removed from Windows 10.)

Interesting note: Explorer is a morphing tool. It changes depending on what you click. For example, in Windows 10 if you click the C: drive in the left pane, you will see options at the top of the screen including Copy, Paste, Delete, and so on. However, if you click **This PC**, the options change to things such as Properties, Map network drive, and Manage. If you click **Network**, you get options that deal with networking, such as the Network and Sharing Center. So, Explorer becomes a great place to go to initiate all kinds of different work with files, and has plenty of links to other places where you would configure Windows.

Windows Update

As with any OS, Windows should be updated regularly. Microsoft recognizes deficiencies in the OS—and possible exploits that could occur—and releases patches to increase OS performance and protect the system. These patches can be downloaded and installed automatically or manually depending on the user's needs, or the organization's needs, and are controlled via the Windows Update program.

Windows Update can be accessed in Windows 10 by going to **Settings > Update and Security > Windows Update** (or by searching for it). In Windows 8 and 7 it is located within the Control Panel. There is no executable name for it, because Windows Update is a service, not an application. However, you can update the system from the command line if necessary.

From within Windows Update you can decide how updates will be delivered and installed. In Windows 7 and 8 you can disable checking for updates altogether, but with Windows 10 you can only defer updates—unless you do one of the following: stop and disable the Windows Update service in the Services console window (or in the command line); disable it with the Group Policy Editor; disable it within the registry; or otherwise turn it off programmatically. Sometimes, larger organizations will do this—in a more enterprise manner—so that Windows is not randomly updating computers on the network and causing functionality issues between systems.

At times, individual Windows updates, or the Windows Update program itself, can fail. To troubleshoot an issue, use the Windows Update Troubleshooter program, which can be downloaded from Microsoft's website. Also, view the Windowsupdate.log file (located in %windir%) to see the failure errors. See the following links for more information about Windows Update troubleshooting and a list of error codes:

https://docs.microsoft.com/en-us/windows/deployment/update/
windows-update-troubleshooting

https://docs.microsoft.com/en-us/windows/deployment/update/
windows-update-error-reference

Patch Management

Larger organizations with a lot of computers will be concerned with *patch management*, which is the patching of many systems from a central location. Microsoft updates can be pushed out to multiple clients from a Windows Server system with System Center Configuration Manager (SCCM) or Windows Server Update Services (WSUS). Third-party tools can be used as well. The patch management process should be considered thoughtfully. Typically, a patch management strategy will consist of four steps: planning, testing, implementing, and auditing. So before actually pushing the updates out, you should carefully consider what you will be updating and test it thoroughly on a couple of systems on a separate, isolated test network. After you implement the patch across the network, you should analyze whether the patch took to the systems, and audit the systems periodically. By using this four-step process, you can minimize errors in Windows updating within the enterprise.

System Information/Msinfo32

Another tool that Windows offers for device analysis is the System Information tool. This can be accessed in all versions of Windows by opening the Run prompt and typing **msinfo32.exe**. (Typing **.exe** actually isn't necessary by default.) From here, you can view and analyze information about the hardware components, the software environment, and the hardware resources used, but you cannot make any changes. You view this information for the local computer and for remote computers as well by typing the name or IP address of the system you want to analyze.

System Restore

This tool can be used to create a snapshot of the state of the operating system and store it for later retrieval. It can be very helpful when troubleshooting the system.

System Restore can fix issues caused by defective hardware or software by reverting to an earlier point in time. Registry changes made by hardware or software are reversed in an attempt to force the computer to work the way it did previously. Restore points can be created manually and are also created automatically by the operating system before new updates, applications, or hardware is installed.

To create a restore point in Windows:

1. Go to **Control Panel > All Control Panel Items > System**, and then click the **System Protection** link. This displays the System Protection tab of the System Properties dialog box, as shown in Figure 27.3. Alternatively, you could go to **Run** and type **systempropertiesprotection**.

FIGURE 27.3   The System Protection tab of the System Properties dialog box

2. Click the **Create** button. This opens the System Protection dialog box.

3. Type a name for the restore point, and then click **Create**.

If System Restore is not available, it might be turned off. There are several reasons why a person might turn it off (for example, if the system had been scanned for viruses recently).

To enable or disable System Restore in Windows, click the **Configure** button within the System Protection tab of the System Properties dialog box. From here you would click the radio button for **Turn on system protection** in Windows 10 and 8. In Windows 7, you would click **Restore system settings and previous versions of files** (on the system drive, usually C:) or you would click **Restore previous versions of files** (on other drives containing data only).

System Restore is kind of like using a time machine (if one actually existed). It allows you to reset the computer to an earlier configuration—hopefully, one that functioned properly. To actually restore the computer to an earlier point in time, just click the **System Restore** button on the System Properties/ System Protection dialog box and then follow the instructions. But beware, some applications might be removed, and drivers might be uninstalled.

> **Note**
>
> If the system won't boot normally, you can also attempt to run System Restore from Safe Mode or you can use the Windows Recovery Environment/System Recovery Options. We'll talk about those troubleshooting techniques in the troubleshooting section of this book.

> **ExamAlert**
>
> Understand how to enable and disable System Restore, how to create restore points, and how to restore the system to an earlier point in time.

Remote Desktop Connection/MSTSC

Remote Desktop Connection is a Microsoft tool used to control and work on remote Windows systems. It displays the remote OS in a window on your desktop. It works as a client and a host in Windows Pro and higher editions, but only as a client in Home editions. The executable name is **mstsc**, so you can use that in the Run prompt or command line to open the program, and to connect directly to systems. We'll discuss this more in Chapter 42, "Basic Scripting and Remote Access Technologies." Remote Desktop Connection is included in Windows, but you can also download a more robust and organized version of the program called Remote Desktop Connection Manager. Technicians often simply refer to these as RDP, which is short for Remote Desktop Protocol—the underlying networking protocol that supports the program.

DxDiag

When it comes to making sure your devices work properly, one of the most important devices is the video card; a utility you can use to analyze and diagnose the video card is the DirectX Diagnostic Tool (also known as DxDiag). To run this, open the **Run** prompt and type **dxdiag**. Depending on the version of Windows and the configuration, the utility might ask if you want it to check whether the corresponding drivers are digitally signed. A digitally signed driver means it is one that has been verified by Microsoft as compatible with the operating system. After the utility opens, you can find out what version of DirectX you are running. DirectX is a group of multimedia programs that enhance video and audio, including Direct3D, DirectDraw, DirectSound, and so on. With the DxDiag tool, you can view all the DirectX files that have been loaded, check their date, and discern whether any problems were found with any files. You can also find out information about your video and sound cards, including what level of acceleration they are set to, and you can test DirectX components such as DirectDraw and Direct3D. The DirectX feature is important to video gamers and multimedia professionals. Figure 27.4 shows an example of the Display tab within the DirectX Diagnostic Tool running on a Windows 10 Pro computer that has DirectX 12 installed.

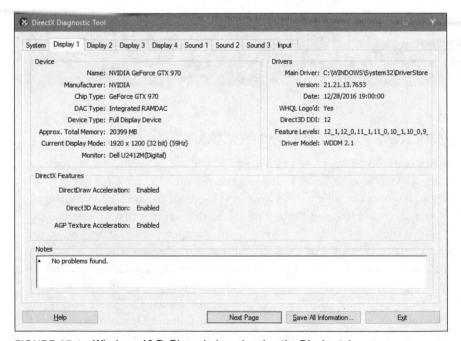

FIGURE 27.4   **Windows 10 DxDiag window showing the Display tab**

Driver Signing

Windows device driver files are digitally signed by Microsoft to ensure quality. The digital signature ensures that the file has met a certain level of testing and that the file has not been altered. By default, in Windows, driver signing is configured automatically, and only administrators can install unsigned drivers. Driver signing can be turned off, but doing so is not recommended because it can pose a tremendous security risk.

The Windows Registry

Left this one for last! The Windows registry is a database that stores the settings for Windows. It contains hardware and software information and user settings. If you cannot make the modifications that you want in the Windows GUI, the registry is the place to go (aside from the command line). To modify settings in the registry, use the Registry Editor, which can be opened by typing **regedit.exe** at the Run prompt. This displays a window like the one shown in Figure 27.5.

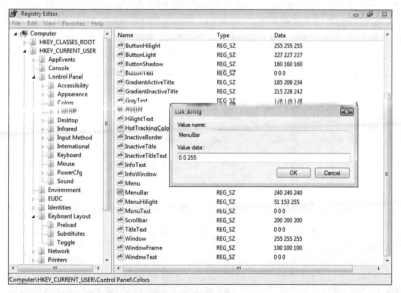

FIGURE 27.5 **The Registry Editor in Windows**

The registry is divided into several sections, known as hives, and these hives begin with the letters HKEY. Table 27.1 describes the five visible hives in the Registry Editor.

TABLE 27.1 **Description of Registry Hives in Windows**

Registry Hive	Description
HKEY_CLASSES_ROOT	Stores information about applications' file associations and Object Linking and Embedding (OLE).
HKEY_CURRENT_USER	Stores settings that concern the currently logged-on user. It is common to make changes in this hive.
HKEY_LOCAL_MACHINE	Stores hardware and software settings that are specific to the computer. This is where the bulk of a PC technician's registry edits are made. One example of data stored here are the programs that run when the OS starts.
HKEY_USERS	Stores data corresponding to all users who have ever logged on to the computer.
HKEY_CURRENT_CONFIG	Contains information that is gathered every time the computer starts up.

Hives are also known as keys that contain other keys and subkeys. This forms the organizational system for the registry. It is similar to folders and subfolders within Windows Explorer or File Explorer. However, the registry does not store actual data files; it stores settings. Inside the keys and subkeys are registration entries that contain the actual settings. These can be edited or new entries can be created. The types of entries include

▶ String values, which are used for decimal numbers

▶ Binary values, which are used for binary entries

▶ DWORD and QWORD entries, which are used for binary and hexadecimal entries

▶ Multistring values, which can have a variety of information

Registry hives are stored in \%systemroot%\System32\Config.

Many users fear the registry, but the technician need not. Just follow a couple simple rules: 1) Back up the registry before making changes and 2) don't make modifications or additions until you have a thorough understanding of the entry you are trying to modify or add.

Figure 27.5 shows a registry entry called MenuBar within HKEY_CURRENT_ USER\Control Panel\Colors. By double-clicking the MenuBar entry, an Edit String window appears (as shown). Again, the beauty of the registry is that you can make modifications to things that normally can't be modified in the Windows GUI. MenuBar is one of these examples. In the figure, the entry's string value has been changed to 0 0 255, which means the color blue. To effect this change, click **OK**, close the Registry Editor (no saving necessary), and then log off and log back on. Some registry changes require a reboot of the system.

As previously mentioned, you need to know how to back up the registry. You can back up any individual key or the entire registry. Say a user wanted to back up the Colors subkey before making changes to the MenuBar entry. The proper procedure would be to click the **Colors** subkey, click **File** on the Menu bar, and then select **Export**. Then it's as simple as selecting a location to save the registry entry and naming it. It exports as a .reg file.

A typical subkey like this is about 2 KB in size. Backing up the entire registry can be done in two ways. First, you can right-click **Computer**, select **Export**, and save the file. The other option is to right-click any registry key, select **Export**, and in the Export Registry File window, select the **All** radio button in the Export range box.

Later, individual keys or the entire registry can be imported with the Import option on the File menu. You might need to do this if a registry modification caused a problem with the system. For example, certain changes to the registry could cause the GUI to fail to load. Or audio could become disabled. Again, be sure to make a backup before playing around with the registry. To repair a missing graphical interface or audio issue that is registry-related, attempt a System Repair from the Windows DVD or, if possible, restore an older version of a backed-up registry. (You will learn more about System Repair in the Windows troubleshooting section of this book.)

Finally, the Registry Editor enables you to connect to remote computers to gain partial access to their respective registries. To do this, select **File** and then select **Connect Network Registry**. You can then browse for computers that are members of the same network your computer is a member of, connect to them, and then make modifications to those remote registries. Of course, you need to have administrative privileges on the remote computer.

ExamAlert

Know how to open the Registry Editor, modify entries, export the registry, and connect to remote registries.

Note

Don't forget, I made that table of Run commands for you. For example, **regedit.exe** opens the Registry Editor. It's available at this link:

https://dprocomputer.com/blog/?p=3010

Cram Quiz

Answer these questions. The answers follow the last question. If you cannot answer
these questions correctly, consider reading this chapter again until you can.

1. You have been tasked with repairing a magnetic-based hard drive that is running
   sluggishly. Which of the following tools should you use to fix the problem? (Select
   the best answer.)

   ○ **A.** Disk Management

   ○ **B.** Optimize Drives

   ○ **C.** Storage Spaces

   ○ **D.** Mount point

2. What is HKEY_LOCAL_MACHINE considered to be?

   ○ **A.** A registry entry

   ○ **B.** A subkey

   ○ **C.** A string value

   ○ **D.** A hive

3. Which of the following system utilities should be used to create a text file with no
   formatting?

   ○ **A.** Notepad

   ○ **B.** Explorer

   ○ **C.** msinfo32

   ○ **D.** Registry

4. A customer is having a problem connecting to mapped network drives but can
   connect to the Internet just fine. You are tasked with fixing that system. Which tool
   should you use to take charge of the system and analyze it?

   ○ **A.** dxdiag

   ○ **B.** mstsc

   ○ **C.** msinfo32

   ○ **D.** dfrgui

   ○ **E.** diskpart

   ○ **F.** System Restore

5. What must you do first to a basic disk to create spanned, striped, mirrored, or RAID-5 volumes in Disk Management?

○ **A.** Extend it.

○ **B.** Shrink it.

○ **C.** Split it.

○ **D.** Initialize it.

○ **E.** Convert it to dynamic.

Cram Quiz Answers

1. **B.** Use the Optimize Drives (Disk Defragmenter) utility. This will attempt to defragment the drive and place the files in a contiguous order so that the hard drive doesn't behave so sluggishly. Of course, there could be other causes for the poor hard drive performance, such as malware, capacity issues, and so on. Disk Management is where you go to configure the hard drive but not to repair it—at least not directly. Storage Spaces is used to build software-based hard drive arrays. A mount point is a drive that is mapped to an empty folder; it is not a utility.

2. **D.** HKEY_LOCAL_MACHINE is one of the five visible hives that can be modified from within the Registry Editor. This hive is where hardware and software settings that are specific to the computer are stored.

3. **A.** Use Notepad to create basic unformatted text files for use in programming, web design, batch files, and so on. Explorer is Windows' graphical file manipulation tool. The **msinfo32** executable opens the System Information window. The registry is a database of settings in Windows; it is not a utility. To modify the registry, use the Registry Editor.

4. **B.** Use **mstsc**. That is the executable that opens the Remote Desktop Connection program, which allows you to connect to the customer's computer and take control of it—and hopefully analyze it and fix the problem! The **dxdiag** executable opens the DirectX Diagnostics Tool. The **msinfo32** executable opens the System Information window. The **dfrgui** executable opens the Optimize Drives utility. Diskpart is the command-line version of Disk Management. System Restore is used to restore a Windows system to a previous point in time. By the way, mstsc stands for Microsoft Terminal Services Client—the original name for the program long ago. Know those utilities!

5. **E.** Convert the disk to dynamic. Once this is done, the volume can be extended, shrunk, or split. You would initialize a drive if it is not recognized by Windows immediately. For example, if it is a new or foreign drive that has been installed to a computer that already had Windows functioning.

CHAPTER 28

Windows Control Panel Utilities

This chapter covers the following A+ 220-1002 exam objective:

▶ **1.6** – Given a scenario, use Microsoft Windows Control Panel utilities.

This chapter focuses on the Control Panel. We'll be discussing many of the utilities that are stored in the Windows Control Panel, and we'll be digging through a bunch of dialog boxes and other utility windows. Take some time to look at your Windows system's Control Panel, and familiarize yourself with the various icons that are displayed—in Category mode, and in icons mode. Let us begin.

Note

Some of the items listed in this CompTIA A+ objective are covered elsewhere in the book.

As always, I highly recommend opening and working on programs and utilities within a virtual machine, or on a system that is located on an isolated test network (or both!).

1.6 – Given a scenario, use Microsoft Windows Control Panel utilities

ExamAlert

Objective 1.6 concentrates on the following Control Panel utilities: Internet Options, Display Settings, User Accounts, Folder Options, System, Windows Firewall, Power Options, Credential Manager, Programs and Features, HomeGroup, Devices and Printers, Sound, Troubleshooting, Network and Sharing Center, Device Manager, BitLocker, and Sync Center.

The Control Panel is where a user would go to make system configuration changes; for example, changing the color scheme, making connections to networks, installing or modifying new hardware, and so on. The Control Panel can be opened in a variety of ways. For example, in Windows 10 go to **Start > Windows System > Control Panel**. In Windows 8, you can use the Charms bar or right-click **Start**. In Windows 7, you can click **Start > Control Panel**. Or in any Windows OS, you can type **control** in the Search field or Run prompt. By default, the Control Panel shows up in Category view. For example, in Windows 10, 8, and 7, System and Security is a category. To see all the individual Control Panel icons, click the drop-down arrow next to View by: Category, and then select either Large icons or Small icons. That will change the path to **Control Panel > All Control Panel Items**, which we will be using often.

Get used to working in the Control Panel, but keep in mind that for Windows 10 some of the icons have been moved to the Settings area. Either way, be ready to operate these tools—for the exam, and for the real world.

> **ExamAlert**
>
> The CompTIA A+ exams expect you to know the individual icons in the Control Panel. In Windows, this is also referred to as All Control Panel Items. Study them!

Internet Options

Internet Options is where you go if you want to make configuration changes for Internet Explorer (IE) or Edge. These changes can also carry over to other browsers that ride along on top of IE/Edge. If you open the Internet Options applet in the Control Panel of Windows, it will bring up the Internet Properties dialog box, as shown in Figure 28.1. You can also open it by going to **Run** and typing **inetcpl.cpl**.

Here we have seven tabs. The names are pretty self-explanatory, but let's discuss each one briefly. These are just the basics for now, but you should know the tabs well because we will be returning to many of them as we progress through the book.

▶ **General:** In this first tab you can set the home page (or pages) to whatever you want. You can see that I set it to the TechNet website. You can also configure how pages are displayed, delete the browsing history, and change the appearance of the browser.

FIGURE 28.1 **Internet Properties dialog box opened to the General tab.**

▶ **Security:** Here you can create and modify security zones—including the Internet—and change the security levels for each zone; this checks for ActiveX controls, unsafe content, and has other safeguards. The higher you set the slider, the more security there will be, and the less you will be able to connect to. We'll discuss this concept more in the security section of this book.

▶ **Privacy:** In this tab you can block or allow specific websites (domains) and enable/configure the pop-up blocker.

▶ **Content:** Use this tab to find out what security certificates have been installed that IE/Edge can use, and to import new certificates. You can get more in-depth information about certificates in the Certificate Manager (certmgr.msc). In this tab you can also change the setting for AutoComplete, which suggests full words and phrases based on the first couple of letters that you type into the URL bar and text fields.

▶ **Connections:** Here you can set up different connections to the Internet, including broadband and dial-up, and manage LAN settings, including the ability to connect to websites via a proxy server.

▶ **Programs:** Use this tab to select how links will be opened, manage add-ons, use an HTML editor, and set programs and associations with IE/Edge.

▶ **Advanced:** This tab is the catch-all for the rest of the settings that don't fit in the other tabs, as well as advanced settings such as international settings, multimedia, and security settings.

> **ExamAlert**
>
> Be able to describe each of the Internet Properties tabs for the exam.

Display

Display is where we can modify how our monitor outputs the image of the OS, change the size of items, calibrate color, project to other screens, and make use of ClearType text, which is a Microsoft technology designed to automatically make displayed text appear clearer. These are pretty straightforward settings, but three concepts require a little more discussion: resolution, refresh rate, and color depth.

> **Note**
>
> In Windows 10, Display has moved from the Control Panel to Settings.

Resolution

Display resolution is described as the number of pixels (picture elements) on a screen. It is measured horizontally by vertically (H×V). The more pixels that can be used on the screen, the bigger the desktop becomes and the more windows a user can fit on the display. The word *resolution* is somewhat of a misnomer and will also be referred to as pixel dimensions. Table 28.1 shows several typical resolutions used in Windows.

TABLE 28.1 **List of Display Resolutions**

Resolution Type	Full Name	Pixel Dimension	Aspect Ratio
VGA*	Video Graphics Array	640×480	4:3 (1.333:1)
WXGA min. (720p)	Widescreen eXtended Graphics Array minimum	1280×720	16:9 (1.78:1)
HD Ready	High Definition similar to WXGA (primarily used on laptops)	1366×768	16:9 (1.78:1)
WSXGA+	Widescreen Super eXtended Graphics Array Plus	1680×1050	16:10 (1.6:1)
WUXGA	Widescreen Ultra eXtended Graphics Array	1920×1200	8:5 (1.6:1)
HD 1080p and 1080i	Full High Definition	1920×1080	16:9 (1.78:1)
UHD 4K	Ultra High Definition	3840×2160	16:9 (1.78:1)

* VGA mode is usually seen only when you attempt to boot the system into Safe Mode or another advanced boot mode, or when the video driver has failed.

Aspect ratio can be defined as an image's width divided by its height (for example, VGA's resolution is 640×480). When you divide the width (640) by the height (480), the result is 1.333. You also hear this referred to as a four-to-three ratio (4:3). This means that for every 4 pixels running horizontally, there are 3 pixels running vertically. Wider resolutions have a higher first number (for example, 16:9). Most current laptops and desktop LCD screens use a widescreen format by default (16:9, 8:5, or 16:10). Take a look at your own computer's resolution setting and figure out which aspect ratio it uses.

Display resolutions continue to get larger. Keep in mind, however, that the maximum resolution of a monitor can be achieved only if the video card—and cable—can support it.

ExamAlert

Know the high-def resolution modes and understand the difference between the 16:9, 16:10, 8:5, and 4:3 aspect ratios.

To modify screen resolution in Windows 8/7, right-click the desktop and select **Screen resolution**. The Resolution drop-down menu is within that window. Or go to **Control Panel > All Control Panel Items > Display** and click the **Adjust resolution** link. In Windows 10, right-click the desktop and select **Display settings**, or go to **Settings > Display**. Remember that there are usually several ways to navigate to the same configuration Window—use whatever works best for you!

Sometimes a user might set the resolution too high, resulting in a scrambled or distorted display. This can happen when video cards support higher resolution modes than the monitor supports. When this happens, reboot the computer into either Enable Low-Resolution Video or Safe Mode, and then adjust the resolution setting to a level that the monitor can support.

A video card's amount of memory dictates the highest resolution and color depth settings. You can multiply the resolution by the color depth to find out how much memory will be needed. For example, if a user wants to run a 1920×1080 resolution at 32-bit color (4 bytes of color), the equation is 1920×1080×4, which would equal approximately 8 MB—easily covered by today's video cards. But keep in mind that this is the bare minimum needed to display Windows and that more will be necessary for advanced display settings. Much more video memory is necessary to run games and graphics programs. Some desktop computers and laptops have integrated video, which uses shared video memory. This means that instead of the video device having its own memory, it shares the motherboard's RAM. Motherboard RAM will usually be slower than a video card's memory, and there will probably be less available. Due to this, a PCI Express video card is recommended over integrated video for computers that run resource-intensive applications such as CAD, virtualization, video editing, and games.

> **Note**
>
> Another related concept is video scaling. Windows allows for scaling, which makes icons, text, and images appear bigger on the screen without having to adjust the resolution. For example, Windows 10 allows custom scaling between 100 and 500 percent of the original. This can be very helpful for educators and presenters, for people with poor vision, or for technicians who remotely control systems that have very high resolutions.

Color Depth

Color depth (also known as bit depth or color quality) is a term used to describe the number of bits that represent color. For example, 1-bit color is known as monochrome—those old screens with a black background and one color for the text, like Neo's computer in *The Matrix*! But what is 1-bit color? 1-bit color in the binary numbering system means a binary number with one digit. This digit can be a zero or a one, for a total of two values: usually black and white. This is defined in scientific notation as 2^1 (2 to the 1st power equals 2). Another example would be 4-bit color, which is used by the ancient but awesome Commodore 64 computer. In a 4-bit color system you can have 16 colors total. In this case, $2^4 = 16$. Of course, 16 colors aren't nearly enough for today's applications; 16-bit, 24-bit, and 32-bit are the most common color depths used by Windows. For example, 24-bit color allows for 16,777,216 different shades. 8-bit color is used in VGA mode, which is uncommon for normal use, but you might see it if you boot into Safe Mode or other advanced modes that disable the normal video driver.

Why is all this important? Two reasons:

▶ First, backward compatibility. A user might need to use an older program that doesn't display well in 32-bit color. You might choose to reduce the color depth to 16-bit from within the monitor's properties window or run the program in compatibility mode with a lesser color depth.

▶ Second, to reduce the amount of computer resources needed. Usually a computer has enough video resources to run 32-bit, but you never know when you will work on an older computer that has a low-end video card and limited RAM. Reducing the color depth can help the system to perform better.

To modify color depth, do the following:

► **Windows 8/7:** Go to **All Control Panel Items > Display > Adjust Screen Resolution** (or right-click the desktop and select **Screen resolution**). Then click the **Advanced settings** link. This brings up the Display Adapter Properties dialog box. Next, go to the **Monitor** tab and locate the Colors drop-down menu.

► **Windows 10:** Go to the **Display Adapter Properties** dialog box **Adapter** tab, and click **List All Modes**. Navigating to this dialog box can vary depending on third-party software. In Windows 10, one way is to go to **Settings > System > Display**, then click the **Advanced display settings** link, and finally locate the **Display adapter properties** link.

Note

In Windows—especially Windows 10—be prepared for 32-bit color depth options only. If you can't change color depth, consider using Program Compatibility mode instead. We'll discuss that later in this chapter.

Refresh Rate

Refresh rate is generally known as the number of times a display is "painted" per second. It is more specifically known as *vertical refresh rate*. On an LCD, the liquid-crystal material is illuminated at a specific frequency. This is usually set to 60 Hz and is not configurable on most LCDs. (The configuration can be found in the monitor's properties window.) However, there are some computer monitors (and some televisions) that can go to 120 Hz and 240 Hz and beyond. If it *can* be configured, you would do so in the Display Adapter Properties dialog box within the Monitor tab.

Don't confuse the refresh rate with frames per second (frames/s or fps). Although the two are directly related, they are not the same thing. For example, a digital video camera might record video at 30 fps. When played back or edited, this will run fine on a 60-Hz monitor. However, if a user is playing a video game that is set to run at 90 fps, the game attempts to send those frames of video data from the video card to the monitor. If the monitor is limited to a 60-Hz refresh rate, the video card will attempt to display the additional frames within the given refresh rate, potentially causing a blur, which might or might not be acceptable to the user. For many users in the gaming community, the higher the frames per second, the better. But to actually attain a higher frame rate (beyond 60 fps), a higher refresh rate will also be necessary.

User Accounts

There are three main types of user accounts you should know for the exam:

▶ The Administrator account has full (or near full) control of an operating system. It is usually the most powerful account in Windows and has access to everything.

▶ The Standard User account (also simply referred to as the User) is the normal account for a person on a network. The user has access to (owns) his/her data but cannot access the data of any other user and by default cannot perform administrative tasks (such as installing software).

▶ The Guest account has limited access to the system. A Guest cannot install software or hardware, cannot change settings or access any data, and cannot change the password.

Within Windows you can add or remove accounts, change passwords, change group associations, and so on. To make modifications to the users, do the following:

▶ In all versions of Windows (if the edition supports it) go to **Local Users and Groups**, either from within **Computer Management** or directly via **Run > lusrmgr.msc**. Of the listed options, this is the preferred method for administrators.

▶ Windows 10: Go to **Settings > Accounts > Family & other people** (or similar name).

▶ Windows 8/7: Go to **Control Panel > User Accounts > Manage accounts**.

We'll be discussing user accounts more (especially user security) as we move through the book.

Folder Options

Folder Options is where you can modify how folders display information, whether or not certain data is visible, and how indexes are searched. This is available as a Control Panel icon in Windows 8/7, but in Windows 10 you will either have to use the File Explorer Options icon or go a different way; for example, open File Explorer—make sure you have This PC or a folder clicked—then on the menu bar click **View** then **Options** and then click **Change folder and search options**.

The General tab gives you the option to change how folders are browsed. By default, each folder is opened in the same window, but you could modify this so that each clicked folder opens in a separate window; just be careful, because this could result in a lot of open windows and confusion. You can also choose whether to single-click or double-click to open items as a preference. You can also increase privacy by deselecting the two options for showing recently used files and folders in the Quick access areas.

The View tab offers some more specific options. Take a look at Figure 28.2 for an example.

FIGURE 28.2   Folder Options dialog box opened to the View tab

For example, hidden files are not displayed by default. But if you select the **Show hidden files, folders, and drives** radio button, then hidden files will be displayed in Explorer. Another option is a couple of lines below that, called **Hide protected operating system files (Recommended)**. This is check marked by default, but if you were to deselect that, then system files would become visible to you. If you were to do both of these things, then files such as bootmgr and pagefile.sys would become visible in the root of C:. You can also deselect the **Hide extensions for known file types** checkbox so that you can see all of the extensions associated with files. All of these are great options for the administrator, but they are not set up by default so that the typical user doesn't get any more information than he or she needs. Spend a little time configuring the various Folder Options and consider what would be best for the typical user and what would be best for the admin.

Performance (Virtual Memory)

Virtual memory makes a program think that it has contiguous address space, when in reality the address space can be fragmented and often spills over to a hard drive. RAM is a limited resource, whereas virtual memory is, for most practical purposes, unlimited.

There can be a large number of processes, each with its own virtual address space. When the memory in use by all the existing processes exceeds the amount of RAM available, the operating system moves pages of information to the computer's hard drive, freeing RAM for other uses. In Windows, virtual memory is known as the paging or page file, specifically, pagefile.sys, which exists in the root of C:. To view this file, you need to unhide it. As previously mentioned, this can be done within the Folder Options dialog box in the View tab. Select the **Show hidden files, folders, and drives** radio button, and then, a few lines below, deselect the **Hide protected operating system files** checkbox. While you're at it, deselect **Hide extensions for known file types**. This allows you to see not only the filename but the three-letter extension as well. Finally, pagefile.sys should now show up in the root of C:, where pagefile is the filename and .sys is the extension.

Take a look at the size of your page file and jot down what you find. To modify the size and location of the page file, open the System Properties dialog box and click the **Advanced** tab (or try using **Run > systempropertiesadvanced. exe**). Next, click the **Settings** button within the Performance box; this brings up the Performance Options window. Now click the **Advanced** tab and then click **Change** in the Virtual memory box. In the Virtual Memory dialog box that opens, you can let Windows manage the virtual memory for you or select a custom size for the page file. The paging file has the capability to increase in size as needed. If a user runs a lot of programs simultaneously, then increasing the page file size might resolve performance issues. Another option would be to move the page file to another volume on the hard drive or to another hard drive altogether. It is also possible to create multiple paging files or stripe a paging file across multiple drives to increase performance. Of course, nothing beats adding physical RAM to the computer, but when this is not an option, possibly because the motherboard has reached its capacity for RAM, optimizing the page file might be the solution. For more information about configuring virtual memory in Windows, visit the following web page:

https://docs.microsoft.com/en-us/previous-versions/technet-magazine/ ff382717(v=msdn.10)

Note

We cover remote settings in Chapter 29, "Windows Networking and Application Installation," and system protection and the Windows Firewall in Chapter 27, "Microsoft Operating System Features and Tools, Part 2," as well as in the security portion of this book.

Power Management

Part of optimizing an operating system is to manage power wisely. You can manage power for hard drives, the display, and other devices; you can even manage power for the entire operating system.

To turn off devices in Windows after a specified amount of time, navigate to **Control Panel > All Control Panel Icons > Power Options**. From here, you can select a power plan such as Balanced, eco, Power Saver, or High Performance—it will vary from one computer to the next. There are a lot of settings within these power plans; here's one example. Select **Balanced** and click **Change plan settings**. The display is set to turn off after a certain amount of time; it can be set from 1 minute to 5 hours, or it can be turned off. Going a little further, if you click the **Change advanced power settings** link, the Power Options dialog box appears. From here, you can specify how long before the hard drive turns off and set power savings for devices such as the processor, wireless, USB, PCI Express, and so on. Take a few minutes looking through these options and the options for the other power plans.

Some users confuse the terms standby and hibernate; let's try to eliminate that confusion now. Standby means that the computer goes into a low power mode, shutting off the display and hard drives. Information that you were working on and the state of the computer are stored in RAM. The processor still functions but has been throttled down and uses less power. Taking the computer out of standby mode is a quick process; it usually requires the user to press the Power button or a key on the keyboard. It takes only a few seconds for the CPU to process the standby information in RAM and return the computer to the previous working state. Hard drives and other peripherals might take a few more seconds to get up to speed. Keep in mind that when there is a loss of power, the computer will turn off and the contents of RAM will be erased, unless it is a laptop (which has a built-in battery) or the computer is connected to a UPS; but either way, uptime will be limited. Note that some laptops still use a fair amount of power when in standby mode.

Hibernate is different from standby in that it effectively shuts down the computer. Hibernation consumes the least amount of power of any power state except for when the computer is turned off. All data that was worked on is stored to the hard drive in a file called hiberfil.sys in the root of C:. This will usually be a large file. Because RAM is volatile and the hard drive is not, hibernate is a safer option when it comes to protecting the data and the session that you were working on, especially if you plan to leave the computer on for an extended period of time. However, because the hard drive is so much slower than RAM, coming out of hibernation will take longer than coming out of standby mode. Hibernation has also been known to fail in some cases and cause various issues in Windows.

Standby is known as "Sleep" in Windows and is accessible in the same location as the shutdown options. Either use the **Start** button (click or right-click) or press **Alt+F4** (after all other programs have been closed).

Hibernation, however, might need to be turned on before it can be used. To enable hibernation in Windows, open the Command Prompt as an administrator. Then type **powercfg.exe/hibernate on**. Next, you need to turn off Hybrid sleep in the Power Options dialog box that you accessed previously. Expand **Sleep**, expand **Allow hybrid sleep**, and then set it to **Off**. Finally, expand the **Hibernate after** option and set it to the number of minutes you desire. Now check the **Start** menu again; the Hibernate option should be there just below Sleep.

> **ExamAlert**
>
> Know the differences between standby, sleep, and hibernate.

Credential Manager

The Windows Credential Manager is where login-based information is stored. These could be basic credentials such as usernames and passwords, or more complex credentials that use certificates. From this program you can add, remove, and edit the credentials that give you access to networks and websites.

You can open this directly from **Control Panel > All Control Panel Items**. (You can also go to Run and type **control /name Microsoft. CredentialManager**.)

By default, when you first open the program you will see Web Credentials and Windows Credentials. A web credential could be a login to a social media site that you allowed Windows to save for you. An example of a Windows credential could be a login to a Microsoft domain or to a local system.

Open a credential by clicking the arrow; from here you can remove the credential or edit it (for example, editing the password). You can also add new credentials, back them up, and restore them.

Another window with the same content (called Stored User Names and Passwords) can be accessed from the command line by typing the following:

rundll32.exe keymgr.dll, KRShowKeyMgr

Once again, here you can add or remove—and back up and restore—credentials for programs, websites, and networks; but the data is organized differently.

Take a look at both programs, and analyze the stored passwords. You might be surprised by some of the credentials that are stored there—especially Web Credentials. Be ready to remove these if they are unwanted, or pose a security risk.

Programs and Features

Programs and Features is used to modify Windows applications and features, as well as third-party applications and features, and to repair them or uninstall them.

You can get to the list of options under Programs and Features from the Control Panel (in Category view) by selecting **Programs**. From there you will see options to uninstall programs, turn Windows features on or off, view the installed updates for Windows and other programs, and run programs made for previous versions of Windows. Except for that last one, these options are also available if you go to **Control Panel > All Control Panel Items > Programs and Features**. (Go directly there by accessing **Run** and typing **appwiz.cpl**.)

So, if you need to uninstall or repair a program, or if you need to add features (such as Hyper-V or the .NET Framework), then use Programs and Features.

> **ExamAlert**
>
> Know how to access Programs and Features to uninstall programs or turn Windows features on or off.

Program Compatibility

Most applications run properly on Windows. However, some applications that were designed for older versions of Windows might not run properly on your version of Windows. To make applications written for older versions of Windows compatible with Windows 10/8/7, use the Program Compatibility utility or the Compatibility tab of a program file's Properties window.

To start the wizard in Windows, open the Control Panel and then click the **Programs** icon (in Category view). Then, under Programs and Features, click the link called **Run programs made for previous versions of Windows**. That brings up the Program Compatibility Troubleshooter. This program asks you which program you want to make compatible, asks which OS it should be compatible with, and (depending on the version) inquires as to the resolution and colors that the program should run in. Windows will attempt to "fix" programs automatically if possible. The Program Compatibility Troubleshooter can also be run from the Compatibility tab of an individual program's Properties window.

To use the Compatibility tab, right-click the program you want to make compatible from within Explorer and then click **Properties**. From there, click the **Compatibility** tab. You can select which OS compatibility mode you want to run the program in and define settings such as resolution, colors, and so on. An example of this is displayed in Figure 28.3, which was taken from a Windows 10 Pro computer. It shows an older version of an application that I have set to run in compatibility mode for Windows 7 and at reduced color (16-bit).

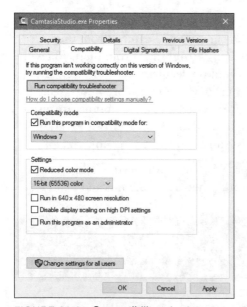

FIGURE 28.3 **Compatibility tab of a program's Properties window**

Windows incorporates the Program Compatibility Assistant (PCA), which automatically attempts to help end users run applications that were designed for earlier versions of Windows. If for some reason this assistant were to cause a program to fail, then its service can be disabled in services.msc or in the Group Policy Editor. For more information on some common PCA scenarios visit:

https://docs.microsoft.com/en-us/windows/desktop/w8cookbook/pca-scenarios-for-windows-8

> **ExamAlert**
>
> Know how to use the Program Compatibility utility and the Compatibility tab in a program's Properties window.

Devices and Printers

This is where you can add, configure, troubleshoot, and remove your printers and other devices such as monitors, UPS, wireless devices, mice, and audio/multimedia devices. Most technicians use Devices and Printers for printers, and if you do, you'll find that it can be a good launching point for the configuration of other devices on the system. We discuss this Control Panel utility more in Chapter 15, "Printers and Multifunction Devices," and elsewhere in the book.

> **Note**
>
> Although HomeGroup has been removed as of Windows 10, we discuss it in Chapter 29, as well as the Network and Sharing Center, another Control Panel utility listed under Objective 1.6.

Sound

Audio takes a back seat in the A+ certification somewhat, but in some environments—for example, in my line of work—it is crucial. To troubleshoot audio problems, the best place to go is **Control Panel > All Control Panel Items > Sound**, which displays a dialog box similar to Figure 28.4. You can also get to this by right-clicking the sound icon in the Notification Area and selecting **Sounds**, or by going to **Run** and typing **mmsys.cpl**.

FIGURE 28.4   **Sound dialog box in Windows**

Here you can modify which audio devices are used for playback and recording, as well as select specific sound themes for Windows. You can also modify what happens with the volume of Windows and programs when communications are detected (for example, video chatting or webinars).

In Figure 28.4, you'll note that the device simply called "Speakers" is check marked; that means it is the default device that will be used for the playback of audio. On my system, that happens to be a USB headset. In addition to that, there is a Focusrite USB device that is "Ready." If I needed to output audio from that device, I would right-click its icon and select **Set as default device**. The same process is necessary in the Recording tab if you are using multiple microphones and recording devices. For people such as technicians, educators, presenters, and video bloggers who want to incorporate better microphones than the ones that are included with a system, the Recording tab of the Sound dialog box becomes critical. However, if you have a custom audio processor with its own software, you might have to access that instead of the Sound dialog box to get full functionality, or possibly to have any functionality at all.

> **ExamAlert**
>
> Know how to enable and disable audio devices in the Playback and Recording tabs of the Sound dialog box.

Troubleshooting

Windows comes with a built-in troubleshooting system that can automatically attempt to fix problems with the system related to programs, hardware, Internet connections, network connectivity, system settings, security, and more. If a program, device, or setting fails, the troubleshooter (by default) will try to help with the problem. Or you can click the **Troubleshooting** icon in the Control Panel and look for help for your specific problem, be it hardware or software related. You can also disable the automatic troubleshooter here (if it interferes with your software), and perform a remote assistance request (shown as a link called Get help from a friend) to have others aid with the problem.

You can also initiate specific troubleshooters from the command line (or Run). For example, let's say that you were having issues with a UPS that is connected to your computer via USB. If you wanted to have Windows troubleshoot your power system, then you could type **msdt.exe /id PowerDiagnostic**. That will bring up the Power troubleshooter window. The msdt.exe (Microsoft Support Diagnostic Tool) is pretty powerful. There are a lot of IDs that you can use to troubleshoot different parts of the system. See the following link for a list of those Troubleshooting Pack IDs:

https://docs.microsoft.com/en-us/previous-versions/windows/it-pro/windows-server-2008-R2-and-2008/ee424379(v=ws.10)

In addition, if you have engaged in a tech support communication of some sort with Microsoft, they might give you a passkey to be used with msdt so that they can further analyze your system. Simply type **msdt** in the Run prompt, and type in the passkey to get additional support for the computer.

Sync Center

The Sync Center is valuable when you are dealing with files that you work on that are stored locally as well as on file servers. This tool keeps the data between the two files synchronized as you update on one location or another. If you work on data that is stored on the cloud, a tool such as this becomes less commonly used. But if you need to work on files locally and from other locations or from a network drive and the file has to exist in multiple locations, then the Sync Center might be necessary. The Sync Center utility allows you to view any partnerships that you currently have, and any conflicts that might occur. If you want to keep copies of your work stored on a file server, you might need to enable offline files, which you can do from here by clicking **Manage offline files**. If the file server goes down, then files that have been configured as offline files can still be worked on, and when the server comes back up, they will be synchronized (if synchronization has been configured properly). Offline files can be viewed once they are enabled in the Offline Files folder and are stored in C:\Windows\CSC (permissions are required to view this folder).

> **Note**
>
> We discuss the Device Manager in Chapter 26, "Microsoft Operating System Features and Tools, Part 1," and BitLocker in Chapter 33, "Windows Security Settings and Best Practices."

Cram Quiz

Answer these questions. The answers follow the last question. If you cannot answer these questions correctly, consider reading this chapter again until you can.

1. You have been tasked with verifying the certificates that are in use on a computer that is configured to use Microsoft Edge. Which tab of the Internet Properties dialog box should you access?

   ○ **A.** General
   ○ **B.** Security
   ○ **C.** Privacy
   ○ **D.** Content
   ○ **E.** Connections
   ○ **F.** Programs
   ○ **G.** Advanced

2. Which window would you navigate to in order to modify the virtual memory settings in Windows? (Select the best answer.)

   ○ **A.** Device Manager
   ○ **B.** Performance Options
   ○ **C.** System
   ○ **D.** Folder Options
   ○ **E.** System Properties

3. Which power management mode stores data on the hard drive?

   ○ **A.** Sleep
   ○ **B.** Hibernate
   ○ **C.** Standby
   ○ **D.** Pillow.exe

4. What should you modify if you need to change the number of pixels that are displayed horizontally and vertically on the screen?

   ○ **A.** Color depth

   ○ **B.** Refresh rate

   ○ **C.** Resolution

   ○ **D.** Scaling

5. You are about to start troubleshooting a Windows system. You need to be able to view the bootmgr file in the C: root of the hard drive. Which of the following should you configure to make this file visible? (Select the two best answers.)

   ○ **A.** Hidden files and folders

   ○ **B.** Extensions for known file types

   ○ **C.** Encrypted or compressed NTFS files in color

   ○ **D.** Protected operating system files

6. A customer's computer has many logins to websites saved within Windows. Some of these are security risks. Where can you go to remove those login usernames and passwords? (Select the two best answers.)

   ○ **A.** Programs and Features

   ○ **B.** Credential Manager

   ○ **C.** Devices and Printers

   ○ **D.** MSDT

   ○ **E.** Store User Names and Passwords

   ○ **F.** Sync Center

Cram Quiz Answers

1. **D.** Go to the Content tab of the Internet Properties dialog box (also known as Internet Options) to find out about the certificates that are in use within Microsoft Edge or Internet Explorer—and any other browsers that piggyback the Internet Properties settings.

2. **B.** Navigate to the Performance Options dialog box and then click the **Advanced** tab to modify virtual memory in Windows. You access that window from the System Properties window, clicking the **Advanced** tab, selecting the **Performance** section, and then clicking the **Settings** button. Although System Properties is essentially correct, it is not the best, or most accurate, answer.

3. **B.** When a computer hibernates, all the information in RAM is written to a file called hiberfil.sys in the root of C: within the hard drive.

4. **C.** Modify the screen resolution to change how many pixels are displayed on the screen (HxV). For example, change from 1280x720 to 1920x1200, or vice versa. Scaling is similar in that it will make text and images appear larger or smaller depending on how you set it, but it doesn't actually change the amount of pixels that are displayed on the screen.

5. **A and D.** In **Folder Options > View** tab, configure Hidden files and folders and set it to **Show hidden files, folders, and drives**, and configure protected operating system files by deselecting the check mark for the setting **Hide protected operating system files**. Files such as bootmgr are hidden and protected by default; you need to unhide them in both ways in order to see them.

6. **B and E.** Use the Credential Manager utility or the similar Store User Names and Passwords utility to remove login credentials to websites and networks that are considered to be security risks. The less passwords that are lying around, the better!

CHAPTER 29

Windows Networking and Application Installation

This chapter covers the following A+ 220-1002 exam objectives:

▶ **1.8** – Given a scenario, configure Microsoft Windows networking on a client/desktop.

▶ **1.7** – Summarize application installation and configuration concepts.

To a certain extent Windows networking is automated—in a lot of scenarios the technician doesn't have to configure very much. However, the larger and/or more complicated a network becomes, the more configuration is usually required.

This chapter goes over some of the basics of Windows networking including network types, sharing and connecting to data, establishing different networking connections, and modifying additional networking settings. It might seem like a lot, but the great thing about TCP/IP, and computer networking in general, is that it works in essentially the same manner across the board, regardless of the operating system that is installed to the computer. So, the more you learn about networking, the easier it becomes to network *any* operating systems together.

At the end of the chapter we'll briefly cover some application installation and configuration concepts and a couple of best practices. The objective order is backwards because I place a lot more importance on Objective 1.8.

Let's continue on our quest toward the A+ certification.

1.8 – Given a scenario, configure Microsoft Windows networking on a client/desktop

> **ExamAlert**
>
> **Objective 1.8** focuses on network types and settings (domain, workgroup, HomeGroup), shares and mapping, networking connections, proxy settings, Remote Desktop Connection, firewall settings, alternative IP address, and network card properties.

Workgroup, HomeGroup, and Domain

After you have configured your network adapter, you are ready to join a network. There are a few choices; in the business world, it's either workgroup or domain. A home or home office that is inhabited by some Windows computers might be configured for HomeGroup, which is another type of workgroup. However, the HomeGroup option was removed from Windows 10 as of update 1803. You might still see it used in Windows 7 or 8, and potentially as part of Windows 10 computers that have not been updated.

Workgroups and domains are logical groupings of computers. A workgroup (sometimes also referred to as peer-to-peer) is usually a small group of computers that share the same network name. No one computer controls the network, and all systems are considered equal. One of the disadvantages is that a computer storing data can be accessed only by a maximum of 20 other systems simultaneously. A domain builds on this by having one or more computers that are in control of the network and enabling more computers, more simultaneous access, and centralized administration. Domains also get a name, such as dprocomputer.com, and are sometimes also referred to as client/server networks. You can select whether your computers will be part of a workgroup or a domain by opening the **System Properties** dialog box and selecting the **Computer Name** tab. (Or go to **Run** and type **systemPropertiesComputerName**.) Then click the **Change** button. This displays the Computer Name/Domain Changes dialog box, as shown in Figure 29.1.

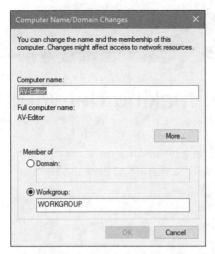

FIGURE 29.1   **Computer Name/Domain Changes dialog box**

From here, you can join a workgroup (which is the default, by the way)
or attempt to join a domain. Your SOHO network will probably not have
a domain, but who knows. If you are anything like me, you might end up
running multiple domains, which is entirely possible even in a SOHO network.
However, most SOHO networks in the field will not use domains; they are
more commonly found in larger organizations. The domain is controlled by
a Microsoft server known as a domain controller. To connect to the domain
from a client computer, you need to know the domain name (for example,
dpro42.com) and the DNS server IP address for that domain. You also need
an account on the domain and need to log on to that domain with a username
and password assigned to you by the systems administrator or network
administrator. It's also a good idea to make sure that the workstation's time and
server's time are synchronized.

> **Note**
>
> The HomeGroup element of Windows 7 and 8 offers SOHO users a quick-and-dirty
> way to accomplish networking; it uses a single alphanumeric password for people to
> join, as opposed to workgroups that have individual user accounts and passwords.
> The HomeGroup is aimed at easily sharing files, multimedia, printers, and so on. To
> configure HomeGroup, go to **Control Panel > All Control Panel Items > Home-
> Group**, or go to the **Network and Sharing Center > View your active networks**.
> From either location, you can create, join, and leave HomeGroups.

> **ExamAlert**
>
> Be able to define the differences between a workgroup, domain, and HomeGroup.

Sharing Resources and Making Network Connections

Before anyone can view the amazing things you have to offer on your computer, you need to *share* them. Let's discuss the sharing of data and then the sharing of printers.

Data Sharing and Access

First, sharing needs to be turned on in the **Network and Sharing Center > Advanced sharing** settings (or the **HomeGroup Advanced Settings**). From here you can turn on folder and printer sharing for private networks only, guest or public networks only, or all networks. You can also enable or disable password-protected sharing. What you select will depend on your environment, the kind of network you have, and the security level you desire. We are not overly concerned with these settings in a domain environment (other than turning sharing off for the client computers), but in a workgroup environment you might opt to have sharing enabled on one or more network types. Some small offices will turn off password-protected sharing to make it easier to share resources with other users on other computers, but there is a potential security risk in doing this.

> **Note**
>
> Some companies with small networks avoid Windows sharing altogether, and instead install a network-attached storage (NAS) device that has print server capabilities.

After sharing has been configured for the computer that will host the data, sharing can then be enabled for *individual* resources. For example, let's say we had a folder named "data" and we wanted to share the contents of that folder to other users and computers. We would need to locate the folder, right-click it, and either select **Share with** or select **Properties** and then click the **Sharing** tab. Figures 29.2 and 29.3 show both of these options.

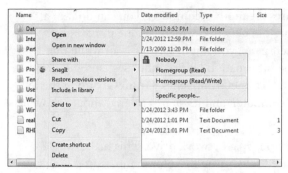

FIGURE 29.2 **Right-clicking a folder and selecting Share with**

FIGURE 29.3 **The Sharing tab of the Data folder Properties window**

In Figure 29.2, you can see that folders are locked by default and are shared with no one. However, you can opt to have other users in the workgroup or HomeGroup read the data or be able to read and modify the data. Figure 29.3 shows that we can share here as well; plus, we can enable Advanced Sharing and set custom permissions for users.

You can also create hidden shares, which can be seen by administrators but not by typical users. To do this, add a dollar sign (**$**) to the end of the share name. Drive letters are automatically shared as administrative shares (for example, C$). An example of a built-in Windows administrative share is admin$, which is the share name for C:\Windows.

Now, if you want to access shares on another computer, you can do it in a couple of ways. First is browsing the network, which is done in Explorer. Simply click **Network** in the left pane; you might have to wait while the computer browser refreshes the information before other systems and devices will show up. (If you are part of a HomeGroup, click **HomeGroup** in the left pane.) Click to open a remote computer, and its shares (if any) should show up there.

Another way to access shares is to map a network drive. This makes a permanent connection to a shared folder using Explorer and assigns it a drive letter. These network drives are mapped according to Microsoft's universal naming convention (UNC), which is \\computername\sharename.

To map a drive, do the following:

1. Locate the Map Network Drive window.

   ▶ **In Windows 10/8:** Open **File Explorer**, select **This PC** in the left pane, and then click **Map network drive**.

   ▶ **In Windows 7:** Open **Windows Explorer**, click **Tools** on the Menu bar, and then click **Map network drive**. (If the Menu bar is not visible, press **Alt+T** on the keyboard.)

2. Select a drive letter (for example, F:).

3. Type the entire path to the share you want to map to. Use the naming convention mentioned previously or connect by *IPaddress\sharename*.

4. Click **Finish**.

Figure 29.4 shows an example. You'll note the computer name is *nasbox1* and the share name is *datashare*. In this case I mapped a drive to a NAS device instead of a Windows computer, but it works the same way. In the figure I used Y:. Some organizations like to use F: or M: or Z:, but it's more of a preference. The key is to be consistent. If ten computers are going to map a drive to the same resource, consider using the same letter to do so; this makes it easier for the administrator to recognize where mapped drives are connecting to.

Note that **Reconnect at sign-in** is check marked. This way, the user won't have to reconnect and supply credentials every time that user wants to get to the data. There is another option, **Connect using different credentials**, which may be necessary if the remote share, or network policy, requires it. If this is selected, then the system will prompt the user to enter a username and password.

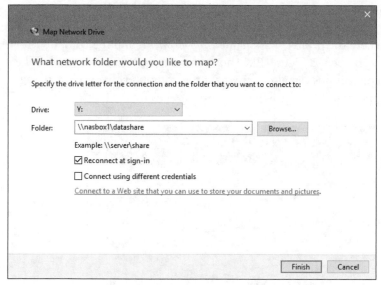

FIGURE 29.4 **Map Network Drive window**

Mapping network drives can also be done in the Command Prompt with the **net use** command. For example, to map the same drive as shown in Figure 29.4, the syntax would be **net use y: \\nasbox1\datashare**. We discuss this more in Chapter 25, "Microsoft Command Line Tools."

ExamAlert

Know how to map network drives in the GUI and in the Command Prompt.

Printer Sharing and Access

To share a printer, first make sure that printer sharing has been enabled in the Network and Sharing Center (click the **Change advanced sharing settings** link to check). Then, you can share the individual printer. Go to **Devices and Printers**, then locate the printer you want to share, right-click it and select **Printer properties**, and access the **Sharing** tab. From there, check mark **Share this printer** and give it an easy-to-remember share name; preferably without spaces. (We discuss this more in Chapter 15, "Printers and Multifunction Devices.")

To connect to the printer from a remote computer, users can attempt to browse for it, or add the printer by connecting via UNC. To do this, once again go to **Devices and Printers** (this time on the remote system) and click **Add a printer**. If Windows doesn't find the printer on the network automatically, then click **The printer that I want isn't listed**. You then have some options. First, you can select the shared printer by name; for example, \\av-editor\ hp-printer1, where the printer share name is *hp-printer1*, and the computer it is connected to is *AV-Editor*. Figure 29.5 shows this configuration screen. HTTP and HTTPS connections can also be made if the computer that is controlling the printer supports it.

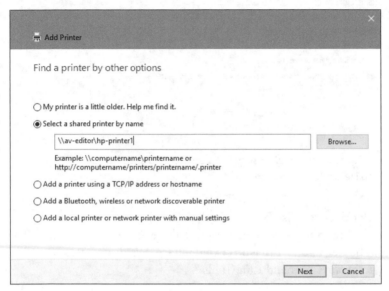

FIGURE 29.5 **The Add Printer window**

You can also connect via TCP/IP by clicking the **Add a printer using a TCP/IP address or hostname** radio button. From here you can connect to a standalone network printer by IP address directly, or utilize Web Services for Devices (WSD) to connect to a printer. WSD is a Microsoft API used to enable programming connections to web service–enabled devices, such as printers, scanners, and file shares.

> **ExamAlert**
>
> Know how to connect (map) to a network printer by printer share name or IP address.

Establishing Networking Connections

From within Windows a user can connect to a variety of networks. For the most part, the best way to do this is to go to the Network and Sharing Center and click the link **Set up a new connection or network**. This displays a window similar to Figure 29.6.

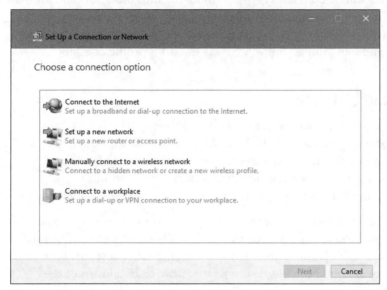

FIGURE 29.6   **The Set Up a Connection or Network window**

From here you can do several things. First, you can make Internet connections via broadband or dial-up. You can also create a new network by configuring a SOHO router (if available). In addition, you can manually connect to a wireless network, which might be necessary if the AP is not broadcasting the SSID. And then you can connect to the workplace via direct dial-up (which is uncommon) or virtual private network (VPN). To establish a wireless wide area network (WWAN)/cellular connection, you would usually rely on third-party software that comes with the WWAN adapter. You also can make many of these connections in Windows 10 by going to **Settings > Network & Internet**.

For the most part, what you need to know is the IP address (or name) of the gateway or server that you need to connect to, as well as the appropriate passwords to get into the network, and possibly to establish encrypted networking sessions.

In general, whenever you establish a new networking connection, you will be asked to provide a *network location*. Windows 10 and 8 will ask you whether you want it to be private or public. A private profile means that network discovery is turned on (and that the system is searchable on the network) and file and printer sharing are enabled. Private is good for home connections or when connecting to a workplace where you trust the systems that you are connecting to (and their surrounding systems). A public profile means that network discovery and file/print sharing is turned off; this connection is good for when you need to connect to public networks that you don't trust because you don't know what computers will be on that network. Windows 7 uses the additional profile terms "home" and "work," which are essentially the same as the private profile in Windows 10/8; the difference between the two is that a home profile allows you to create and join HomeGroups, whereas the work profile does not.

Proxy Settings

Some organizations use proxy servers to cache HTTP, HTTPS, FTP, and other information. To connect to the Internet in this scenario, the client workstations must have the Proxy server setting configured. This allows the client to access the proxy server, which then forwards requests out to the Internet and to the corresponding web servers, or other types of servers.

The setting is located within the Internet Properties window, which can be opened from the browser, or by going to **Control Panel > Internet Options**. From there, access the **Connections** tab and click the **LAN settings** button. Click the **Proxy server** check box, and type the name or IP address of the proxy server that is being used. Figure 29.7 shows an example of this. Here you can see that the proxy server's IP address is 172.18.0.105, and that we are using port 80. Even though the proxy server is usually stored on the LAN, this could be a security risk and you might want to consider using HTTPS and port 443. We discuss proxy servers more in Chapter 7, "Networked Hosts and Network Configuration."

FIGURE 29.7 **Proxy server setting in the LAN Settings dialog box**

By default, the IP address and port selected are used for all protocols. But you can modify this by clicking the **Advanced** button, deselecting the checkbox named **Use the same proxy server for all protocols**, and then manually selecting separate servers and ports for different protocols.

ExamAlert

Know how to navigate to and configure the proxy settings in Windows!

Note

Remote Desktop Connection and Remote Assistance are covered in Chapter 42, "Basic Scripting and Remote Access Technologies."

Firewall settings are covered in Chapter 31, "Physical and Logical Security."

Configuring an Alternate IP Address in Windows

I mentioned alternate IP addresses earlier in the book. Let's expand on that a little bit and show how to configure them.

An alternate IP configuration allows you to have a secondary connection. For example, a user might work from home the bulk of the time, but once in a while the user is required to report to a satellite office that does not have a DHCP server. The primary TCP/IP configuration would be used when working at home, but an alternate configuration could be created for those uncommon visits to the office.

To do this, navigate to the IPv4 Properties dialog box for the network adapter to be configured. Access the Network and Sharing Center and click the **Change adapter settings** link. That opens the Network Connections window. You can get to this screen directly by accessing Run and typing **ncpa.cpl**. Right-click the appropriate network adapter—for example **Ethernet**, or **Wi-Fi**—and select **Properties**. In the Properties dialog box select **Internet Protocol Version 4** and click **Properties**. Once there, click the **Alternate Configuration** tab. This is shown in Figure 29.8. By the way, this tab will only be visible if the primary configuration is obtaining an IP address automatically.

The alternate configuration can be set up to use an automatic private IP address (APIPA, usually not desirable), or can be configured statically (manually) as is the case in Figure 29.8. Here we have a classless IP address, 10.252.38.147, using the 255.255.0.0 subnet mask. If the user wishes to connect to the Internet or domain-based resources, a gateway address and a DNS server address would have to be configured as well; we are using 10.252.0.1 as the gateway and the primary DNS, and 10.252.0.2 as a secondary DNS.

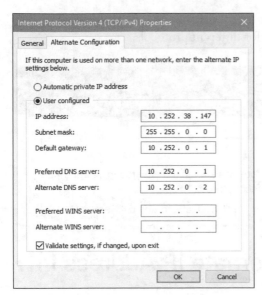

FIGURE 29.8   Alternate Configuration tab of the IPv4 Properties dialog box

So, when the user is at home, the computer connects to the primary network and obtains an IP address automatically from a DHCP server. When not at home, the system will still search for a DHCP server as part of its primary configuration, but when at the satellite office, it won't find one (because one doesn't exist), and then the static configuration will kick in.

> **Note**
>
> This is not a very common configuration, because DHCP is available almost everywhere, and the Windows registry can store multiple profiles for a single network adapter's TCP/IP configurations. If you are interested, these are stored in:
>
> **HKEY_LOCAL_MACHINE\SYSTEM\CurrentControlSet\Services\Tcpip\ Parameters\Interfaces**
>
> You might actually troubleshoot there one day.

Network Card Properties

There are some advanced network adapter properties that can be configured in Windows, such as duplex settings, Wake-on-LAN, QoS, and so on. These can be accessed from the network adapter's **Properties** dialog box > **Advanced** tab. You can access a network adapter's Properties dialog box from the Device Manager—which is preferred—by simply right-clicking the network adapter and selecting **Properties**. Or, you can go to **Network Connections**, right-click the network connection and select **Properties**, then select **Configure**.

How well your network adapter operates depends on several factors (for example, the duplex setting it is configured for). There are two duplex settings that a network adapter can be set for: half duplex and full duplex. Half duplex means that your network adapter can send or receive data but not at the same time; full duplex means that the adapter can do both simultaneously, thus doubling the maximum data throughput. This can be configured by clicking the **Speed & Duplex** setting (or like name). This is normally set to Auto Negotiation, but you can modify the speed or duplexing settings to take full advantage of your network. Of course, this depends on the type of device your network adapter connects to and how that device is configured. If your router is capable of 1000 Mbps in full duplex mode, by all means select this on the network adapter! That will enable it to send *and* receive 1000 Mbps at the same time.

ExamAlert

Know the difference between half duplex and full duplex.

You might also decide to configure other settings, such as Wake-on-LAN (WoL), Power over Ethernet (PoE), and quality of service (QoS)—if your network adapter supports them. WoL is used so that the computer can be woken up by a remote computer when that remote system sends data to the network adapter. (This can be a special packet known as a *magic packet*.) This is great for small networks when you store data on one computer that is set to sleep after, say, 15 minutes. The data sent to the network adapter will wake up the computer, allowing the remote user to get the data required. (I have a video showing how to implement WoL on my website if you are interested.) As mentioned in Chapter 5, "Ports, Protocols, and Network Devices," PoE is when a device is supplied power by the Ethernet networking connection. The power travels along the network cable along with the data. This is common for IP-based devices, such as WAPs, IP cameras, VoIP phones, and so on. As mentioned in Chapter 6, "SOHO Networks and Wireless Protocols," QoS attempts to prioritize streaming media and other types of data. There are a ton of settings here that go beyond the A+ objectives, but try to familiarize yourself with what we covered so far.

Note

If you are interested in more of these advanced properties and their descriptions, go to Intel's website and search for **"Advanced Settings for Intel Ethernet Adapters"** (include the quote marks).

Sometimes, settings need to be configured in the BIOS if you have an integrated network adapter or "on-board NIC." This might be instead of, or in addition to, Windows. For example, sometimes there are options to configure whether PXE is functional, whether the NIC can boot from the network, and/or whether WoL will function. In some cases you might configure an IP address for remote administration such as Intelligent Platform Management Interface (IPMI), which allows an administrator to remotely control the entire system (OS, BIOS, and all) within a browser or other program. And that's just the beginning, so, be ready to configure the BIOS.

> **Note**
>
> I deferred the Cram Quiz until after the next brief objective.

1.7 – Summarize application installation and configuration concepts

> **ExamAlert**
>
> **Objective 1.7** focuses on system requirements, OS requirements, methods of installation and deployment, local user permissions, and security considerations.

If you are designing a system to use a particular program such as virtualization, graphic design, CAD, A/V editing, gaming, and so on, then it is important to carefully analyze the main program that will be used, and plan carefully for its installation and configuration—making sure that it will run properly within your hardware configuration and the operating system that is running.

Application Requirements

First we have to plan out system and OS requirements for the application. Some applications have versions for Windows and for Mac, but it's important to think about platform compatibility regarding the main application you want to use. Many applications have a set of minimum requirements, but also have a set of *recommended* requirements. With any specific applications that will be resource intensive, I suggest you go with the recommended requirements (or more); otherwise, you could experience slow performance.

For example, on the PC side of things, an application might *require* Windows 7 SP1 or higher, .NET 4.6, 2 GB of hard drive space, a dedicated Windows-compatible audio device and speakers, and display resolution of at least 1024 × 768. But those are minimums. The application could *recommend* a 2.8-GHz quad-core CPU, 16 GB of RAM, and a discrete PCIe video card that can be used for hardware acceleration. However, even the recommended requirements might not be quite enough, depending on your system and environment. For instance, I wish that every program I use would run faster. As of the publishing of this book, I run my programs on a system with a hex-core 3.3-GHz CPU, 32 GB of RAM, a powerful GPU, an M.2 drive for storage, and Windows 10 Pro; and I still wish I had more power—even though I am well past the *recommended* requirements of any programs that I use. That's partially because I run so many other powerful applications simultaneously.

On the Mac side of the spectrum, you might find that a program wants macOS 10.12 or higher, and essentially the same type of hardware. Remember: compatibility is key. And, when planning your system, you have to over-engineer. Make sure you have plenty of resources (and then some) based on the *recommended* requirements of an application.

> **Note**
>
> Recommended requirements will change over time, and new versions of applications are always being released, which usually consume more resources! Be ready.

Method of Installation and Deployment

Many applications are simply downloaded and run through the installer for Windows, macOS, or Linux. But in some cases, the application you wish to install might be stored on a USB flash drive, or an optical drive, or perhaps it is located somewhere on the network. You might have to connect to a mapped network drive, or an FTP server, and possibly extract the content from a .zip file or other compressed group of files. How the application will be installed should play into your planning stage. Be ready for multiple installation and deployment types. For instance, in the case of a program such as Microsoft Office, you might use a server to deploy the program (or new version of the program) to multiple clients at once. Finally, know where you are installing the program to. If you are using Windows, for example, a 32-bit version of the program will go to C:\Program Files (x86), and a 64-bit version of the program will be installed to C:\Program Files. In essence, know the source, but also know the target.

User Permissions

When you install an application in Windows, Windows will usually ask who you want to have access to the program. Quite often, the options are: the user who is installing the application only, or everyone on the computer. That can be somewhat limiting, especially if you have several users that share the system. Later, you can assign permissions to users/groups on the folder that contains the application's executable file. Be ready to navigate to C:\Program Files (x86) and C:\Program Files to do this for 32-bit and 64-bit applications, respectively.

As an administrator, you might be called upon to install a special application to a user's computer, where only that user may use the application—even you aren't allowed, regardless of the fact that you are an admin. In that case, you would have to change permissions appropriately, or give the user permissions to install the application. Be ready to be called upon to make changes to ownership and permissions in Windows.

Security Considerations

I'd like you to consider this: every installed application increases the target surface of an operating system. The application in question could open up networking connections, or open ports on the firewall, or create backdoors, each of which can be inviting to attackers. Plus, the availability of the rest of the system could be reduced by some applications that are not coded well. Consider running evaluation versions of software on a testbed (isolated network or VM network) before installing to live clients. Test the security of an application by scanning the system for malware, scanning for open ports, and run other applications side-by-side to find out if there will be any conflicts. Then, check how the application updates. You may or may not want it to auto-update. If it does not auto-update, then you should periodically check for updates that will address security vulnerabilities, and increase the functionality of the program. Depending on your organization's policies, that could be every 6 months or less. The installation of the program and the program's updates could also affect the network. The larger the program, the more the network will be affected. So, after you have tested an application thoroughly, be sure to run installations and upgrades off-hours, unless they are absolutely necessary!

Cram Quiz

Answer these questions. The answers follow the last question. If you cannot answer these questions correctly, consider reading this chapter again until you can.

1. Which of the following are administrative share names? (Select the two best answers.)

   ○ **A.** C$

   ○ **B.** C:\Windows

   ○ **C.** ADMIN$

   ○ **D.** System32

   ○ **E.** $print

2. Which of the following requires a Windows-created password to gain access to it?

   ○ **A.** Workgroup

   ○ **B.** Client/server

   ○ **C.** HomeGroup

   ○ **D.** Domain

3. You want to connect to a share on \\server1\data-share. Which of the following should be used to accomplish this?

   ○ **A.** HomeGroup

   ○ **B.** Right-click the folder and select **Share with**

   ○ **C.** ipconfig

   ○ **D.** net use

4. You have been tasked with setting up a client Windows computer. It needs to gain access to the Internet, but all web traffic is cached and filtered by a go-between server on the LAN. What should you configure to enable Internet access for the Windows client?

   ○ **A.** Alternate IP address

   ○ **B.** Proxy server

   ○ **C.** Duplex

   ○ **D.** WSD

5. Which of the following are important considerations when planning the installation of a new application? (Select the three best answers.)

   ○ **A.** CPU speed

   ○ **B.** Windows location

   ○ **C.** Program Files location

   ○ **D.** User permissions

   ○ **E.** Warranty

6. In Windows 10, which network location profile setting should you choose if you are not sure what computers will be on the network or if you can trust them?

   ○ **A.** Private

   ○ **B.** Home

   ○ **C.** Work

   ○ **D.** Public

Cram Quiz Answers

1. **A and C.** Every volume gets an administrative share by default including the C: drive, which is assigned C$. ADMIN$ is another administrative share; it is the share name for C:\Windows. System32 is simply a folder name within C:\Windows. $print is not an administrative share, but it could be used as a share name. An actual administrative share is print$.

2. **C.** HomeGroup connections require an alphanumeric password that was created by Windows automatically. Joining or creating a workgroup does not require a password. Client/server networks such as Microsoft Active Directory domains require a username and password, but these are created by the administrator of the network or selected by the user.

3. **D.** The **net use** command can connect to shares such as \\server1\data-share or any other share on the network. Of course, you could also do this by mapping a network drive in Explorer. HomeGroup uses a more user-friendly approach to sharing and connecting to shares. Right-clicking the folder and selecting **Share with** will share the folder but won't make a connection to the share. **ipconfig** is used in the Command Prompt to find out the IP configuration of the network adapter.

4. **B.** Within **Internet Properties > Connections > LAN Settings**, configure a proxy server by entering the IP address of the proxy server and the port to be used. An alternate IP address allows a system to connect to a separate network while away from the primary network. The duplex setting is where you can configure a network adapter to send or receive data one at a time (half duplex) or simultaneously (full duplex). WSD stands for Web Services for Devices, which is what Windows uses by default to connect to remote printers.

5. **A, C, and D.** When installing a new application, we should consider the CPU speed (and other minimum/recommended hardware requirements), the Program Files location (is it 64-bit or 32-bit), and user permissions. The Windows location isn't really important; by default, it will be C:\Windows, but its location doesn't really impact the installation of the application. The warranty (if there is one) can be important if there is a failure, but doesn't play into the installation of the software.

6. **D.** A public profile means that network discovery and file/print sharing is turned off; this connection is good for when you need to connect to public networks that you don't trust because you don't know what computers will be on that network. Private is good for networks where you trust the systems. Windows 7 uses the additional profile terms "home" and "work," which are essentially the same as the private profile in Windows 10/8.

CHAPTER 30

Linux and macOS Tools

This chapter covers the following A+ 220-1002 exam objective:

▶ **1.9** – Given a scenario, use features and tools of the macOS and Linux client/desktop operating systems.

Although Windows dominates the desktop and laptop market, there are other operating systems you can choose from as well. macOS is a favorite with users who need to manipulate audio and video media. Also, some people just prefer macOS to Windows. On the desktop side, Linux is used mostly by enthusiasts and techies. Both have a small business market share, but even a small share of the market is still a substantial number of computers. Because macOS has a larger market share than Linux, we'll begin with that.

1.9 – Given a scenario, use features and tools of the macOS and Linux client/desktop operating systems

> **ExamAlert**
>
> **Objective 1.9** focuses on macOS and Linux best practices, tools, features, and basic commands.

macOS

Apple is credited with making the graphical user interface (GUI) that people manipulate with a mouse and keyboard—the mainstream way of working with the computer. Today's macOS takes this to a new level by using antialiasing, ColorSync, Retina display, and drop-shadow technologies to create a more exciting and fluid interface. macOS uses control panels (windows with icons) to configure, troubleshoot, and maintain the computer. This is similar to the Microsoft Windows Control Panel, though different functions have varying names and locations. Some applications are ported for macOS (for example, Microsoft Office for Mac); however, macOS uses its own web browser (Safari) as opposed to Internet Explorer or Microsoft Edge. Web browsers such as Chrome and Firefox can be run on macOS as well.

macOS's desktop has a user-friendly design that includes a basic menu bar at the top, which includes the Apple menu, the currently opened application, and standard options (such as File, Edit, and so on). There are icons on the bottom (in the "Dock") used for commonly used applications, such as Safari, Mission Control, Mail, and FaceTime. The *Dock* is a major feature of the macOS GUI used to launch common applications and switch between running apps.

> **ExamAlert**
>
> Use the Dock to open common applications and switch between running apps.

macOS Features

There are many, many features in macOS that make it a user-friendly environment. The CompTIA exams focus on a few of those; let's discuss them now.

The best way to open applications or files is to use *Finder*, a program similar to Explorer but designed in such a way as to make finding applications easy. This is available on the menu bar as well as within the Dock. Applications and files can also be stored on the Dock and anywhere on the desktop, but if you don't see the application or file you want, use the Finder program. If you still can't find what you are looking for or you aren't even sure if it is on your computer, use the *Spotlight* search tool. This is displayed as a spyglass in the menu bar on the top right of the desktop and can also be accessed by pressing and holding the Command and Spacebar keys simultaneously on the keyboard. This search tool searches through files, e-mails, apps, songs, printers, and so on. It can also search other computers on the network (which it discovers using Bonjour—a networking technology used by macOS to locate networked computers and devices). Plus, it looks through external sources such as Wikipedia, Bing, and iTunes, to name a few. The goal is to receive a media-rich, definitive set of results to your query.

> **ExamAlert**
>
> Understand what the Finder and Spotlight programs are in macOS.

Let's get into what you see on a Mac and how it is displayed. First, you can modify how the desktop is displayed or you can set up multiple desktops. This is done within *Mission Control*. Mission Control zooms away from the desktop, giving you a larger perspective of apps, "spaces," and virtual desktops. It acts as an application switcher and window manager. Mission Control can be launched in a variety of ways, including swiping up on the Trackpad with three fingers, double-tapping the Magic Mouse (which is an Apple mouse that allows for special clicking and gesturing, making it easier to navigate through macOS), clicking the Mission Control icon on the Dock, or pressing the Mission Control key on the keyboard. Now you can have multiple desktops by dragging windows to the upper-right corner or you can add windows to already existing desktops by dragging them to the appropriate desktop at the top of the window. The Dashboard is available here as well; it has some default functions, such as the clock, calendar, and calculator. You can also add special programs to the Dashboard by clicking the + sign. This technology has great implications for the researcher, student, programmer, A/V editor, and so on. It allows a user to highly customize the user interface. But be careful, because too many desktops and too many open applications will cause the system to run sluggishly. Also, users will sometimes forget that they have applications open in other desktops; a quick, three-finger swipe up will reveal anything that is currently running.

Speaking of three-finger swipes, there are all kinds of *gestures* and multitouch gestures that can make you a more efficient macOS user. If you have the supporting hardware (such as a Magic Trackpad or Magic Mouse), you can make use of things such as tapping, scrolling, pinching, and swiping, similar to the same functions on a mobile device. For example, a two-finger swipe up or down will scroll content; a two-finger double tap will perform a smart zoom, and you can do it again to return; and, of course, there is the pinch out to zoom. The list goes on and on. For a complete list of these multitouch gestures, visit https://support.apple.com/en-us/HT204895.

You can also allow users on other Macs to view your screen and even take control of your computer with a tool called *Screen Sharing* (similar to Windows Remote Desktop). To enable this, go to the **Apple** menu **> System Preferences**, click **Sharing**, then select **Screen Sharing**. For a step-by-step procedure on how to do this, and how to connect from another system, visit https://support.apple.com/guide/mac-help/share-the-screen-of-another-mac-mh14066/mac. It gets a little more complicated when you want a Windows computer to control (or just see) a Mac. Third-party VNC software (such as RealVNC) can help with this. VNC works cross-platform between Windows, macOS, Linux, and mobile OS versions. VNC can also be used to view a Mac that has Screen Sharing enabled.

Sometimes you might need to share the screen with a second display or to a projector. Many Mac computers come with a secondary DisplayPort (DP) port to enable duplication of the screen. This works in a fashion similar to that which was described previously in the book in the laptops and video sections.

> **ExamAlert**
>
> Know how to configure multiple desktops, Screen Sharing, and the replication of the display to a secondary monitor.

Ah, the dual-booters! It's amazing how many people want to run Windows on their Mac. Apple offers a utility called *Boot Camp* that allows you to do just this with Windows 7 and higher (64-bit versions). However, more powerful Mac hardware will be required for newer versions of Windows. After the Windows OS is installed, you can reboot the computer to switch from one OS to the other.

Boot Camp can be found in **Finder > Applications > Utilities** and then select **Boot Camp Assistant**. You then need to download the supporting software, create a partition (to be used by Windows), and preferably install the OS from a disk image (ISO). This image can be created with third-party programs such as PowerISO. Then follow the Boot Camp prompts, complete the installation of Windows, and reboot the system. You can switch from macOS to Windows by making use of the Startup Disk preference pane or you can switch from Windows to macOS by accessing the Boot Camp icon in the Notification Area. For more details on how to install Windows on your Mac with Boot Camp, visit https://support.apple.com/en-us/HT201468.

As you can imagine, there are some security concerns when it comes to dual-booting. Now the computer is potentially open to attacks on the macOS *and* the Windows side. Both OSes (especially Windows) should be carefully secured if you are a Mac owner with a dual-boot system.

Speaking of security, passwords need to be protected in macOS just as they are in any other OS. Apple provides the *Keychain* utility, a password management system that can contain not only passwords but private keys and certificates. It can be accessed from **Finder > Applications > Keychain Access**.

Managing and Maintaining macOS

Once again, for the locating and managing of files and running applications, macOS uses Finder. The program will open up automatically whenever you access a drive or file listing. From here, you can create files, copy and paste files, access "Favorites" (such as Applications, Downloads, and so on), access removable drives, and tag files/applications with various colors. Files can also be manipulated in the command line. macOS possesses a shell utility called *Terminal* that allows you to manipulate data and make configuration changes similar to the Command Prompt in Windows. However, the syntax is different and is based off of Linux. (We'll cover several commands you can use in the upcoming "Linux Command Line" section.) To open the Terminal, go to **Finder > Applications > Utilities > Terminal**. You can also open up applications such as this by using the Spotlight tool and simply typing the name of the application.

Aside from locally stored data, you can view remote discs on other Mac computers by sharing them in the System Preferences, and you can view them from the local computer by selecting the **Remote Disc** option in **Finder > Devices**. This is required sometimes, especially when the user is working at a MacBook that does not have an optical drive. Data can also be stored on the cloud—Apple's version is called *iCloud*. To back up data to iCloud, go to the **Apple** menu > **System Preferences** and click **iCloud**, click **Manage**, and then select **Backups**.

For backing up the state of the computer, macOS utilizes the *Time Machine* backup program. To enable this, go to the **Apple** menu and select **System Preferences**. Then select the **Time Machine** icon and turn it on to enable automatic backing up of any drive. From here, you can back up drives locally or to iCloud. Restoring data also happens from this program. Essentially, you can select the point to which you want to restore—be it a day ago or a year ago. To do this, simply select the desired "snapshot" from a timeline in the program. This is similar to Windows System Restore. Because the program saves multiple states of files over time, a separate backup method (such as a USB flash drive or other external media) is also recommended for important files.

Although Macs are known for their resilience, their drives should still be maintained. The built-in *Disk Utility* is used for verifying and repairing the hard drive, repairing drive permissions, and possibly booting from the recovery partition (which all Macs have). Disk Utility can also be used to create an image or to recover a system from that image.

Sometimes you might encounter the *spinning pinwheel*, also known as the spinning pinwheel of death (SPOD). This multicolored spinning wheel is a variation of the mouse pointer arrow; it appears when an application either becomes temporarily unresponsive or enters an infinite loop and cannot recover. If an application freezes or is otherwise not responding properly, you can force that app to close by using the *Force Quit* application. This is located on the Apple menu; once you open Force Quit, you can select the application you want to force to close. This is similar to using the Task Manager in Windows. You can also use the keyboard combination **Command+Option+Esc**, which is similar to **Ctrl+Alt+Del** on a Windows PC. However, be ready to troubleshoot further; launching the application again may result in another SPOD.

> **ExamAlert**
>
> Know how to use the Time Machine, Disk Utility, and Force Quit tools in macOS.

General system maintenance includes system updates, anti-malware updates, driver updates, and firmware updates. macOS can be updated by going to the **Apple** menu and selecting **Software Update**. It can also be updated from the App Store. Anti-malware updates should of course be done within the third-party application you are using; we discuss malware in more depth in Chapter 32, "Wireless Security, Malware, and Social Engineering." The video driver is built into macOS, so it can only be updated by upgrading to a new version of the operating system. Keyboards, mice, and many other devices need to be approved for use with Mac computers, so if you buy an Apple-approved device, it should work with macOS. Unfortunately, if the device requires a higher version of macOS, you'll have to upgrade. Most printers work with macOS also, but if a printer driver needs to be downloaded, macOS will automatically run the AirPrint program to locate and download the driver. In general, macOS is designed to simplify the process of installing devices. Finally, firmware updates are usually done automatically when you upgrade to a newer version of macOS. If you are unsure if an EFI firmware update is necessary, you can find out by going to the **Apple** menu > **Software Update**. (For older systems, navigate to **Finder > Applications > Utilities** and open the **System Information** app.) For more about firmware updates, see this link: https://support.apple.com/en-us/HT202040.

Although macOS is not a derivative of Linux, it is definitely similar in many ways. The two are certainly linked, from their architectural structure to their respective command lines. Let's move into the world of Linux now.

Linux

Linux users have the option of using one of several GUIs that are similar to the macOS GUI. One popular GUI environment is GNOME, which stands for GNU Network Object Model Environment. A GUI that runs on top of the Linux operating system, GNOME consists solely of free and open-source software. Its emphasis is on simplicity and accessibility while endeavoring to use a low amount of resources.

There are programs for Linux available that are close to the equivalent of Microsoft applications. For example, OpenOffice and LibreOffice are free software applications that can be used to create word processing documents, spreadsheets, and so on. Newer versions of Microsoft Office are offering a limited amount of compatibility with these documents.

The command-line functionality in most Linux distributions is in-depth and well documented, allowing a user to configure, and troubleshoot, just about anything from within the "shell" or command line. To help you learn more about any commands, the operating system usually has built-in manual (MAN) pages that are also accessible online.

Linux Desktop Distributions

Overall, the most common types of Linux by far include Android (for mobile devices), Google Chrome OS, and various derivatives of Linux used by gaming consoles. However, this section concentrates on desktop computers and the types of Linux that can be loaded on them.

There are literally hundreds of Linux desktop distributions. Most are used by PC enthusiasts and gamers, as well as some programmers. You'll hear of all kinds of distributions of Linux, including openSUSE, Linux Mint, Kali, and many more. There are so many Linux distributions that we could probably fill a book describing them, and more are being released every week. That's the beauty of the license for Linux. It is free to use and develop. People at home can make their very own version of Linux if they so desired. One popular distribution (or "distro" as they are called) is Ubuntu. As far as Linux goes, it is commonly used for a variety of purposes. Figure 30.1 shows an example of the Ubuntu GUI.

FIGURE 30.1 **Ubuntu desktop**

Figure 30.1 shows a basic information bar on the top that shows the active window that is running—in this case, Terminal. In the Terminal window I ran a couple of commands. The first is **cat /etc/os-release**, which results in the version number of Ubuntu that I am running (18.04.1 LTS). The second is **uname -r**, which tells me the Linux kernel version (4.15.0). Commands such as these work on most distributions of Linux.

> **Note**
>
> For practice with Ubuntu, consider creating an Ubuntu bootable USB stick within Windows. For details, visit https://tutorials.ubuntu.com/tutorial/tutorial-create-a-usb-stick-on-windows#0. This enables you to boot Linux from the flash drive, and practice Linux commands using the built-in Terminal application. Or, consider downloading the latest version of Ubuntu and installing it to a virtual machine. For details, visit https://www.ubuntu.com/download/desktop.

Linux Partition Scheme and File System

Linux uses the GUID Partition Table (GPT) to list and control the partitions on the systems. GPT supports UEFI, 128 partitions, and partition sizes beyond 2 TB, and is stored in multiple locations, making it superior to master boot record (MBR) technology. Most commonly, Linux uses the ext4 file system.

> **Note**
>
> By the way, Apple's macOS version 10.4 and higher require GPT. In this respect (and many others), it is similar to Linux. Older versions of macOS used the Apple Partition Map, though it is unlikely that you will see that today.

Linux Command Line

The command line is also referred to as a "terminal" (and as the "shell"). In some versions of Linux, the terminal is available by navigating the menu system. In others, it is accessed by using the Search tool and searching for **terminal**, or by pressing **Ctrl+Alt+T**. And in still others, it runs automatically, as is the case in versions of Linux that don't use a GUI.

Table 30.1 describes several commands you should know for the exam. Know that when working in the Linux directory structure, you always use a slash (/) to separate directory levels. (In Windows, a backslash [\] is used.) So, you might have a path such as **/downloads/music/mp3s**. If there is ever any confusion as to which is the slash and which is the backslash on the keyboard, remember this: the backslash (\) is the one near the backspace key. Use the slash **/** for Linux, which usually shares the key with the question mark.

TABLE 30.1 **List of Linux-based Commands**

Command	Description
ls	Lists directory contents. Similar to **dir** in Windows.
cd	Changes directory. Same as Windows **cd** command.
mv	Moves files. Similar to Windows **move** command.
cp	Copies files and directories. Similar to Windows **copy** command.
rm	Removes files or directories. Similar to Windows **del** and **rd** commands.
dd	Converts and copies a file.
chmod	Modifies the read and write permissions for a file or folder.
chown	Changes the file owner and group.
ps	Displays information about a process/lists running processes.
kill	Used to terminate processes.
apt-get	Used to handle packages (installing, updating, or upgrading).
sudo	Allows a user to execute a single command as another user (such as a root). **su** lets you run the shell/Terminal session as another user (root or any other user) altogether.
vi	Opens the text editor shell. Normally followed by a filename. Press **q** or **q!** to exit. You may have to press the colon (**:**) key first.
passwd	Used to update a user's password.
pwd	Displays the full path/filename of the working directory. Don't confuse with **passwd**!
grep	Searches for matching information in specified files and displays that information.
ifconfig	Shows the TCP/IP properties of the network connections. Similar to Windows **ipconfig** command but can also be used to configure network interfaces. Figure 30.2 shows an example of **ifconfig**. Newer versions of Linux also use the **ip a** command.
iwconfig	Shows the TCP/IP properties of the wireless network connections and can configure them. (Not available in macOS.)
shutdown	Brings the system down but can be modified in a variety of ways to gracefully shut down the system, notify users, and many more options.

```
sysadmin@Ubuntu-18-A:~$ ifconfig
ens32: flags=4163<UP,BROADCAST,RUNNING,MULTICAST>  mtu 1500
        inet 172.18.0.122  netmask 255.255.0.0  broadcast 172.18.255.255
        inet6 fe80::63dd:d1c:eead:edff  prefixlen 64  scopeid 0x20<link>
        ether 00:0c:29:26:b9:c6  txqueuelen 1000  (Ethernet)
        RX packets 82078  bytes 121480348 (121.4 MB)
        RX errors 0  dropped 19  overruns 0  frame 0
        TX packets 32580  bytes 2253178 (2.2 MB)
        TX errors 0  dropped 0 overruns 0  carrier 0  collisions 0

lo: flags=73<UP,LOOPBACK,RUNNING>  mtu 65536
        inet 127.0.0.1  netmask 255.0.0.0
        inet6 ::1  prefixlen 128  scopeid 0x10<host>
        loop  txqueuelen 1000  (Local Loopback)
        RX packets 697  bytes 63201 (63.2 KB)
        RX errors 0  dropped 0  overruns 0  frame 0
        TX packets 697  bytes 63201 (63.2 KB)
        TX errors 0  dropped 0 overruns 0  carrier 0  collisions 0

sysadmin@Ubuntu-18-A:~$ ▊
```

FIGURE 30.2   ifconfig command

In Figure 30.2, the command **ifconfig** has been issued, displaying the network configuration of the network adapter. The IP address (172.18.0.122) is displayed for the primary network adapter (ens32). Older common names for network adapters in Linux included eth0, eth1, wlan0, and so on, but those have been replaced with "predictable" network interface names, such as *en* for Ethernet, *sl* for serial line IP, *wl* for WLAN, and *ww* for WWAN. This will help you to quickly identify what type of network adapters are installed to the system, simply by typing **ifconfig**. What kind of adapter do we have in the figure? That's right, Ethernet. That and wireless adapters are what you will most often see. The other adapter is called lo, which is short for loopback; the same exact internal IP address used by Windows for testing—it is 127.0.0.1. All systems running TCP/IP version 4 use this loopback testing address.

The last line shows the prompt. *Sysadmin* is the username, and *Ubuntu-18-A* is the computer name. The default administrative account in most versions of Linux is root, but it's always a good idea to create a working admin account, keeping the root account as a backup, but making sure they both have strong, complex passwords.

> **Note**
>
> To use **ifconfig** and other networking tools, they first have to be installed. If necessary, you can do this by typing **sudo apt-get install net-tools**.

> **ExamAlert**
>
> Know your Linux commands! Practice them on a distribution such as Ubuntu or in macOS—or both!

This command-line information is accessible and available in most versions of Linux. Remember, you can learn more about most of these commands by typing **man** and then the command; for example, **man dir**. You can also learn about them online at https://linux.die.net/man/ and various other places—just use your favorite search engine.

> **Note**
>
> Another operating system, called FreeBSD, is a common Unix-like OS that has a variety of uses. For example, pfSense uses it for its open-source firewalling software. It is very similar to Linux (yet not Linux), and is a derivative of Berkeley Software Distribution. Most commands work in the same manner on Linux and FreeBSD because they are both ultimately Unix-based.

Basic Linux Troubleshooting

Let's discuss a couple of common issues that can occur in Linux. Let's say you boot the OS, and instead of booting normally, the GUI fails to load. Instead you see a basic command-line prompt. This could mean a couple of things. It could be that the GUI shell has failed and needs to be reinstalled or updated. It could be that the system booted to a special mode or an application made it boot to the command line. Or perhaps the video driver failed.

The first thing you should try is one of the many **start** commands. This will vary according to your version of Linux. For example, you might use the **startx** command in an attempt to bring up the GUI. Or, if you're using Ubuntu or a similar distro, you might use the command **sudo service lightdm start**. In the case that a graphical desktop is not installed, you might have to install it by typing something similar to **sudo apt-get install ubuntu-desktop**. As mentioned in the previous table, the **apt-get** command is used to install/uninstall Linux packages—but a working network connection is required. If you suspect that a driver has failed, you will need to install the appropriate package with the **apt-get** command. Of course, I am assuming that you have already ruled out a hardware or connectivity issue. You might also find that a recently installed application is causing the failure. Again, the **apt-get** command will be instrumental in removing undesirable applications. Or, perhaps some of the packages need to be upgraded. Most distributions have a GUI-based updater, but you could check which packages have existing upgrades, and upgrade them with the **sudo apt-get upgrade** command.

Of course, you might boot the system and see a worse error, such as the kernel panic error. This is akin to the Windows BSOD, and the system won't be able to boot properly. Similar to this, but less disastrous, is the kernel "oops," which is when a particular process causes a problem but the kernel kills (terminates) the process successfully. However, watch for these errors, as they might lead to full-blown kernel panic errors. One possible solution to kernel panic is to reboot to rescue media, or to a fully bootable Linux OS from a flash drive (or optical drive). The **apt-get --reinstall** command might be instrumental in the solution as well.

Bootloader files such as GRUB and LILO can fail as well and the system won't boot. (These are similar to bootmgr in Windows.) Once again, third-party bootable utilities can help with the problem, or in the case of Ubuntu, the specially designed Boot Repair utility can help. That would have to be installed from the command line of an externally running Linux OS, and then it will require some configuration. Be ready to have an extra flash drive just for booting special Linux-based repair OSes.

One of the great things about Linux is that many of the distributions are incredibly well documented on the Internet—and by very talented people. Support pages and forums are available for most distros. Use these resources; chances are, the error you are encountering has been seen before, described online, and *solved*.

Cram Quiz

Answer these questions. The answers follow the last question. If you cannot answer these questions correctly, consider reading this chapter again until you can.

1. Which of the following is the built-in web browser for macOS?

   ○ **A.** Safari

   ○ **B.** Chrome

   ○ **C.** Firefox

   ○ **D.** Internet Explorer

2. Which program should you use to access Utilities in macOS? (Select the two best answers.)

   ○ **A.** Mission Control

   ○ **B.** Finder

   ○ **C.** Spotlight

   ○ **D.** Safari

1.9 – Given a scenario, use features and
tools of the macOS and Linux client/desktop
operating systems

CramQuiz

3. Which of the following should be enabled when you want a user at another Mac to take control of your computer?

   ○ **A.** Remote Desktop

   ○ **B.** Remote Assistance

   ○ **C.** Screen Sharing

   ○ **D.** Screen Mirroring

4. Which utility allows a Mac user to dual-boot macOS and Windows?

   ○ **A.** Ubuntu

   ○ **B. apt-get**

   ○ **C. bootrec**

   ○ **D.** Boot Camp

5. You want to save the state of the Mac running macOS. Which tool should be used?

   ○ **A.** System Restore

   ○ **B.** Time Machine

   ○ **C.** Force Quit

   ○ **D.** Disk Utility

6. Which program handles installing a printer's driver automatically in macOS? (Select the best answer.)

   ○ **A.** Bonjour

   ○ **B.** Magic Mouse

   ○ **C.** AirPrint

   ○ **D.** iCloud

7. A customer reports that a spinning wheel appears on her screen whenever she tries to run a specific application. What does this represent? (Select the best answer.)

   ○ **A.** A failing CPU

   ○ **B.** An Apple macOS proprietary crash screen

   ○ **C.** A Microsoft Windows proprietary crash screen

   ○ **D.** A Linux proprietary crash screen

8. Which command in Linux will show the directory contents?

   ○ **A. ls**

   ○ **B. pwd**

   ○ **C. cd**

   ○ **D. mv**

9. Which command should be used to change the permissions of a file?
   - ○ **A. ps**
   - ○ **B. chown**
   - ○ **C. NTFS**
   - ○ **D. chmod**

10. Which command will show the configuration details of a wireless connection in Linux?
    - ○ **A. ifconfig**
    - ○ **B. ipconfig**
    - ○ **C. iwconfig**
    - ○ **D. grep**

Cram Quiz Answers

1. **A.** Safari is Apple's web browser. It is used in macOS and iOS. Chrome is developed by Google and can be added on to macOS. Firefox (Mozilla) can also be added to macOS. Internet Explorer is the built-in browser that Windows uses.

2. **B and C.** Finder is the application to use when looking for applications and files. Utilities is located in **Finder > Applications.** Spotlight can be used to locate just about anything on the Mac, including Utilities. Mission Control allows you to modify the desktop (and run multiple desktops). Safari is Apple's web browser.

3. **C.** Use Screen Sharing in macOS to allow another user to view and take control of your Mac. (The remote user could also use VNC.) Remote Desktop and Remote Assistance are similar programs used in Windows. Screen mirroring is a technology (common in mobile devices) that allows the display to be mirrored to a TV or to another computer.

4. **D.** Use the Boot Camp Assistant to dual-boot macOS and Windows on a Mac. Ubuntu is a distribution of Linux. **apt-get** is a command run in Linux to install, uninstall, and upgrade applications. **bootrec** is a command used in Windows to troubleshoot Boot Manager and data store issues.

5. **B.** Use the Time Machine to save the state of the computer or to restore to that computer's earlier state. This is similar to the Windows System Restore utility. Force Quit is a utility in macOS that will close a nonresponsive application. Disk Utility is used to verify and repair macOS drives.

6. **C.** AirPrint is the technology used to install printers automatically into macOS (as long as the printer is compatible with macOS). Bonjour is a networking technology used by macOS to locate networked computers and devices. The Magic Mouse is an Apple mouse that allows for special clicking and gesturing, making it easier to navigate through macOS. iCloud is Apple's cloud infrastructure, where a Mac user can store and back up data. While AirPrint might locate the printer driver on iCloud, iCloud is not the best answer.

7. **B.** A pinwheel, otherwise known as the spinning pinwheel of death (SPOD), is an Apple macOS proprietary crash screen. An example of a Microsoft Windows proprietary crash screen is the Blue Screen of Death (BSOD). Linux is an open-source operating system. Although there are crash screens in Linux, they are not considered proprietary. A spinning wheel could possibly be *caused* by a failing CPU, but it is more likely caused by a stalled or frozen application.

8. **A. ls** will list the directory contents in Linux and macOS. It is similar to the **dir** command in Windows (which can also be used in Linux). **pwd** is used to display the full path of the working directory (for example, /home/root). **cd** is used to change directories. It is very similar to the Windows command of the same name. **mv** is used to move files.

9. **D.** Use the **chmod** command to change permissions in Linux and macOS. **ps** displays information about a given process. **chown** changes ownership of a file. NTFS is the file system used by Windows that allows for file-level security assigned by the user or group.

10. **C. iwconfig** is used to display the configuration settings of a wireless adapter in Linux (but not in macOS). It can also be used to configure that adapter. **ifconfig** shows the configuration details for wired connections. **ipconfig** shows the configuration details of network connections in Windows. **grep** is used to search for matching information in specified files.

CORE 2 (220-1002)

Domain 2.0: Security

CHAPTER 31

Physical and Logical Security

This chapter covers the following A+ 220-1002 exam objectives:

▶ **2.1** – Summarize the importance of physical security measures.

▶ **2.2** – Explain logical security concepts.

Welcome to the first chapter on security. Everyone should have some basic knowledge of information security. Computers and computer networks are constantly at risk, and new risks are always rearing their ugly heads.

This chapter is broken into two parts: physical security and logical security. Simply stated, an attacker might try to break into a facility physically, or hack into a system logically. And I use the terms "break" and "hack" loosely—the methods used to accomplish those ends can vary. The goal of this chapter is to present some basic options for securing against a person who would: 1. Attempt to unlawfully enter a building or other location; and 2. Attempt to unlawfully gain access to a computer network, and individual systems. We're also securing against the tools, software, and computers that a person might employ.

Know this: *Nothing is 100 percent secure*. It is impossible to completely secure something. Attackers and hackers are always finding ways to get around security solutions—it just takes time and persistence. So, what we are interested in are solutions that are *relatively* secure. We need powerful security methods that are within budget, but not so cumbersome that they will bring our computers and networks to a crawl. That's the essence of a good security plan. To repeat, nothing is 100 percent secure. Keep that in mind as we progress through these security chapters.

Note

Remember that the CompTIA A+ is not a security certification, but because security is such an important part of the IT world, it is given a substantial percentage of the exam. As such, we will spend several chapters on security topics.

2.1 – Summarize the importance of physical security measures

Physical security has to do with the tangible, visible, and hands-on methods of preventing access to a home, building, server room, data center, or any other location. There are lots of ways to accomplish an acceptable level of physical security. Let's start with one of the most important—yet often overlooked—methods: the lock.

Physical Locks

The physical lock and key is one of the oldest security methods used as a deterrent against unlawful entry. In addition to main entrances, you should always lock server rooms, wiring closets, labs, and other technical rooms when not in use. It should be documented who has the keys to server rooms, data centers, and wiring closets. Locks should be changed out and rotated with other locks every so often. This keeps things dynamic and harder to guess at. Another type of lock is the cipher lock, which uses a punch code to unlock the door. These physical methods might be used by themselves or combined with an electronic system.

It's important to use a lock for the room that the servers are in, but the servers themselves can also be locked up. Consider placing them in a well-ventilated, lockable cabinet. Special cable locks can also be installed for PCs, laptops, and servers. Some PC cases come with built-in locks. Configure the BIOS to log when someone opens the case of the computer. This is logged as a chassis intrusion notification. Use a USB lock to stop people from removing USB devices or to block the physical ports.

Entry Systems

The most common electronic entry system is the cardkey system. These use proximity-based door access cards that you simply press against, or near, a transmitter next to the door handle. They are often RFID-based. Although these are common, they are not the most secure option (smart cards can be more secure, as we will discuss in a moment). But because they are less expensive than other systems, you will see them quite often. Other electronic systems use key cards that incorporate a photo ID (a worker's badge). These can contain information about the identity of the user, which in combination with a *badge reader* ultimately authenticates the user. These don't have to be cards; they can come in smaller form factors, such as *key fobs*, which can be attached right to a user's keychain. These systems will sometimes offer entry control, which will limit someone's ability to enter or exit during certain times of the day and identify and check names against an authenticated roster or an *entry control roster*.

Moving on to the next level of security, let's talk briefly about the smart card. These are cards that have a nano-processor and can actually communicate with the authentication system. Examples of these include the Personal Identity Verification (PIV) card used by U.S. government employees and contractors and the Common Access Card (CAC) used by Department of Defense (DoD) personnel. These cards identify the owner, authenticate them to areas of the building and to computers, and can digitally sign and encrypt files and e-mail with the RSA encryption algorithm (using an RSA token). Because these are physical items a user carries to gain access to specific systems, they are known as *hardware-based tokens*. A token might also display a code that changes, say, every minute or so; these are known as one-time password (OTP) tokens. When a person wants access to a particular system, such as the accounting system or other confidential system, that person would have to type the current code that is shown on the token into the computer. This is a powerful method of authentication but can be expensive as well.

Some organizations will design what is known as a *mantrap*, which is an area with two locking doors. A person might get past a first door by following someone else in (tailgating/piggybacking), but might have difficulty getting past the second door, especially if there is a security guard in between the two doors. If the person doesn't have proper authentication, he or she will be stranded in the mantrap until authorities arrive.

Biometrics

Biometrics is the science of recognizing humans based on one or more physical characteristics. Biometrics is used as a form of authentication and access control. It is also used to identify persons who might be under surveillance.

Biometrics falls into the category of "something a person is." Examples of bodily characteristics that are measured include fingerprints, retinal patterns, iris patterns, and even bone structure. Biometric readers (for example, fingerprint scanners) are becoming more common in door-access systems and can be found integrated with mobile devices or used as external USB devices that connect to the computer. Biometric information can also be combined with smart card technology. An example of a biometric door-access system is Suprema, which has various levels of access systems, including some that incorporate smart cards and biometrics, together forming a multifactor authentication system. There are also less expensive consumer-grade biometric locks that often include a fingerprint reader as well as a key code or a key lock. One example of biometric hardware for a local computer is a USB-based fingerprint scanner, which is used to authenticate users during the login process.

Biometrics can be seen in many movies and TV shows. However, some biometric systems are easily compromised. It has only been of late that readily available biometric systems have started to live up to their hype. Thorough investigation and testing of a biometric system is necessary before purchase and installation. In addition, it should be used in a multifactor authentication scheme. The more factors, the better, as long as your users can handle it. (You would be surprised what a little bit of training can do.) Voice recognition software has made great leaps and bounds since the turn of the millennium. A combination of biometrics, voice recognition, and pin access would make for an excellent three-factor authentication system. But, as always, only if you can get it through budgeting!

Protecting Data Physically

Confidential documents should never be left sitting out in the open. They should either be properly filed in a locking cabinet or shredded and disposed of when they are no longer needed. Passwords should not be written down and definitely not left on a desk or taped to a monitor where they can be seen. Many organizations implement a clean desk policy that states each user must remove all papers from his or her desk before leaving for lunch, breaks, or at the end of the day. Anything that shows on the computer screen can be protected in a variety of ways. To protect data while the person is working, you can use a privacy screen, or install a privacy filter, which is a transparent cover for PC monitors and laptop displays. It reduces the cone of vision, usually to about 30 degrees, so that only the person in front of the screen can see the content shown on the screen. Many of these are also antiglare, helping to reduce eye stress of the user. Also, users should lock their computers whenever they leave their workstations. Windows can also be automatically set to lock after a certain amount of time, even if users forget to do so manually.

Cram Quiz

Answer these questions. The answers follow the last question. If you cannot answer these questions correctly, consider reading this section again until you can.

1. Which of the following is the science of recognizing humans based on physical characteristics?

   ○ **A.** Mantraps

   ○ **B.** Biometrics

   ○ **C.** Tailgating

   ○ **D.** CAC

2. You have been tasked with preventing unwanted removal of a webcam. Which of the following tools should you implement?

   ○ **A.** Smart card

   ○ **B.** USB fingerprint scanner

   ○ **C.** USB lock

   ○ **D.** Privacy filter

Cram Quiz Answers

1. **B.** Biometrics is the science of recognizing humans based on physical characteristics. In the authentication world, it falls into the category of "something a person is." Mantraps are areas of a building implemented in an effort to stop tailgating. CAC stands for Common Access Card, used by defense personnel such as DoD employees.

2. **C.** Use a USB lock to prevent the removal of USB-based devices such as external USB hard drives, keyboards, mice, and webcams. Smart cards and USB-based fingerprint scanners are ways to authenticate a user to the computer or network. A privacy filter is used to prevent shoulder surfing—when a person attempts to watch what a user is typing/performing in the system—by reducing the viewing angle.

2.2 – Explain logical security concepts

Logical security has to do with operating systems, programs, and data. It will be less tangible than physical security, but when combined with the physical, and if implemented properly, can provide for a high level of security. A lot of what we will discuss is within the realm of authentication. Let's start with that.

Authentication

Unauthorized access can be prevented through the use of authentication, which is the verification of a person's identity. It is a preventive measure that can be broken down as the following categories:

- ▶ Something the user knows (for example, a password or PIN). These are known as *knowledge factors*.

- ▶ Something the user has (for example, a smart card or other security token). These are known as *possession factors*.

- ▶ Something the user is (for example, the biometric reading of a fingerprint or retina scan). These are known as *inherence factors*.

- ▶ Something the user does (for example, a signature or speaking words). These are known as *behavioral factors*.

- ▶ Somewhere the user is (for example, at work or at home). These are known as *location-based factors*.

The first three categories (or factors) are the most common. A powerful security methodology is to combine two or more of these factors together. When this is done, it is known as *multifactor authentication (MFA)*. An example of this is the combination of a password (knowledge factor) and a smart card (possession factor). Or, combining a fingerprint (inherence factor) with a software token that has been installed to a user's smartphone (possession factor). Both of these are two-factor authentication schemes that you will probably see in the field. The beauty of MFA is that if one factor is defeated or compromised by a malicious person, then the second factor still stands. Think about it for a couple of minutes. Imagine some scenarios where two-factor authentication can help to prevent a security breach. Of course, efficient and effective multifactor user authentication only works well if it is strong: complex passwords, powerful biometric systems, and updated smart card systems.

> **ExamAlert**
>
> When two or more authentication factors are combined, the result is multifactor authentication (MFA).

Principle of Least Privilege

This principle says that a user should have access to only what is required. If a user needs to update Excel files and browse the Internet, that user should not be given administrative access. You might think of this as common sense, but it should not be taken lightly. When user accounts are created locally on a computer and especially on a domain, great care should be taken when assigning users to groups. Also, as many programs are installed, they request who can use and make modifications to the program; quite often, the default is All Users. Some technicians just click Next when hastily installing programs, without realizing that the user now has full control of the program—control that you might not want to provide them. Just remember, keep users on a need-to-know basis; give them access only to what they specifically need to do their job.

One example of a Microsoft technology that is based on this principle is User Account Control (UAC). It is a security component of Windows that keeps every user (besides the actual Administrator account) in standard user mode instead of as an administrator with full administrative rights—even if the user is a member of the administrators group. It is meant to prevent unauthorized access and avoid user error in the form of accidental changes. With UAC enabled, users perform common tasks as non-administrators and, when necessary, as administrators, without having to switch users, log off, or use Run As.

Basically, UAC was created with two goals in mind: first, to eliminate unnecessary requests for excessive administrative-level access to Windows resources, and second, to reduce the risk of malicious software using the administrator's access control to infect operating system files. When a standard end user requires administrator privileges to perform certain tasks (such as installing an application), a small pop-up UAC window appears, notifying the user that an administrator credential is necessary. If the user has administrative rights and clicks Continue, the task will be carried out; if the user does *not* have sufficient rights (and can't provide an administrative password), the attempt fails. Note that these pop-up UAC windows do not appear if the person is logged on with the actual Administrator account.

Active Directory

We don't cover too much concerning servers in this book, but this is an exception. Get ready for a crash course on Active Directory!

A Microsoft *domain* is a network of Windows computers that is controlled by a Windows Server which has Active Directory installed—that server is a *domain controller*. Active Directory (AD) is a Microsoft directory service that centralizes the management of user accounts, computer accounts, and so on, for the domain.

> **ExamAlert**
>
> Know that a domain is Microsoft's implementation of a client/server network. It centralizes the management of users and computers.

For a user to log on to the domain, that person must have a user account on the domain controller, and the user must know the username, password, and the domain to be logged on to; for example, dpro42.com. In addition, the Windows client computer must have been configured to connect to the domain previously.

The user account is stored within the domain in one of two places: within the Users folder (which is the default) or within an organizational unit that the administrator has created. Figure 31.1 shows an example of this.

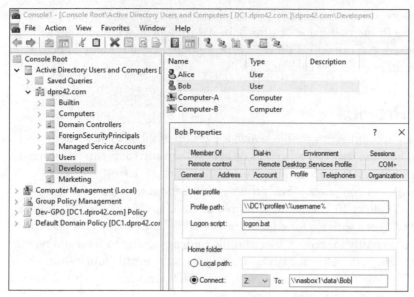

FIGURE 31.1   **User account stored on a domain controller in Active Directory**

I packed a lot of stuff into Figure 31.1. Here we have a Windows Server that is acting as a domain controller (which means it has AD installed). We are working within Active Directory Users and Computers, which, as the name implies, is where you would go to add, remove, and configure user accounts and computer accounts. I actually added it to an MMC along with a few other snap-ins. By default, users are created within the Users folder, which you can find by following the path **Active Directory Users and Computers > *Domain Name* > Users**. Dpro42.com is the domain name I chose for this Microsoft network (I own the domain as well). The Users folder has lots of built-in users and groups for you to work with.

However, as I mentioned, you can also add users to an *organizational unit (OU)*, which is a container that you can use to categorize your users and computers. Also, you can apply separate group policies for each OU. This allows you to configure different rules for each set of users, groups, and computers, from one OU to the next. There's a *lot* more to it, but that should suffice for the A+ exam.

Generally, I set up OUs to mimic an organization's departments. So, as shown in Figure 31.1, I've created two OUs: Developers and Marketing. The Developers OU is selected, and on the right you can see that there are two users and two computers within that OU: Alice, Bob, Computer-A, and Computer-B; all of which I created.

Furthermore, the user account "Bob" is selected, and you can see that I have opened the Properties dialog box for Bob. We are looking at the Profile tab. This is where you can set up a profile path, logon script, and home folder for the account. Let's discuss each one briefly.

User Profiles

Every user account gets a profile, which is a group of folders and settings based on how the user configures his or her desktop environment: Start menu options, desktop icons, background color, and so on. By default, when a user first logs on to a computer, a *local* profile is created and stored on that computer. In Windows 10, this profile is stored in C:\Users*%userprofile%*, where *%userprofile%* is a variable for whichever user is currently logged on. You can get to the currently logged-on user's profile folder by going to **Run** and typing **%userprofile%**, or **%homepath%**. That displays the profile folders and—if you are showing hidden files—the NTUSER.DAT file, which is what Windows actually uses to store the profile data.

Now, if you would like a user's profile to follow the user from one computer to the next on a domain, what you want is a *roaming* profile. That's a profile that is stored on a server. And that's where the Profile path field in Figure 31.1 comes in. In the figure we have configured the location of this user's roaming profile as \\DC1\profiles\%username%. *DC1* is the computer where the profile is stored. In this case it is the domain controller that we are working on, but it might be stored somewhere else, and it's probably a good idea to do so. *profiles* is the share name for the folder where all the user profiles are stored. *%username%* is another variable, which takes the place of the account name. (We could have used "Bob" if we wanted to, with the same result, but you can appreciate the power of a variable, especially if you will be working with a lot of accounts.) As long as the path to the profile is valid, the domain controller will store it there, and the user can log on to various computers on the network while the profile follows the user around.

Logon Script

A logon script is used to assign tasks that are executed when the user logs on to the domain. It could include running programs, mapping network drives, setting variables, updating anti-malware applications, running commands, and calling other scripts. The idea is to automate the configuration process of a user's environment and workflow so that the user can simply sit down, log on, and start working. In Figure 31.1 the script is called logon.bat. Who knows, maybe some command-line functionality is included in the script; for example, a static ARP entry is created to a server (**arp -s**), or perhaps a particular program such as Excel is opened up. Imagine the power of scripting! In the figure we chose logon.bat as the name, which means it is a batch file, but you could use Visual Basic or the PowerShell to create scripts. Whatever you use, the file has to be stored; either in the default location on the server (NETLOGON), or elsewhere, in which case the path to the file location must be entered into the field in addition to the filename.

Home Folder

The home folder is where a user will store documents by default. Looking again at Figure 31.1, if you select the **Local path** option, then stored documents will end up at the local computer that the user is sitting at. However, the idea behind having a Microsoft domain is so that you can centrally store files. So, in many cases you will select **Connect:** and use a mapped network drive (such as Z:) to a path. In Figure 31.1, we are mapping Z: to *nasbox1*, which has a share called *data*, and finally to a folder named *Bob*. This way, regardless of the computer that Bob logs on to, data will be stored to that Z: drive.

> **Note**
>
> The last three concepts (profile, logon script, and home folder) can be used on a local Windows system as well. Just go to **Computer Management > System Tools > Local Users and Groups > Users**, right-click the user in question and select **Properties**, then go to the **Profile** tab. The same options are there, but they will be limited without the use of a domain. The whole concept here is that having a domain allows you to centralize data, profiles, and home folders—everything is more organized and more easily monitored, and that *usually* equates to more security.

Group Policy

Group policies are part of Windows, whether you are working at a local system or within a domain. They house all of the rules that users must abide by within the OS; for example, what programs they can use, and when passwords have to be changed. There are hundreds of policies that can be modified to secure the system. In a domain environment, there is a default domain policy which is stored on the domain controller; it affects all typical users that are created. However, you can create separate policies for users that are organized into OUs. In Figure 31.1 you will see in the left pane a policy named Dev-GPO [DC1.dpro42.com] Policy. That is a policy that I created just for the Developers OU, with its two users and two computers. It could be that I want those users to have even longer passwords than the rest of the users on the domain. That can be accomplished by modifying the Dev-GPO Policy.

On the local system you can modify the group policy by going to **Run** and typing **gpedit.msc**, which opens the Group Policy Editor. Some of the most common policies that you will modify include the Password Policy and Account Lockout Policy (to name a couple). These can be accessed quicker by going to **Run** and typing **secpol.msc**, which brings you to the Local Security Policy console window, a subset of the entire Group Policy. Figure 31.2 shows an example of this window on a Windows 10 Pro computer, with the Password Policy opened. Policy modification is essentially the same regardless of whether the policy is stored on a local Windows client or on a Windows domain controller.

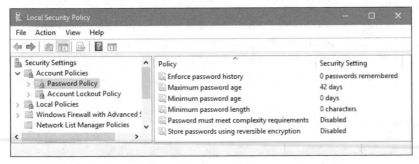

FIGURE 31.2   **Local Security Policy opened to the Password Policy**

> ### ExamAlert
>
> Know how to access and configure the Group Policy Editor (**gpedit.msc**) and the Local Security Policy (**secpol.msc**).

A Quick Word About AD

This is just the tip of the iceberg when it comes to Active Directory; that's why there are loads of Microsoft certifications dealing with Windows Server. It should be enough for the A+ exam, but if you are interested in learning more, then I recommend you check out the following links:

▶ Getting Started with Windows Server 2019:
   https://docs.microsoft.com/en-us/windows-server/get-started-19/get-started-19

▶ Windows Server 2019 Free Trial:
   https://www.microsoft.com/en-us/cloud-platform/windows-server-trial

Firewalls

The Windows Defender Firewall is meant to protect client computers from malicious attacks and intrusions, but sometimes it can be the culprit when it comes to certain applications failing. You can access the firewall in Windows by going to **Control Panel > Windows Defender Firewall** or by accessing the **Run** prompt and typing **firewall.cpl**. From here you can enable or disable the firewall for the Private network profile and the Public/Guest network profile. By default, these are on, or "connected."

When the firewall is on, the default setting is to shield all inbound ports (effectively closing them). This is a type of default *port security*, and it means that certain applications that need to communicate with a remote host might not work properly. Or if the client computer wanted to host some services (such as FTP or a web server), the firewall would block them. That's where exceptions come in. You can still use the firewall, but you can specify applications that are exceptions to the rule. Figure 31.3 shows an example of exceptions made on a Windows 10 Pro computer. To create exceptions, click the **Allow an app or feature Through Windows Defender Firewall** link.

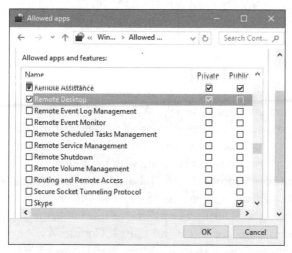

FIGURE 31.3   **Firewall exceptions**

In this example, we have two applications that are not blocked from incoming connections. Remote Assistance is not blocked at all, not on the Private profile nor on the Public profile. However, Remote Desktop is allowed only on the Private profile (listed as Home/Work Private Network in Windows 7). So, as long as the firewall is enabled, this computer can make Remote Assistance calls to other users on the Internet. But if a person wanted to connect to this system through Remote Desktop without an invitation, that person would have to be on the LAN. This way, we aren't sacrificing the entire security of the system. All other incoming connections will be blocked.

We can get more in-depth with the firewall settings. By clicking the **Advanced Settings** link, we can make use of the Windows Defender Firewall with Advanced Security (also available in Administrative Tools and as a snap-in in the MMC). You can also get to this by opening the **Run** prompt and typing **wf.msc**. From here, you can create inbound and outbound rules for individual applications based on the private network, the public network, or both. You can also configure the firewall with the **netsh** command or within the PowerShell. For more information follow this link: https://tinyurl.com/WFDAS.

If the firewall gives you errors when attempting to either update the firewall settings, add exceptions, or access the advanced settings, make sure the Windows Firewall service is enabled and running in services.msc.

Essentially, the firewall is a packet filter which uses *access control lists (ACLs)* to specify what packets can pass through. ACLs are composed of source and destination IP addresses and ports, as well as the type of packets to be allowed or denied. ACLs are written differently depending on what device or program you are using. In Windows they can be written using the PowerShell, or configured graphically using the Windows Defender Firewall with Advanced Security.

VPN

We discussed virtual private networks (VPNs) briefly in Chapters 7, "Networked Hosts and Network Configuration," and 29, "Windows Networking and Application Installation." In essence, a VPN is a way of tunneling through the Internet securely, instead of relying on the security (or lack thereof) of your ISP. Microsoft Windows VPN connections can be made with the following protocols: Point-to-Point Tunneling Protocol (PPTP), Layer Two Tunneling Protocol (L2TP), Secure Socket Tunneling Protocol (SSTP), or Internet Key Exchange version 2 (IKEv2) protocols. During the writing of this book, the preferred methods for Windows clients are SSTP and IKEv2. Certain Windows VPN security features only work with IKEv2, such as LockDown VPN, which secures the computer in a way where traffic can only flow over the VPN connection, and no other network connections or adapters, while the VPN session is active. You can also configure traffic filtering rules based on protocols, and using port and IP address ranges.

When signing into a VPN from a Windows client, you need to know the server name or its IP address (often a public IP), and you need to configure the VPN type (IKEv2 and so on). Then you have to specify the sign-in information, which could be the typical username and password, or it might use a smart card, an OTP, or a certificate.

ExamAlert

Know that VPNs use secure tunneling protocols to connect secure private networks (or devices) together through the public (unsecured) Internet.

Note

Some organizations use VPN servers or appliances that are not quite compatible with the Windows VPN client. In those cases, always-on VPN services such as OpenVPN can be used, but a separate client has to be downloaded and installed to the Windows computer.

Note

We'll be covering antivirus, anti-malware, MAC filtering, and e-mail filtering in Chapter 32, "Wireless Security, Malware, and Social Engineering."

Additional Security Considerations in Windows

This is a catch-all for the remainder of the topics in this objective, so we'll be jumping from one concept to the next quickly. Let's start with data loss prevention.

DLP

Are you concerned with the risk of data loss? Enter DLP. Not me! (I just happen to share the same initials.) Data loss prevention (DLP) is a concept that refers to the monitoring of data in use, data in motion, and data at rest. A DLP system performs content inspection and is designed to prevent unauthorized use of data as well as prevent the leakage of data outside the computer (or network) that it resides in. DLP systems can be software- or hardware-based solutions that are installed on the client computer, on storage devices, or as part of the network (or cloud). Cloud-based DLP solutions are offered by most cloud providers to protect against data breaches and misuse of data. These often integrate with software, infrastructure, and platform services, and can include any of the systems mentioned previously.

Microsoft has a variety of DLP-based technologies depending on the software used (for example, Windows Server or Exchange Server). For Windows 10 (as of version 1607), Microsoft offers Windows Information Protection (WIP), which protects against the accidental leakage of data. However, it is not designed to protect against malicious attackers. The usage of this and several other security tools from Microsoft requires Intune or the System Center Configuration Manager (SCCM).

MDM Policies

For large organizations that have many mobile devices, a *mobile device management (MDM)* suite can be implemented. An MDM solution can take care of pushing updates and configuring hundreds of mobile devices from a central location. Decent quality MDM software will secure, monitor, manage, and support multiple different types of mobile devices across the enterprise.

Let's not forget that Windows 10 runs on many mobile devices, and they can be administered from a centralized MDM solution such as Microsoft Intune, VMware AirWatch, Cisco Meraki, and SOTI MobiControl. Elements that you might administer and enforce include device setup, policy acceptance, profile distribution, device tracking, roaming mitigation, remote lock, remote wipe, and so on. We'll discuss MDM more in Chapter 34, "Mobile Device Security."

Trusted and Untrusted Software Sources

There are trusted and untrusted examples of all kinds of software, from OSes to applications, and more. Some organizations trust more software than others. But when it comes to Windows, it's important to think about applications and drivers.

You can block untrusted software using a variety of approaches. You can use tools from third parties or tools built into Windows. For example, in Windows 10 (version 1703 and higher), go to **Settings > Apps > Apps & Features**. At the top you will see a drop-down menu with some options where you can specify what apps are allowed (from the Microsoft Store only, warn before installing apps, and allow from anywhere). In a smaller environment, you can also use Microsoft Family and Safety to block apps and games from being installed.

A good administrator should also think along the lines of policies, directory permissions, and user account types, and not allow a typical user to install programs at all. One way to do this is to block users from installing and running programs in the Local Group Policy Editor (**gpedit.msc**). Navigate to **Computer Configuration > Administrative Templates > Windows Components > Windows Installer**. From here you can disable the Windows Installer altogether, prevent users from working with the Windows Installer, and so on.

In addition, make sure that UAC is enabled on the computer so that it will require administrative privileges to open particular programs. Going beyond this, an admin can block specific applications. One way to do this is in **Local Security Policy (secpol.msc) > Software Restriction Policies**. By creating a new policy here, you can whitelist applications, set enforcement rules, designate file extension types, and set rules for trusted publishers of programs.

Finally, programs such as Windows Defender and Intune can be instrumental in blocking the installation of unwanted programs from unknown sources.

I mentioned previously in the book that driver signing is important because it helps to eliminate the chance of installing device drivers that might interfere with, or crash, the operating system. So, driver signing is enabled by default in Windows, and it will prevent the installation of unsigned drivers. However, you might find a computer where driver signing has been disabled. Unless the computer is being used by a professional (engineer, developer, and so on), and it was turned off for a reason, then you will want to enable it. To do this in Windows 10, reboot the computer to Startup Settings, enter the Command Prompt, and type **bcdedit /set nointegritychecks off**. That's a double-negative, and so it will enable driver signing. We'll discuss Startup Settings in Chapter 36, "Troubleshooting Microsoft Windows."

Certificates

Certificates are used to encrypt data sessions that are initiated by a web browser or other application. Certificates are stored on the client computer—without them, the corresponding applications will either display an error or run in an insecure manner.

Certificates for IE/Edge can be viewed, imported, and removed from within the **Internet Properties** dialog box > **Content** tab > **Certificates** button. Other web browsers—such as Firefox—will access them differently. For example,

Firefox version 65.0.2 (March 2019) allows import/export and other modifications at **Settings > Privacy & Security > Certificates > View Certificates**.

To view all certificates installed to Windows, go to the Certificate Manager (**Run > certmgr.msc**). From here you can view Trusted Root Certification Authorities, Trusted Publishers, and so on. Certificates can be deleted, exported, and more. If there is a security issue with a program or connection to the Internet, and the corresponding certificate, this is one place where you would go to fix the problem.

Train users to avoid websites that do not use a valid certificate. For example, a user might attempt to connect to a website, and receive a message that says, "Your connection is not private." This means either the certificate is invalid or there is no certificate, and an HTTPS session cannot be initiated. That means that any information that passes through from the client to the server can be captured by an attacker. See an example of this at the innocuous site https://untrusted-root.badssl.com/. A user can get past this by clicking Advanced and allowing the session, but they should be trained otherwise. In addition, you can configure the browser (or anti-malware program) to block access altogether if this and similar errors occur. Note that some browsers will allow these connections by default (if the user goes to Advanced and proceeds through). This is an example of an inherent lack of security, which will always exist to some extent. That's why user education is so important. Train your users!

Cram Quiz

Answer these questions. The answers follow the last question. If you cannot answer these questions correctly, consider reading this section again until you can.

1. When is a Windows 10 computer completely secure?

   ○ **A.** When you have updated to the latest version.

   ○ **B.** When you have locked down the Local Security Policy.

   ○ **C.** When Microsoft releases the latest update.

   ○ **D.** Never.

2. Which of the following is a built-in security component of Windows 10?

   ○ **A.** UAC

   ○ **B.** Firefox

   ○ **C.** Active Directory

   ○ **D.** MFA

3. You have been tasked with configuring a user account so that its folders and settings will follow the user to whatever computer the user logs on to within the domain. Which of the following should you configure?

   ○ **A.** OU

   ○ **B.** Roaming profile

   ○ **C.** Logon script

   ○ **D.** Home folder mapped to a network drive

4. You need to block users from installing programs in Windows 10. Of the following, what tool should you select?

   ○ **A. wf.msc**

   ○ **B.** IKEv2

   ○ **C.** WIP

   ○ **D. gpedit.msc**

   ○ **E. certmgr.msc**

Cram Quiz Answers

1. **D.** Neither Windows 10 nor any other technology is ever completely secure. It is impossible. But we can reduce risk to a certain extent by configuring the system properly and by using technology wisely—ultimately providing *relative security*. Updating to the latest version is often a good idea (if done according to company policy), but we can't rely on software updates alone. Using the Local Security Policy you can mold to "lock down" the system to a certain extent, but again, it is only one method. It's the combination of security updates, security configurations, and user education that should be part of an overall security plan.

2. **A.** User Account Control (UAC) adds a layer of security to Windows to protect against malware and user error and conserve resources. Firefox is considered by many to be a secure web browser, but it is not included in Windows 10, nor can it be called a "security component"; it is a browser. Active Directory runs on Windows Server (though it can be accessed remotely from a Windows 10 client); while it can increase the security of an organization's Windows network, it isn't a security component per se. Multifactor authentication (MFA) is when two or more types of identification are required to be authenticated to a system, network, or facility. MFA is not a built-in security component of Windows 10, but it can be accomplished on a Windows 10 system—for example, by using the default username/password scheme (something the person knows), adding a USB-based fingerprint scanner (something the person is), and configuring them to both be used during logon to Windows.

3. **B.** Configure a roaming profile for the user. The roaming profile is configured at the domain controller and allows the user to move from one computer to the next, while the user profile follows—as long as the user is logging on with the same username and password, and logging on to the domain. Refer to Figure 31.1 for the paths and naming conventions. OU stands for organizational unit—a way of

organizing users, computers, and policies. The logon script is designed to execute programs, features, and actions when the user logs on. As long as the user logs on to the domain, it will be initiated. The home folder is simply the default location where a user will save and download files; it can be either local or mapped to a network drive, the latter of which is preferred on a domain.

4. **D.** Use the Group Policy Editor (**Run > gpedit.msc**) to make modifications to how (and if) programs are installed to Windows. (There are a variety of other ways as well.) **Run > wf.msc** brings up the Windows Defender Firewall with Advanced Security. Internet Key Exchange version 2 (IKEv2) is a preferred protocol for use with the Windows VPN client. Windows Information Protection (WIP) protects against accidental data leakage; it's a type of DLP. **Run > certmgr.msc** brings up the Certificate Manager, where you can import, export, and delete encryption certificates.

Yowza, that was a lot of content. Great job so far!

CHAPTER 32

Wireless Security, Malware, and Social Engineering

This chapter covers the following A+ 220-1002 exam objectives:

▶ **2.3** – Compare and contrast wireless security protocols and authentication methods.

▶ **2.4** – Given a scenario, detect, remove, and prevent malware using appropriate tools and methods.

▶ **2.5** – Compare and contrast social engineering, threats, and vulnerabilities.

You can't get enough security! That's because nothing is ever 100 percent secure, as I mentioned in the previous chapter. However, we need to temper our vigilance and security aggressiveness by using prioritization. Always be thinking in terms of the most urgent threats and vulnerabilities to your organization, and continue the list of risks from there. Secure these accordingly, starting from the top.

This chapter continues on our security journey by discussing wireless security and authentication, how to prevent malware, and some different social engineering and technical attacks that you should know. It's a bit of a catch-all chapter due to the number of varying concepts covered, but I'll try to make it as pleasant as possible by breaking it up into manageable sections. Let's go!

2.3 – Compare and contrast wireless security protocols and authentication methods

ExamAlert

Objective 2.3 concentrates on the following: protocols and encryption (WEP, WPA, WPA2, TKIP, and AES), and authentication (single-factor, multifactor, RADIUS, TACACS).

Wi-Fi connections are used by PCs, laptops, tablets, smartphones, industrial devices, and the list goes on. However, with ease of use comes additional security considerations. The plain truth is that a signal traveling in the air is going to be more insecure than one traversing a cable. So, we need to use proper wireless protocols and encryption protocols. Let's talk about some of those now.

Wireless and Encryption Protocols

We discussed wireless connectivity and wireless encryption protocols in Chapter 6, "SOHO Networks and Wireless Protocols." Let's review those protocols now. Table 32.1 shows the protocols you should know for the exam.

TABLE 32.1 **Wireless Encryption Methods**

Wireless Protocol	Description	Encryption Level
WEP	Wired Equivalent Privacy	64-bit
	Deprecated and vulnerable to IV attack	
WPA	Wi-Fi Protected Access	128-bit
WPA2	Version 2	256-bit
TKIP	Temporal Key Integrity Protocol	128-bit
	Deprecated encryption protocol used with WEP or WPA	
AES	Advanced Encryption Standard	128-, 192-, and 256-bit
	Encryption protocol used with WPA/WPA2	

ExamAlert

Know the differences between WEP, WPA, WPA2, TKIP, and AES.

At the writing of this book (2019) the best option is to go with WPA2 for wireless connectivity, and AES for data encryption over that wireless connection. In fact, it may be your only option depending on the client used. For example, in Windows 10 Pro, if you select WPA2 (personal or enterprise), you will be forced by default to use AES. Figure 32.1 shows an example of this.

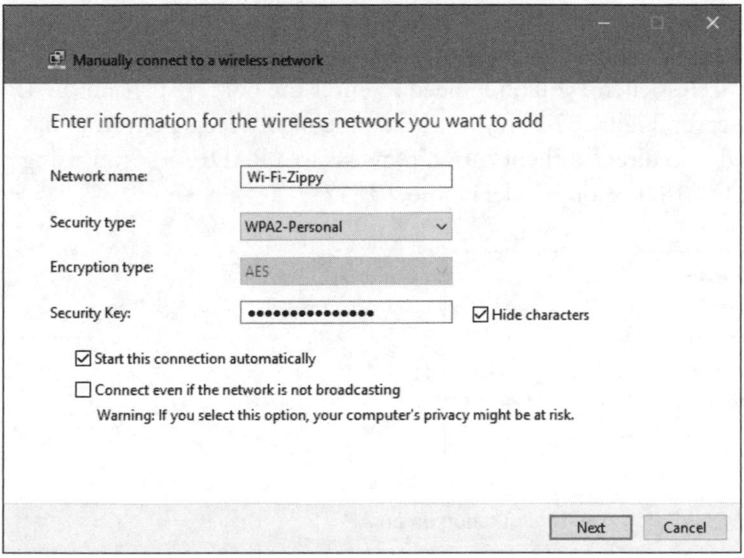

FIGURE 32.1   **Manual wireless network connection in Windows**

The Encryption type field is grayed out, and while you could modify that in the Group Policy Editor or in the Registry Editor, it's usually not wise. What would be wise is to check the **Hide characters** checkbox for the Security Key—by default on some systems the box is not checked and it displays what is typed.

In the figure, our security type is WPA2-Personal. That means that we are connecting to a basic Wi-Fi access point, and that there is a pre-shared key (PSK) that allows access. It is stored on the AP. However, there are other options; some less secure, and some more secure. The no authentication (Open) option has no key, no security, but you might use that to temporarily make a network connection and download the required software. Many larger organizations will disable this option so that users and admins cannot connect without encryption. WEP is also listed, which is generally not recommended because it can be compromised.

The more secure options include WPA2-Enterprise and 802.1X. WPA2-Enterprise, as the name implies, is designed for larger networks; ones that use an authentication server of some sort. That could be a RADIUS server or a Terminal Access Controller Access-Control System Plus (TACACS+) server. These can be used as centralized authentication platforms for wireless connections and a variety of other authentication purposes, and can be used as a single sign-on (SSO) server as well. The more common Remote Authentication Dial-In User Service (RADIUS) provides centralized administration of dial-up, VPN, and wireless authentication and can be used with 802.1X as well. It uses ports 1812 and 1813 by default, and when connecting to a RADIUS server from a wireless client, you often need to enter the port (1812) and the IP address of the server. Figure 32.2 shows an example of an access point that has been configured to redirect authentication requests to a RADIUS server using the IP address 172.18.0.13 on the default port 1812.

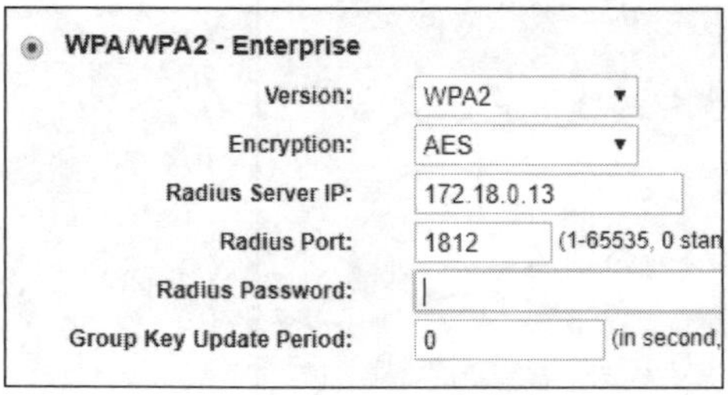

⦿ **WPA/WPA2 - Enterprise**		
Version:	WPA2 ▼	
Encryption:	AES ▼	
Radius Server IP:	172.18.0.13	
Radius Port:	1812	(1-65535, 0 stan
Radius Password:		
Group Key Update Period:	0	(in second,

FIGURE 32.2   WPA2-Enterprise Configuration on an AP

RADIUS can be run on a variety of devices and servers including Windows Server. RADIUS can also be used as a multifactor authentication tool, or as part of an MFA scheme. This can be much more secure when compared to a single-factor authentication scheme such as a typical WPA2-PSK connection.

> **Note**
>
> 802.1X is an IEEE standard that defines port-based network access control (PNAC). Not to be confused with 802.11x WLAN standards, 802.1X is an authentication technology used to connect hosts to a LAN or WLAN. 802.1X allows you to apply a security control that ties physical ports to end-device MAC addresses, and prevents additional devices from being connected to the network. It is a good way of implementing port security, better than simply setting up MAC address filtering.

Cram Quiz

Answer these questions. The answers follow the last question. If you cannot answer these questions correctly, consider reading this section again until you can.

1. Which of the following is the strongest form of wireless encryption?

   ○ **A.** WPA

   ○ **B.** WEP

   ○ **C.** AES

   ○ **D.** TKIP

2. You have been tasked with connecting wireless clients to a server that supports SSO and 802.1X. Which of the following technologies should you implement? (Select the two best answers.)

   ○ **A.** WPA2-PSK

   ○ **B.** WPA2-ENT

   ○ **C.** WEP

   ○ **D.** TKIP

   ○ **E.** RADIUS

Cram Quiz Answers

1. **C.** Advanced Encryption Standard (AES) is the strongest form of wireless encryption (given the listed answers). WPA is a wireless encryption protocol that is not bad, but WPA2 is recommended. WEP and TKIP are deprecated, have been compromised, and should be avoided. Only use WEP, TKIP, or the no authentication option if you are temporarily connecting a device to a Wi-Fi network in an attempt to update it to a newer protocol, or if you are initiating testing. And even then, use extreme caution!

2. **B and E.** To take advantage of single sign-on (SSO) and 802.1X, you would need a special authentication device (such as RADIUS) on the server side, and WPA2-Enterprise on the client side (sometimes abbreviated as WPA2-ENT). And what port does RADIUS use by default? Remember?

   WPA2-PSK uses a pre-shared key that is stored on the AP, and doesn't support the other technologies. WEP and TKIP are outdated and should be avoided.

2.4 – Given a scenario, detect, remove, and prevent malware using appropriate tools and methods

> **ExamAlert**
>
> **Objective 2.4** focuses on malware (ransomware, Trojan, keylogger, rootkit, virus, botnet, worm, spyware) and the tools and methods for mitigating malware issues (antivirus, anti-malware, recovery console, backup/restore, end user education, software firewalls, DNS configuration).

Malicious software, or *malware*, is software designed to infiltrate a computer system and possibly damage it without the user's knowledge or consent. Malware is a broad term used by computer professionals to include viruses, worms, Trojan horses, spyware, rootkits, keyloggers, adware, and other types of undesirable software.

Malicious Software Types

Of course, we don't want malware to infect our computer systems, but to defend against it, we first need to define it and categorize it. Then we can put preventative measures into place. It's also important to locate and remove/quarantine malware from a computer system in case it does manifest itself. Table 32.2 summarizes the various malware threats you should know for the exam.

TABLE 32.2 **Malware Types**

Malware Threat	Definition
Virus	Code that runs on a computer without the user's knowledge; it infects the computer when the code is accessed and executed.
Worm	Similar to viruses except that it self-replicates, whereas a virus does not.
Trojan horse	Appears to perform desired functions but is actually performing malicious functions behind the scenes.
Spyware	Malicious software either downloaded unwittingly from a website or installed along with some other third-party software with the intention of spying on the user's work.
Rootkit	Software designed to gain administrator-level control over a computer system without being detected.

Malware Threat	Definition
Ransomware	Restricts access to a computer system or locks the system until a ransom is paid. Often propagated by a Trojan, and uses RSA encryption keys to "lock" the files.
Keylogger	Captures all of the keystrokes made by a user on a computer keyboard.
	Software-based: Loaded into a computer knowingly or without the user's knowledge using a Trojan.
	Hardware-based: Connected physically to the keyboard's cable inline, storing data, and possibly transmitting it wirelessly.

> **ExamAlert**
>
> Know the difference between a virus, worm, Trojan horse, rootkit, ransomware, and the other various malware threats!

Malware can be spread in a variety of ways, including removable media, e-mail attachments, downloaded programs, malicious hyperlinks, and the dreaded botnet. A *botnet* is a group of compromised computers that are controlled by a master computer which directs them to attack particular servers and routers on the Internet. It is called a botnet because it is a network of computers—robots, or bots for short—that work as a collective. Usually, the computer is infected with a Trojan that contains the code to connect the system to the botnet. Unless the anti-malware program detects this, the user has no knowledge of it happening; it all occurs behind the scenes. Take a look at the Looking Glass Threat Map (https://map.lookingglasscyber.com/) to see current botnet attacks around the world. We'll discuss botnets a little more later in this chapter.

Preventing Malicious Software

Now that we know the types of malware, let's talk about how to stop them before they happen.

In a nutshell, prevention of malware infection can be performed by using anti-malware programs, updating the OS and apps, scanning the system, policies, and user education. But that's just in a nutshell. Let's dive a little deeper.

Preventing Viruses, Worms, and Trojans

There is some confusion among people about the difference between viruses, worms, and Trojans; even among some hackers and antivirus software developers. That's because there are literally thousands of strains of malware (possibly many more), and they can be quite difficult to classify. To a certain extent, the distinction doesn't matter. The bottom line is this: for the most part, prevention is the same for viruses, worms, and Trojans.

We can do several things to protect a computer system from these. First, every computer should have antivirus (AV) software running on it. Companies that provide antivirus and anti-malware solutions often call them endpoint protection platforms. Second, that software should be updated. If the AV software is bundled with the OS—for example, Windows Defender—then the OS updates will take care of that. If it is third-party AV software, then it means that the software will require a current license; this is renewed yearly with most providers. Or if it is free AV software, you need to periodically check if it is still a full version of the software. If it isn't already set to auto-update, set the AV software to automatically update at periodic intervals (for example, every day or every week). It's a good idea to schedule regular full scans of the system within the AV software.

As long as the definitions have been updated, antivirus systems will usually locate viruses along with worms and Trojans. However, these systems will usually not locate rootkit activity. Keep in mind that AV software is important, but it is not a cure-all.

Next, we want to make sure that the computer has the latest updates available. This goes for the operating system and applications such as Microsoft Office. Backdoors into operating systems and other applications are not uncommon, and the OS manufacturers often release fixes for these breaches of security. For example, Windows offers the Windows Update program. This should be enabled, and you should either manually check for updates periodically or set the system to check for updates automatically. It might be that your organization has rules governing how Windows Update will function. If so, configure Automatic Updates according to your company's policy. You can check whether your Windows computer is up to date by going to **Control Panel > Windows Update,** or **Settings > Update & Security > Windows Update**.

It's also important to make sure that a firewall is available, enabled, and updated. A firewall closes all the inbound ports to your computer (or network) in an attempt to block intruders. The Windows Defender Firewall is a built-in feature of Windows, and you might also have a SOHO router with a built-in firewall. By using both, you have two layers of protection from viruses and other attacks. You can access the Windows Defender Firewall by navigating to the Control Panel or going to **Run > firewall.cpl**. Keep in mind that you might need to set exceptions for programs that need to access the Internet.

This can be done by the program or the port used by the protocol and can be configured in the Exceptions tab, enabling specific applications to communicate through the firewall while keeping the rest of the ports closed.

> **Note**
>
> Another good technique when trying to prevent viruses (and just about any malware) is to disable AutoPlay/Autorun for USB-connected devices and optical drives. Plus, remember to disable these devices in the BIOS! We'll discuss this more in Chapter 33, "Windows Security Settings and Best Practices."

From a more generalized perspective, preventing malware is done through the use of a concept called *defense in depth* or layering of security, and by monitoring the system, as well as end user education.

Educate users as to how viruses can infect a system. Instruct them on how to screen (or filter) their e-mails and tell them not to open unknown attachments. Show them how to scan removable media before copying files to their computers or set up the computer to scan removable media automatically. Sometimes user education works; sometimes it doesn't. One way to make user education more effective is to have a technical trainer educate your users instead of doing it yourself. This can provide for a more engaging learning environment. During this training you might opt to define an organization's acceptable use policy (AUP). This is a document stipulating constraints and practices that a user must agree to before being granted access to a corporate network or the Internet. Sometimes, the AUP can be a bit difficult for the average non-techie to understand. However, the document is usually designed to not only stipulate constraints but to educate the user, so it is in the user's best interest to learn what policies are within the AUP.

By using these methods, virus infection can be severely reduced. However, if a computer is infected by a virus, you want to know what to do to troubleshoot the problem. We'll get into that as well as the CompTIA A+ malware removal process in Chapter 37, "Troubleshooting PC Security Issues and Malware Removal."

Worms and Trojans can be prevented and troubleshot in much the same manner as viruses. There are scanners for Trojans as well (for example, Microsoft's Malicious Software Removal Tool). In some cases, AV software scans for worms and Trojans in addition to viruses. Both of these tools can easily detect *known* Trojans, regardless of whether it is the actual attacker's application or any .exe files that are part of the application and are used at the victim computer.

However, if the Trojan or worm is brand new, a hot fix or individual scanner might become available from your anti-malware provider. New Trojans and variants of Trojans are created every day. Until the anti-malware provider finds out about them, they are known as zero-day attacks (covered in more detail later in the chapter). The only way to prevent these is to stick to the fundamentals that we've discussed throughout this section.

Preventing and Troubleshooting Spyware

Preventing spyware works in much the same manner as preventing viruses in that spyware prevention includes updating the operating system and using a firewall. Also, because spyware has become much more common, antivirus companies have begun adding anti-spyware components to their software. Here are a few more things you can do to protect your computer in the hopes of preventing spyware:

▶ Download and install anti-spyware protection software. Your system might already have a program (for example, Windows Defender); if not, there are plenty of third-party programs available on the Internet. Be sure to keep the anti-spyware software updated. If you are using Windows, consider enabling SmartScreen for Microsoft Edge, which checks web content and protects from malicious sites and downloads.

▶ Adjust web browser security settings. Enable a phishing filter if you have one and turn on automatic website checking. This attempts to filter out fraudulent online requests for usernames, passwords, and credit card information, which is also known as web-page spoofing. Enable checking of certificates. If a certificate (a secure encrypted connection on the web) has been revoked or is otherwise invalid, you want to know about it—a message such as "invalid certificate (trusted root CA)" will only be received when the browser is checking for it. If not, you could inadvertently stumble on to a disreputable website. Additional security settings can also help to fend off session *hijacking*; that is, the act of taking control of a user session after obtaining or generating an authentication ID. Another attack similar to session hijacking is browser redirection. This is when a user's web browser is automatically redirected to one or more malicious websites. It can be done when a user inadvertently accesses a malicious website from a search; it can be caused by a Trojan that modifies a computer's DNS entries (for example, DNSChanger); or it can be caused by spyware or a virus that configures a proxy server address within the browser and/or modifies the "hosts" file. Refer to Figure 29.7 in Chapter 29, "Windows Networking and Application Installation," for an example of a proxy configuration on a Windows client. If this proxy server is not authorized, then it should be removed—after which you should restart the computer and verify that it is still disabled. Trojans such as these (and the ensuing spyware) can be avoided by increasing a browser's security settings, updating antivirus programs, and by educating users. It can be fixed by scanning the system with antivirus software, removing the proxy server address from the browser's settings, and deleting and rewriting the hosts file, which is located in %systemroot%\System32\ drivers\etc.

> **ExamAlert**
>
> Understand how to disable or remove a proxy server configuration in the web browser.

▶ Uninstall unnecessary applications and turn off superfluous services (for example, turn off Telnet and FTP if they are not used).

▶ Educate users on how to surf the Web safely. User education is actually the number one method of preventing malware! Access only sites believed to be safe, and download only programs from reputable websites. Don't click OK or Agree to close a pop-up window; instead, press Alt+F4 on the keyboard to close that window. Be wary of file-sharing websites and the content stored on those sites. Be careful of e-mails with links to downloadable software that could be malicious.

▶ Consider technologies that discourage spyware. For example, use a browser that is less susceptible to spyware. Consider running the browser (or the entire OS) within a virtual machine, or recommend a tablet or basic Internet appliances to users who use a computer to access the Internet only.

Preventing Rootkits

A successfully installed rootkit enables unauthorized users to gain access to a system, acting as the root or administrator user. Rootkits are copied to a computer as a binary file; this binary file can be detected by signature-based and heuristic-based antivirus programs. However, after the rootkit is executed, it can be difficult to detect. This is because most rootkits are collections of programs working together that can make many modifications to the system.

When subversion of the operating system takes place, the OS can't be trusted, and it is difficult to tell whether your antivirus programs run properly or any of your other efforts have any effect. Although security software manufacturers attempt to detect running rootkits, they are not always successful.

One good way to identify a rootkit is to use rescue removable media (a USB flash drive or optical disc) to boot the computer. This way, the operating system is not running, which means the rootkit is not running, making it much easier to detect by the external media.

Unfortunately, because of the difficulty involved in removing a rootkit, sometimes the best way to combat rootkits is to wipe the drive and reinstall all software. Generally, upon detecting a rootkit, a PC technician will do this because it usually is quicker than attempting to fix all the rootkit issues and it can verify that the rootkit has been removed completely—as long as there is a backup for the data.

However, software isn't the only method of defense and repair when it comes to rootkits. Newer motherboards equipped with a UEFI/BIOS take advantage of Secure Boot technology, which can help to protect the preboot process against rootkit attacks. This way, a rootkit can potentially be stopped *before* it actually causes any damage.

Backup/Restore and Recovery Environments

A good plan includes not only prevention methods, but also solid backup procedures. Back up as often as you can. This could be done on a file-by-file basis, using built-in Windows programs such as File History and Backup and Restore (Windows 7) as well as third-party programs; but it can also include the imaging of hard drives, creating a single file that incorporates the entire hard drive and all of its contents. Snapshots can be taken as well to mark a point in time, for example, using System Restore. Any system that has important data should have a backup plan. Consider this whenever you build or deploy new systems. We'll be discussing backup plans more later in the book.

In the case that malware does infect a system, we have to quarantine it, remove it, and recover the system. A great way to do this is to "think outside the box" and boot the system to some type of recovery environment. This could be a Linux-based repair disc/drive, or we could use the built-in Windows Recovery Environment (RE). For more on this topic, see Chapter 36, "Troubleshooting Microsoft Windows."

Cram Quiz

Answer these questions. The answers follow the last question. If you cannot answer these questions correctly, consider reading this section again until you can.

1. Which of the following types of malware self-replicates?

   - ○ **A.** Virus
   - ○ **B.** Worm
   - ○ **C.** Trojan
   - ○ **D.** Rootkit

2. Which of the following types of malware is designed to gain administrative-level control of a system?

   - ○ **A.** Ransomware
   - ○ **B.** Keylogger
   - ○ **C.** Rootkit
   - ○ **D.** Spyware

3. You have been tasked with implementing a virus prevention plan on a group of Windows client computers. Which of the following should you carry out? (Select all that apply.)

   - ○ **A.** Update AV software.
   - ○ **B.** Configure File History.
   - ○ **C.** Update Microsoft Office.
   - ○ **D.** Install a rootkit scanner.
   - ○ **E.** Verify that a firewall is installed.

Cram Quiz Answers

1. **B.** A worm will self-replicate, whereas a virus will not; otherwise, the two are very much the same. Trojans perform malicious functions behind the scenes and allow remote access to systems. Rootkits are designed to gain administrator (or root) level access to the computer.

2. **C.** A rootkit is designed to get administrative control of a computer system. The word "root" is synonymous with administrator in many systems (Linux, Unix, etc.). Ransomware is malware that encrypts a person's files so that they are not accessible. Keyloggers capture the keystrokes a person makes on a keyboard. They are used to steal passwords and other confidential information. Spyware is malware that is used to watch (and possibly record) what a person is doing on the system and on the Internet.

3. **A, C, and E.** First off, update everything. Then, verify that AV software and a firewall are installed and updated. Be sure to update the OS and apps as well. Microsoft Office is especially susceptible to malware, so if you run it, you have to keep a close eye on it. Configuring File History or any other backup methods won't prevent malware from occurring, but it is important to perform, nonetheless. Remember, backup is not prevention. A rootkit scanner won't scan for viruses, and won't prevent them; in fact, it won't prevent rootkits, but it might find them.

2.5 – Compare and contrast social engineering, threats, and vulnerabilities

Social engineering is the act of manipulating users into revealing confidential information or performing other actions that are detrimental to users. Almost everyone gets e-mails nowadays from unknown entities making false claims or asking for personal information (or money!); this is one example of social engineering. Here are the social engineering techniques you should know for the exam.

Phishing

Phishing is the attempt to fraudulently obtain private information. A phisher usually masquerades as someone else, perhaps another entity. Phishing is usually done by electronic communication/phone. Little information about the target is necessary. A phisher may target thousands of individuals without much concern as to their backgrounds. An example of phishing would be an e-mail that requests verification of private information. Clicking a link in the e-mail will probably lead to a malicious website that is designed to lure individuals into a false sense of security to fraudulently obtain information. The website will often look like a legitimate website. A common phishing technique is to pose as a vendor (such as an online retailer or domain registrar) and send individuals e-mail confirmations of orders that they supposedly placed.

Specific groups of people might be targeted with more streamlined phishing campaigns; this is known as *spear phishing*. A campaign can even target specific individuals. This is common when targeting senior executives of corporations, a concept known as *whaling*.

As you can imagine, several different types of social engineering are often lumped into what is referred to as phishing, but actual phishing for private information is normally limited to e-mail and websites. To defend against this, a phishing filter or add-on should be installed and enabled on the web browser. Also, individuals should be trained to realize that reputable institutions and businesses will not call or e-mail requesting private information. If individuals are not sure whether they're being targeted, they should hang up the phone or simply delete the e-mail. A quick way to find out if an e-mail is phishing for information is to hover over a link (but don't click it!). You will see a URL domain name that is far different from the institution that the phisher is claiming to be—probably a URL located in a distant country.

Shoulder Surfing

Shoulder surfing is when a person uses direct observation to find out a target's password, PIN, or other such authentication information. The simple resolution for this is for the user to physically shield the screen, keypad, or other authentication-requesting devices. A technical method is to use a screen filter. A more aggressive approach is to courteously ask the assumed shoulder surfer to move along. Also, private information should never be left on a desk or out in the open. In fact, many organizations will have a "clean desk policy" that states this explicitly. Computers should be locked or logged off when the user is not in the immediate area. Shoulder surfing and the methods described in the following several sections are examples of no-tech hacking.

> **ExamAlert**
>
> Use a screen filter to protect against shoulder surfing.

Piggybacking/Tailgating

Piggybacking is when an unauthorized person tags along with an authorized person to gain entry to a restricted area—usually with the person's consent. Tailgating is essentially the same, yet with one difference: it is usually without the authorized person's consent. Both of these can be defeated through the use of mantraps. A mantrap is a small space that can usually fit only one person. It has two sets of interlocking doors; the first set must be closed before the other will open, creating somewhat of a waiting room where people are identified (and cannot escape).

Multifactor authentication is often used in conjunction with a mantrap. Multifactor authentication is when two or more types of authentication are used when dealing with user access control (for example, using a proximity card and PIN at the first door and then using a biometric scan at the second). A mantrap is an example of a preventive security control. Turnstiles, double entry doors, and employing security guards are other less expensive solutions to the problem of piggybacking and tailgating and help address confidentiality in general.

Dumpster Diving

Dumpster diving is when a person scavenges for private information in garbage and recycling containers. Any sensitive documents should be stored in a safe place as long as possible. When they are no longer necessary, they should be shredded. (Some organizations incinerate their documents.) Information might be found not only on paper, but also on hard drives or removable media. Proper recycling and/or destruction of hard drives is covered later in the book. Another way to deter a person from attempting dumpster diving is to use security cameras and good lighting in the area where the dumpsters are stored; some organizations will keep their dumpsters indoors in a warehouse or similar area.

Impersonation

Impersonation is to present oneself as another person, imitating that other person's characteristics. By impersonating the appropriate personnel or third-party entities, a person hopes to obtain records about an organization, its data, and its personnel. IT people and employees should always be on the lookout for impersonators and always ask for identification. If there is any doubt, the issue should be escalated to your supervisor and/or a call should be made to the authorities. Impersonation is often a key element in what is known as pretexting—the inventing of a scenario in the hopes that a key person will reveal confidential information.

> **Note**
>
> This objective covers more than just social engineering, but the following techniques are sometimes used by attackers and malicious insiders in addition to social engineering, and are therefore somewhat related.

Additional Attacks and Security Vulnerabilities

Because there are so many types of threats and vulnerabilities in today's computers and networks, there are many types of attacks as well. Let's briefly examine a couple more types of attacks and common vulnerabilities that a typical organization might have to face.

Network-based Attacks

A *spoofing* attack is when an attacker masquerades as another person by falsifying information. This can be done as a social engineering attack, such as in the previously mentioned phishing method, or it can be performed as a more technical attack, such as the *man-in-the-middle (MITM) attack*. This is when an attacker intercepts all data between a client and a server. It is a type of active interception. If successful, all communications are diverted to the MITM computer. The attacking computer can at this point modify the data, insert code, and send it to the receiving computer. This type of eavesdropping is only successful when the attacker can properly impersonate each endpoint.

Then there are attacks that exploit vulnerabilities that haven't even been discovered yet or have been discovered but have not been disclosed through the proper channels so that security administrators can be aware of them. These are known as *zero-day attacks*. An attacker will exploit a vulnerability in an operating system or a network security device in such a way that makes it almost impossible to defend against. Because of this, zero-day attacks are a severe threat. Actually, most vulnerabilities are discovered through zero-day attacks, and the first group of systems that are attacked have very little defense. But once the attack is detected, the development of a solution is not far behind (it could be days or even hours); the vulnerability (and attack) becomes known and is no longer zero-day.

Most of the attacks and malware we have reviewed so far can be initiated by *zombies*: computers that distribute the malware or participate in an attack without the knowledge of the owner. These zombies (or robots or bots) can be grouped together by a central attacker to form a *botnet*. This is done to perpetuate large-scale attacks against particular servers. The distributed denial-of-service (DDoS) is an example of an attack committed by a botnet; it is designed to bring down a server or website.

ExamAlert

In a DDoS attack, multiple systems are used to attack a server, website, or network.

Password Cracking

One way that attackers attempt to gain access to systems is by way of password cracking. This is usually done with the aid of password-cracking software. Two common methods of password cracking are the dictionary attack and the brute-force attack.

A dictionary attack uses a prearranged list of likely words, trying each of them one at a time. It can be used for cracking passwords, passphrases, and keys. It works best with weak passwords and when targeting multiple systems. The power of the dictionary attack depends on the strength of the dictionary used by the password-cracking program.

A brute-force attack is when every possible password instance is attempted. This is often a last resort because of the amount of CPU resources it might require. It works best on shorter passwords but can theoretically break any password, if given enough time and CPU power.

A cryptanalysis attack uses a considerable set of precalculated encrypted passwords located in a lookup table. These tables are known as rainbow tables, and the type of password attack is also known as precomputation, where all words in the dictionary (or a specific set of possible passwords) are hashed and stored. This is done in an attempt to recover passwords quicker. This attack can be defeated by implementing salting, which is the randomization of the hashing process. It usually incorporates key stretching, which is adding bits of information to the password to make it stronger.

Once again, a complex and long password is the best way to prevent these types of attacks from succeeding. But a system and its network should also be protected with the Internet security appliances mentioned previously.

ExamAlert

Know the differences between dictionary and brute-force attacks, as well as rainbow tables.

Security Best Practices

Most organizations have policies regarding security best practices. The biggest vulnerability to an organization is the violation of those best practices (namely, non-compliant systems). For example, an organization might have rules stating that all systems must be updated at particular intervals: operating systems, anti-malware applications, and so on. If a single computer fails to be updated, it is no longer in compliance with policy. This one computer could be used by a hacker or malicious insider to cause all kinds of harm, even on systems that are updated, simply because the nonupdated system is behind the firewall (on the LAN) with the rest of the computers. When updating systems, double-check that everything has indeed been updated. Use scanning software to find all systems on the network, and review network documentation to make sure no systems have "fallen through the cracks."

> **Note**
>
> This section was a bit of a catch-all. Remember, the CompTIA A+ is not a security exam, but it does require that you know some of the basics about these concepts.

Cram Quiz

Answer these questions. The answers follow the last question. If you cannot answer these questions correctly, consider reading this section again until you can.

1. Which of the following describes an attempt to guess a password by using a combination of letters and numbers?

   - ○ **A.** Brute-force
   - ○ **B.** Social engineering
   - ○ **C.** Dictionary
   - ○ **D.** Zero-day

2. A user clicked a link in an e-mail that appeared to be from his bank. The link led him to a page that requested he change his password to access his bank account. It turns out that the webpage was fraudulent. What is this an example of?

   - ○ **A.** Impersonation
   - ○ **B.** Dumpster diving
   - ○ **C.** Phishing
   - ○ **D.** Shoulder surfing

3. Several hundred infected computers simultaneously attacked your organization's server, rendering it useless to legitimate users. What kind of attack is this an example of?

   ○ **A.** Botnet

   ○ **B.** MITM

   ○ **C.** Tailgating

   ○ **D.** DDoS

   ○ **E.** Rainbow table

Cram Quiz Answers

1. **A.** Brute-force attacks use a combination of letters, numbers, and symbols to guess passwords, PINs, and passcodes; as opposed to dictionary attacks, which use a list of words. Social engineering is an attempt to manipulate people into providing confidential information. A zero-day attack is one that occurs that has not been seen or documented before—the most difficult to prepare against.

2. **C.** This is an example of phishing. Phishers will use e-mail to trick a person into divulging confidential information. While it could be said that the website that was accessed is impersonating the actual banking website, that would be more of a spoof; true impersonation is when a person mimics another person. Dumpster diving is when a person hunts through garbage or recycling to find confidential information. Shoulder surfing is when a person attempts to get information by sight by, for example, looking over a person's shoulder as that person types in a password.

3. **D.** A distributed denial-of-service (DDoS) attack is one where many computers (zombies) work together In an attempt to bring down a server or router. While it makes use of a botnet, not all botnets are necessarily bad, nor is the botnet the attack. A man-in-the-middle (MITM) attack is a type of spoof, where a person uses a computer to intercept and either use or change data that is captured. Tailgating is a type of social engineering attack where a person attempts to enter a secure area by following another person in without that person's knowledge. A rainbow table is set of precalculated encrypted passwords located in a lookup table.

Now, some of things we talked about in this chapter may sound far-fetched, but they are real, and need to be proactively secured against. Continue!

CHAPTER 33

Windows Security Settings and Best Practices

This chapter covers the following A+ 220-1002 exam objectives:

▶ **2.6** – Compare and contrast the differences of basic Microsoft Windows OS security settings.

▶ **2.7** – Given a scenario, implement security best practices to secure a workstation.

More security? Yes, three more chapters to be sure, including this one, but it doesn't end there. You should always be thinking with your information security hat on.

This chapter gets into some basic Windows security settings as well as some computer security best practices. Some of these best practices can be used on any OS, but we'll be focusing on Windows for most of this chapter. Begin.

2.6 – Compare and contrast the differences of basic Microsoft Windows OS security settings

ExamAlert

Objective 2.6 focuses on users and groups, NTFS vs. share permissions, shared files and folders, system files and folders, user authentication, Run as administrator vs. standard user, BitLocker, BitLocker To Go, and EFS.

The main goals of information security are to keep data *Confidential*, and keep the *Integrity* of data intact—all while preserving the *Availability* of data. That is the *CIA triad* of computer security—consider it whenever you are securing hardware, software, data, and people. In this chapter we'll contemplate security as it relates to files, folders, users, permissions, and encryption.

Users and Groups

Users are what it's all about when it comes to Windows security. On a Windows client computer, you can accomplish basic user account creation from within Settings or the Control Panel, but in this section we will be focusing on the more useful Local Users and Groups, which you can access from Computer Management or directly by going to **Run** and typing **lusrmgr.msc**.

There are four main types of user account levels you should know for the exam:

▶ Administrators have full (or near full) control of an operating system. They are the most powerful accounts in Windows and have access to everything.

▶ Standard Users (also simply referred to simply as users) are the normal accounts for people who can log on to the network. This user account has access to (owns) data but cannot access the data of any other user and by default cannot perform administrative tasks (such as installing software).

▶ Guests have limited access to the system. A Guest cannot install software or hardware, cannot change settings or access any data, and cannot change the password. The Guest account is sometimes used for temporary workers or vendors who may need temporary access. The Guest account is disabled by default.

▶ Power Users are included in Windows for backward compatibility with older versions of applications.

ExamAlert

Know the Windows user accounts and groups including Administrator, Power User, Guest, and Standard User. Know what they can and cannot do!

All of these are actually groups within Windows client operating systems (such as Windows 10). If you access the Local Users and Groups window and click the **Groups** folder, then you will see these groups and many more; for example, Backup Operators, Remote Desktop Users, and so on. There are, however, individual Administrator and Guest accounts (located in the Users folder) that are built into the system.

You can create users by clicking the **Users** folder and then clicking **Action > New User**, or by right-clicking in the user list work area and selecting **New User**. This brings up a window as shown in Figure 33.1.

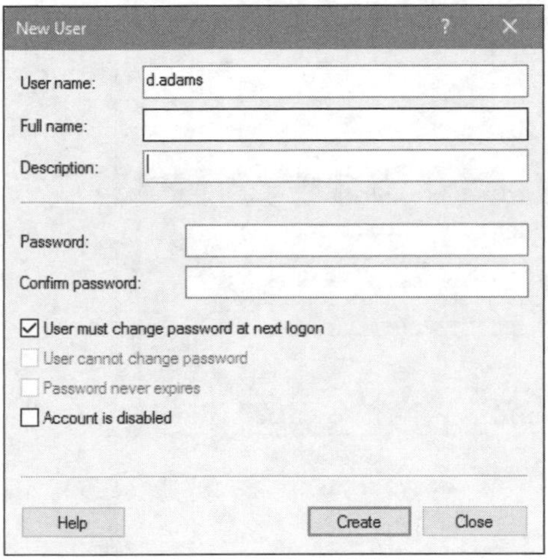

FIGURE 33.1   **New User window**

Try going through the process now. At the bare minimum, you'll be required to type a username. You can fill out other information as well, including the user's full name and a description of the user. By default, the **User must change password at next logon** option is selected, so you don't have to select a password. In some scenarios the systems administrator supplies the password. If so, then you as the admin would have to type the password (and confirm it), then deselect the first checkbox, and then select **User cannot change password**. The password will have to comply with any password policy that has been set (length, complexity, etc.). Keep in mind that this is not the most secure way to do things, but might be necessary in some cases. You'll also note that there is a checkbox called Account is disabled. You can disable an account temporarily from here, but generally you would work with that setting after the account is created (from the account **Properties** dialog box > **Account** tab). For example, if a user fails to log on with the correct password after *x* number of attempts (set in a Group Policy), then the account will become disabled and the administrator will have to deselect the checkbox to enable the user to log on. Conversely, if a person leaves an organization or is terminated, then you should immediately disable the account so that the user cannot log on anymore.

By default, when a user is first created, the user is automatically given group membership to the Users group, and performs as a standard user. But, you can add memberships to other groups if you need to; for instance, if you needed to have a second administrator. To do this, right-click the user account and select **Properties**, then click the **Member Of** tab. The Select Groups dialog box pops up, shown in Figure 33.2, where you can either type the name of the group you want to make the user a member of, or browse for it.

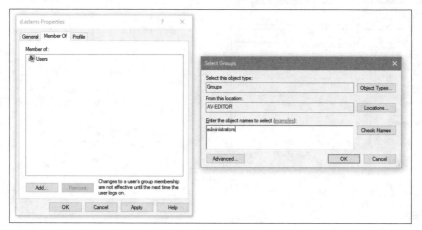

FIGURE 33.2 **Group membership in Windows**

In the figure, the user d.adams is currently a member of the Users group, but I am in the process of adding that user to the Administrators group. But be careful who you add as an admin—that person will now get full control!

Note

You can also configure Windows users for single sign-on (SSO) authentication. This generally requires a domain, Microsoft Identity Manager, Azure, or OpenID Connect (often a combination of those). For more information on this, see the following link:

https://docs.microsoft.com/en-us/azure/active-directory/manage-apps/what-is-single-sign-on

---

Permissions

Folders and files can be assigned permissions, which allow users a particular level of access to the data. There are two levels of permissions, which are configured in the Properties window of a folder or a file:

▶ Share permissions can be accessed from the Sharing tab. By default, the Everyone group has Read (read-only) access. The other two permissions available are Change and Full Control.

▶ NTFS permissions are accessed from the Security tab. Here we have six default levels of permissions, from Read to Write to Full control, as shown in Figure 33.3. If you happen to be using both share and NTFS permissions together, the most restrictive of the two will take precedence. So, for example, if a user was given Full Control access in the Share permissions and only Read in the NTFS permissions, the user would ultimately have only the Read permission.

FIGURE 33.3 Security tab of a folder's Properties window

ExamAlert

NTFS permissions are modified in the Security tab of the folder's Properties window.

The weakest of the NTFS permissions is Read and the strongest, of course, is Full control. Administrators have Full control by default. However, typical users have only Read, List folder contents, and Read & execute by default. You also note that we have the option to Allow access or Deny access and that this can be done by the user or by their user group, thus the term user-level security. Generally, when you want users to have access to the folder, you add them to the list and select Allow for the appropriate permission. When you don't want to allow them access, normally you simply don't add them. But in some cases, an explicit Deny is necessary. This could be because the user is part of a larger group that already has access to a parent folder, but you don't want the specific user to have access to this particular subfolder.

Permission Inheritance and Propagation

If you create a folder, the default action it takes is to inherit permissions from the parent folder. So any permissions that you set in the parent will be inherited by the subfolder. To view an example of this, locate any folder within an NTFS volume (besides the root folder), right-click it, select **Properties**, access the **Security** tab, and click the **Advanced** button. An example of this in Windows 10 is shown in Figure 33.4. (Names and navigation will be slightly different in other versions of Windows.)

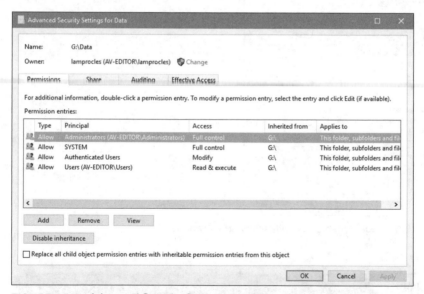

FIGURE 33.4 **Advanced Security Settings window**

What this all means is that any permissions added or removed in the parent folder will also be added or removed in the current folder. In addition, those permissions that are inherited cannot be modified in the current folder. To make modifications in this case, click the **Disable inheritance** button (or deselect the corresponding checkbox in earlier versions of Windows). When you do so, you have the option to copy the permissions from the parent to the current folder or remove them entirely. So, by default, the parent is automatically propagating permissions to the subfolder and the subfolder is inheriting its permissions from the parent. You can also propagate permission changes to subfolders that are not inheriting from the current folder. To do so, select the **Replace all child object permission entries with inheritable permission entries from this object** checkbox. (Again, names will vary according to the version of Windows.)

This might all seem a bit confusing; you will probably not be asked many exam questions on the subject. Just remember that folders automatically inherit from the parent unless you turn inheriting off—and you can propagate permission entries to subfolders at any time by selecting the **Replace...** option.

> **Note**
>
> One other concept you should know that is not on the objectives is *ownership*. By default, Windows uses the discretionary access model (DAC), which means that the creator of a file or folder is the owner—and that means that only that person can assign permissions to that file or folder. However, an administrator can change who the owner is simply by clicking the **Change** link that is shown in Figure 33.4. So, the administrator can take ownership, and subsequently change permissions if he or she needs to.

Moving and Copying Folders and Files

This subject (and the previous one) is actually an advanced Microsoft Windows concept, so we'll try to keep this simple. *Moving* and *copying* folders and files have different results when it comes to permissions. Basically, it breaks down like this:

▶ When you copy a folder or file on the same volume or to a different volume, it *inherits* the permissions of the parent folder it was copied to (known as the target directory).

▶ When you move a folder or file to a different location on the same volume, it *retains* the original permissions.

▶ When you move a file to another volume, it *inherits* the permissions of the parent folder.

> **Note**
>
> Keep in mind that when you move data within a partition, the data isn't actually relocated; instead, the pointer to the file or folder is modified.

File Security

To start, files can be assigned four different attributes in Windows: read-only, hidden, compression, and encryption. To access these, right-click any file and select **Properties**. On the General tab you will see the Read-only checkbox; if this is checked, no one can save modifications to the file, but a new file can be saved with the changes. Checking the **Hidden** checkbox makes the file invisible to all users except the user who created the file. Admins can unhide files individually or for the entire system, as I will explain in a moment. When you click the **Advanced** button, you see two checkboxes: **Compress contents to save disk space**, which allows you to convert the file to a smaller size that takes up less space on the drive; and **Encrypt contents to secure data**, which scrambles the file content so only the user who created the file can read it. We'll discuss encryption later in this chapter.

> **Note**
>
> The **attrib** command in the Command Prompt can modify the read-only, archive, system, and hidden attributes for files and display the attributes for each file. This older command is still available in Windows but is not used often. For more information about this command, see this link:
>
> https://dprocomputer.com/blog/?p=811

System files and folders are hidden from view by the OS to protect the system. In some cases, you can simply click the **Show the contents of this folder** link, but to permanently configure the system to show hidden files and folders, navigate to the Folder Options dialog box. Then select the **View** tab and, under Hidden files and folders, select the **Show hidden files, folders, and drives** radio button. To configure the system to show protected system files, deselect the **Hide protected operating system files** checkbox, located shortly below Show hidden files and folders. This enables you to view files such as bootmgr, pagefile.sys, and hiberfil.sys.

Administrative Shares

Folders and files need to be shared so that other users on the local computer and on the network can gain access to them. Windows operating systems use an access control model for securable objects like folders. This model takes care of rights and permissions, usually through discretionary access control lists (DACLs) that contain individual access control entries (ACEs). All the shared folders can be found by navigating to **Computer Management > System Tools > Shared Folders > Shares**, as shown in Figure 33.5. You can see that I have shared a folder named Data, which is also known as a local share.

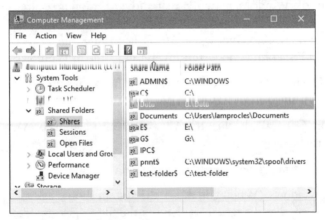

FIGURE 33.5   **Windows shares**

Here we also see the hidden *administrative shares*, which can be identified by the $ on the end of the share name. These shares cannot be seen by standard users when browsing to the computer over the network; they are meant for administrative use. Note that every volume (C:, E:, and G:, for example) has an administrative share. Although it is possible to remove these by editing the registry, it is not recommended because it might cause other networking issues. You should be aware that only administrators should have access to these shares. Hidden shares can be created by simply adding $ to the end of the share name when enabling the share. Administrative/hidden shares can be accessed only if the user knows the exact network path to the folder and has permissions to access it.

> **ExamAlert**
>
> Hidden/administrative shares can be identified by the $ on the end of the share name.

Encrypting File System

Encryption is the process of converting information with the use of a cipher (algorithm), making it unreadable by other users unless they have the correct "key" to the information. Cryptography is the practice of hiding information. In a cryptosystem, information is protected by disguising it.

There are a few different encryption technologies used in Windows. For example, whenever you log on to a Windows network, that authentication is secured with the Kerberos protocol. Another example is when you want to encrypt one or more files or folders. In this case, Windows uses the Encrypting File System (EFS), a component of NTFS. Follow these steps to encrypt a file in Windows:

1. Locate the file, right-click it, and select **Properties**. This brings up the General tab within the file's Properties window.

2. At the bottom of the General tab, click the **Advanced** button. This brings up the Advanced Attributes window.

3. Check the box labeled **Encrypt contents to secure data**.

4. Click **OK** for both windows. (When you do so, the system should ask whether you want to encrypt the parent folder and the file or just the file. It's recommended that the file's parent folder be encrypted as well.)

To unencrypt the file and return it to normal, simply deselect the checkbox.

> **Note**
>
> You can color code encrypted and compressed NTFS files. This is done in the Folder Options dialog box by clicking the **View** tab and selecting **Show encrypted or compressed NTFS files in color**. After you select that, a green filename indicates an encrypted file and a blue filename indicates a compressed file.

If a file needs to be decrypted and the original user (owner of the key or certificate) isn't available, an EFS recovery agent will need to be used. In many cases, the default recovery agent is the built-in Administrator account. It is important to note a couple more items: One is that EFS isn't designed to protect data while it is transferred from one computer to another; the other is that EFS is not designed to encrypt an entire drive.

> **Note**
>
> File-sharing connections are also encrypted in Windows 7 and higher. You can modify this setting via **Network and Sharing Center > Change advanced sharing settings** or **HomeGroup > Change advanced sharing settings**. Either way, 128-bit encryption is recommended.

BitLocker Encryption

To encrypt an entire disk, you need some kind of full disk encryption software. There are several currently available on the market. One developed by Microsoft is called BitLocker, which is available only on select editions of Windows (Pro, Enterprise, and so on). This software can encrypt the entire disk, which, after it's completed, is transparent to the user. However, there are some requirements for this, including

- ▶ A Trusted Platform Module (TPM), which is a chip residing on the motherboard that actually stores the encrypted keys.

  or

- ▶ An external USB key to store the encrypted keys.

  and

- ▶ A hard drive with two volumes, preferably created during the installation of Windows. One volume is for the operating system (most likely C:) that will be encrypted; the other is the active volume that remains unencrypted so that the computer can boot. If a second volume needs to be created, the BitLocker Drive Preparation Tool can be of assistance and can be downloaded from https://www.microsoft.com/en-us/download/details.aspx?id=7806.

ExamAlert

Know the components necessary for BitLocker.

BitLocker software (as well as EFS) is based on the Advanced Encryption Standard (AES) and uses a 128-bit key by default, though it can be increased to 256-bit in the Group Policy Editor. Keep in mind that a drive encrypted with BitLocker usually suffers in performance compared to a nonencrypted drive and could have a shorter shelf life as well. By default, BitLocker is used to encrypt the internal drive of a system. However, you can also encrypt USB drives and other removable devices by using BitLocker To Go.

Note

Need to increase the BitLocker's AES cipher strength to 256-bit? Open the Local Group Policy Editor (**Run > gpedit.msc**) and go to **Computer Configuration > Administrative Templates > Windows Components > BitLocker Drive Encryption**, then enable and configure the policy for your version of Windows.

Run As

Remember that standard users can't do very much in Windows. You need to run a lot of these configuration programs as an administrator—meaning in elevated mode. Generally, right-clicking the app and selecting **Run as administrator** is enough. For more options, see Chapter 25, "Microsoft Command Line Tools."

Cram Quiz

Answer these questions. The answers follow the last question. If you cannot answer these questions correctly, consider reading this section again until you can.

1. You have been tasked with setting up encryption for a Windows computer. You are required to encrypt several shared folders within a partition, so that they can't be read by other users. What tool should you use?

   ○ **A.** BitLocker

   ○ **B.** TPM

   ○ **C.** Administrative share

   ○ **D.** EFS

2.6 – Compare and contrast the differences
of basic Microsoft Windows OS security
settings

CramQuiz

2. One of the users on your network is trying to access files shared on a remote computer. The file's share permissions allow the user Full Control but the NTFS permissions allow the user Read access. Which of the following will be the resulting access for the user?

  ○ **A.** Full Control

  ○ **B.** Modify

  ○ **C.** Read

  ○ **D.** Write

3. You are the administrator for your network and you set up an administrative share called Data$. Which of the following is necessary in order for another user to access this share? (Select the two best answers.)

  ○ **A.** The user must be part of a HomeGroup.

  ○ **B.** The user must have permissions to access the share.

  ○ **C.** The user must know the decryption key.

  ○ **D.** The user must know the exact network path to the share.

  ○ **E.** The user must enable File Sharing in the Network and Sharing Center.

4. Which Windows account would you create for someone who needs to regularly install software, change settings, and take ownership?

  ○ **A.** Power User

  ○ **B.** Standard User

  ○ **C.** Guest

  ○ **D.** Root

  ○ **E.** Administrator

Cram Quiz Answers

1. **D.** Use the Encrypting File System (EFS). This is easily done: right-click the folder(s), select **Properties**, click the **Advanced** button, and checkmark **Encrypt contents to secure data**. At this point, other users will not be able to read the files contained in those folders. BitLocker is used to encrypt an entire hard drive (or volume), but in the scenario you only need to encrypt several folders. A Trusted Platform Module (TPM) is a chip that is required for using BitLocker, but it is not necessary for EFS. By creating an administrator share, you will effectively hide the contents from typical users, unless they know an admin password. If they do know the password, then they could read the files. Regardless, administrative shares do not encrypt data.

2. **C.** The user will get only Read access. If you are using both sets of permissions, those most restrictive will take precedence. In this case, NTFS permissions are more restrictive than share permissions.

3. **B and D.** The user needs to have permissions to the share and must know the exact path to the network share because it is an administrative share. HomeGroup does not play into this scenario. Also, the question does not mention whether the file is encrypted. The user doesn't need to enable sharing; the person is trying to access a share.

4. **E.** Administrators have full control of an operating system. Power Users are included in Windows for backward compatibility with older versions, and are seldom used. Standard Users are the normal default accounts for people who can log on to the network. Guests have limited access to the system. A Guest cannot install software or hardware, cannot change settings or access any data, and cannot change the password.

2.7 – Given a scenario, implement security best practices to secure a workstation

As systems administrators we have to make sure that users can only get access to what they need, and that no one else can masquerade as a legitimate user. User accounts can be secured through a combination of strong passwords, password policies, restrictions, account lockouts, and, in general, good account management, which requires not only solid configuration but also monitoring and auditing of user accounts. While many of the techniques in this chapter are designed for Windows, some of the concepts can be easily incorporated into any operating system.

Usernames and Passwords

The username/password combination is the most common type of authentication for gaining access to computers. The username is known to all parties involved and can be seen as plain text when typed. In some cases, the user has no control over what the username will be; in other cases, the username might be a name or e-mail address (and the username could be selected by the user). For example, you might use a sign-in to access the Windows Store for apps; in this case, it is typical to use your e-mail address as your username. You can see it, it shows up on the screen, and you can be identified by it. The password is either set by the user or created automatically for the user. This password, however, is not something we want anyone else to know or see.

It is common knowledge that a strong password is important for protecting a user account, whether the account is with a bank, at work, or elsewhere. But what is a strong password? Many organizations define a strong password as a password with at least 8 characters, including at least one uppercase letter, one number, and one special character. The best passwords have similar requirements but are 15 characters or more. Many password-checker programs are on the Web for you to get an idea of what is considered "strong." Table 33.1 shows a strong password and a "best" password.

TABLE 33.1 **Strong and Stronger Passwords**

Password	Strength of Password
|Ocrian7	Strong
This1sV#ryS3cure	Very strong or "best"

Notice the first password is using the | (pipe) symbol instead of the letter L. This is a special character that shares the \ (backslash) key on the keyboard. The second password uses 16 characters, including three capital letters, two numbers, and a partridge in a pear tree, um, I mean one special character. (Just checking whether you are still with me!) Although a partridge wouldn't help your password security, the other methods make for an extremely strong password that would take a super computer a long time to crack. (Of course, the passwords in the table now are weak, because they have been mass printed and are *known*. They are just examples and should not be used on a system.)

ExamAlert

Understand what is required for a strong complex password.

Note

As mentioned in Chapter 11, "Motherboards and Add-on Cards," BIOS/UEFI passwords are also very important, especially the administrative password. The same basic rules described here apply to BIOS passwords as well.

Password Policies

Changing your password at regular intervals is important as well. The general rule of thumb is to change your password as often as you change your toothbrush. However, because this is a subjective concept (to put it nicely!), many organizations have policies concerning your password. It might need to meet certain requirements, or it might need to be changed at regular intervals, among other policies. Figure 33.6 shows an example of the default password policy within the Local Security Policy window on a Windows computer. To open the Local Security Policy window, go to **Run > secpol.msc**. Then navigate to **Security Settings > Account Policies > Password Policy**.

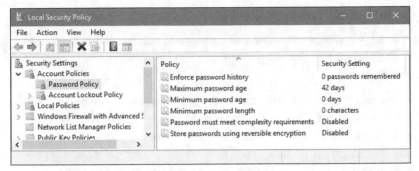

FIGURE 33.6   **Default password policy in Windows**

As shown in the figure, there are several items that we can configure (or can be configured by the network administrator centrally if the computer is part of a domain). The five important ones for the exam include

▶ **Enforce password history:** When this is defined, users cannot use any of the passwords that are remembered in the history. If you set the history to 3, the last three passwords cannot be used again when it is time to change the password.

▶ **Maximum password age and Minimum password age:** These settings define exactly how long a password can be used. The maximum is initially set to 42 days but does not affect the default Administrator account. To enforce an effective password history, the minimum must be higher than 0 days.

▶ **Minimum password length:** This requires that the password must be at least the specified number of characters. For a strong password policy, set this to between 8 and 14.

▶ **Password must meet complexity requirements:** This means that passwords must meet three of these four criteria: uppercase characters, lowercase characters, digits between 0 and 9, and nonalphabetic characters (special characters).

> **Note**
>
> For more information on some password best practices, visit
> https://www.microsoft.com/en-us/research/publication/password-guidance/

Account Management

Now that we have a secure password and a password policy in place, let's talk about securing the user accounts for Windows. There are a few things we can do to secure these:

1. **Rename and password protect the Administrator account:** To configure this account, navigate to **Computer Management > System Tools > Local Users and Groups > Users** and locate the Administrator account. By right-clicking the account, you see a drop-down menu in which you can rename it and/or give it a password. (Just remember the new username and password!) It's great to have this additional administrator account on the shelf just in case the primary account fails. If the account is disabled you can enable it if necessary. Right-click the account and select **Properties**. In the **General** tab, deselect the **Account is disabled** checkbox. Alternatively, open the Command Prompt (Admin) and type **net user administrator /active:yes**. Of course, you have to have administrative privileges to perform these actions.

2. **Verify that the Guest account (and other unnecessary accounts) are disabled:** Navigate again to **Local Users and Groups > Users**, right-click the account in question, select **Properties**, and then select the checkbox named **Account is disabled** (it is disabled by default in most versions of Windows). You can also delete accounts (aside from built-in accounts, such as the Guest account); however, companies usually opt to have them disabled so that the company can retain auditing information that is linked to the account.

3. **Restrict user permissions:** Users are created as standard users by default, but it's always a good idea to audit the user accounts and make sure that they don't have any unnecessary group memberships that could give them more power than they require. This is part of the principle of least privilege—the less a user can do, the more secure the system will be.

4. **Set logon time and computer restrictions:** In a Windows domain, you can allow and disallow certain hours of the day that a user can log on to the network. In the user's Properties dialog box, go to the Account tab, then click the Logon Hours button. From there you can configure when the user is allowed to log on. For example, in Figure 33.7 Bob can only log on to the domain Monday through Friday from 8 AM to 6 PM. You can also specify individual computers that the user can log on to by

clicking the **Log On To** button in the Properties dialog box. For temporary employees and contractors, it's a good idea to configure account expiration, which is at the bottom of the Account tab page.

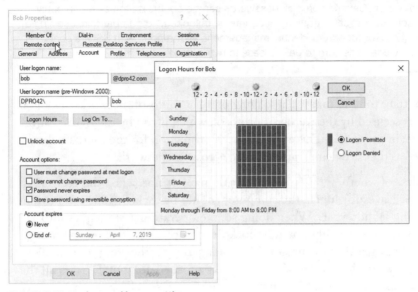

FIGURE 33.7 **Logon Hours setting**

5. **Set the Account lockout threshold:** If a user attempts to log on to a system and is unsuccessful (after a specified number of attempts), the user will be locked out of the system. The settings and thresholds for this can be configured in the Local Security Policy window. Navigate to **Security Settings > Account Policies > Account Lockout Policy**. From here, you can set the Account lockout threshold to a certain number of invalid logons, set how long the user will be locked out, and set how long until the lockout counter is reset. If an account is locked out and you need to unlock it immediately, follow one of the options at the end of step 1.

> **Note**
>
> Lockouts due to forgotten passwords are common in organizations. Sometimes a user will use several passwords to gain access to various systems, making the problem worse. Several complex passwords can be confusing to users and cause many tech support calls requiring accounts be unlocked. To combat this, use *single sign-on (SSO)* or federated identity management. Remember, with SSO, a user needs only one password to gain access to two or more systems.

It's important to note that when logging on to a Microsoft network, the logon process is secured by the Kerberos protocol, which is run by the Active Directory domain controller. This adds a layer of protection for the username and password as they are being authenticated across the network.

Regardless of whether a user is part of a domain or not, when the user takes a break or leaves for lunch, the computer should be locked. This can be done by pressing Windows+L. When doing so, the operating system goes into a locked state, and the only way to unlock the computer is to enter the username and password of the person who is logged in to the computer. The difference between this and logging out is that a locked computer leaves all the session's applications and files open; logging out closes all open applications and files.

Aside from locking the computer manually, the user can opt to put the computer to sleep after a certain period of time or enable a password-protected screensaver, both of which will force the user to log on when returning to the computer. Sleep settings can be accessed in Windows 10 by navigating to **Settings > Power & Sleep**, or by navigating to **Control Panel > All Control Panel Items > Power Options > Edit Plan Settings**. Further configuration can be performed within the **Power Options** dialog box, by clicking the **Change advanced power settings** link. To set the screen saver to require a password when the system resumes in Windows 10, for example, go to **Settings > Personalization** (or right-click the desktop and select **Personalize**). Then go to **Lock screen > Screen saver settings**. In the dialog box, checkmark **On resume, display logon screen**.

Disabling AutoPlay/Autorun

If you disable AutoPlay, removable media won't automatically start its Autorun application (if it has one), and any embedded malware won't have a chance to infect the system before you scan the media. To disable AutoPlay/Autorun in Windows, complete the following steps:

1. Go to the **Run** prompt and type **gpedit.msc**. This opens the Local Group Policy Editor. (This is not available in some editions of Windows.)

2. Navigate to **Computer Configuration > Administrative Templates > Windows Components > AutoPlay Policies**.

3. Double-click the **Turn off Autoplay** setting. This displays the Turn off Autoplay configuration window.

4. Click the **Enabled** radio button, and then click **OK**. You are actually enabling the policy named Turn off Autoplay.

Another way to do this in Windows 10 is to open **Settings** and then click **Devices**. Next, select **AutoPlay** from the left side. Finally, set the AutoPlay slider button to **Off**.

> **Note**
>
> We discuss data encryption earlier in the chapter and patch management in Chapter 27, "Microsoft Operating System Features and Tools, Part 2."

The Information Security Field Is Enormous

As you can see, we could configure security for Windows all day—and still have more to do. That's one of the reasons why the computer security field is so massive; and this is just Windows. Remember, these last couple of chapters have been an overview of how to secure Windows and Windows networks. Keep reading and learning, because there is so much work to do when it comes to computer and data security!

Cram Quiz

Answer these questions. The answers follow the last question. If you cannot answer these questions correctly, consider reading this section again until you can.

1. Which of the following is the strongest password?

   ○ **A.** |ocrian#

   ○ **B.** Marqu1sD3S0d

   ○ **C.** This1sV#ryS3cure

   ○ **D.** Thisisverysecure

2. Your boss is concerned about people that have been terminated coming back in the building and attempting to log on to the network using passwords that they used in the past. What should you do to help protect against this? (Select the two best answers.)

○ **A.** Set up a password length policy.

○ **B.** Configure an account lockout threshold.

○ **C.** Immediately disable the accounts of people who have been terminated .

○ **D.** Set logon time restrictions.

○ **E.** Disable the Guest account.

3. A customer complains that while he was away at lunch, someone used his computer to send e-mails to other co-workers without his knowledge. Which of the following should you recommend?

○ **A.** Enable a screensaver.

○ **B.** Unplug the network cable before leaving for lunch.

○ **C.** Use the Windows lock feature.

○ **D.** Enable the out-of-office message in e-mail when leaving for lunch.

4. Which of the following best describes encryption?

○ **A.** Prevents unauthorized users from viewing or reading data

○ **B.** Prevents unauthorized users from deleting data

○ **C.** Prevents unauthorized users from posing as the original source sending data

○ **D.** Prevents unauthorized users from decompressing files

5. How can you prevent applications from automatically executing, and possibly infecting a computer with malware, when removable media is inserted?

○ **A.** Enable the account lockout threshold policy.

○ **B.** Turn on BitLocker.

○ **C.** Turn off BitLocker To Go.

○ **D.** Disable AutoPlay.

Cram Quiz Answers

1. **C.** This1sV#ryS3cure incorporates case-sensitive letters, numbers, and special characters and is 16 characters long. That makes it the strongest password of the listed answers. |ocrian# has special characters but is missing uppercase letters and numerals—plus it is only 8 characters long. Marqu1sD3S0d does not have any special characters. Thisisverysecure is 16 characters long and has one capital letter but does not have any numerals or special characters.

2. **B and C.** The best answers are to configure an account lockout threshold and immediately disable the accounts of anyone who has been terminated. A common method is to use the "three strikes and you're out" rule for account lockout, meaning that a person can attempt to log on three times before the account is locked out. But more importantly, disable (or lock) the accounts of people who have been offboarded or terminated. The other options are all good security options in general, but won't help much with disgruntled past employees who are attempting to get into the system. Also, some type of authentication system should be in place so that these people cannot get access to the building.

3. **C.** Tell the customer to lock the computer (by pressing Windows+L or by using the Start menu) before leaving for lunch. As long as there is a strong password, other co-workers should not be able to access the system. Screensavers by themselves do not secure the system, but a user can enable the password-protected screensaver feature (be aware that there is a delay before the screensaver turns on). Unplugging the network cable is not a legitimate answer; plus, it can always be plugged back in. The out-of-office message will reply only to people e-mailing the user; it won't stop outgoing e-mails.

4. **A.** Encryption prevents unauthorized users from viewing or reading data. Properly configured permissions prevent unauthorized users from deleting data or attempting to decompress files. A strong logon password prevents unauthorized users from posing as the original source sending data.

5. **D.** If you disable AutoPlay, removable media won't automatically start its Autorun application (if it has one), and any embedded malware won't have a chance to infect the system before you scan the media. The account lockout threshold specifies the amount of times a user can attempt to log on to Windows before being logged off. BitLocker and BitLocker To Go are used for encryption, not for blocking removable media from automatically executing files.

CHAPTER 34

Mobile Device Security

This chapter covers the following A+ 220-1002 exam objective:

▶ **2.8** – Given a scenario, implement methods for securing mobile devices.

Mobile devices need to be secured just like any other computing devices. But due to their transportable nature, some of the security techniques will be a bit different, and can be more of a challenge for the systems administrator. I recommend that you prepare for the possibility of a stolen, lost, damaged, or compromised device. The methods in this chapter can help you to recover from these problems and also aid you in preventing them from happening.

2.8 – Given a scenario, implement methods for securing mobile devices

ExamAlert

Objective 2.8 focuses on screen locks, remote wipes, locator applications, remote backup applications, failed login attempts restrictions, antivirus/anti-malware, patching/OS updates, biometric authentication, full device encryption, multifactor authentication, authenticator applications, trusted sources vs. untrusted sources, firewalls, and policies and procedures.

Because mobile devices are expensive and could contain confidential data, they become a target for thieves. Plus, they are small and easy to conceal, making them easier to steal. However, there are some things you can do to prevent theft or loss, protect your data, and attempt to get the mobile device back in the case it is *misplaced*.

Screen Locks

The first thing a user should do when receiving a mobile device is to configure a screen lock. Locking the device makes it inaccessible to everyone except experienced hackers (or someone who knows your unlock method). To unlock the device the user has to be authenticated in one of several ways. There are several types of screen locks that a user can choose from to be authenticated. The screen lock can be something a user *knows* such as a PIN or a password. It could also be based on something the person *is*; it might use fingerprint, voice, or facial recognition technology, which are collectively known as *biometrics*. Or, it could be something the person *does*, such as a basic swipe (which has no inherent security by itself), or a pattern that is drawn on the display, or a series of taps or knocks on the phone. Finally, in a secure environment, it could be a combination of these different methods—this is known as *multifactor authentication (MFA)*. Figure 34.1 shows an example of an Android smartphone's screen lock options.

FIGURE 34.1 **Android screen lock options**

The complex password will often be the accepted secure form of screen lock. See Chapter 33, "Windows Security Settings and Best Practices," for more information about complex passwords. You can also select how long the device will wait after inactivity to lock (part of the screen timeout). In a confidential environment, you might set this to the lowest setting—10 or 15 seconds.

Speaking of passwords, some devices have the option to make the password visible (or the last character typed visible). This is almost never recommended because it makes the mobile device vulnerable to shoulder surfers (people looking over your shoulder to find out your password); it should be deselected. When deselected, only asterisks (*) are shown when the user types a password.

ExamAlert

Know how to configure a screen lock using fingerprint, face, swipe, and password locks. Also, know how to disable visible passwords.

Aside from the default timeout, devices can also be locked by pressing the Power button quickly. If configured, the passcode must be supplied whenever a mobile device comes out of a sleep or lock state and whenever it is first booted.

Some devices may have an account lockout threshold. That means if a user fails to be authenticated after a certain number of attempts (typically three or five), the device locks temporarily and the user has to wait a certain amount of time before attempting to authenticate again. After that, if the user fails to be authenticated again, the timeout increases (on most devices). After a certain number of attempts, the device either needs to be connected to the computer it was last synced to or it must be restored to factory condition with a hard reset (which can wipe the data). Many companies utilize a mobile device management (MDM) solution. In an MDM-controlled environment, the device and/or account might be locked in this scenario, and only an administrator will be able to unlock it.

ExamAlert

Understand the consequences of entering an incorrect passcode or other authentication information too many times.

Some devices have a setting where the device will be erased automatically after a certain number of incorrect authentication attempts. There are also third-party apps available for download for most mobile devices that can wipe the data after *x* number of attempts. Some apps configure the device to automatically take a picture after three failed attempts and e-mail the picture to the owner.

Authenticator Applications

Authenticator apps can be installed to a mobile device to help in the process of authenticating an individual. They might be used as the only method of authentication, or as part of a two-step authentication process. The latter is common. For example, let's say you are logging in to a service provider, such as Google. Let's further suppose that you have initiated two-step authentication, where you have to supply not only a username and password, but also, in the second step, a code that was sent to you on your mobile device (often by way of text message or e-mail). The authenticator app can be used to take the place of that second step by making use of a QR code or something similar. The code is preinstalled to the mobile device, but it can allow a person to log on to a service or be otherwise authenticated to something, even if Internet access is not currently available on the mobile device.

Two-Step Authentication

Two-step authentication is quite common, but not necessarily the most secure. Don't mistake two-*step* authentication with two-*factor* authentication. Two-step authentication normally requires that the person logging in have two pieces of information that the person *knows*. True multifactor authentication requires two or more different *factors* of information, such as something a person *knows* and something a person *is*.

Theft and Loss of Mobile Devices

There's an app for virtually everything. Imagine that a device is lost or stolen. If the user had previously installed a locator application and the GPS/location service was enabled on the device, the user could track where the device is. At that point, the organization would decide whether to get the police involved. One example is Google's *Find My Device*, but there are plenty of other locator and tracker apps available for Android and iOS.

Even if you track your mobile device and find it, it might be too late. A hacker can get past passcodes and other screen locks. It's just a matter of time before the hacker has access to the data. So, an organization with confidential information should consider a remote wipe program. As long as the mobile device still has access to the Internet, the remote wipe program can be initiated from a desktop computer, which will delete all the contents of the remote mobile device. In some cases, the command that starts the remote wipe must be issued from an MDM server.

You should also have a backup plan in place as well so that data on the mobile device is backed up to a secure location at regular intervals. This way, if the data needs to be wiped, you are secure in the fact that most of the data can be recovered. The type of remote wipe program, backup program, and policies regarding how these are implemented will vary from one organization to the next. Be sure to read up on your organization's policies to see exactly what is allowed from a mobile security standpoint.

> **ExamAlert**
>
> Know what locator/tracker applications are, and how remote wipes are used to erase confidential data in the event of a stolen device.

Compromised and Damaged Devices

Theft and loss aren't the only risks a mobile device faces. We should protect against the chance that a mobile device is damaged or that its security is compromised. The device could be the victim of unauthorized account access, root access, leaked files, location tracking, camera/microphone activation, and so on. These could be due to a rogue application, malware installation, or other hijacking of the mobile device. You need to be prepared before these things happen.

Backup

Many organizations implement backup and remote backup policies. iOS devices can be backed up to a PC via USB connection and by using iTunes. Also, they can be backed up remotely to iCloud. In addition, you can use third-party apps for remote backup. Information can even be restored to newer, upgraded iOS devices. Various manufacturers of Android devices have their own proprietary backup programs to the cloud. Otherwise, almost all Android data and settings can be backed up in a collection of ways. First, Google Cloud can be used to back up e-mail, contacts, and other information. If you use Gmail, then e-mail, contacts, and calendars are backed up (and synchronized) to Google servers automatically. If a mobile device is lost, the information can be quickly accessed from a desktop computer or other mobile device. Android applications can be backed up as long as they are not copy-protected. If you choose not to use Google Cloud to back up files or not to use the synchronization program that came with the device, there are plenty of third-party apps that can be used to back up via USB to a PC or to back up to the cloud.

Updates

One way to protect mobile devices from compromise is to patch or update the operating system. By default, you will be notified automatically about available updates on Android- and iOS-based devices. However, you should know where to go to manually update these devices as well. For Android, this is generally in the About Device section, though actual navigation can change from version to version. You are usually notified of updates in the notification panel/status screen.

If you find that there are system updates or security updates available for download, you should probably install them right away. Security patches are a large percentage of system updates because there are a lot of attackers around the world who want to compromise the Android operating system. But let's be real—attackers will go for any OS if it catches their fancy, be it Android or iOS or any other operating system! Updates for iOS can be located at **Settings > General > Software Update** (or similar path).

> **Note**
>
> Remember that the exact path to the update feature in a mobile OS can be different from one device to the next and from one manufacturer to the next. In addition, new versions of the software are constantly being released, resulting in changed paths and modified settings names. However, you can find out the path you need by consulting the software manufacturer's website (visit the following links), by going to the device manufacturer's website, or even by going to your cellular provider's website.
>
> ▶ iOS: https://support.apple.com/ios
>
> ▶ Android: https://support.google.com/android

> **ExamAlert**
>
> Know how to check for, and perform, Android and iOS updates.

Antivirus/Anti-malware/Firewalls

Updates are great, but they are not created to specifically battle viruses and other malware. So, just like there is antivirus/firewall software for PCs, there is AV/FW software for mobile devices. These are third-party applications that need to be downloaded (and possibly paid for) and installed to the mobile device. Some examples for Android include Lookout (built into many devices), McAfee, Avast, Bitdefender, Sophos, and the list goes on. Different terms are used to describe the various protective software that is installed to a mobile device: antivirus, anti-malware, firewall, endpoint protection platform, and mobile intrusion prevention system (MIPS). Be ready to install and configure any of these on mobile devices.

iOS, on the other hand, is a tightly controlled operating system. One of the benefits of being a closed-source OS is that it can be more difficult to write viruses for; however, there is no OS that can't be compromised. For the longest time, there was no antivirus software for iOS. That is, until 2011, when a type of jailbreaking software called *jailbreakme* used a simple PDF to move insecure code to the root of the device, causing a jailbreak. Ever since, AV software became a reality for iOS-based devices.

iOS *jailbreaking* is the process of removing the limitations that Apple imposes on its devices that run iOS. This enables users to gain root access to the system and allows the download of previously unavailable applications and software not authorized by Apple.

In the Android world, the act of gaining "superuser" privileges is known as *rooting*. Note that performing either rooting or jailbreaking could be a breach of the user license agreement. It can also be dangerous. These types of hacks might require a user to wipe out the device completely and/or install a special application that may or may not be trustworthy. Many phones are rendered useless or are compromised when attempting this procedure. Applications that have anything to do with rooting or jailbreaking should generally be avoided.

> **ExamAlert**
>
> Understand the terms *jailbreaking* and *rooting*.

MDM

Any AV software for Android or iOS should be checked regularly for updates—if the device is not configured to automatically download updates, that is. Also, as previously mentioned, for large organizations that have many mobile devices, an MDM suite can be implemented. An MDM server can take care of pushing updates and configuring hundreds of mobile devices from a central location. Decent quality MDM software will secure, monitor, manage, and support multiple different types of mobile devices across the enterprise.

Full Device Encryption

If a device is stolen or lost, and the authentication method is defeated, then the attacker (or other person) will have access to the data, unless some kind of remote wipe is initiated. However, sometimes, remote wipe will not function; for example, if the device is out of range of a radio tower, or the attacker brings it into a shielded area such as a Faraday cage. This is when encryption can be helpful to avoid data loss.

Some mobile device manufacturers allow for encryption of the entire storage area for select devices. In other cases, you will have the option to encrypt the SD card only. This is something to consider when deciding on the type of mobile devices to use in your organization. Careful planning is required when implementing encryption—not only planning the selection of the software to be used, but also planning the process, and knowing what to do in the case that decryption is necessary. For example, in many cases, if you encrypt an entire smartphone, the encryption process can be lengthy, even an hour or two—it depends on the speed of the device, the software used, and the amount of data to encrypt. One way around this is to only encrypt new data, instead of all the data, as shown in Figure 34.2. That might be a viable time-saver in a bring your own device (BYOD) environment. Another consideration: it's important not to interrupt the encryption process or files could be corrupted. A lot of the time, you'll simply encrypt new devices before they are given to a user, but that's not always the case; regardless, have the device fully charged before starting the process. Finally, if the files need to be decrypted, you might need to initiate a factory reset, or provide the key to the data, so be sure to have a decryption plan in place.

FIGURE 34.2 **SD card encryption screen on an Android-based smartphone**

The beauty of encryption is that it will make it very difficult to make sense of the files. If the proper encryption methods are used—for instance, AES-256—then a hacker would require a team of supercomputers working for a near infinite number of years to crack the cipher and decrypt the content (as of the writing of this book, of course). So, it is unlikely that a hacker will attempt to decrypt files unless the hacker guesses that a weak or compromised cipher has been employed. Instead, the hacker will use...*other* methods. (And don't ask me what "near infinite" means...)

Remember that encryption and any other techniques used to secure a device or data are not foolproof. A good security person will create a *threat model*; in essence, determine what the threats and vulnerabilities are within a particular system or data set, and prioritize them from most threatening to least. After the threat model has been established, you can then decide on the security techniques to be implemented.

> **Note**
>
> If you liked that last paragraph, then you might be interested in pursuing the CompTIA Security+ certification or other computer security–related certifications.

Policies and Procedures

Well, at some point we had to talk about rules, and who sets them. Sometimes it's the systems administrator, and many times, it is an executive, upper management, or a committee. Whoever it is, you can bet that there will be policies and procedures to follow at your organization. Generally, these are designed to be helpful, but it can be somewhat of a challenge in a BYOD or COPE environment.

> **Note**
>
> Remember, BYOD = bring your own device, and COPE = corporate owned personally enabled.

BYOD environments are ones where a person can use his or her personal mobile device for work purposes. As you can imagine, this can create a lot of logistical problems. For example, an organization adopting BYOD has to carefully plan how data is to be separated; devices will require different partitions, data access policies, DLP methods, and so on, not to mention data encryption. User agreements must be drawn up and signed by employees to acknowledge they understand what they can and can't do with their devices while on company premises or during work hours. The organization should consider use of an MDM for the addition and removal of devices.

From a user perspective, what we are most concerned with is the loss of employee privacy. From a company perspective, we are concerned with the leakage of data, or any other security breach related to the mobile device. As an entry point to a network, mobile devices have historically been less secure than a typical workstation computer. That's a generalized statement, but what I am suggesting is caution whenever configuring mobile devices. There are a lot of other issues that can present themselves whenever you mix business and personal. However, what is more important is what we can do about it.

First, I mentioned using an MDM solution, which can remotely administer a host of devices. It gives the administrator the ability to lock down devices and create those separate partitions, perhaps virtual partitions, or utilize containerization. These should completely separate the work data *and* apps from the personal data and apps. The MDM solution can also be used to limit how and when a user works, defining the time and the place where work can be done. Second is the user agreement, in which the organization clearly explains that the work data on a mobile device can be accessed and monitored by the organization at any time. Next, is to organize. Keep a log of all the BYOD devices on the network; it should be collected separately from any MDM software that is running. This is done to limit mobile device sprawl. Then, enact the best practices we have talked about in this book, such as complex passwords, automatic locks, DLP, encryption, MFA, and so on. Finally, carefully decide upon who will be administering the devices, and keep that list short!

In a COPE environment, the order is reversed. Instead of a person bringing in a device that is already in use and having it adjusted for work, COPE is when the organization owns the device, prepares it for work, and then offers it for personal use as well; kind of like having a company car. This can make it easier for the organization to administer devices (especially at the outset), but it can lock the user into a certain type of device for personal use. So, you will also see the acronym CYOD (choose your own device) bandied about. That means that the organization has a group of different devices, possibly including both iOS- and Android-based options, and the users can choose which one they prefer. However, remember the rule: the more platforms you have, the more administration that is required, and the more security concerns you will have. Some organizations offer a specific device across the board (such as Microsoft Surface) for work, and give the user the option of whether or not to use it personally, because some people would rather not be bothered with a dual-function device. Otherwise, most of the BYOD concepts we talked about also apply to COPE/CYOD.

Profile Security Requirements

For mobile device security, a good practice is to create *security profiles*, templates that you can use on multiple devices, as long as they are on the same platform. Then create a template (or set of templates) for each type of mobile device. For the most part, that means using an MDM solution. MDMs often come with prebuilt profiles for administration, but they are usually not secured—especially for your organization's particular needs. So, it's best to start with a built-in profile, and then build out the security from there, based on your overall security plan, threat model, and vulnerability assessment.

Once you have begun creating a profile, start configuring it securely. For example, choose the mode that it will use, such as authenticated (which might use Transport Layer Security [TLS]) or encrypted (which might use TLS and AES). Then select a certificate that will be used when the mobile device communicates with the MDM server; be sure that it is a valid certificate with the proper bit level of encryption. Configure endpoint protection, which might include Windows Defender and BitLocker (for Microsoft devices) or other endpoint protection software. Your organization might also require identity protection services be installed on the mobile devices. Think about kiosk settings (whitelisting) to limit what a user can do on the mobile device, and give the user access to the functionality that is required. Then, it's all about configuring services securely that we have talked about previously: e-mail, VPN, Wi-Fi, DLP, and certificates. For example, Microsoft Intune supports Simple Certificate Enrollment Protocol (SCEP) and Public Key Cryptography Standards (PKCS) certificates to help with the authentication of users via Wi-Fi and VPN. Profiles can also be configured to govern how people utilize data through a cellular provider, and whether or not hotspots can be created.

As mentioned, you can initiate whitelisting and blacklisting to allow certain programs or disallow certain programs, respectively. Plus, consider configuring trusted and untrusted application sources for the mobile devices. For example, an administrator might configure an Android-based profile that only allows users to download apps from the Google Play Store or, better yet, doesn't allow users to install apps *at all*. Ultimately, the idea is to lock down the devices as much as possible but still allow the user to perform his or her work. The more you can automate this process through the use of templates and scripts, the better.

> **Note**
>
> We'll be discussing policies and procedures more in the operational procedures section later in this book.

Cram Quiz

Answer these questions. The answers follow the last question. If you cannot answer these questions correctly, consider reading this chapter again until you can.

1. You want to prevent a user from accessing your phone while you step away from your desk. What should you do?

   ○ **A.** Implement remote backup.

   ○ **B.** Set up a remote wipe program.

   ○ **C.** Configure a screen lock.

   ○ **D.** Install a locator application.

2. Which of the following can be described as removing limitations on iOS?

   ○ **A.** Rooting

   ○ **B.** Jailbreaking

   ○ **C.** Geotracking

   ○ **D.** AV software

3. Your organization is concerned about a potential scenario where a mobile device with confidential data is stolen. Which of the following should be recommended first? (Select the best answer.)

   ○ **A.** Remote backup application

   ○ **B.** Remote wipe program

   ○ **C.** Passcode locks

   ○ **D.** Locator application

4. You are concerned about the possibility of jailbreaks on your organization's iPhones and viruses on the Android-based devices. Which of the following should you implement? (Select the two best answers.)

   ○ **A.** AV software

   ○ **B.** Firewall

   ○ **C.** Mobile device management

   ○ **D.** Device reset

5. There are Android-based smartphones in your organization that are part of the BYOD infrastructure. They need to be able to connect to the LAN remotely using a VPN. Which of the following should you incorporate into the MDM profile for the smartphones to connect to the VPN securely? (Select the best answer.)

○ **A.** AV software

○ **B.** Certificate

○ **C.** Remote wipe

○ **D.** Authenticator app

○ **E.** Microsoft Intune

Cram Quiz Answers

1. **C.** You should configure a screen lock (either a pattern drawn on the screen, a PIN, a password, biometric recognition, etc.). Remote backup, remote wipe, and locator applications will not prevent a user from accessing the phone.

2. **B.** Jailbreaking is the process of removing the limitations of an iOS-based device so that the user gets super-user abilities. Rooting is a similar technique used on Android mobile devices. Geotracking is the practice of tracking a device over time. AV software is antivirus software, which is used to combat malware.

3. **B.** The remote wipe program is the most important one listed. This will prevent a thief from accessing the data on the device. Afterward, you might recommend a backup program (in case the data needs to be wiped), as well as passcode locks and a locator application.

4. **A and D.** You should implement antivirus (AV) software on the local mobile device and consider MDM for deploying antivirus updates to multiple mobile devices remotely. This can protect against viruses and other malware as well as jailbreaks on Apple devices. As of the writing of this book, firewalls for mobile devices are not common, but that could change in the future. Device resets are used to restart the mobile device or to reset it to factory condition, depending on the type of reset and the manufacturer of the device. We'll discuss those more in Chapter 38, "Troubleshooting Mobile Operating Systems."

5. **B.** Use an encryption certificate to secure the VPN connection process from the mobile devices to the LAN. Consider powerful VPN technologies such as Open-VPN, IKEv2, RADIUS servers, and so on. Antivirus software is important for mobile devices, but won't impact secure VPN connectivity. Remote wipe is an important theft/loss solution. Authenticator apps are used to verify a user to a system and are often used in place of the second step of two-factor authentication, but are not as secure as using a certificate. Microsoft Intune can be used to administer mobile devices, but is not inherently secure; the profiles therein need to be configured in a secure way.

CHAPTER 35

Data Destruction and SOHO Security

This chapter covers the following A+ 220-1002 exam objectives:

▶ **2.9** – Given a scenario, implement appropriate data destruction and disposal methods.

▶ **2.10** – Given a scenario, configure security on SOHO wireless and wired networks.

Hey! This is the last chapter on security. Or is it? We should always be thinking in terms of security, as you will see while we progress through the rest of the book. But as far as Domain 2.0: Security, this is the last chapter.

Here we'll cover how to properly repurpose, recycle, dispose of, and destroy hard drives. And by the way, we'll be focusing on internal hard drives, but some of the methods herein can be applied to other devices that store data: USB flash drives, memory sticks, and so on. Be ready to protect all data, wherever it exists! Then we'll discuss some SOHO router security, including physical and logical security measures. There's lots to do, so *let's go already!*

2.9 – Given a scenario, implement appropriate data destruction and disposal methods

> ExamAlert
>
> **Objective 2.9** focuses on physical destruction (shredder, drill/hammer, electromagnetic [degaussing], incineration, certificate of destruction) and recycling or repurposing best practices (low-level format vs. standard format, overwrite, drive wipe).

Hard drives that contain an organization's data can be a security threat. When a hard drive is removed from a computer, it needs to be either stored, repurposed within the company, recycled for use by another entity, or disposed of in a proper manner. Sanitizing the hard drive is a common way of removing data, but it's not the only way. The manner in which data is removed might vary depending on its proposed final destination. Proper data removal goes far beyond file deletion or the formatting of digital media. The problem with high-level formats done within the operating system is the data remanence (or the residue) that is left behind; with the help of third-party software, that residue can be used to re-create files. So, we have to plan how the drive will be repurposed and use some quality tools to make sure any data has been removed properly.

> **Warning**
>
> The tools and procedures described in the following sections will either remove all data on a drive or render a hard drive unusable! Proceed with extreme caution and at your own risk. Consider using virtual machines for testing.

Formatting Drives

Recall that we talked about formatting back in Chapter 24, "Operating System Installation." As mentioned in that chapter, Windows can perform a quick format and a full format, both of which are known as *high-level* formats, but have different results. A quick format in Windows simply removes access to the files, but a full format writes zeros to the entire partition (zeroing out the drive). So, for repurposing a drive, the full format is the better option. It is a form of overwriting.

However, there is also the term *low-level format* in the CompTIA A+ objectives. Also known as a physical format, the low-level format is something that is done to mechanical drives by the manufacturer. Modern hard drives are low-level formatted at the factory, and it is a technique that should only be done once to a drive under normal circumstances; it physically creates the tracks and sectors on a hard disk drive. Older hard drives (from the 1980s and 1990s) could be low-level formatted from the BIOS in an effort to extend the lifespan of the drive, but it can be damaging to the drive. Today, the term "low-level format" or "LLF" has taken on a little more meaning for some people. Commands such as **dd** (which can zero out the drive) and **hdparm**, programs such as GParted, and some other third-party tools are considered by some to be LLF tools. But, the reality is that they either zero out the drive or simply remove and create partitions, so they are not really low-level formatting the drive. However, some of these tools *can* be more effective than a basic Windows format.

Regardless, all of these processes have to be performed from outside of the partition and file system that is to be formatted or overwritten. So, for example, to rewrite a Windows system partition, you could boot the computer to a live Linux flash drive (running Ubuntu or other distro) and run the command or program required on the target Windows system partition.

Overwriting Drives

Let's talk about deleting versus overwriting for a moment. If you delete a file on a hard drive, the OS will not be able to access it anymore. However, in most systems, the file remains until it is overwritten, either by another file or through another process. So, deleting data is not nearly enough to secure a drive that will be repurposed or recycled. Overwriting is a better option. This can be done with programs that write various data to the drive, but a common method is to *zero out* the drive. This means that you write binary zeros over every sector, and all the data, that is on the drive.

You can zero out a drive in Windows in a few ways. First, with the full format option in the GUI that we mentioned previously. Second, with the **format** command in the Command Prompt. For example, the following command will format the E: drive as NTFS and will zero out every sector of the drive in two passes, meaning that it will run the process twice. You have to be in elevated mode in the Command Prompt to perform this procedure.

```
format E: /fs:NTFS /p:2
```

You can increase the number of passes by changing the parameter **p:2** to whatever number you wish. Some companies require x number of passes, perhaps three. It all depends on the organization you are working for, and the policies that have been put in place. But remember, the more passes, the more time it will take, and the more stress that will be put on the hard drive.

> **Note**
>
> For more information about the **format** command and all of its parameters, type **format /?** in the Command Prompt and/or see the following link:
>
> https://docs.microsoft.com/en-us/windows-server/administration/windows-commands/format

The third option is to use **diskpart**, but this utility will wipe the entire drive, including any existing partitions, leaving you with unallocated space. To do this, enter the **diskpart** utility (again in elevated mode), list the disks (with the **list disk** command), then select the disk you want to zero out (for example, **select disk 1**), then type **clean all**. (You will have to type the name of the volume to proceed.) To use the drive again, it will have to be initialized, partitioned, and formatted.

For all three of these options, the process can be very lengthy. It depends on the size of the drive, the speed of the drive, and the amount of data on it. To test these commands quickly, use a virtual machine with a small secondary virtual drive, say around 8 GB. Remember, you have to be outside of the partition or drive that you want to zero out. So, if you want to zero out the E: partition, do it from C:, and so on.

We can also zero out the drive in Linux and macOS. I mentioned that it can be done graphically with the GParted application (which has to be installed first), but you can also do it in Terminal with the **dd** command. For example:

```
sudo dd if=/dev/zero of=/dev/sdb1
```

Replace "sdb1" with whatever drive and partition you want to zero out. This particular command will zero out the first partition of the drive *sdb* (a second drive in the system). There are no warnings and the process can take a long time. To watch the progress of the procedure, use the **status=progress** parameter. Afterward, you will have to reformat the partition to the file system of your choice. Be very careful not to zero out the system partition. Use with extreme caution!

So, zeroing out the drive can be a potentially secure way of overwriting all of the data so that the drive can be repurposed within an organization. But what if the drive is to be recycled for use by another organization, or what if you wanted to sell a personal computer? You might want to go further. And if your organization has highly sensitive data, or personally identifiable information (PII), then a higher standard should be employed.

For example, the DoD 5220.22-M standard specifies *sanitizing* the drive. One implementation of this standard is to perform three passes: first, overwriting the entire drive with binary zeroes; second, overwriting the entire drive with binary ones; and third, overwriting the entire drive with a random bit pattern, and verifying that final overwrite and logging that verification.

However, newer standards are more secure, such as NIST 800-88 Rev. 1, *Guidelines for Media Sanitization* (published in 2014). 800-88 is actually broken down into three categories: clear, purge, and destroy.

Clear

This is the removal of data with a certain amount of assurance that it cannot be reconstructed. However, the data is actually recoverable with special techniques. In this case, the media is repurposed and used within the company again. Zeroing out the drive and using bit-erasure software are examples of clearing. However, this method is not recommended for sensitive data.

Purge

Purging, or wiping the data of, a drive *is* recommended for sensitive data and drives that will leave the organization. It can be done in two ways: with the Secure Erase option (or similar technique) or by degaussing the drive.

Secure Erase is a command that can be run from the firmware of an ATA drive (accessed from the UEFI/BIOS or elsewhere). Or, you can use tools from Seagate (SeaTools), Western Digital (SSD Dashboard), or Samsung (Magician). Third-party tools such as Blancco Drive Eraser are also available. If you use any of these tools, the drive will still function. The question is this: Will the tools meet the standards and policies set forth by your organization? Always follow your organization's guidelines, and if there are no guidelines, or you are not sure, then purge the drive to the best of your ability, document the procedure, and store the drive in a secure location.

> **Note**
>
> Third-party tools such as DBAN can also wipe a drive, but they are designed for personal use and do not meet the requirements of NIST standards, and so are not recommended for drives with sensitive data.

It is also possible to degauss a hard disk drive, which will render the data unreadable, and in most cases will render the drive unusable, which is why some people will refer to it as a method of "destruction." Machines such as electromagnetic degaussers and permanent magnet degaussers can be used to permanently purge information from a disk. The process rearranges the magnetic field of the disk so that the data is destroyed. This process is necessary for disks that cannot be accessed from a computer—if the drive can't be accessed, then zeroing-out methods cannot be performed. If a drive is designated to leave the organization, and the drive is damaged, this process might be used first before physical destruction. Some IT destruction companies will always degauss first before physical destruction. Keep in mind that degaussing is primarily used on magnetic-based drives.

Destroy

This is when the storage media is physically destroyed. This could be done in a very basic way by using a hammer or similar tool, or by drilling holes through the platters. But for drives with sensitive data, a more robust destruction technique should be employed. Electromagnetic degaussing is one option, but as previously mentioned, that will often be used in conjunction with a complete physical destruction process, such as incineration or the more common hard drive shredding (also known as pulverization). At this point—if there is anything left of the drive—the media can be disposed of in accordance with municipal guidelines.

Some organizations require a certificate of destruction to show that a drive has indeed been destroyed; in fact, the certificate is often required because of data privacy laws. This is obtained from the third party that performs the drive destruction. A typical organization does not have the equipment necessary to perform proper destruction. That's why an outside vendor will be contracted to do the work—those vendors have the mechanical degaussers and hard-drive shredders designed specifically to meet NIST and DoD standards. Some of these vendors will come onsite to perform the process of destruction in front of the appropriate company personnel. Then the personnel sign off on the procedure. It's not recommended that hard drives be mailed or otherwise transported to the vendor, but if they are, the organization should use properly insured and tracked postal options or couriers, and the entire process should be documented utilizing a chain of custody or similar process.

> **ExamAlert**
>
> Know the differences between clearing, purging, and destruction.

The type of data removal used will be dictated by the data stored on the drive. If there is no PII or other sensitive information, it might simply be cleared. But in many cases, organizations will specify purging of data if the drive is to leave the building and be reused. In cases where a drive previously contained confidential or top-secret data, the drive will usually be destroyed. Again, always follow the policies that have been developed by your organization. If they are unclear, ask for additional interpretation from the appropriate personnel.

> **Note**
>
> The actual NIST SP 800-88 document can be obtained at this link:
>
> https://csrc.nist.gov/publications/detail/sp/800-88/rev-1/final

Cram Quiz

Answer these questions. The answers follow the last question. If you cannot answer these questions correctly, consider reading this section again until you can.

1. A hard drive needs to be disposed of in such a way that no one can access the data. Which method should be used?

    ○ **A.** Degaussing

    ○ **B.** Clearing

    ○ **C.** diskpart

    ○ **D.** Destruction

2. A drive is to be repurposed within your company. You have been tasked with zeroing out the drive three times from within Windows. Which of the following methods will accomplish this?

    ○ **A.** Degaussing

    ○ **B.** format C: /fs:fat32 /p:3

    ○ **C.** diskpart > select disk 1 > clean all

    ○ **D.** dd if=/dev/zero of=/dev/sda1

3. You have been tasked with purging a hard drive so that it can be recycled to a sister company. Which of the following should you perform before sending the hard drive out?

    ○ **A.** Clear the drive.

    ○ **B.** Degauss the drive.

    ○ **C.** Run Secure Erase.

    ○ **D.** Pulverize the drive.

Cram Quiz Answers

1. **D.** You should destroy the hard drive. Before physical destruction, sanitize it and/or degauss it. Clearing is the removal of data from a drive that is to be repurposed and used again within the organization. The **diskpart** utility can be used to clear the drive, but it is not appropriate for hard drive disposal.

2. **B.** The only option listed that will zero out the drive three times (from Windows) is **format C: /fs:fat32 /p:3**. This procedure formats the drive as FAT32 and runs the process three times (p:3). Degaussing a hard disk drive will render the data unreadable and, in most cases, will make the drive unusable. By default, the **diskpart** and **dd** processes listed will only zero out the drive once. They would have to be run with an additional parameter, or run manually two more times to meet the criteria. Also, **dd** is run from Linux, not from Windows, so that is another reason that answer is incorrect. But be very careful: note that the drive listed in the **dd** command is *sda1*. That will most likely be the system drive; if the command is run on that drive, the OS will be erased, which is what you want in this case—just remember to use caution when erasing drives. Double-check what you are doing before you run any commands.

3. **C.** At the bare minimum, run the Secure Erase program (or comparable program) to sanitize the drive. The rest of the answers are not examples of sanitizing or purging. Clearing the drive by formatting or zeroing out does not meet the requirements for sending the drive out to another company as standardized by NIST and the DoD. Degaussing the drive will render it useless. Pulverizing the drive (shredding it) will destroy it and will also render it unusable.

2.10 – Given a scenario, configure security on SOHO wireless and wired networks

ExamAlert

Objective 2.10 concentrates on wireless-specific configurations (changing default SSID, setting encryption, disabling SSID broadcast, antenna and access point placement, radio power levels, and WPS), change default usernames and passwords, enable MAC filtering, assign static IP addresses, firewall settings, port forwarding/mapping, disabling ports, content filtering/parental controls, update firmware, and physical security.

In Chapter 6, "SOHO Networks and Wireless Protocols," we discussed the setup of a small office/home office (SOHO) network. But without securing the network, we may as well just call up a hacker and ask that person to invade the network. The core of the SOHO network is the SOHO router. This device actually acts as a switch, router, firewall, and wireless access point. For the rest of this section, we'll talk about how to secure this device and we'll refer to it simply as a router. Before you make any security configurations, it is highly recommended that you update the firmware, and don't forget to save the configuration when you are done!

Note

Remember that you can access online emulators for several different kinds of routers. It's good to run through these configurations on your own router or an emulator of some sort.

Changing Default Passwords

The first thing we should do to secure the router is to change the password. Most routers come with a blank password, or have a basic password, such as *admin*. Connect to the router by opening up your favorite browser (your favorite should be the most secure one), typing the IP address of the router (for example, 192.168.0.1 or 192.168.1.1), and logging in. If the router has the option to create another admin account (or at least change the name), do it, and keep the original administrator account as the backup. But no matter what the router, you will definitely be able to change the password—and you should change it! Make it something complex, based on the rules we discussed in Chapter 33, "Windows Security Settings and Best Practices." Save the settings (which will log you out) and then log in with the new password to make sure it took effect.

> **ExamAlert**
>
> Remember to change the admin password first before anything else!

Many routers also have a user password. Change this as well but change it to a different password from the admin password.

Wireless-Specific Security Settings

Now we'll move on to some core radio and broadcasting security concepts, including the SSID, encryption, antennas, radio power levels, and WPS.

Changing and Disabling the SSID

The Service Set Identifier (SSID) is used to name a wireless network. Default SSIDs are usually basic; it is wise to change the name of the wireless network before enabling wireless on the router. Names that include uppercase letters, lowercase letters, and numbers will be more challenging for casual wireless passersby to memorize.

After all wireless clients are connected to the network, consider disabling the SSID. Though it is not a perfect solution, it will mask part of the SSID broadcast, making it impossible to see with normal wireless locating software. Figure 35.1 shows a modified SSID named *Neptune8Network* and that it is not enabled. By the way, given the channel and mode listed, what frequency is this router transmitting on? The channel is 165, so its center frequency is 5.825 GHz.

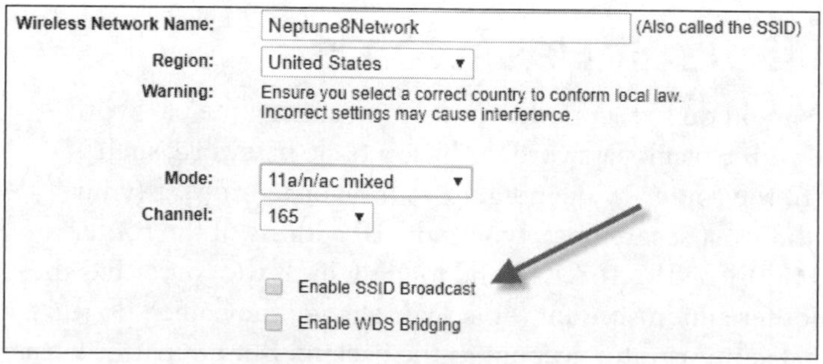

Wireless Network Name:	Neptune8Network	(Also called the SSID)
Region:	United States ▾	
Warning:	Ensure you select a correct country to conform local law. Incorrect settings may cause interference.	
Mode:	11a/n/ac mixed ▾	
Channel:	165 ▾	
	☐ Enable SSID Broadcast	
	☐ Enable WDS Bridging	

FIGURE 35.1 **Renamed and disabled SSID**

When the SSID is disabled, wireless clients won't be able to scan for it. If you need to connect additional wireless clients, you will either have to enable the SSID broadcast or enter the wireless SSID manually when connecting. For example, to connect manually in Windows, open the Network and Sharing Center and select **Set up a new connection or network**. Then select **Manually connect to a wireless network**. (The wireless adapter must be installed with correct drivers to see this link.) You will have to type the SSID (known as Network name), the security type, the encryption type, and the security key to get into the network. We talk more about this type of connection, as well as setting encryption on a SOHO router and on the client, in Chapter 32, "Wireless Security, Malware, and Social Engineering."

Antennas and Radio Power Levels

Strategically place your access point. Usually, the best place for an AP is in the center of the building—if at all possible. This way, equal access can be given to everyone on the perimeter of the organization's property, and there is the least chance of the signal bleeding over to other organizations. If needed, attempt to reduce the transmission power levels of the antenna, which can reduce the broadcast range of the AP. For example, Figure 35.2 shows the transmission power of an AP set to Low, which for small offices is usually enough. The other options are medium and high, or you might actually get a numerical option on some routers (measured in dBm). Test it by connecting with a laptop or other mobile device and moving to the perimeter of the building. If the lowest setting still allows access from the mobile device with a decent data transfer rate then there is no need to increase the power level.

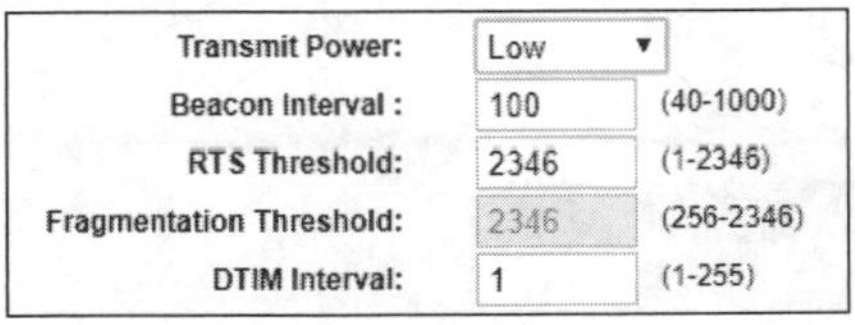

Transmit Power:	Low ▾	
Beacon Interval :	100	(40-1000)
RTS Threshold:	2346	(1-2346)
Fragmentation Threshold:	2346	(256-2346)
DTIM Interval:	1	(1-255)

FIGURE 35.2 **Power level of an access point set to Low**

Also, to avoid interference in the form of EMI or RFI, keep WAPs away from any electrical panels, cables, devices, motors, or other pieces of equipment that might give off an electromagnetic field. If necessary, shield the device creating the EM field.

An AP's antennas can be rotated so that they are parallel to each other, or at an angle to each other. For example, if you have two antennas, then 180 degrees is often a good orientation to sweep the area for wireless transmissions. The more antennas the better (usually), especially if they incorporate MIMO technology (described in Chapter 6) to combine multiple data streams.

By placing the AP and adjusting the antennas appropriately, and lowering the radio power levels as far as possible, you can further secure your wireless network while still providing decent service to your users.

> **ExamAlert**
>
> Strategically place your access points and know how to adjust radio power levels and AP antennas.

Disabling WPS

Wi-Fi Protected Setup was originally intended to make connecting to a wireless access point easier for the average user. However, anything that is made simpler is often less secure as well. Case in point, WPS is vulnerable to brute-force attacks, which can lead to intrusions on the network. Brute-force attacks are used to guess passwords and codes by trying combinations of letters, numbers, and symbols. The WPS code is usually 8 to 10 digits long, which is not very difficult to crack. So, your best bet is to disable WPS on the router to help secure the network. Figure 35.3 shows WPS as disabled (the Enable box is not checked). You can also see the basic 8-digit PIN code that is used. Sometimes, the WPS configuration is deep within the advanced settings or parameters of an AP.

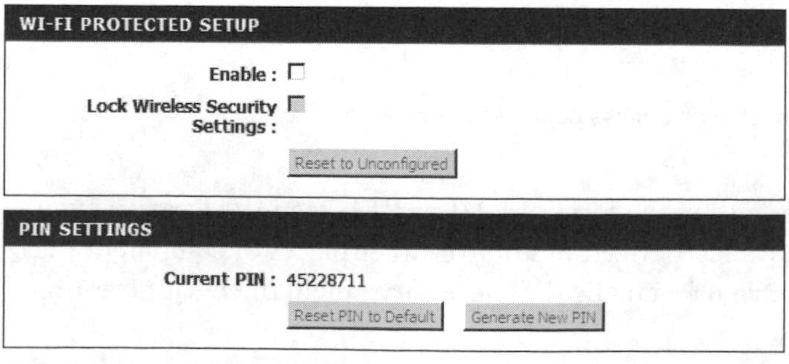

FIGURE 35.3   Disabled Wi-Fi Protected Setup on a common router

Enabling MAC Filtering

The wireless access point might also have the capability to be configured for MAC filtering (a basic form of network access control), which can filter out which computers can (or cannot) access the wireless network (and wired network). The AP does this by consulting a list of MAC addresses that have been previously entered. For example, take a look at Figure 35.4. If you used the Allow option as selected in the figure, then only the network adapters with those corresponding MAC addresses can connect; everyone else cannot join the wireless network.

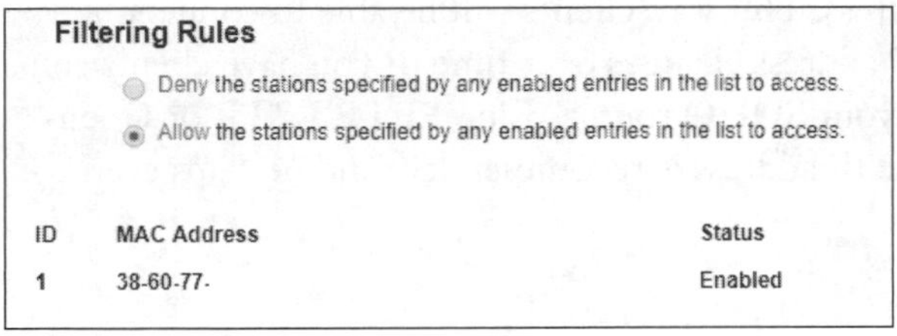

Filtering Rules

     ○ Deny the stations specified by any enabled entries in the list to access.

     ◉ Allow the stations specified by any enabled entries in the list to access.

ID	MAC Address	Status
1	38-60-77·	Enabled

FIGURE 35.4   **MAC filtering rules on an AP**

In some cases, a device might broadcast this MAC table. If this is the case, look for an update for the firmware of the access point and attempt to fine-tune the broadcast range of the device so that it does not leak out to other organizations. Because MAC filtering and a disabled SSID can be fairly easily circumvented using a network sniffer, it is important to also use strong encryption and possibly consider other types of network access control (such as 802.1X) and external authentication methods (such as RADIUS).

> **ExamAlert**
>
> MAC filtering can filter out which computers can (or cannot) access the wireless network (and wired network). Know how to enable MAC filtering.

Assigning Static IP Addresses

A SOHO router can be set to limit the number of dynamic addresses it hands out. If there are not enough to go around, you might find that certain hosts (such as servers or printers) lose connectivity when there are more client computers on the network. First, consider increasing the scope of addresses that the router is configured to hand out to clients. Second, try assigning static IP addresses to the servers and printers—essentially, any hosts that share information or services. If more clients obtaining dynamic addresses are added in the future, the servers and printers will not be affected.

By default, the SOHO router itself uses a static IP address on the LAN side; however, on the WAN side it is usually set to obtain an IP address from an ISP dynamically, though you can change this to static if you wish. If you have servers that the SOHO router is port forwarding to, and you have clients connecting to those servers from the Internet, then you might consider requesting a bank of static IPs from your ISP, and configure the SOHO router's WAN port to use one of those static IPs. Or at the very least, use a service such as DynDNS to forward your Internet domain name to your SOHO router's dynamically assigned IP address. This way, clients will be able to connect by domain name, even if the IP address changes over time. If you have clients connecting via a VPN through your SOHO router, using PPTP, L2TP, or Open-VPN, then the use of a static IP address is recommended, and perhaps even required.

Disabling Physical Ports and Physical Security

Many routers come with the capability to disable the physical ports on the switch portion of the device. This is a wise precaution. If you disable unused physical ports, a rogue computer can be plugged into the router physically but won't have any hopes of accessing the network. This concept is a policy in most organizations. Unused router or switch ports are disabled so that a person can't connect a laptop to any old RJ45 jack on the premises.

> **ExamAlert**
>
> Disable any physical ports that are not in use!

Consider the physical security of the SOHO router as well. Can anyone in the building put their hands on it? That would be inappropriate, so you need to physically secure the device. That means keeping it in a locked area such as a wiring closet, or if that is not possible, consider placing it above a drop ceiling (mounted properly), or on the ceiling if there is no drop ceiling. This way the device will at least be more difficult to reach—as long as you don't have a ladder lying around. Being as it is a *SOHO* router, then chances are that the organization does not have a server room, but if it does, then that is another excellent location.

Note

We discuss various firewall settings and port forwarding in Chapter 6.

Content Filtering/Parental Controls

Most SOHO routers come with a parental control section where content can be filtered on a very basic level. The "parent" can select the MAC address of a computer, and specify what domain names that computer is allowed to connect to—and when. Figure 35.5 shows an example of this.

MAC Address of Child PC:	D0-D2-B0-EE-21-CB
All MAC Address In Current LAN:	D0-D2-B0-EE-21-CB(192.168.41.103) ▼
Website Description:	D Pro
Allowed Domain Name:	dprocomputer.com
	davidlprowse.com
Effective Time:	Sched-1 ▼

FIGURE 35.5 **Parental control entry**

In the figure you can see that the MAC address D0-D2-B0-EE-21-CB has access to two domains (dprocomputer.com and davidlprowse.com, of course) and that there is an Effective Time using Sched-1, a schedule I preconfigured which allows the "child" to connect from 8 AM to 4 PM on weekdays; scheduling is usually a component of parental control.

Because the MAC address of a computer can't be changed (by a typical user), this configuration follows the computer, even if it gets a new IP address later. That's also the concept behind MAC filtering, and in fact some Parental Control sections will have a MAC filter built in.

A Final Word on SOHO Routers

To round out this section, make sure that the router's firmware is up to date. Also, always make sure the built-in firewall is enabled. This firewall is going to be much more important than the Windows firewalls on the individual computers, though both are recommended. Most routers' firewalls are on by default, but you should always check. If you do any kind of port forwarding, port triggering, DMZ configurations, or remote connections, make sure the firewall is allowing traffic only through the specific port or ports you require and that everything else is blocked. Check for updates every month or so, and while you are at it, change the administrator password for good measure.

Cram Quiz

Answer these questions. The answers follow the last question. If you cannot answer these questions correctly, consider reading this section again until you can.

1. Which of the following helps to secure a SOHO router? (Select the three best answers.)

   ○ **A.** Change default passwords.

   ○ **B.** Enable SSID.

   ○ **C.** Enable MAC filtering.

   ○ **D.** Enable WPS.

   ○ **E.** Enable WPA2.

2. You want to prevent rogue employees from connecting a laptop to the SOHO router and accessing the network. How can you accomplish this? (Select the two best answers.)

   ○ **A.** Enable MAC filtering.

   ○ **B.** Create a DMZ.

   ○ **C.** Configure a complex SSID.

   ○ **D.** Disable physical ports.

3. You want to prevent certain users from accessing particular websites. What should you configure on the SOHO router?

   ○ **A.** MAC filtering

   ○ **B.** Disable unused ports

   ○ **C.** Port forwarding

   ○ **D.** Parental controls

   ○ **E.** Power levels

Cram Quiz Answers

1. **A, C, and E.** Changing default passwords, enabling MAC filtering, and enabling WPA2 can all increase the security of a SOHO router. Enabling the SSID broadcast makes it visible. Enabling WPS makes it easier to connect to but has security implications.

2. **A and D.** By enabling MAC filtering, you can create a list of MAC addresses that the SOHO router will accept. Any other computers with different MAC addresses will not be allowed access to the network. This works for wired and wireless connections. You can also disable physical ports on the router; this blocks any physical signal from being sent to those unused ports. A demilitarized zone (DMZ) is used to host servers and acts as a separate area between the LAN and the Internet. A complex SSID is great but won't matter to a user connecting a laptop physically to the router because the SSID affects only wireless access.

3. **D.** By enabling parental controls, you can select computers—by MAC address—
and select what websites (domains) those computers are allowed to connect to.
MAC filtering by itself simply allows or denies computers access to the router
based on the MAC address of the computer. Disabling unused ports is a good
idea, but will simply stop a computer from accessing the SOHO router if it is connected on that port. Port forwarding is when you configure the router to forward
Internet-based IPs and ports to a computer or server that is on the LAN or DMZ.
Power levels refers to the broadcasting power of the AP's radio. The lower the
better, as long as people on the perimeter (of the building) can still communicate
with the router.

Domain 3.0: Software Troubleshooting

CHAPTER 36

Troubleshooting Microsoft Windows

This chapter covers the following A+ 220-1002 exam objective:

▶ **3.1** – Given a scenario, troubleshoot Microsoft Windows OS problems.

Welcome to the first chapter of Domain 3.0: Software Troubleshooting.

Now for the toughest part of working with Windows: troubleshooting. Before beginning this chapter, I recommend that you review the six-step troubleshooting methodology in Chapter 17, "Computer Troubleshooting 101." As I mentioned in Chapter 17, troubleshooting is probably the most important skill for a computer technician to possess. There are many different things that can go wrong in a computer; the majority of them are software-related. This chapter endeavors to give you the tools, utilities, and skills necessary to troubleshoot the various boot errors, stop errors, and other Windows problems that you might encounter.

We'll start with how to access and use the Windows Recovery Environment. Then we'll move into some boot issues and stop errors and demonstrate how to fix those. And throughout the chapter we'll discuss various issues and symptoms and the techniques and tools used to combat them. It's a super-important chapter, so let's get right to it.

3.1 – Given a scenario, troubleshoot Microsoft Windows OS problems

> **ExamAlert**
>
> **Objective 3.1** concentrates on common symptoms, including slow performance, limited connectivity, failure to boot, no OS found, application crashes, blue screens, black screens, printing issues, services fail to start, slow bootup, and slow profile load; it also covers common solutions, including defragment the hard drive, reboot, kill tasks, restart services, update network settings, reimage/reload OS, roll back updates, roll back devices drivers, apply updates, repair application, update boot order, disable Windows services/applications, disable application startup, Safe boot, and rebuild Windows profiles.

Windows Recovery

There are many tools included with Windows designed to help you troubleshoot and repair just about any issue that might come up. Before getting into the exact issues you might face, let's discuss some of these advanced repair and preinstallation environment repair tools, what they do, and where you can access them. We'll start with the Windows Recovery Environment.

Windows Recovery Environment (Windows RE)

Windows RE (or WinRE) is a set of tools included in Windows whose purpose is to recover Windows from errors that prevent it from booting; these tools can also be instrumental in fixing issues that cause a computer to "freeze up." There are several possible ways to access Windows RE; each method varies according to the version of Windows being used.

In Windows 10 and 8, Windows RE is accessed through the Boot Options menu. You can get to Boot Options in a variety of ways, including the following:

- ▶ Right-click the **Start** button, select **Shut down** or **sign out**, and while holding the **Shift** key, select **Restart**.
- ▶ In the Command Prompt, type **shutdown /r /o** and then press **Enter**.

▶ In Windows 10, go to **Start > Settings > Update & security > Recovery**, and under **Advanced Startup** click **Restart now**.

▶ Boot to various recovery or boot media; for example, a recovery partition, a Windows USB flash drive or DVD, or the Windows Preinstallation Environment (WinPE), which can be booted from flash drive, disc, and via the Preboot eXecution Environment (PXE). WinPE can be used to run recovery tools such as WinRE, as well as for running drive-cloning utilities. To use WinPE you must first download the Windows Assessment and Deployment Kit (ADK), and then the Windows PE add-on. You can get them from this link:

https://docs.microsoft.com/en-us/windows-hardware/manufacture/desktop/download-winpe--windows-pe

> **Note**
>
> In Windows 7, you either boot from the installation media or boot to a special partition on the hard drive that has Windows RE installed. We'll be focusing on Windows 10 and 8 for this section.

Once the system has rebooted, you should see the Choose an option screen. Selecting **Troubleshoot** will present several options, including

▶ **Refresh your PC** (Windows 8 only), which saves personal files but removes all programs installed to the desktop and resets PC settings.

▶ **Reset your PC**, which in Windows 8 removes all files and essentially performs a factory reset. In Windows 10 it allows you to keep personal files *or* remove everything.

▶ **Advanced Options**. Selecting Advanced Options brings up the main tools that a technician will use to troubleshoot a system.

Figure 36.1 shows the Advanced options screen in Windows 10 (version 1803), where the main recovery tools are available. In Windows 7 the equivalent is called System Recovery Options. Table 36.1 describes these options in more depth.

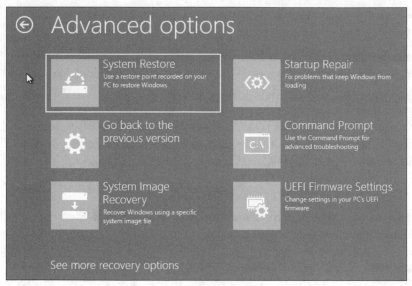

FIGURE 36.1 The Windows 10 Advanced options screen

TABLE 36.1 **Description of the Windows Recovery Options**

Recovery Option	Description
System Restore	Restores the computer's system files to an earlier point in time. It's a way to undo system changes to your computer without affecting your personal files, such as e-mail, documents, or photos. Note: If you use System Restore when the computer is in Safe Mode, you cannot undo the restore operation. However, you can run System Restore again and choose a different restore point, if one exists.
Go back to the previous version	(Windows 10 only.) This allows you to go back to an earlier build of Windows; for example, going back to Windows 10 version 1607 from version 1803. You can also do this from Settings in Windows.
System Image Recovery	These programs are used to restore a hard drive from a backup in select editions of Windows.
Startup Repair	When clicked, this automatically fixes certain problems, such as missing or damaged system files that might prevent Windows from starting correctly. When you run Startup Repair, it scans your computer for the problem and then tries to fix it so your computer can start correctly.
Command Prompt	Advanced users can use Command Prompt to perform recovery-related operations and also run other command-line tools for diagnosing and troubleshooting problems. You will have to log on as an administrator.
UEFI Firmware Settings	(Windows 10 and 8.) Allows a user to access the UEFI from the OS to make changes. (Requires UEFI compatible BIOS.)

Recovery Option	Description
Startup Settings	(Windows 10 and 8.) Enables booting to a variety of modes that are explained later in the chapter. To access this in Windows 10, click **See more recovery options**. This is known as the Advanced Boot Options menu in Windows 7.
Windows Memory Diagnostic	(Windows 7 only.) Scans the computer's memory for errors. In Windows 10 and 8 this can simply be run from the Command Prompt option with the **mdsched** command.

ExamAlert

Memorize the different Windows RE options in Windows.

Note

To learn more about WinRE for Windows 10, see this link:

https://docs.microsoft.com/en-us/windows-hardware/manufacture/desktop/windows-recovery-environment--windows-re--technical-reference

To learn more about WinRE for Windows 8, see this link:

https://docs.microsoft.com/en-us/previous-versions/windows/it-pro/windows-8.1-and-8/hh825173(v=win.10)

One thing to keep in mind is that Windows will attempt to do a self-repair if it senses a boot issue. This will occur first when you start, or restart, the system. If this automatic repair does not fix the problem, the Windows Recovery Environment is your next stop. But in some cases, you need to boot the system in a different *way* in order to fix a problem. Let's discuss advanced booting now.

Startup Settings and Advanced Booting

If Windows is not functioning properly, the culprit might be a video driver, new configuration, or other system issues. There are several startup options—such as Safe Mode—that can aid in fixing these problems. Historically, these options were accessed by pressing the F8 key immediately after the computer starts up. When you do so it displays the Windows Advanced Boot Options menu, which is what you need to use in Windows 7. These are effectively the same options as shown in the WinRE Startup Settings in Windows 10/8, with slight name changes and rearrangement.

While the F8 keypress is still supported by Microsoft, and it works in Windows 7 by default, it does not work in Windows 10/8 by default. To enable F8 functionality in Windows 10 and 8, type the following into the Command Prompt (as an admin):

```
bcdedit /set {default} bootmenupolicy legacy
```

That effectively replaces the Startup Settings version. To disable it, and go back to the Startup Settings version, use the same command but replace **legacy** with **standard**.

The Startup Settings window and the Advanced Boot Options menu have essentially the same options, with one difference—the Advanced Boot Options menu includes the **Repair Your Computer** option, which will automatically attempt to fix Windows issues for you. That's not included in the Startup Settings window because there are several automated repair options elsewhere in WinRE. You will most likely use Startup Settings more often, so let's show and describe that. Figure 36.2 shows an example of the Startup Settings window as displayed in Windows 10. Table 36.2 describes the options as listed in the Startup Settings window. Note that you can use the F1–F9 function keys to select the corresponding startup options.

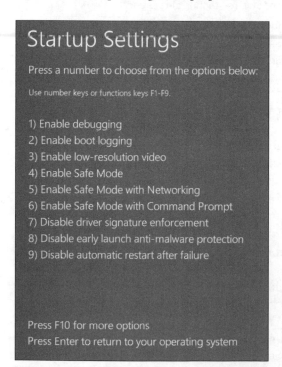

FIGURE 36.2 The Windows 10 Startup Settings screen

TABLE 36.2 **Description of the Windows Startup Settings**

Startup Setting	Description
1) Enable debugging	Enables the use of a debug program to examine the system kernel for troubleshooting.
2) Enable boot logging	Logs the boot process and creates a ntbtlog.txt file. This is stored in the %systemroot%.
3) Enable low-resolution video	Uses a standard VGA driver in place of a GPU-specific display driver but uses all other drivers as normal, typically at 640×480 resolution.
4) Enable Safe Mode	Starts system with a minimal set of drivers; used in case one of the drivers fails. Safe Mode is a good option when attempting to use System Restore and when scanning systems for viruses. It is also a good option if you encounter a Blue Screen of Death (BSOD) error, and you need to roll back a driver.
	You can also initiate Safe Mode (and its derivatives) by opening the System Configuration utility (**Run > msconfig**), accessing the **Boot** tab, checking **Safe boot**, and restarting the computer.
5) Enable Safe Mode with Networking	Starts system with a minimal set of drivers and enables network support.
6) Enable Safe Mode with Command Prompt	Starts system with a minimal set of drivers but loads Command Prompt instead of the Windows GUI.
7) Disable driver signature enforcement	Enables drivers containing improper signatures to be installed
8) Disable early launch anti-malware protection	(Windows 10/8 only.) Rootkits can infect a system early on as it boots and some anti-malware programs are designed to check for these early on in the boot process. But in some cases, you need to disable these anti-malware programs to diagnose and fix the system; for example, when using System Restore.
9) Disable automatic restart after failure	Prevents Windows from automatically restarting, if an error causes Windows to fail. Choose this option only if Windows is stuck in a loop in which Windows fails, attempts to restart, and fails again repeatedly.

ExamAlert

Know the various Startup Settings (such as Safe Mode) and know what they do.

Boot Errors

There are various reasons why a computer will fail to boot. If it is operating system-related, you usually get some type of message that can help you to troubleshoot the problem. Windows uses the bootmgr and BCD files during the startup process. If these files are corrupted or missing, you will get a corresponding error message. Two common errors are "Bootmgr is missing" and "The Windows Boot Configuration Data file is missing required information." Let's talk about each of these now.

Bootmgr is missing

This message displays if the Windows Boot Manager file (bootmgr) is missing or corrupt. This black screen probably also says Press **Ctrl+Alt+Del** to Restart; however, doing so will probably produce the same results.

By default, the bootmgr file should be located in the root of C:. There are a few methods to repair this error. The first is to boot to the Windows Recovery Environment and select the **Startup Repair** option. This should automatically repair the system and require you to reboot. If this doesn't work, try the second method, which is to rebuild the Boot Configuration Data (BCD) store. Again, boot to the Windows RE, select the **Command Prompt** option, and then type the command **bootrec /rebuildbcd**. That rebuilds the data store and might fix the problem. You might also need to run System Restore from the Windows RE to fix the problem.

Sometimes, you might find that the C: partition needs to be set to active. Or the 100-MB special partition (which houses important boot information) is missing. Check these as well when troubleshooting this error.

Finally, in some cases, the commands **bootrec /fixboot** and **bootrec /fixmbr** can help. These rewrite the boot sector and master boot record (MBR), respectively. (One scenario in which you might need to do this is when the Windows computer was configured to dual-boot with an older version of Windows.) Note that **bootrec /fixmbr** is ineffective on GPT-based systems because they do not use an MBR.

> **Note**
>
> For more information about fixing this error, visit the following links. They are written for Windows 7, but most of the information applies to newer versions of Windows as well.
>
> https://support.microsoft.com/en-us/help/2622803/
> bootmgr-is-missing-press-ctrl-alt-del-to-restart-error-when-you-start
>
> https://support.microsoft.com/en-us/help/927392/
> use-bootrec-exe-in-the-windows-re-to-troubleshoot-startup-issues

> **ExamAlert**
>
> Make sure you understand that **bootrec** can be used to troubleshoot and repair a boot sector, a Boot Configuration Data (BCD) store, and, less commonly, the master boot record (MBR).

The Windows Boot Configuration Data file is missing required information

This message means that either the Windows Boot Manager (bootmgr) entry is not present in the BCD store or the Boot\BCD file on the active partition is damaged or missing. Additional information you might see on the screen includes File: \Boot\BCD and Status: 0xc0000034. Unfortunately, this means that the BCD store needs to be repaired or rebuilt. Hold on to your hat; there are three methods of repair for this error. The first two are the same as with our "Bootmgr is missing" error. Let's review those again. Chances are you'll be called on to perform these in the field or perhaps on the exam, so know them well.

The first method of repair is to boot to WinRE, go to Advanced options, and select the **Startup Repair** option. This should automatically repair the system and require you to reboot. If not, move on to the second method.

The second method of repair is to boot to WinRE and select the **Command Prompt** option. Type **bootrec /rebuildbcd**. At this point, the bootrec.exe tool either succeeds or fails. If the bootrec.exe tool runs successfully, it displays an installation path to a Windows directory. To add this entry to the BCD store, type **Yes**. A confirmation message appears that indicates the entry was added successfully.

If the bootrec.exe tool can't locate any missing Windows installations, you have to remove the BCD store and then re-create it. To do this, type the following commands:

```
Bcdedit /export C:\BCD_Backup
ren c:\boot\bcd bcd.old
Bootrec /rebuildbcd
```

These methods usually work, but if not, there is another method that is more in depth and requires rebuilding the BCD store manually.

> **Note**
>
> For more information, you can find this step-by-step process and learn more about fixing BCD store issues at:
>
> https://support.microsoft.com/en-in/help/2004518/error-message-when-you-start-windows-7-the-windows-boot-configuration

> **ExamAlert**
>
> Know how to recover from Windows boot errors!

Improper and Spontaneous Shutdowns

You've probably seen a Windows computer fail and reboot with a message such as **Windows was shut down improperly**. Improper shutdowns and spontaneous shutdowns could happen for a variety of reasons: brownouts or blackouts, power surges, hardware failures, a user inadvertently unplugging the computer, or perhaps a virus or other malware. It can be a disturbing phenomenon to users and one that could be going on for a while, so be patient with the user (and the computer) when troubleshooting this problem.

Some of the methods you can use to troubleshoot these issues include

▶ **Check the Event Viewer:** Look in the System log to see if there are any alerts about hardware failures, service failures, and so on. If there is an alert, consider upgrading the driver for the affected hardware or upgrading the software that the service is dependent on. Ensure the computer is running the latest updates.

▶ **Use MSConfig (System Configuration utility):** On the General tab, select the **Selective startup** checkbox and the **Load startup items** checkbox. To weed out third-party program issues, click the **Services** tab, click the **Hide all Microsoft services** checkbox, and then click **Disable all**. Restart the system and see if the same issues return or if events are still written to the Event Viewer. Remember to restore Normal startup in MSConfig when finished troubleshooting.

▶ **Boot into Safe Mode:** Use Safe Mode to further investigate the problem. Safe Mode uses only the most basic drivers, so if it is a driver issue, this could help you find out about it. Don't forget, you can also use Safe boot in MSConfig.

► **Run a virus scan:** Run a scan for malware and quarantine anything unusual. Update the antivirus software when you are finished.

► **Check power:** Make sure the AC outlet is wired properly and is supplying clean power. Verify that the power plug is firmly secured to the computer. If necessary, you might have to check the power supply. Intermittent and unexplainable shutdowns can sometimes be linked to power supplies or other hardware failures.

► **Use Windows RE:** If necessary, use the Windows Recovery Environment to troubleshoot spontaneous shutdowns.

Stop Errors

A stop error (also known as a Blue Screen of Death [BSOD]) is the worst type of error that can happen while Windows is operating. It completely halts the operating system and displays a blue screen with various text and code. (In Window 10, you might see a sad face with a QR code, among other things.) Anything you were working on is, for the most part, lost. In some cases, it reboots the computer after a memory dump has been initiated. (This is also known as auto-restart.) If not, you need to physically turn off the computer off with the Power button and turn it back on. Some BSODs happen only once, and if that is the case, you need not worry too much. But if they happen two or three times or more, you should investigate. Quite often they are due to a hardware issue, such as improperly seated memory or a corrupt driver file. If you see two columns of information with a list of drivers and other files, a driver issue could be the culprit. Look at the bottom of the second (or last) column and identify the driver that has failed (for example, ntfs.sys). These drivers can become corrupt for a variety of reasons and would need to be replaced when you boot into Windows. Or if you can't boot into Windows and Windows does not auto-repair the file, you can replace the driver from within Windows RE's Command Prompt. Less commonly, a BSOD might be caused by a memory error that will have additional code that you can research on Microsoft's websites (Microsoft Support and TechNet).

By default, three things happen when a stop error occurs:

1. An event will usually be written to the System log within the Event Viewer, if that option has been selected in the Startup and Recovery window, as shown in Figure 36.3. When a stop error is written to the System log, it may be listed as an Information entry, not as an Error entry. The stop error will be listed as "The computer has rebooted from a bugcheck. The bugcheck was: *error number*." Use the error number to look up the

problem—and hopefully find a solution—on Microsoft Support and/or TechNet.

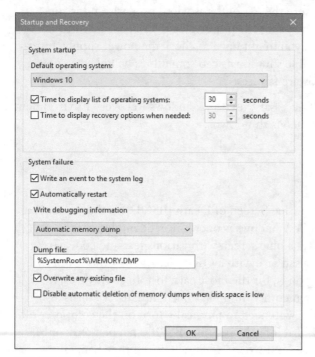

FIGURE 36.3   **The Startup and Recovery window**

The settings shown in Figure 36.3 can be accessed from the Advanced tab in the System Properties dialog box (which you can access directly via **Run > SystemPropertiesAdvanced.exe**). Click the **Settings** button in the Startup and Recovery area to access the Startup and Recovery window.

2. Windows will write debugging information to the hard drive for later analysis with memory dump debugging programs; this debugging information is essentially the contents of RAM. The default setting in Windows is to only write a portion of the contents of RAM, known as a Kernel Memory Dump. The Kernel Memory Dump is saved as the file %SystemRoot%\Memory.dmp. You can also select a Small Memory Dump; this is written to %SystemRoot%\Minidump. Windows supports the option for a Complete Memory Dump, which dumps the entire contents of RAM to a file again named Memory.dmp. To support the Complete Memory Dump, the paging file must be large enough to hold all the physical RAM plus 1 MB.

> **Note**
>
> For more information about the various dump files, visit
>
> https://docs.microsoft.com/en-us/windows-hardware/drivers/debugger/varieties-of-kernel-mode-dump-files

3. The computer automatically restarts (if that option is selected, which is the default in Windows).

> **ExamAlert**
>
> Know how stop errors occur and how memory dumps function.

Restoring Windows

Beyond even stop errors, a complete system failure is when a system cannot be repaired. When this happens, the only options are to reinstall Windows or to restore Windows. There are several methods for restoring Windows, including

▶ **All Windows:** Boot to the Windows installation media (USB flash drive, DVD, etc.), then click the repair option. At the main Windows RE Advanced options (or System Recovery Options) window, select **System Image Recovery**. Provide backup media.

▶ **Windows 7:** Boot to the Windows installation media, then click the repair option, and at the first System Recovery Options window (with the possible list of operating systems), select the **Restore your computer using a system image that you created earlier** option (you will be required to provide the backup media).

▶ **All Windows:** Reset the system to a factory image stored on a separate partition of the hard drive. This is common on laptops, especially ones that do not have optical drives. Or use third-party tools such as Symantec Ghost or Acronis True Image. Remember, the image needs to be created *before* the disaster!

There are various other ways to access the utilities mentioned. Refer to earlier parts of this chapter for details or refer to the documentation that came with your third-party software.

Common Windows Symptoms and Solutions

We mentioned a lot of issues and solutions already, but there are a good number of other symptoms that you will encounter when working on Windows. What makes troubleshooting difficult is that there are often several potential solutions to a problem. Let's fill the gaps by listing some of those symptoms and potential solutions in Table 36.3.

> **ExamAlert**
>
> You will likely be tested on the common symptoms and solutions listed in Table 36.3. Given a scenario, know how to troubleshoot Windows OS problems well for the exam and in the field!

TABLE 36.3 **Windows Symptoms and Solutions**

Symptom	Potential Solutions
Slow performance/ Slow bootup	▶ Use the Troubleshooter. Go to **Control Panel > System and Security**, and click the **Troubleshoot common computer problems** link under Security and Maintenance. Or, in Windows 10 click **Start > Settings > Update & Security > Troubleshoot**. ▶ Clean up and defragment the hard drive. ▶ Reboot often. ▶ Watch for numerous tabs opened in a web browser. ▶ Uninstall unused programs. ▶ Limit programs that run at startup. View the Notification Area to see what is running. Use the **Task Manager > Startup** tab to disable programs. ▶ Scan for malware. ▶ Increase RAM (if not possible, see the next bullet). ▶ Increase the virtual memory: **Run > systempropertiesadvanced.exe > Advanced** tab > click the **Settings** button under Performance to open the Performance Options dialog box > **Advanced** tab > **Change** button. ▶ End tasks in the **Task Manager > Processes** tab or with the **taskkill** command.

Symptom	Potential Solutions
Limited or no connectivity	▶ Restart the system. ▶ Reboot your router or modem. ▶ Update the network settings: IP address, gateway address, run an **ipconfig /release** and **ipconfig /renew**. ▶ Update the wireless network settings: SSID, encryption type, and so on. ▶ Check if the system is in airplane mode. ▶ If necessary, boot into Safe Mode and roll back the network driver. ▶ Check the patch cable and look for a link light! ▶ Use the Network and Internet Troubleshooter (**Control Panel > All Control Panel Items > Troubleshooting > Network and Internet**).
No OS found/ Failure to boot	▶ Update the BIOS boot order. ▶ Repair master boot record or boot files in system partition (see various repair options earlier in the chapter). ▶ Check hardware connections (hard drive cables, etc.). If necessary, roll back any changes, or reimage/reload the OS.
Application crashes	▶ Apply updates to the OS. ▶ Apply updates to the application. ▶ Repair the application: **Control Panel > All Control Panel Items > Programs and Features**, then right-click the application in question and select **Repair** (or reinstall if necessary). ▶ Run the application in program compatibility mode. Use the Program Compatibility Troubleshooter (**Control Panel > All Control Panel Items > Troubleshooting**, and click the link **Run programs made for previous versions of Windows**). Or, right-click the program executable and change the compatibility settings. ▶ Temporarily disable the application from startup if it is interfering with other programs and the OS: **Task Manager > Startup** tab.
Blue screen/black screen	See the sections "Windows Recovery," "Boot Errors," and "Stop Errors" earlier in the chapter.
Printing Issues	▶ Use the Troubleshooter: **Control Panel > All Control Panel Items > Troubleshooting > Hardware and Sound > Printer**. ▶ Configure settings in **Control Panel > All Control Panel Items > Devices and Printers**. ▶ Roll back device drivers. (This applies to any devices that fail in Windows as a potential solution.) (See Chapter 21, "Troubleshooting Printers," for more information.)

Symptom	Potential Solutions
Device issues	▶ Use the Troubleshooter: **Control Panel > All Control Panel Items > Troubleshooting**.
	▶ Use the Device Manager to troubleshoot (**Run > devmgmt. msc**). Know the Device Manager icons:
	▶ Black arrow pointing down = device is disabled. Simply re-enable it to use the device. In rare cases, a hardware conflict can be caused by I/O settings or IRQs (for example, serial COM ports).
	▶ Exclamation point = incorrect driver or hardware conflict. Try removing the device, let Windows reinstall. If that does not work, download correct drivers from manufacturer's website.
	To troubleshoot further, open the Properties window for the device and locate the error code on the General tab or Events tab. Cross-reference with the codes listed at this link: https:// support.microsoft.com/en-us/help/310123/error-codes-in-device-manager-in-windows
Services fail to start	▶ Start or restart services: **Run > services.msc**, right-click the service in question and choose **Properties**, and stop and start it within the Properties window. Or, use the **net start** and **net stop** commands. Check for issues with other services that the affected service is dependent on.
	▶ Verify that they have not been disabled in msconfig or the Services console window.
Slow profile load	▶ Clean up temp files and cookies with cleanup programs and manually. For example:
	c:\Users\%username%\AppData\Local\Microsoft\Windows\ Temporary Internet Files
	c:\Users\%username%\AppData\Roaming\Microsoft\ Windows\Cookies
	▶ Verify that the workstation's time is synchronized to the domain controller (if on a domain). Use the **net time** command. For example, log on locally and type **net time \\\domaincontroller/ set**.
	▶ Check the User Profile Service for issues.
	▶ Watch for too many programs loading at startup.
	▶ Configure policies via **gpedit.msc: Computer Configuration > Administrative Templates > System > Group Policy**, and similar policies.
	▶ Run the Windows Troubleshooter.
	▶ Roll back updates (if necessary).
	In uncommon cases, try the options listed in the next row: Corrupted profile.
	Bonus: Sometimes, this issue is misanalyzed and it isn't the profile at all. In some cases, the video driver needs to be updated, or there is a separate issue concerning the GUI and desktop.

Symptom	Potential Solutions
Corrupted profile	▶ Copy the profile over to a new account. Do this at **Run > systempropertiesadvanced.exe**, then click the **Settings** button in the User Profiles section. Or, copy the entire folder, or just the ntuser.dat file as required. ▶ Repair the user profile within the Registry Editor. ▶ Otherwise remove, rename, and/or rebuild the profile.

A Final Word on Windows Troubleshooting

Here's the thing about troubleshooting—it goes on and on. There are many problems and, usually, there are multiple potential solutions to each problem. And what works today on one version of Windows might not work tomorrow on another version of Windows. Be ready to think outside the box, and use that six-step troubleshooting methodology. This will guide you while you prioritize the list of probable causes, and the list of potential solutions. Also, visit https://support.microsoft.com and https://technet.microsoft.com often.

Cram Quiz

Answer these questions. The answers follow the last question. If you cannot answer these questions correctly, consider reading this chapter again until you can.

1. Which option starts the operating system with a minimal set of drivers?

   ○ **A.** Windows RE

   ○ **B.** System Restore

   ○ **C.** Safe Mode

   ○ **D.** Debugging Mode

2. Which tool should be used if you want to do Startup Repair in Windows?

   ○ **A.** File History

   ○ **B.** Windows RE

   ○ **C.** System Restore

   ○ **D.** Safe Mode

3. Which command repairs the bootmgr file in Windows? (Select the best answer.)

   ○ **A.** msconfig

   ○ **B.** bootrec /fixboot

   ○ **C.** bootrec /rebuildbcd

   ○ **D.** boot\bcd

4. One of your customers updated the software for a wireless adapter on a PC. After rebooting, the user logged in and the computer displayed a blue screen. What should you do?

   ○ **A.** Install the device on a known good computer.

   ○ **B.** Reboot the computer and access debugging mode.

   ○ **C.** Purchase a new wireless adapter.

   ○ **D.** Roll back the device drivers in Safe Mode.

5. You are running Windows 8.1 and want to save personal files and remove all programs installed to the desktop while resetting PC settings. Which of the following should you select?

   ○ **A.** Reset your PC

   ○ **B.** Refresh your PC

   ○ **C.** System Recovery Options

   ○ **D.** Command Prompt

6. A stop error could manifest itself as what?

   ○ **A.** A BSOD

   ○ **B.** An Event Viewer error

   ○ **C.** An Action Center notification

   ○ **D.** An Internet Explorer error

7. Which tools can be used to restore a computer? (Select all that apply.)

   ○ **A.** File History

   ○ **B.** System Restore

   ○ **C.** System Image Recovery

   ○ **D.** Msconfig

8. Which of the following might cause a blue screen?

   ○ **A.** A faulty DVD-ROM

   ○ **B.** A CPU without a fan

   ○ **C.** Bad drivers

   ○ **D.** A program compatibility issue

9. An application is frozen and cannot be closed. However, the rest of the operating system works fine. Which tool can be used to close the application?

   ○ **A.** tasklist

   ○ **B.** taskkill

   ○ **C.** shutdown

   ○ **D.** convert

10. You are tasked with repairing an issue with a Windows client computer that is attempting to log on to a domain. The user informs you that it takes 5 minutes to log on to the domain, but logging in to the local machine only takes 15 seconds. What steps should you take to fix the problem? (Select the two best answers.)

    ○ **A.** Clean up temp files.

    ○ **B.** Disable unnecessary services in msconfig.

    ○ **C.** Update the BIOS boot order.

    ○ **D.** Synchronize the Windows client's time to the domain.

    ○ **E.** Run **ipconfig /release** and **ipconfig /renew**.

Cram Quiz Answers

1. **C.** Safe Mode starts the operating system with a minimal set of drivers. Windows RE (WinRE) is the recovery environment used to repair Windows; it exists outside the operating system. System Restore is used to revert back to an earlier point in time of the OS. Debugging mode is one of the Advanced boot options.

2. **B.** Windows RE includes Startup Repair. File History is the backup and restore feature of Windows 10 and 8. Safe Mode is part of the Startup Settings screen (Windows 10 and 8) and the Advanced Boot Options menu (Windows 7). System Restore is a different tool that is also available in Windows RE; it can be used to restore the computer's settings to a previous point in time.

3. **O. bootrec /rebuildbod** is one of the methods you can try to repair bootmgr in Windows. **Msconfig** is used to modify how the OS starts up but cannot repair bootmgr.exe. **Bootrec /fixboot** is used to repair the boot sector. In rare cases, it might be able to fix the bootmgr file. **Boot\bcd** is where the boot configuration store is located.

4. **D.** You should boot into Safe Mode and roll back the drivers of the device in the Device Manager. The drivers that the customer installed were probably corrupt and caused the stop error. There's no need to remove the device and install it anywhere just yet. Debugging mode probably won't be necessary for this; it is more commonly used to analyze issues during boot. Never purchase new equipment until you have exhausted all other ideas!

5. **B.** You should select Refresh your PC. In Windows 8.1 this removes programs that were installed and resets PC settings but it saves personal files. When you select Reset your PC (in Windows 8.1), all files are removed and the system is reset to the original state. In Windows 10, Reset your PC gives you both options. System Recovery Options in Windows 7 is where the Windows Recovery Environment tools are found. The Command Prompt is used to run specific commands (either from within the OS or from Windows RE) and isn't the best answer for this scenario.

6. **A.** A BSOD (Blue Screen of Death) is what results from a stop error in Windows. The proper name for it is a stop error.

7. **B and C.** System Restore is the tool used to restore a computer to an earlier point in time. While this doesn't completely restore from an image, it is still a form of restoration. System Image Recovery is the Windows 7 solution for restoring an image. File History is used in Windows 10 and 8 to locate files from backup and restore them to the system. Msconfig is used to modify how Windows boots and which services are run.

8. **C.** Bad drivers could cause a blue screen error (stop error). Blue screens could also be caused by improperly seated RAM, among other hardware issues. A faulty DVD-ROM drive would not cause a blue screen. A CPU installed without a fan would overheat, causing the system to shut down. Incompatible programs simply don't run.

9. **B. Taskkill** ends the underlying process of an application, closing the application. **Tasklist** is used to view which processes are running, their process IDs, and the memory used by each. **Shutdown** is a command used to turn off the computer in a variety of ways. **Convert** is used to alter a FAT32 partition to NTFS.

10. **A and D.** Try cleaning up temp files and cookies (either with a cleanup program or manually). Then, make sure that the client computer's time is synchronized to the domain controller. Disabling unnecessary services is always a good idea, but it is unlikely that doing so will slow the logon process to the domain that much, especially if the local logon is quick. Updating the BIOS boot order isn't necessary because the system is booting to Windows just fine. Releasing and renewing the IP address shouldn't be necessary in this scenario, but it can be helpful when troubleshooting no (or limited) connectivity issues. Remember, troubleshooting is what we do. It's all about persistence—keep searching for the answer!

CHAPTER 37

Troubleshooting PC Security Issues and Malware Removal

This chapter covers the following A+ 220-1002 exam objectives:

▶ **3.3** – Given a scenario, use best practice procedures for malware removal.

▶ **3.2** – Given a scenario, troubleshoot and resolve PC security issues.

In Chapter 32, "Wireless Security, Malware, and Social Engineering," we discussed the types of malicious software you should know for the exam. Now that we've covered a lot more security, and some Windows troubleshooting methods, let's get into how to resolve malware-based security issues and discuss proper malware removal.

For this chapter I've combined both objectives together because they are closely related. We'll be covering 3.3 first so that we can discuss the malware removal process. Keep one thing in mind while going through this chapter: some organizations don't want to troubleshoot malware at all. They will simply wipe the system and re-image it, restoring the data afterward. That method has its place in the IT field, but in this chapter, for the most part, we will be concentrating on the resolution of malware issues by way of removal. You might hear the terms "antivirus software," "anti-malware program," "endpoint protection platform," and other similar terms. They are all essentially the same thing, and I will for the most part refer to this as anti-malware.

We'll also discuss some closely related security issues that may or may not be malware related. Sometimes, a security issue may appear to be malware related, but really it is something different, or something that was designed to look like malware. So be ready to troubleshoot with an open mind (as always) and look for alternative causes for the problems you will face.

3.3 – Given a scenario, use best practice procedures for malware removal

> **ExamAlert**
>
> **Objective 3.3** concentrates on the steps involved with identifying, researching, quarantining, and remediating malware, including end-user education.

3.2 – Given a scenario, troubleshoot and resolve PC security issues

> **ExamAlert**
>
> **Objective 3.2** focuses on common symptoms of malware, including pop-ups, browser redirection, security alerts, slow performance, Internet connectivity issues, PC/OS lockup, application crash, OS updates failures, rogue antivirus, spam, renamed system files, disappearing files, file permission changes, hijacked e-mail, responses from users regarding e-mail, automated replies from unknown sent e-mail, access denied, invalid certificate (trusted root CA), and system/application log errors.

The CompTIA A+ Seven-Step Malware Removal Procedure

As much as you try to protect computers from malware, it will eventually affect—or *infect*—one or more systems on your network. At that point, it is important to think logically and methodically. CompTIA offers up some best practices when it comes to malware removal. Now, if you do encounter what you believe to be malware, or an anti-malware platform informs you of an infection, then that system or systems should be taken off the network, and isolated right away.

Here is the CompTIA recommended procedure for the removal of malware:

1. Identify and research malware symptoms.

2. Quarantine the infected systems.

3. Disable System Restore (in Windows).

4. Remediate the infected systems.

    a. Update the anti-malware software.

    b. Scan and use removal techniques (Safe Mode and preinstallation environment).

5. Schedule scans and run updates.

6. Enable System Restore and create a restore point (in Windows).

7. Educate the end user.

> **ExamAlert**
>
> Know the CompTIA A+ malware removal procedure.

Malware Removal Scenario

Let's take a look at an example using the step-by-step process. In this scenario, a user in the marketing department contacts you and says he thinks his computer is infected. You initiate a trouble ticket, and then walk over to the person's computer to investigate. Now, while you are implementing the best practices for removing malware, remember to also incorporate the six-step troubleshooting methodology detailed in Chapter 17, "Computer Troubleshooting 101." To start, that means gathering information: analyzing the computer and talking to the user. Let's go through the steps now.

1. Identify and research malware symptoms

When you arrive at the user's computer, the user tells you that since this morning the system boots, and runs, much more slowly than usual. Also, you witness that he cannot open a couple of important applications that are stored locally. Based on this information, you decide that there is a chance that the computer is infected with a virus, as these are common symptoms of viruses.

> **Note**
>
> Before making any changes, make sure you back up any critical data!

2. Quarantine the infected systems

At this point, the computer should be quarantined—logically, and possibly physically. The system should be taken off the network. If it is wired to the network, disconnect it. If it is wireless, enter airplane mode, or disable the wireless adapter in the Device Manager. In some cases, you will work on the computer where it is located, but if possible, shut it down and physically isolate it by bringing it to the computer bench, or other lab environment, where it can be worked on further.

> **Note**
>
> An organization might have a policy that states the system should be isolated immediately at the slightest mention of a virus or malware. So, depending on the situation, you might have remotely shut down the system, taken it off the network, or otherwise quarantined it, before you even started this malware removal process.

3. Disable System Restore (in Windows)

System Restore can get in the way of proper analysis of a system, so it is recommended that you disable it before doing anything else. Do this by accessing the System Protection tab of the System Properties dialog box (**Run > systempropertiesprotection.exe**). Highlight any drives that have protection turned on (one at a time) and then click the **Configure** button. That opens the System Protection dialog box for that particular volume, as shown in Figure 37.1. Click the **Disable system protection** radio button, (**Turn off system protection** in Windows 7). Do this for each volume that has system protection enabled.

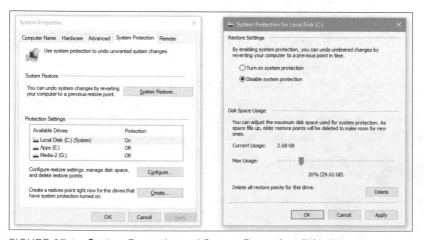

FIGURE 37.1 **System Properties and System Protection dialog boxes**

Other systems such as macOS and Linux should have similar restoration programs disabled (if any). The idea is to disable any programs that might interfere with your upcoming scans.

4. Remediate the infected systems

First, check and update the anti-malware software. Is it running properly? Can it update? Verify that the update brings it to the latest version. Next, it's time to scan the system. This is best done from Safe Mode in Windows, or from a preinstallation environment such as WinRE (see Chapter 36, "Troubleshooting Microsoft Windows," for details on how to access those), or from a bootable USB flash drive with its own OS or repair/recovery environment. These modes and environments reduce the chance that the virus (or other malware) will be able to interfere with your scans and remediation techniques.

> **Note**
>
> At this point, you might encounter problems performing the tasks required. Tougher malware is designed to stop a person from disabling System Restore, or from updating (or even using) the anti-malware program. The toughest malware slows down Safe Mode to a crawl, or makes it difficult otherwise to use the system. If this happens, you should seriously consider re-imaging the system.

Once the anti-malware program has been updated, initiate a full scan of each volume systematically. These can be time consuming, so be prepared to multitask. (Don't we always?) You might also opt to scan the system from a separate OS running on a USB flash drive or on another system altogether (you might have removed and isolated the target hard drive). This can be a powerful way to resolve problems, as you are working from an external system, and is a common practice. Either way, scan each volume individually, and log the results.

Chances are that you will find one or more pieces of malware. If that is the case, quarantine, remove, and/or delete them based on the anti-malware program (or programs) that you are using, and according to organizational policy.

Scan the system again to verify that all malware is taken care of. Then boot the system and make sure that it does not have the same symptoms as before. The system should boot at the appropriate speed, and the programs that were mentioned should now run properly. If not, then additional measures will have to be taken, and once again, you should consider re-imaging.

> **ExamAlert**
>
> Remember that the remediate step for removing malware includes using scanning and removal techniques in Safe Mode or from a preinstallation environment such as WinRE.

In less common scenarios you might need to remove registry entries that were added by malware. In the case of a boot sector virus, you'll have to boot the system to external media, or slave off the hard drive to your testing computer for full analysis.

5. Schedule scans and run updates

If the system has been given the thumbs up and it is now certified for use, then access the anti-malware program again and schedule periodic scans of the system. Also make sure that scheduled updates are turned on and are defined based on company policy. Many organizations use corporate-level, centrally managed antivirus solutions—known as endpoint protection platforms. These can push out updates to all the computers on the network at once. Create a profile for all the computers within a group that should be affected by these updates.

This is all part of the preventative maintenance stage, and there are lots of other things we can do to make a PC stronger. For example, we can enable Secure Boot in the UEFI/BIOS. We can enable No-eXecute (NX) bit technology in the BIOS (for compliant CPUs), which can help stop viruses from infecting code. Update the OS, and so on. Be ready to *harden* the computer system as described elsewhere in this book.

6. Enable System Restore and create a restore point (in Windows)

Turn System Restore back on for all drives that require it. Then, create a restore point. Look at Figure 37.1. In the System Properties dialog box, you would do this by clicking the **Create** button toward the bottom of the window. This way, if a problem does occur in the future, you can go back in time, so to speak, to the point where the malware was removed and the system was functioning normally.

7. Educate the end user

At this point, the computer is ready for use. Reconnect the system to the network, and advise the end user as to what you performed and why. Explain what happened to the system. In this particular scenario, there wasn't much that the user could do to prevent the problem. However, sometimes end users will click unknown links, or attempt to install untrusted software. Explain in an amicable way how this is not good for the computer. Educate the end user on how to safely operate the system.

> **Note**
>
> Educate users to watch out for rogue antivirus programs. These are actually malicious programs that appear to be antivirus programs, using similar names and logos as the real thing. Keep a sharp eye out for programs masquerading as other programs!

Symptoms of Viruses

The previous scenario gave a couple typical symptoms of viruses, but there are more. If a computer is infected by a virus, you want to know what to look for so that you can "cure" the computer. Here are some additional typical symptoms of viruses:

- ▶ Slow performance: the computer runs slower than usual.

- ▶ The computer/PC operating system locks up frequently or stops responding altogether.

- ▶ The computer restarts on its own or crashes frequently.

- ▶ Hard drives and applications are not accessible or don't work properly.

- ▶ Applications crash (this could also be a sign of a Trojan that has exhausted the resources needed to run the application).

- ▶ Windows Update fails.

- ▶ Permission to specific files and folders is denied, with access denied errors.

- ▶ Internet access is blocked or is redirected.

- ▶ Strange sounds occur.

- ▶ You receive unusual error messages or security alerts (which are most likely false).

- ▶ Display or print distortion occurs.

- ▶ New icons appear or old icons (and applications) disappear.

- ▶ There is a "double extension" on a file attached to an e-mail that was opened (for example, .txt.vbs or .txt.exe). These are designed to trick a user into thinking the file attachment is a text file, when in reality it is a potentially dangerous script or executable.

- ▶ Antivirus programs will not run, can't be installed, or can't be updated.

- ▶ Files disappear, have been renamed or corrupted, or folders are created automatically.

Symptoms of Spyware

Spyware is another bane of computers. It is designed to spy on the user and attempt to gain confidential information. Be on the lookout for it. Here are some common symptoms of spyware:

- ▶ The web browser's default home page has been modified. This is a type of browser redirection.

- ▶ A particular website comes up every time you perform a search.

- ▶ Excessive pop-up windows appear. Rogue antivirus applications and security alerts seem to appear out of nowhere, supposedly scanning the system.

- ▶ The network adapter's activity LED blinks frequently when the computer shouldn't be transmitting data.

- ▶ The firewall and antivirus programs turn off automatically.

- ▶ New programs, icons, and favorites appear.

- ▶ Odd problems occur within Windows (the system is slow, applications behave strangely, and so on).

- ▶ The Java console appears randomly.

Preventing and Troubleshooting Spam

We've all heard of spam. Spam is the abuse of electronic messaging systems such as e-mail, broadcast media, and instant messaging. The key is to block as much spam as possible, report those who do it, and train your users. Here are several ways that spam can be reduced:

▶ **Use a strong password:** E-mail accounts can be hijacked if they have weak passwords. This is especially common with web-based e-mail accounts, such as Gmail. After obtaining access, the hijacker sends spam to everyone on the user's contact list. Use a complex password and change it often to prevent e-mail hijacking.

▶ **Use a spam filter:** This can be purchased for the server side as software or as an appliance. These appliances monitor spam activity and create and update whitelists and blacklists, all of which can be downloaded to the appliances automatically. On the client side, you can configure Outlook and other mail programs to a higher level of security against spam; this is usually in the Junk E-mail Options area. Many popular anti-malware suites have built-in spam filtering. Make sure it is enabled!

▶ **Use whitelists and blacklists:** Whitelists are lists of e-mail addresses or entire e-mail domains that are trusted, whereas blacklists are those that are not trusted. These lists can be set up on e-mail servers, e-mail appliances, and within mail client programs such as Outlook.

▶ **Train your users:** Instruct users to create and use free e-mail addresses whenever they post to forums and newsgroups; they should not use their company e-mail addresses for anything except company-related purposes. Make sure that they screen their e-mail carefully; this is also known as e-mail vetting. E-mail with attachments should be considered volatile unless the user knows exactly who sent the e-mail. Train your users and customers never to make a purchase from an unsolicited e-mail.

Hijacked E-mail

Going beyond spam, sometimes an e-mail account is hijacked. The user might be sharing access with the hijacker or lose access altogether. This could have been caused by a virus, a Trojan, the user clicking a malicious script, or a malicious insider. One way to tell that this is happening is when other users on the network respond to the hijacked user's alleged e-mails—which are actually coming from the hijacker. You can also watch for automated replies from unknown sent e-mails and look at the e-mail trail and the e-mail headers. The original hacked e-mails will often look "spammy" or otherwise suspicious.

The headers of the e-mail can be very telling when it comes to the source of the e-mail and the way it was delivered. You can find out the mail servers used and IP addresses, protocols and encryption used, and so on. For example, to see the headers of an e-mail within Outlook, you could double-click the e-mail in question so that it opens in its own window. Then, click **File > Properties**. This brings up a Properties window for the e-mail, which supplies a lot of information, but we are most interested in the Internet headers section. Here's an example snippet of an Internet header:

```
Envelope-to: webmaster@dpro42.com
Delivery-date: Wed, 13 Mar 2019 06:36:06 -0700
Received: from maile-da.domainname.com ([8.174.6.201]:51959)
by server.domainname.com with esmtps (TLSv1.2:ECDHE-RSA-AES256-GCM-
  SHA384:256)
```

Here we can see who the recipient is (Envelope-to) as well as the server name and IP address of the mail server that the e-mail was received from, plus the outgoing port that was used. (Domain names and IPs were changed to protect the innocent.) If hijacking is going on, this can be some key information. We can block those IPs and domains as we see fit. From the header information we also see that TLSv1.2 and AES256 are being used in GCM mode with an SHA cryptographic hash applied. And there is a lot more we can find out by scrolling down. Plus, there are a variety of other methods for viewing headers on the client side and the server side.

To resolve a hijacked e-mail account issue, the first thing the admin should do is change the user password, and then make sure that the user's account is affected by a policy which requires complex and lengthy passwords that are changed periodically. If necessary, back up the e-mail from the account, delete (or disable) the account, and create a new one for the user. Then, reset any other passwords for other accounts on the network that the user might have—chances are that the person uses the same password. Caution the user that his or her password has been compromised, and to never use it again...anywhere... ever. Consider multifactor authentication (MFA) for e-mail, adding a layer of security such as biometrics or a smart card in addition to a password. This is one of those times when single sign-on (SSO) MFA can really be beneficial. When you have separate individual systems, the chance of a weak password is greater than an SSO scenario. Plus, if an SSO account is compromised, it is only one account that has to be fixed. But the MFA side of things will reduce the risk of account compromise.

More Symptoms of PC Security Issues and Potential Solutions

There are some symptoms within Objective 3.2 that we have not covered yet. Those symptoms and some potential solutions to them are listed in Table 37.1.

TABLE 37.1 **PC Security Symptoms and Solutions**

Symptom	Potential Solutions
Browser redirection	▶ Check for a redirect in the browser **properties > home page** setting. For example, for IE and Edge, go to the **Control Panel > Internet Options > General** tab. ▶ Check for redirects in the hosts file (located in C:\Windows\system32\drivers\etc). ▶ Check if websites have been added to the Trusted Sites section of the browser. ▶ Run anti-malware scans. Watch for spyware and viruses. ▶ If running DNS on the server side, consider running DNSSEC (Domain Name System Security Extensions).
Invalid certificate issue/ trusted root CA	▶ Analyze and verify installed certificates in the trusted root of the **Certificate Manager (Run > certmgr.msc) > Trusted Root Certification Authorities**. ▶ Analyze the Security log file in the Event Viewer for information on individual events concerning invalid certificates. ▶ Delete, export, revoke, and otherwise modify the certificates that are invalid, and import new trusted certificates from a trusted CA.
Invalid e-mail certificate	If there is no malicious activity: ▶ Import a new certificate for all parties concerned. For example, in Outlook go to **File > Options > Trust Center > Trust Center Settings > E-mail Security**. Then import a new Digital ID (certificate). (Be sure to select the **Add digital signature to outgoing messages** checkbox.) ▶ Publish the certificate appropriately if a certificate server is being used that is not properly integrated with other platforms on the network (for example, Microsoft Exchange Server). If there is potential malicious activity: ▶ Analyze the Event Viewer: System, Application, and Security logs. ▶ Consider revoking the current certificate, creating a new one, and importing it to all parties concerned. ▶ Scan the system and change account passwords.
Computer is being remotely controlled by an unknown entity	▶ Scan for malware, especially Trojans. ▶ Disable Remote Desktop and Remote Assistance, and any third-party remote-control software such as RealVNC.
Ransomware hoax alerts	If it is real, then files are encrypted and locked. We discuss this elsewhere in the book. But there are many ransomware hoaxes as well that occur when a person stumbles onto an infected or malicious website. If this happens: ▶ Block websites and domains where the web pages are initiated from. ▶ Check for browser redirection. ▶ Train users not to click the × button to close the browser. Instead, end the application or underlying background process within the Task Manager.

ExamAlert

Know the common symptoms of malware and how to troubleshoot and resolve them.

Cram Quiz

Answer these questions. The answers follow the last question. If you cannot answer these questions correctly, consider reading this chapter again until you can.

1. Which of the following are symptoms of viruses? (Select the three best answers.)

   ○ **A.** A computer runs slowly.

   ○ **B.** A computer locks up.

   ○ **C.** Excessive pop-up windows appear.

   ○ **D.** A strange website is displayed whenever a search is done.

   ○ **E.** Unusual error messages are displayed.

2. Which of the following is the best mode to use when scanning for viruses?

   ○ **A.** Safe Mode

   ○ **B.** Reset this PC

   ○ **C.** Command Prompt only

   ○ **D.** Boot into Windows normally

3. You have been tasked with repairing a computer that is exhibiting the following symptoms:

   ▶ Excessive pop-up windows appear.

   ▶ A particular website comes up every time the user searches.

   What is the most likely cause?

   ○ **A.** Spam

   ○ **B.** Virus

   ○ **C.** Social engineering

   ○ **D.** Trojan

   ○ **E.** Spyware

4. A co-worker technician is using certmgr.msc to analyze a problem with a computer. Which of the following issues is the technician most likely troubleshooting?

   ○ **A.** Trusted root CA

   ○ **B.** Hijacked e-mail

   ○ **C.** Spam

   ○ **D.** Browser redirection

5. Several computers were infected with malware because the end users clicked unknown links embedded in e-mails. You have successfully applied the first six steps of the best practice procedures for malware removal. What should you do next?

   ○ **A.** Schedule scans and run updates.

   ○ **B.** Enable System Restore and create a restore point.

   ○ **C.** Document findings, actions, and outcomes.

   ○ **D.** Educate the corporate users.

Cram Quiz Answers

1. **A, B, and E.** Some symptoms of viruses are a computer running slowly, a computer locking up, and unusual error messages. Excessive pop-ups and strange websites displaying after searches are symptoms of spyware.

2. **A.** Safe Mode should be used (if your anti-malware software supports it) when scanning for viruses. Safe Mode is found in the Startup Settings or the Advanced Boot Options menu. Other options found there include: Command Prompt only, which offers command-line access only; and the option to boot into Windows normally. Reset this PC is a WinRE option that will reinstall Windows: in Windows 8 it will delete the user data; in Windows 10 it can delete the data or keep it during the reinstall.

3. **E.** The computer is most likely suffering from spyware. Spam is the abuse of e-mail or other messaging system. A virus will infect a system and have symptoms that might include slow performance, application crashes, and computer lockups. Social engineering is a group of attacks done on a social level; for example, shoulder surfing, dumpster diving, tailgating, and so on. A Trojan is malware that is often used to gain access to remotely control a system, or acts as a container for the actual malware payload.

4. **A.** The technician is most likely investigating a certificate issue—that's why the tech is using the Certificate Manager (certmgr.msc). The Trusted Root CA (Certificate Authority) section within the Certificate Manager contains all of the certificates that were issued to the computer by third-party companies, as well as certificates that were created on the computer itself. When double-clicked, each certificate will display the issuer and the validation dates. Make sure certificates are still valid! If not, delete them, and notify the appropriate companies or personnel.

5. **D.** You should educate the corporate users next. This is step 7 (the final step) of the CompTIA best practice procedures for malware removal. In this scenario, the end users clicked unknown links. Explain to them why this is a bad idea and what the result was—downtime and loss of productivity. Then consider proposing written policies, security controls, and training programs to prevent the issue from happening again. "Schedule scans and run updates" is step 5. "Enable System Restore and create a restore point" is step 6. "Documenting findings, actions, and outcomes" is a great idea! However, that is step 6 (final step) of a separate process—the CompTIA troubleshooting methodology, as detailed in Chapter 17.

CHAPTER 38

Troubleshooting Mobile Operating Systems

This chapter covers the following A+ 220-1002 exam objectives:

▶ **3.4** – Given a scenario, troubleshoot mobile OS and application issues.

▶ **3.5** – Given a scenario, troubleshoot mobile OS and application security issues.

Okay, here's the last chapter on troubleshooting. The number of mobile devices in the workplace has been steadily growing for a long time now, and with more devices come more problems that will need your attention. There is a bit of overlap between this chapter and Chapter 3, "Smartphones, Tablets, and Other Mobile Devices, Part 1," and Chapter 4, "Smartphones, Tablets, and Other Mobile Devices, Part 2." That's because the hardware and the software of a mobile device are so closely linked; a problem that occurs could be due to software, hardware, or both! So, you might want to refer back to those chapters to get a little refresher on mobile device hardware and communications. Let's get troubleshooting!

Note

For this chapter we will cover the two objectives together, because they are so heavily intertwined.

ExamAlert

Objective 3.4 focuses on the following common symptoms of mobile OS and application issues: dim display, intermittent wireless, no wireless connectivity, no Bluetooth connectivity, cannot broadcast to external monitor, touchscreen non-responsive, apps not loading, slow performance, unable to decrypt e-mail, extremely short battery life, overheating, frozen system, no sound from speakers, inaccurate touch screen response, system lockout, and app log errors.

> **ExamAlert**
>
> **Objective 3.5** concentrates on the following common symptoms of mobile OS and application security issues: signal drop/weak signal, power drain, slow data speeds, unintended WiFi connection, unintended Bluetooth pairing, leaked personal files/data, data transmission over limit, unauthorized account access, unauthorized location tracking, unauthorized camera/microphone activation, and high resource utilization.

Wi-Fi Troubleshooting

When troubleshooting mobile device wireless connections, always perform the following basic wireless troubleshooting techniques:

- ▶ The device is within range.

- ▶ The correct SSID was entered (if manually connecting).

- ▶ The device supports the encryption protocol of the wireless network.

- ▶ The device is not in airplane mode.

- ▶ The user didn't inadvertently connect to an unintended Wi-Fi network. It happens more often than you might think with the number of today's open Wi-Fi networks available.

- ▶ Tethering and mobile hotspots are not conflicting with the wireless connection.

- ▶ The cellular connection is not conflicting with the wireless connection.

If you still have trouble, here are a few more methods that can help to connect or reconnect to a wireless network:

- ▶ Power cycle the mobile device.

- ▶ Power cycle Wi-Fi.

- ▶ Remove or "forget" the particular wireless network and then attempt to connect to it again.

- ▶ Consider using a Wi-Fi analyzer app to locate the wireless network in question. Sometimes these analysis apps can give you more information that can help to solve the connectivity problem. They're also a great security tool to check your own WAP. Just be careful because some can use up a good deal of system resources and possibly cause the battery to run hot.

▶ Access the advanced settings and check whether there is a Wi-Fi sleep policy, whether Wi-Fi scanning has been turned off, whether there is a proxy configuration, or whether a static IP is used. Also, Wi-Fi Direct and WPS might need to be configured properly, or disabled. Any of these could possibly cause a conflict. You might also try renewing the lease of an IP address, if the device is obtaining one from a DHCP server (which it most likely will be). Some devices also have an option for Best Wi-Fi Performance, which uses more power but might help when connecting to distant WAPs. Another possibility is that the mobile device needs to have an encryption certificate installed, which is usually done from here as well. The advanced settings will vary from device to device, but an example is shown in Figure 38.1. Note the IP address and MAC address at the bottom of the figure; if you ever need to know either of those addresses, this is a good place to go.

FIGURE 38.1 **Advanced wireless settings**

One of these methods usually works when troubleshooting a wireless connection, but if all else fails, a hard reset can bring the device back to factory settings. (Always back up all data and settings before performing a hard reset.) And if the mobile device still can't connect to any of several known good wireless networks, consider accessing the Developer options and the *super* advanced wireless settings (more on Developer options later), or take the device to an authorized service center.

You might also encounter issues where the device can connect to Wi-Fi but has a slow connection. In that case, check the signal strength, as well as the distance to the nearest AP, whether or not the device is connecting to the *correct* AP (in case there is more than one option), and if there are any obstructions.

> **ExamAlert**
>
> Know your Wi-Fi troubleshooting techniques!

Bluetooth Troubleshooting

If you have trouble pairing a Bluetooth device and connecting or reconnecting to Bluetooth devices or personal area networks (PANs), try some of the following methods:

- ▶ Make sure the phone or other mobile device is Bluetooth-capable.

- ▶ Verify whether Bluetooth is enabled on the mobile device. Also, if applicable, verify whether it is enabled on the target device (for example, an automobile sound system).

- ▶ Verify whether your devices are fully charged, especially Bluetooth headsets.

- ▶ Check whether you are within range. For example, Class 2 Bluetooth devices have a range of 10 meters.

- ▶ Restart the mobile device and attempt to reconnect.

- ▶ Check for conflicting Wi-Fi frequencies. Consider changing the channel used by the Wi-Fi network (if it is on 2.4 GHz).

- ▶ Use a known good Bluetooth device with the mobile device to make sure that the mobile device's Bluetooth is functional.

- ▶ Remove or "forget" the particular Bluetooth device, turn off Bluetooth in general, restart the mobile device, and then attempt to reconnect.

▶ Check that the user didn't make an unintended Bluetooth connection. If a Bluetooth device doesn't have a passcode or other security methods implemented, it can easily be connected to another mobile device, and vice versa.

ExamAlert

Know your Bluetooth troubleshooting techniques!

Troubleshooting E-mail Connections

If you have trouble connecting an e-mail account, try some of the following methods:

▶ Make sure the mobile device has Internet access. If connecting through the cellular network, make sure there is a decent reception.

▶ Verify that the username, password, and server names are typed correctly. Remember that the username is often the e-mail address itself.

▶ Check the port numbers. See Chapter 5, "Ports, Protocols, and Network Devices," for a list of ports. Be aware, however, that network administrators might decide to use non-default port numbers!

▶ Remember that secure e-mail ports are preferred most of the time. Double-check whether security is required in the form of Secure Sockets Layer (SSL) or Transport Layer Security (TLS). For nonstandard port numbers and security configurations, check with your network administrator.

ExamAlert

When troubleshooting e-mail connections on mobile devices, double-check all settings such as username, password, server name, and port number.

You might also encounter issues where a user cannot decrypt e-mail communications. Encryption issues can happen on several levels, including at the server, during the e-mail session, the individual e-mails themselves, and attachments. Today, e-mail sessions are based on SSL or TLS. The user's e-mail account needs to log in to a secure server making use of the correct protocol and port. We discuss that more in Chapter 5; however, if individual e-mails (or attachments) cannot be decrypted, then it is probably a certificate issue. If the problem only affects one user, then the certificate should be checked at the mobile device; a new one will potentially have to be imported. In Figure 38.1 you saw an option in Android for installing certificates from storage. It can also be done from Encryption & credentials, as shown in Figure 38.2.

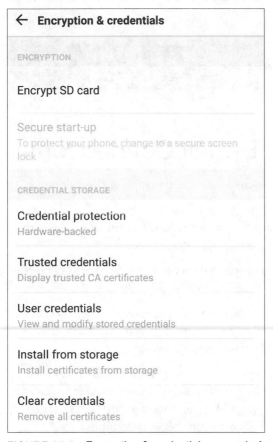

FIGURE 38.2   Encryption & credentials screen in Android

From this screen you can clear and install certificates, and check trusted credentials. So, you could check if a certificate has expired or has been revoked and import the new one as need be. Note that attachments might use a separate certificate from the main e-mail certificate. With some mobile device management (MDM) solutions, certificates can be exported directly to the mobile device; just make sure to use an encrypted session between the MDM and the device to prevent the certificate from being compromised!

ExamAlert

If individual e-mails (or attachments) cannot be decrypted, then it is probably a certificate issue.

Troubleshooting and Stopping Applications

Applications that are opened on a mobile device will continue to run in the background unless they are specifically turned off within the app or within the OS, or the device is restarted.

To turn off apps (or services) that are running on a typical Android-based system, go to App info, or the Application Manager (or similar name). That displays all the currently running applications and services, though the services portion might be within a different tab of that screen. As with PCs, mobile device apps use RAM. The more RAM that is used by the mobile device, the worse it will perform; it will slow it down and eat up battery power. So, to close an app, you would simply locate it on the list, tap it, and on the next screen tap **Force stop**. Figure 38.3 (left) shows an example of an app info screen with the Force stop option. You can also stop services or processes in this manner. If you are not absolutely sure what the service is, do not initiate a Stop because it can possibly cause system instability. In the past, due to that instability, force stops were reserved only for services; they are now an option on many devices for applications as well. Just remember that force stops can cause the OS to behave erratically. You can also clear the storage data and cache by tapping **Storage**. This also is shown in Figure 38.3 (right). By clearing the data and cache, you can fix a lot of issues with applications.

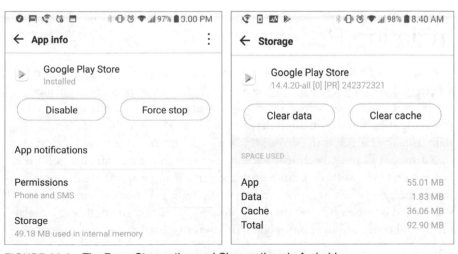

FIGURE 38.3 The Force Stop option and Clear options in Android

To force quit an app on iOS-based devices, follow these steps:

1. On an iPhone X or later or an iPad with iOS 12, from the Home screen, swipe up from the bottom of the screen and pause slightly in the middle of the screen. On an iPhone 8 or earlier, double-tap the **Home** button to show your most recently used apps.

2. Swipe right or left to find the app that you want to close.

3. Swipe up on the app's preview to close the app.

> **Note**
>
> For older iOS devices, you may have to press and hold the **Sleep/Wake** button for a few seconds until a red slider appears. Then press and hold the **Home** button until the app quits.

> **ExamAlert**
>
> Understand how to stop apps on Android and Apple devices.

There are third-party apps that can close down all of the apps in one shot if you need to save time. However, these can cause erratic behavior as well. Finally, if an application is causing the device to lock up and you can't stop the app normally or through a force stop, then a soft reset or a hard reset will be necessary.

Initiating Resets

Sometimes, mobile devices are the victims of a frozen screen; tapping on the screen and pressing any buttons has no effect. To fix this problem, consider a soft reset. A *soft reset* is done by simply powering off the mobile device and powering it back on. (You might have to hold the Power button for longer than usual.) This resets the drivers and the OS. Soft resets are similar to shutting down a PC and powering it back up. Some technicians will also call this a power cycle. The soft reset can help when certain applications are not functioning properly or when network connectivity is failing. When a smartphone is still locked up when it is restarted, try pulling the battery (if applicable), replacing it, and restarting the phone again, or attempt a hard reset.

iOS-based devices can do a variety of more advanced software resets beyond a simple power cycle, such as Reset All Settings, Erase All Content and Settings, Reset Network Settings, and so on. These are available by tapping **Settings > General > Reset**.

A *hard reset* should be initiated only when things have gone terribly wrong; for example, when hardware or software has been compromised or has failed and a soft reset does not fix the problem. You want to make sure that all data is backed up before performing a hard reset because some hard resets will reset the mobile device back to the original factory condition.

> **Warning**
>
> All data will be wiped when a hard reset is initiated!

Hard resets vary from one device to the next. They can be initiated from within the OS (for example, within the Backup and Reset settings screen). Or they can be initiated by pressing a special combination of buttons, possibly while restarting the device. For example, you might press and hold the Power button, Volume Up button, and Home button until you access Recovery Mode. Or you might have to press the Volume Down button and press and release the Power button at the same time to access reset options such as Clear Storage and Recovery.

> **Note**
>
> On some devices, pressing and holding the Volume Down button and the Power buttons simultaneously will bring up Safe Mode. This turns off user-installed apps and can be very helpful when troubleshooting.

At the recovery location, follow the prompts to initiate a hard reset. Again, all data should be backed up prior to starting a reset—I can't say it enough! At this point, the device will be reset and you will have to restore data and settings from backup.

> **ExamAlert**
>
> Know how to perform soft and hard resets on Android devices.

Unlike many other mobile devices, hard resets on iOS-based devices do not delete data. They instead stop all apps and reset the OS and drivers. This can be accomplished with the following steps:

1. Make sure that the device has at least 20 percent battery life remaining. (This process could take some time, and you don't want the battery to discharge completely in the middle of it.)

2. Press the **On/Off** or **Sleep/Wake** button *and* the **Home** button simultaneously for 10 seconds or until the Apple logo appears. (Ignore the red slider.)

3. When the logo appears, the hard reset has been initiated. It may take several minutes to complete.

To fully reset an iOS-based device such as an iPad to factory condition, you need to go to **Settings > General > Reset > Erase all Content and Settings**. Another way to do this is to connect the iOS device to a computer via USB and open iTunes on the computer. Then select the **iPad** option, click **Summary**, and then click **Restore**. Regardless of the method you choose, initiate a hard reset to complete the procedure.

> **Note**
>
> For more information on how to restart your iPhone X (or later) and your iPhone 8 (or earlier) and iPad, visit https://support.apple.com/en-us/HT201559
>
> For more information on how to restore your iPhone or iPad to factory settings visit https://support.apple.com/en-us/HT201252

> **ExamAlert**
>
> Know how to reset settings and erase all content on iOS devices.

As you have seen with Android and Apple, the types of resets vary from one device to the next, so be sure to go to the manufacturer's website to find out exactly what the various resets do for your mobile device and how you can perform them—and one more time, back up your data!

Additional Mobile Device Troubleshooting

Let's discuss a little more about troubleshooting mobile devices, namely display issues, application issues, overheating, and radio connectivity issues. We previously discussed some touchscreen and battery issues in Chapter 20, "Troubleshooting Video Issues and Mobile Devices," so we won't repeat those things here.

Mobile Device Application and OS Troubleshooting

The operating system and the loaded applications can give users some heart-ache, too—especially given how some people truly *love* their smartphones and tablets.

We talked about keeping the device updated; in general, this is true, especially for anti-malware applications. But sometimes, an update is not a good idea. For example, the latest version of a mobile OS might not work well on your device (even if the experts say it will). The older the device, the slower the CPU; and the newer the OS version, the more CPU resources it requires. Ultimately, the new version of an OS will not function as well. The same goes for the latest versions of apps, though not to such an extent. In the case that a device is updated and it starts to work sluggishly, a downgrade may be necessary. This means going back to the original factory image for the device and usually requires a USB connection to a desktop computer, with USB debugging enabled. In order to enable USB debugging, some devices require you to "become a developer," which can be done, for example, by tapping the build number (in About) seven times or some other similar technique. Once you are in developer mode, you can enable USB debugging from Settings. Other devices allow you to select USB debugging when you first plug in the device via USB. You'll need to have a full battery before initiating a downgrade. Check your device documentation for more information, or go to the manufacturer's website to find out how to enable USB debugging for your specific device.

Applications can also cause a mobile device OS to perform slowly or freeze the system altogether. If this happens, first restart the device. If that does not work, consider force stopping the application in question, uninstalling unnecessary apps, and possibly resetting the device. If you have previously enabled developer mode, you can access that and see a list of all running services, and modify them from there.

Apps might also fail to load or might load very slowly. That could be because there are too many apps open, or perhaps the web browser has too many tabs open. It could also be a sign that there is no space left on the device. Remove and/or relocate apps to see if it fixes the problem. On most Android devices, you can also clear the cache memory for the system and for individual apps. To clear the system cache, reboot the device into recovery mode (usually with a simultaneous button combination, such as Power, Volume Up, and Home), and then select "wipe cache partition" or similar name. Just be very careful not to select the factory reset option! It is often very close in proximity on the menu. Individual app cache (and app data) can be cleared on the same screen where force stops are performed.

External Monitor Issues

Earlier in the book I said you can connect anything to anything else, if you have the right adapter. That holds true for mobile devices as well. However, some adapters are made better than others. For example, it is wise to use an adapter made by Apple for connecting, say, an iPad's Lightning port to an HDMI input. For Android devices, seek out quality adapters for connecting from USB-C equipped Android devices to HDMI, or to the USB port of an automobile. For both iOS and Android, make sure there is a solid connection and that you are using the correct adapter. Generally, this just works out of the box, even if screen sharing or screen mirroring is turned off, because it relies on a cabled connection, not a wireless connection. The troubleshooting side of it is usually at the TV, monitor, or projector where the image is to be mirrored. Always remember to check the input option being used; it is usually part of the on-screen display (OSD).

On the software side of things, make sure that screen mirroring is enabled. Different Android devices will have this setting in different places. One example is to go to **Network > Screen Sharing** (it could also be in General, Display, or elsewhere depending on the device). Verify that screen sharing is enabled. On the other end, make sure the device that is being shared to is accepting the connection. There could be a passcode required if you are connecting to some kind of casting device (Amazon Fire TV, Google Chromecast, Apple TV, and so on). Don't forget to check the volume on the mobile device as well. iOS devices use the Screen Mirroring option, which by default only connects to Apple TV devices, but there are third-party software offerings that can allow iOS devices to mirror to computer systems. Screen Mirroring can easily be found by double-tapping the **Home** button, or swiping up from the bottom of the display.

> **Note**
>
> If a physical cable is connecting the iOS device to an external display, then the Screen Mirroring name changes to Dock Connector. If you were to press **Stop mirroring**, then you might need to restart the iOS device in order to enable the mirror again.

Troubleshooting Mobile Device Security Issues

Some of the most important security concerns are unauthorized access, loss of *authorized* access, and compromised or lost data—that's what we need to protect against. In other words, we want to keep the bad guys out, and the employees in, all while preserving the data.

We can implement a variety of security measures, but we have to be careful not to *over-secure*. Too many hurdles for users can cause an unacceptable number of system lockouts. That means a loss of productivity for the users, and increased tech support calls to have the accounts and/or devices unlocked. Over time, this costs the organization money and slows down projects.

That's why the "three strikes and you're out rule" is a good middle ground. It allows enough attempts for the user who makes some typos during the login process, but it provides a lockout for an attacker who tries to guess a user's password. This rule can be set up as a policy within an MDM, affecting all mobile devices within the group. With a typical standalone mobile device, the lockout might last for 15 minutes, and subsequent lockouts can be longer. However, when configuring this within an MDM, the lockout should be more severe, most likely locking the account until an administrator confirms the user's identity and perhaps runs a quick interview. Even that might not be enough, however. Just because an account was locked out today doesn't necessarily mean it wasn't compromised previously. The simple fact that the lockout occurred should be a red flag. Many organizations will then launch an investigation at some level or at least a basic analysis of the account. Logs should be checked for anomalous activity, resource usage should be looked into, and the admin should double-check for any unauthorized usage of the device, apps, or the data.

Speaking of logs, always try to view log files to ascertain if any security issues have occurred within the mobile device's OS or the applications. Some applications have their own logs that you can view. Many MDMs have log files that you *definitely* should review periodically. Finally, you can go deep into an individual mobile device programmatically. For example, with Android, use the Android SDK (system developer kit) and make use of the Android Debug Bridge (ADB) from a PC or other system—with USB debugging enabled on the mobile device. What you are looking for are errors and anomalous activity that might indicate a security breach.

> **ExamAlert**
>
> Always try to view log files to ascertain if any security issues have occurred within the mobile device's OS or the applications.

It's those apps that can be a real target. Remember I mentioned that every program installed to a computer increases the attack surface? One reason so many mobile devices get hacked is that there are so many apps out there, each of which poses a security risk to some extent. Remember to limit the number of apps that a person has access to. An attacker might attempt to gain information from an employee of a company by initiating unauthorized location tracking. This can be done with an app or through a backdoor of the OS, or with malware, often a Trojan. If you suspect this, then disable location services until the problem is resolved.

Attackers will also attempt to take control of the camera/webcam and microphone of a mobile device to spy on a user. One way to tell if this is happening is by listening for shutter noises occurring even when the user is not taking pictures. The temporary solution is to disable (or unplug) the camera/webcam or cover it with masking tape, and force stop any unknown applications. Another basic preventive action is to have the webcam indicate when it is in use, either with a light, tone, or message. Along those lines, you can also check application permissions. For instance, the Camera app will allow certain programs to make use of the camera. If there are any on the list that are not expected, are not desirable, or are potentially malicious, then disable them. For example, in Android a typical navigation path would be **General > Apps & Notifications > App permissions**. From there you will see the Camera app; tap it to find out which applications are using it and disable them as necessary.

As a security person, what you are looking for is high resource utilization on the mobile device, or a power drain. These can indicate that a Trojan has been installed that has taken control of the webcam or is working in a remote desktop manner. Another indicator is high data usage. When the data transmission for a device goes over the limit set by the cellular provider—or over a wireless transmission quota that your organization has set—it could be that the mobile device has been compromised and is working as a bot. Not to mention the fact that the user will lose productivity.

If you suspect that there is unauthorized usage, then the mobile device should be taken offline, isolated, scanned, and otherwise analyzed. In many cases, the device will have to be wiped (as per company policy) and re-imaged. If the device is used in a BYOD environment, re-imaging the company partition might be enough, but with some organizations the device might be banned until the personal side is also re-imaged.

Primarily, we want to try to prevent all of these things from happening. Remember I mentioned "an ounce of prevention is worth a pound of cure"? That means updating anti-malware and firewalls, requiring strong passwords, disallowing public and open Wi-Fi hotspot connections, using DLP to prevent leaked data, and, in general, locking down devices at the MDM workstation. Those are some preventive measures we can take to protect the integrity of the data and keep it confidential, while maintaining productivity of authorized users.

Cram Quiz

Answer these questions. The answers follow the last question. If you cannot answer these questions correctly, consider reading this chapter again until you can.

1. An application won't close on an Android smartphone. You've tried to force stop it, to no avail. What should you do?

   ○ **A.** Hard reset the device.

   ○ **B.** Stop the underlying service in Running Services.

   ○ **C.** Soft reset the device.

   ○ **D.** Take the device to an authorized service center.

2. Which of the following are valid Wi-Fi troubleshooting methods? (Select the two best answers.)

   ○ **A.** Power cycle the device.

   ○ **B.** Restart Bluetooth.

   ○ **C.** Use a static IP.

   ○ **D.** Make sure the device is within range.

   ○ **E.** Rename the SSID.

3. You are troubleshooting a mobile device's e-mail connection. Your company requires the latest in security when it comes to e-mail sessions. The e-mail client is a separate app that is not browser based. How should the mobile device's e-mail client program be configured? (Select the two best answers.)

   ○ **A.** SSL on port 25

   ○ **B.** TLS on port 443

   ○ **C.** POP3 with TLS using port 995

   ○ **D.** SMTP using port 995

   ○ **E.** IMAP using SSL on port 110

   ○ **F.** SMTP using TLS on port 587

4. You suspect that a mobile device has been compromised and is now part of a botnet. What are some of the indicators that this has happened? (Select the two best answers.)

   ○ **A.** High resource usage

   ○ **B.** Notification of camera/webcam usage

   ○ **C.** Apps were force stopped

   ○ **D.** Power drain

   ○ **E.** Log files are unavailable

   ○ **F.** The user's account was locked out

Cram Quiz Answers

1. **C.** If you've already tried to stop the application within Running Services, attempt a soft reset. Hard resets on Android devices should be used only as a last resort because they will return the device to factory condition—wiping all the data. The question indicated that the application won't close, not that a service won't stop, though you could try finding an underlying service that might be the culprit. But try resetting the device before doing this or taking it to an authorized service center.

2. **A and D.** Valid Wi-Fi troubleshooting methods include power cycling the device and making sure that the mobile device is within range of the wireless access point. Bluetooth could possibly cause a conflict with Wi-Fi. If you suspect this, simply turn off Bluetooth. Static IP addresses are one thing you can check for when troubleshooting. Normally, the mobile device should obtain an IP address dynamically from a DHCP server. Renaming the SSID of the access point could cause problems for all clients trying to connect. However, you should make sure that the correct SSID was typed (if the connection was made manually).

3. **C and F.** A common configuration is to use POP3 for receiving mail utilizing TLS on port 995, and SMTP for sending mail utilizing TLS on port 587. You might also use SSL and possibly port 465 for SMTP. SSL is not designed to run on port 25 by default. TLS can run on port 443, but that is primarily used for HTTPS or any other browser-based systems (in the question, the e-mail client is not browser based). SMTP uses port 25 (insecure) or 587 or 465. IMAP uses port 143 (insecure) or 993 by default. Take a look at your mobile device and see what protocols and ports are used by your e-mail application.

4. **A and D.** If a mobile device has been compromised and added to a botnet, the user might never know, other than the potential for high resource usage, a power drain on the battery, and, less commonly, high data usage. You should check all of these things as well as any available logs. (If the logs are not available, then that could indicate other foul play.) Take the device off the network, isolate it, then run a scan of the device; you are on the hunt for Trojans especially. A notification of camera/webcam usage either means that it is being used properly by the user or an attacker is attempting to spy on the user, but it doesn't mean that the mobile device has joined a botnet; it is possible, but unrelated. If apps were force stopped, it could have been by the user, or by a rogue app, or by an attacker who has taken control of the mobile device, but this is also a separate problem. If the user account was locked out, it could simply be that the user forgot the password and had too many failed attempts. Or, it could be that a hacker was attempting to guess the password, either directly or through covert means. Again, that's a separate problem. In all of these cases, the image should be preserved for later analysis, and the device should most likely be re-imaged to be sure that any bad apps, malware, and so on have been removed.

And that does it for the security section of this book. Well done. But remember, always have security on your mind! As technicians, it should be a primary consideration for any of the technology that we work with.

CORE 2 (220-1002)

Domain 4.0: Operational Procedures

CHAPTER 39

Documentation, Change Management, and Disaster Recovery

This chapter covers the following A+ 220-1002 exam objectives:

▶ **4.1** – Compare and contrast best practices associated with types of documentation.

▶ **4.2** – Given a scenario, implement basic change management best practices.

▶ **4.3** – Given a scenario, implement basic disaster prevention and recovery methods.

Welcome to the first chapter of Domain 4.0: Operational Procedures. While this domain comprises the smallest percentage of the exam, it's not by much. So as with all of the domains, it is important that you understand the content.

Now we'll be shifting gears to the organizational, operational, and facilities side of things, so prepare for a bit of a different mindset. Because it is an A+ exam, we won't be going very deep into operational procedures, but you should know the basics.

In this chapter we will cover the fundamentals of documentation, change management, and disaster recovery. As you progress to other certifications, and if you progress into management, these concepts become more crucial.

4.1 – Compare and contrast best practices associated with types of documentation

Proper documentation is a key element of any organization. Without it, we have chaos. With it, we can at least bring some semblance of order to our networks, policies, and decisions. For us techs, the most important reason to have solid documentation is that it helps us to troubleshoot problems. If a person on the team documents properly, then it makes troubleshooting that much easier for anyone else who encounters the same problem. If everyone documents well, then it means increased productivity for the entire team. And one other thing: leave it better than you found it. That means if something is not accurate, make it so. Others will thank you, and you never know, you might thank yourself one day. (We all know that we technicians talk to ourselves sometimes!)

Network Topology Diagrams

To develop quality network documentation, an administrator should use network diagramming software, perhaps in conjunction with network mapping software. A good network diagram should show how computers and network devices are connected together—their *topology* so to speak. Figure 39.1 shows a basic example of a network diagram.

In the figure you can see network switches, a couple of SOHO routers, a workstation, a cable modem and the cloud/Internet. A topology is just one way of documenting the network; it doesn't show *where* the systems are, but it shows *how* they are connected. For example, there is a master switch that connects out to the Internet, and has two other connections to separate firewalled LANs. My main workstation, *AV-Editor*, has access to both networks because it is a multi-homed computer, meaning it has two NICs. In general, we're not overly concerned with the client computers, but particular workstations might be important to list in the network diagram.

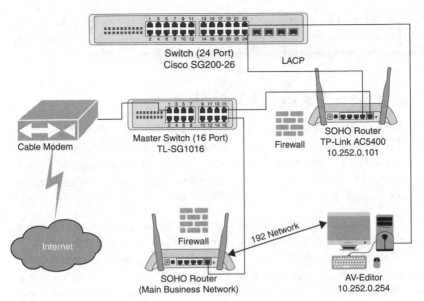

FIGURE 39.1 **Network diagram**

Figure 39.1 displays more of a high-level logical topology diagram: IP addresses used by the LAN and certain systems, and to which devices groups of computers are connected. However, you might get a little more detailed about the individual ports on switches and the actual physical connections; at that point, it might be referred to as a physical network diagram. It all depends on what you are focusing on: the physical or the logical, or both.

You can build your own network diagram with tools such as Microsoft Visio or ConceptDraw, or use network mapping software that will automatically search the network for hosts, including servers, routers, and switches; for example, SolarWinds' Network Topology Mapper. Combine both together and you can come up with some pretty powerful network documentation.

ExamAlert

Network topology diagrams identify network components and how they are physically and/or logically connected together.

You might also opt to use a spreadsheet to sort computers by name or IP address. Some companies use virtual notebooks or custom-made Wikis for their documentation to supplement a network diagram. And of course, there are plenty of vendors that offer network documentation software solutions.

The whole point is to have solid documentation that you can refer to in the case that there is a problem, or if you need to reconfigure network components or add or remove components to or from the network.

Knowledge Bases/Articles

Well, I've been referencing knowledge base articles throughout the book, especially Microsoft-related articles. But a knowledge base (KB) is more than articles written by a company; the information is also spread among community support, forums and blogs. Regardless, it's important to know *where* and *how* to find the information you seek.

The "where" I can answer with this: Go to the source! I say it often—use the websites created by the manufacturers of the hardware and the developers of the software. For example, if you are supporting Windows 10 clients, use the Microsoft support sites. If you are using Western Digital hard drives, use the Western Digital support site. Remember this when using an Internet search engine. Often, you will get third-party results which may or may not contain accurate data. So always start by going to the source.

The "how" might differ depending on which vendor's site you visit, but for the most part, vendors' sites are internally searchable by phrase or by KB number. Once you get the knack for searching, you can learn how to do most everything with a product using the support website—from installation and configuration, to security and troubleshooting. Let's take a look at a couple of examples, starting with Microsoft since it is so prevalent on the A+ exams.

The Microsoft Knowledge Base is spread among multiple websites and has hundreds of thousands of articles and posts from Microsoft employees and from the Microsoft "community." To search the Knowledge Base, simply go to one of the following sites and type in the search term or KB article number.

- ▶ **Microsoft Support:** https://support.microsoft.com. This is the main support site that Microsoft offers for end users and for IT professionals. Over the years, a lot of content from other Microsoft sites has been redirected here. Also, Microsoft has moved away from the term "Knowledge Base" to a certain degree, and often uses terms such as "help" or "support" instead. For example, the page at https://support.microsoft.com/en-us/help/322756 demonstrates how to back up and restore the registry in Windows. In the past, this article would have been called KB #322756, and it is still searchable that way, but Microsoft has moved toward more easily searchable URLs, as you will see if you follow the previous link. (Once you access the link, it will append it with the post name, which is what makes it more search engine friendly.) You'll find in your journeys that you sometimes end up at Microsoft Docs (https://docs.microsoft.com) as well.

► **Microsoft TechNet:** https://technet.microsoft.com. Historically, this was the support site designed with the IT professional in mind. The Microsoft Knowledge Base can be found here: https://technet.microsoft.com/en-us/ms772425.aspx. From this location, you can search for solutions within a mini-search engine or by the KB article number, plus there is community support, labs, a Wiki, and blogs. However, a lot of content has been redirected over to support.microsoft.com over the years, so be ready to search both.

Here are a couple of other examples:

► **Apple:** https://support.apple.com/. Here you can find support articles and community support for Apple products including macOS-based systems and iOS-based mobile devices.

► **Android:** https://support.google.com/android/. Here you can learn about the Android OS, and also redirect to the major manufacturers that use it on their mobile devices.

► **Intel:** https://www.intel.com/content/www/us/en/programmable/support/support-resources/knowledge-base. This KB contains articles, posts, and discussions about all of Intel's products. Intel has a separate developer KB as well.

► **Western Digital:** https://support.wdc.com/knowledgebase/. This site supplies written articles for the various hard drives and other products that WD manufacturers, along with community support.

Try accessing some of these links and spend some time searching around the knowledge bases so that you get a feel for how they work. Think about some of the products and software that you use at home or at work and locate their support sites and knowledge bases. You will find that some companies have better support and KBs than others—some have superior technical documentation specialists, and a more efficiently structured community platform. Over time, this kind of product documentation often leads to a higher level of customer satisfaction as well as trusted name recognition. This is the model to follow if your organization currently makes, or decides to create, its own knowledge base.

ExamAlert

Know how to research knowledge bases! If you can research within these, you can research pretty much anywhere.

Incident Documentation

Incident documentation is something that you maintain during the incident response process. It should be initiated at the onset of an event and continued through to its conclusion. If you know, or even suspect, that there is an incident, start recording all facts and information that you encounter. Use some type of logbook (hardcopy or digital, though I prefer hardcopy for this type of procedure), plus a mobile device with webcam, other digital camera, audio recorder, or a combination of those to record all of the data that you can.

Incident documentation is just a piece of the incident response procedure. We'll be discussing that in more depth in Chapter 41, "Incident Response, Communication, and Professionalism."

Compliance and Regulatory Policy

Compliance is the process of making sure an organization and its employees follow the policies, procedures, regulations, standards, laws, and ethical practices that have been written by, or apply to, the organization. In a nutshell, the resulting documentation is called a *compliance policy*. Most corporations have one, and they are usually quite similar. This documentation is available to all employees, and will often include principles of business conduct; for example, no discrimination, integrity in business dealings, fair competition, proper record keeping, environmental sustainability, cooperation with authorities, and so on. Additional documentation will detail how this is to be accomplished by way of policies and procedures. Generally, this type of documentation, or at least the overview, is publicly available via the Internet (as a PDF) and in print form.

There are organizations that create standardized policies and procedures. One example is the International Organization for Standardization (ISO). An organization that follows a particular ISO standard can be certified as ISO-compliant for that standard, such as ISO 9001:2015, *Quality management systems – Requirements*, or ISO/IEC 27002:2013, *Information technology – Security techniques*. An organization has to be examined and accredited by an accrediting certification body to state that it is ISO certified. This is a rigorous process that an organization should not take lightly. Also, keeping up the standard can create *too much* documentation and could possibly bog the organization down in details and minutia if it doesn't have the appropriate compliance personnel. These personnel must be well trained in the day-to-day operations of the organization and its procedures; have a strong understanding of information technology; and be well versed in how to read, update, and publish technical documentation.

For an organization that doesn't have the necessary personnel or wherewithal to certify to, or use, the ISO standards, it can still incorporate individual guidelines such as NIST SP 800-88 (*Guidelines for Media Sanitization*), which we spoke of in Chapter 35, "Data Destruction and SOHO Security." The National Institute of Standards and Technology (NIST) has plenty of guidelines such as this that an organization can use to model its IT infrastructure and overall security plan. These guidelines are freely available and can be integrated with an organization's documentation.

Regulatory policies of an organization attempt to achieve compliance with a government's objectives through laws and regulations. Now we're going beyond standards and moving into the realm of law. For example, in many organizations, compliance personnel will confirm that certain laws are being followed, especially as they pertain to personally identifiable information (PII)—for instance, the Privacy Act of 1974 (2015 edition), which establishes a code of fair information practice, and the Sarbanes-Oxley Act (SOX), which governs the disclosure of financial and accounting information. Most industries are regulated to some extent, so it falls to the compliance people to know a little bit about the law as well.

> **Note**
>
> As a technician, you should take a look at these regulatory laws to get a better idea of what is expected of an organization, and what an organization might expect from you and any other employees and contractors. Also, consider looking at some of the compliance management software suites available on the Internet.

Acceptable Use Policy

Acceptable use policies (AUPs) define the rules that restrict how a computer, network, or other system may be used. They state what users are allowed to do when it comes to the technology infrastructure of an organization. Often, the AUP must be signed by the employees before they begin working on any systems.

An AUP protects the organization, but it also defines to employees exactly what they should, and should not, be working on. If a director asks a particular employee to repair a particular system that is outside the parameters of the AUP the employee signed, the employee should know to refuse. If employees are found working on a system that is outside the scope of their work, and they signed an AUP, it could be grounds for termination. As part of an AUP, employees enter into an agreement acknowledging they understand that the unauthorized sharing of data is prohibited. Also, employees should understand that they are not to take any information or equipment home without express permission from the various parties listed in the policy. The idea behind this is to protect the employee, the sensitive data (especially PII), the company systems (from viruses and network attacks), and the organization itself (from legal action).

Password Policy

In Chapter 33, "Windows Security Settings and Best Practices," we discussed some basic password policies that can be configured on a Windows client or server. However, every organization should have a comprehensive written password policy that states how passwords—and configured password policies—should function, and how they are implemented and used. This should be a part of the policies and procedures of an organization's overall documentation. In fact, it should be planned and developed before any configuration of a system's password policies. This document will state all of your rules for password configuration, usage, storage, and cryptographic hashing.

For example, as part of your new password policy plan, you might decide to have a high limit for characters and state that users can pick up to 64 characters. This might sound like a lot, but with several organizations (including NIST) recommending length over complexity, and the fact that NIST recommends longer passphrases over pass*words*, it actually can make for fewer forgotten passwords with more security due to length, which ultimately translates to bit strength. It's the mandatory minimum that is even more important, at the very least eight characters, but if you are using pass*phrases*, it should be more. NIST also doesn't necessarily recommend special characters anymore either. The concept here is to increase security while fostering usability. Once again, we are looking for the balance between confidentiality and availability.

Your organization's password policy might also state that users have to change passwords every three months, and might recommend checking for blacklisted (or *pwned*) passwords. As part of the document, you should describe what absolute secrecy is, and that employees need to abide by it for their own protection and for the organization's sake. The written document should be well structured and be easy to read, with an overview, a scope of purpose, and procedures for the creation of passwords, the creation of policies, and the enforcement of the written policies. Keep in mind that the password is only one factor of authentication. It should be incorporated into a multifactor authentication (MFA) scheme. Using MFA enhances security much more than just having a strong password policy, but both are important.

> **Note**
>
> Take a look at NIST SP 800-63, which delves into digital identity guidelines, including credentials such as passwords:
>
> https://www.nist.gov/itl/tig/projects/special-publication-800-63

Inventory Management

Inventory management, or should we say *IT asset* inventory management, is the supervision, tracking, and auditing of IT equipment within the organization's infrastructure. All companies are at risk of technology sprawl—meaning the disorganization of IT equipment and software that can occur over time. To reduce this risk, an organization should use written and software-based documentation to track all assets. This includes tracking the lifecycle of client computers, servers, switches, routers, mobile devices, IoT devices, and other hardware, as well as tracking software that is installed, uninstalled, and updated. It also includes any items that are stored for later use. You might use asset tags for physically stored items. These could be written or printed tags, barcode stickers, or RFID tags. There are a variety of software packages available that can track all of this information. Most inventory tracking systems can read all of those types of tags, and can communicate with handheld wireless and USB-based devices used to scan the tags. This software is part of your overall technical documentation.

> **ExamAlert**
>
> Asset tags and barcodes are used by inventory management systems and software to identify and keep records of company assets.

Documentation might also include things that you collect, such as licenses for software. For example, Microsoft has used the certificate of authenticity (COA) and the client-access license (CAL) for ages. These commercial licenses come with software that is purchased and they prove that the organization paid for the software or the additional client licenses to connect to that software (as is the case with Windows Server products). Many types of software use a standard end-user licensing agreement (EULA), a personal license which might be on paper or stored on the computer (or online) and might be a personal single license or commercial multiple licenses.

Let's not forget about the virtual side of things. VMs should be documented and tracked the same way that physical computers are. This VM management helps us to avoid virtualization sprawl.

Documentation Is Key

The bottom line is this: Document everything that you possibly can—within reason. Know how to access all the written and digital documentation. If the process for finding the information is not written, ask your manager or human resources department to help you, and ask to put the process in writing. And remember to leave the documentation better than you found it!

Cram Quiz

Answer these questions. The answers follow the last question. If you cannot answer these questions correctly, consider reading this section again until you can.

1. You have been tasked with fixing a problem on a Windows Server. You need to find out which switch it connects to and how it connects. Which of the following types of documentation should you consult?

   ○ **A.** Microsoft Knowledge Base

   ○ **B.** Network topology diagram

   ○ **C.** Incident documentation

   ○ **D.** Compliance policy

   ○ **E.** Inventory management

2. You work for an enterprise-level organization that is certified as ISO 27002:2013. You have been tasked with adding a group of Windows client computers with a new image configuration to the IT asset inventory database, and this task has a standard procedure. You must furnish a document to be signed off by two people. Who should you approach for signatures? (Select the two best answers.)

   ○ **A.** Your manager

   ○ **B.** Compliance officer

   ○ **C.** IT director

   ○ **D.** Owner of the company

   ○ **E.** CISO

3. What do inventory management systems and software use to keep track of assets? (Select the two best answers.)

   ○ **A.** Regulatory policies

   ○ **B.** AUPs

   ○ **C.** Asset tags

   ○ **D.** Barcodes

Cram Quiz Answers

1. **B.** Use a network topology diagram (if one is available). This documentation should graphically map out what switch the server connects to and how. An automated network map would work as well. While the Microsoft Knowledge Base is great for answering questions about Windows Server, Microsoft has no way of knowing exactly how *your* organization has set up the network; nor do you want Microsoft to know—unless perhaps you initiate a tech support call to Microsoft for another issue. Incident documentation is used during the incident response process. Compliance policy deals with adhering to guidelines, standards, and possibly law. Inventory management will help you to find out things such as when the server was installed, and possibly where it is physically located, but the best documentation to find out how network devices and servers are connected is the network topology diagram documentation.

2. **A and C.** Before you perform any work where ISO compliance requires signatures, always obtain the signature of your manager, and any other parties that should be aware of what you are about to do. In this case, the IT director (or other similar title) should be aware of anything substantial being added to the network as assets. You might also have a project manager, or someone in asset management or other departments, sign off as well. If hardcopy, make copies and store the documents in the appropriate location. If digital, make sure that the signatures are properly validated and store the e-docs in the proper secure locations. The compliance officer need not be involved unless there is a change concerning processes and procedures—yes, that would be a procedure to change a procedure. The owner of the company shouldn't be bothered with these types of day-to-day operations, other than it should be part of your weekly report. Also, an enterprise-level company will more likely have a group of executives, instead of an owner. One of those might be the Chief Information Security Officer (CISO); however, this person will usually not be included, because the IT director will either report to that person directly or be working closely with them.

3. **C and D.** Asset tags and barcodes are used by inventory management systems and software to identify and keep record of company assets. Regulatory policies of an organization attempt to achieve compliance with a government's objectives through laws and regulations. Acceptable use policies (AUPs) state what users are allowed to do with respect to the technology infrastructure of an organization.

4.2 – Given a scenario, implement basic change management best practices

Change management is a structured way of changing the state of a computer system, network, policy, procedure, or process. The idea behind this is that change is necessary, but an organization should adapt with that change, and be knowledgeable of it throughout its lifecycle. Any change that a person wants to make should be introduced to each of the leaders of the various departments that it might affect. Those personnel must approve the change before it goes into effect. Before this happens, department managers will most likely make recommendations and/or give stipulations. There might even be a committee involved. When the necessary people have signed off on the change, it should be tested and then implemented. During implementation, it should be monitored and documented carefully.

In a larger organization that complies with various certifications such as ISO 9001:2015, this whole process can be a complex task. IT people should have charts of personnel, project managers, and department heads. There should also be current procedures in place that show who needs to be contacted in the case of a proposed change.

The typical A+ technician doesn't need to know everything about change management but should understand the basics, including the basic plan for change, how to work within a change management system, and how to implement basic change management best practices. To that end, Table 39.1 gives definitions for change management terms that you should know for the exam. It also includes some examples that assume a scenario where you as an IT technician see a need to update the firewall software for a group of client computers.

TABLE 39.1 **Change Management Terms**

Term	Description
Documented business processes	Most likely, there will be forms involved that require the technician to state the reason for a proposed change. These are known as *change control forms*. The technician should fill out the forms as accurately as possible in plain English with little or no jargon.
Purpose of the change	This is where the technician gives a basic description of the change and why the change should come about (though these might be separated on some forms). For example: "It is my contention that computers 251 through 299 are vulnerable to a certain type of attack that could be prevented by updating their firewalls."
Scope the change	This is where the technician goes into detail about what systems will be updated and the procedure that will take place, including who it will affect and when; for example, expanding or reducing the functionality of a technology. This is also known as *scope change*.
Risk analysis	Risk analysis (risk assessment) is the attempt to determine threats that could occur with computers and networks. It's a big topic, but here the technician would simplify based only on the change that is proposed. The technician should state any vulnerabilities that can be mitigated as part of the change and any that could potentially occur due to that change. For example, the firewall update could possibly interfere with other installed applications, and therefore should be tested in an isolated environment first before deployment.
End-user acceptance	How will the end user be affected, and what are the chances that they will accept the change gracefully? This also applies to customers of the company if they are affected. The idea behind most of IT is that it should be transparent to the user—in this scenario, that is what the technician is hoping for. Also, the firewall update should take place off-hours to prevent a loss of productivity.
Change board	Also known as a change control board or change advisory board, this group includes department heads, subject matter experts (SMEs), and project managers that will decide on whether or not a proposed change should be approved. In some cases, this group's approval is not necessary; for example, a technician might only need a manager signature to update a single computer's anti-malware platform. But in the scenario, there are 50 computers and users that will be affected, so it will probably go to committee.
Backout plan	This is a set of procedures that will reverse any changes made quickly and efficiently. It should be enacted only if the change failed. It should also include the contact information of all parties involved and a communications plan to make sure the backout goes smoothly. The failure should be well documented. We reduce the chance of a backout plan ever being necessary by performing our risk analysis and testing.
Document changes	Once approval is made, the technician should carefully document any changes that are made and when. Forms or a database are often used to facilitate this. The technician should note each step taken during the update of the firewalls, and detail any anomalies or unexpected events during the process.

> **ExamAlert**
>
> Know the change management terms and definitions for the exam.

Remember that some changes require more attention to change management than others. A basic change to a system might not even require a signature, or it might simply require a form template with a manager's signature. But a more complex change that affects multiple systems and users will need a more developed change management approach. It might consist of stages, including planning, awareness, analysis and learning, and finally adoption. Keep an open mind. The point where advanced change management planning should occur, and the particular procedures and naming conventions used, will vary from one organization to the next.

> **Note**
>
> Here's a Microsoft-related example strategy for change management:
>
> https://docs.microsoft.com/en-us/microsoftteams/change-management-strategy

> **Note**
>
> The Cram Quiz at the end of the chapter covers the material for both objectives 4.2 and 4.3.

4.3 – Given a scenario, implement basic disaster prevention and recovery methods

> **ExamAlert**
>
> **Objective 4.3** concentrates on backup and recovery, backup testing, UPS, surge protector, cloud storage vs. local storage backups, and account recovery options.

There's no need to go looking for disasters; they will come looking for you—that is if…you don't plan well, and if you don't incorporate fault tolerance and redundancy whenever possible. The more we secure and provide redundancy, the more we reduce the risk of disaster. However, a disaster can happen. In the *unlikely* event that it does, we need to be ready. Be prepared with a disaster recovery plan (DRP).

The objective of a DRP is to ensure that an organization can respond quickly to an emergency and minimize the effects of the disaster on the organization, its employees, and its technology. A DRP could be a simple one-page document (for small offices) or an entire set of documentation including profiles, processes, and procedures; more likely the latter.

> **Note**
>
> The following link leads to NIST SP 800-34 Rev. 1, *Contingency Planning Guide for Federal Information Systems*. Study it, and also do a search for DRPs from large companies such as IBM.
>
> https://csrc.nist.gov/publications/detail/sp/800-34/rev-1/final

For the A+ exam, we are concerned with a couple of concepts within the realm of disaster prevention and disaster recovery: backup and recovery, cloud versus local backups, and account recovery. Let's discuss those now.

Backup and Recovery

Backing up data is critical for a company. It is not enough to rely on a fault-tolerant array of hard drives, or other redundancy methods. Individual files or the entire system can be backed up to another set of hard drives, or to optical discs, or to tape. Windows 10/8 and Windows 7 use separate programs for backing up data. They are each accessed differently, but they work in similar ways. Let's discuss File History and Windows Backup.

Using Windows 10/8 File History and Recovery

File History is a file backup program that can be accessed from the Control Panel. After you turn it on, it automatically searches for accessible drives on the local computer or network that are potential candidates for backups. By default, it copies files from the Libraries location, Desktop, Contacts, and Favorites. You can select the copy destination that the File History program will use. You can also restore personal files from here. To initiate a file copy within the File History program:

1. Start File History by accessing **Control Panel > File History**. (If in Category view of the Control Panel, go to **System and Security > File History**.)

2. Enable File History by clicking the **Turn on** button. That will automatically initiate a backup. Or click the **Select a drive** link to select or add a network location to back up to. Click **OK** when finished. This returns you to the main File History window and initiates the backup.

3. Subsequent backups can be made by clicking the **Run now** link or by selecting the **Advanced Settings** link and configuring when the files are to be saved.

If File History is no longer needed or desired, click the **Turn off** button.

In some cases, you might want to back up more than just personal files from specific locations, and you might want to back up the entire system. One way to do this is to use the **System Image Backup** option (linked to the bottom-left corner of the File History window). This is actually a re-creation of the older Backup and Restore program from Windows 7 (located directly in the Control Panel in Windows 7). This program can create an image of your system drive and user data files, from which you can restore later on. You can also manually select additional information, such as the entire C: drive as shown in Figure 39.2. There are third-party imaging products as well (for example, Symantec Ghost). Many organizations prefer to use these.

ExamAlert

Know the difference between a file-level backup and an image-level backup.

Larger companies will use more elaborate backup systems, which often back up to tape drives with large capacities, such as Linear Tape-Open (LTO). A typical LTO-8 tape can hold 12 TB of raw data. These drives come with their own programs that will allow you to select various types of backups and verify those backups in several ways. Two methods of backup include the full backup and the incremental backup.

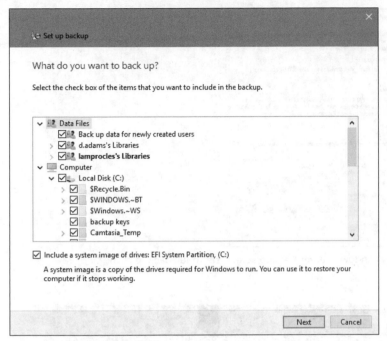

FIGURE 39.2   Windows Backup screen with the C: drive selected

▶ **Full backup:** This method backs up the entire contents of a folder or drive, whichever is selected. The full backup can be stored on one or more tapes. If more than one is used, the restore process would require starting with the oldest tape and moving through the tapes chronologically one by one. Full backups can use a *lot* of space, causing a backup operator to use a lot of backup tapes, which can be expensive. Full backups can also be time-consuming if there is a lot of data. So, often, incremental (or differential) backups are used with full backups as part of a backup plan.

▶ **Incremental backup:** This method backs up only the contents of a folder that has changed since the last full backup or the last incremental backup. An incremental backup must be preceded by a full backup. Restoring the contents of a folder or volume would require a person to start with the full backup tape and then move on to each of the incremental backup tapes chronologically, ending with the latest incremental backup tape.

Windows Server has a built-in program called Windows Server Backup (wbadmin.msc). After adding it as a feature in Windows Server, you can then back up data how you wish, optimize the backup performance, and select either full or incremental backups for individual volumes, as shown in Figure 39.3.

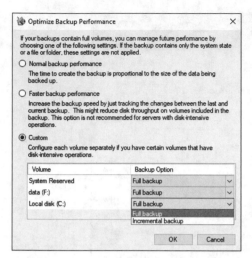

FIGURE 39.3 Windows Server Backup screen set to full backup of the C: drive

---

ExamAlert

Know how to use File History and Windows Server backup.

Backup Testing

After a backup is complete it should be verified or validated in some way. Manufacturers of backup software and hardware solutions usually include some kind of verification mechanism that you can select during the backup process. This will verify that the backup was written properly to the backup media.

However, this isn't enough to satisfy a DRP. A backup operator needs to periodically test backups by actually restoring hand-picked backup jobs to test systems. This might seem like a shot in the dark, but you can logically select what to test by being included in the change management loop. Any substantial change proposals might need to notify the backup group, so that those changes can be tested by way of a new backup/restoration.

When initially backing up a system, such as a Windows Server, that backup should be *thoroughly* tested via a restoration and in-depth comparison of the original data to the restored data. But it goes further than that; restores should be tested on simulated systems with simulated *failures*. So, for example, if we are concerned that the server's system drive (or array) could fail, then we could test that by setting up a test server with the same configuration and hard drive array and restore the system data or image to that test system. Or, if the IT budget doesn't allow for this, we could at least test it virtually. Quality virtu-alization software is a must in this case because it needs to emulate hardware appropriately.

> **ExamAlert**
>
> Perform backup testing to ensure that backups are actually being performed and that data can actually be restored!

> **Note**
>
> See the following NIST links for guidelines on the backup (CP-9) and recovery (CP-10) of data. These are part of SP 800-53.
>
> Backup: https://nvd.nist.gov/800-53/Rev4/control/CP-9
>
> Recovery: https://nvd.nist.gov/800-53/Rev4/control/CP-10

Cloud Storage vs. Local Storage Backups

Most of what we have discussed so far has been based on the backup of data to local storage. The beauty of local storage is that you own it. (Or your organiza-tion does!) That means that you can access it when you wish, it is physically available to you, and can most likely be secured more easily. In addition, if there is a failure, the time to repair will usually be less than if you back up data to the cloud. Plus, simulations and testing can be run faster as well (in most cases). So being local has its advantages. However, it can be costly: servers, racks, tape drives, *electricity*, and so on can make an IT person wonder if backing up to the cloud is a better solution—and sometimes it is.

The big platforms such as Amazon Web Services (AWS), Microsoft Azure, Google Cloud, and so on have various cloud services plus storage, syncing, and backup solutions. These tend to be more secure than services such as Dropbox, Microsoft OneDrive, and Google Drive because they are designed for business use, especially enterprise-level business, where security is paramount. The key is speed. We need to have a fast backup solution (and more importantly, a rapid restoration process) in spite of the location of the backup.

Regardless of the solution you use, the backups should be well documented, and backup accounts should have strong passwords/passphrases. This is all part of a data backup strategy where we are concerned with having onsite backups (for easy restoration), offsite backups (for disastrous situations), backup testing, and an organized storage system that is properly documented.

Account Recovery Options

The first thing to remember is this: Don't delete accounts! Accounts may need to be accessed several years later for a variety of reasons. Instead of deletion, accounts should be *disabled*. If you refer to Chapter 33, Figure 33.1 shows the option to disable an account. Beyond this, archive old accounts to another location, and back up *any* account folders.

Going a bit further, on the domain side of things you can protect objects from accidental deletion. For example, Figure 39.4 shows a user account within a Windows domain that has been protected from accidental deletion within the Object tab. On a Windows Server this tab is only accessible if you enable the viewing of Advanced Features. This technique is best used on accounts that exist within an organizational unit (OU)—in the figure we are working within the Marketing OU.

FIGURE 39.4 **Protecting a user account from accidental deletion**

At some point accounts may need to be recovered. This might be as simple as a folder restoration, or it might get more in depth if the account profile was corrupted.

Folder restoration implies that there is a backup of the user accounts. On a Windows client, user accounts (and their profiles) are stored in C:\Users. This entire folder can (and should) be backed up. On a Windows domain controller, accounts (such as admin accounts) are stored in C:\Users by default, but generally, you will be using roaming profiles for domain users, so in that case, the accounts are stored wherever you create the profiles folder—which should usually be on another partition, drive, or system altogether. An example of this is shown in Figure 31.1 in Chapter 31, "Physical and Logical Security." Either way, those folders should be backed up.

When it comes time to restore the folders (if they have been accidentally deleted or were corrupted), restore from backup, copy the accounts to the appropriate folders, and then, if necessary, re-create or repair the user accounts within the appropriate user group or OU: For Windows client computers this is done in Local Users and Groups; for Windows domain controllers this is done in Active Directory Users and Computers. If necessary, set a profile path or copy profiles to new accounts. On a Windows domain controller, you can also use the **Ntdsutil.exe** command-line utility to incorporate the users.

> ### ExamAlert
>
> Know how to restore accounts in Windows.

In the case of corruption, you can attempt to copy the profile to a new account, as mentioned in Chapter 36, "Troubleshooting Microsoft Windows." Sometimes, you might need to go a bit further and modify the registry and security identifiers (SIDs), and perform additional configuration, but this goes a bit beyond the A+ certification.

> ### Note
>
> You don't want to get caught without a backup—it can seriously affect your job security. User accounts are at the top of the list when it comes to backups.

> ### Note
>
> We cover the Objective 4.3 topics UPS and surge protector in Chapter 40, "Safety Procedures and Environmental Controls."

> ### Note
>
> The following cram quiz combines this section and the previous section related to Objectives 4.2 and 4.3.

Cram Quiz

Answer these questions. The answers follow the last question. If you cannot answer
these questions correctly, consider reading this chapter again until you can.

1. In a change management board meeting you are discussing any vulnerabilities that
   can be mitigated as part of a recommended change and anything that could potentially occur due to that change. What best describes what you are discussing?

   ○ **A.** Purpose of change

   ○ **B.** Scope the change

   ○ **C.** Backout plan

   ○ **D.** Document changes

   ○ **E.** Risk analysis

2. You have been tasked with backing up new user profiles in an enterprise environment. You propose to back up these user accounts to a new tape backup
   device. Which of the following procedures should you follow? (Select the two best
   answers.)

   ○ **A.** Change management

   ○ **B.** End-user acceptance

   ○ **C.** File History

   ○ **D.** Incremental backup

   ○ **E.** Backup testing

3. You have been contracted to perform some work at a small office. There is a
   problem with a Windows 10 computer and the user accounts folder has been
   corrupted. "Luckily" the company has a backup. Where should you restore the
   accounts to? (Select the two best answers.)

   ○ **A.** C:\Users

   ○ **B.** Ntdsutil

   ○ **C.** Active Directory Users and Computers

   ○ **D.** Local Users and Groups

   ○ **E.** ISO-compliant array

Cram Quiz Answers

1. **E.** You are discussing risk analysis, which is the attempt to determine threats that could occur with computers and networks. Purpose of change is where you give a basic description of the change and why the change should come about. Scope the change is when you go into detail about what systems will be updated. The backout plan is a set of procedures that will reverse any failed changes made quickly and efficiently. Documenting changes happens once approval is made; the technician should carefully document any changes that are made and when.

2. **A and E.** Because this is a change (backing up to a new tape device), a change management document will probably be needed, listing procedures for usage of the new backup device, and the backup of the new accounts. Backup testing should be done often, or at least periodically, but definitely when it comes to new data, as is the case in this scenario with new user profiles. We are not concerned with the end-user acceptance aspect of change management because the users should not be affected by this—it should be transparent to them—but if we were, that would be part of change management. File History is a Windows 10/8 tool; in enterprise environments we would use Windows Server Backup or a comparable third-party tool. Because these are new user profiles, we would want to do a full backup, not an incremental backup.

3. **A and D.** First, you will have to restore from backup and copy the user accounts to the C:\Users folder. Then, you'll need to make sure the accounts exist within Local Users and Groups. You might have to add them and then specify the profile path for the user, or perhaps copy profiles to new users. It depends on the scenario and the scope of the damage. Ntdsutil.exe and Active Directory Users and Computers are tools that work on Windows Servers, not Windows clients. A small office will probably not be ISO compliant, nor will it use an array of hard drives to store user accounts; the accounts will most likely simply be stored on the Windows 10 client as they were before.

CHAPTER 40

Safety Procedures and Environmental Controls

This chapter covers the following A+ 220-1002 exam objectives:

▶ **4.4** – Explain common safety procedures.

▶ **4.5** – Explain environmental impacts and appropriate controls.

Health, safety, recycling, environment—that's what this chapter is all about. The subject at hand is protection; protecting yourself, your fellow co-workers, the organization's data and systems, and the environment. Do this, and you will have made the world a better place. Let's begin.

4.1 – Explain common safety procedures

> **ExamAlert**
>
> **Objective 4.4** concentrates on the following: equipment grounding, proper component handling and storage, toxic waste handling, personal safety, and compliance with government regulations.

Safety first! Remember to put safety on the top of your priority list when dealing with computers, power, networking, and people. Protect yourself, protect others, and protect your computer. Proper grounding, electrical safety, physical safety, and fire prevention are the keys to a happy and healthy career.

We'll start with electrostatic discharge (ESD) prevention. Guard those components! By using antistatic methods, you protect your computer's parts and keep *it* safe. Let's discuss that now.

ESD Prevention and Equipment Grounding

Electrostatic discharge (ESD) occurs when two objects of different voltages come into contact with each other. The human body is always gathering static electricity, more than enough to damage a computer component (for example, that $500 video card you just purchased!). ESD is a silent killer. When you touch a component without proper protection, the static electricity could discharge from you to the component, most likely damaging it, but with no discernible signs of damage. Worse yet, it is possible to discharge a small amount of voltage to the device and damage it to the point at which it works intermittently, making it tough to troubleshoot. It takes only 30 volts or so to damage a component. On a dry winter day, you could gather as much as 20,000 volts when walking across a carpeted area! However, you can equalize the electrical potentials in several ways, allowing you to protect components from ESD, including the following:

▶ **Use an antistatic wrist strap:** These are inexpensive and take only a moment to put on and connect. In addition, almost all antistatic wrist straps come equipped with a resistor (often 1 megaohm) that protects the user from shock/electrocution hazards.

▶ **Use an antistatic mat:** Place the computer on top of the mat. Connect the mat via the antistatic cable the same way you do the antistatic wrist strap. You can also stand on a mat, and connect that one in the same manner.

▶ **Self-grounding (touch the chassis of the computer):** To further discharge yourself, do this before handling any components. This is also a good habit to get into when an antistatic strap is not available.

▶ **Use antistatic bags:** Adapter cards, motherboards, and the like are normally shipped in antistatic bags; hold on to them! When installing or removing components, keep them inside the bag until you are ready to work with them. Keep the bag itself on top of the antistatic mat.

▶ **Handle components properly:** If you are sitting at your desk without any ESD protection, there is no reason to be handling components, so don't. Handle components only when you are fully protected. When you do handle components, try to hold them at the edge. For example, when installing RAM, hold the module at the sides. This will inhibit any direct handling of the chips, contacts, and other circuitry. Adapter cards should be held by the metal plate (bracket) or by the edge of the fiberglass board but never by the contacts. Never touch a CPU's lands/pins or the CPU cap if at all possible.

Some other ways to prevent ESD include using antistatic wipes, sprays, and gloves, keeping your feet stationary (to reduce friction), working in a uncarpeted area, and raising the humidity.

> **Note**
>
> Take a look at the various standards for static control at the following link:
>
> https://www.esda.org/standards/

> **ExamAlert**
>
> Remember the main ways to avoid ESD: wearing an antistatic strap, using an antistatic mat, self-grounding (touching the computer case), and using antistatic bags.

Warning! Be Careful with Electricity!

Remember, the whole idea here is to equalize the electric potentials between the person and the equipment so that you reduce the risk of a discharge. But you have to be careful with electrical circuits. If you are not sure what you are doing, *hire a qualified and certified electrician* to help you. In my lab, I take off the alligator clips of the antistatic wrist strap and mats, and connect them to a common point ground connector, which then plugs into a dedicated grounding outlet (though any properly wired AC outlet will do). In a bench or lab environment, it goes much further—there will be dedicated grounding outlet strips, and/or the entire bench is grounded, plus all kinds of other techniques are used such as antistatic gloves, lab coats, special flooring, and so on. Be sure to follow whatever procedures your organization has set forth.

If you are still unsure or are concerned, simply take the electricity out of the mix. Connect the alligator clips of the antistatic strap and mat to the chassis of the computer, then touch an unpainted portion of the case before handling components. This is not as good as a properly grounded setup, but it does help to equalize the potentials.

It is also possible to equalize the potentials with the computer plugged in, but I do *not* recommend it, for a variety of reasons. For example, you might not know whether the AC outlet (or circuit) is wired properly. So, remember to keep the computer unplugged—disconnect the power or hit the kill switch on the back of the computer (if there is one)—before working on the system. This way, you reduce the chance of an electrical shock.

It's also important to ground network racks in a server room or data center. This can be done by installing grounding bars to the racks/equipment, and by using a thick, low-gauge grounding wire (for example, 6 AWG) and connecting it from the grounding bars to a grounded location. That might be the building's main ground wire, or an I-beam, and so on. Check your municipality's code to find out what is acceptable. The key is to provide a path for electricity in the case of a power-related issue.

Electrical Safety

Electricity is a great energy that should be treated as such. Before working on any computer component, turn off the power and disconnect the device from the AC outlet. If a device such as a power supply or video monitor has a label that reads No Serviceable Components Inside, take the manufacturer's word for it and send the component to the proper repair facility, or simply replace the component. The message on the device is intended to keep a person out, usually because the internal components might hold an electrical charge.

Be sure to use your power supply tester, receptacle tester, and other power testing equipment properly. If you do not know how to use these, escalate the issue to the facilities department, or another person in your company. If you find issues with AC outlets or other type of AC equipment, refer this to your manager or building supervisor. Do not try to fix these issues. If you find an issue like this in a customer's home, tell the customer about the problem and recommend that the AC outlet be repaired by an electrician before going any further.

Do not open power supplies. As far as the A+ exam is concerned, if a power supply goes bad, replace it, even if you think it is just the fan and would be an easy repair. It is known as a *field replaceable unit (FRU)* for a reason. Although it is possible to repair power supplies, it should be done only by trained technicians. Remember that the power supply holds a charge; this alone should be enough to keep you away from the internals of the power supply. But in addition to that, the amount of time it would take a person to repair a power supply would cost more to a company than just buying a new one and installing it. However, be sure to recycle the old one according to municipal guidelines.

LCD monitors can also be dangerous. I can't actually tell you *not* to work on them, especially because laptops integrate them. Regardless, it is again recommended that the failed monitor (or laptop) be sent to the proper repair organization or to the manufacturer if the device is within warranty. However, if you do decide to work on the LCD, one thing to be careful of is capacitors; these are normally near the LCD power supply and hold a charge. Also, make sure that the device is turned off and unplugged; if it is a laptop, make sure the battery has been removed. One of the items that can fail on an LCD monitor is the backlight inverter. The inverter is usually mounted on a circuit board, and if it fails, either a fuse needs to be replaced or the entire inverter board needs to be replaced. The inverter is a high-voltage device; try not to touch it, and be especially sure not to touch it when the LCD device is on. (Keep in mind that LED-based LCD monitors don't have inverters, and these monitors are much more common as of the writing of this book in 2019.) A lot of this is common sense, but it is worthwhile to always be sure—like measuring twice before you cut.

> **Note**
>
> In the uncommon scenario that you come across a CRT monitor, don't open it. These carry a lethal charge. Instead, refer these monitors to a company that specializes in monitor repair. If you need to dispose of CRTs, there are some monitor repair companies that will buy them or simply accept them without charge. Otherwise, they need to be recycled in compliance with local government regulations and/or municipal ordinances.

Another device that you need to make sure you turn off and unplug is the laser printer. Extremely dangerous high voltages are inside a laser printer. On a related note, if the printer was recently used, watch out for the fuser; the fuser runs hot!

Finally, it is important to match the power requirement of your computer equipment with the surge protector or uninterruptible power supply (UPS) that it connects to. Verify that the number of watts your computer's power supply requires is not greater than the amount of power your surge protector can provide; the same goes for the watts (or volt-amps) that the UPS can provide. In addition, be sure that you do not overload the circuit that you connect to. For additional information about electrical safety, see the electrical safety and health topics at the Occupational Safety and Health Administration (OSHA) website:

https://www.osha.gov/SLTC/electrical/index.html

Electrical Fire Safety

Let's talk a little about electrical fire safety. The safest measures are preventive ones. Buildings should be outfitted with smoke detectors and fire extinguishers. The proper type of fire extinguisher for an electrical fire is a Class C extinguisher. For example, CO_2-based BC fire extinguishers are common and relatively safe to humans, but they can cause damage to computers. If equipment needs to be protected by more than a CO_2-based BC fire extinguisher, an ABC Halotron extinguisher should be used. Server rooms and data centers will often be protected by a larger special hazard protection system such as FM-200, which is based on the gaseous suppression agent, heptafluoropropane. This clean agent won't cause damage to servers and other expensive equipment.

If you see an electrical fire, use the proper extinguisher to attempt to put it out. If the fire is too big for you to handle, then the number one thing to do is dial 911. Then evacuate the building. Afterward, you can notify building management, your supervisor, or other facilities people.

Hopefully, you will never come near a live electrical wire. But if you do, you want to attempt to shut off the source. Do not attempt to do this with your bare hands, and make sure that your feet are dry and that you are not standing in any water. Use a wooden stick, board, or rope. If this is not possible, you need to contact your supervisor or building management so that they can shut down power at another junction. If you find an apparently unconscious person underneath a live wire, do not touch the person! Again, attempt to move the live wire with a wooden stick or similar object. Never use anything metal, and do not touch anything metal while you are doing it. After moving the wire, call 911 and contact your superiors immediately. While waiting, attempt to administer first aid to the person.

> **Note**
>
> For more information about fire extinguisher types and operation, see the following link:
>
> https://www.osha.gov/SLTC/etools/evacuation/portable_about.html

Physical Safety

Physical safety considerations include the following:

- ▶ Securing cables
- ▶ Using caution with heavy items
- ▶ Not touching hot components
- ▶ Using safety equipment
- ▶ Considering workplace ergonomics

Cables can be a trip hazard. Employ proper cable management by routing cables away from high-traffic areas and keeping computer cables stowed away and tie-wrapped. Network cables should have been installed permanently within the walls and ceiling, but sometimes you might find a rogue cable. If you discover a cable on the floor or hanging from the ceiling, alert your network administrator or your manager. Do not attempt to reroute the network cable. You don't know what data is transferred on the cable. Because network cabling is monitored by municipalities the same way other electrical work is monitored, only qualified, trained technicians should take care of network wiring.

Lifting heavy items incorrectly can cause many types of injuries. As a general rule, if an item is heavier than one quarter of your body weight, you should ask someone else to help. When lifting items, stand close to the item, squat down to the item by bending your knees, grasp the item firmly, keep your back straight, and slowly lift with your legs, not your back. Be sure not to twist your body; keep the item close to your body. This helps to prevent back injuries. When moving items, it is best to have them stored at waist level so that minimal lifting is necessary. OSHA has plenty of guidelines and recommendations for physical safety at the workplace. Its website is https://www.osha.gov/.

Be careful when handling components that might be hot. The best method when dealing with hot items (such as a laser printer's fuser, a burned-out power supply, or a CPU or hard drive that needs to be replaced) is to wait until they have cooled. To be safe, before replacing items, wait 15 minutes for them to cool. Servers and networking equipment can get quite hot as well, even when they are stored in a climate-controlled room. Take great care when working with these devices. Also, be careful with items that hold a charge. For the A+ certification, know that if a device has the possibility of holding a charge, you should not open it. This includes power supplies and CRT monitors. These types of electronics can be recycled in most municipalities. Programs might include curb-side pickup, drop-off centers, or recycling events. Usually these are free. There are also many donation programs for equipment that still functions.

Use safety equipment whenever necessary. This includes safety goggles, hard hats, air filter masks, fluorescent clothing, and so on. Whenever you enter a work area, lab, construction site, or any other nonoffice environments in the field, be sure to follow safety instructions.

You probably won't get any questions on the exam about this, but ergonomics are important when operating the computer. Ergonomics can affect the long-term health of the computer operator. It is important to keep the wrists and hands in-line with the forearms and to use proper typing technique. Keep the elbows close to the body and supported if possible. The lower back should be supported, your head and neck should be straight and in line with your back, and your shoulders should be relaxed. Keep the top of the monitor at or just below eye level. Take breaks at least every two hours to avoid muscle cramps and eyestrain. To further reduce eyestrain, increase the refresh rate of the monitor if possible.

> **Note**
>
> For more information on ergonomics, see OSHA's information on computer workstations at the following link:
> https://www.osha.gov/SLTC/etools/computerworkstations/index.html

Cram Quiz

Answer these questions. The answers follow the last question. If you cannot answer these questions correctly, consider reading this section again until you can.

1. If a power supply fails, what should you do?
   - ○ **A.** Replace it.
   - ○ **B.** Repair it.
   - ○ **C.** Use a different computer.
   - ○ **D.** Switch it to a different voltage setting.

2. Which of the following are ways to avoid ESD? (Select three.)
   - ○ **A.** Use an antistatic wrist strap.
   - ○ **B.** Use a vacuum cleaner.
   - ○ **C.** Use an antistatic mat.
   - ○ **D.** Touch the chassis of the computer.

3. You walk into the server room and see a person lying on the floor with a live electrical wire draped over. What should you do first?
   - ○ **A.** Run out and call 911.
   - ○ **B.** Grab the wire and fling it off the person.
   - ○ **C.** Grab the person and drag him out from under the wire.
   - ○ **D.** Grab a piece of wood and use it to move the wire off the person.

Cram Quiz Answers

1. **A.** Replace the power supply. Trying to repair it can be dangerous and is not cost-effective to the company.

2. **A, C, and D.** Using antistatic wrist straps and mats and touching the chassis (self-grounding) of the computer are all ways to stop ESD. Vacuum cleaners can cause damage to components.

3. **D.** The first thing you should do is get a wooden stick, rope, or something similar (every server room should have one) and use it to CAREFULLY move the wire off of the person. In reality, the first thing you should do is breathe and not make any rash decisions because in the heat of the moment, you might think a bit less clearly than you are right now. Anyway, after the wire is removed, you should call 911 and then attempt to offer first aid to the victim. DO NOT ever touch a live wire or anything that the live wire is coming into contact with.

4.5 – Explain environmental impacts and appropriate controls

ExamAlert

Objective 4.5 focuses on MSDS documentation for handling and disposal; temperature, humidity level awareness, and proper ventilation; power surges, brownouts, and blackouts; protection from airborne particles; dust and debris; and compliance with government regulations.

Environmental factors vary from one organization to the next. For the exam, you need to know how and why to control temperature and humidity, what an MSDS is and how to use it, and how to deal with dust and debris when it comes to computers. You should also have a basic understanding of some of the procedures that a typical organization puts into practice in order to meet government-based guidelines and regulations.

Temperature, Humidity, and Air

You should be aware of the temperature and humidity measurements in your building. You should also be thinking about airborne particles and proper ventilation. Collectively, OSHA refers to this as "air treatment," which is the removal of air contaminants and/or the control of room temperature and humidity. Though there is no specific government policy regarding this, there are recommendations, including a temperature range of 68 to 76 degrees Fahrenheit (20 to 24 degrees Celsius) and a humidity range of between 20 percent and 60 percent. Remember, the higher the humidity, the less chance of ESD, but it might get a bit uncomfortable for your co-workers; they might not want to work in a rainforest, so a compromise will have to be sought. If your organization uses air handlers to heat, cool, and move the air, it will be somewhat difficult to keep the humidity any higher than 25 to 30 percent. That brings us to ventilation. An organization should employ the use of local exhaust (to remove contaminants generated by the organization's processes) and the introduction of an adequate supply of fresh outdoor air through natural or mechanical ventilation.

For air treatment, organizations should make use of filtration devices, electronic cleaners, and possibly chemical treatments activated with charcoal or other sorbents (materials used to absorb unwanted gases). Most filtration systems make use of charcoal and HEPA filters. These filters should be replaced at regular intervals. Air ducts and dampers should be cleaned regularly. And ductwork insulation should be inspected now and again. If there still is a considerable number of airborne particles, portable air filtration enclosures can be purchased that also use charcoal and HEPA filters; you can also utilize ultraviolet light to eliminate particles. These are commonly found in PC repair facilities due to the amount of dust, debris, and dirt sitting in PCs that are waiting for repair. Some organizations even foot the bill for masks or respirators for their employees. Many PC workbenches will be equipped with compressed air systems and vacuum systems (incorporating HEPA filters). This way, the PC tech can blow out the dust and dirt from a computer and vacuum it up at the same time. Otherwise, it is usually best to take the computer outside (unless it is windy).

> **ExamAlert**
>
> Protect yourself from airborne particles with air filtration enclosures and masks!

MSDS and Disposal

Products that use chemicals require material safety data sheets (MSDSs). These are documents that give information about particular substances (for example, the ink in inkjet cartridges). Information in the MSDS includes

▶ Proper treatment if the substance is ingested or comes into contact with the skin

▶ How to deal with spills and other hazards

▶ How to dispose of the substance

▶ How to store the substance

It's easy to find MSDSs; most companies have them online. You can search for them at the manufacturer's website or with a search engine. An MSDS identifies the chemical substance, possible hazards, fire-fighting measures, handling and storage, and so on. Make sure you have Adobe Acrobat Reader installed because most MSDSs are in PDF format.

It's important to know what to do if someone is adversely affected by a product that has chemicals. A person might have skin irritation due to coming into contact with toner particles or with a cleaner that was used on a keyboard or mouse. As a technician, your job is to find out how to help the person. If you do not have direct access to the MSDS, you should contact your facilities department or building management. Perhaps the cleaning crew uses a particular cleaning agent that you are not familiar with and only the facilities department has been given the MSDS for this. It's better to review all MSDS documents and be proactive, but in this case, you probably won't have access to the document. Collaborate with the facilities department to get the person who was affected the proper first aid and, if necessary, take the person to the emergency room. Finally, remove the affected device (such as a keyboard or mouse). Replace it with a similar device until you can get the original device cleaned properly.

> **ExamAlert**
>
> Know that an MSDS contains warnings and safety information about chemical substances and hazards.

Generally, substances that contain chemicals should be stored in a cool, dry place, away from sunlight. "Cool" means the lower end of the OSHA guideline, approximately 68 degrees F (20 degrees C). Often, this will be in a storage closet away from the general work area and outside of the air filtration system. This also allows the items to be stored in a less humid area.

Recycling and proper disposal are also important. Batteries should not be thrown away with normal trash because they contain chemicals. First, you should check your local municipal or EPA guidelines for proper disposal of batteries and, in some cases, you will find that there are drop-off areas for these—either at the town municipal center or sometimes at office and computer supply stores. This applies to alkaline, lithium (for example, CR2032), lithium-ion, and other types of batteries.

> **ExamAlert**
>
> Check your local municipal and EPA guidelines for disposal of batteries and other equipment.

Ink and toner cartridges can usually be sent back to the manufacturer, or office supply stores and printer repair outfits often will take them for later recycling. Some municipalities have a method for recycling electrical devices in general.

Speaking of recycling and disposal, cell phones, smartphones, and tablets should be disposed of properly as well. However, these will contain data, as opposed to the devices we have spoken of so far. First off, internal memory,

SD cards, and SIMs should be wiped, and if necessary destroyed (as described in Chapter 35, "Data Destruction and SOHO Security"). If destroyed, the remains will be recycled by the vendor that provided the destruction services, or by the organization in accordance with municipal guidelines. Phones and tablets that have been wiped properly—but not destroyed—might also be donated to various charities or given to electronics recycling companies, or recycled at a county-wide recycling event.

Power Devices

Many of the issues that you see concerning power are due to lack of protection and improper planning, and as such you will see several questions (if not more) on the A+ exam regarding this subject.

Utilizing proper power devices is part of a good preventive maintenance plan and helps to protect a computer. You need to protect against several things:

▶ Surges

▶ Spikes

▶ Sags

▶ Brownouts

▶ Blackouts

A *surge* in electrical power means that there is an unexpected increase in the amount of voltage provided. This can be a small increase or a larger increase known as a spike. A *spike* is a short transient in voltage that can be due to a short circuit, tripped circuit breaker, power outage, or lightning strike.

A *sag* is an unexpected decrease in the amount of voltage provided. Typically, sags are limited in time and in the decrease in voltage. However, when voltage reduces further, a brownout could ensue. During a *brownout*, the voltage drops to such an extent that it typically causes the lights to dim and causes computers to shut off. This reduction in power can be damaging to devices that aren't properly protected.

A *blackout* is when a total loss of power for a prolonged period occurs. Another problem associated with blackouts is the spike that can occur when power is restored. In the New York area, it is common to have an increased number of tech support calls during July; this is attributed to lightning storms! Quite often this is due to improper protection.

> **ExamAlert**
>
> A power surge is an unexpected increase in voltage. A brownout is a drop in voltage that can cause computers to shut off. A blackout is a total loss of power for a prolonged time.

Some devices have specific purposes and others can protect against more than one of these electrical issues. Let's describe a few of these devices.

Surge Protectors

A *surge protector* or *surge suppressor* is a power strip that also incorporates a metal-oxide varistor (MOV) to protect against surges and spikes. Most power strips that you find in an office supply store or home improvement store have surge protection capability. The word *varistor* (sometimes spelled varsistor) is a blend of the terms *variable* and *resistor*.

> **ExamAlert**
>
> To protect against surges and spikes, use a surge protector!

Surge protectors are usually rated in joules, which are a way to measure energy; essentially, the more joules, the better. For computer systems, 1000 joules or more is recommended. This joule rating gives you a sense of how long the device can protect against surges and spikes. Surges happen more often than you might think, and every time a surge happens, part of the varistor is burned out. The higher the joule rating, the longer the varistor (and therefore the device) should last. Most of today's surge protectors have an indicator light that informs you if the varistor has failed.

Because surges can occur over telephone lines, RG-6 cable lines, and network lines, it is common to see input and output ports for any or all these on a decent surge protector. Higher-quality surge protectors have multiple MOVs not only for the different connections (such as AC and phones), but for the individual wires in an AC connection.

Uninterruptible Power Supplies

An *uninterruptible power supply (UPS)* takes the functionality of a surge suppressor and combines that with a *battery backup*. So now, our computer is protected not only from surges and spikes, but also from sags, brownouts, and blackouts.

> **ExamAlert**
>
> Use a UPS/battery backup to protect your computer from power outages! It can keep your computer running long enough to save your work and properly shut it down if necessary.

But the battery backup can't last indefinitely! It is considered emergency power and typically keeps your computer system running for 5 to 30 minutes, depending on the model you purchase, and the load being placed on the UPS. Workstation UPSes often have two types of outlets on the device: one group that is marked for battery backup and surge protection, and one marked for surge protection only. Server room rack-mountable UPSes often only have battery backup outlets.

Most UPS devices also act as line conditioners, protecting from over- and under-voltage; they condition (or regulate) the voltage sent to the computer. If you happen to see a customer's lights flickering, this could indicate dirty power, and you should consider recommending a UPS for the customer's computers and networking equipment. Most UPS devices today have a USB-based connection so that your computer can communicate with the UPS. When there is a power outage, the UPS sends a signal to the computer telling it to shut down, suspend, or stand by before the battery discharges completely. Most UPSes come with software that you can install that enables you to configure the computer with these options.

UPS devices' output power capacity is rated in volt-amps (VA) and watts. Although you might have heard that volt-amps and watts are essentially the same, this is one of those times that they are somewhat different. The volt-amp rating is slightly higher due to the difference between apparent power (when in battery backup mode) and real power (when pulling regular power from the AC outlet). For example, a typical UPS device might have a volt-amp rating of 350 VA but a wattage rating of 200 watts. Generally, this is enough for a computer, monitor, and a few other devices, but a second computer might be pushing it given the wattage rating. The more devices that connect to the UPS, the shorter the battery lasts if a power outage occurs; if too many devices are connected, there might be inconsistencies when the battery needs to take over. Thus, many UPS manufacturers limit the amount of battery backup-protected receptacles. Connecting a laser printer to the UPS is not recommended due to the high current draw of the laser printer; also, to protect the UPS from being overloaded, never connect a surge protector or power strip to one of the receptacles in the UPS.

> **ExamAlert**
>
> Do *not* connect laser printers to UPS devices.

The UPS has a battery (often lead-acid) that, when discharged, requires several hours to recharge. This battery is usually shipped in a disconnected state. Before charging the device for use, you must first either flip over the battery or otherwise make sure that the battery leads connect to the UPS; if the battery ever needs to be replaced, a red light usually appears and is accompanied by a beeping sound. Beeping can also occur if power is no longer supplied to the UPS by the AC outlet. The "power" of a UPS can't be denied. It is a required component in server rooms, and is very useful at users' computers as well, especially custom workstations. It's interesting to note that most power outages last for 15 minutes or less—often they are short blips. Just remember that to continue using a desktop computer during any length power outage, the user will need to have not only the computer, but also the monitor and some peripherals connected to the battery backup outlets of the UPS.

> **ExamAlert**
>
> For custom workstations, make sure that computers, monitors, and powered USB hubs are all plugged into the UPS.

Cram Quiz

Answer these questions. The answers follow the last question. If you cannot answer these questions correctly, consider reading this section again until you can.

1. What document can aid you if a chemical spill occurs?

   ○ **A.** HEPA
   ○ **B.** MSDS
   ○ **C.** OSHA
   ○ **D.** EPA

2. A co-worker complains that after the cleaning crew has come through, the keyboard irritates his hands and leaves some green residue. What should you do?

   ○ **A.** Call the fire department.
   ○ **B.** Contact the facilities department.
   ○ **C.** Contact the manufacturer of the keyboard.
   ○ **D.** Call OSHA and complain.

3. You are concerned with power outages that occur infrequently and for short periods of time. You don't want your users' computers to suffer from potentially harmful restarts. What device should you install for the users' computers?

   ○ **A.** Surge protector

   ○ **B.** Line conditioner

   ○ **C.** MSDS

   ○ **D.** UPS

4. You want a *cost-effective* solution to the common surges that can affect your computer. Which device offers the best solution?

   ○ **A.** UPS

   ○ **B.** Surge suppressor

   ○ **C.** Power strip

   ○ **D.** Line conditioner

Cram Quiz Answers

1. **B.** The material safety data sheet (MSDS) defines exactly what the particular chemical substance is, what the potential hazards of it are, and how to deal with them. HEPA stands for high-efficiency particulate air, as in a HEPA filter. OSHA stands for the Occupational Safety and Health Administration. EPA stands for the Environmental Protection Agency.

2. **B.** Contact the facilities department to see if they have the MSDS for the cleaner. You and/or the facilities department should then treat the irritation according to the MSDS. If this does not work and the problem gets worse, take the co-worker to the emergency room. Remove the keyboard from the work environment.

3. **D.** Use an uninterruptible power supply (UPS) to protect a computer from ungraceful shutdowns and restarts that can occur as a result of brownouts and blackouts. A surge protector (suppressor) is a power strip that also incorporates a metal-oxide varistor (MOV) to protect against surges and spikes. A line conditioner can level out dirty power but won't protect against a power outage. An MSDS defines what a particular chemical substance is and how to deal with related hazards.

4. **B.** A surge suppressor (or surge protector) is the right solution at the right price. A UPS is a possible solution but costs more than a surge protector and is not necessary in this scenario. A line conditioner also would be a viable solution but, again, is not necessary. And a power strip doesn't necessarily have surge protection functionality—it is simply a strip of outlets for additional connectivity.

CHAPTER 41

Incident Response, Communication, and Professionalism

This chapter covers the following A+ 220-1002 exam objectives:

▶ **4.6** – Explain the processes for addressing prohibited content/ activity, and privacy, licensing, and policy concepts.

▶ **4.7** – Given a scenario, use proper communication techniques and professionalism.

How will you respond to incidents? How will you communicate with customers? How will you deal with the best practices, regulations, and laws that your organization complies with? We'll answer these questions and more as we progress through this chapter.

A good technician not only knows how to work with technology, but also how to deal with customers, tough problems, and imminent threats. It's the well rounded technician that enjoys the most job security.

4.6 – Explain the processes for addressing prohibited content/ activity, and privacy, licensing, and policy concepts

ExamAlert

Objective 4.6 concentrates on the following: incident response, licensing/ DRM/EULA, regulated data, and following all policies and security best practices.

One of the goals of policies and procedures, best practices, and regulations is to prevent incidents from occurring. However, it is inevitable that incidents will happen. As people we are imperfect, and therefore we create imperfect technologies. When the right criteria are met, small imperfections can pave the way for incidents to transpire. The important part is how we respond to these incidents and how we limit the damage.

Incident Response

First of all, we have to differentiate between an event and an incident. An *event* is simply something that happens within your computer or on the network. It could be good or bad. For example, an event could be an administrator connecting a system to another system through a mapped network drive according to the organization's procedures. This is an occurrence that is positive. But there are adverse events as well, where negative consequences result; for example, unauthorized privilege escalation, or execution of malware. Rev it up further to the computer security *incident*. This is when there is an imminent threat or an outright violation of security policies, and a security breach has occurred. A technician, or team of techs, is expected to respond to incidents quickly and efficiently. One example of an incident is when an attacker initiates a DDoS attack (using a master system and a botnet) against a server, perhaps causing that server to crash. Or, if an attacker locks files on a computer with ransomware.

How you follow up on an incident is a good measure of your ability to an organization. *Incident response* is the set of procedures that any investigator follows when examining a technology incident. How you first respond, how you document the situation, and your ability to establish a chain of custody are all important to your investigating skills.

First Response

When you first respond to an incident, your first task will be to identify exactly what happened. You must first recognize whether this is a simple problem that needs to be troubleshot or whether it is an incident that needs to be escalated. For example, if you encounter a person who has prohibited content on a computer, this can be considered an incident and you will be expected to escalate the issue to your supervisor, reporting on exactly what you have found. Copyrighted information, malware, inappropriate content, and stolen information could all be considered prohibited. So, before you do anything, you should report your findings to the proper channels and then make sure that the data and affected devices are preserved. This often means making a backup of the computer's image. However, this will depend on your organization's policies. You might be told to leave everything as is and wait for a computer forensics expert or a security analyst; it will depend on the scenario. The idea here is that the scene will be preserved for that other person so that he or she can collect evidence.

> **ExamAlert**
>
> As a first responder you will identify the incident, report through the proper channels and escalate if necessary, ensure data/device preservation, and document everything!

Remember: Documentation Is Key

The bottom line is this: You want to document everything that you find and anything that happens after that. If your organization doesn't have any other methodology, write it down! When you leave the scene, you will be required to divulge all information to your supervisor. If you fixed the problem and no other specialists were required, the documentation process will continue through to the completion of the task and beyond when you monitor the system. You should also document any processes, procedures, and user training that might be necessary for the future.

Incident Response Life Cycle

Let's take it a bit further and discuss actual computer security incident response. Different organizations will have different views on how incident response should be handled. One common method is to incorporate a four-phase life cycle:

1. **Preparation:** An organization with a well-planned incident response procedure (in advance), a strong security posture, and a knowledgeable chief information security officer (CISO) will be able to limit damage caused during an incident. Good communication is required, and the technician(s) should have access to secure storage facilities, digital forensic workstations, forensic software, and plenty of documentation on hand.

2. **Detection and analysis:** This includes the identification of exactly what is happening during the incident. Because there are literally thousands of attack vectors (perhaps much more), we can't create step-by-step procedures for every type of incident. However, we can categorize incidents to a certain extent, and then take the appropriate steps based on what type of incident we have detected. For example, categories could include DDoS/brute-force attacks, web-based attacks, spoofing/MITM, and theft. Once we know what the attack is, we can then analyze it with the right tools

and methods. Of course, there will be a certain amount of thinking on your feet involved; a technician should be ready to adjust his or her mindset and methodologies in real time. However, the process has to be quick, so that we can contain the problem rapidly.

3. **Containment, eradication, and recovery:** First isolate the problem: quarantine systems, isolate networks, place attackers' processes in padded cells or other holding areas (if at all possible), remove devices, and so on. Then, remove the threat with other mitigation techniques that are necessary. After that, retrieve data, re-enable systems, and recover images and backups. Some organizations will break this down into multiple phases.

4. **Post-incident activity:** Here a technician(s) reviews what happened and why, finalizing documentation, getting signatures, and contemplating as a team the lessons learned.

Note

This life cycle is documented in *great* detail within the NIST SP 800-61 Rev. 2, *Computer Security Incident Handling Guide*:

https://csrc.nist.gov/publications/detail/sp/800-61/rev-2/final

The CompTIA A+ won't go far into the depths of this document, but if you are interested in a career that involves incident response, consider reading this, and have it on hand.

Remember that an organization might have more phases, or break them up differently. In addition, the incident response process will be in much greater detail than what is shown here. Be ready to study your organization's documentation carefully!

Chain of Custody

If you are required to preserve evidence, one way to do this is to set up a chain of custody. This is the chronological documentation or paper trail of evidence. It should be initiated at the start of any investigation. It documents who had custody of the evidence all the way up to litigation (if necessary), and logs the transfer of evidence from person to person. It also verifies that the evidence has not been modified or tampered with. The log should include identifying information for systems such as serial numbers, IP addresses, MAC addresses, and so on; the names, titles, and phone numbers of everyone who collected, analyzed, and handled evidence; the time and date (universal); and where and how the evidence is stored.

> **ExamAlert**
>
> The chain of custody is a chronological, verifiable paper trail documenting who possessed evidence.

As an A+ tech, you will probably not get too involved with incident investigations, but you should know the basic concepts of first response, documentation, and chain of custody for the exam, as well as if you find yourself in a situation where you have found prohibited content or illegal activities. The bottom line is that many times your job will be to *escalate the issue* to the appropriate personnel.

Licensing/DRM/EULA

There are various types of licensing for software, hardware, support, and services. Let's focus on software licensing here. Licensing could be free or paid for. For example, we mentioned Microsoft Windows client licenses previously in the book. It's important to have this licensing well organized and accessible. Most proof of licensing today is digital, so it should be stored in a safe place, possibly encrypted, backed up, and digitally validated.

Licensing is also important during incident response. Depending on the situation, you might need to locate licenses (or lack thereof) for software, client connections, and hardware; for example, the client access licenses (CALs) being used to access a Windows Server. License compliance violation can have legal ramifications, not to mention availability and integrity repercussions.

There are two terms related to licensing that you should know for the exam:

▶ **EULA:** An end-user licensing agreement is a contract or agreement that is made between a proprietary software vendor and the end user. In most cases, the end user is required to agree to the EULA before using the product. The EULA primarily defines the ways that the software can be used, and asserts that the vendor has limited liability for issues and damages that occur through the use of the product. These are usually lengthy documents, but if a company plans to use software products that require an EULA, then the appropriate personnel should have a working legal understanding of them.

▶ **DRM:** Digital Rights Management (DRM) is a group of security controls designed to restrict the usage or proliferation of copyrighted software and products. For example, various DRM controls can prevent illegal copying of software.

ExamAlert

EULA is a licensing agreement between a software vendor and the end user. DRM restricts usage or proliferation of copyrighted software and products.

Essentially, if a technician finds that a user or company is illegally copying, circumventing, or modifying software, is using software without the appropriate licensing, or is otherwise breaching the EULA or DRM agreement, then the technician should report that finding to the appropriate personnel or authorities and log and document the situation in accordance with incident response procedures.

Software licenses can be commercial—for example, licenses for Microsoft or Apple software—or open source, as is the case with the GNU General Public License (GPL) used for Linux software. In the case of commercial or closed-source licensing, the user, or corporation, is usually not allowed to share or modify the software.

There are also personal and enterprise-level licenses. So, for example, a home user might have a computer with a paid personal license to use Microsoft Windows 10 Home Edition, but a midsized to large organization will have enterprise-level licenses that are usually bought in bulk—for example, Windows 10 Enterprise Edition.

Software with open-source licensing is usually free to use. With open-source licensing, the user is allowed to study, modify, and share the software, or even create new distributions of it, and sell it for a profit.

ExamAlert

Know the difference between open-source vs. commercial licenses. And, know the difference between personal license vs. enterprise licenses.

Be sure to *organize* and store licensing properly according to organizational policy, and know how to *find* licenses for your own organization, or for a customer if you are contracted to perform work for a customer.

Regulated Data

There are several types of data regulations that are covered on the A+ exam. These regulations are designed to protect personal information and the people themselves. Here we'll briefly discuss PII, PHI, PCI-DSS, and GDPR.

PII

Personally identifiable information (PII) is something that every organization and technician should be concerned with, because it affects us all. PII is information used to uniquely identify, contact, or locate a person. This type of information could be a name, birthday, Social Security number, biometric information, and so on. In Chapter 39, "Documentation, Change Management, and Disaster Recovery," I mentioned the Privacy Act of 1974 and other laws, regulations, and guidelines. These are designed to protect PII in a standardized way, but organizations often have their own privacy policies (which may be based off of these best practices) that go further to define how users' identities will be protected in a procedural manner.

PHI

Protected health information (PHI) is information that is protected under the HIPAA Privacy Rule. The Health Insurance Portability and Accountability Act (HIPAA) is a wide-ranging act, passed in 1996, that governs the protection of all kinds of health information. Any organization in the United States that requests, stores, or accesses health information must abide by the rules within HIPAA.

Best practices for PII and PHI are quite similar, so let's discuss a couple of these as they relate to digital records:

▶ Appoint a security admin (with compliance experience) to oversee the access and storage techniques of PII and PHI records.

▶ Physically secure computers, servers, server rooms, data centers, and network connections where the records are being stored.

▶ Store records in an encrypted format, and transmit records from one system to another or from a system to the cloud using end-to-end encrypted sessions. This way, data at rest, data in motion, and data in transit can be protected.

Otherwise, make use of the many security best practices that we have documented within this book's security chapters, and keep in mind that PII and PHI records are at the top of the list when it comes to logging, auditing, and monitoring.

PCI-DSS

The payment card industry (PCI) encompasses anything that concerns credit cards, debit cards, ATMs, point-of-sale (POS) machines, and so on, that organizations use or transact with when dealing with user cardholder data. The PCI Security Standards Council (PCI-SSC) developed a compliance program known as the Payment Card Industry Data Security Standards (PCI-DSS). These standards, and the varying levels of compliance, define how credit card data is to be transacted and stored.

The best practices for PCI-DSS include a lot of the security methods we have discussed previously in this book, but from a more high-level viewpoint, the PCI-SSC is looking for: a sustainable security program; compliant policies and procedures; performance metrics (such as those defined in NIST SP 800-55 Rev. 1, *Performance Measurement Guide for Information Security*); specific assignments to qualified personnel (perhaps who certify to PCI-DSS); proper risk assessment and management techniques, monitoring of security controls (which is a big part of the compliance); maintaining evidence; incident response procedures; and generally maintaining security awareness.

PCI-DSS is important whether your organization is a small, five-employee office or an enterprise-level corporation.

> **Note**
>
> You can view the entire best practices document (updated to version 2.0 in 2019) as set forth by the PCI-SSC at the following link:
>
> https://www.pcisecuritystandards.org/documents/PCI_DSS_V2.0_Best_Practices_for_Maintaining_PCI_DSS_Compliance.pdf

GDPR

The General Data Protection Regulation (GDPR) is a European Union regulation that deals with data protection and privacy for people who live in the EU; but it has wide-ranging implications for companies around the world (especially in the United States) that have transactions with EU citizens, requiring them to adopt the policies and best practices that support the regulation.

805
4.6 – Explain the processes for addressing prohibited content/activity, and privacy,
licensing, and policy concepts

One common example of an industry that was "turned upside down" by GDPR is the e-mail/mailing list industry. This was due to the fact that these lists contained personal data—meaning any information relating to an identified or identifiable natural person—which in many cases was not compliant with the GDPR. The GDPR defines how transparency should function, the proper securing of data, the awareness of what data is being collected, and citizen rights such as the right to access and request erasure of personal data. This regulation was enforceable as of May 25, 2018, and at the time, it seemed that technical changes, written policies, and proper opt-in/opt-out lists became realities almost overnight for many companies. It affects my own business and every single company that I deal with.

ExamAlert

Know the types of regulated data, including PII, PCI, GDPR, and PHI.

However, as far as GDPR best practices, they are very similar to what we have mentioned already in this chapter, and the security methods include much of what we have discussed in the security sections of this book. These best practices focus on: the auditing of data; secure management of data; assessing risk of data that is stored; assigning a Data Protection Officer (for companies with 250 employees or more); training employees about GDPR best practices; and having a data breach and incident response plan in place.

Note

For more information on the GDPR, see the following link:

https://ec.europa.eu/info/law/law-topic/data-protection_en

Don't Be Too Alarmed by Data Regulations!

An A+ technician should know what these regulations and best practices are, and be ready to abide by them when employed by an organization. However, the simple truth is that most A+ technicians will have very little to do with the creation, modification, or enforcement of these regulations. The bottom line is that we should concentrate on identifying the threat model for our organization's data, and implement strong security measures that hopefully will prevent data breaches, while monitoring the data carefully for any changes, anomalies, or attacks. If you are ever confused by a regulation, best practice, or written organizational policy, then see the appropriate compliance or human resources personnel to get the record straight.

Cram Quiz

Answer these questions. The answers follow the last question. If you cannot answer these questions correctly, consider reading this section again until you can.

1. You find illegal materials on a customer's computer. Your boss commands you to preserve computer evidence until he gets to the scene. What is your boss asking you to begin?

   ○ **A.** Documentation

   ○ **B.** Chain of custody

   ○ **C.** First response

   ○ **D.** GDPR compliance

2. Which of the following is not one of the steps of the incident response process?

   ○ **A.** Eradication

   ○ **B.** Recovery

   ○ **C.** Containment

   ○ **D.** Non-repudiation

3. You are the security administrator for your organization. You have just identified a malware incident. Of the following, what should be your first response?

   ○ **A.** Containment

   ○ **B.** Removal

   ○ **C.** Recovery

   ○ **D.** Monitoring

4. Which type of regulated data is specifically protected under the HIPAA Privacy Rule?

   ○ **A.** PII

   ○ **B.** PCI

   ○ **C.** GDPR

   ○ **D.** PHI

Cram Quiz Answers

1. **B.** Your boss is asking you to begin the process of a chain of custody: the chronological paper trail of evidence. It is a form of documentation, but a specific one. You were the first responder. These cases will be rare, but you should understand the terminology and what to do if you find illegal materials.

4.6 – Explain the processes for addressing
prohibited content/activity, and privacy,
licensing, and policy concepts

CramQuiz

2. **D.** Non-repudiation, although an important part of security, is not part of the incident response process. Non-repudiation means that you have irrefutable proof that a person did something—it might include logs, audit trails, and so on. Eradication, containment, and recovery are all parts of the incident response process

3. **A.** Of the listed answers, most organizations' incident response procedures specify that containment of the malware incident should be first. Next would be the removal of the malware, then recovery of any damaged systems, and finally monitoring (which should actually be going on at all times). But before all of this is the preparation phase, and of course, in the scenario, identification was already performed.

4. **D.** Protected health information (PHI) is information that is protected under the HIPAA Privacy Rule. The Health Insurance Portability and Accountability Act (HIPAA) is a wide-ranging act that governs the protection of all kinds of health information. Personally identifiable information (PII) is information used to uniquely identify, contact, or locate a person. The payment card industry (PCI) encompasses anything that concerns credit cards, debit cards, ATMs, or point-of-sale (POS) machines. The General Data Protection Regulation (GDPR) is a European Union regulation that deals with data protection and privacy.

4.7 – Given a scenario, use proper communication techniques and professionalism

Mind your customer service skills. You might be a super-tech, but without people skills, your job market will be limited. By being professional and utilizing good communication skills, you increase the chances of receiving a good customer reaction. Also, these skills help you to get to the heart of the issue and can help to make you more efficient, saving time as you repair computer problems. Throughout the rest of the book, you learned how to repair the computer. Now put those abilities together with a professional demeanor and good communication skills and there should be no lack of new customers in the future.

Communication Techniques and Professionalism

For the CompTIA A+ 220-1002 exam, communication and professionalism consist of nine categories:

▶ **Use proper language and avoid jargon, acronyms, and slang, when applicable:** Speak slowly, clearly, and professionally so the customer can fully understand what you are saying. Refrain from slang and profanity. Avoid computer jargon and acronyms (for example, WPA2 or TCP/IP). If you use computer jargon, the customer might think that you are insecure and cannot clearly explain things. Stay away from the techno-babble. The customer expects you to know these things technically but to explain them in a simple manner. That's the essence of a good teacher!

▶ **Maintain a positive attitude/project confidence:** Even if the customer thinks the situation is hopeless or the customer is frustrated, be positive. Sometimes problems that appear to be the worst have the easiest solutions! And there is *always* a solution. It's just a matter of finding it. Also, as part of being positive, try to project confidence. Be calm and assure your customer that the problem will be solved.

▶ **Actively listen (taking notes) and avoid interrupting the customer:** The more you listen, the better you will understand the problem. Write down key points related to the problem the customer is having. Don't interrupt the customer, even if you think you know what the problem is before the customer has fully explained the situation. Be respectful and allow the customer to completely explain the problem. The customer's tale just might give you clues as to what the *real* problem is. Listen carefully but be assertive when eliciting answers.

▶ **Be culturally sensitive:** Understand that customers come from all walks of life. Be aware that cultural differences and similarities exist. Be respectful and kind. Use appropriate professional titles when applicable and when possible. Make an effort to ensure that both you and the customer understand each other and work toward a common goal. If you don't at first understand the customer or if there is a language barrier, kindly ask the customer to repeat themselves.

▶ **Be on time (if late, contact the customer):** It's all about punctuality. Be on time! If a customer has to wait, the situation might become difficult before you even begin. If you are running late, contact the customer, apologize, and let the customer know that you will be late.

▶ **Avoid distractions:** Phone calls should be screened and left to go to voicemail unless it is an emergency. The same goes for e-mails that arrive on your smartphone and text messages on the phone. If other customers call, explain to them that you are with a customer and will call them back shortly (or have your manager or co-worker take care of them if they are available). Avoid talking to co-workers when dealing with customers. The customer wants to feel valued and wants to get the problem fixed in a timely manner. Try to avoid personal interruptions in general. And avoid using those social media sites.

▶ **Deal with difficult customers or situations:** By being patient, understanding, and respectful, you show customers that you are a professional and serious about fixing their computer problems. Never argue with customers or take a defensive or offensive stance. This is another one of those times in which I like to think of Mr. Spock. Approach customers' computer problems and complaints from a scientific point of view. Try not to make light of a customer's computer issues, no matter how simple they might seem, and avoid being judgmental of any possible user error. Try not to ask things such as "What did you do?" or "Who was working on this?" because these questions can come across as accusations. Ask computer-oriented, open-ended questions when eliciting answers from the customers (for example, ask "What is wrong with the computer?" or "What can you tell me about this computer?"). Stick with the senses; questions such as "What type of strange behavior did you see from the computer?" keeps customers more relaxed and can help you to narrow down the cause of the problem. Again, if a customer doesn't come across clearly, restate what you believe to be the issue or repeat your question so that you can verify your understanding so both of you will be on the same page. Clarify the customer's statements. Ask concise questions to the customer to further identify what the issue is and narrow the scope of the problem. After you think you understand what the problem is, you should always clarify by repeating the problem back to the customer. Restate the issue to verify everyone understands the problem. And again, do not disclose experiences via social media outlets.

▶ **Set and meet expectations/timeline and communicate status with the customer.** When you have a clear idea of what the customer's trouble is, set a timeline; offer a reasonable assessment of how long it will take to fix the issue and what will be involved. Stay in contact with the customer, giving him or her updates at certain intervals—every half hour for smaller jobs and perhaps two or three times a day for larger jobs. If applicable, offer different repair or replacement options as the job progresses. At first, you might inform a customer that it appears a power supply needs to be changed. Later, you might find that an optical drive also needs to be replaced. Keep the customer up to date and offer options. Whatever the service, be clear as to the policies of your company and provide the proper documentation about the services you will be performing. After you finish the job, follow up with the customer to verify that the computer runs smoothly and that he or she is satisfied.

▶ **Deal appropriately with customers' confidential and private materials:** Do not look at or touch confidential information. Ask the customer to move the confidential items to another area where you cannot see them. Do not look at or touch the confidential materials located on a computer, desktop, printer, and so on. This could include bank statements, accounting information, legal documents, and other top-secret company information. Going beyond this, don't disclose any work experiences you had with an organization on social media outlets.

Always *remember to do the right thing*. If a customer asks you to do something that you think is inappropriate, be sure to verify exactly what it is the customer wants you to do. Then take appropriate action. For example, if a customer asks you to install company software on his personal laptop, you should verify that the installation is allowed under the company's licensing agreements. If so, no harm is done. If not, you will have to politely refuse the customer. This type of customer behavior, while rare, should be reported to your manager.

> **ExamAlert**
>
> Be professional, punctual, positive, and practice all the other skills mentioned in this section. They are important for the exam—and much more important in the computer field.

Cram Quiz

Answer these questions. The answers follow the last question. If you cannot answer these questions correctly, consider reading this section again until you can.

1. How will speaking with a lot of jargon make a technician sound?

   - ○ **A.** Competent
   - ○ **B.** Insecure
   - ○ **C.** Smart
   - ○ **D.** Powerful

2. A customer experiences a server crash. When you arrive, the manager is upset about this problem. What do you need to remember in this scenario?

   - ○ **A.** Stay calm and do the job as efficiently as possible.
   - ○ **B.** Imagine the customer in his underwear.
   - ○ **C.** Avoid the customer and get the job done quickly.
   - ○ **D.** Refer the customer to your supervisor.

3. Which of the following are good ideas when dealing with customers? (Select two.)

   - ○ **A.** Speak clearly.
   - ○ **B.** Ignore them.
   - ○ **C.** Avoid distractions.
   - ○ **D.** Explain to them what they did wrong.

4. You are a field technician working at a customer's site. One of the workers asks you to load a copy of an organization's purchased software on a personal laptop. What should you do first?

   ○ **A.** Verify that the installation is allowed under the company's licensing agreement.

   ○ **B.** Act as though you are distracted and ignore the user.

   ○ **C.** Leave the premises and inform the police.

   ○ **D.** Tell the worker that installing unlicensed software is illegal.

   ○ **E.** Notify the worker's manager of a security breach.

5. You have been asked by a customer at a hospital to perform routine maintenance on a laser printer. Before you begin, you notice PHI has printed out. What should you do first?

   ○ **A.** Ensure the paper tray is full so that everything can print.

   ○ **B.** Place the printed output in a secure recycle bin and begin maintenance.

   ○ **C.** Kindly warn the customer that printing PHI at work is a HIPAA violation.

   ○ **D.** Ask the customer to move the printed output to another area.

Cram Quiz Answers

1. **B.** Too much computer jargon can make an end user think that you do not have the qualifications needed and are masking it with techno-babble.

2. **A.** There isn't much you can do when a customer is upset except stay calm and fix the problem!

3. **A and C.** Speak clearly so that customers understand you, and avoid distractions so that the customers know they have your complete attention.

4. **A.** You should first check whether the company allows installations of paid software on personal computers or laptops. If it is allowed, go ahead and do the installation. If not, then you should refuse and notify your manager of the occurrence. Refusal can be tough at times, so be strong, and think about the consequences of your actions. They could directly affect you in a negative way.

5. **D.** Ask the customer to move the confidential information. Protected health information (PHI) is information that is protected under the HIPAA Privacy Rule. Before ensuring that the paper tray is full, you should first ask the customer to remove the private information. You should never throw away or recycle customer printed output unless they ask you to. Printing PHI at a hospital is routine and not a HIPAA violation. Remember to always behave professionally and protect people's privacy. If you make this a regular practice, you will often receive a customer's gratitude, and as time goes on, you will increase your job security.

CHAPTER 42

Basic Scripting and Remote Access Technologies

This chapter covers the following A+ 220-1002 exam objectives:

▶ **4.8** – Identify the basics of scripting.

▶ **4.9** – Given a scenario, use remote access technologies.

Here we have the last of the 220-1002 chapters. Let's get away from the operational procedures and end the book with some more hands-on technology. In this chapter we'll cover some basic scripting with the use of tools such as PowerShell, and demonstrate how to make various remote connections to computers to view and control them. Let's do this!

4.8 – Identify the basics of scripting

ExamAlert

Objective **4.8** concentrates on the following: script file types (such as .bat, .ps1, .vbs, .sh, .py, and .js); environment variables; comment syntax; basic script constructs, such as basic loops and variables; and basic data types, such as integers and strings.

The goal of this section is to cover the basics of scripting construction and to give some examples of common scripting types used. This section is not designed to make you a programmer; however, you should be able to identify different types of scripts, and break down the components of some basic scripts. One of the goals of scripting is to make things faster and more efficient by automating processes, ultimately making your job as a technician easier.

Basic Data Types

There are two basic data types listed in the A+ objectives that you should know: integers and strings. In computer programming and scripting, an integer is essentially the same as in mathematics. An integer is a whole number (no fractions or decimal point) that can be positive, negative, or zero.

Integer types can have different sizes, and you have no doubt heard of some of them—for example, the byte of information. Typically, a byte can be between 0 and 255. In binary, this would be 00000000 through 11111111. So, it can have 2^8 (or 256) values. But there are more integral data types, like the nibble (which is 4 bits) or a word (which is 16 bits), or the doubleword (which is 32 bits).

All programming languages from C++ and Java to Python and JavaScript use integers, because all programming languages are based in mathematics.

> **ExamAlert**
>
> Know that an integer is a whole number that can be positive, negative, or zero. For example, 2, –2, 0, 201, and –201.

> **Note**
>
> By the way, if you need fractions or decimal places (real numbers), then you need floating-point numbers.

A string is a sequence of characters, used as a constant (such as a "word" like *cat*) or as a variable (such as *x*). A constant is something that remains the same. A variable is something that can change over time, but we reference it with something that does not change (for example, *x* or *y*). As opposed to an integer, a string is designed to represent text instead of numbers. You'll also hear strings referred to as alphanumeric strings, which can include letters in the alphabet, digits, blank space, and special characters and punctuation.

> **ExamAlert**
>
> Know that a string represents text (characters) rather than numbers.

Collectively, these data types are the building blocks for data within programming languages. However, let's focus on using these data types within scripting.

Basic Script Constructs

Scripting construct methods are essentially the same from one scripting language to the next. Let's use PowerShell as our example as we discuss some basic scripting constructs.

IF

One basic construct to use while scripting is the *if* statement. Here's an example of general syntax:

```
if (conditional_expression) {
  statement_list
}
```

We use parentheses around the conditional expression, which can include things such as basic math—for example, (1 + 1)—or can point to code blocks, which would be contained in alligators—for example, <test1>. If the conditional expression is true, then the statement list runs. For example, you might have the script write something to the screen or perform some kind of function within the OS, using a module from within PowerShell such as Write-Host or GetBitLockerVolume. Whatever it is, it should be confined within the curly braces.

This is a form of an IF-THEN statement. While many programming languages use IF-THEN statements, PowerShell doesn't actually incorporate the term "then." Instead, if a condition is true, the code runs. If not, then we use the "Else" option to specify that other code runs.

Other constructs in PowerShell include *switch*, *for*, *break*, *continue*, *while*, and *do*.

Let's say that we want to repeat a task ten times. It would be silly to type the code ten times, so instead we can incorporate a loop. Two of the constructs we can use for looping in PowerShell include *for* and *while*.

For and While

For loops are used to repeat a block of code as needed. These repetitions are also known as *iterations*. A for loop has two parts: a header specifying the iteration, and a body which is executed once per iteration. Look at the following general syntax:

```
for (init; condition; repeat)
    {command_block}
```

Init is the command that is run before the loop begins. Generally, it is used to initialize a variable. *Condition* is whether the expression is true or false. If it is true, then the command will continue to repeat until the loop is exhausted and the condition is changed to false. This is based on how many iterations, which is also included. *Repeat* reads the value of the variable and increments it…one at a time. The *command_block* is the command or group of commands that will repeat. Here's an example of a for loop in PowerShell that will count to 10:

```
for ($i=1; $i -le 10; $i++)
    {Write-Host $i}
```

PowerShell will always place a $ before a variable—for example, $i. In this case, the init is $i=1, so the variable *i* has been set to 1. That's where the counting starts. It will repeat ten times as set in the condition.

Try that last script and the following one in PowerShell. I recommend using the PowerShell Integrated Scripting Environment (ISE), which you can open via **Run > powershell_ise**, but the regular PowerShell will work as well. Both of these scripts will count off from 1 to 10, with a slight difference between them. Can you spot the difference?

```
for ($i=1; $i -le 10; $i++) {$i,"`n"}
```

Remember, we are using the **for** construct to create the loop, and the **$i** variable for the integers to be displayed.

Next, a while loop is similar to a for loop; it runs a command block based on the results of a conditional test. If the condition is true, the loop begins and the block of statements in the loop will repeat until the condition is no longer true. Here's an example of a while loop in PowerShell that will count to 10:

```
while ($val -ne 10)
    { $val++ ; Write-Host $val }
```

One of the main differences between for and while is that while is more flexible when it comes to the number of iterations and the way that they are defined. Counting to 10 is better done with a for statement; in this case, you have to create a new variable (such as $i = 1), but if you are using existing variables in a program, the while statement might make for a more efficient and cleaner way to write the code.

ExamAlert

Basic loops let a program execute the same statement several times. Each time a loop executes a block of statements, it is called an iteration.

Environment Variables

We have mentioned environment variables previously in the book; for example, %systemroot% (which is usually C:\Windows) and %username% (which is whatever user or users you are referring to). If you are working in the GUI, the Registry Editor, or scripting in the Command Prompt, the *%variable-name%* syntax is what you use. However, PowerShell has its own variables that start with $ (similar to many other scripting languages); for example, **$Env:*variablename***. An actual value is **$Env:Path**.

Path is a variable in Windows. Its purpose is to allow us to run programs from various locations in Windows without having to type the entire folder path to the executable. For example, a default path in Windows 10 is C:\Windows\ system32. Programs that reside within system32 can simply be run in the Run prompt, Command Prompt, or PowerShell just by typing the executable name. You can find out all of these path locations by executing the following in PowerShell:

```
Get-Item Env:Path
```

That will display any paths that have been added to the Path variable. However, this isn't only functional within the shell—it, and other variables, can be added programmatically to scripts as well, which has a wide range of implications, from administration to development. Be ready to work with environment variables in Windows and in Linux.

Comment Syntax

Sometimes, you will want to add descriptions, warnings, links, or other information to your scripts that do not actually *do* anything other than give information to the person reading the script. These things can be accomplished by adding comment syntax to the code. You can also *comment out* certain lines of code if you want them to stop functioning temporarily for testing purposes.

Using comment syntax in PowerShell and Bash is as easy as adding a number sign (**#**) before each line. For example:

```
# this script will count to 100.
for ($i=1; $i -le 100; $i++) {$i,"`n"}
```

Other types of scripts, such as JavaScript, use the double slash (**//**) before each line, which I'll demonstrate in the JavaScript section.

> **ExamAlert**
>
> For the exam, know how to comment out syntax with # (in PowerShell and Bash) or
> // (in other commonly used scripting languages).

Script File Types

Six script types are listed in the A+ objectives. Probably the most important
of these for the exam are Windows-based PowerShell scripts (.ps1) and
Linux-based Bash scripts (.sh). Let's start with those.

ps1

PowerShell ISE is Microsoft's integrated scripting environment for Windows.
It is a much more powerful shell than the Command Prompt, and is the preferred method for administration, scripting, and developing. You can open it
in a variety of ways, as mentioned previously in the book, but the easy way is
via **Run > powershell_ise**. Try opening it now in your version of Windows.
It's recommended that you use Windows 8 or higher (Pro edition or higher)
or Windows Server 2012 or higher to get the full functionality of PowerShell.
Once you open it, you will see that there is a scripting area (the top area with
the white background) and a working shell (the bottom area with the blue
background) as well as a Commands tab where you can copy and paste every
option within PowerShell. For the exam and for the field, I recommend using
version 5 or higher (as of the writing of this book in 2019). To find out the
version of PowerShell, type the following in the shell:

```
$PSVersionTable
```

For example, I am using Windows 10 Pro version 1803. For this version of
Windows, the PowerShell version (PSVersion) is 5.1.17134.590. You get a lot of
other great information from this command as well.

> **Note**
>
> You can accomplish a lot of scripting within the regular PowerShell, and if you
> open that by accident, you can simply type **ise** to access the PowerShell ISE. Did
> I mention I love the command line yet?

Once you open ISE, it automatically starts an untitled file with the .ps1 extension. From here you can write multiline scripts and run them in the shell by clicking the Run Script button (which is a green arrow within the toolbar) or by pressing **F5**. Then you can save them for later use or modification, or for sharing with other admins. For those of you with high resolutions, you might find that the text is a bit small—simply press **Ctrl** and roll the mouse wheel to dial in the right scaling.

ExamAlert

Know that PowerShell files are identified by the .ps1 extension!

One of the main reasons to use PowerShell is to automate processes, or at least make them faster. For example, if you wanted to create a user in Windows 10, you would have to go through a lengthy process in Settings, or in Local Users and Groups, all the while using both the keyboard and the mouse. However, you can also create users in the PowerShell. Take a look at the following command:

```
New-LocalUser "user1" -FullName "Test User" -Description "Test user
account."
```

This command would result in a new user being created, called *user1*, with the name *Test User*. PowerShell would then ask you to type a password for the account, after which the account is created and placed in the Users folder; you can easily test it by typing **net user**, which will display the users on the computer (though you do get verification from PowerShell after the command is run).

Boom, done, and we never had to go through the GUI once—so already PowerShell is a boon for sys admins. But take it a step further by using variables and tables (arrays) of information, and then adding more and more lines to the script. And then save the whole adventure for later use. Figure 42.1 demonstrates an example of some of this.

And that's just the tip of the iceberg with PowerShell. Plus, if you can't remember commands or the syntax used for a specific command, then you simply search the Commands tab, find the command you want, and access its details. Then you can type the information that you need in a GUI format and insert it into the shell and test it, or simply copy it to the scripting window.

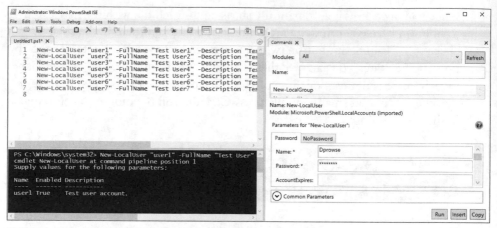

FIGURE 42.1 **PowerShell ISE example with new local users**

In the example, we added the password during user creation. To create the password first and store it securely, you could use the following syntax:

```
$Password = Read-Host -AsSecureString
```

And type the password that you want. Then reference it later during the user creation process with the following:

```
-Password $Password
```

-Password is the parameter and **$Password** is, wait for it...a *variable*. That will grab the password that you previously stored. In PowerShell, a variable name always begins with a dollar sign ($).

Want to test whether multiple computers are alive on the network? You could do a series of pings, but the PowerShell comes with the **Test-Connection** command that enables you to test many systems, in many ways, and of course save the whole script for later use.

.bat and Batch Files

For a long time, Windows users (and DOS users) would write complicated (and temperamental) batch scripts, for example, to map network drives or perform a series of pings, and then save them as .bat files. You can still create batch files today within Notepad, and some Windows users still do, but PowerShell makes the process much easier, and more configurable.

To add comment information or to temporarily comment out syntax, add a number sign (#) before each line. To quickly comment out multiple lines at the same time, click at the beginning of the first line to be commented. Then press and hold **Alt+Shift**, and arrow down as far as you need to go, then press **Shift+#**.

Once we are done creating our scripts, we can save them as .ps1 files for later use. Store them in an appropriate folder that only authorized people can access!

Note

For more information about PowerShell, start here:

https://docs.microsoft.com/en-us/powershell/scripting/overview?view=powershell-6

If you are going to be working in a Windows environment, then I strongly recommend that you learn how to use PowerShell.

ExamAlert

Know how to use PowerShell ISE for the exam!

.sh

In the Linux world, we can create scripts with a text editor (such as the built-in **vi**). In most Linux environments we do this within the Terminal. Terminal is a shell called Bash (which is an extremely common shell also used by Unix systems and macOS). Bash is also where you can save scripts by default: the path is /bin/bash, though you can save them elsewhere if you wish. Normally, scripts are saved with the .sh extension (short for shell).

ExamAlert

Know that .sh file extensions represent Linux/Unix shell scripting files.

Let's build a basic and traditional "Hello World" script. First, we need to access the Terminal. A nice shortcut to open the terminal in Linux is **Ctrl+Alt+T**. Once that is done, open the text editor where we will build our scripts by typing **vi**. That brings up a basic text editor that requires special key strokes to perform certain actions. For example, take a look at Table 42.1 for some basic commands in vi.

TABLE 42.1 **Common vi Tasks and Keystrokes/Commands**

Task	Keystroke
To enter edit mode (you must do this before you can write a script)	Press **Esc** and type **I**
To go to command mode	Press **Esc**
To save a file	Press **Esc** and type :w *filename*
To quit	Press **Esc** and type :q

Keep in mind that you will need sudo (superuser or equivalent) access to perform some of these actions.

1. Press **Esc** and type **I** to enter editing mode.

2. Type the following syntax:

```
#!/bin/bash
echo "Hello, World!"
```

3. Save the file by pressing **Esc** and typing :w *filename* (for example, :w **helloworld.sh**), and pressing **Enter**.

4. Quit out of vi by pressing **Esc** and typing :q and pressing **Enter**. This will bring you back to the standard Bash terminal.

5. Now, set permissions so that the script will run. For example:

```
chmod +x helloworld.sh
```

6. Run the script by typing **./helloworld.sh**.

You should now see the text that you placed in quotes within the script, **Hello, World!** Great job! That is an example of the most basic of Linux-based scripts.

Here's a script that will utilize looping and display the quoted text five times:

```
#!/bin/sh
for i in 1 2 3 4 5
do
  echo "Looping $i"
done
```

If you typed it exactly, chmodded it, and performed a sudo, you should see the looped results. It also makes use of the variable **$i**, which changes from 1 to 2 to 3 to 4 to 5 on each line.

Now, here's an example of an IF-THEN statement:

```
if <condition>;
then <commands>
fi
```

This uses an if-then-fi statement—also known as if…fi—to make decisions and execute statements conditionally. The condition is based on what you type in *condition*, and the *commands* are what will occur if the condition is met. These are often run automatically as cron jobs in Linux. Cron jobs can be created by using the **cron** utility, which is a time-based job scheduler.

To comment out in Bash, we add the number sign (#) before each line that we want commented out, just as we did in PowerShell.

Keep in mind that scripts can be used for productive or malicious purposes, so they should be tightly controlled.

> **Note**
>
> For more information, here's a good tutorial on Linux Bash and scripting within Ubuntu Linux:
>
> https://help.ubuntu.com/community/Beginners/BashScripting
>
> Also, if you find vi to be somewhat cumbersome, consider a Linux text editor such as Atom or Sublime Text.

> **ExamAlert**
>
> Know how to use Bash: the Terminal and vi for the exam!

.js

If you are going to have a powerful and interactive front end to your website, you will most likely be using JavaScript. Though it can be used in other environments, JavaScript is best known for use within the development of web pages. A good web developer will know the following: HTML to define the content of web pages, CSS to work with the layout of web pages, and JavaScript to program how the web pages will behave and to add functionality. For example, if you wanted to have a quiz on your website or a calculator, you could use JavaScript.

Here's an example of a script written in JavaScript:

```
<p id="testdemo"></p>
<script>
function myFunction(a, b) {
  return a * b;
}
document.getElementById("testdemo").innerHTML = window.myFunction(10, 2);
</script>
```

In this example, the number 20 will be displayed to the user in a window. We are *defining* a function called myFunction, which is essentially multiplying the variables *a* times *b*. Later we are *invoking* the function with document.getElementById and using the numbers 10 and 2 for the equation.

When finished building a JavaScript script, save it as a .js file.

JavaScript can use whatever variables you like to store data values with the **var** statement. For example:

```
var x = 2
var y = 3
var z = x + y
```

If we were to invoke z somewhere in the page, it would display the number 5. But we could define the variables with whatever letter assignment we like.

Don't forget, to comment out code, use the double-slash method (*//*), by adding the double-slash before each line to be commented out. *//* is designed for single lines of code. For multiple lines, use *\/** at the beginning of the comment and **/* at the end. JavaScript will ignore any text between them. By the way, if you are scripting in JavaScript, you will probably also be working in HTML. If you are working on an HTML web page and you want to leave a comment or comment something out, you would use **<!--   -->**. For example:

```
<!-- This is a comment -->
```

Replace "This is a comment" with whatever you wish. You could also surround any code that you want to disable temporarily (comment out) with the same characters, placing **<!--** at the beginning and **-->** at the end. Just remove the comment-out syntax when you need the code again. Works great for testing!

You'll find that all scripting is based on math and common sense, once you get past the syntax and naming conventions, that is!

Note

For a good tutorial on JavaScript, with embedded testing, see the following link:
https://www.w3schools.com/js/default.asp

ExamAlert

Remember, JavaScript files use a .js file extension.

.py

Python is a high-level object-oriented programming language. While it can be used for scripting, it is a general-purpose programming language that can be used to build in-depth programs, making it more powerful than JavaScript or VBScript, but slightly less powerful than languages such as C++ and Java, because it requires an interpreter.

To use Python in Windows or Linux, you first have to install it; you can grab it from here: https://www.python.org/. When scripting in Python, you save the script as a .py file.

> **ExamAlert**
>
> Python scripting files have a .py file extension.

Python uses statements similar to other languages such as if, for, and while, and makes use of variables in a similar fashion. Here's an example of a Python "Hello World" script that makes use of the *write* method:

```
import stdio
# Write 'Hello, World' to standard output.
stdio.writeln('Hello, World')
```

Python will make use of variables such as **foo**; for example, foo =10. But the value of foo can change as necessary. This is similar to C++ language, but don't run away just yet. Remember that Python is designed for small and large projects, and therefore can be a great scripting tool in Windows and Linux, regardless of its differences compared with JavaScript and PowerShell.

> **Note**
>
> To learn more about Python, see the following link:
>
> https://docs.python.org/3/

.vbs

A file with the extension .vbs indicates a Visual Basic script, or VBScript. VBScript is known as an object-based scripting language, which was historically used in Windows environments (.NET and Office) and within web pages. You can build VBScript scripts within the Windows Notepad program or with any other text editor (such as Notepad++). Then, simply save the script as a .vbs file.

Visual Basic is also heavily used in Microsoft Office (namely Excel) with the included Visual Basic Editor.

ExamAlert

A file with the .vbs extension indicates a Visual Basic script, or VBScript.

VBScript uses variables such as **Dim Var** that hold values in memory which can be changed by the script later on as need be by calling a function. For example, we might set two variables like this:

```
Dim Var1
Dim Var2
```

And then call a function like this:

```
Function add()
Var1 = 10
       Var2 = 20
```

Historically, VBScript was used to work with Windows configurations. For example, here's the beginning of a VBScript script that would create a user in Active Directory:

```
strComputer = "DC1"
strComputerUser = "dpro42\Bob"

Const ADS_UF_PASSWD_NOTREQD = &h0020
```

Of course, there is more to the actual script (a whole lot more), and PowerShell can do it *much* quicker and easier. But what we see here is the variable **strComputer**, which means the computer name—in this case, I'm using my server name *DC1*. Then we have another variable, **strComputerUser**, which defines the username (*Bob*) and the domain that it is being created within (*dpro42*). A constant (declared with the Const statement) is a meaningful name that takes the place of a number or a string of information—in this case **0020**, which deals with the password for the user.

VBScript can also be used on web pages. Here's an example of a basic "Hello World" script written in VBScript that is embedded within HTML. The VBScript script itself starts with <script.... and ends with </script>.

```
<html>
    <body>
        <script language = "vbscript" type = "text/vbscript">
            document.write("Hello World!")
        </script>
    </body>
</html>
```

The actual VBScript script is **document.write("Hello World!")**, which will simply place the words "Hello World!" on the screen. It uses the Document Object and the write method to write text on the screen. You can use the same method with JavaScript and other scripting languages, but here you can see we are selecting "vbscript" as our script language.

> **Note**
>
> In Windows, a lot of what was once done in VBScript is now done with PowerShell. On the Internet, it is more likely that you would use JavaScript or some other tool. However, VBScript still has a place in .NET (though many developers prefer C#) and especially within Microsoft Office. See this link for a tutorial about using the Visual Basic Editor within Microsoft Office—known as Visual Basic for Applications (VBA):
>
> https://docs.microsoft.com/en-us/office/vba/library-reference/concepts/getting-started-with-vba-in-office

A Final Word on Scripting

Scripting is new to the 220-1002 A+ exam. The typical A+ tech won't be doing much scripting in object-based scripting languages such as JavaScript, Python, and VBScript. You should be able to identify the various types of scripts and file extensions, but I suggest that you focus primarily on PowerShell and Bash as those are specifically designed for systems administration with Windows and Linux, respectively.

Cram Quiz

Answer these questions. The answers follow the last question. If you cannot answer these questions correctly, consider reading this section again until you can.

1. What should you type to comment out syntax in JavaScript?
   - A. $
   - B. #
   - C. //
   - D. <!-- -->

2. Which of the following is an integer? (Select the two best answers.)
   - A. 16
   - B. cat
   - C. string
   - D. 00000001

3. You want to list a variable number 16 times but don't want to type 16 lines of code. Which of the following techniques should you use?

- ○ **A.** If-Then
- ○ **B.** Looping
- ○ **C.** Environment variables
- ○ **D.** Comment syntax

4. A technician just finished scripting a sequence of code and saved the file as a .sh. What system is the technician working in?

- ○ **A.** PowerShell
- ○ **B.** Linux
- ○ **C.** JavaScript
- ○ **D.** Python
- ○ **E.** Batch file

Cram Quiz Answers

1. **C.** Use the double-slash (//) to comment out individual lines of code in JavaScript. The $ is used to denote a variable in many languages and scripting tools, including PowerShell and Bash. # is used to comment out lines of code in PowerShell and Bash. <!-- --> is used to comment out syntax in HTML.

2. **A and D.** The number 16 is an integer (any whole number is), and the binary number 00000001 is an integer that is equal to one 8-bit byte of information. Cat is an example of a string, which is a sequence of characters.

3. **B.** Make use of looping, which allows you to write one line of code based on math that will output the 16 lines of code required. If-Then statements are used as conditional expressions. Environment variables are variables that define items within the system such as the environment path. Comment syntax is used to temporarily disable lines of code.

4. **B.** The technician is working on a Linux system and making use of Bash (perhaps vi). When you work in Bash, it is accepted as a best practice to save the scripts as .sh files. PowerShell uses .ps1 by default. JavaScript is .js. Python is .py. Batch files are used for scripting in Windows and are saved with the .bat extension, but remember, PowerShell is recommended over batch files.

4.9 – Given a scenario, use remote access technologies

Why walk or drive to another computer when you can control it remotely? Unless there is a networking or hardware issue, always try to remote into a system to repair it. It will be faster and more efficient. As a sys admin, tools such as RDP, SSH, and RealVNC are some of your best friends.

Remote Desktop

Remote Desktop software, included with Windows, enables a user to see and control the GUI of a remote computer. This enables users to control other computers on the network or over the Internet without leaving their seats; this aids technicians in their attempts to repair computers because they don't have to go to the system that needs repair. But first, to have a Remote Desktop session, you need to configure the software. To do so, open the System Properties window and select the **Remote** tab (**Run > systempropertiesremote**). From here, there are two boxes of information:

▶ **Remote Assistance:** The **Allow Remote Assistance connections to this computer** checkbox is selected by default. This means that connections can be made via Remote Assistance invitations, by e-mail, or via instant messaging. These invitations can ask for help or offer help. This is often implemented in help-desk scenarios in which a user invites a technician to take control of his or her computer so that it can be repaired. Invitations are made by accessing the Windows Remote Assistance program (simply type it into the Search field). For this to function, in addition to having the checkbox checked, Remote Control must be enabled by clicking the **Advanced** button and selecting the **Allow this computer to be controlled remotely** checkbox. When the proper settings are enabled, Remote Assistance calls flow right through the Windows Firewall.

▶ **Remote Desktop Connection:** This is where you can select whether other users can connect to, and control, your computer at any time without an invitation from you. There are options to disable remote connections, enable connections with any version of Remote Desktop, and enable connections running Remote Desktop with Network Level

Authentication for security. This is disabled by default, but if enabled, the remote users can make connections to your computer by computer name or by IP address. Finally, you can select the users who are allowed to connect to your computer. If your network is a workgroup, then the local user account(s) you select is just that: local. For the remote user to connect, the remote computer must have an identical account (the same username and password) as the one you selected on your computer and the remote user must know the username/password. If the network is a domain, this is not an issue due to centralized administration of accounts.

> **ExamAlert**
>
> Be able to explain the difference between Remote Assistance and Remote Desktop.

To make a Remote Desktop connection to a remote computer, first make sure that the remote computer has Remote Desktop enabled. Next, open the program. In any version of Windows, simply type **remote** in the Search field and select Remote Desktop Connection. In Windows 10 go to **Start > Windows Accessories**. Consider using Windows 10 Pro edition or higher. In Windows 7, you can click **Start > All Programs > Accessories**. Click **Show Options** for more logon settings, as shown in Figure 42.2. To make the connection, you need to supply a computer name or the IP address of the remote computer and a username and password of an account on the remote computer.

FIGURE 42.2   **The Remote Desktop Connection window**

Click **Connect** and the screen of the other computer should show up on your local display. At this point, you can control the remote computer as if you were sitting locally at it. By default, when you connect, the remote computer's physical screen locks; it can be unlocked only with a username/password.

> **Note**
>
> Remote Desktop is based off the Remote Desktop Protocol (RDP, which it is often referred to by techs). When Remote Desktop is enabled, this protocol is allowed through the Windows Firewall using TCP port 3389 (by default), a well-known port. Give *strong consideration* to using Network Level Authentication when allowing Remote Desktop connections. And, for further security, consider implementing FIPS 140 compliance, with TLS and making use of port 443 (configured in Group Policy).

You can also use the **mstsc** command in the Command Prompt to make Remote Desktop connections, edit existing Remote Desktop configuration files, and migrate old connection files to newer systems. This command can be used in the Command Prompt or in the Run prompt. For example, if you wanted to remotely control another system with the **mstsc** command in full-screen mode, you would type

```
Mstsc.exe /v:computername /f
```

> **Note**
>
> For more information on the **mstsc** command, visit
>
> https://docs.microsoft.com/en-us/windows-server/administration/windows-commands/mstsc

Need to control more than one computer remotely at the same time? Consider using the Remote Desktop Connection Manager. I use it all the time. It's an extra download for Windows available here:

https://www.microsoft.com/en-us/download/details.aspx?id=44989

SSH

We briefly discussed the Secure Shell (SSH) protocol, way back in Chapter 5, "Ports, Protocols, and Network Devices." Consider reviewing the protocol before continuing.

There are lot of protocols and programs that make use of SSH. SSH is typically considered to be a secure way to connect to remote Linux systems, network devices, and more (as long as it is configured properly). Once you connect via SSH, and log in as an administrator, you can control the remote system from the command line.

For example, from time to time I will securely connect to a pfSense firewall (which is FreeBSD based) from my Windows 10 client using PuTTY, a common SSH client program. Take a look at Figure 42.3.

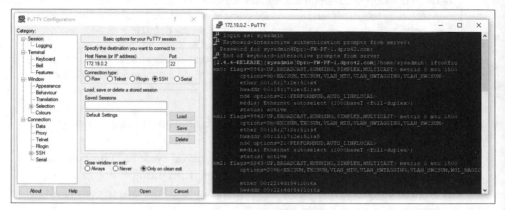

FIGURE 42.3   SSH connection using PuTTY to a FreeBSD system

On the left you see the PuTTY client program configured to connect to the host 172.19.0.2 on port 22 (the default port for SSH). When you click the Open button, you get a text window like the one on the right in the figure. From the top down it shows that I logged in as sysadmin, and then I typed the command **ifconfig** just to show some information in the command line. That's it—full remote control from the command-line. When done, type **exit** to end the session.

There are plenty of other SSH clients available, but note these two important things: 1. You have to have SSH *installed* on the target device (consider OpenSSH if nothing is already installed); and 2. The SSH service has to be turned on at the computer (or network device) that you want to remote into. Further, make sure you are using good passwords, and consider additional forms of security such as certificates, timeouts, and so on, as described in the security portion of this book.

> ### Note
>
> You might opt to run RDP or SSH through a VPN for added security, especially if you are remoting to a computer on the Internet. Some people use OpenSSH with OpenVPN tunneling!

> **ExamAlert**
>
> Know how to use Remote Desktop and SSH client software to make connections to remote computers.

SSH is one example of a secure replacement for the older and deprecated Telnet. Telnet makes use of port 23, and can be used on many different systems, but because of its security vulnerabilities, it is disabled by default. In the rare case that you need to use it in Windows, you can enable it by going to the Windows Features dialog box and selecting **Telnet Client**.

> **ExamAlert**
>
> Know that Telnet (port 23) is insecure and has been replaced by SSH (port 22).

More Third-Party Tools

There are plenty of other tools that are available for the remote control of systems. I routinely make use of a Virtual Network Computing (VNC) product such as RealVNC to remotely control Linux computers, macOS systems, and Android-based smartphones and tablets. Other remote control tools include TeamViewer, AnyDesk, LogMeIn, Chrome Remote Desktop, and the list goes on. (I do not endorse any of these tools, and as always, you should use third-party tools with caution.)

You can also share your screen with other systems, which works well for collaboration and education. For example, use Miracast on Windows 10 Surface systems, or utilize a web-based webinar system such as Cisco Webex. Just make sure that the remote users cannot take control of your system (unless you want them to and give them permission to do so).

The key with any of these tools is to make sure that they are secure. If you are connecting over the Internet, you need a secured session. Whether that is done by way of VPN for direct connections or by using an encrypted certificate when connecting via a browser (with TLS, RSA, and AES, for example), you want to make sure that the session is secure and that passwords are lengthy and hard to guess.

Cram Quiz

Answer these questions. The answers follow the last question. If you cannot answer these questions correctly, consider reading this section again until you can.

1. Which program enables a user to invite a technician to help repair their computer remotely?

   ○ **A.** Remote Desktop Connection

   ○ **B.** Remote Assistance

   ○ **C.** RDP

   ○ **D.** Remote connectivity

2. You have been tasked with making a command-line-based, remote connection to an Ubuntu Linux computer located on your LAN, so that you can run two scripts on it as an administrator. What protocol should you use? (Select the best answer.)

   ○ **A.** RDP

   ○ **B.** mstsc

   ○ **C.** SSH

   ○ **D.** VPN

3. You are in charge of setting up the administrators' connections to remote Windows 10 computers located at satellite offices using RDP. What are some of the ways to make the connections more secure? (Select the three best answers.)

   ○ **A.** Use strong passwords

   ○ **B.** Use OpenSSH

   ○ **C.** Use Network Level Authentication

   ○ **D.** Use PuTTY

   ○ **E.** Use L2TP and IKEv2

Cram Quiz Answers

1. **B.** Remote Assistance calls can be made from users to invite other users to help fix a problem for them. Remote Desktop Connections are the connections that a computer makes to a remote computer to control it.

2. **C.** Use Secure Shell (SSH) to connect (on port 22) to the Ubuntu Linux computer, take control, and run the scripts as required (within vi or your favorite text editor). You could also incorporate a VPN, but if both systems are on the LAN, this is usually not necessary. RDP is the protocol (and commonly used name) behind Windows' Remote Desktop Connection software. mstsc is the command-line executable for Remote Desktop Connection.

3. **A, C, and E.** Always use strong passwords (whether that is length, complexity, or a mixture of the two), as well as Network Level Authentication, which requires the user's credentials from the client computer. Also, since the connections are to remote offices, consider using a virtual private network (VPN). Layer 2 Tunneling Protocol (L2TP) is decent solution for a VPN (if configured properly), but OpenVPN, or another always-on VPN service, is usually better. Internet Key Exchange Version 2 (IKEv2) is the preferred VPN protocol on Windows 10 computers. OpenSSH and PuTTY might be used together for Linux and similar connections, but they wouldn't be used in this Windows-based scenario because the task requires RDP—meaning the Remote Desktop Connection program.

Great Job!

If you have come this far, I congratulate you! This is the last chapter of actual CompTIA A+ objective-based content. Somehow it *coincidentally* ended on the number 42.... Anyway, directly following this chapter you will find the 220-1002 practice exam, and then the final chapter where I give some tips for passing the exam, and close out the book. Take a break (you deserve it), and then continue on to the practice exam!

If you are planning on taking the actual CompTIA A+ Core 2 (220-1002) exam, be sure to go through the 220-1002 checklist, located in "Introduction to Core 2 (220-1002)," just before Chapter 23.

A+ Core 2 (220-1002) Practice Exam

The 80 multiple-choice questions provided here help you to determine how prepared you are for the actual exam and which topics you need to review further. Write down your answers on a separate sheet of paper so that you can take this exam again if necessary. Compare your answers against the answer key that follows this exam. Read through the explanations and also the incorrect answers very carefully. If there are any concepts that you don't understand, go back and study them more.

1. Which of the following commands will display the MAC address of a computer?

   ○ **A. ping**

   ○ **B. netstat**

   ○ **C. ipconfig /all**

   ○ **D. ipconfig /renew**

2. You want to perform a network installation of Windows. Which of the following must be supported by the client computer?

   ○ **A.** PCIe

   ○ **B.** PXE

   ○ **C.** BitLocker

   ○ **D.** Multiboot

3. Which command is used to list the contents of a directory in the Command Prompt?

   ○ **A. cd**

   ○ **B. dir**

   ○ **C. ping**

   ○ **D. ver**

4. One of your customers runs Windows on a laptop. A new security flaw and fix has been published regarding Windows. Which of the following can prevent exploitation?

   ○ **A.** Encrypting the hard drive

   ○ **B.** Training the customer

   ○ **C.** Implementing a patching policy

   ○ **D.** Configuring screen locks

5. Your company has multiple users who work with the same commercial software. What is the best type of license to purchase so that it is in compliance with the EULA?

   ○ **A.** Seat license

   ○ **B.** Commercial license

   ○ **C.** Enterprise license

   ○ **D.** Open source license

6. Which of the following is a risk of implementing BYOD?

    ○ **A.** Encryption mismatches

    ○ **B.** Higher risk of phishing attacks

    ○ **C.** Introduction of malware onto the network

    ○ **D.** DHCP failures

7. One of your co-workers tells you that whenever she returns to her desk she has to type her username and password to unlock the computer. She says she cannot modify the screensaver. After analyzing the system, you notice that the screensaver and the screen lock options are indeed grayed out. Which of the following is the most likely reason for this?

    ○ **A.** Incorrect local-level user policies

    ○ **B.** Domain-level group policies

    ○ **C.** Antivirus domain-level policies

    ○ **D.** Corrupted registry

8. Which of the following features in Windows allows the following command to run? (Select the two best answers.)

`$PSVersionTable`

    □ **A.** Compatibility mode

    □ **B.** OneDrive

    □ **C.** Windows Firewall

    □ **D.** PowerShell

    □ **E.** ISE

9. You have been tasked with printing a group policy configuration report to an HTML file for offline review. Which of the following commands will enable you to do this?

    ○ **A.** gpresult

    ○ **B.** gpupdate

    ○ **C.** gpedit.msc

    ○ **D.** secpol.msc

10. Which of the following tasks is automatically added to the Windows Task Scheduler to improve hard disk performance?

    ○ **A.** cleanmgr

    ○ **B.** defrag

    ○ **C.** diskpart

    ○ **D.** chkdsk

11. Which of the following is the maximum addressable RAM limit for a system running a 32-bit version of Windows?

   ○ **A.** No limit

   ○ **B.** 4 GB

   ○ **C.** 8 GB

   ○ **D.** 32 GB

   ○ **E.** 256 TB

12. One of the users in your company frequently leaves her workstation and wants to make sure that her confidential data is not accessed by anyone else. However, the user does not want to turn off the computer when she leaves work in the evening. Which of the following is the best solution for securing the workstation?

   ○ **A.** Implement a password and fingerprint lock for after-hours login.

   ○ **B.** Set a strong password that requires a renewal every 30 days.

   ○ **C.** Apply a screen lock after 5 minutes of nonuse and set login time restrictions for after hours.

   ○ **D.** Run a screensaver after 1 minute of nonuse and a fingerprint lock for after hours.

13. A manager suspects that a user has obtained movies and other copyright-protected materials through the use of a BitTorrent client. The incident response tech confirms the suspicion, and as such, the user is in violation of company policy. What should the incident response technician do next?

   ○ **A.** Immediately delete all unauthorized materials.

   ○ **B.** Secure the workstation in a limited-access storage facility.

   ○ **C.** Reprimand the user and apply a content filter to the user's profile.

   ○ **D.** Document the incident and purge all policy-violating materials.

14. A new user in your company has been given permission to connect to the corporate network with a smartphone that he owns. Which of the following should you perform before configuring the smartphone for actual access to the network?

   ○ **A.** Check the phone for unauthorized root access.

   ○ **B.** Erase all personal data from the phone.

   ○ **C.** Check the phone for location tracking.

   ○ **D.** Disable Bluetooth.

15. You work for an organization that uses various permissions for individual user accounts. One of the managers with a restricted user account receives the following message:

Windows Update cannot currently check for updates because the service is not running.

The manager contacts your organization's help desk to report the error. You connect to the manager's computer and identify the problem. What action should you take next to quickly resolve the problem?

- ○ **A.** Reboot the computer.
- ○ **B.** Roll back the device drivers.
- ○ **C.** Restart the network services.
- ○ **D.** Rebuild the Windows profile.

16. Which of the following usually incorporates an eight-digit code that can be found on the bottom of a SOHO router?

- ○ **A.** Port forwarding
- ○ **B.** WPS
- ○ **C.** Wireless encryption
- ○ **D.** Port triggering

17. You have been asked to set up a new networking closet and you notice that the humidity level in the room is very low. Which of the following tasks should be done before rack-mounting any networking equipment?

- ○ **A.** Install grounding bars.
- ○ **B.** Set up a dehumidifier.
- ○ **C.** Use an ESD strap.
- ○ **D.** Implement a fire suppression system.

18. Which of the following security techniques is most closely related to when a user enters a username and password once for multiple applications?

- ○ **A.** Propagation
- ○ **B.** MFA
- ○ **C.** SSO
- ○ **D.** Inheritance

19. Jason from accounting reports that when pressing Ctrl+Alt+Del to log on to a Windows workstation, he is asked for a PIN. Which of the following should you tell Jason?

- ○ **A.** "Enter all the passwords that you have used previously."
- ○ **B.** "Reboot the computer."
- ○ **C.** "Check the network cable."
- ○ **D.** "Please verify that you are using your smart card."

20. A surge suppressor safeguards connected equipment by directing surges to the

   ○ **A.** path of least resistance.

   ○ **B.** path of shortest conductance.

   ○ **C.** path of lowest inductance.

   ○ **D.** path of highest voltage.

21. By default, a file or folder will receive its NTFS permissions from the parent folder. This process is known as which of the following terms?

   ○ **A.** Permission propagation

   ○ **B.** Single sign-on (SSO)

   ○ **C.** Client-side virtualization

   ○ **D.** Proxy settings

   ○ **E.** Recovery image

   ○ **F.** Inheritance

22. Which of the following are examples of physical security? (Select the two best answers.)

   ☐ **A.** Directory permissions

   ☐ **B.** OTP hardware tokens

   ☐ **C.** Principle of least privilege

   ☐ **D.** Privacy filters

23. You have been given technical documentation from the network administrator which details the switch ports that you will need to use for an upcoming network upgrade. Which of the following documents did you receive?

   ○ **A.** Logical topology diagram

   ○ **B.** Process diagram

   ○ **C.** Physical network diagram

   ○ **D.** Fiber backbone diagram

24. Which of the following will help to protect an organization from further data exposure *after* a list of passwords has already been leaked due to a policy breach? (Select the two best answers.)

   ☐ **A.** Require strong passwords.

   ☐ **B.** Use multifactor authentication.

   ☐ **C.** Educate end users.

   ☐ **D.** Enable file encryption.

   ☐ **E.** Restrict user permissions.

25. A user is reporting that his web browser is not going to the site he is trying to access. Which of the following statements describes the best way to resolve this?

   ○ **A.** Ensure the user is not utilizing a proxy server.

   ○ **B.** Remove all Internet shortcuts.

   ○ **C.** Delete all Internet cookies.

   ○ **D.** Clear all Internet cache.

26. Which of the following Windows features has undergone the most significant changes from Windows 7 to Windows 10 and has also greatly simplified the OS installation process?

   ○ **A.** Metro interface

   ○ **B.** User Account Control

   ○ **C.** Driver detection

   ○ **D.** PXE installation

27. Which of the following terms best describes the Apple utility used with iOS devices for synchronizing and upgrading?

   ○ **A.** Safari

   ○ **B.** iMac

   ○ **C.** iTunes

   ○ **D.** Bluetooth

28. Which of the following is a way to remove data from a hard drive through destruction? (Select the two best answers.)

   ☐ **A.** Disabling ports

   ☐ **B.** Shredding

   ☐ **C.** Drilling

   ☐ **D.** Using low-level formatting

   ☐ **E.** Purging

29. Which of the following Internet Options tabs should you access to enable TLS 1.2 in Internet Explorer?

   ○ **A.** Security

   ○ **B.** Privacy

   ○ **C.** Advanced

   ○ **D.** Connections

30. You are attempting to install a Windows 10 64-bit OS within a VM but you keep receiving errors. The specifications for the VM include

    ○ Two 1-GHz CPUs

    ○ 2 GB of RAM

    ○ 15 GB hard drive space

    ○ 800 × 600 screen resolution

    Which of the following should you do to resolve this issue?

    ○ **A.** Increase the number of CPUs.

    ○ **B.** Increase the amount of memory.

    ○ **C.** Increase the amount of hard drive space.

    ○ **D.** Increase the screen resolution.

31. Your organization's network consists of 25 computers. Your boss is interested in employing a file server with network shares and a print server. Which of the following Windows network setups should you recommend?

    ○ **A.** Workgroup

    ○ **B.** Ad hoc

    ○ **C.** Star

    ○ **D.** Domain

32. Which of the following is the best example of the use of chain of custody?

    ○ **A.** The technician notes the date, time, and who was given the computer.

    ○ **B.** The technician remembers when and who he or she gave the computer to.

    ○ **C.** The technician uses a third party to hand over the computer to the proper authorities.

    ○ **D.** The technician calls the supervisor after the computer has been transferred.

33. You just installed a new updated driver for a network interface card (NIC). Now you want to test its data transfer rate. What tool should you use to run your test?

    ○ **A.** Device Manager

    ○ **B.** Local Security Policy

    ○ **C.** Performance Monitor

    ○ **D.** Component Services

34. You just got your first IT job working at a help desk. You get a call from a user about an issue you have never seen before, and you are not sure where to begin troubleshooting. What is the first course of action you should take?

- ○ **A.** Tell the customer that this is the first time you have encountered this problem and to please be patient.
- ○ **B.** Tell the customer that the problem needs to be escalated to a higher-tier technician.
- ○ **C.** Tell the customer to please hold while a senior technician is consulted regarding the problem.
- ○ **D.** Ask the customer if he or she would mind holding for no more than two minutes to check resources.

35. One of your company's users just purchased an Android smartphone and is attempting to access a public hotspot. The user receives a message that a page cannot be displayed. The user notices a question mark (?) in the radio icon in the toolbar. The user has activated Bluetooth, and verified that airplane mode is off. Tethering is turned on. The user is using the smartphone to call in to the help desk for assistance. Which of the following is the most likely issue?

- ○ **A.** The user has exceeded the data allowance.
- ○ **B.** There is unauthenticated wireless connectivity.
- ○ **C.** It is an un-rooted smartphone.
- ○ **D.** The SIM card is not activated.
- ○ **E.** The smartphone is only 3G capable.
- ○ **F.** A data plan was not purchased.

36. Which Windows utility can be used to see which user is currently logged on?

- ○ **A.** MSConfig
- ○ **B.** Disk Management
- ○ **C.** Task Manager
- ○ **D.** Administrative Tools

37. Which of the following tools are commonly used to remove dust from the inside of a computer? (Select the two best answers.)

- ☐ **A.** Compressed air
- ☐ **B.** Cotton and alcohol
- ☐ **C.** Feather duster
- ☐ **D.** Antibacterial surface cleaner
- ☐ **E.** Vacuum

38. You have been tasked with installing Windows 10 on 100 computers to a new subnet on your network. You are required to remove system-specific identifiers. Which of the following should be used to accomplish this?

- ○ **A.** System Preparation tool
- ○ **B.** Windows Deployment Services
- ○ **C.** Remote Installation Services
- ○ **D.** Unattended installation

39. Which of the following is a common symptom of a problem that can occur while starting up the Windows operating system?

- ○ **A.** Spontaneous shutdown/restart.
- ○ **B.** Invalid boot disk.
- ○ **C.** WinRE won't start.
- ○ **D.** The optical disc failed.
- ○ **E.** The emergency repair disk doesn't boot.
- ○ **F.** Regsvr32 has failed.

40. Which of the following are possible symptoms of malware? (Select all that apply.)

- ☐ **A.** Security alerts
- ☐ **B.** Windows Update failures
- ☐ **C.** Pre-installation environment
- ☐ **D.** Renamed system files
- ☐ **E.** Rogue antivirus
- ☐ **F.** User error

41. One of your company's users complains that his smartphone is making shutter noises even when he is not taking pictures. What should you do first to determine the cause of the problem?

- ○ **A.** Update all applications on the smartphone.
- ○ **B.** Run OS updates.
- ○ **C.** Uninstall the camera installation.
- ○ **D.** Check the application permissions.
- ○ **E.** Reset the phone to factory settings.

42. You are troubleshooting a Windows system suffering from poor performance. The Event Viewer states that the file system is corrupt. What should you do next?

- ○ **A.** Reload the OS using FAT32 instead of NTFS.
- ○ **B.** Run **chkdsk** with the **/R** option and reboot the system.

    ○ **C.** Open the **defrag** utility and run the drive analysis.

    ○ **D.** Change the drive from basic to dynamic.

43. Which type of fire extinguishing technology should be used during an electrical fire?

    ○ **A.** Overhead sprinkler systems

    ○ **B.** Water-based fire extinguishers

    ○ **C.** Class B fire extinguishers

    ○ **D.** Non-water-based fire extinguishers

44. You attempt to install a legacy application on a computer running Windows 8. You receive an error that says the application cannot be installed because the OS is not supported. Which of the following describes the first step you should take to continue installing the application?

    ○ **A.** Install the latest service pack.

    ○ **B.** Install the application in Safe Mode.

    ○ **C.** Install the application in compatibility mode.

    ○ **D.** Install the latest security updates.

45. A user tells you that his new smartphone is suffering from poor battery life. The user has been using the phone for a short time and has installed several apps lately. Which of the following is the most likely cause of the problem?

    ○ **A.** Unauthorized root access

    ○ **B.** Battery needs to be replaced

    ○ **C.** Defective SD card

    ○ **D.** Signal drop or weak signal

    ○ **E.** Slow data speeds

46. You have been tasked with setting up a SOHO wireless network in a small healthcare office that cannot afford a server. The wireless users require the highest level of security available, and various other levels of desktop authentication for access to cloud-based resources. Which of the following protocols and authentication methods should you implement? (Select the two best answers.)

    ☐ **A.** WEP

    ☐ **B.** WPA

    ☐ **C.** WPA2

    ☐ **D.** TKIP

    ☐ **E.** RADIUS

    ☐ **F.** TACACS

    ☐ **G.** SSO

    ☐ **H.** Multifactor

47. A customer calls to report that when she walks away from her laptop for an extended period of time, she has to reconnect to wireless upon her return. Which of the following will most likely correct this issue?

   ○ **A.** Replace the wireless card.

   ○ **B.** Install a higher capacity battery.

   ○ **C.** Adjust the power settings.

   ○ **D.** Disable the screensaver.

48. You are required to remove the ability for standard users to shut down or restart a shared computer. Which command should be used to accomplish this task?

   ○ **A. shutdown.exe**

   ○ **B. bootrec.exe**

   ○ **C. gpedit.msc**

   ○ **D. services.msc**

49. Which of the following commands should be used to search for a specific string in a filename?

   ○ **A. sudo**

   ○ **B. grep**

   ○ **C. chmod**

   ○ **D. wget**

50. You are working on a computer that is displaying a black screen. You restart the computer but the operating system will not load. After inquiring with the user, you find out that the operating system was patched the previous evening. Which of the following should you attempt next?

   ○ **A.** Repair the Windows registry.

   ○ **B.** Configure boot options in the BIOS.

   ○ **C.** Reboot into Safe Mode and roll back the updates.

   ○ **D.** Disable Windows services.

51. You are required to replace a desktop power supply. Which of the following tasks should be performed first?

   ○ **A.** Remove your watch and jewelry.

   ○ **B.** Review local regulations for disposal procedures.

   ○ **C.** Read the MSDS.

   ○ **D.** Check for environmental concerns.

52. Your customer has a computer (named comp112) that has been infected by a worm. The worm has propagated to at least 30 other computers on the network. Which of the following tasks should be performed before attempting to remove the worm from the comp112 computer?

   - ○ **A.** Log the user off the system.
   - ○ **B.** Boot the system in Safe Mode.
   - ○ **C.** Run a full virus scan.
   - ○ **D.** Disconnect the network cable from the computer.

53. You are working at a computer and see the following syntax in the beginning of a script:

   `#!/bin/bash`

   What type of system are you working at?

   - ○ **A.** Windows
   - ○ **B.** Linux
   - ○ **C.** iOS
   - ○ **D.** JavaScript

54. Which of the following tools will allow you to change the number of CPU cores that Windows uses?

   - ○ **A.** perfmon
   - ○ **B.** dxdiag
   - ○ **C.** msconfig
   - ○ **D.** taskmgr

55. A user is unable to view office network files while working from home. Which of the following is the most likely cause of the problem?

   - ○ **A.** Outdated anti-malware protection
   - ○ **B.** Inactive VPN
   - ○ **C.** MDM policies
   - ○ **D.** Untrusted software

56. One of your co-workers is attempting to access a file on a share located on a remote computer. The file's share permissions are set to allow the user full control; however, the NTFS permissions allow the user to have read access. Which of the following will be the user's resulting access level for the file?

   - ○ **A.** Read
   - ○ **B.** Write
   - ○ **C.** Modify
   - ○ **D.** Full Control

57. You are installing a 32-bit program on a 64-bit version of Windows. Where does the program get installed to?

   ○ **A.** C:\

   ○ **B.** C:\Program Files

   ○ **C.** C:\Windows

   ○ **D.** C:\Program Files (x86)

58. A home user needs to reinstall Windows on a home computer but cannot find the operating system disc that came with the computer. Which of the following would allow the home user to install the operating system?

   ○ **A.** System Restore

   ○ **B.** Recovery partition

   ○ **C.** Linux rescue boot disc

   ○ **D.** Primary partition

59. You have been tasked with running updates on a Windows computer. Some of the updates go through fine, but another fails. While troubleshooting, you restart the computer and attempt to install the failed update, but it continues to fail. Which of the following should you do first?

   ○ **A.** Analyze the Event Viewer for more information about the failures.

   ○ **B.** Download the failed updates to install it manually.

   ○ **C.** Visit the Microsoft Update website to see if there is an issue with a specific update.

   ○ **D.** Look up the error number associated with the failed update.

60. You are working on a client computer and receive a message that says the trust relationship to the domain has been broken. Which of the following steps should be taken to resolve this problem from the client computer?

   ○ **A.** Update the BIOS using the latest version.

   ○ **B.** Run **chkdsk**.

   ○ **C.** Rejoin the computer to the domain.

   ○ **D.** Reboot the PC as the domain will automatically rebuild the relationship.

61. You are configuring a friend's iPad. He needs to access his work e-mail. In order to do this, you require information from the IT department. Which information should you ask for?

   ○ **A.** Server and gateway

   ○ **B.** IP address and domain

   ○ **C.** IP address and DNS

   ○ **D.** Server and domain

62. Which of the following file formats does Android use for application installation?

    ○ **A.** .api

    ○ **B.** .exe

    ○ **C.** .ipa

    ○ **D.** .apk

    ○ **E.** .sdk

63. A co-worker has asked for a solution that will prevent file corruption by ensuring a graceful shutdown in the case of a power outage. The user would like at least one hour of uptime if the power goes out. Which of the following should you recommend?

    ○ **A.** Surge protector

    ○ **B.** Power strip

    ○ **C.** Uninterruptible power supply

    ○ **D.** Power distribution unit

64. Which command in Windows can initiate **chkdsk** at boot time?

    ○ **A. convert**

    ○ **B. ipconfig**

    ○ **C. chkntfs**

    ○ **D. netdom**

65. A customer reports to you that a file shared on her computer for another user is not accessible to that third party. The customer says that the third party was given Allow rights for Read and Write access to the file. Which of the following could be a reason as to why the third party cannot access the file?

    ○ **A.** The parent folder has explicit Allow rights set for the third-party user.

    ○ **B.** The parent folder has explicit Deny rights set for the third-party user.

    ○ **C.** The user forgot to share the parent folder and only shared the specific file.

    ○ **D.** The parent folder likely has the archive attribute enabled.

66. Which of the following tools is used to type recovery commands into a Linux box?

    ○ **A.** Backup/Time Machine

    ○ **B.** Shell/Terminal

    ○ **C.** Restore/Snapshot

    ○ **D.** Command/CMD

67. You are part of a security team that is auditing an organization's server room. You find that a USB drive was previously inserted into three of the servers. There were many attempts to log in that were successfully performed using common login information. What should you do to prevent the vulnerability from being exploited again? (Select the two best answers.)

☐ **A.** Remove admin permissions.

☐ **B.** Modify the Autorun settings.

☐ **C.** Install a software-based firewall.

☐ **D.** Disable the Guest account.

☐ **E.** Change default credentials.

☐ **F.** Run operating system security updates.

68. Which Windows command can stop a single process from the command-line?

○ **A. taskkill**

○ **B. shutdown**

○ **C. tasklist**

○ **D. del**

69. In a SOHO wireless network, which of the following prevents unauthorized users from accessing confidential data?

○ **A.** Enabling MAC filtering

○ **B.** Changing the SSID name

○ **C.** Setting encryption

○ **D.** Reducing broadcast power

70. Which Control Panel utility is best used to remove a Windows application?

○ **A.** Disk Cleanup

○ **B.** Administrative Tools

○ **C.** Folder Options

○ **D.** Programs and Features

71. You receive a tech support call from a user on your corporate network about an Internet connection that is not working. You analyze the system and find out that the user's system has a valid IP address, can connect to network shares, and can view local intranet pages in her web browser. However, when you attempt to access a public website, the connection times out. Which of the following should you investigate next?

○ **A.** Proxy settings

○ **B.** IPv6 settings

○ **C.** Hosts file

○ **D.** DNS server

72. You have been tasked with setting up an AP in a small office that is in the middle of a crowded building. What should you do to increase the security of the wireless network? (Select the two best answers.)

    ☐ **A.** Configure WPA encryption.

    ☐ **B.** Disable the DHCP server.

    ☐ **C.** Reduce the transmit power.

    ☐ **D.** Reduce channel availability.

    ☐ **E.** Enable QoS management.

    ☐ **F.** Disable the SSID broadcast.

73. A computer has been infected with multiple viruses and spyware. Which of the following tasks should be performed before removing this malware?

    ○ **A.** Disable System Restore.

    ○ **B.** Disable network cards.

    ○ **C.** Run Windows Update.

    ○ **D.** Run the **chkdsk /R** command.

74. One of your customers has set up a perimeter firewall and has implemented up-to-date AV software. She asks you what else she can do to improve security. Which of the following will have the greatest impact on her network security? (Select the two best answers.)

    ☐ **A.** Conduct a daily security audit.

    ☐ **B.** Use strong passwords.

    ☐ **C.** Install additional antivirus software.

    ☐ **D.** Assign security rights based on job roles.

    ☐ **E.** Disable screensavers.

75. Which of the following statements describe how to demonstrate professionalism when dealing with a customer? (Select the three best answers.)

    ☐ **A.** Avoid distractions.

    ☐ **B.** Retain a chain of custody.

    ☐ **C.** Avoid being judgmental.

    ☐ **D.** Leave documentation to the customer.

    ☐ **E.** Meet expectations that the customer sets for you.

76. You previously installed a new application for a customer, adding three new services. Today, the customer informs you that the application will not start. You find out that one of the three new services has failed to start and manual attempts

to start it fail. Where should you look next for information? (Select the two best answers.)

- ☐ **A.** Registry
- ☐ **B.** Event Viewer
- ☐ **C.** %systemroot%\System32\Drivers
- ☐ **D.** Log files for the new application
- ☐ **E.** Task Manager

77. Your organization has hired a new IT firm to manage its switches and routers. The IT firm is out of state and will need to be able to remotely access the devices. Which of the following should be implemented to provide secure access from the IT firm to the switches and routers?

- ○ **A.** RDP
- ○ **B.** Telnet
- ○ **C.** SSH
- ○ **D.** VNC

78. Which of the following is the best way to maintain data security for a mobile device that has been lost or stolen?

- ○ **A.** Passcode lock
- ○ **B.** GPS
- ○ **C.** Remote wipe
- ○ **D.** Login attempt restrictions

79. Look at the following syntax:

```
net use Z: \\servername\sharename
```

Which of the following file types would you expect that syntax to be located in?

- ○ **A.** .vbs
- ○ **B.** .bat
- ○ **C.** .js
- ○ **D.** .py

80. One of your customers connected a tablet computer to her personal mobile hotspot device for Internet access to be used in a public location. The device running the hotspot shows that there are two connections instead of just one. Which of the following actions can she perform to prevent this unauthorized access to the device *immediately*? (Select the two best answers.)

- ☐ **A.** Access the intruder's device and shut it down.
- ☐ **B.** Add the intruding device to a blocked access list.
- ☐ **C.** Set up a Wi-Fi analyzer to identify the intruding device.
- ☐ **D.** Change the SSID to a different broadcast name.
- ☐ **E.** Shut down the device until the intruder is no longer in the area.

Answers at a Glance

1. C	**35.** B	**69.** C
2. B	**36.** C	**70.** D
3. B	**37.** A, E	**71.** A
4. C	**38.** A	**72.** C, F
5. C	**39.** B	**73.** A
6. C	**40.** A, B, D	**74.** B, D
7. B	**41.** D	**75.** A, C, E
8. D, E	**42.** B	**76.** B, D
9. A	**43.** D	**77.** C
10. B	**44.** C	**78.** C
11. B	**45.** A	**79.** B
12. C	**46.** C, H	**80.** B, D
13. B	**47.** C	
14. A	**48.** C	
15. C	**49.** B	
16. B	**50.** C	
17. A	**51.** A	
18. C	**52.** D	
19. D	**53.** D	
20. A	**54.** C	
21. F	**55.** B	
22. B, D	**56.** A	
23. C	**57.** D	
24. B, C	**58.** B	
25. A	**59.** D	
26. C	**60.** C	
27. C	**61.** D	
28. B, C	**62.** D	
29. C	**63.** C	
30. C	**64.** C	
31. D	**65.** B	
32. A	**66.** B	
33. C	**67.** B, D	
34. D	**68.** A	

Answer Explanations

1. Answer: **C**. **ipconfig /all** will display the MAC address of a computer. Whereas a simple **ipconfig** will show the IP address, subnet mask, and gateway address, an **ipconfig /all** gives you more information: the MAC address (called the physical address), the DNS server IP address, whether or not DHCP is enabled, and additional information. See Chapter 25, "Microsoft Command-Line Tools," for more information.

   Incorrect answers: **ping** is used to test whether other computers are available on the network. **netstat** displays all the network sessions to remote computers. **ipconfig /renew** is used with **/release** to reissue DHCP-obtained IP addresses.

2. Answer: **B**. To perform a network installation, a network adapter in the target computer must be PXE-compliant. Also, there must be some type of server acting as a repository for the Windows installation files. See Chapter 24, "Operating System Installation," for more information.

   Incorrect answers: PCIe is an expansion bus. The network adapter will make use of this expansion bus if it is an actual network interface card (NIC) or if it is embedded in the motherboard. BitLocker is a full drive encryption feature included with select editions of Windows. Multiboot technology means that the computer can boot to two or more operating systems.

3. Answer: **B**. **dir** is used to list the contents of a directory in the Command Prompt. You might also use the **tree** command to show the tree of directories. See Chapter 25, "Microsoft Command Line Tools," for more information.

   Incorrect answers: **cd** is short for change directory and is used to navigate. **ping** is used to verify if another computer is available on the network. **ver** shows the version number of the Windows operating system (though **winver** gives more information in a graphical format).

4. Answer: **C**. Every company should have a patching policy and a plan for how to implement patches for security fixes. The policy will dictate what a technician should do in the event of a published security fix. By patching the laptop, you decrease the chances of exploitation. See Chapter 27, "Microsoft Operating System Features and Tools, Part 2," for more information.

   Incorrect answers: Hard drive encryption and user training are also excellent ideas, but they won't necessarily help with this particular security flaw. Screen locks can help to deter a user who would attempt to use another user's computer, but again, they have little to do with the new security flaw.

5. Answer: **C**. You would want to get an enterprise license. This allows multiple users to install the software on their systems, and each can accept the end-user licensing agreement (EULA) individually. See Chapter 41, "Incident Response, Communication, and Professionalism," for more information.

   Incorrect answers: The terms "seat" and "commercial" licensing might be used for other types of licenses, but generally, the term "enterprise" is widely used when there are many end user licenses required (for example, when you are dealing with Microsoft operating system and Office software). An open source license doesn't require a purchase. It can be downloaded and freely modified, based on the rules of the open source licensing agreement.

6. Answer: **C**. The most common issue when implementing bring your own device (BYOD) as a policy to your organization is the possibility that malware from someone's smartphone, tablet, or laptop could be introduced to the network and spread to other systems. So, every BYOD device needs to be equipped with anti-malware software and kept up to date. Also, it would be wise to remotely administer these devices with a mobile device management (MDM) solution so that anti-malware updates can be streamed from a central source. See Chapter 34, "Mobile Device Security," for more information.

Incorrect answers: If you implement the system correctly, encryption of company-owned data can be the same across the board, and should be. Devices in general will probably become more secure because they are initiated into a corporate BYOD network, so the level of phishing attacks should be the same or be reduced. DHCP failures should not increase unless your IP scope (range of IP addresses) can't handle the additional devices on the network. As always, you should consult your network documentation and see if your DHCP server's IP scope can handle all the clients that you plan to introduce onto the network.

7. Answer: **B**. The most likely reason for this is that domain-level group policies have been implemented by the administrator. This is by design so that end users cannot enable screensavers. This cannot be changed by the end user. See Chapter 31, "Physical and Logical Security," for more information.

Incorrect answers: As mentioned, these domain-level group policies are by design; they are not incorrect policies, although it is possible to implement a similar security feature with the local computer policy of a system. Antivirus policies that are instituted at the domain level would affect the antivirus software of a group of systems on the network but should not affect Windows settings. A corrupted registry could cause problems with the logon, but what is happening in the scenario is a specific setting designed to secure the workstations on the domain.

8. Answers: **D** and **E**. PowerShell—and the PowerShell Integrated Scripting Environment (ISE)—is an advanced command line in Windows that goes beyond the Command Prompt. It is designed for administrators so that they can run scripts, batch commands, and snippets, and save the work as .ps1 files (by default). The command **$PSVersionTable** will tell you the version of PowerShell, Windows version, and more. The "PS" in the command stands for "PowerShell"! See Chapter 42, "Basic Scripting and Remote Access Technologies," for more information.

Incorrect answers: Compatibility mode is a mode in Windows that allows you to run older programs within newer versions of Windows. OneDrive is Microsoft's cloud service. The Windows Firewall is the built-in software-based firewall that blocks unwanted intrusion.

9. Answer: **A**. Use the **gpresult** command; this allows you to view the results of the Microsoft Group Policy configuration and print it to various file formats if you wish. See Chapter 25, "Microsoft Command-Line Tools," for more information.

Incorrect answers: **gpupdate** takes care of updating settings on a computer regarding the computer policy configuration. **gpedit.msc** opens the Local Group Policy Editor window. **secpol.msc** opens the Local Security Policy window.

10. Answer: **B**. The **defrag.exe** utility (which is the Disk Defragmenter, otherwise known as Optimize Drives) can be automatically added to the Task Scheduler in Windows in an effort to improve hard disk performance. See Chapter 27, "Microsoft Operating System Features and Tools, Part 2," for more information.

   Incorrect answers: **cleanmgr.exe** is the Disk Cleanup program. **diskpart** is the text-based Command Prompt version of the Disk Administrator utility. **chkdsk** is short for check disk, another text-based Command Prompt utility used to check whether the drive is healthy. Any programs (executables) can be added to the Task Scheduler. However, the more programs you add (and the more often they run), the more resources your system will use, so make sure you use the Task Scheduler sparingly, and make sure that the **defrag** option is not run too often; that will use a lot of resources and could damage the drive if run too much.

11. Answer: **B**. The maximum amount of RAM that any 32-bit operating system can use is 4 GB, because 32-bit CPUs can only address 4 GB of RAM. That's why the bulk of the systems that you will work with will be 64-bit. See Chapter 23, "Operating System Types and Windows Versions," for more information.

   Incorrect answers: "No limit" is not a possibility when it comes to a computer's RAM at this time. To have, and use, more than 4 GB, a 64-bit CPU, and a 64-bit version of Windows would be required. 32 GB is common for workstations as of the writing of this book (2019), but the amount of RAM that computers can use is always on the rise! 256 TB is the typical maximum amount of RAM that a 64-bit system can address, though we rarely come anywhere close to that.

12. Answer: **C**. The screen lock and login time restrictions are your best bet. This way, the computer will look after 5 minutes, even if the user forgets to lock it manually (with a quick Windows+L on the keyboard). Set the login restriction hours within the system or on the domain so that no one can log in after a certain time (such as 5 PM). See Chapter 33, "Windows Security Settings and Best Practices," for more information.

   Incorrect answers: Every system should have a password, but by default, that is only needed when the computer is first turned on or if the person logs off and logs back on. To avoid logging off and losing work, use the screen lock option. That will require the password when the user comes back to the computer. A strong password is important but does not meet the requirements when it comes to the person leaving the workstation frequently and the issue of not turning off the computer. A screensaver is not enough because this does not necessarily require a password. The screen lock is a much more secure method in general.

13. Answer: **B**. The incident response technician should secure the workstation in a limited-access storage facility until the matter is sorted out. A company can be liable for what its employees download, so the workstation should be securely stored and not disturbed until the matter has been investigated thoroughly. The incident response technician should also contact the network administrator (or network security administrator) and inform him or her that the user was able to download a BitTorrent client and figure out a way to block the usage of those. See Chapter 41, "Incident Response, Communication and Professionalism," for more information.

Incorrect answers: Because there are legal ramifications (for the user and for the company), the incident response tech should not delete anything and should store the computer securely for the time being. At some point, the tech will probably be called upon to image the drive, from which investigation can then be carried out. Reprimanding the user is up to the manager, but applying a content filter would probably be done for the entire network, not just that individual user's profile. The tech should definitely document the incident—that is of utmost importance—but the tech should not purge the downloaded materials. Instead, quarantine the computer in a safe location until the investigation is complete. If the user was working with a BitTorrent client, there is the chance that the user was performing other illegal acts, so the computer should be thoroughly analyzed, and the hard drive should be stored indefinitely in a secure place for future reference.

14. Answer: **A**. Before actually giving access to a smartphone (or any other BYOD device) to the computer network, make sure that it has not been rooted or jail-broken. When this is done to a mobile device, it makes it much more susceptible to malicious attack—which could spread to the rest of the network. In fact, the simple fact that the device is rooted could mean that it was already infected, as is often the case. See Chapter 34, "Mobile Device Security," for more information.

Incorrect answers: You have no authority to erase personal data from a user's phone. You might also want to check your policy for GPS and location tracking before giving the phone access. Regardless, if your BYOD environment is being properly controlled by an MDM, you would be able to set whether GPS or location tracking is enabled by way of group policy and disable it remotely within the MDM. Bluetooth might be necessary to the user, so there is no reason to disable it unless your organization's policy expressly forbids it.

15. Answer: **C**. It is likely that the Windows Update service stopped. It can be restarted (along with RPC which it is dependent on) within the Services console window in Computer Management (or **Run > services.msc**), or within the Command Prompt by typing **net start wuauserv**. However, it might be that Windows Update was disabled on purpose as part of company policy. Always check your organization's policies and procedures first before starting services. See Chapter 34, "Mobile Device Security," for more information. See Chapter 27, "Microsoft Operating System Features and Tools, Part 2," for more information.

Incorrect answers: Rebooting the computer will most likely result in the same issue later on when Windows Update needs to update the OS. There are no device drivers that will affect the Windows Update service. Rebuilding the user profile is also not necessary here; plus, it is a lengthy process, and definitely not a quick solution.

16. Answer **B**. Wi-Fi Protected Setup (WPS) is a standard used by many router manufacturers to make connecting to a wireless network easier for the user. It usually consists of an 8- to 10-digit PIN and is located on the bottom of the router. It can also be viewed within the router's firmware. There have been several problems with WPS and most manufacturers recommend that you disable it within the firmware. See Chapter 35, "Data Destruction and SOHO Security," for more information.

Incorrect answers: Port forwarding forwards an external network port to an internal IP address and port. Wireless encryption is a method of rearranging wirelessly transferred data so that it is hard to decode. Examples include WPA and WPA2. Port triggering enables you to specify outgoing ports that your computer uses for special applications; their corresponding inbound ports will be opened automatically when the sessions are established.

17. Answer: **A**. All networking racks should be grounded, either to grounding bars, an I-beam in the ceiling, or other methods of grounding. This should be done before installing any equipment to the racks in order to prevent any damage from electrostatic discharge (ESD). See Chapter 40, "Safety Procedures and Environmental Controls," for more information.

Incorrect answers: A dehumidifier would make the problem worse by removing additional humidity from the air. An ESD strap will provide some protection to the devices while you work on them but it won't help once you disconnect. Fire suppression systems are important but they won't protect against ESD.

18. Answer: **C**. Single sign-on (SSO) is when a user account's username and password can be used to gain access to multiple applications, systems, or networks (instead of the user having to memorize multiple passwords). SSO is often used within a federated identity management system. See Chapter 33, "Windows Security Settings and Best Practices," for more information.

Incorrect answers: Propagation and inheritance deal with NTFS permissions. By default, child objects (such as subfolders) inherit their NTFS permissions from the parent folder—conversely, the parent folder propagates those permissions to the child folder. MFA stands for multifactor authentication; for example, when a user is required to log on with two types of identification such as a password and a fingerprint.

19. Answer: **D**. You should tell Jason to make sure he is using his smart card. In a multifactor authentication system, you might have a combination of a physical smart card requiring that a personal identification number (PIN) be typed, and then the password. So, you want to make sure that users are swiping (or inserting) their smart card before entering the PIN code. Of course, all this depends on the type of authentication (or MFA) system that is in place. In this scenario, and with the answers listed, verification of the user's smart card is the best answer. See Chapter 31, "Physical and Logical Security," for more information.

Incorrect answers: The user probably hasn't gotten to the authentication stage where the password needs to be entered, but regardless, it is not a good idea to suggest entering all past passwords. Rebooting the computer can fix many problems, but in situations such as these it will simply result in the same issue. The network connection shouldn't play into the PIN requirement.

20. Answer: **A**. Surge suppressors (otherwise known as surge protectors) safeguard the equipment that is connected to them by directing surges to the path of least resistance. Electrical resistance is the measure of difficulty to pass an electric current through a conductor and is measured in Ohms (Ω). It will usually mean redirecting the current to ground. So, the metal-oxide varistor (MOV) within the surge suppressor will normally redirect to the ground wire of the AC circuit because there is no resistance on that wire. See Chapter 40, "Safety Procedures and Environmental Controls," for more information.

Incorrect answers: Electrical conductance deals with current and how easily it flows; it is the inverse quantity of resistance. Inductance deals with changes in current flowing through a circuit. The path of highest voltage is just that—for example, the hot wire of an AC circuit (120 V). You would not want a surge to be redirected to high-voltage areas, and you should always redirect surges and spikes to the ground.

21. Answer: **F**. Inheritance is when a file or folder receives its NTFS permissions from the parent folder. It is the default setting of the Advanced configuration dialog box within the Security tab of a file or folder. In Windows, it is shown as a button that can enable or disable inheritance (also described as "Include inheritable permissions from this object's parent" in older versions of Windows). See Chapter 33, "Windows Security Settings and Best Practices," for more information.

    Incorrect answers: This is different from permission propagation in that propagation is when a parent folder forces the permissions to the subfolder. It can be initiated by the user, is a separate configuration, and is not necessarily configured to work by default. SSO is a type of authentication method where a single username/password combination (or other single authentication scheme) is used to gain access to multiple different resources. Client-side virtualization is when a client operating system (such as Windows 10) is run in a virtual machine. The virtual software applications that house VMs have their own set of requirements, as do the VMs themselves. For example, Windows running within a VM will not require as many resources as Windows running on a physical computer in a standard installation. Proxy settings are Internet connectivity settings that are set up on a computer running an OS such as Windows. The proxy setting is usually an IP address of a special computer on the network that acts as a go-between for the client computer and the Internet. It stores web information so that the client computer can gain access to the information faster while conserving Internet bandwidth. A recovery image is an image file that can recover an operating system. It is created by the manufacturer or by the user as a form of preventive maintenance in the event of a system crash and can be saved to an optical disc, to a USB flash drive, or to a special partition on the hard drive.

22. Answers: **B** and **D**. One-time password (OPT) tokens are usually implemented as hardware-based tokens that a person carries with them. The passcode changes periodically (for instance, every 60 seconds). A privacy filter is a filter placed in front of a monitor to reduce the viewing angle and make it more difficult for shoulder surfers (social engineers) to discern information from the screen. Another example is an RSA token. An RSA token can be a physical device, either located within a smart card or a key fob. This is intelligent technology that communicates with the security system, transferring information such as identification, dynamic passcodes, and more, allowing for a more secure authentication method. See Chapter 31, "Physical and Logical Security," for more information.

    Incorrect answers: Directory permissions are the rights granted to users within Windows, allowing them (or denying them) access to files, folders, printers, and other resources. The principle of least privilege is a technical term that states that a person should only have access to what is absolutely necessary; the concept "need to know" is part of this principle.

23. Answer: **C**. A physical network diagram will show switches and their individual ports (among other things.) This documentation is designed to help describe where computers and other networking equipment should connect, on a port to port basis. See Chapter 39, "Documentation, Change Management, and Disaster Recovery," for more information.

Incorrect answers: A logical topology diagram is a network diagram also, but it usually shows things on more of a high level; for example, the IP addresses used by a LAN and what device that group of computers connects to. A process diagram is one that shows a step-by-step procedure, or troubleshooting process. A fiber backbone diagram is one that shows high-speed connections, often from one network to another. It wouldn't be required for the upgrade that concerns switch ports, which most likely implies standard 1-Gbps switches.

24. Answers: **B** and **C**. You should implement a multifactor authentication system (such as one that uses usernames/passwords and also a smart card). You should also educate end users as to company policies regarding the usage and storage of files and databases that can include passwords and personally identifiable information (PII). See Chapter 31, "Physical and Logical Security," for more information.

Incorrect answers: The strength of the password was not the problem here. The organization might have already instituted a policy that requires complex passwords; it's the password file or database that was leaked (most likely by an employee, possibly a malicious insider). But strong passwords are nonetheless important. File encryption is also a good idea, but it won't help with authentication strength. Restricting user permissions is important, too, but if the password list that was leaked includes administrator passwords, well then, game over. You would need to implement an organization-wide password reset (and right away).

25. Answer: **A**. Make sure the user is not using a proxy server within the browser before attempting anything else. A proxy address (whether added by malware or by the user himself) can redirect the browser to unwanted websites (often malicious in nature). See Chapter 29, "Windows Networking and Application Installation," for more information.

Incorrect answers: Internet shortcuts that were added without the user's knowledge could also be a culprit, so these should be checked and the browser should also be cleared of cookies and cache if necessary. But check that proxy setting first!

26. Answer: **C**. Of the listed answers, driver detection has undergone the most significant changes from Windows 7 to Windows 10, and has simplified the OS installation process. This is usually the case when it comes to new versions of an OS—they can "see" new hardware better. See Chapter 23, "Operating System Types and Windows Versions," for more information on Windows versions.

Incorrect answers: The Metro interface was incorporated into Windows 8 and 8.1, but was removed for Windows 10. User Account Control (UAC) has been around since before Windows 7, but has worked essentially the same way over the years, plus it doesn't play into the installation process. Preboot Execution Environment (PXE) installation means that you are installing an OS over the network. PXE is something that a network adapter must be compliant with to do this; it is outside of the Windows install process.

27. Answer: **C**. iTunes is used with Apple iOS devices to synchronize them with a computer, upgrade them, or restore them to factory defaults. See Chapter 30, "Linux and macOS Tools," and Chapter 4, "Smartphones, Tablets and Other Mobile Devices, Part 1," for more information.

    Incorrect answers: Safari is the iOS web browser. iMac is Apple's desktop/laptop computer. Bluetooth is a way of transmitting data wirelessly between devices and smartphones or PCs. Apple iOS devices generally synchronize to computers via USB or Wi-Fi.

28. Answers: **B** and **C**. A hard drive shredder or drill can be used to physically tear the drive into multiple pieces or to make holes in the platters of a hard drive, thus making it inoperable. It can then be disposed of according to municipal guide-lines. It is one of several types of ways to physically destroy a hard drive and is only performed when the drive has met the end of its lifecycle, is not going to be recycled within the organization, and is to be disposed of. However, shredding (or pulverizing) is the best way to do this; vendors offer services to perform this work and provide a certificate of destruction when complete. See Chapter 35, "Data Destruction and SOHO Security," for more information.

    Incorrect answers: Disabling ports is done on a firewall or SOHO router to block access into (or out of) the network. A low-level format is a type of formatting pro-cedure done in the UEFI/BIOS of a system (on older drives), through the use of special removable media, or is done at the manufacturer. It removes more data than a standard operating system format but does not destroy the drive (though it can cause damage to particular sectors if performed too often). Many techni-cians also refer to data wiping as a method of low-level formatting.

29. Answer: **C**. Use the Advanced tab to enable TLS 1.2 (and other security proto-cols) within Internet Explorer. See Chapter 28, "Windows Control Panel Utilities," for more information.

    Incorrect answers: This was a bit of a trick question. At first glance, you would think that TLS 1.2 is a *security* feature; and while it is, the Security tab deals more with zone security, not specific protocol-based security options. The Privacy tab deals with blocking cookies. The Connections tab concerns setting up Internet connections, VPNs, and proxy server connections.

30. Answer: **C**. Windows 10 64-bit installations require 32 GB of hard drive space. 15 GB is not enough for that or for 32-bit installations, which require 16 GB of space. This holds true for physical installations and virtual installations. The vir-tual machine (VM) installation will fail until the VM's hard drive space is increased. In fact, 15 GB is not enough for Windows 8 or Windows 7 either. See Chapter 23, "Operating System Types and Windows Versions," for more information.

    Incorrect answers: Windows 10 64-bit requires a 1-GHz CPU, 2 GB of RAM, and at least 800×600 resolution, so the rest of the answers are incorrect because they *do* meet the minimum requirements.

31. Answer: **D**. You should recommend the Microsoft Domain setup. This means installing a server that acts as a domain controller where all logon authentica-tion is centralized. This way, all access to network shares and print servers is also centralized. A domain controller is a server that is running a version of the Windows Server operating system and has Active Directory Domain Services

running. See Chapter 29, "Windows Networking and Application Installation," for more information.

Incorrect answers: A workgroup is a good choice for networks with 20 computers or less. Once you exceed 20 computers, it becomes wise to configure a domain. The main reason for this is that a single Windows 10/8/7 client computer can handle only 20 connections simultaneously. Storing all your data on one computer for every user to access is fine for networks with 10 to 15 computers. But as you increase your network to 20 computers or more, you are forced to store resources on multiple computers, which can create confusion. Ad hoc means that no one computer is in control; this especially applies to wireless networks and is sufficient for a few systems but definitely not for 25 computers. Star refers to the network topology or how computers are connected. This isn't covered in the A+ objectives but it essentially means that the computers are wired in such a way that all of them physically connect to a central connecting device (such as a switch) or wirelessly connect to a wireless access point. This is easily the most common way that computers connect to the network. While you could recommend this as well, it is basically accepted that this will be the network configuration in the vast majority of scenarios. The question was assessing your understanding of the Windows solution for how the data will be shared.

32. Answer: **A**. Chain of custody is the chronological documentation (written) of evidence pertaining to a computer or other technical device that has prohibited content or has been confiscated. The technician should write (or type) the date, time, and who took custody of the computer next. It's important for the technician to adhere to the chain-of-custody rules when storing the computer or data. It's also important to verify that the chain of custody remains intact, so as to ensure evidence is admissible in legal proceedings. See Chapter 41, "Incident Response, Communication, and Professionalism," for more information.

Incorrect answers: Committing such important facts to memory is not enough; this will not stand up in court as evidence. A "third party" will break the chain of custody. Calling the supervisor is part of first response; it's not part of chain of custody.

33. Answer: **C**. Use the Performance Monitor (**Run > perfmon.exe**) to analyze a device. In this example, you can find out how many bits per second the NIC can transfer—the data transfer rate. You can also use this tool to monitor all of the other devices (objects) on the system and save and report on those findings in a variety of ways. See Chapter 26, "Microsoft Operating System Features and Tools, Part 1," for more information.

Incorrect answers: Device Manager is where you would go to install or uninstall a device, or roll back the driver for that device. Local Security Policy (**Run > secpol.msc**) is where you would go to enable or disable rules (policies) on a Windows client computer. Component Services is used to configure Component Object Model (COM) elements (such as ActiveX controls) and Microsoft Distributed Transaction Coordinator (MSDTC) (for example, working with .NET).

34. Answer: **D**. Most help desks' standard policy is to have their techs research new problems for a couple minutes before escalating them to higher-level techs. Oftentimes this proves to be the right course because the technician is often able to find the answer within two or three minutes. Of course, if you do place

the customer on hold, watch the time (I suggest a timer app), and be sure to get back to that person when that time is up. See Chapter 41, "Incident Response, Communication, and Professionalism," for more information.

Incorrect answers: It's better to tell the customer that you are checking resources than to tell the customer that you have never encountered the problem before because it instills more confidence. If you can't find the answer in two minutes, then inform the customer that you will have to escalate the problem.

35. Answer: **B**. The question mark (?) on the icon or elsewhere in the wireless connection properties will normally indicate an unauthenticated connection, meaning that the user is connecting to an "open" public hotspot; which in turn means that the user did not have to log on, and might not be using any encryption to connect via Wi-Fi. When this is the case, certain web pages and sites may not open. For example, if the user was trying to connect to the company VPN or something similar, the company's infrastructure might see that the smartphone does not have an authenticated connection, and deny access. The same can happen with some websites. See Chapter 32, "Wireless Security, Malware, and Social Engineering," for more information.

Incorrect answers: Data allowance has to do with a cellular connection, not a Wi-Fi connection. In addition, many providers offer "unlimited" data transfer, which really means that you can send and receive x amount of data (for instance, 20 GB) before the connection is throttled down—but again, that is based on cellular connectivity, not Wi-Fi connectivity. Un-rooted is what we want! That is a normally functioning phone. A rooted phone, on the other hand, is one that has been configured to gain root-level access in order to run certain programs and make changes to the phone. However, that shouldn't affect data usage or connectivity (unless the rooting led to a hack). If the SIM card was not activated, then the user would not have been able to call in to the help desk. 3G is a cellular data technology, not Wi-Fi. A user normally can't purchase a smartphone without a data plan, but even if the user could, that plan deals with cellular data, not Wi-Fi connections. As you can see, most of the incorrect answers concern cellular data, but the scenario refers to a Wi-Fi connection.

36. Answer: **C**. In Windows, the Task Manager Users tab will show any currently logged-on users and their status. The Windows 10 Task Manager will show the percentage of resources that are being used by each user. See Chapter 26, "Microsoft Operating System Features and Tools, Part 1," for more information.

Incorrect answers: MSConfig (System Configuration) is used to change boot settings and disable services. Disk Management is used to monitor the status of drives and to work with partitioning/formatting. Administrative Tools is a collection of tools used to configure the OS but it does not offer a quick way to see which users are logged in to the system.

37. Answers: **A** and **E**. Compressed air and a vacuum are common tools used to remove dust and debris from inside a computer. Of course, when you use compressed air, consider doing this outside because the dust and dirt will fly all over the place. Use a vacuum to clean up after you are done. If you do use a vacuum inside the computer, make sure it is an antistatic, computer-ready vacuum, and more importantly, don't touch any of the components inside the system! See Chapter 40, "Safety Procedures and Environmental Controls," for more information.

Incorrect answers: Cotton and alcohol (or a 50/50 mix of alcohol and water) might be used to clean a printer's rubber rollers, the bottom of an ink cartridge (if it is very dirty), or a display. A feather duster would cause electrostatic discharge (ESD) and should be avoided; it is not a good tool for the job. Antibacterial surface cleaner should only be used on the outside of a computer case.

38. Answer: **A**. You should use the System Preparation tool (Sysprep) to remove system-specific identifiers (IDs). Chances are you are cloning a system or running the installations over the network from a single image. By default, that image will have a Security Identifier (SID), which will be copied to each system. That will cause conflicts, which you don't want; therefore, use the Sysprep tool to eliminate the problem, giving different SIDs to each computer. Chances are that you are using Windows Deployment Services (WDS) if you are imaging 100 computers with Windows; it requires Windows Server 2008 or higher. See Chapter 24, "Operating System Installation," for more information.

Incorrect answers: Remote Installation Services (RIS) was used with older versions of Windows Server and is deprecated in favor of WDS. You most likely *are* doing an unattended installation (or installations) and have probably created the answer files already, during which time you would use the Sysprep tool. But just having a single answer file alone (without using Sysprep) would result in all computers receiving the same SID.

39. Answer: **B**. An invalid boot disk error is a common symptom of a problem loading the Windows operating system. It could be caused by removable media inserted into the computer (an optical disc or USB flash drive) that is not bootable. This could be avoided by setting the hard drive to first in the BIOS boot order. Another possible symptom of problems loading the operating system would be if a RAID array was not detected during bootup or during installation of the OS. Either way, the hard drive, or RAID array of hard drives, should be inspected for faulty connections. See Chapter 36, "Troubleshooting Microsoft Windows," for more information.

Incorrect answers: A spontaneous shutdown and restart indicates either a problem with the power supply or the possibility of malware on the system. Note that the question refers to "starting up" Windows; a shutdown or restart can only happen when the system has already booted. WinRE is the Windows Recovery Environment, which includes System Recovery Options such as Startup Repair and System Restore. WinRE is not accessible during a routine bootup of Windows but can be initiated by booting from the Windows DVD or from a special partition on the hard drive or by booting from a USB flash drive. If it won't start, there could be a problem with the DVD, the DVD drive, the boot order, or how it was installed to the partition on the hard drive. If the optical disc fails, it shouldn't stop the startup of Windows because Windows will most likely be located on the hard drive. An emergency repair disk (or disc) should only be booted to in the event that there is a problem with Windows. A failure to boot to an emergency repair disk is not a common symptom of a problem starting Windows, but we might use a recovery disc to fix the problem. REGSVR32 (sometimes misrepresented as REG*SRV*32) is a tool used in the Command Prompt to activate or deactivate ActiveX controls, none of which should stop Windows from booting.

40. Answers: **A**, **B**, and **D**. Malware can have many symptoms. Viruses are especially prevalent in today's society; there are millions of different kinds. Fake security alerts, failure to update Windows, and renamed system files are all possible symptoms of malware—more specifically, symptoms of a virus. See Chapter 37, "Troubleshooting PC Security Issues and Malware Removal," for more information.

Incorrect answers: Windows has a preinstallation environment known as Windows PE or simply WinPE; this is a lightweight version of Windows that is often used to deploy the operating system. It can be booted from optical disc, USB flash drive, over the network via PXE, or by the hard drive. It is an add-on to Windows available with the Windows Automated Installation Kit (WAIK). It can be used to run recovery tools such as Windows RE, and for running drive-cloning utilities. Rogue antivirus programs are not symptoms of malware; they *are* malware! A rogue antivirus program can often be something that appears to be a legitimate when it is not. Or it could be a part of a rogue security software suite, which deceives the user into paying for fake malware protection. User error is not a symptom of malware but it could very well be the cause. If a user surfs to a malicious website or opens an unknown e-mail attachment without verifying the source of the e-mail first, malware could be—and often is—the result. Educate the end user when it comes to screening e-mails and surfing the Web. Show the user how to be responsible when accessing online information.

41. Answer: **D**. It could be that another program (quite possibly malicious) is using the camera on its own without user intervention. So, the first best thing to do is to check the application permissions. For example, in Android a typical navigational path would be **General > Apps & Notifications > App permissions**. From there you will see the Camera app; tap it to find out which applications are using it. Then, you can deselect whichever apps you need to. You might also find a malicious or unwanted program is on the list and enabled for camera usage—if so, it should be removed. See Chapter 38, "Troubleshooting Mobile Operating Systems," for more information.

> **Note**
>
> You can also check for permissions programmatically (via the Android Debug Bridge, ADB) by calling the **ContextCompat.checkSelfPermission(...)** code snippet using an **if** statement. If you are interested in Android development, check out this link:
>
> https://developer.android.com/training/permissions/requesting

Incorrect answers: Updating all applications is a bit premature. You may want to do that at some point though, as long as company policy allows it. OS updates should be checked as well at some point, but not first, because that does not get to the root of the problem. Uninstalling the camera application won't change how other apps can use the camera. You will simply be preventing the user from using the camera. Resetting the phone is one of the last options, but it could be a reality if the smartphone has been compromised, which is a distinct possibility in this scenario. If resetting is necessary, your company might also require a few overwrites of data first.

42. Answer: **B**. The only option that would help the situation would be to run the **chkdsk** command with the **/R** option. **/R** locates bad sectors and recovers readable information, which is the only option listed that might fix the file system corruption (keyword *might*). **/R** implies **/F** as well, which fixes basic errors on the drive. See Chapter 25, "Microsoft Command Line Tools," for more information.

   Incorrect answers: Reloading the OS would wipe all data (on the system partition at least), so it is not recommended. In addition, you wouldn't normally go from NTFS to FAT32; it's recommended to use NTFS. Plus, if the file system was corrupt, a reinstall of the OS (using NTFS again) would fix those issues. Opening the **defrag** utility and running a drive analysis doesn't really change the drive; it simply tells you if the drive is fragmented. Changing the drive from basic to dynamic is done so that you can resize partitions.

43. Answer: **D**. Non-water-based fire extinguishers should be used during an electrical fire. This could be a CO_2-based fire extinguisher such as a Class C extinguisher, a Halotron fire extinguisher, or an FM-200 overhead system. See Chapter 40, "Safety Procedures and Environmental Controls," for more information.

   Incorrect answers: Standard overhead sprinkler systems use water. They should not be present where expensive computer equipment is located (for example, in server rooms). Regular water-based fire extinguishers should not be used. Class B extinguishers are meant for burning gases and liquids, whereas Class C are meant for electrical fire (think "C" for "copper," like the copper inside electrical wiring).

44. Answer: **C**. Attempt to install legacy (older) applications in compatibility mode. Select the older OS that the application was originally written for. See Chapter 28, "Windows Control Panel Utilities," for more information.

   Incorrect answers: It is less likely that updates or the latest service pack (SP) will help in this situation. In fact, Windows 8 and higher don't use service packs, but it is wise to update to Windows 8.1. Service packs are used in Windows 7 and earlier. Security updates probably won't have an effect on this scenario either.

45. Answer: **A**. The most likely cause in this scenario is that there has been unauthorized root access. Whether this was done by the user on purpose or without his knowledge by one of the newly installed apps is still something you need to discover. Unauthorized root access by an app or by a user could cause the phone to perform unwanted actions, which would most likely drain the battery quickly. See Chapter 38, "Troubleshooting Mobile Operating Systems," for more information.

   Incorrect answers: It is unlikely that the battery needs to be replaced seeing as how it is a new phone, but it is something you can investigate after checking if the phone has been rooted. A defective SD card probably won't affect the battery. Weak signal could cause a battery drain (especially if the user is in a basement or other unfavorable wireless location), but short battery life is more likely caused by root access, by powerful apps pulling too much power, or by a bright display that has been configured to not shut off. Slow data speeds are an annoyance, but they're not something that should cause the battery to drain quickly.

46. Answers: **C** and **H**. For the highest level of wireless security, use WPA2 (and AES). For authentication, select multifactor authentication (MFA). Many healthcare providers are required to log on with a username/password and a smart card (or biometric). See Chapter 32, "Wireless Security, Malware, and Social Engineering," for more information.

    Incorrect answers: Out of WEP, WPA, and WPA2, WPA2 is the most secure. WEP is especially vulnerable. TKIP is an outdated example of an encryption protocol; AES is a much better choice. RADIUS and TACACS are example of authentication servers—the scenario mentioned that the company cannot afford a server. It is unknown what the cloud contains; who knows, there is probably an authentication server there (connected to via secure VPN), but it is not something that *you* would implement at the SOHO office. Also, it is more likely that a company would use TACACS+, not the older TACACS. SSO stands for single sign-on, and it quite possibly is already set up in the cloud, as it is very common in the healthcare industry.

47. Answer: **C**. Try adjusting the power settings so that wireless connections will not time out as quickly. This can be done in Windows by accessing **Control Panel > Hardware and Sound > Power Options > Change plan settings > Change advanced power settings** and, in the Power Options dialog box, modifying the Wireless Adapter Settings. See Chapter 28, "Windows Control Panel Utilities," for more information.

    Incorrect answers: If the wireless card was faulty, the customer would never be able to get onto a wireless network, so there is no reason to replace the wireless card. The capacity of the battery will not affect wireless connections. Disabling the screensaver will also not affect the wireless connection; however, you can get to some of the power options necessary to solve the wireless problem indirectly from the screensaver window.

48. Answer: **C**. Use **gpedit.msc** in the Run prompt or the Command Prompt. This will display the Local Group Policy Editor window, where you can make changes to the OS, such as remove the Shut Down button. See Chapter 31, "Physical and Logical Security," for more information.

    Incorrect answers: **shutdown.exe** is used to shut down the computer automatically or modify programmatically how the computer shuts down. **bootrec.exe** is a tool used to repair problems such as an error in the boot sector (fixing this requires the syntax **bootrec /fixboot**). **services.msc** can be executed from the Run prompt; it brings up the Services window, where you can start/stop services.

49. Answer: **B**. **grep** is the Linux command used to search for matching information in a file, files, or filename. See Chapter 30, "Linux and macOS Tools," for more information.

    Incorrect answers: Other Linux commands include **sudo**, which is used to allow a user to execute a command as another user (for example, an administrator); **chmod**, which is used to change the permissions of a file or folder; and **wget**, which retrieves content from web servers (as opposed to the **get** command, which is often used to obtain files from an FTP server).

50. Answer: **C**. Chances are that the update caused an issue with the computer; perhaps the video driver or another driver was updated, resulting in the black screen. Booting into Safe Mode can help to figure out the problem. If Safe Mode displays properly than you can be fairly certain that there is a video driver issue (which can then be rolled back) or some other driver issue. If you aren't sure what was affected, you can roll back the entire update. See Chapter 36, "Troubleshooting Microsoft Windows," for more information.

Incorrect answers: The registry is rarely the first place to go when troubleshooting problems, and definitely not in this case. That is where you go to make advanced configuration changes to the OS. Many times, when you take exams, two answers will look plausible; that's the case here with "Configure boot options in the BIOS." Often, if there is a black screen, it might be accompanied by a message, such as "invalid boot device" or "No OS found." If that is the case, then it could very well be that the BIOS boot priority needs to be changed. However, in the scenario, there is no mention of a message of any sort (it could be that the video card is simply displaying a black screen), but you did get information that there was an update the night before. Disabling Windows services is a possibility, but you would want to boot into Safe Mode first and diagnose the system further before you had a reason to disable any services.

51. Answer: **A**. Remove watches, jewelry, and any other metals when working on a computer so they are out of the way and do not pose any threats while working on the computer. See Chapter 40, "Safety Procedures and Environmental Controls," for more information.

Incorrect answers: You should review local regulations and check for environmental concerns when disposing of hard drives, batteries, and toner cartridges. Read the MSDS (material safety data sheet) when you encounter a fluid spill or other unknown chemical.

52. Answer: **D**. Before you do anything else, disconnect the network cable from comp112. This can help to isolate the problem. You might also decide to disconnect the network cables from any other systems that were infected by this worm. Sometimes, it is easier to do this at the server room. See Chapter 37, "Troubleshooting PC Security Issues and Malware Removal," for more information.

Incorrect answers: After the network cable is disconnected, the computer should be shut down (which will log off the user anyway) and rebooted into Safe Mode. Then the worm should be isolated and quarantined. Finally, a full virus scan should be run. This, of course, is just a quick example; you probably need to do more to resolve this problem on all computers concerned.

53. Answer: **B**. This is a Linux, Unix, or macOS system. When it comes to Linux and Unix and similar systems, a lot of technicians simply refer to them as *nix, meaning anything ending in "nix." Linux uses the Bash shell by default. This is where scripts are run. This default line tells the system the path and how to interpret the upcoming script. See Chapter 42, "Basic Scripting and Remote Access Technologies," for more information.

Incorrect answers: Windows uses the PowerShell. Saved scripts (such as .ps1 files) don't use this type of line to identify the shell interpreter. iOS doesn't use

Bash or Terminal the way that macOS or Linux does. JavaScript is not a system at all; instead, it is a type of scripting language, often used with websites.

54. Answer: **C**. The System Configuration utility (**msconfig**) can be used to change the total number of CPU cores used by Windows. This can be found by going to the **Boot** tab and clicking the **Advanced options** button. From there, checkmark the **Number of processors** checkbox and select the number of CPU cores (or actual number of CPUs if you have more than one). This is usually done to troubleshoot the CPU or Windows; in most cases, Windows will use all CPU cores available to it by default. See Chapter 26, "Microsoft Operating System Features and Tools, Part 1," for more information.

Incorrect answers: The Performance Monitor (**perfmon.exe**) is used to analyze system performance and can view each core in real time, as can the Task Manager (**taskmgr.exe**). The DirectX Diagnostics tool (**dxdiag.exe**) is used to analyze audio and video DirectX components in the system.

55. Answer: **B**. The most likely cause (of the listed answers) is an inactive virtual private network (VPN) connection. If the user did not log in through the VPN, or if the VPN session timed out, then the user will not be able to get access to the files stored at the office LAN. See Chapter 31, "Physical and Logical Security," for more information.

Incorrect answers: Outdated anti-malware protection could possibly allow a virus to get into the system, a symptom of which might be missing or renamed files on the local computer. Mobile device management (MDM) policies are designed to configure or restrict mobile devices. However, we don't know what type of computer the person is using from home, but we can guess it is a laptop, and not a smartphone or tablet. Untrusted software is any application that an organization does not trust, and does not want installed to systems. It's possible that untrusted software could cause the VPN connection to fail, but it is less likely as an indirect cause of the problem.

56. Answer: **A**. The user will have only read access to the file. Remember that the more restrictive permissions take precedence, so in this case, the NTFS "Read" permission level takes effect. See Chapter 33, "Windows Security Settings and Best Practices," for more information.

Incorrect answers: It is possible for the user to get write, modify, or full control access, but only if the NTFS permissions are configured to allow the user to do so. As it stands, the user only has read access.

57. Answer: **D**. The program would be installed to C:\Program Files (x86). This is the default folder for 32-bit programs when installed to a 64-bit version of Windows. This works in the same manner in Windows 7, 8, and 10. See Chapter 23, "Operating System Types and Windows Versions," for more information.

Incorrect answers: 64-bit programs are installed to the C:\Program Files folder. The operating system is installed to C:\Windows. Finally, C:\ is the root of the hard drive. A few system files are placed in the root, but otherwise the OS and applications are installed to folders within the root. x86 is the general term applied to 32-bit computers, whereas x86-64 (or simply x64) is the term applied to 64-bit computers.

58. Answer: **B**. If the computer has a recovery partition, then the reinstallation of Windows can be accomplished from there. This is often a partition that was placed on the hard drive by the computer manufacturer for just this type of scenario. See Chapter 24, "Operating System Installation," for more information.

Incorrect answers: System Restore is an example of Windows functionality that can bring the system back to an earlier point in time but does not reinstall the entire OS. A Linux rescue boot disc might work, but only if a Windows image is available somewhere, so the answer is not specific enough. (You might also use a flash drive with a Windows image.) The primary partition is where Windows is installed *to*. It will not normally contain recovery data or a recovery Windows image.

59. Answer: **D**. The first thing you should do is look up the error number. If an item fails during Windows Update, an error log called WindowsUpdate.log should be written to the %systemroot%; usually C:\Windows. An example of an error code is 0x80243FFF, which is a user interface error. (It might show up in the log without the 0x.) You might also need to access the CBS.log file, which is located in %systemroot%\Logs. See Chapter 27, "Microsoft Operating System Features and Tools, Part 2," for more information.

> ## Note
>
> Here's a link to a list of Windows Update error codes:
>
> https://docs.microsoft.com/en-us/windows/deployment/update/windows-update-error-reference

Incorrect answers: While the Event Viewer can be very handy for analyzing system file, application, and security issues, it is not the first and best place to go when troubleshooting Windows Update errors. The Event Viewer is more generic (problem-wise), whereas the WindowsUpdate.log and CBS.log files are very specific. Downloading the failed update and installing it manually will probably result in the same error. You need to dig deep and find out what the real cause of the problem is. You do want to visit the Microsoft website, but you will most likely be going to https://support.microsoft.com or https://docs.microsoft.com (or both); there is no Microsoft Update website per se (as of the writing of this book).

60. Answer: **C**. You must rejoin the computer to the domain. This can be done by navigating to the **Computer Name** tab of the System Properties dialog box, which is accessed from the **Advanced settings** link from the System window or by executing **systempropertiescomputername.exe** at the Run prompt. You might also use the **netdom** command in the Command Prompt if you have Remote Server Administration Tools (RSAT) installed to the Windows client or are working directly on a Windows server. See Chapter 29, "Windows Networking and Application Installation," for more information.

Incorrect answers: Updating the BIOS to the latest version will help with any firmware issues but won't have any effect on trust relationships within Windows. Running **chkdsk** will check for errors on the hard drive. Rebooting the PC will not automatically rebuild the relationship; you must manually rejoin the computer to the domain.

61. Answer: **D**. Your friend might have an address such as thomasR@abc-company.com. To enable iPad access to this e-mail account, you'll need the type of server that handles e-mail (be it SMTP, POP3, IMAP, or an Exchange server) and the domain name that the server resides on. Often, this will be the same domain name as the e-mail address, but not always. An example of an SMTP mail server might be mail.abc-company.com. A POP3 server might be pop.abc-company.com. See Chapter 38, "Troubleshooting Mobile Operating Systems," for more information.

Incorrect answers: IP addresses aren't necessary when configuring an e-mail account within an iPad, an Android device, a PC, or any computer, really. This is because the e-mail account software will automatically attempt to resolve the mail server name to the IP address, in the same manner a web browser does when you type in a web address. The gateway address and DNS server are only necessary when attempting to connect a device to the Internet. This most likely won't be an issue with an iPad, but it can be configured in the networking settings if necessary.

62. Answer: **D**. Android uses the extension .apk for application installations and upgrades. It loosely stands for Android application package. See Chapter 23, "Operating System Types and Windows Versions," for more information.

Incorrect answers: An API is an application program interface, which the .apk would go through; it's not normally used as an extension. .exe is short for executable, the most commonly used application extension in Windows. .ipa is an iOS application archive file. An SDK is a software development kit. You would use this, for example, if you wanted to program or analyze an Android device or if you wanted to build applications for Windows. SDK is not normally used as a file extension, although you might see it used with less common computer-aided drafting software.

63. Answer: **C**. You should recommend an uninterruptible power supply (UPS). This meets both requirements: 1. That the system gracefully shuts down in the case of a power outage, which protects files from corruption; and 2. Can provide an hour of uptime (though that will require a fairly powerful UPS of at least 1500 VA). See Chapter 40, "Safety Procedures and Environmental Controls," for more information.

Incorrect answers: A surge protector and power strip don't meet either of the two requirements. A power strip simply allows for more outlets, while a surge protector can help protect a computer with surges or spikes. A power distribution unit (PDU) is a device with multiple outlets that can come in many forms including as a strip; however, it is much more than a power strip in that it can be monitored and controlled. PDUs are often used in data centers and server rooms and are also known as main distribution units (MDUs).

64. Answer: **C**. **chkntfs** is the command utility that can be used to initiate **chkdsk** at bootup. For example, **chkntfs /d** will check drives at boot time. If a drive is judged to be "dirty," **chkdsk** is run automatically on that drive. A "dirty" drive is one that causes a system hang or has open files. For more information on **chkntfs**, type **chkntfs /?**. See Chapter 25, "Microsoft Command Line Tools," for more information.

Incorrect answers: **convert** enables a partition change from FAT32 to NTFS without losing data. **ipconfig** is used to analyze the configuration of a network adapter. **netdom** enables administrators to manage active directory domains and trust relationships from the Command Prompt. For example, it could be used to join a Windows 7 computer to a domain. It is used primarily on Windows Server operating systems.

65. Answer: **B**. The best answer listed is that the parent folder has explicit Deny rights set for the third-party user. If this is the case, then by default, that permission will *propagate* to any subfolders and files within the parent. This can also be expressed as the default action for a subfolder (also known as a child folder) to *inherit* its permissions from the parent. Basically, you should remember two things: one, that a folder inherits its permissions from the parent; and two, that Deny rights will always override Allow rights. See Chapter 33, "Windows Security Settings and Best Practices," for more information.

Incorrect answers: If the folder was set with Allow rights, the third party should be able to access the data. If the user forgot to share the folder, the third party would not be able access the data. However, it's the second part of that answer that is impossible because you can't share a specific file; you can only share folders. The archive attribute would simply create a backup copy of a file or folder. Permissions questions can be some of the toughest on the A+ exam, but if you remember a few basic rules (such as the ones mentioned here), you should survive them!

66. Answer: **B**. The most common Linux shell program is the Terminal utility, which uses the Bash shell. (This is also available in macOS.) This utility allows the user to enter commands of all types—including recovery commands—to be executed by Linux. See Chapter 30, "Linux and macOS Tools," for more information.

Incorrect answers: The equivalent of the Terminal utility in Windows is the Command Prompt, often referred to as CMD or cmd because it can be opened with the **cmd.exe** executable. Backup and restoration programs, such as macOS's Time Machine, Windows System Restore, and so on, cannot have recovery commands typed into them. You require some kind of text interface to do so.

67. Answers: **B** and **D**. Modify the Autorun settings and disable the Guest account. Modify AutoPlay/Autorun by disabling it in the Group Policy Editor. (Also, the use of USB drives and other removable media should be disabled in the UEFI/BIOS.) Disable the Guest account within Local Users and Groups (or within Active Directory Users and Computers if on a domain). The problem with the Guest account is that it has no password by default. It could be used to attempt privilege escalation. See Chapter 33, "Windows Security Settings and Best Practices," for more information.

Incorrect answers: Removing admin permissions is somewhat vague. An administrative account has administrative permissions for a reason: so that the admin can access the server. Removing a user from the Administrators group would result in a standard user account, which is great from a principle of least privilege perspective, but that person could no longer log in to the server, making it pointless. A software-based firewall would not have prevented this exploit because the user was local (behind the firewall) using a USB stick. You could change the default credentials of the Guest account, but it is better to either give it a strong password (if you have to use it), or better yet, disable the account altogether.

OS security updates should be run on a regular basis, but this is an issue that goes beyond updates.

68. Answer: **A**. **taskkill** is the command in Windows that can stop a single process from the command line. See Chapter 25, "Microsoft Command Line Tools," for more information.

Incorrect answers: **shutdown** is a command used to shut down the entire system either right away or at a designated time. **tasklist** provides a list of all processes running in the command line. It associates each process with an ID. This is integral when running the **taskkill** command—you need to know the executable or the process ID (PID) of the task you want to stop. **del** is short for the **delete** command, which is used to delete files.

69. Answer: **C**. Encryption (for example, WPA2 with AES) will prevent unauthorized users from accessing confidential data that is transmitted over the wireless network. One of the best ways to protect confidentiality of data in general is through encryption. Use the highest level of encryption possible on a SOHO wireless network to eliminate this threat. See Chapter 35, "Data Destruction and SOHO Security," for more information.

Incorrect answers: Enabling MAC filtering looks like a good answer. However, this is used to stop unauthorized computers from accessing the wireless network. While a good idea, it does nothing to protect the actual data itself. Plus, a good hacker can get past MAC filtering. If that happens, encryption is going to be the savior anyway. While anything is hackable, the AES cipher will require a powerful computer and a long time to break. Changing the SSID name only modifies the name of the wireless network. However, by default, the SSID is broadcast from most SOHO routers, which is easily found by various wireless scanning software packages. Reducing the broadcast power is a smart idea as well, but this simply reduces the distance the SOHO router sends its wireless signal. If the hacker is within this range, they will have access to the network. The key here is confidential. To protect confidentiality, use encryption.

70. Answer: **D**. Programs and Features is the place to go in the Control Panel (CP) to remove an application in Windows. You can also open this by entering **appwiz.cpl** in the Command Prompt. See Chapter 28, "Windows Control Panel Utilities," for more information.

Incorrect answers: Disk Cleanup is used to remove temporary files; it's not used to remove applications. Administrative Tools is a group of tools, such as Computer Management and the Task Scheduler. Folder Options is where you can go to change how folders are displayed.

71. Answer: **A**. Check the proxy server settings in the browser. Many large networks use a proxy server to facilitate the caching of web pages—often this is for external, or *public*, websites only. It could be that the proxy server was not configured properly or wasn't configured at all. In Internet Explorer, the proxy server settings can be accessed by going to the Internet Properties dialog box (either from the browser menu bar or from **Control Panel > Internet Options**), navigating to **Connections > LAN settings**, and configuring the bottom half of the window where it says Proxy server. It is done in a similar fashion in other browsers. See Chapter 29, "Windows Networking and Application Installation," for more information.

Incorrect answers: You shouldn't have to modify the IPv6 settings because the question says the system has a valid IP address. The hosts file is an older text file used to statically resolve hostnames to IP addresses. Although this file still exists in some versions of Windows, it is rarely used, except for malicious purposes. If it was used for malicious purposes, the browser probably wouldn't be able to connect to *any* websites, be they external or internal. A DNS server performs domain name to IP address resolutions; if other pages are working on the intranet, then chances are that the DNS server is not the issue.

72. Answers: **C** and **F**. Of the listed answers, you should reduce the transmitting power of the AP and disable the SSID broadcast. Reducing the power prevents signal bleed to other offices; usually this can be set to "low" or something similar. Disabling the SSID or network name of the AP makes it so a typical user cannot scan for and locate the wireless network. Other smart ideas are to put a strong password on the admin account, use WPA2/AES, implement MAC filtering, and disable WPS. See Chapter 35, "Data Destruction and SOHO Security," for more information.

Incorrect answers: WPA is generally avoided as WPA2 is better. Disabling the DHCP server won't do much for security, but it will hamper availability, because most end users' computers will obtain IP addresses automatically. Most SOHO routers can modify the channel width, but can't reduce the channel *availability*. Users can either connect or not. When enabled, Quality of Service (QoS) can help to prioritize traffic from specific computers or applications.

73. Answer: **A**. For proper quarantining and removal of malware, you will usually have to disable System Restore first because it can get in the way of the anti-malware scanning and removal processes. See Chapter 37, "Troubleshooting PC Security Issues and Malware Removal," for more information.

Incorrect answers: You might ask, "Well, what about disabling the network cards so that the malware doesn't spread?" While this might work, the best way is to physically disconnect the computer from the wired network and turn off any wireless on/off switches if at all possible. Or remove the wireless antenna from the computer. It's just impossible to tell if a virus or other type of malware is playing tricks on the Windows option to disable a networking card. Windows Update should be run after quarantining and removal processes are complete. You can run **chkdsk /R** to locate bad sectors and recover readable information, if necessary, after the malware removal is complete.

74. Answers: **B** and **D**. Among other things, you should recommend using strong passwords and assigning security rights based on job roles. Strong passwords are important on routers, wireless devices, switches, computers, and anything else that can be logged into. Role-based access control is when rights and permissions are assigned based on the person's job in a company: accounting, marketing, and so on. See Chapter 33, "Windows Security Settings and Best Practices," for more information.

Incorrect answers: Daily security audits might be a good idea, but they do not increase security; they only determine whether there is a threat or vulnerability that needs to be attended to. The customer already said that her antivirus software is up to date, so additional AV software should not be necessary. In fact, you shouldn't run any more than one type of AV software because they can have conflicting results that can slow down the system. Disabling screensavers doesn't really increase the security of the network, but setting up a password lock within the screensaver can make the individual systems more secure.

75. Answers: **A**, **C**, and **E**. Professionalism comes in many forms. When dealing with a customer, you should avoid distractions, avoid being judgmental, and meet expectations that are set. Also, avoid arguing, talking to co-workers, and personal interruptions. Be positive and listen to the customer. See Chapter 41, "Incident Response, Communication and Professionalism," for more information.

Incorrect answers: It is important to retain a chain of custody, but this has more to do with tracking evidence and less to do with professionalism. Documentation is important as well and should be developed by you as the technician; it should not be left to the customer.

76. Answers: **B** and **D**. You should look in the Event Viewer (Application log) and look for any other log files that are created by that new application. These might contain clues as to why the service won't start. Perhaps the service is dependent on another service or perhaps a particular file needs to be replaced. See Chapter 26, "Microsoft Operating System Features and Tools, Part 1," for more information.

Incorrect answers: The registry contains all of the parameters of the operating system but it won't give you error information. %systemroot%\System32\Drivers contains drivers for hardware. Who knows, the log file might lead you to believe that a driver needs to be replaced, but it isn't the first place you should look. Task Manager shows the performance of the CPU and RAM and shows what services are running. You might have attempted to start the service from there (or the Services Console) as part of the scenario.

77. Answer: **C**. The Secure Shell (SSH) is the best of the listed answers. It allows for secure sessions from a client to a server or to a network device. SSH will need to be installed and enabled on the switches and routers, and then the IT firm employees will need to connect with a secure SSH client (such as PuTTY or something similar). See Chapter 42, "Basic Scripting and Remote Access Technologies," for more information.

Incorrect answers: RDP stands for Remote Desktop Protocol—it is a commonly used term to refer to Microsoft's Remote Desktop Connection program—which can only be used to connect to Windows clients and servers. Telnet is an insecure protocol that was the predecessor to SSH. It is disabled on most client systems, and some switches and routers don't incorporate its functionality at all. Virtual Network Computing (VNC) is used most often to connect to remote client computers such as Windows, macOS, Linux, and Android, but SSH is the preferred method for connecting to network devices such as switches and routers.

78. Answer: **C**. The best answer to maintain data security is to initiate a remote wipe on a device that has been lost or stolen. That will delete the data and make it very difficult to reconstruct. See Chapter 38, "Troubleshooting Mobile Operating Systems," for more information.

Incorrect answers: Passcode locks and login attempt restrictions will only hamper a hacker who has appropriated the device. GPS (or location services) can help to find the device; however, if a device has been stolen or lost, time is of the essence, and the data should be remotely wiped right away.

79. Answer: **B**. The syntax shown is one way of mapping a network drive in Windows. **net use** is the command, the drive letter to be used is Z: and the path to the share is \\servername\sharename. This type of command would historically be found in a batch file in Windows; it uses the .bat extension. However, PowerShell is the newer, and better, tool to work with—it uses the .ps1 file extension by default. See Chapter 42, "Basic Scripting and Remote Access Technologies," for more information.

Incorrect answers: .vbs means Visual Basic script, which can be used in Windows, but is not necessary for basic networking procedures such as mapping network drives. .js is JavaScript, which is often used within websites. .py is Python, which is used for a variety of things, but again, is not necessary for mapping network drives.

80. Answers: **B** and **D**. To immediately prevent unauthorized access from the intruder, you could add the intruding device to a blocked access list. This might be done by IP or MAC address and can be accomplished within some mobile devices directly within the hotspot configuration settings or with a third-party app. The other correct answer is to change the SSID. By changing the SSID, the other user will be disconnected in a short period of time. However, that other user could always scan for networks and try to connect again. So, the best thing to do is to require encryption (WPA2 and AES) and use a strong password (although this will take more time). You could also disable the SSID broadcast altogether on some devices. This would stop the average user from connecting, but if the person has a Wi-Fi analyzer, he or she might still be able to connect. In addition, disabling the SSID can have unforeseen consequences. For example, your own mobile device that is connecting to the hotspot might be kicked off, and then you would have to reconnect it manually. See Chapter 35, "Data Destruction and SOHO Security," for more information.

Incorrect answers: Accessing the intruder's device and shutting it down is not a good idea for a variety of reasons, especially if the intruder is malicious or experienced with technology. Also, it is not an *immediate* solution. Neither is setting up a Wi-Fi analyzer to identify the intruding device; in fact, that might not be a solution at all. Shutting down the device is not a solution because now you, the user, have lost access as well. However, if you find you are in a situation in which you can't block the intruder, even with strong encryption, then shutting down the device might be your only option.

A Final Word About the 220-1002 Exam

After taking this practice exam, if you are unsure or unconfident in any way, then I urge you to step back, and continue studying the 220-1002 objectives before attempting the real exam.

Be ready for anything! I can't tell you *exactly* what will be on the exam, because that would violate the CompTIA NDA, and more importantly, the questions can change at any time! But the bottom line is this: if you know the concepts, you can pass any test. Use the official CompTIA A+ objectives as your guide. Review this book thoroughly. Finally, I challenge you to study in a hands-on manner on real computers, and investigate all the concepts to the best of your ability. This will help you not only for the exam, but also for the real world!

CHAPTER 43

Getting Ready for the Exams, and Farewell

This chapter provides some additional tools and information to help you be successful when preparing for and taking the CompTIA A+ Core 1 (220-1001) and Core 2 (220-1002) exams:

▶ Getting ready for the exams

▶ Tips for taking the real exams

▶ Beyond the CompTIA A+ certification

ExamAlert

Warning! Don't skip this chapter!

I impart some of the most vital things you need to know about taking the real exams here.

Getting Ready for the Exams

The CompTIA A+ certification exams can be taken by anyone; there are no prerequisites, but CompTIA recommends one year of experience as an IT support specialist. For more information on CompTIA and the A+ certification, visit https://certification.comptia.org/.

Also visit my A+ page at https://dprocomputer.com for information, additions, and updated errata.

To acquire your A+ certification, you need to pass two exams: the Core 1 (220-1001) and the Core 2 (220-1002). These exams are administered by Pearson VUE (https://home.pearsonvue.com/). You need to register with Pearson VUE to take the exams.

ExamAlert

I strongly suggest that you *do not* take both exams on the same day. Instead, take them a week or so apart (at least). Trust me on this.

Note

If you haven't already, make use of the step-by-step checklists for each exam, located in the 220-1001 and 220-1002 introductions in this book.

Each exam consists of two types of questions:

▶ **Multiple-choice:** These pose a question to you and ask you to select the correct answer (or answers) from a group of four or more choices. They are quite similar to the questions you've seen throughout this book.

▶ **Performance-based:** These ask you to answer a question, complete a configuration, or solve a problem in a hands-on fashion. The questions might ask you to drag and drop information to the correct location or complete a simulation in an emulated or virtual system.

To master both types of questions, you will need to have a deep understanding of the theory, but you will also need hands-on skills. So, use the companion website materials (described in the Introduction), and practice on your actual computers as much as possible. This is, of course, imperative for the exams, but it is even more important for the real world. The more you install, configure, and troubleshoot real systems, the more you will be prepared for the job interview, as well as whatever comes your way once you have acquired a position within an organization.

ExamAlert

You've been warned! Practice as much as possible on the following:

▶ Real desktop/laptop computer hardware and software
▶ A SOHO router
▶ Smartphones and tablets
▶ Printers, displays, and other peripherals

An Important Note Regarding Exam Questions

This book does not offer the exact questions that are on the exam. There are two reasons for this:

1. CompTIA reserves the right to change the questions at any time. Any changes, however, will still reflect the content within the current A+ objectives.

2. The contents of the CompTIA A+ exams are protected by a nondisclosure agreement (NDA); anyone who sits an exam has to agree to this before beginning a test. The NDA states that the questions within the exams are not to be discussed with anyone.

So, I cannot tell you exactly what is on the exams, but I do cover all of the objectives within this book in order to give you the best chance of passing the exams.

In addition to the tear-out cram sheet in the beginning of this book (print version), one great way to study is to compile and use a "cheat sheet." I am not saying to cheat (nor do I condone it); this is more of a *key facts* document, containing things that you want to memorize, or have a hard time memorizing, such as numbers, acronyms, procedures, minimum requirements, and so on. Include whatever you feel would help you best.

Table 43.1 provides a partial example of a cheat sheet that you can create to aid in your studies. Fill in the appropriate information in the right column. For example, the first step of the six-step troubleshooting methodology is "Identify the problem."

TABLE 43.1   Example Cheat Sheet

Concept	Fill in the Appropriate Information Here
The six-step troubleshooting methodology	1.
	2.
	3.
	4.
	5.
	6.
List of commonly used ports	
The laser imaging process	
The malware removal process	
Windows startup files	
Commands and descriptions (For example, **ping** tests to see whether other systems on the network are live.)	
Etc. *	

* Continue Table 43.1 in this fashion on paper. The key is to write down various technologies, processes, step-by-step procedures, and so on to commit them to memory.

Tips for Taking the Real Exams

Some of you will be new to exams. This section is for you. For other readers who have taken exams before, feel free to skip this section or use it as a review.

The exams are conducted on a computer and are composed of multiple-choice and performance-based questions. You have the option to skip questions. If you do so, be sure to mark, or "flag," them for review before moving on. Feel free to mark any other questions that you have answered but are not completely sure about. This is especially recommended for the performance-based questions. In fact, you might choose to leave all of the performance-based questions until the end. That, of course, is up to you.

When you get to the end, there will be an item review section, which shows you any questions that you did not answer and any that you flagged for review. Be sure to answer any questions that were not completed.

The following list includes tips and tricks that I have developed over the years. I've taken at least 20 certification exams in the past decade and the following points have served me well.

General Practices for Taking Exams

▶ **Pick a good time for the exam:** It would appear that the fewest number of people are at test centers on Monday and Friday mornings. Consider scheduling during these times. Otherwise, schedule a time that works well for you, when you don't have to worry about anything else. Keep in mind that Saturdays can be busy. Oh, and don't schedule the exam until you are ready. I understand that sometimes deadlines have to be set, but in general, don't register for the exam until you feel confident you can pass. Things come up in life that can sometimes get in the way of your study time. Keep in mind that most exams can be canceled as long as you give 48 hours' notice. (To be sure, check that time frame when registering.)

▶ **Don't over study the day before the exam:** Some people like to study hard the day before; some don't. My recommendations are to study off the Cram Sheet and your own cheat sheets, but in general, don't overdo it. It's not a good idea to go into overload mode the day before the exam.

▶ **Get a good night's rest:** A good night's sleep (7 to 9 hours) before the day of the exam is probably the best way to get your mind ready for an exam.

▶ **Eat a decent breakfast:** Eating is good! Breakfast is number two when it comes to getting your mind ready for an exam, especially if it is a morning exam. Just watch out for the coffee and tea. Too much caffeine for a person who is not used to it can be detrimental to the thinking process.

▶ **Show up early:** The testing agency recommends that you show up 30 minutes prior to your scheduled exam time. This is important; give yourself plenty of time and make sure you know where you are going. Know exactly how long it takes to get to a testing center and account for potential traffic and construction. You don't want to have to worry about getting lost or being late. Stress and fear are the mind killers. Work on reducing any types of stress the day of and the day before the exam. By the way, you do need extra time because when you get to the testing center, you need to show ID, sign forms, get your personal belongings situated, and be escorted to your seat. Have two forms of ID (signed) ready for the administrator of the test center. Turn your cell phone or smartphone off when you get to the test center; they'll check that, too.

▶ **Bring ear plugs:** You never know when you will get a loud testing center or, worse yet, a loud test taker next to you. Ear plugs help to block out any unwanted noise that might show up. Just be ready to show your ear plugs to the test administrator.

▶ **Brainstorm before starting the exam:** Write down as much as you can remember from the Cram and cheat sheets before starting the exam. The testing center is obligated to give you something to write on; make use of it! By getting all the memorization out of your head and on "paper" first, it clears the brain somewhat so that it can tackle the questions. I put paper in quotation marks because it might not be paper; it could be a mini dry-erase board or something similar.

▶ **Take small breaks while taking the exam:** Exams can be brutal. You have to answer a lot of questions (typically anywhere from 65 to 90) while staring at a screen for an hour or more. Sometimes these screens are old and have seen better days; these older flickering monitors can cause a strain on your eyes. I recommend small breaks and breathing techniques. For example, after going through every 25 questions or so, close your eyes and slowly take a few deep breaths, holding each one for five seconds and then releasing each one slowly. Think about nothing while doing so. Remove the test from your mind during these breaks. It takes only about half a minute but can help to get your brain refocused. It's almost a Zen type of thing; but for me, when I have applied this technique properly, I have gotten a few perfect scores. It's amazing how the mindset can make or break you.

► **Be confident:** You have studied hard, gone through the practice exams, created your cheat sheet—you've done everything you can to prep. These things alone should build confidence. But actually, you just have to be confident for no reason whatsoever. Think of it this way: You are great... I am great... (to quote Dr. Daystrom). But truly, there is no disputing this! That's the mentality you must have. You are not being pretentious about this if you think it to yourself. Acting that way around others...well, that's another matter. So, build that inner confidence and your mindset should be complete.

Smart Methods for Difficult Questions

► **Use the process of elimination:** If you are not sure about an answer, first eliminate any answers that are definitely incorrect. You might be surprised how often this works. This is one of the reasons why it is recommended that you not only know the correct answers to the practice exam questions, you also know why the wrong answers are wrong. The testing center should give you something to write on; use it by writing down the letters of the answers that are incorrect to keep track. Even if you aren't sure about the correct answer, if you can logically eliminate anything that is incorrect, the answer will become apparent. To sum it up, the character Sherlock Holmes said it best: "When you have eliminated the impossible, whatever remains, however improbable, must be the truth." There's more to it, of course, but from a scientific standpoint, this method can be invaluable.

► **Be logical in the face of adversity:** The most difficult questions are when two answers appear to be correct, even though the test question requires you to select only one answer. Real exams do not rely on "trick" questions. Sometimes you need slow down, think logically, and compare the two possible correct answers. Also, you must imagine the scenario that the question is a part of. Think through step by step what is happening in the scenario. Write out as much as you can. The more you can visualize the scenario, the better you can figure out which of the two answers is the best one.

▶ **Use your gut instinct:** Sometimes a person taking a test just doesn't know the answer; it happens to everyone. If you have read through the question and all the answers and used the process of elimination, sometimes gut instinct is all you have left. In some scenarios, you might read a question and instinctively know the answer, even if you can't explain why. Tap into this ability. Some test takers write down their gut instinct answers before delving into the question and then compare their thoughtful answers with their gut instinct answers.

▶ **Don't let one question beat you!** Don't let yourself get stuck on one question, especially the performance-based questions. Skip it and return to it later. When you spend too much time on one question, the brain gets sluggish. The thing with these exams is that you either know it or you don't. And don't worry too much about it; chances are you are not going to get a perfect score. Remember that the goal is only to pass the exams; how many answers you get right after that is irrelevant. If you have gone through this book thoroughly, you should be well prepared. You should have plenty of time to go through all the exam questions with time to spare to return to the ones you skipped and marked.

▶ **If all else fails, guess:** Remember that the exams might not be perfect. A question might seem confusing or appear not to make sense. Leave questions like this until the end. When you have gone through all the other techniques mentioned, make an educated, logical guess. Try to imagine why the test would bring up this topic, as vague or as strange as it might appear.

Wrapping Up the Exam

Review all your answers. If you finish early, use the time allotted to you to review the answers. Chances are you will have time left over at the end, so use it wisely! Make sure that everything you have marked has a proper answer that makes sense to you. But try not to overthink! Give it your best shot and be confident in your answers. You don't want to second-guess yourself!

Beyond the CompTIA A+ Certification

CompTIA started a policy on January 1, 2011. A person who passes the A+ exams will be certified for 3 years. To maintain the certification beyond that time, you must either pass the new version of the exams (before the three years are up), pass a higher level CompTIA exam (such as the Network+ or

Security+), or enroll in the CompTIA Continuing Education (CE) Program. This program has an annual fee and requires that you obtain Continuing Education Units (CEUs) that count toward the recertification. There are a variety of ways to accumulate CEUs. See CompTIA's website for more information.

After you pass the exams, consider thinking about your technical future. Not only is it important to keep up with new technology and keep your technical skills sharp, but technical growth is important as well; consider expanding your technical horizons by learning different technologies.

Usually, companies wait at least six months before implementing a newly released version of an OS or application on any large scale, but you will have to deal with it sooner or later—most likely sooner. Windows, Linux, macOS, Android, and iOS are always coming out with new versions. Consider keeping up with the newest versions and obtaining access to the latest software and operating systems. Practice installing, configuring, testing, securing, maintaining, and troubleshooting them.

To keep on top of the various computer technologies, think about subscribing to technology websites, RSS feeds, and periodicals, and read them on a regular basis. Check out streaming video tech channels on the Internet. Join computer Internet forums and attend technology conventions. After all, a technician's skills need to be constantly honed and kept up to date.

The best advice I can give is for you to do what you love. From an IT perspective, I usually break it down by technology, as opposed to by the vendor or certification. For example, you might want to learn more about e-mail systems, or securing internetworks, or you might prefer to work on databases, build websites, develop apps—who knows! You are limited only by your desire. Whatever the field, learn as much as you can about that field and all its vendors to stay ahead.

Final note: I wish you the best of luck on your exams and in your IT career endeavors. Please let me know when you pass your exams. I would love to hear from you! Also, remember that I am available to answer any of your questions about this book via my website:

https://dprocomputer.com

Sincerely,

David L. Prowse

Index

Numbers

A

T

U

To receive your 10% off Exam Voucher, register your product at:

www.pearsonitcertification.com/register

and follow the instructions.